GAAP

INTERPRETATION AND APPLICATION
1992 EDITION

Patrick R. Delaney, PhD, CPA
Northern Illinois University
DeKalb, Illinois

James R. Adler, PhD, CPA
Checkers, Simon & Rosner
Chicago, Illinois

Barry J. Epstein, PhD, CPA
Checkers, Simon & Rosner
Chicago, Illinois

Michael F. Foran, PhD, CPA, CMA, CIA
Wichita State University
Wichita, Kansas

JOHN WILEY & SONS

New York Chichester Brisbane Toronto Singapore

About the Authors

Patrick R. Delaney, PhD, CPA, is the Arthur Andersen & Co. Alumni Professor of Accountancy at Northern Illinois University. He received his PhD in Accountancy from the University of Illinois. Professor Delaney served as a Faculty Resident with Arthur Andersen & Co. He is the coauthor of *CPA Examination Review*, 2-volume and 3-part sets, both published by John Wiley & Sons, Inc. He is past president of the Rockford Chapter, Institute of Management Accountants; serves on Illinois CPA Society Committees (currently as a member of the Accounting Principles Committee and previously as Vice-President and member, Board of Directors; Chairman of Accounting Principles Committee; and member of Relations with Accounting Educators and Students Committee); and has served on numerous other professional committees. He is a member of the American Accounting Association, American Institute of Certified Public Accountants, and the National Association of Accountants. Professor Delaney has published in *The Accounting Review* and is the recipient of NIU's Excellence in Teaching Award and the Illinois CPA Society's Outstanding Educator Award.

James R. Adler, PhD, CPA, is partner in charge of Investigative Accounting and senior technical partner at Checkers, Simon & Rosner. He is a member of the Small Business Advisory Group at the Financial Accounting Standards Board Emerging Issues Task Force and is a past chairman of the Accounting Principles Committee and other committees at the Illinois CPA Society. He earned his BS, MBA, and PhD at New York University. Dr. Adler has been an expert accounting witness and provided litigation and investigative services to various business and law firms. He has served as a consultant to public accounting firms, financial institutions, and other enterprises and was a university professor. A frequent speaker and writer on accounting topics, he has authored articles in *Crain's Chicago Business*, and *Cashflow* and won awards for teaching excellence.

Barry J. Epstein, PhD, CPA, is partner-in-charge of quality control for Checkers, Simon & Rosner. He previously held quality control and technical research positions with other local and national CPA firms and has taught at several universities. The author of two other books and numerous articles in professional and academic journals, he has also served as an expert witness and taught at many continuing professional education programs. Dr. Epstein currently is chairman of the Illinois CPA Society's Accounting Principles Committee. He received his PhD in Management Information Systems and Finance from the University of Pittsburgh.

Michael F. Foran, PhD, CPA, CMA, CIA, is a Professor of Accountancy at Wichita State University. He received his PhD in Accounting from the University of Washington. He is a member of the American Accounting Association, the Financial Executives Institute, the Institute of Internal Auditors (IIA), and the Institute of Management Accounting. He has served as chairman and/or a member of many national, regional, and local committees in these organizations. He has spoken on numerous occasions to various academic and professional groups. He is a past President of the Wichita Chapter of the IIA. Dr. Foran has published in *The Accounting Review, Accounting Horizons, Journal of Accountancy, Management Accounting, The Tax Advisor, The National Public Accountant,* and many other academic and professional journals.

Contributors

Michael L. Baker, MBA, Price Waterhouse, Indianapolis. He served as a major contributor to the first edition (1985). He prepared the chapters: Inventories, Accounting for Leases, Earnings Per Share, and Accounting Changes and Correction of Errors.

John C. Borke, MAS, CPA, Associate Professor of Accounting at the University of Wisconsin-Platteville. Professor Borke prepared the chapter: Interim and Segment Reporting.

Bill Griesenauer, MAS, CPA, Forsythe-McArthur Associates, Inc., Skokie, Illinois. Mr. Griesenauer prepared the chapter: Long-Term Debt.

William Hartig, MBA, CPA, Allstate Insurance Company, Northbrook, Illinois. Mr. Hartig prepared the chapter: Special Revenue Recognition Areas.

John R. Simon, PhD, CPA, Alumni Professor of Accountancy at Northern Illinois University. He received his PhD from the University of Illinois and is a recipient of NIU's Excellence in Teaching Award. Professor Simon prepared the chapter: Foreign Currency.

Bernadette Tallitsch, MAS, CPA, Price Waterhouse. Ms. Tallitsch prepared the chapter: Statement of Cash Flows.

Additionally, the following employees of our DeKalb office also assisted in the preparation and review of the manuscript. They are: Jody Latta, Rebecca Hoger, David Czerniewski, and Dee Wolter.

Acknowledgements

The authors are deeply indebted to all of those who assisted in the production of this book for without them there would be no book to publish. Our heartfelt thanks go out to Charles C. Bowie, III, David Czerniewski, Lee Gampfer, Greg Graber, Karen Klein, Jonathan Koosed, Pam Miller, Margaret Paul, Kay Poormehr, Norma Rodriguez, and Barbara Stagner for your many hours of dedication and effort.

Preface

GAAP: Interpretation and Application provides an analytical explanation and illustration of those generally accepted accounting principles having the most widespread applicability. This book integrates the principles promulgated by the FASB and its predecessors into a usable topical format.

The focus of this book is on the practitioner and the practical problems faced in applying GAAP. However, a major strength of this book is its ability to address and explain the theory and application of GAAP in sufficient detail so as to supplement accounting textbooks. This book is not merely a reiteration of current promulgated GAAP. Using our combined expertise, we have addressed the problems faced by both the practitioner and the student in applying and understanding GAAP. Understandability is enhanced through the use of detailed examples, diagrams, and lucid explanations which emphasize the practical application of GAAP.

Each chapter (or major section therein) of this book provides a discussion of the perspective and issues relative to the topics covered; a listing of the sources of GAAP; the promulgated concepts and rules with examples of implementation; and the required financial statement disclosures for the topical areas. Additionally, the book has a comprehensive index that provides a quick reference to each pronouncement; it serves as a reference to other sources of information on specific accounting problems, it serves as an index to the FASB's system of coding pronouncements (i.e., the Current Text); and it provides a simplified checklist of required disclosures under generally accepted accounting principles.

We hope that this book serves as a reliable reference tool for practitioners, faculty, and students in working through the complexities of the authoritative literature. Comments from users concerning materials contained in or omitted from this work would be appreciated (see the form containing our address at the back of this book).

Patrick R. Delaney
James R. Adler
Barry J. Epstein
Michael F. Foran

October 15, 1991

TABLE OF CONTENTS

AUTHORITATIVE ACCOUNTING PRONOUNCEMENTS

Listed below are all of the authoritative accounting pronouncements **currently in effect** as we go to press. The current text refers to the FASB's *Accounting Standards - Current Text* which is divided into two volumes: General Standards and Industry Standards. These may be ordered from the AICPA or FASB. Places in this text where the pronouncements are discussed may be found by referencing the last column in the listings below.

Pronouncement Abbreviations

The following is a key to the abbreviations used throughout the book to refer to authoritative pronouncements:

Pronouncement	*Abbreviation*
Accounting Principles Board Opinion	APB
Accounting Research Bulletin	ARB
Statements of Financial Accounting Concepts	SFAC
Statements of Financial Accounting Standards	SFAS
Financial Accounting Standards Board Interpretation	FASB I
FASB Technical Bulletin	FASB TB
AICPA Accounting Interpretation	AICPA AIN
Emerging Issues Task Force Issue	EITF

Accounting Research Bulletins (ARBs), Accounting Procedures Committee, AICPA (1953-1959)

Number	Title	*Current text reference*	*GAAP Interp. & Applic. page reference*
43	Restatement and Revision of Accounting Research Bulletins Nos. 1-42, (originally issued 1939-1953)		
	Ch. 1 Prior Bulletins	A31, B50, CO8, C23, R36, R70, R75	535
	Ch. 2 Form of Statements	F43	44
	Ch. 3 Working Capital	B05, I78	35, 38, 106, 115, 120, 327, 328
	Ch. 4 Inventory Pricing	I78	123, 128-131, 133, 144-146, 154
	Ch. 7 Capital Accounts	C20, Q15	549
	Ch. 9 Depreciation	D40	
	Ch. 10 Taxes	T10	331, 332
	Ch. 11 Government Contracts	Co5	663
	Ch. 12 Foreign Operations and Foreign Exchange	C51, F65	

Number	Title	Current text reference	GAAP Interp. & Applic. page reference
20	Accounting Changes	A06, A35	68, 110, 133, 160, 177, 601-604, 606, 607, 609-611, 615-617, 620, 621
21	Interest on Receivables and Payables	I69	34, 329, 339, 343-345, 348, 375
22	Disclosure of Accounting Policies	A10	43, 121
23	Accounting for Income Taxes-Special Areas	I42, I25 Bt7	420, 459, 460, 467, 661
25	Accounting for Stock Issued to Employees	C47	18, 294, 527, 539, 546
26	Early Extinguishment of Debt	D14	297, 348, 350
28	Interim Financial Reporting	I73	13, 154, 466, 476, 585, 587, 590, 591, 620
29	Accounting for Nonmonetary Transactions	N35, C11	230, 233, 323, 530, 532
30	Reporting the Results of Operations	E09, I13, I17, I22	52, 53, 62, 67, 68, 515, 592

Financial Accounting Standards Board (FASB)
Statements of Financial Accounting Standards (1973-1991)

Number	Title	Current text reference	GAAP Interp. & Applic. page reference
2	Accounting for Research and Development Costs	R50, Co2	244, 245, 662
3	Reporting Accounting Changes in Interim Financial Statements	I73	585, 620
4	Reporting Gains and Losses From Extinguishment of Debt	D14, I17	67, 298, 331, 350, 391
5	Accounting for Contingencies	C59, I50, In6, R70	45, 46, 161, 177, 197, 333, 334, 339, 354, 513, 664
6	Classification of Short-Term Obligations Expected to be Refinanced	B05	107, 348

Number	Title	Current text reference	GAAP Interp. & Applic. page reference
79	Elimination of Certain Disclosures for Business Combinations by Nonpublic Enterprises	B50	325
80	Accounting for Futures Contracts	F80	120, 647
81	Disclosure of Post-Retirement Health Care and Life Insurance Benefits	P50	667
83	Designation of AICPA Guides and Statement of Position on Accounting by Brokers and Dealers in Securities, by Employee Benefit Plans, and by Banks as Preferable for Purposes of Applying APB Opinion 20	Bt7, A06, Em6, St4	661, 663, 666, 667
84	Induced Conversions of Convertible Debt	D10, D14	360
85	Yield Test for Determining Whether a Convertible Security is a Common Stock Equivalent	E09	564
86	Accounting for the Costs of Computer Software to be Sold, Leased, or Otherwise Marketed	R50, Co2	662
87	Employers' Accounting for Pensions	P16, C59, I67, Re6	496, 500, 502-504, 506, 509-515, 517, 519-521
88	Employers' Accounting for Settlements and Curtailments of Defined Benefit Pension Plans and for Termination Benefits	P16	496, 502, 513-515, 519
89	Financial Reporting and Changing Prices	C28	
90	Regulated Enterprises--Accounting for Abandonments and Disallowances of Plant Costs	Re6	666
91	Accounting for Nonrefundable Fees and Costs Associated with Originating or Acquiring Loans	L10, L20, D22, I89, Bt7, Fi4 In6, Mo4	367, 661
92	Regulated Enterprises--Accounting for Phase-in Plans	Re6, D40	666
93	Recognition of Depreciation by Not-For-Profit Organizations	D40, No5	665
94	Consolidation of All Majority Owned Subsidiaries	C51, I82, L10	248, 257, 274, 321, 322
95	Statement of Cash Flows	AO6, A10, C25, De4, EO9, I25, I28, I73, Oi5, S20, F60, F80	36, 79, 84, 97

Financial Accounting Standards Board (FASB)
Interpretations (1974-1991)

Number	Title	Current text reference	GAAP Interp. & Applic. page reference
1	Accounting Changes Related to the Cost of Inventory (APB 20)	A06	604
4	Applicability of FASB Statement No. 2 to Purchase Business Combinations	B50	
6	Applicability of FASB Statement No. 2 to Computer Software	R50	
7	Applying FASB Statement No. 7 in Statements of Established Enterprises	De4	
8	Classification of a Short-Term Obligation Repaid Prior to Being Replaced by a Long-Term Security (SFAS 6)	B05	331
9	Applying APB Opinions No. 16 and 17 when a Savings and Loan or Similar Institution is Acquired in a Purchase Business Combination (APBs 16 and 17)	I60, B50, Bt7	661
11	Changes in Market Value After the Balance Sheet Date (SFAS 12)	I89	253
12	Accounting for Previously Established Allowance Accounts (SFAS 12)	--	
13	Consolidation of a Parent and Its Subsidiaries Having Different Balance Sheet Dates (SFAS 12)	I89	
14	Reasonable Estimation of the Amount of a Loss (SFAS 5)	C59	333
16	Clarification of Definitions and Accounting for Marketable Equity Securities That Become Non-marketable (SFAS 12)	I89	
18	Accounting for Income Taxes in Interim Periods (APB 28)	I73	466, 469, 474, 585
19	Lessee Guarantee of the Residual Value of Leased Property (SFAS 13)	L10	374
20	Reporting Accounting Changes Under AICPA Statements of Position (APB 20)	A06	606
21	Accounting for Leases in a Business Combination (SFAS 13)	L10	390
23	Leases of Certain Property Owned by a Governmental Unit or Authority (SFAS 13)	L10	393

Number	Title	Current text reference	GAAP Interp. & Applic. page reference
85-5	Issues Relating to Accounting for Business Combinations	B50	
85-6	Accounting for a Purchase of Treasury Shares at a Price Significantly in Excess of the Current Market Price of the Shares and the Income Statement Classification of Costs Incurred in Defending Against a Takeover Attempt	I60, C23, I17	67
86-2	Accounting for an Interest in the Residual Value of a Leased Asset: • Acquired by a Third Party or • Retained by a Lessor that Sells the Related Minimum Rental Payments	L10	392, 393
87-1	Accounting for a Change in Method of Accounting for Certain Postretirement Benefits	P50	515
87-2	Computation of a Loss on an Abandonment	I42, Re6	666
87-3	Accounting for Mortgage Servicing Fees and Rights	Mo4	664
88-1	Issues Relating to Accounting for Leases	L10	373, 379, 393, 405, 409
88-2	Definition of a Right of Setoff - (Reference APB Opinion No. 10, para 7)	B10	98, 327
90-1	Accounting for Separately Priced Extended Warranty and Product Maintenance Contracts		

Financial Accounting Standards Board (FASB)
Statements of Financial Accounting Concepts (1978-1991)

Number	Title	Current text reference	GAAP Interp. & Applic. page reference
	Issued		
1	Objectives of Financial Reporting by Business Enterprises	--	3, 21, 22, 79
2	Qualitative Characteristics of Accounting Information	--	3, 23, 548
4	Objectives of Financial Reporting by Nonbusiness Organizations	--	
5	Recognition and Measurement in Financial Statements of Business Enterprises	--	3, 26, 54, 57, 79, 80, 161, 180

Number	Title	Current text reference	GAAP Interp. & Applic. page reference
6	Elements of Financial Statements		3, 30, 31, 32, 52, 53, 55-58, 99, 347, 348, 352, 417, 421, 422, 435, 525

Emerging Issues Task Force Issues (1984-1991)

Issues Considered by The Emerging Issues Task Force

Disposition of Issues

Resolved by the FASB	42
Resolved by the SEC	8
Resolved by the AICPA	2
FASB staff work in progress	1
AICPA committee work in progress	1
Issue to be addressed within an existing FASB major project	6
Consensus was reached on the accounting	152
No resolution	10
Further discussion by the Task Force is pending	5
Total	227

Issues Grouped by Type

Income taxes	22
Financial institutions	35
Financial instruments	54
Off-balance-sheet financing	12
Pensions/employee benefits	23
Business combinations/new basis	30
Inventory/fixed assets/leases	21
Real Estate	9
Other	21
Total	227

Number	Topic	Status
	INCOME TAXES (22)	
84-1	Tax Reform Act of 1984; Deferred Income Taxes of Stock Life Insurance Companies	Resolved by FTB 84-3, which is superseded by FAS 96.
84-2	Tax Reform Act of 1984; Deferred Income Taxes Relating to Domestic International Sales Corporations	Resolved by FTB 84-2, which is superseded by FAS 96.
84-27	Deferred Taxes on Subsidiary Stock Sales	Resolved by FAS 96.
84-33	Acquisition of a Tax Loss Carryforward-- Temporary Parent-Subsidiary Relationship	Consensus reached.
84-43	Income Tax Effects of Asset Revaluations in Certain Foreign Countries	Consensus nullified by FAS 96.
85-5	Restoration of Deferred Taxes Previously Eliminated by Net Operating Loss Recognition	Resolved by FAS 96.
85-15	Recognizing Benefits of Purchased Net Operating Loss Carryforwards	Consensus nullified by FAS 96.
86-1	Recognizing Net Operating Loss Carryforwards	Consensus nullified by FAS 96.
86-3	Retroactive Regulations regarding IRC Section 338 Purchase Price Allocations	Consensus partially nullified by FAS 96.
86-4	Income Statement Treatment of Income Tax Benefit for Employee Stock Ownership Plan Dividends	Consensus nullified by FAS 96.
86-9	IRC Section 338 and Push-Down Accounting	Consensus reached. Additional guidance provided by FAS 96.
86-11	Recognition of Possible 1986 Tax Law Changes	Resolved by FTB 86-1, which is superseded by FAS 96.
86-33	Tax Indemnifications in Lease Agreements	Consensus reached.
86-37	Recognition of Tax Benefit of Discounting Loss Reserves of Insurance Companies	Consensus nullified by FAS 96.
86-41	Carryforward of the Corporate Alternative Minimum Tax Credit	Consensus nullified by Issue 87-8. See EITF Abstracts.
86-42	Effect of a Change in Tax Rates on Assets and Liabilities Recorded Net-of-Tax in a Purchase Business Combination	Consensus nullified by FAS 96.
86-43	Effect of a Change in Tax Law or Rates on Leveraged Leases	Consensus reached. See Issue 87-8.
86-44	Effect of a Change in Tax Law on Investments in Safe Harbor Leases	Consensus reached.
86-46	Uniform Capitalization Rules for Inventory under the Tax Reform Act of 1986	Consensus reached.

Number	Topic	Status
87-8	Tax Reform Act of 1986: Issues Related to the Alternative Minimum Tax	Consensus partially nullified by FAS 96.
87-28	Provision for Deferred Taxes on Increases in Cash Surrender Value of Key-Person Life Insurance	Resolved by FAS 96.
88-4	Classification of Payment Made to IRS to Retain Fiscal Year	Consensus reached.

FINANCIAL INSTITUTIONS (35)

Number	Topic	Status
84-4	Acquisition, Development, and Loans	Resolved by AICPA Notice to Practitioners, issued 2/10/86.
84-9	Deposit Float of Banks	Consensus reached.
84-19	Mortgage Loan Payment Modifications	Consensus reached.
84-20	GNMA Dollar Rolls	Resolved by AICPA Statement of Position 85-2.
84-21	Sale of a Loan with a Partial Participation Retained	Consensus reached.
84-22	Prior Years' Earnings per Share Following a Savings and Loan Association Conversion and Pooling	Consensus reached.
84-31	Equity Certificates of Deposit	Consensus reached.
85-3	Tax Benefits Relating to Asset Dispositions Following an Acquisition of a Financial Institution	Consensus nullified by FAS 96.
85-7	Federal Home Loan Mortgage Corporation Stock	Resolved by FTB 85-1.
85-8	Amortization of Thrift Intangibles	Consensus reached.
85-13	Sale of Mortgage Service Rights on Mortgages Owned by Others	Consensus reached.
85-18	Earnings-per-Share Effect of Equity Commitment Notes	Consensus reached.
85-20	Recognition of Fees for Guaranteeing a Loan	Consensus reached. Additional guidance provided by FAS 91 and SEC Staff Accounting Bulletin No. 60. Disclosure guidance provided by FAS 105.
85-24	Distribution Fees by Distributors of Mutual Funds That Do Not Have a Front-End Sales Charge	Consensus reached.
85-26	Measurement of Servicing Fee under FASB Statement No. 65 When a Loan is Sold with Servicing Retained	Resolved by FTB 87-3.

Number	Topic	Status
85-31	Comptroller of the Currency's Rule on Deferred Tax Debits	Consensus reached.
85-33	Disallowance of Income Tax Deduction for Core Deposit Intangibles	Consensus nullified by FAS 96.
85-41	Accounting for Savings and Loan Associations under FSLIC Management Consignment Program	Consensus reached.
85-42	Amortization of Goodwill Resulting from Recording Time Savings Deposit at Fair Values	Consensus reached.
85-44	Differences between Loan Loss Allowances for GAAP and RAP	Consensus reached.
86-21	Application of the AICPA Notice to Practitioners regarding Acquisition, Development, and Construction Arrangements to Acquisition of an Operating Property	Consensus reached.
86-38	Implications of Mortgage Prepayments on Amortization of Servicing Rights	Consensus reached; consensus partially nullified by Issue 89-4.
86-39	Gains from the Sale of Mortgage Loans with Servicing Rights Retained	Consensus reached.
87-5	Troubled Debt Restructurings: Interrelationship between FASB Statement No. 15 and the AICPA Savings and Loan Guide	Consensus reached.
87-22	Prepayments to the Secondary Reserve of the FSLIC	Consensus reached.
87-34	Sale of Mortgage Servicing Rights with a Subservicing Agreement	Consensus reached.
88-17	Accounting for Fees and Costs Associated with Loan Syndications and Loan Participations	Consensus reached.
88-19	FSLIC-Assisted Acquisitions of Thrifts	Consensus reached. Additional guidance provided by SEC Staff Accounting Bulletin No. 82.
88-20	Difference between Initial Investment and Principal Amount of Loans in a Purchased Credit Card Portfolio	Consensus reached.
88-25	Ongoing Accounting and Reporting for a Newly Created Liquidating Bank	Consensus reached. Additional guidance provided by SEC Staff Accounting Bulletin No. 82.
89-3	Balance Sheet Presentation of Savings Accounts in Financial Statements of Credit Unions	Consensus reached.
89-9	Accounting for In-Substance Foreclosures	Consensus reached.

Number	Topic	Status
90-11	Accounting for Exit and Entrance Fees Incurred in a Conversion from the Savings Association Insurance Fund to the Bank Insurance Fund	Further discussion pending.
90-18	Effect of a "Removal of Accounts" Provision on the Accounting for a Credit Card Securitization	Consensus reached.
90-21	Balance Sheet Treatment of a Sale of Mortgage Servicing Rights with a Subservicing Agreement	Further discussion pending.

FINANCIAL INSTRUMENTS (54)

Number	Topic	Status
84-3	Convertible Debt "Sweeteners"	Resolved by FAS 84.
84-5	Sale of Marketable Securities with a Put Option	Consensus reached. See Issue 85-40.
84-7	Termination of Interest Rate Swaps	Consensus reached.
84-8	Variable Stock Purchase Warrants Given by Suppliers to Customers	Resolved by SEC Staff Accounting Bulletin No. 57.
84-14	Deferred Interest Rate Setting	Consensus reached.
84-16	Earnings-per-Share Cash-Yield Test for Zero Coupon Bonds	Resolved by FAS 85.
84-36	Interest Rate Swap Transactions	No resolution.
84-40	Long-Term Debt Repayable by a Capital Stock Transaction	Resolved by SEC. See EITF Abstracts.
85-6	Futures Implementation Questions	Resolved by FASB. See FASB Highlights, issued 6/85.
85-9	Revenue Recognition of Options to Purchase Stock of Another Entity	Consensus reached. To be addressed in FASB project on financial instruments.
85-17	Accrued Interest upon Conversion of Convertible Debt	Consensus reached.
85-23	Effect of a Redemption Agreement on Carrying Value of a Security	Consensus reached.
85-25	Sale of Preferred Stocks with a Put Option	Consensus reached. See Issue 85-40.
85-28	Consolidation Issues Relating to Collateralized Mortgage Obligations	Consensus reached.
85-29	Convertible Bonds with a "Premium Put"	Consensus reached.
85-30	Sale of Marketable Securities at a Gain with a Put Option	Consensus reached. See Issue 85-40.
85-34	Bankers' Acceptances and Risk Participations	Resolved by SEC. See EITF Abstracts.
85-38	Negative Amortizing Loans	Resolved by FAS 91.
85-39	Implications of SEC Staff Accounting Bulletin No. 59 on Noncurrent Marketable Equity Securities	Resolved by SEC. See EITF Abstracts.

Number	Topic	Status
85-40	Comprehensive Review of Sales of Marketable Securities with Put Arrangements	Consensus reached.
86-5	Classifying Demand Notes with Repayment Terms	Consensus reached.
86-8	Sale of Bad Debt Recovery Rights	Consensus reached.
86-15	Increasing-Rate Debt	Consensus reached. Additional guidance provided by SEC Staff Accounting Bulletin No. 77.
86-18	Debtor's Accounting for a Modification of Debt Terms	Consensus reached.
86-24	Third-Party Establishment of Collateralized Mortgage Obligations	Consensus reached. Also will be addressed as part of the recognition phase of the FASB project on financial instruments.
86-25	Offsetting Foreign Currency Swaps	Consensus reached.
86-26	Using Forward Commitments as a Surrogate for Deferred Rate Setting	Resolved by SEC. See EITF Abstracts.
86-28	Accounting Implications of Indexed Debt Instruments	Consensus reached.
86-30	Classification of Obligations When a Violation Is Waived by the Creditor	Consensus reached.
86-32	Early Extinguishment of a Subsidiary's Mandatorily Redeemable Preferred Stock	Consensus reached.
86-34	Futures Contracts Used as Hedges of Anticipated Reverse Repurchase Transactions	Consensus reached.
86-35	Debentures with Detachable Stock Purchase Warrants	Consensus reached.
86-40	Investments in Open-End Mutual Funds That Invest in U.S. Government Securities	Consensus reached.
86-45	Imputation of Dividends on Preferred Stock Redeemable at the Issuer's Option with Initial Below-Market Dividend Rate	Resolved by SEC Staff Accounting Bulletin No. 68. May be addressed in FASB project on financial instruments.
87-1	Deferral Accounting for Cash Securities That Are Used to Hedge Rate or Price Risk	No Consensus reached. However, guidance provided by EITF and FASB.
87-2	Net Present Value Method of Valuing Speculative Foreign Exchange Contracts	Consensus reached.
87-12	Foreign Debt-for-Equity Swaps	Consensus reached.
87-18	Use of Zero Coupon Bonds in a Troubled Debt Restructuring	Consensus reached.

Number	Topic	Status
87-19	Substituted Debtors in a Troubled Debt Restructuring	Consensus reached.
87-20	Offsetting Certificates of Deposit against High Coupon Debt	Consensus reached.
87-25	Sale of Convertible, Adjustable-Rate Mortgages with Contingent Repayment Agreement	No resolution.
87-26	Hedging of Foreign Currency Exposure with a Tandem Currency	Consensus reached.
87-30	Sale of a Short-Term Loan Made under a Long-Term Credit Commitment	Consensus reached.
87-31	Sale of Put Options on Issuer's Stock	Consensus reached.
88-8	Mortgage Swaps	Consensus reached.
88-9	Put Warrants	Consensus reached.
88-11	Allocation of Recorded Investment When a Loan or Part of a Loan Is Sold	Consensus reached.
88-22	Securitization of Credit Card Portfolios	Consensus reached.
89-4	Accounting for a Purchased Investment in a Collateralized Mortgage Obligation Instrument or in a Mortgage-Backed Interest-Only Certificate	
89-5	Sale of Mortgage Loan Servicing Rights	Consensus reached.
89-15	Accounting for a Modification of Debt Terms When the Debtor is Experiencing Financial Difficulties	Consensus reached.
89-18	Divestitures of Certain Investment Securities to an Unregulated Commonly Controlled Entity under FIRREA	Consensus reached.
90-2	Exchange of Interest-Only and Principal-Only Securities for a Mortgage-Backed Security	Consensus reached.
90-17	Hedging Foreign Currency Risks with Purchased Options	Further discussion pending.

OFF-BALANCE-SHEET FINANCING (12)

Number	Topic	Status
84-11	Offsetting Installment Note Receivables and Bank Debt ("Note Monetization")	Consensus reached.
84-15	Grantor Trusts Consolidation	No resolution.
84-23	Leveraged Buyout Holding Company Debt	Guidance provided by SEC Staff Accounting Bulletin No. 73. Disclosure guidance provided by FAS 105. To be addressed in FASB project on consolidations.
84-25	Offsetting Nonrecourse Debt with Sales-Type or Direct Financing Lease Receivables	Resolved by FTB 86-2 and SEC Staff Accounting Bulletin No. 70.
84-26	Defeasance of Special-Purpose Borrowings	Resolved by FASB.

Number	Topic	Status
84-30	Sales of Loans to Special-Purpose Entities	To be addressed in FASB project on consolidations.
84-41	Consolidation of Subsidiary after Instantaneous In-Substance Defeasance	Resolved by FAS 94.
84-42	Push-Down of Parent Company Debt to a Subsidiary	Guidance provided by SEC Staff Accounting Bulletin No. 73. To be addressed in FASB project on consolidations.
85-11	Use of an Employee Stock Ownership Plan in a Leveraged Buyout	No resolution.
85-16	Leveraged Leases • Real Estate Leases and Sale-Leaseback Transactions • Delayed Equity Contributions by Lessors	Consensus reached. Additional guidance provided by FAS 98.
86-36	Invasion of a Defeasance Trust	Consensus reached.
87-7	Sale of an Asset Subject to a Lease and Non-recourse Financing: "Wrap Lease Transactions"	Consensus reached. Additional guidance provided by FTB 88-1.

PENSION/EMPLOYEE BENEFITS (23)

Number	Topic	Status
84-6	Termination of Defined Benefit Pension Plans	Consensus nullified by FAS 88.
84-18	Stock Option Pyramiding	To be addressed in FASB stock compensation project.
84-34	Permanent Discount Restricted Stock Purchase Plans	To be addressed in FASB stock compensation project.
84-44	Partial Termination of a Defined Benefit Pension Plan	Resolved by FAS 88.
85-10	Employee Stock Ownership Plan Contribution Funded by a Pension Plan Termination	Consensus nullified by FAS 88.
86-19	Change in Accounting for Other Postemployment Benefits	Resolved by FTB 87-1. Also will be addressed in FASB project on other postemployment benefits.
86-27	Measurement of Excess Contributions to a Defined Contribution Plan or Employee Stock Ownership Plan	Consensus reached.
87-13	Amortization of Prior Service Cost for a Defined Benefit Plan When There Is a History of Plan Amendments	Resolved by FASB. See EITF Abstracts.
87-23	Book Value Stock Purchase Plans	Consensus reached. Also see Issue 88-6.
87-33	Stock Compensation Issues Related to Market Decline	Consensus reached.

Number	Topic	Status
88-1	Determination of Vested Benefit Obligation for a Defined Benefit Pension Plan	Consensus reached.
88-5	Recognition of Insurance Death Benefits	Consensus reached on principal issue. Guidance on second issue provided by FAS 96 Q & A.
88-6	Book Value Stock Plans in an Initial Public Offering	Consensus reached.
88-23	Lump-Sum Payments under Union Contracts	Consensus reached.
89-1	Accounting by a Pension Plan for Bank Investment Contracts and Guaranteed Investment Contracts	No consensus reached. However, guidance provided by FASB. See EITF Abstracts. Also will be addressed in FASB project on pension plan accounting for guaranteed investment and similar contracts.
89-8	Expense Recognition for Employee Stock Ownership Plans	Consensus reached.
89-10	Sponsor's Recognition of Employee Stock Ownership Plan Debt	Consensus reached.
89-11	Sponsor's Balance Sheet Classification of Capital Stock with a Put Option Held by an Employee Stock Ownership Plan	Consensus reached.
89-12	Earnings-per-Share Issues Related to Convertible Preferred Stock Held by an Employee Stock Ownership Plan	Consensus reached.
90-3	Accounting for Employers' Obligations for Future Contributions to a Multi-employer Pension Plan	Consensus reached.
90-4	Earnings-per-Share Treatment of Tax Benefits for Dividends on Stock Held by an Employee Stock Ownership Plan	Consensus reached.
90-7	Accounting for a Reload Stock Option	Consensus reached.
90-9	Changes to Fixed Employee Stock Option Plans as a Result of Restructuring	Consensus reached.

BUSINESS COMBINATIONS (30)

Number	Topic	Status
84-13	Purchase of Stock Options and Stock Appreciation Rights in a Leveraged Buyout	Consensus reached.
84-35	Business Combinations • Sale of Duplicate Facilities • Accrual of Liabilities	Resolved by FTB 85-5. Partially resolved by FAS 87 and SEC Staff Accounting Bulletin No. 61.

Number	Topic	Status
84-38	Identical Common Shares for a Pooling of Interests	Consensus nullified by FTB 85-5.
85-2	Classification of Costs Incurred in a Takeover Defense	Consensus nullified by FTB 85-6.
85-4	Downstream Mergers and Other Stock Transactions between Companies under Common Control	Resolved by FTB 85-5.
85-14	Securities That Can Be Acquired for Cash in a Pooling of Interests	Consensus reached.
85-21	Changes in Ownership Resulting in a New Basis of Accounting	To be addressed in FASB project on consolidations.
85-45	Business Combinations: Settlement of Stock Options and Awards	Consensus reached. May be addressed in FASB project on stock compensation.
86-10	Pooling with 10 Percent Cash Payout Determined by Lottery	Consensus reached.
86-14	Purchased Research and Development Projects in a Business Combination	Resolved by FASB. See EITF Abstracts.
86-16	Carryover of Predecessor Cost in Leveraged Buyout Transactions	Consensus superseded by Issue 88-16.
86-20	Accounting for Other Postemployment Benefits of an Acquired Company	Consensus reached. Also will be addressed in FASB project on other postemployment benefits.
86-31	Reporting the Tax Implications of a Pooling of a Bank and a Savings and Loan Association	Consensus reached. Additional guidance provided by FAS 96.
87-11	Allocation of Purchase Price of Assets to be Sold	Consensus reached.
87-15	Effect of a Standstill Agreement on Pooling-of-Interests Accounting	Consensus reached.
87-16	Whether the 90 percent Test for a Pooling of Interests is Applied Separately to Each Company or on a Combined Basis	Consensus reached.
87-21	Change of Accounting Basis in Master Limited Partnership Transactions	Consensus reached.
87-27	Poolings of Companies That Do Not Have a Controlling Class of Common Stock	Consensus reached.
88-14	Settlement of Fees with Extra Units to a General Partner in a Master Limited Partnership	No resolution. May be addressed by the AICPA.
88-16	Basis in Leveraged Buyout Transactions	Consensus reached.
88-26	Controlling Preferred Stock in a Pooling of Interests	Consensus reached.

Number	Topic	Status
88-27	Effect of Unallocated Shares in an Employee Stock Ownership Plan on Accounting for Business Combinations	Consensus reached.
89-19	Accounting for a Change in Goodwill Amortization for Business Combinations Initiated Prior to the Effective Date of FASB Statement No. 72.	Consensus reached.
90-5	Exchanges of Ownership Interests between Entities under Common Control	Consensus reached.
90-6	Accounting for Certain Events Not Addressed in Issue No. 87-11 Relating to an Acquired Operating Unit to Be Sold	Consensus reached.
90-10	Accounting for a Business Combination Involving a Majority-Owned Investee of a Venture Capital or LBO Fund	Further discussion pending.
90-12	Allocating Basis to Individual Assets and Liabilities for Transactions within the Scope of Issue No. 88-16	Consensus reached.
90-13	Accounting for Simultaneous Common Control Mergers	Consensus reached.
90-14	Unsecured Guarantee by Parent of Subsidiary's Lease Payment in a Sale-Leaseback Transaction	Consensus reached.
90-16	Accounting for Discontinued Operations Subsequently Retained	Further discussion pending.

INVENTORY/FIXED ASSETS/LEASES (21)

Number	Topic	Status
84-10	LIFO Conformity of Companies Relying on Insilco Tax Court Decision	No resolution.
84-12	Operating Leases with Scheduled Rent Increases	Consensus nullified by FTB 85-3. Additional guidance provided by FTB 88-1.
84-24	LIFO Accounting Issues	Resolved by SEC Staff Accounting Bulletin No. 58.
84-28	Impairment of Long-Lived Assets	FASB staff work in progress.
84-29	Gain and Loss Recognition on Exchanges of Productive Assets and the Effect of Boot	Consensus reached. See Issue 86-29.
84-37	Sale-Leaseback Transaction with Repurchase Option	Partially resolved by FAS 98.
85-32	Purchased Lease Residuals	Consensus nullified by FTB 86-2.
86-13	Recognition of Inventory Market Declines at Interim Reporting Dates	Consensus reached.
86-17	Deferred Profit on Sale-Leaseback with Lessee Guarantee of Residual Value	Consensus reached. Additional guidance provided by FAS 98.

Number	Topic	Status
86-29	Nonmonetary Transactions: Magnitude of Boot and the Exceptions to the Use of Fair Value	Consensus reached. See Issue 87-29.
87-27	Poolings of Companies that Do Not Have a Controlling Class of Common Stock	Consensus reached.
88-10	Costs Associated with Lease Modification or Termination	Consensus reached. Also see FTB 88-1.
88-21	Accounting for the Sale of Property Subject to the Seller's Preexisting Lease	Consensus reached.
89-7	Exchange of Assets or Interest in a Subsidiary for a Noncontrolling Equity Interest in a New Entity	Consensus reached.
89-13	Accounting for the Cost of Asbestos Removal	Consensus reached.
89-16	Consideration of Executory Costs in Sale-Lease-back Transactions	Consensus reached.
89-17	Accounting for the Retail Sale of an Extended Warranty Contract in Connection with the Sale of a Product	Consensus reached. Also will be addressed in FASB project on separately priced warranty and service contracts.
89-20	Accounting for Cross Border Tax Benefit Leases	Consensus reached.
90-8	Capitalization of Costs to Treat Environmental Contamination	Consensus reached.
90-15	Impact of Nonsubstantive Lessors, Residual Value Guarantees, and Other Provisions in Leasing Transactions	Consensus reached.
90-20	Impact of an Uncollateralized Irrevocable Letter of Credit on a Real Estate Sale-Leaseback Transaction	Consensus reached.

REAL ESTATE (9)

Number	Topic	Status
84-17	Profit Recognition on Sales of Real Estate with Graduated Payment Mortgages and Insured Mortgages	Consensus reached. See Issue 87-9.
85-27	Recognition of Receipts from Made-up Rentals Shortfalls	Consensus reached.
85-37	Recognition of Note Received for Real Estate Syndication Activities	AICPA committee work in progress.
86-6	Antispeculation Clauses in Real Estate Sales Contracts	Consensus reached.
86-7	Recognition by Homebuilders of Profit from Sales of Land and Related Construction Contracts	Consensus reached.
87-9	Profit Recognition on Sales of Real Estate with Insured Mortgages or Surety Bonds	Consensus reached.
88-12	Transfer of Ownership Interest as Part of Down Payment under FASB Statement No. 66	Consensus reached.
88-24	Effect of Various Forms of Financing under FASB Statement No. 66	Consensus reached.

Number	Topic	Status
89-14	Valuation of Repossessed Real Estate	Consensus reached.
	OTHER (21)	
84-39	Transfers of Monetary and Nonmonetary Assets among Individuals and Entities under Common Control	No resolution.
85-1	Classifying Notes Received for Capital Stock	Consensus reached.
85-12	Retention of Specialized Accounting for Investments in Consolidation	Consensus reached.
85-22	Retroactive Application of FASB Technical Bulletins	Resolved by FASB. See FASB Status Report, No. 175, issued 4/22/86.
85-35	Transition and Implementation Issues for FASB Statement No. 86	Resolved by FASB. See FASB Highlights, issued 2/86.
85-36	Discontinued Operations with Expected Gain and Interim Operating Losses	Consensus reached.
85-43	Sale of Subsidiary for Equity Interest in Buyer	Consensus reached under Issue 86-29.
85-46	Partnership's Purchase of Withdrawing Partners' Equity	No resolution.
86-2	Retroactive Wage Adjustments Affecting Medicare Payments	Consensus reached.
86-12	Accounting by Insureds for Claims-Made Insurance Policies	Consensus reached.
86-22	Display of Business Restructuring Provisions in the Income Statement	Resolved by SEC Staff Accounting Bulletin No. 67.
87-4	Restructuring of Operations: Implications of SEC Staff Accounting Bulletin No. 67	Consensus reached.
87-6	Adjustments Relating to Stock Compensation Plans	Consensus reached.
87-10	Revenue Recognition by Television "Barter" Syndicators	Consensus reached.
87-17	Spin-Offs or Other Distributions of Loans Receivable to Shareholders	Consensus reached.
87-24	Allocation of Interest to Discontinued Operations	Consensus reached.
88-3	Rental Concessions Provided by Landlord	Resolved by FTB 88-1.
88-15	Classification of Subsidiary's Loan Payable in Consolidated Balance Sheet when Subsidiary's and Parent's Fiscal Years Differ	No resolution. May be addressed in FASB project on consolidations.
88-18	Sales of Future Revenues	Consensus reached.
89-2	Maximum Maturity Guarantees on Transfers of Receivables with Recourse	Consensus reached.
90-22	Accounting for Gas-Balancing Arrangements	No resolution. Referred to AICPA industry group for consideration.

1 Researching GAAP Problems

Accounting principles have developed through both official pronouncements by authoritative bodies empowered to create and select accounting principles and evolution by accepted historical practice. Accounting principles developed when rule-making bodies perceived a need and promulgated opinions and standards or, in their failure to act, when conditions arose requiring solutions, by practicing accountants and academicians.

Development of GAAP

Primarily as a result of external pressures, the American Institute of Accountants, later to become the American Institute of Certified Public Accountants (AICPA), created a committee in 1930 to cooperate with the New York Stock Exchange in creating standards for accounting procedures. The widespread growth in the activities of the Exchange had led to expanded ownership and trading activities by an underinformed public. This lack of information, more than the stock market crash of 1929, caused the accounting profession to become involved in the concept of generally accepted accounting principles. Although the profession had, through various committees, made previous contributions toward creating uniform accounting standards prior to 1930, the creation of this special committee was different because of the recognition that complexities in business activities and in ownership dispersion required consistency in accounting measurements and in the selection of accounting procedures. This special committee recommended five rules to the Exchange which later in 1938 were published as Accounting Research Bulletin (ARB) 1 of the Committee on Accounting Procedure.

The Committee published 51 such bulletins, including Accounting Research Bulletin 43 which consolidated and restated Bulletins 1-42. The Committee was also instrumental in attempting to make accounting terminology uniform. However, the Committee's method of operation came into question in the late 1950s as the need for research into accounting principles became obvious. The result was the substitution of the Accounting Principles Board (APB) for the Committee in order to promulgate principles based primarily on the research of the Accounting Research Division. The Division was to undertake extensive and exhaustive research, publish the results, and allow the Board to lead the discussions which would ensue concerning accounting principles and practices. The Board's authority was enforced primarily through prestige and Rule 203 of the Code of Professional Ethics. However, approval by the Securities and Exchange Commission (SEC) of Board issuances gave additional support to its activities.

During the 14 years of the Board, 31 opinions and 4 statements were issued. These dealt with amendments of Accounting Research Bulletins, opinions on the form and content of financial statements, and issuances requiring changes in both the measurement and disclosure policies of the profession. However, the Board did not utilize the Accounting Research Division, which published 15 research studies during its lifetime. Both the Board and the Division acted independently in selecting topics for their respective agendas. The Board issued pronouncements in areas where little research had been done, and the Division performed research studies without seeking to be all-inclusive or exhaustive in analysis. The Accounting Principles Board did not operate differently than the Committee on Accounting Procedure.

As a result of these operational problems and the conclusions of the Wheat Study Group, the Financial Accounting Standards Board (FASB) was formed in 1972. The Board consists of seven full-time members; four are chosen from public practice of accounting, and the remaining three are knowledgeable in financial matters but need not be CPAs. Although there is some controversy and disagreement as to its activities and pronouncements, the FASB continues to operate with the confidence of accounting practitioners and various business organizations.[*]

Conceptual Framework

The FASB has issued six pronouncements called Statements of Financial Accounting Concepts (SFAC) in a series designed to constitute a foundation of financial accounting standards. The framework is designed to prescribe the nature, function, and limits of financial accounting and to be used as a guideline that will lead to consistent standards. These conceptual statements do not establish accounting standards or disclosure practices for particular items. They are not enforceable under the Rules of Conduct of the Code of Professional Ethics.

Of the six SFACs, the fourth, *Objectives of Financial Reporting by Nonbusiness Organizations*, is not covered here due to its specialized nature.

---

[*] *To date, the FASB has issued 106 Statements on Financial Accounting Standards, various Interpretations and Technical Bulletins, and devoted substantial time and resources towards developing a Conceptual Framework for Financial Accounting.*

SFAC 1, *Objectives of Financial Reporting by Business Enterprises*, identified three objectives of financial reporting. These were to provide useful information for economic decisions, to provide understandable information capable of predicting cash flows, and to provide relevant information about economic resources and the transactions, events, and circumstances that change them.

SFAC 2, *Qualitative Characteristics of Accounting Information*, identifies the qualities which make information useful. Under a cost benefit constraint, the primary qualities of useful information are that it be relevant and reliable. Relevant information is timely and either aids in predicting the future or in providing knowledge of the past (feedback value). Reliable information is verifiable and neutral and it faithfully represents events. In addition, such information must be comparable, consistent, and understandable.

SFAC 3, *Elements of Financial Statements of Business Enterprises*, has been replaced by SFAC 6. This statement has been amended by SFAC 6 to include financial reporting by not-for-profit organizations.

SFAC 5, *Recognition and Measurement in Financial Statements of Enterprises*, sets forth recognition criteria which determines what information should be in financial statements and the timing of when that information will appear. A full set of such statements would show financial position at the end of a period, earnings, comprehensive income and cash flows for the period, and investments by and distributions to owners during the period.

SFAC 6, *Elements of Financial Statements of Business Enterprises*, defines ten elements as the basic components of financial statements. Three of these elements (assets, liabilities, and equity) relate to the balance sheet and are discussed in depth in Chapter 2. The remaining elements (comprehensive income, revenue, expenses, gains, losses, investments by owners, and distributions to owners) relate to the performance of an entity over time and are discussed in Chapter 3. These would be displayed on the income statement, statement of changes in financial position, and statement of changes in equity.

The appendix to this chapter discusses SFAC 1, 2, and 5 in greater detail.

Generally Accepted Accounting Principles

Generally accepted accounting principles are concerned with the measurement of economic activity, the time when such measurements are made and recorded, the disclosures surrounding these activities, and the preparation and presentation of summarized economic activities in financial statements. These principles are a product of the economic environment in which they are developed. Complicated business activities usually result in complex accounting principles.

In APB Statement 4, the Board stated:

> *Generally accepted accounting principles* therefore is a technical term in financial accounting. Generally accepted accounting principles encompass the conventions, rules, and procedures necessary to define accepted accounting

practice at a particular time. The standard of "generally accepted accounting principles" includes not only broad guidelines of general application, but also detailed practices and procedures.

Generally accepted accounting principles are conventional--that is, they become generally accepted by agreement (often tacit agreement) rather than by formal derivation from a set of postulates or basic concepts. The principles have developed on the basis of experience, reason, custom, usage, and, to a significant extent, practical necessity.

Accounting principles are usually directed toward solutions that are objective, conservative, and verifiable. There are two broad categories of accounting principles-- measurement and disclosure. Measurement principles determine the timing and basis of items which enter the accounting cycle and impact the financial statements. These are quantitative standards which require numerically precise answers to problems and activities subject to large amounts of uncertainty.

Disclosure principles deal with factors that are not always numerical. Such disclosures involve qualitative features that are essential ingredients of a full set of financial statements. Their absence would make the financial statements created by measurement principles misleading by themselves. Disclosure principles complement measurement standards by explaining these standards and giving other information on accounting policies, contingencies, uncertainties, etc. which are essential ingredients in the analytical process of accounting.

Hierarchy of GAAP

The Auditing Standards Board (ASB) is the senior authoritative organization in the promulgation of generally accepted auditing standards. These standards include and the auditors' standard report specifically includes the phrase "present fairly in conformity with generally accepted accounting principles." With this responsibility and authority, the ASB has undertaken to define the meaning of the above phrase and to delineate the sources of GAAP. The determination of which accounting principle is applicable under a particular set of conditions may be difficult or even impossible without such a determination of the hierarchy of GAAP by an authoritative body.

In AU 411 (SAS 5, 43, and 52), the ASB identified the following as the sources of established generally accepted accounting principles:

a. Accounting principles promulgated by a body designated by the AICPA Council to establish accounting principles, pursuant to Rule 203 (ET section 203.01) of the AICPA Code of Professional Conduct

b. Pronouncements of bodies composed of expert accountants that follow a due process procedure, including broad distribution of proposed accounting principles for public comment, for the intended purpose of establishing accounting principles or describing existing practices that are generally accepted

    c.   Practices or pronouncements that are widely recognized as being generally accepted because they represent prevalent practice in a particular industry or the knowledgeable application to specific circumstances of pronouncements that are generally accepted

    d.   Other accounting literature

Category (a) refers to officially established principles by the Financial Accounting Standards Board (FASB) and the predecessor organizations: Accounting Principles Board and the Committee on Accounting Procedure. The pronouncements included are as follows:

    1.   FASB Statements of Financial Accounting Standards

    2.   FASB Interpretations

    3.   AICPA Accounting Principles Board Opinions

    4.   AICPA Accounting Research Bulletins

For financial statements of state and local governments, the Governmental Accounting Standards Board (GASB) statements and interpretations would also belong in the first category. If the GASB has not issued a pronouncement on a specific transaction or event, then the FASB pronouncements would apply.

Under category (a), an auditor would be precluded from expressing an unqualified opinion if the financial statements contained a material departure from such pronouncements, unless, due to unusual circumstances, adherence to the pronouncements would cause the financial statements to be misleading.

If the accounting treatment is not specified by any pronouncement in category (a), that is covered by Rule 203, the searcher should next proceed to category (b). The "expert accountants using due process procedures" includes AICPA Industry Audit and Accounting Guides, AICPA Statements of Position, and Technical Bulletins of the FASB and GASB.

The third category, (c), consists of pronouncements or prevalent practices of industry and would include AICPA Accounting Interpretations as well as practices that are widely recognized and utilized in an industry. Under category (b) or (c), the auditor could still issue an unqualified opinion in the instance of a material departure from the recommended accounting treatment, but would have to be prepared to justify the treatment used. In other words, categories (b) and (c) are preferable but not mandatory GAAP.

The final source of GAAP, (d), is utilized in the absence of any source of established principles when other accounting literature may be referred to. These would include APB Statements, AICPA Issues Papers, AcSEC Practice Bulletins, minutes of the FASB Emerging Issues Task Force, FASB Statements of Financial Accounting Concepts, Concept Statements of the GASB, International Accounting Standards Committee Statements of International Accounting Standards, pronouncements of other professional associations or regulatory agencies, and accounting textbooks and articles. The use of these other sources depends upon their relevance to particular circumstances, the specificity of the guidance, and the general recognition of the author or issuing organization as an authority. This would mean that FASB issuances in this category would be more influential in establishing an acceptable accounting practice than would an accounting textbook. Guidance in this category would require more judgment and a broader search of literature than would be true in the other three categories.

In an exposure draft issued on May 31, 1991, with comment expiration date of August 1, 1991, the Auditing Standards Board proposed an amendment to "The Meaning of Present Fairly in Conformity With Generally Accepted Accounting Principles in the Independent Auditor's Report." This revision would amend the guidance concerning the hierarchy of generally accepted accounting principles.

Under the revisions there would be five categories of generally accepted accounting principles. For nongovernmental entities, the highest category would be as currently existing, FASB Statements and Interpretations, APB Opinions and AICPA Accounting Research Bulletins. For state and local governments, GASB Statements and interpretations plus AICPA and FASB pronouncements, if made applicable by a GASB Statement or interpretation would be the highest category.

Category B, for nongovernmental entities, would consist of FASB Technical Bulletins, and those AICPA Industry Audit and Accounting Guides and AICPA Statutes of Position cleared by the FASB. For state and local governments, Industry Audit and Accounting Guides and Statements of Position cleared by the FASB and made specifically applicable by the GASB.

Category C, for nongovernmental entities would be represented by consensus positions of the Emerging Issues Task Force of the FASB and FASB cleared AcSEC Practice Bulletins. For state and local governments, this third category would include consensus positions of the GASB Emerging Issues Task Force (a group not yet in existence) and these FASB cleared AcSEC Practice Bulletins specifically made applicable by the GASB.

The fourth category of generally accepted accounting principles for nongovernmental entities consists of AICPA accounting interpretations, questions and answers published by the FASB staff, uncleared AICPA Industry Audit and Accounting and Statements of Position, and industry practices widely recognized and prevalent. This category for state and local governments includes questions and answers published by the GASB staff, state and local government practices widely recognized and prevalent and those AICPA Statements of Position and Industry Audit and Accounting Guides not yet cleared by the FASB but specifically made applicable by the GASB.

The fifth and final category of nongovernmental entity generally accepted accounting principles is other accounting literature including FASB Concepts Statements, APB Statements, AICPA Issues Papers, International Accounting Standards Committee Statements, GASB Statements, interpretations and technical bulletins, pronouncements of other professional associations for regulatory agencies, AICPA Technical Practice Aids and accounting textbooks, handbooks and articles. The state and local government generally accepted accounting principles includes GASB Concepts Statements as well as all items listed in the hierarchy for nongovernmental agencies that were not specifically made applicable to state and local governments.

The major changes in the hierarchy are the specific separation of nongovernmental generally accepted accounting principles from state and local government generally accepted accounting principles, the raising of the level of Emerging Issues Task Force pronouncements and AcSEC practice bulletins from the final category in the old hierarchy to the third category in the proposed listing and the separation of FASB cleared AICPA issuances from ones not cleared or acted upon by the FASB.

Of course, in all accounting theory, the substance of a transaction rather than legal form should guide the accounting treatment, and materiality is a factor that must be considered in the selection of an appropriate method.

The FASB

Since 1973 the FASB has been the designated authoritative organization that establishes standards of financial accounting and is recognized as authoritative through Financial Reporting Release No. 1 by the Securities and Exchange Commission and through Rule 203, Rules of Conduct by the AICPA.

The FASB is an independent body relying on the Financial Accounting Foundation for selection of its members and receipt of its budgets. Funds are raised from contributions made to the Foundation. The Board of Trustees of the Foundation is made up from members of:

> American Accounting Association
> American Institute of Certified Public Accountants
> Financial Analysts Federation
> Financial Executives Institute
> Government Finance Officers Association
> National Association of Accountants
> National Association of State Auditors, Comptrollers, and Treasurers
> Securities Industry Association

There is also a Financial Accounting Standards Advisory Council that has responsibility for consulting with the Board on major areas of inquiry and analysis.

The Board issues several types of pronouncements. Statements of Financial Accounting Standards are the most important of these setting forth mandatory accounting principles. Interpretations are used to classify or elaborate on existing Standards or pronouncements of predecessor bodies. Interpretations are submitted for comment to the Standards Advisory Council. Technical Bulletins usually address issues not covered directly by existing standards and are primarily used to provide guidance where it is not expected to be costly or create a major change. Bulletins are discussed at Board meetings and subject to Board veto. Both Bulletins and Interpretations are designed to be responsive to implementation and practice problems on relatively narrow subjects.

Emerging Issues Task Force (EITF)

The Emerging Issues Task Force (EITF) was formed in 1984 by the FASB in order to assist the Board in identifying current or emerging issues and implementation problems that may need to be placed on the agenda of the Board. Membership on the Task Force consists of persons selected from wide ranging backgrounds who would be aware of issues and practices that should be considered by the group. The Task Force meets on almost a monthly basis throughout the year with persons representing the SEC and FASB in attendance for discussion but not voting purposes.

For each agenda item, an issues paper is developed by members, their firms, or the FASB staff. After discussion by the Task Force, a consensus can be reached on the issue in which case further action by the FASB is not needed. However, the FASB may include a narrow issue in the scope of a broader project and reaffirm or supersede the work of the Task Force. If no consensus is reached, the problem may end up on the Board agenda or be resolved by the SEC or AICPA. It is also possible that no consensus is reached and the issue remains unresolved with no organization currently working on the problem. These may be in especially narrow areas having little broad based interest.

The FASB publishes a volume of EITF Abstracts which are summaries of each issue paper and the results of Task Force discussion. The Status Report issued by the FASB on a recurring basis throughout the year follows up on the subsequent developments after a Task Force decision on an issue. A listing of the Issues Considered by the Emerging Issues Task Force grouped by type in which the status concerning resolution of each issue is indicated appears in the front of this book immediately following the Table of Contents.

The EITF has been severely criticized for promulgating GAAP without sufficient due process procedures. Only a limited audience is aware of each issue, and the time period of exposure is often very brief, one month or so. However, the Task Force resolves problems in an environment where delay would often result in widespread divergent practices of accounting becoming entrenched. The guidance provided is often on narrow issues that are of immediate interest and importance.

Mandatory and Preferable GAAP

The first category above constitutes mandatory GAAP. This book is concentrated almost exclusively on GAAP in this category. Any deviation from accounting principles specified by the designated rule-making body would require an auditor to either qualify the opinion or explain in the body of the report the reasons and effects of the departures.

Departures from positions given by publications in the second and third categories would require auditors to document and justify their conclusions. Although the positions constitute GAAP, they represent preferable viewpoints, not mandatory ones. Preferable accounting principles have historically been specialized principles of particular industries which may not be transferable to other industries or to general business accounting policies.

Certain preferable accounting principles have become mandatory principles by the actions of the FASB. In Statement 32, the Board indicated that accounting principles and practices in certain AICPA Statements of Position and Accounting and Auditing Guides were preferable accounting principles. This recognition by the Board raised the status of these pronouncements which at that time had been somewhat uncertain. Then the Board began to extract those principles and practices and issue Statements to adopt these preferable principles. Such steps by the Board had the effect of promoting principles from preferable to mandatory.

The Board also amended Statement 32 to retroactively include Statements of Position 81-1 and 81-2 and Audit and Accounting Guide for Construction Contractors as preferable accounting principles. The appendix of Statement 32 contains certain remaining Statements of Position, Industry Guides, and projects in process at the AICPA. All of these items listed have been granted the status of preferability by this action of the Board. Since the Board is the only authority in category one of SAS 43, items selected by the Board for inclusion in SFAS 32 are automatically preferable. Complications arise when SAS 43 grants such preferability status, since the Auditing Standards Board (ASB) is not empowered to create generally accepted accounting principles. The ASB, however, carefully defined such preferability in terms of the audit function in determining fairness in conformity with GAAP which is clearly within its authority.

The concept that auditors should express an opinion on the preferability of a change in accounting principles undertaken by an entity whose financial statements are being examined has been extremely controversial. Preferability in these circumstances has been sometimes modified in terms such as "preferable in the circumstances" or the term "preferability" is avoided altogether. When the Securities and Exchange Commission proposed making such a preferability statement mandatory, certain members of the profession actually filed suit to stop such a proposal from being implemented.

As accounting principles continue to be promulgated, developed, and evolved, other problems concerning preferability will surely surface again. Many accountants will argue that unless a definite stand on accounting principles is taken by an authoritative body, they will have no reason or justification for choosing one accounting procedure over another.

Materiality

Materiality as a concept has great significance in understanding, researching, and implementing GAAP. Each Statement of Financial Accounting Standards (SFAS) issued by the FASB concludes by stating that the provisions of the statement are not applicable to immaterial items.

Materiality is both a qualitative and quantitative concept. Certain events or transactions are material because of the nature of the item regardless of the dollar amounts involved. The enactment of prohibition outlawing the sale of most alcoholic beverages was a significant event to companies that produce and sell such products. Offers to buy or sell assets for more or less than book value, litigation proceedings against the company for price fixing or antitrust allegations, and active negotiations involving future profitability are all examples of items not capable of being evaluated for materiality based upon numerical calculations.

Quantitatively, materiality has been defined in APB 15, Earnings per Share, and SFAS 14, Financial Reporting for Segments of a Business Enterprise. In the first case, reduction of earnings per share for potential and/or probable dilution need not be disclosed if it aggregates less than 3%. In the second case, a material segment or customer is defined as 10% or more of revenues.

The Securities and Exchange Commission has in several of its pronouncements defined materiality as 1% of total assets for receivables from officers and stockholders, 5% of total assets for separate balance sheet disclosure of items, and 10% of total revenues for disclosure of oil and gas producing activities.

Material information is that whose absence makes the financial statements misleading. This is not a definition of materiality nor does it sufficiently explain the concept to provide guidance in distinguishing material information from immaterial information. Until further research is performed or the FASB acts to provide such guidance, the individual accountant must exercise professional judgment in evaluating information and concluding on its materiality.

Standards Overload

Another complexity in the search for accounting principles has arisen in recent years with the complaint that there are too many accounting standards and too many organizations issuing pronouncements that create accounting standards. Solutions are needed to reduce and simplify existing GAAP either for all entities or at least for those entities where enforcement of such standards is not cost justified. Both the FASB and the AICPA have undertaken studies in order to seek to simplify or eliminate certain accounting principles.

A list of items identified as needing attention by standard setters will vary, depending upon personal preferences and problems. Generally, standards which are complicated, such as those on leases and income taxes, will find their way onto nearly everyone's list.

The search for simplicity is not an easy process. Complex business and economic activities may not lend themselves to simple accounting standards to measure and disclose them. If simplicity means having to make an incorrect measurement, many users will have to choose between erroneous financial statements, which do not reflect economic reality, and complicated accounting standards. A reduction in standards could ultimately reduce the quality of financial reporting.

Differential accounting principles for different entities may create additional complexities. Different disclosure standards may reduce the quantity of financial information available for certain entities selected, but this may also reduce the quality of such information. Different measurement standards again may create erroneous financial statements in terms of economic reality.

Differential standards require a selection of a system by which to categorize entities by the standards they should follow. Some recommend a size test with big firms following complete standards and small firms following a simpler set of standards. Size might be determined by assets, sales, net worth, or number of owners. Another possibility is an ownership test, with public companies following a different and more comprehensive set of standards than privately owned businesses. The difficulty in making such a selection and the added complexity caused by two sets of different standards obviously compounds the standard overload problem instead of reducing it.

The search for simpler accounting standards is not hopeless, however. Where research shows that disclosures are not utilized or understood by the users of financial data, such disclosures can easily be dropped. Where measurement standards are created to differentiate between events that are clearly not different from an economic viewpoint, such standards add nonessential complications and can be amended. For example, all business combinations constitute an economic union and the terms **purchase** and **pooling** have no meaning in economic theory. Also, all leases give rise to liabilities, as future obligations, and assets, as future economic benefits. The differentiation of some leases as capital and others as operating may be a highly subjective concept.

The search for easier, simpler, and fewer accounting standards will continue. Certain differential standards in terms of disclosures have already been adopted, allowing nonpublic entities to avoid disclosing earnings per share, segment data, and retroactive effects of a business combination. As the FASB considers future pronouncements on accounting standards, the issue of cost-benefit and applicability to all segments of the profession will be prime considerations. The standards overload issue will not fade away because there are numerous problems with the potential solutions that have been suggested.

Researching Published GAAP

The search for written GAAP consists primarily of analysis of the publications of various organizations concerned with accounting principles and practices. Accounting policies are established by these authorities in order to limit discretion and create uniformity, to the extent practical, for information and reporting purposes.

The FASB publishes two sets of books (both looseleaf and bound) which can assist in researching accounting issues. The *Current Text* integrates all of the currently recognized standards in alphabetical order. The AICPA Research Bulletins, APB Opinions, and FASB Standards and Interpretations are combined in topical order. Supplemental guidance from the AICPA Accounting Interpretations and FASB Technical Bulletins are also incorporated. The materials have been edited down from the original pronouncements and may lack the clarity that can be obtained only from the unedited version. Descriptive material including reasons for conclusions are missing. Each paragraph in the current text is indexed back to the original pronouncement for research or follow up referencing. The first volume of the *Current Text* deals with general standards while the second volume contains industry standards for specialized industries.

The *Original Pronouncements* contains all of the AICPA Accounting Research Bulletins, Interpretations and Terminology Bulletins, the APB Opinions, Statements and Interpretations, the FASB Standards, Interpretations, Concepts, Technical Bulletins, and Exposure Drafts. These are in five volumes in the order of their issuance. Paragraphs containing accounting principles that have been superseded or dropped are shaded in order to make the user aware. Such changes are identified in detail by a status page placed at the beginning of each pronouncement which can reference the user to other areas and pronouncements.

Essentially, if you need a quick answer to a specific question, the *Current Text* can be accessed very fast. If you need to understand the answer, the *Original Pronouncements* will afford you the opportunity to study the area in depth.

The Securities and Exchange Commission issues Staff Accounting Bulletins and makes rulings on individual cases that come before it, which create and impose accounting standards on those whose financial statements are submitted to the Commission. The SEC, through acts passed by Congress, has broad powers to prescribe accounting practices and methods for all statements filed with it. Although it has usually preferred to encourage the development of standards in the private sector by deferring to the AICPA and FASB, the SEC has occasionally adopted policies that conflict with established standards. In each case, the result has been a veto by the SEC of the standard, as the AICPA or FASB has withdrawn or amended the standard to conform to SEC policy. Usually SEC disclosure standards require far more information. However, the history of the SEC is one of cooperative assistance in the formulation of accounting standards. Congressional committees have been critical of the SEC in instances where they felt that too much power was ceded to the profession itself without adequate oversight by the Commission.

The search for authoritative guidance at the AICPA goes beyond Industry Audit and Accounting Guides and Statements of Position. The Auditing Standards Board may issue a pronouncement which affects GAAP similar to SAS 43 on the hierarchy of accounting principles. In its issuance of SAS 6, Related Party Transactions, in July 1975, the ASB set standards for auditing and disclosing such related party transactions. Not until the FASB issued Standard 57 in 1982, which was consistent with SAS 6, did the ASB amend its standard deferring to the FASB. Also, accounting interpretations are given by the AICPA Technical Information Service. Certain answers to inquiries made of it are published in a volume of Technical Practice Aids. These items constitute preferable GAAP to the extent that they are not amended or superseded by later pronouncements. Also, AICPA Issues Papers may be relied upon depending upon the circumstances to provide relevant information about alternative accounting treatments. Other publications of committees at the AICPA or information published in the *Journal of Accountancy* may give rise to understanding and interpreting accounting standards in areas where clarity is needed. The status of all AICPA publications not adopted by the FASB as mandatory or preferable is unclear. They are, however, issuances of the professional parent organization of the accounting profession and, therefore, must be considered as authoritative. Those who depart from them must be prepared to justify that departure based upon the facts and circumstances available in the particular situation.

The American Accounting Association is an organization consisting primarily of accounting educators. It is devoted to encouraging research into accounting theory and practice. The issuances of the AAA tend to be normative, that is, prescribing what GAAP ought to be like, rather than explaining current standards. However, the monographs, committee reports, and *The Accounting Review* published by the AAA may be useful sources for research into applicable accounting standards.

Other governmental agencies such as the Government Accounting Office and the Cost Accounting Standards Board (now out of existence) have offered certain publications which may assist in researching written standards. Also, industry organizations and associations may be other helpful sources.

In the absence of any clear-cut and definite pronouncements covering the issues that require answers, a different approach may be useful. The AICPA publishes an annual survey of the accounting and disclosure policies of many public companies in *Accounting Trends and Techniques* and maintains a library of financial statements which can be accessed through a computerized search process (NAARS). Through selection of key words and/or topics, these services can provide information on whether other entities have had similar problems and the methods used in accounting for them.

The lack of specificity can create problems in attempting to adhere to a highly flexible standard. For example, in adhering to APB 28 on Interim Financial Reporting, assume a problem arises in how to account for an annual catalogue expense. The cost of the catalogue can be allocated based on a time expired basis, benefit received, or other activity to each interim period. However, the Opinion also states that an arbitrary allocation of costs should not be made. Since any method of allocation chosen may be deemed as arbitrary and since other allocation formulas would yield different results, the Opinion is not explicit. Therefore, different entities might expense the catalogue in different periods based upon different allocation schemes. The result is not uniform accounting or even faithfulness to the principles in APB 28. Obviously, almost any accounting for the catalogue could be justified as being consistent with that Opinion.

Extremely detailed standards can, on the other hand, lead to answers which are clearly misleading. APB 15 states that all warrants are common stock equivalents and should be used in computing primary earnings per share unless antidilutive. Assume that warrants issued contain a put option, whereby the holder of the warrant may either convert it into stock or put the warrant to the company at a defined price. If the economic situation was such that the holder would be better off financially to exercise the put rather than convert into common, then obviously the marketplace would treat the warrant as debt and not as a dilutive security. However, there is no alternative under APB 15 but to treat the warrant as dilutive in earnings per share calculations. An accountant may allow the entity to report on an economic basis rather than a GAAP basis, but clearly, whether justified or not, that would create a deviation from an accounting standard.

These are but two examples of the difficulties of dealing with written GAAP. Pronouncements may not be explicit enough, or they may be too explicit, to provide definitive answers to a particular accounting problem. Researching GAAP may not end with finding a pronouncement on the topic. Careful reading of the publication and analysis of the underlying rationale for the transaction and activity are essential to insure compliance with the spirit and intentions of GAAP and not just its written word.

Researching Using this Book

This book can assist in researching generally accepted accounting principles in order to find technical answers to specific inquiries. A listing of all Authoritative Accounting Pronouncements in numerical order appears in the front of this book immediately following the table of contents. These are then referenced both to the Current Text published by the FASB and sections in this book. Accordingly, the entire original pronouncement can be found in the FASB Original Pronouncement books or traced to or from this book to both the original pronouncements and/or the current text. The reader can therefore find more detail on each and every topic covered in this book and also be aware of which topics and pronouncements are not covered within this book at all. This should make research cross referencing quick and reliable.

With respect to the EITF pronouncements, this book does not directly analyze most of them. Therefore, the text provides a listing of the pronouncements in topic order and within that by date order. Each issues paper is then identified as to the current status whether superceded, resolved, or consensus reached by the EITF. Within each of the topical areas, the reader will be able to identify any or all of the EITF issues papers that would be relevant to the current research. The reader then will have to go to the relevant EITF issuances published by the FASB. The topical updating of the EITF pronouncements does not appear elsewhere in the accounting literature, including the looseleaf services by the FASB.

The reader, therefore, can be directed by this book to the specific professional authoritative literature concerning the area of inquiry. In a like manner, the reader of the professional literature can use the listing of Authoritative Accounting Pronouncements to quickly locate the pages in this book relevant to each specific pronouncement.

Nonpromulgated GAAP

Not all GAAP came about because of a deliberation process and issuance of pronouncements by authoritative bodies. Certain principles and practices evolved into current acceptability without adopted standards. Depreciation methods such as straight-line and declining balance are both acceptable as are inventory costing methods such as LIFO and FIFO. There are, however, no definitive pronouncements that can be found to state this. There are many disclosure principles that evolved into general accounting practice because they were required by the SEC in documents submitted to them. Among these are reconciling the actual rate with the statutory rate used in determining income tax expense, when not otherwise obvious from the financial statements themselves. Even much of the form and content of balance sheets and income statements has evolved over the years.

The FASB through the Conceptual Framework Project, discussed more fully in the appendix of this chapter, has attempted to build a constitution of accounting theory for the evaluation of concepts by accounting principles researchers. Previously, the Accounting Principles Board in Statement 4 attempted to accomplish similar results. The underlying general standards from which all accounting concepts can be derived have proven to be elusive, but accounting standard authorities seem destined to continue their search for them.

Researching nonpromulgated GAAP consists of reviewing pronouncements in areas similar to those being researched, and careful reading of the relevant portions of the Conceptual Framework. Understanding concepts and intentions espoused by the deliberative authorities can give the essential clues to a logical formulation of alternatives and conclusions regarding problems that have not yet been addressed by these authorities.

Many of what are now promulgated accounting principles evolved through successful accounting practice. Two interesting and widely debated issues impact on this concept. First is the issue of whether promulgated GAAP consists of a codification of successful practice. In areas where a diversity of practice had previously existed, and pronouncements resolved the problem by selecting among the alternatives, the issue of which caused the success--practice or the pronouncement--is essentially unresolvable. The issue is certain to have supporters on both sides claiming that theory emulates practice or that successful practice came from the standards. In nonpromulgated GAAP, the methods may have evolved or may have benefited from other pronouncements in similar areas. The second issue is whether accounting research impacts on promulgated GAAP. Since its formation, the FASB has supported empirical research in an attempt to measure the cost and benefits of accounting pronouncements. Traditionally, research has been prescriptive in nature, describing what accounting could be under a different system. It, therefore, does not lend itself to impact technical pronouncements. However, research into capital markets and into social and economic consequences of accounting policy has impacted and will continue to impact future accounting principles. Unfortunately, the reverse will also become true. Accounting principles may be developed because of political, social, and economic reasons unrelated to accounting theory. The impact of such a development might well mean the end of the use of accounting theory as a problem-solving method.

Solving GAAP Problems

The methods that are employed in solving existing accounting problems can be summarized in the following steps:

1. Research published GAAP. A search should be initiated at the highest level of published accounting standards, following the levels and sources of principles according to Statement on Auditing Standards 43. The researcher should look for specific pronouncements and issuances level by level. In the absence of pronouncements directly applicable to the topic, the investigation should be broadened to include related and analogous topics. Analysis of the economic factors influencing the transaction will help in the broader search.

2. Research other literature. Other literature beyond that recognized by SAS 43 may consist of periodical literature and general industry publications. These may be important since not all principles are promulgated and successful practice is a source of accounting standards.

3. Research practice. Inquiries of other entities regarding the accounting practices they follow may indicate a potential solution or at least allow consideration of alternatives.

4. Use theory. When published standards, other literature, and practice fail to provide the answers to problems, the researcher must fall back on accounting theory. Textbooks, appendices to official pronouncements, FASB discussion memorandums, and the like are sources of theory to be analyzed. The use of theory constrained by the economic factors underlying the problem being researched may succeed in clarifying issues and alternatives when no other guidance is available.

Examples of unsolved accounting problems and potential solutions follow.

Example Involving Equity Method

The equity method of accounting for investments in partnerships and significantly influenced and controlled corporations is in accordance with accounting principles stated in APB Opinion 18. However, there is no clearly defined solution to the problem of how to account for issuances of additional shares or interests by the investee. Assume the following:

A Company forms B Company by depositing $100,000. B then sells additional stock to outsiders, reducing A's percentage of ownership to 25%, for a total of $4,900,000. A under the equity method would see its investment account rise from $100,000 to $1,250,000 (or 25% of [$100,000 + $4,900,000]).

A did not do anything that constitutes an earning process. Furthermore, a capital transaction of an investee could have been a capital transaction by the investor. The increase in investment may be seen as a capital transaction and an increase in paid-in capital.

Another argument is that A owned 100% of an entity and now owns only 25%. Essentially, A could have sold its investment directly but chose instead to have the investment sold indirectly by the investee. Under this theory, the increase in investment may be seen as a sale by A of part of its investment, which resulted in a gain, or as a revenue transaction to be reported in the income statement.

There are various writings in accounting literature that speak on both sides of this question. Although, in general, most textbooks show the increase as a capital transaction, the Internal Revenue Service may tax it. The Securities and Exchange Commission in Staff Accounting Bulletin No. 51 states that it will accept both methods, and the AICPA in Issues Paper, Accounting in Consolidation for Issuances of a Subsidiary's Stock, states a preference for the revenue transaction method.

The issue is whether A's original acquisition was a bargain purchase (no revenue to be recognized) or the subsequent sale was an earning process (revenue is realized). The issue may revolve around what activities A pursued prior to B issuing its stock that may have caused the value of B's stock to rise. Such activities may qualify for revenue recognition.

Example Involving Consolidations

In consolidations of less than 100% ownership of a subsidiary, the question arises as to the use of the parent or entity theories of combination. Assume the following:

A Company purchases 80% of B Company for $46,000 when B has total book value of $50,000. Since 80% of $50,000 is $40,000, there is a $6,000 differential to be accounted for. Under the parent theory, since cost exceeds book value by $6,000, the entire amount represents either an identified or unidentified (goodwill) asset to be accounted for in the future. Under the entity theory, since 80% created a $6,000 value, then the entire value must be $7,500, of which $6,000 is attributed to the majority interest and $1,500 belongs to the minority interest.

Under the parent theory, the implied additional value is not acceptable because there is no cost associated with it. Under the entity theory, recognition of only the actual differential denies the market implication of value. There is no authoritative literature that speaks to these issues although the parent theory is derived from the proprietary theory (view everything from the standpoint of the owner), while the entity theory (view everything from the standpoint of the entity as a whole) is a predominant accounting concept.

Generally, if the additional value of $6,000 is unidentified (goodwill), the cost issue becomes persuasive because of the concept of acquisition of unidentifiable intangibles. If the additional value is identified, practice would push the value down to the subsidiary by entering the $7,500 increase in assets and increase in equity. B would then have a total book value of $57,500 and 80% of it would equal the investment of A of $46,000. The accounting then is B's accounting for its own asset. The argument justifying this is that the legal form of the various entities, A and B, is immaterial. A new economic entity began with A's purchase of the stock of B and the same thing could have been accomplished through a partnership to which assets were transferred or by a liquidation of B into a new corporation, with a stepped-up basis for assets. Substance over form would support equal accounting regardless of the form of the transaction.

There are, however, many who would support neither the push down nor the implied value recognition. The answer is not definitive because there has yet to be a pronouncement on the parent and entity theories of consolidation.

Example Involving Cancelable Leases

A lease which is cancelable is not covered by SFAS 13, Accounting for Leases. However, assume that a firm has no intention of canceling the lease; would this intention alone be sufficient to cause capitalization of the asset and obligation, assuming the criteria were met? Most accountants would probably agree that the intention of the pronouncement would be met by such capitalization.

In a peculiar situation, assume a construction company bidding for state projects must maintain a 2:1 current ratio in order to obtain such jobs. The company has various equipment subject to cancelable leases, which otherwise would qualify as capital leases. If the leases are capitalized, the ratio falls below 2 to 1 causing cancelation of the leases due to lack of construction jobs. If the leases are not capitalized, the ratio is above 2 to 1, and the company would intend to keep the equipment for the entire lease without cancelation. Such an accounting dilemma is conceivable, and the solution may not exist. However, since bidding does not guarantee getting a contract, the intention of the lessee with respect to cancelation is unclear at the time of bidding, and most likely, the leases would not be capitalized at that time.

Example Involving Employee Capital Accumulation Plans

Such plans exist when companies reward employees by giving them stock or the right to benefit from the change in market price of the company's stock or both. There are two types of plans: (a) compensatory--the employee gets compensation and the company records an expense and liability, and (b) noncompensatory--no accounting recognition.

If a compensation plan is initiated at the then fair market value of the stock, no compensation can be reported because such compensation is measured only from the amount of the discount (market price less exercise price offered). Therefore, no discount means no accounting even though the plan is compensatory. So the difference between compensatory and noncompensatory plans can be meaningless (APB 25).

However, in practice many plans exist. These include incentive plans, option plans, stock appreciation rights plans, phantom stock plans, restricted plans, and others. Let's look at two examples:

1. A nonqualified stock option plan.
2. A stock appreciation right plan.

The substance of these two plans is essentially the same because economic benefits that may be received by the employee can be identical.

Assume that both plans are issued at an exercise price equal to the market price of the stock and that market price increases over time. Under the nonqualified plan, although compensatory, the compensation is measured at the date of grant which is the date of issuance. No compensation would ever be recorded and the increase in market value would be ignored. The employee could exercise the option and sell the stock, earning the profit while the corporation would ignore the "cost."

Under the stock appreciation right, the employee gets the profit directly from the corporation without buying and then selling the stock. However, when the amount of market appreciation is paid out, the corporation records the compensation as the excess of the market price over the exercise price of the SAR.

These two plans are virtually identical, yet the accounting for them is different. Furthermore, the first plan could give the employee a fixed number of shares while the second plan could be identical except the shares may be reduced based upon some contingency. Obviously, the first plan would be more valuable than the second because of no contingency in it to the employee. The stock plan is a more valuable award to the employee than the stock appreciation right. Under current accounting, the plan would cost zero while the right would cost the entire amount of the employee's gain.

Unfortunately, the form of the transaction prevails over the economic substance, although it clearly shouldn't. The corporation can influence its accounting recognized costs by how the plan is structured. The FASB is working on this problem.

Other Examples

Other problems similar to the previous ones also exist. Should profit sharing and money purchase plans that are substitutes for pension plans be subjected to the accounting and disclosure requirements for pension plans? How should income tax expense allocated to individual companies in a consolidated group be accounted for? The expense could be allocated on the proportion of income or loss, on the proportion of income alone (no credit for losses to those entities that had losses), on the incremental basis of each company with the net benefit or cost of the consolidated tax return accruing to the parent company, or on any other basis. There are no pronouncements stating the methods that are acceptable.

Solutions to GAAP problems may not be definitive and may not be obtainable by looking up a pronouncement. The theory of accounting and analysis of the economic factors may be the path to their solution.

APPENDIX

Conceptual Framework

In 1965, an AICPA Special Committee on Opinions of the Accounting Principles Board (APB) reported that the objectives, concepts, principles, and terminology of accounting should be enumerated and defined. In response to this recommendation, the APB published Statement 4, *Basic Concepts and Accounting Principles Underlying Financial Statements of Business Enterprises*. The purpose of this Statement was to increase the understanding of accounting fundamentals and to provide a basis for the development of accounting. This Statement was descriptive, not prescriptive, because it identified and organized GAAP based on the observation of accounting practice. Although the Statement was intended to contribute to the development of a "more consistent, comprehensive structure of useful financial information," it did not attempt to provide solutions to the problems of accounting nor did it attempt to determine what GAAP should be. In 1971, the AICPA established the Study Group on the Objectives of Financial Statements (known as the Trueblood Committee). This Committee identified twelve objectives of financial statements and seven qualitative characteristics of reporting. In 1976, based upon the Trueblood Report, the FASB issued *Tentative Conclusions on Objectives of Financial Statements of Business Enterprises* and later the same year issued *Conceptual Framework for Financial Accounting and Reporting: Elements of Financial Statements and Their Measurement*. These two pronouncements led to the establishment of Statements of Financial Accounting Concepts.

Components of the conceptual framework. The components of the conceptual framework for financial accounting and reporting include objectives, qualitative characteristics, elements, recognition, measurement, financial statements, earnings, funds flow, and liquidity. The relationship between these components is illustrated in the following diagram taken from a FASB Invitation to Comment, *Financial Statements and Other Means of Financial Reporting*.

In the diagram, components to the left are more basic and those to the right depend on components to their left. Components are closely related to those above or below them.

The most basic component of the conceptual framework is the objectives. The objectives underlie the other phases and are derived from the needs of those for whom financial information is intended. The qualitative characteristics are the criteria to be used in choosing and evaluating accounting and reporting policies.

Elements of financial statements are the components from which financial statements are created. They include assets, liabilities, equity, investments by owners, distributions to owners, comprehensive income, revenues, expenses, gains, and losses. In order to be included in financial statements, an element must meet criteria for recognition and possess a characteristic which can be reliably measured.

Conceptual Framework
For Financial Accounting and Reporting

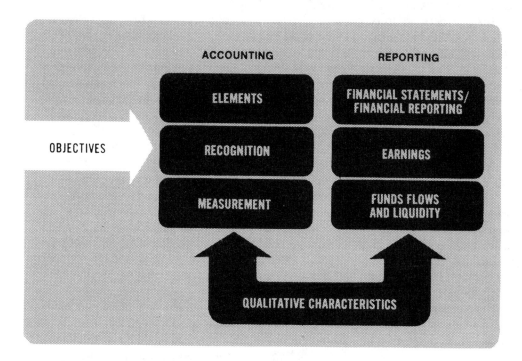

Reporting or display considerations are concerned with what information should be provided, who should provide it, and where it should be displayed. How the financial statements (financial position, earnings, and funds flow) are presented is the focal point of this part of the conceptual framework project.

Unlike a Statement of Financial Accounting Standards (SFAS), a Statement of Financial Accounting Concepts (SFAC) does not establish GAAP. Since GAAP may be inconsistent with the principles set forth in the conceptual framework, the FASB expects to reexamine existing accounting standards. Until that time, a SFAC does not require a change in existing GAAP. SFACs do not amend, modify, or interpret existing GAAP nor do they justify changing GAAP based upon interpretations derived from them.

SFAC 1: Objectives of Financial Reporting by Business Enterprises

SFAC 1 identifies the objectives (purposes) of financial reporting and indicates that these objectives apply to all financial reporting; they are not limited to financial statements. Financial reporting includes the financial statements and other forms of communication that provide accounting information (corporate annual reports, prospectuses, annual reports filed with the Securities and Exchange Commission, news releases, and management forecasts).

SFAC 1 identifies three objectives of financial reporting. The **first objective** of financial reporting is to provide information that is useful in making business and economic decisions. Financial information users are divided into internal and external groups. Internal users include management and directors of the business enterprise. Internal reports tend to provide information which is more detailed than the information available to or used by external users. External users include both those individuals who have or intend to have a direct economic interest in a business and those who have an indirect interest because they advise or represent those individuals with a direct interest. These users include owners, lenders, suppliers, potential investors and creditors, employees, customers, financial analysts and advisors, brokers, underwriters, stock exchanges, lawyers, economists, taxing authorities, regulatory authorities, legislators, financial press and reporting agencies, labor unions, trade associations, business researchers, teachers, students, and the public. SFAC 1 is directed at general purpose external financial reporting by a business enterprise as it relates to the ability of that enterprise to generate favorable cash flows. External users' needs are emphasized because these users lack the authority to obtain the financial information they want and need from an enterprise. Thus, external users must rely on the information provided to them by management.

The **second objective** of financial reporting is to provide understandable information which will aid investors and creditors in predicting the future cash flows of a firm. Investors and creditors want information about cash flows because the expectation of cash flows affects a firm's ability to pay interest and dividends, which in turn affects the market price of that firm's stocks and bonds.

The **third objective** of financial reporting is to provide information relative to an enterprise's economic resources, the claims to those resources (obligations), and the effects of transactions, events, and circumstances that change resources and claims to resources. A description of these informational needs follows:

- **Economic resources, obligations, and owners' equity.** Such information provides the users of financial reporting with a measure of future cash flows and an indication of the firm's strengths, weaknesses, liquidity, and solvency.

- **Economic performance and earnings.** Past performance provides an indication of a firm's future performance. Furthermore, earnings based upon accrual accounting provide a better indicator of economic performance and future cash flows than do current cash receipts and disbursements. Accrual basis earnings are a better indicator because charge for recovery of capital (depreciation/amortization) is made in determining these earnings. The relationship between earnings and economic performance results from the matching of the costs and benefits (revenues) of economic activity during a given period by means of accrual accounting. Over the life of an enterprise, economic performance can be determined by net cash flows or by total earnings since the two measures would be equal.

- **Liquidity, solvency, and funds flows.** Information about cash and other funds flows from borrowings, repayments of borrowings, expenditures, capital transactions, economic resources, obligations, owners' equity, and earnings may aid the user of financial reporting information in assessing a firm's liquidity or solvency.
- **Management stewardship and performance.** The assessment of a firm's management with respect to the efficient and profitable use of the firm's resources is usually made on the basis of economic performance as reported by periodic earnings. Because earnings are affected by factors other than current management performance, earnings may not be a reliable indicator of management performance.
- **Management explanations and interpretations.** Management is responsible for the efficient use of a firm's resources. Thus, it acquires knowledge about the enterprise and its performance which is unknown to the external user. Explanations by management concerning the financial impact of transactions, events, circumstances, uncertainties, estimates, judgments, and any effects of the separation of the results of operations into periodic measures of performance enhance the usefulness of financial information.

SFAC 2: Qualitative Characteristics of Accounting Information

The purpose of financial reporting is to provide decision makers with **useful** information. When accounting choices are to be made by individuals or by standard setting bodies, those choices should be based upon the **usefulness** of that information to the **decision making** process. This SFAC identifies the qualities or characteristics that make information useful in the decision making process. It also establishes a terminology and set of definitions to provide a greater understanding of the characteristics. The following diagram from SFAC 2 summarizes the qualitative characteristics of accounting information:

A Hierarchy of Accounting Qualities

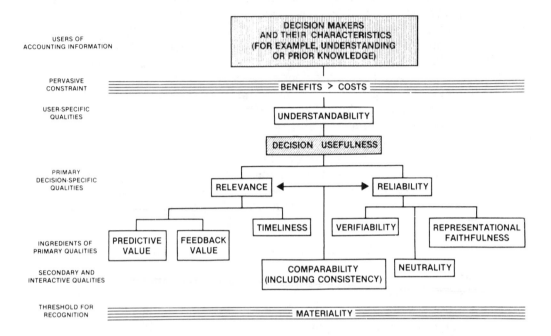

Usefulness for decision making. This is the most important characteristic of information. Information must be useful to be beneficial to the user. To be useful, accounting information must be both relevant and reliable. Both of these characteristics are affected by the completeness of the information provided.

Relevance. Information is **relevant** to a decision if it makes a difference to the decision maker in his/her ability to predict events or to confirm or correct expectations. Relevant information will reduce the decision maker's assessment of the uncertainty of the outcome of a decision even though it may not change the decision itself. Information is relevant if it provides knowledge concerning past events **(feedback value)** or future events **(predictive value)** and if it is **timely**. Disclosure requirement information such as segment reporting and interim earnings reports is relevant because it provides information about past events and it improves the predictability of future events. The predictive value of accounting information does not imply that such information is a prediction. The predictive value refers to the utility that a piece of information has as an input into a predictive model. Although timeliness alone will not make information relevant, information must be timely to be relevant. It must be available before it loses its ability to influence the decision maker.

Reliability. Financial statements are an abstraction of the activities of a business enterprise. They simplify the activities of the actual firm. To be **reliable**, financial statements must portray the important financial relationships of the firm itself. Information is reliable if it is verifiable and neutral and if users can depend on it to represent that which it is intended to represent (**representational faithfulness**).

Information may not be representationally faithful if it is biased. Bias is the tendency for an accounting measure to be consistently too high or too low. Bias may arise because the measurer does not use the measurement method properly or because the measurement method does not represent what it purports to represent.

Verifiability means that several independent measures will obtain the same accounting measure. An accounting measure that can be repeated with the same result (consensus) is desirable because it serves to detect and reduce measurer bias. Cash is highly verifiable. Inventories and depreciable assets tend to be less verifiable because alternative valuation methods exist. The direct verification of an accounting measure would serve to minimize measurer bias and measurement bias. The verification of the procedures used to obtain the measure would minimize measurer bias only. Finally, verifiability does not guarantee representational faithfulness or relevance.

The characteristic of **neutrality** means that accounting information should serve to communicate without attempting to influence behavior in a particular direction. This does not mean that accounting should not influence behavior or that it should affect everyone in the same way (e.g., differential disclosure requirements could be neutral). It does mean that information should not favor certain interest groups. The effect of lease capitalization on leasing firms would not be a valid argument to oppose the requirement that certain leases be recorded as direct financing-type leases.

To be useful, accounting information should be **comparable**. The characteristic of comparability allows the users of accounting information to assess the similarities and differences either among different entities for the same time period or for the same entity over different time periods. Comparisons are usually made on the basis of quantifiable measurements of a common characteristic. Therefore, to be comparable, the measurements used must be reliable with respect to the common characteristic. Noncomparability can result from the use of different inputs, procedures, or systems of classification. Noncomparability can also arise when the data measurements lack representational faithfulness.

The characteristic of **consistency** also contributes to information usefulness. Consistency is an interperiod comparison which requires the use of the same accounting principles from one period to another. Although a change of an accounting principle to a more preferred method results in inconsistency, the change is acceptable if the effect of the change is disclosed. Consistency does not insure comparability. If the measurements used are not representationally faithful, comparability will not be achieved.

Trade-offs. Although it is desirable that accounting information contain the characteristics that have been identified above, not all of these characteristics are compatible. Often, one characteristic may be obtained only by sacrificing another. The trade-offs that must be made are determined on the basis of the relative importance of the characteristics. This relative importance, in turn, is dependent upon the nature of the users and their particular needs.

Constraints. The qualitative characteristics of useful accounting information are subject to two constraints: the **materiality** and the **relative cost benefit** of that information. An item of information is material and should be reported if it is significant enough to have an effect on the decision maker. Materiality requires judgment. It is dependent upon the relative size of an item, the precision with which the item can be estimated, and the nature of the item. No general standards of materiality are provided (although an appendix to SFAC 2 lists several guidelines that have been applied).

Accounting information provides the user with certain benefits. Associated with this benefit, however, is the cost of using that information and of providing it to the user. Information should be provided only if its benefits exceed its cost. Unfortunately, it is difficult to value the benefit of accounting information. It is also difficult to determine whether the burden of the cost of disclosure and the benefits of such disclosure are distributed fairly.

Role of conservatism. Any discussion of the qualitative characteristics of accounting information would be incomplete without some reference to the doctrine of conservatism. Conservatism is a reaction to uncertainty. For many years, accountants have been influenced by conservatism. Conservatism in accounting may mislead users if it results in a deliberate understatement of net assets and net income. Such understatement is undertaken to minimize the risk of uncertainty to outside lenders. Unfortunately, such understatements often lead to overstatements in subsequent years, produce biased financial statements, and conflict with the characteristics of representational faithfulness, neutrality, and comparability.

SFAC 5: Recognition and Measurement in Financial Statements of Business Enterprises

SFAC 5 indicates that financial statements are the principal means of communicating useful financial information. A full set of such statements follows:

- Financial position at end of the period
- Earnings for the period
- Comprehensive income for the period
- Cash flows during the period
- Investments by and distributions to owners during the period

These statements result from simplifying, condensing, and aggregating transactions. Therefore, no one financial statement provides sufficient information by itself and no one item or part of each statement can summarize the information.

A statement of financial position provides information about an entity's assets, liabilities, and equity. Earnings is a measure of entity performance during a period. It is similar to net income but excludes accounting adjustments from earlier periods such as cumulative effect changes in accounting principles. Comprehensive income comprises all recognized changes in equity other than those arising from investments by and distributions to owners. A statement of cash flows reflects receipts and payments of cash by major sources and uses including operating, financing, and investing activities. The investments by and distributions to owners reflect the capital transactions of an entity during a period.

Income is determined by the concept of financial capital maintenance which means that only if the money amount of net assets increases during a period (excluding capital transactions) is there a profit. For recognition in financial statements, subject to both cost-benefit and materiality constraints, an item must meet the following criteria:

1. Definition--meet the definition of an element in financial statements
2. Measurability--have a relevant attribute measurable with sufficient reliability
3. Relevance
4. Reliability

Items reported in these statements are based on historical cost, replacement cost, market value, net realizable value, and present value of cash flows. Price level changes are not recognized in these statements and conservatism guides the application of recognition criteria.

2 Balance Sheet

Perspective and Issues

Balance sheets or statements of financial position present assets, liabilities, and shareholders' equity (net worth, partners' capital). They reflect the financial status of an enterprise in conformity with generally accepted accounting principles. The balance sheet reports the aggregate effect of transactions at a **point in time**, whereas the income statement, statement of retained earnings, and statement of cash flows report the effect of transactions over a **period of time.**

For years, users of financial statements put more emphasis on the income statement than on the balance sheet. Investors' main concern was the short-run maximization of earnings per share. During the late 1960s and early 1970s company growth and desirability was measured by earnings growth. But the combination of inflation and recession during the 1974-75 period and the emphasis in the Conceptual Framework Project on the asset-liability approach to theory brought about a rediscovery of the balance sheet. This shift toward the balance sheet has marked a departure from the traditional transaction-based concept of income toward a capital maintenance concept proposed by economists. Under this approach to income measurement, the amount of beginning net assets would be compared to the amount of ending net assets, and the difference would be adjusted for dividends and capital transactions. Only to the extent that an entity maintained its net assets (after adjusting for capital transactions) would income be earned. By using a capital maintenance concept, investors can better predict the overall profit potential of the firm.

Financial statements should provide information that helps users make rational investment, credit, or economic decisions. The balance sheet must be studied in order to measure a firm's liquidity, financial flexibility and ability to generate profits, pay debts when due, and pay dividends. A firm's liquidity refers to the timing of cash flows in the normal course of business. Liquidity indicates the firm's ability to meet its obligations as they fall due. The concept of financial flexibility is broader than the concept of liquidity. Financial flexibility is the ability to take effective actions to alter the amounts and timing of cash flows so it can respond to unexpected needs and opportunities. Financial flexibility includes the ability to issue new capital or unused lines of credit.

One of the main objectives of financial reporting is to provide information that is useful in assessing the amounts, timing, and uncertainty of future cash flows. There have been two suggestions to make the balance sheet more useful in assessing a firm's liquidity. The first is to make alterations to the balance sheet's format. The second is to provide additional information about liquidity in the notes to the balance sheet.

In many industries, balance sheets are classified into categories. Assets are classified as "current" if they are reasonably expected to be converted into cash, sold, or consumed either in one year or in the operating cycle, whichever is longer. Liabilities are classified as "current" if they are expected to be liquidated through the use of current assets or the creation of other current liabilities.

In some industries, the concept of working capital has little importance and the balance sheet is not classified. Such industries are broker-dealer, investment companies, real estate companies, and utilities. Personal financial statements are unclassified for the same reason.

Sources of GAAP

ARB	*APB*	*SFAS*	*SFAC*	*FASB I*
43, Ch. 2, 3	22	5, 6, 12, 57	6	14

Definitions of Terms

Statement of Financial Accounting Concepts 6 defines ten elements of the financial statements of business enterprises and several other concepts that relate to those elements. Elements are the basic categories which appear on the financial statements. To be included in the financial statements, an item must meet the definitional requirements, recognition requirements, and measurement requirements. Although there may be other elements of the financial statements, this Statement defines only those elements that relate to the status and performance of a business and are relevant to decisions which would require the commitment of resources to the business. Three of the ten elements (assets, liabilities, and equity) are related to the status of an entity at a particular point in time. The other seven elements (comprehensive income, revenues, expenses, gains and losses, investments by owners, and distributions to owners) are related to the performance of an entity over a period of time. The two categories of elements **articulate**. That is, a change in one will affect the other.

Elements of balance sheets.

Assets - *Probable future economic benefits obtained or controlled by a particular entity as a result of past transactions or events (SFAC 6, para 25).*

The following three characteristics must be present for an item to qualify as an asset:

1. The asset must provide probable future economic benefit which enables it to provide future net cash inflows.
2. The entity is able to receive the benefit and restrict other entities' access to that benefit.
3. The event which provides the entity with the right to the benefit has occurred.

Assets remain an economic resource of an enterprise as long as they continue to meet the three requirements identified above. Transactions and operations act to change an entity's assets.

A valuation account is not an asset or a liability. It alters the carrying value of an asset and is not independent of that related asset. Assets have features that help identify them in that they are exchangeable, legally enforceable, and have future economic benefit (service potential). It is that potential that eventually brings in cash to the entity and that underlies the concept of an asset.

> *Liabilities - Probable future sacrifices of economic benefits arising from present obligations of a particular entity to transfer assets or provide services to other entities in the future as a result of past transactions or events (SFAC 6, para 35).*

The following three characteristics must be present for an item to qualify as a liability:

1. A liability requires that the entity settle a present obligation by the probable future transfer of an asset on demand when a specified event occurs or at a particular date.
2. The obligation cannot be avoided.
3. The event which obligates the entity has occurred.

Liabilities usually result from transactions which enable entities to obtain resources. Other liabilities may arise from nonreciprocal transfers such as the declaration of dividends to the owners of the entity or the pledge of assets to charitable organizations.

An entity may involuntarily incur a liability. A liability may be imposed on the entity by government or by the court system in the form of taxes, fines, or levies. A liability may arise from price changes or interest rate changes. Liabilities may be legally enforceable or they may be equitable obligations which arise from social, ethical, or moral requirements. Liabilities continue in existence until the entity is no longer responsible for discharging them. A valuation account is not an independent item. It alters the carrying value of a liability and is directly related to that liability.

Most liabilities stem from financial instruments, contracts, and laws which are legal concepts invented by a sophisticated economy. Enterprises incur liabilities primarily as part of their ongoing economic activities in exchange for economic resources and services required to operate the business. The end result of a liability is that it takes an asset or another liability to liquidate it. Liabilities are imposed by agreement, by law, by court, by equitable or constructive obligation, and by business ethics and custom.

The diagram on the following page from SFAC 6 identifies the three classes of events which affect an entity.

> *Equity - The residual interest in the assets that remains after deducting its liabilities. In a business enterprise, the equity is the ownership interest (SFAC 6, para 49).*

Equity arises from the ownership relation and is the source of enterprise distributions to the owners. Distributions of enterprise assets to owners are voluntary. Equity is increased by owners' investments and comprehensive income and is reduced by distributions to the owners. In practice, the distinction between equity and liabilities may be difficult to ascertain. Securities such as convertible debt and preferred stock may have characteristics of both equity (residual ownership interest) and liabilities (nondiscretionary future sacrifices).

The other elements which change assets, liabilities, and equities will be identified and defined in Chapter 3, Income Statement.

Concepts, Rules, and Examples

Assets and liabilities are recorded in the financial statements under the historical cost principle. Historical exchange prices are used because they are objective and capable of being independently verified. One limitation of the balance sheet is that historical cost does not always reflect current value. When a balance sheet is presented, most assets are reported at cost. However, generally accepted accounting principles allow certain exceptions. Inventories and marketable equity securities may be reported at lower of cost or market, and certain long-term investments may be reported under the equity method. Many accountants believe that the balance sheet would be more useful if the assets were restated in terms of current values. These current values may be market related or may simply be historical cost adjusted for the changing value of the dollar. Although assets are usually stated at historical cost, if market information indicates a permanent and material decline in value, recognition of the economic loss is immediate.

Another limitation of historical cost balance sheets is that estimates are used to determine the carrying/book values of many of the assets. Estimates are used in determining the collectibility of receivables, salability of inventory, and useful life of long-term assets. Depreciation, depletion, and amortization of long-term assets are acceptable practices, but appreciation of assets is not generally recorded. Appreciation of assets is usually recorded only when realized through an arm's-length transaction (sale). Estimates are necessary in order to divide and separate economic events occurring between two distinct accounting periods. However, such estimates require informed judgments for which there is little guidance in accounting literature.

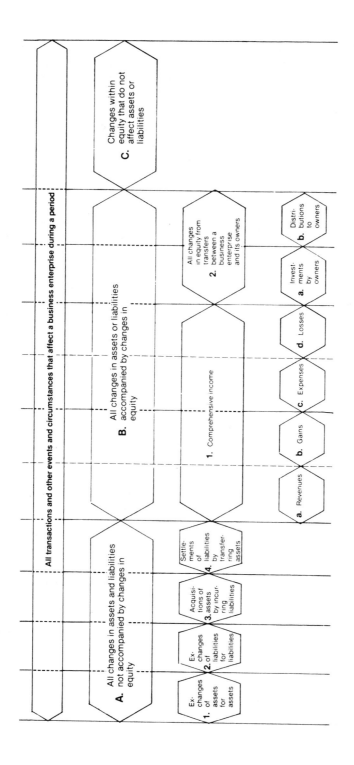

An additional limitation of the balance sheet is that it ignores items that are of financial value to the firm but which cannot be objectively determined. For example, internally generated goodwill, human resources, and secret processes are of financial value, but since these values are not measurable under current accounting principles and practices, they are not recorded on the balance sheet. Only assets obtained in a market transaction are recorded on the books and records of an entity.

A final limitation of the balance sheet is that it ignores the time value of its elements. Although certain receivables and payables may be discounted (APB 21), most items are stated at face value regardless of the timing of the cash flows that they will generate.

The balance sheet has a mixture of historical cost and current value. For some assets and liabilities, cost is a close approximation of current value. Monetary assets such as cash, short-term investments, and receivables closely approximate current value. Current liabilities are payable in a short period, and closely approximate current value. If they were discounted, any discount value would be immaterial because of the short time period before payment. Current liabilities are not classified strictly on the basis of maturity value but on the concept that a current liability is one that requires either a current asset or another current liability to liquidate. Current liabilities should be shown on the balance sheet at face value. Productive assets such as property, plant, and equipment and intangibles are reported at cost less any reduction due to depreciation, depletion, or amortization. Long-term liabilities are recorded as the discounted value of future payments to be made under contract. On the date of issuance, the discount rate equals the market rate. Therefore, current value equals balance sheet cost. However, as time passes and the market rate fluctuates, the recorded cost will not necessarily approximate the current value.

The rights of the common shareholders of a firm and the rights of other capital-supplying parties (bondholders and preferred stockholders) of a firm are many and varied. Both sources of capital are concerned with two basic rights: the right to share in the cash or property disbursements (interest and dividends) and the right to share in the assets in the event of liquidation. The disclosure of these rights is an important objective in the presentation of financial statements.

Form of Balance Sheet

The use of the terms balance sheet, statement of financial position, or statement of financial condition denotes the use of generally accepted accounting principles. If some other comprehensive basis of accounting, such as income tax or cash, is used, the title of the financial statement must be adjusted to reflect this variation. Titles such as "Statements of Assets and Liabilities" would be necessary to differentiate the financial statement being presented from a balance sheet.

The three elements that are displayed in the heading of a balance sheet are:

1. The entity whose financial position is being presented.
2. The title of the statement.

3. The date of the statement.

The entity's name should appear exactly as written in the legal document which created it (e.g., the certificate of incorporation, partnership agreement, etc.). The title should also clearly reflect the legal status of the enterprise as a corporation, partnership, sole proprietorship, or divisions of some other entity. Where the entity's name does not disclose its legal status, supplemental information would have to be added to the title in order to clarify that status. A few examples are as follows:

**ABC Company
(A Partnership)**

**ABC Company
(A Limited Partnership)**

**ABC Company
(A Sole Proprietorship)**

**ABC Company
(A Division of DEF, Inc.)**

The title of the financial statement should be balance sheet unless another name is indicative of the terminology used in the industry. For example, in the securities industry, the title "Statement of Financial Condition" is used.

Finally, the last day of the month should be used as the statement date, unless the entity uses a fiscal reporting period always ending on a particular day of the week such as Friday or Sunday. In these cases, the balance sheet can appropriately be dated accordingly (i.e., December 26, October 1, etc.).

Balance sheets should generally be uniform in appearance from one period to the next. The form, terminology, captions, and pattern of combining insignificant items should be consistent.

Classification of Assets

Assets, liabilities, and stockholders' equity are separated in the balance sheet so that important relationships can be shown and attention can be focused on significant subtotals.

Current assets. Per ARB 43, Chapter 3, current assets are cash and other assets or resources commonly identified as those which are reasonably expected to be realized in cash or sold or consumed during the normal operating cycle of the business. When the cycle is less than one year, the one-year concept is traditionally adopted. However, when the operating cycle exceeds one year, the operating cycle will serve as the proper measurement period for purposes of current asset classification. When the cycle is very long, the usefulness of the concept of current assets diminishes. The following items would be classified as current assets:

1. **Cash** and cash equivalents include cash on hand consisting of coins, currency, undeposited checks; money orders and drafts; and deposits in banks. Anything accepted by a bank for deposit would be considered as cash. Cash must be available for a demand withdrawal. Assets such as certificates of deposit would not be considered cash because of the time restrictions on withdrawal. Also, cash must be available for current use in order to be classified as a current asset. Cash which is restricted in use and whose restrictions will not expire within the operating cycle or cash restricted for a noncurrent use would not be included in current assets. Per SFAS 95, cash equivalents include short-term, highly liquid investments that (a) are readily convertible to known amounts of cash and (b) are so near their maturity (original maturities of three months or less) that they present negligible risk of changes in value because of changes in interest rates. Treasury bills, commercial paper, and money market funds are all examples of cash equivalents.

2. **Short-term investments** are readily marketable securities acquired through the use of temporarily idle cash. If these are equity securities, they would be accounted for under SFAS 12. Other securities may be carried at cost, cost plus accrued interest, or lower of cost or market depending upon their nature and circumstances. The basis of reporting any differences between current market value and cost should be disclosed in the balance sheet presentation as follows:

Marketable securities (carried at lower of cost or market)	$xxx

3. **Receivables** include accounts and notes receivable, receivables from affiliate companies, and officer and employee receivables. The term "accounts receivable" represents amounts due from customers arising from transactions in the ordinary course of business. Allowances due to uncollectibility and any amounts discounted or pledged should be clearly stated. The allowances may be based upon a relationship to sales or based upon direct analysis of the receivables. If material, the receivables should be broken down into their component parts. The receivables section may be presented as follows:

Receivables:		
Accounts	$xxx	
Notes	xxx	
	xxx	
Less allowance for doubtful accounts	(xxx)	
	xxx	
Affiliate companies	xxx	
Officers and employees	xxx	$xxx

4. **Inventories** are goods on hand and available for sale. The basis of valuation and the method of pricing should be disclosed.

> Inventories--at the lower of cost
> or market (specific identification) $xxx

In the case of a manufacturing concern, raw materials, work in process, and finished goods should be disclosed separately on the balance sheet or in the footnotes.

Inventories:
Finished goods	$xxx	
Work in process	xxx	
Raw materials	xxx	$xxx

5. **Prepaid expenses** are assets created by the prepayment of cash or incurrence of a liability. They expire and become expenses with the passage of time, usage or events, e.g., prepaid rent, prepaid insurance, and deferred taxes.

Long-term investments. Investments that are intended to be held for an extended period of time (longer than one operating cycle). The following are the three major types of long-term investments:

1. **Debt and equity securities** are stocks, bonds, and long-term notes. Basis of valuation plus any premium and less any discount or allowance should be clearly shown.

Long-term investments:
Investments in A company stock	$xxx		
Less allowance for excess of cost of long-term equity securities over market value	(xxx)	$xxx	
Notes receivable	xxx		
Less discount on notes receivable	(xxx)	xxx	
Investment in B company bonds		xxx	$xxx

2. **Tangible assets** not currently used in operations.
3. **Investments held in special funds,** e.g., sinking funds, pension funds, amounts held for plant expansion, and cash surrender values of life insurance policies.

Property, plant, and equipment. Assets of a durable nature that are to be used in the production or sale of goods, sale of other assets, or rendering of services rather than being held for sale, e.g., machinery and equipment, buildings, furniture and fixtures, natural resources, and land. These should be disclosed with related accumulated depreciation/depletion as follows:

Machinery and equipment	$xxx	
Less accumulated depreciation	(xxx)	$xxx
or		
Machinery and equipment (net of $xxx		
accumulated depreciation)		$xxx

Accumulated depreciation may be shown in total or by major classes of depreciable assets. In addition to showing this amount on the balance sheet, the notes to the financial statements should contain balances of major classes of depreciable assets, by nature or function, at the balance sheet date and a general description of the method or methods used in computing depreciation with respect to major classes of depreciable assets (APB 12, para 5).

Intangible assets. Noncurrent, nonmaterialistic assets of a business, the possession of which provides anticipative benefits to the owner, e.g., goodwill, trademarks, patents, copyrights, organizational costs, etc. Generally, the amortization of an intangible asset is credited directly to the asset account, although it is acceptable to use an accumulated amortization account.

Other assets. An all-inclusive heading for accounts that do not fit neatly into any of the other asset categories, e.g., long-term prepaid expenses, deferred taxes, bond issue costs, noncurrent receivables, and restricted cash.

Classification of Liabilities

The liabilities are displayed on the balance sheet in the order of payment.

Current liabilities. Per ARB 43, Chapter 3, obligations whose liquidation is reasonably expected to require the use of existing resources properly classifiable as current assets, or the creation of current obligations. Obligations that are due on demand or which are callable at any time by the lender are classified as current regardless of the intent of the entity or lender.

1. Obligations arising from the acquisition of goods and services entering the operating cycle, e.g., accounts payable, short-term notes payable, wages payable, taxes payable, and other miscellaneous payables.
2. Collections of money in advance for the future delivery of goods or performance of services, such as rent received in advance and unearned subscription revenues.
3. Other obligations maturing within the current operating cycle to be met through the use of current assets, such as the current maturity of bonds, and long-term notes.

In two cases, obligations to be paid in the next period should not be classified as current liabilities. Debt expected to be refinanced through another long-term issue and debt that will be retired through the use of noncurrent assets, such as a bond sinking fund, are treated as noncurrent liabilities because the liquidation does not require the use of current assets or the creation of other current liabilities.

Noncurrent liabilities. Obligations that are not expected to be liquidated within the current operating cycle.

1. Obligations arising through the acquisition of assets, such as the issuance of bonds, long-term notes, and lease obligations.
2. Obligations arising out of the normal course of operations, such as pension obligations.
3. Contingent obligations involving uncertainty as to possible losses. These are resolved by the occurrence or nonoccurrence of one or more future events that confirm the amount payable, the payee, and/or the date payable, such as product warranties (see contingency section).

On all long-term liabilities the maturity date, nature of obligation, rate of interest, and any security pledged to support the agreement should be clearly shown. Also, on bonds and long-term notes, any premium or discount should be reported separately as an addition to or subtraction from the bond or note. Long-term obligations where certain covenants exist are classified as current liabilities if any of those covenants have been violated and the lender has the right to demand payment. Unless the lender expressly waives that right or the conditions causing the default are corrected, the obligation is current.

Other liabilities. Items that do not meet the definition of a liability, such as deferred income taxes or deferred investment tax credits. Many times these items will be included in current or noncurrent liabilities even though they technically are not similar.

Classification of Stockholders' Equity

Stockholders' equity is the interest of the stockholders in the assets of a corporation. It shows the cumulative net results of past transactions and other events.

Capital stock. Stock which consists of the par/stated value of preferred and common shares. The number of shares authorized, the number issued, and the number outstanding should be clearly shown. For preferred stock, the preferences and features must also be stated as follows:

> 6% cumulative preferred stock, $100 par value,
> callable at $115, 10,000 shares authorized and outstanding $xxx

> Common stock, $10 par value per share, 2,000,000 shares
> authorized, 1,500,000 shares issued and outstanding $xxx

Preferred stock which is redeemable at the option of the holder is not considered to be part of equity, but is usually shown in a separate caption between liabilities and equity.

Additional paid-in capital. There are two major categories of additional paid-in capital.

1. Paid-in capital in excess of par/stated value which is the difference between the actual issue price and par/stated value. Amounts in excess should be dis-

closed separately for common stock and each issue of preferred stock as follows:

Additional paid-in capital--6% preferred stock	$xxx
Additional paid-in capital--common stock	$xxx

2. Paid-in capital from other transactions which includes treasury stock, retirement of stock, stock dividends recorded at market, lapse of stock purchase warrants, conversion of convertible bonds in excess of the par value of the stock, and any other additional capital from the company's own stock transactions.

Donated capital. Donations of a noncash variety from either stockholders or outside parties, such as land, securities, buildings, and equipment.

Retained earnings. Accumulated earnings not distributed to the shareholders.

1. Appropriated, a certain amount of retained earnings that are not to be distributed to stockholders as dividends.
2. Unappropriated, earnings available to be distributed as dividends.

A balance sheet disclosure should reveal the pertinent provisions, source of restriction, amount subject to restriction, and restrictions on other items, such as working capital and additional borrowings. If a company appropriated retained earnings to satisfy bond indebtedness, the presentation would be as follows:

Retained earnings:		
Appropriated for bond indebtedness	$xxx	
Free and unappropriated	<u>xxx</u>	$xxx

Many corporations do not record the restrictions in appropriated and unappropriated accounts but merely explain the restrictions in the footnotes because financial statement users often believe the appropriation is held as cash. Also included in the equity section of the balance sheet is treasury stock representing issued shares reacquired by the issuer. These are generally stated at their cost of acquisition and as a reduction of shareholders' equity.

Finally, net unrealized losses on noncurrent portfolios of marketable equity securities, the excess of minimum pension liability over unrecognized prior service cost, and unrealized gains (losses) on foreign currency translations will also be shown as adjustments of equity.

Classification of Partners' Capital

In partnership accounting, the net worth section of the balance sheet includes the equity interests of the partners. Although each individual partner's capital need not be displayed, the totals for each class of partner, general or limited should be shown. Loans to or from partners should be displayed as assets and liabilities of the partnership and not as reductions or additions to partners (or stockholders in a corporation) although a separate live item on the balance sheet may be combined with net worth in a separately defined subtotal on the balance sheet. Payments to partners of interest on loans are properly classified as expenses on the income statement. Payments of interest on capital or salaries to partners are considered an allocation of profits and are usually not expensed on the income statement. However, in an attempt to emulate corporate financial reporting, some partnerships with adequate disclosure do display such payments as expenses.

Relation to the Income Statement

The balance sheet and income statement are interrelated through the changes that take place in each as a result of business transactions. Choosing a method of valuing inventory determines the method of calculating cost of goods sold. This articulation enables the users of financial information to use the statements as predictive indicators of future cash flows.

In assessing information about overall firm performance, users are interested in bringing together information in the income statement and the balance sheet. The balance sheet can also be used as a guide to give an indication of a firm's continuing ability to earn income and pay dividends. By combining the two statements, investors can develop some important financial ratios. For example, users may wish to express income as a rate of return on net operating assets.

Supplemental Disclosures

In addition to the measurement accounting principles which guide the values placed on the elements included in the balance sheet, there are disclosure accounting principles which are necessary to make the financial statements not misleading because of their omission.

The following are five techniques of disclosure:

1. Parenthetical explanations
2. Footnotes
3. Supporting schedules
4. Cross references
5. Valuation accounts

Parenthetical explanations. Supplemental information is disclosed by means of parenthetical explanations following the appropriate balance sheet items. For example:

Common stock ($10 par value, 200,000 shares
   authorized, 150,000 issued) $1,500,000

Parenthetical explanations have an advantage over both footnotes and supporting schedules. Parenthetical explanations place the disclosure in the body of the statement. The supplemental information tends to be overlooked when it is placed in a footnote.

Footnotes. If the additional information cannot be disclosed in a relatively short and concise parenthetical explanation, a footnote should be used. For example:

Inventories (see note 1)	$2,550,000

The notes to the financial statements would contain the following:

Note 1: Inventories are stated at the lower of cost or market. Cost is determined on the first-in, first-out method and market is determined on the basis of estimated net realizable value. The market value of the inventory is $2,720,000.

Supporting schedules. In order to adequately present detail about certain balance sheet items, a supporting schedule may be used. Current receivables may be a single line item on the balance sheet, as follows:

Current receivables (see Schedule 2)	$2,500,000

A separate schedule for current receivables would then be presented as follows:

Schedule 2
Current Receivables

Customers' accounts and notes	$2,000,000
Associated companies	300,000
Nonconsolidated affiliates	322,000
Other	18,000
	2,640,000
Less allowance for doubtful accounts	(140,000)
	$2,500,000

Cross references. Cross referencing is used when there is a direct relationship between two accounts on the balance sheet. For example, among the current assets, the following might be shown if $1,500,000 of accounts receivable were required to be pledged as collateral for a $1,200,000 bank loan:

Accounts receivable pledged to bank	$1,500,000

Included in the current liabilities would be the following:

Bank loan payable-secured by accounts receivable	$1,200,000

Valuation accounts are used to reduce or increase the carrying amount of some assets and liabilities found in financial statements. Accumulated depreciation reduces the book value for property, plant, and equipment, and a bond premium (discount) increases (decreases) the face value of a bond payable as shown in the following illustrations:

Equipment	$18,000,000	
Less accumulated depreciation	(1,625,000)	$16,375,000
Bonds payable	$20,000,000	
Less discount on bonds payable	(1,300,000)	$18,700,000
Bonds payable	$20,000,000	
Add premium on bonds payable	1,300,000	$21,300,000

Accounting policies. There are many different methods of valuing assets and assigning costs. Financial statement users must be aware of the accounting policies used by enterprises so that sound economic decisions can be made. Per APB 22, the disclosures should identify and describe the accounting principles followed by the entity and methods of applying those principles that materially affect the determination of financial position, changes in cash flows, or results of operations. The accounting policies should encompass those accounting principles and methods that involve the following:

1. Selection from acceptable alternatives
2. Principles and methods peculiar to the industry
3. Unique applications of GAAP

The accounting policies should be in a separate section called "Summary of Significant Accounting Policies" or be the first note of the notes to the financial statements.

Related Parties. According to SFAS 57, *Related Party Disclosures*, financial statements should include disclosure of material related party transactions other than compensation arrangements, expense allowances, or other similar items in the ordinary course of business.

A related party is essentially any party that controls or can significantly influence the management or operating policies of the company to the extent that the company may be prevented from fully pursuing its own interests. Such groups would include affiliates, investees accounted for by the equity method, trusts for the benefit of employees, principal owners, management, and immediate family members of owners or management.

Disclosures should take place even if there is no accounting recognition made for such transactions (e.g., a service is performed without payment). Disclosures should generally not imply that such related party transactions were on terms essentially equivalent to arm's-length dealings. Additionally, when one or more companies are under common control such that the financial statements might vary from those that would have been obtained if the companies were autonomous, the nature of the control relationship should be disclosed even if there are no transactions between the companies.

The disclosures generally should include:

1. Nature of relationship.
2. Description of transactions and effects of such transactions on the financial statements for each period for which an income statement is presented.

3. Dollar amount of transactions for each period for which an income statement is presented and effects of any change in establishing the terms of such transactions differently than that used in prior periods.
4. Amounts due to and from such related parties as of the date of each balance sheet presented together with the terms and manner of settlement.

Comparative statements. In order to increase the usefulness of financial statements, many companies include in their annual reports 5- or 10-year summaries of condensed financial information. These comparative statements allow investment analysts and other interested readers to perform comparative analysis of pertinent information. ARB 43, Chapter 2 states the presentation of comparative financial statements in annual reports enhances the usefulness of such reports and brings out more clearly the nature and trends of current changes affecting the enterprise. Such presentation emphasizes the fact that the statements for a series of periods are far more significant than those for a single period and that the accounts for one period are but an installment of what is essentially a continuous history.

Subsequent events. The balance sheet is dated as of the last day of the fiscal period, but a period of time may elapse before the financial statements are issued. During this period, significant events or transactions may have occurred that materially affect the company's financial position. These events and transactions are called subsequent events. Significant events occurring between the balance sheet date and issue date could make the financial statements misleading if not disclosed.

There are two types of subsequent events (SAS 1, Subsequent Events). The first type consists of those events that provide additional evidence with respect to conditions that existed at the date of the balance sheet and affect the estimates inherent in the process of preparing financial statements. The second type consists of those events that provide evidence with respect to conditions that did not exist at the date of the balance sheet being reported on but arose subsequent to that date. The first type results in adjustments of the financial statements. The second type does not require adjustment of the financial statements but may require disclosure in order to keep the financial statements from being misleading. Disclosure can be made in the form of footnotes, supporting schedules, and pro forma statements.

Examples of Subsequent Events

1. A loss on an uncollectible trade account receivable as a result of a customer's deteriorating financial condition leading to bankruptcy subsequent to the balance sheet date would be indicative of conditions existing at the balance sheet date, thereby calling for adjustment of the financial statements before their issuance. On the other hand, a loss on an uncollectible trade account receivable resulting from a customer's major casualty, such as a fire or flood subsequent to the balance sheet date, would not be indicative of conditions existing at the balance sheet date and the adjustment of the financial statements would not be appropriate. However, if the amount is material, disclosure would be required.

2. A loss arising from the recognition after the balance sheet date that an asset such as plant and equipment had suffered a material decline in value arising out of reduced marketability for the product or service it can produce. Such a reduction would be considered an economic event in process at the balance sheet date and would require adjustment and recognition of the loss.
3. The second type of events (those not existing at the balance sheet date) which require disclosure but not adjustment include the following:
    a. Sale of a bond or capital stock issue
    b. Purchase of a business
    c. Settlement of litigation when the event giving rise to the claim took place subsequent to the balance sheet date. The settlement is an economic event which would be accounted for in the period of occurrence
    d. Loss of plant or inventories as a result of fire or flood
    e. Losses on receivables resulting from conditions (such as a customer's major casualty) arising subsequent to the balance sheet date
    f. Gains or losses on certain marketable securities

Contingencies. A contingency is defined in SFAS 5 as an existing condition, situation, or set of circumstances involving uncertainty as to possible gain or loss to an enterprise that will ultimately be resolved when one or more future events occur or fail to occur. Resolution of the uncertainty may confirm the acquisition of an asset, the reduction of a liability, the loss or impairment of an asset, or the incurrence of a liability.

An estimated loss from a **loss contingency** shall be accrued by a charge to income and the recording of a liability if **both** of the following conditions are met (SFAS 5, para 8):

1. Information available prior to issuance of the financial statements indicates that it is **probable** that an asset had been impaired or a liability had been incurred at the date of the financial statements.
2. The amount of loss can be **reasonably estimated.**

The likelihood of a loss on a contingency may be broken down into the following three classifications (SFAS 5, para 3):

1. Probable, the future event or events are likely to occur.
2. Reasonably possible, the chance of the future event or events occurring is more than remote but less than likely.
3. Remote, the chance of the future event or events occurring is slight.

If the loss contingency is probable but only a range of estimated values can be made, the minimum point of the range should be accrued and the maximum point should be disclosed.

If the loss contingency is at least reasonably possible, a liability should not be recorded but disclosure is required. If feasible, that disclosure should include an estimate of the loss or range of loss. If a reasonable estimate of the loss cannot be made, that fact should be disclosed.

Certain contingencies are remote, but their disclosure is expected in financial statements because a guarantee has been given. No disclosure is required for unasserted claims or assessments when no act by the potential claimant has transpired. In addition, general or unspecific business risks are neither accrued nor disclosed.

Examples of Loss Contingencies (SFAS 5, para 4)

1. Collectibility of receivables
2. Obligations related to product warranties and product defects
3. Risk of loss or damage of enterprise property by fire, explosion, or other hazards
4. Threat of expropriation of assets
5. Pending or threatened litigation
6. Actual or possible claims and assessments
7. Risk of loss from catastrophes assumed by property and casualty insurance companies including reinsurance companies
8. Guarantees of indebtedness of other entities
9. Obligations of commercial banks under standby letters of credit
10. Agreements to repurchase receivables (or to repurchase the related property) that have been sold

Accrual and disclosure of loss contingencies should be based on an evaluation of the facts in each particular case. Accrual is not a substitute for disclosure and disclosure is not a substitute for accrual.

An estimated gain from a **gain contingency** usually is not reflected in the accounts since to do so might be to recognize revenue prior to its realization. Adequate disclosure of the gain contingency shall be made, but care must be taken to avoid misleading implications as to the likelihood of realization.

Contracts and negotiations. All significant contractual agreements and negotiations should be disclosed in the footnotes to the financial statements. For example, lease contract provisions, pension obligations, requirements contracts, bond indenture convenants, and stock option plans should be clearly disclosed in the footnotes.

Example of Balance Sheet Classification and Presentation

The system of balance sheet classification and presentations is illustrated by the following comprehensive balance sheet:

ABC Corporation
Balance Sheet
December 31, 1992

<u>*Assets*</u>

Current assets:
   Cash and bank deposits:

Restricted to current bond maturity	$xxx	
Unrestricted	<u>xxx</u>	$xxx

   Short-term investments:

Marketable equity securities (at lower of cost or market, market value, $xxx)		xxx
Marketable debt securities (at cost, market value $xxx)		xxx
Refundable income taxes		xxx
Receivables from affiliates		xxx
Accounts receivable	xxx	
Less allowance for doubtful accounts	(xxx)	xxx
Notes receivable due in 1993	xxx	
Less notes receivable discounted	(xxx)	xxx
Dishonored notes receivable		xxx
Installment notes due in 1993		xxx
Interest receivable		xxx
Creditors' accounts with debit balances		xxx
Advances to employees		xxx

   Inventories (carried at lower of cost or market by FIFO):

Finished goods	xxx	
Work in process	xxx	
Raw materials	<u>xxx</u>	xxx

   Prepaid expenses:

Prepaid rent	xxx	
Prepaid insurance	<u>xxx</u>	<u>xxx</u>
Total current assets		$xxx

Long-term investments:
   Investments in equity securities (lower
     of cost or market) $xxx
       Less allowance for excess of cost of
        long-term equity securities over
        market value   (xxx) $xxx
   Investments in equity securities (at cost, plus
    equity in undistributed net earnings since
    acquisition)   xxx
   Investments in bonds (at cost)   xxx
   Investments in unused land and facilities   xxx
   Cash surrender value of officers' life
    insurance policies   xxx
   Sinking fund for bond retirement   xxx
   Plant expansion fund   xxx
       Total long-term investments $xxx
Property, plant, and equipment:
   Land $xxx
   Buildings   xxx
   Machinery and equipment   xxx
   Furniture and fixtures   xxx
   Leasehold improvements   xxx
     Less accumulated depreciation and amortization (xxx)
       Total property, plant, and equipment $xxx
Intangible assets net of amortization:
   Excess of cost over net assets of acquired businesses $xxx
   Patents   xxx
   Trademarks   xxx
   Organization costs   xxx
       Total intangible assets, net $xxx
Other assets:
   Installment notes due after 1993 $xxx
   Unamortized bond issue costs   xxx
       Total other noncurrent assets $xxx
Total assets $xxx

Liabilities and Stockholders' Equity

Current liabilities:

Commercial paper and other short-term notes	$xxx		
Accounts payable	xxx		
Salaries, wages, and commissions	xxx		
Taxes withheld from employees	xxx		
Income taxes payable	xxx		
Dividends payable	xxx		
Rent revenue collected in advance	xxx		
Other advances from customers	xxx		
Current portion of long-term debt	xxx		
Current obligations under capital leases	xxx		
Deferred tax liability	xxx		
Short-term portion of accrued warranty	xxx		
Other accrued liabilities	xxx		
Total current liabilities			$xxx

Noncurrent liabilities:

Notes payable due after 1993	$xxx		
Plus unamortized note premium	xxx	$xxx	
Long-term bonds:			
10% debentures due 2005	xxx		
9-1/2% collateralized obligations maturing serially to 1996	xxx		
8% convertible subordinated debentures due 2010	xxx		
Less unamortized discounts net of premiums	(xxx)	xxx	
Accrued pension cost		xxx	
Obligations under capital leases		xxx	
Deferred tax liability		xxx	
Long-term portion of accrued warranty		xxx	
Total noncurrent liabilities			$xxx
Total liabilities			$xxx

Liabilities and Stockholders' Equity (continued)

Capital stock:

$12.50 convertible preferred stock, $100 stated value, 200,000 shares authorized, 175,000 outstanding	$xxx	
12% cumulative preferred stock, $100 stated value, callable at $115, 100,000 shares authorized and outstanding	xxx	
Common stock, $10 stated value, 500,000 shares authorized, 450,000 issued, 15,000 held in treasury	xxx	
Common stock subscribed 10,000 shares	xxx	
Less: Subscriptions receivable	(xxx)	$xxx

Additional paid-in capital

From 12% cumulative preferred	xxx	
From common stock	xxx	
From treasury stock transactions	xxx	
From stock dividends	xxx	
From expiration of stock options	xxx	
Warrants outstanding	xxx	xxx

Donated capital:

Securities donated by shareholders	xxx	
Land donated by government municipalities	xxx	xxx

Retained earnings:

Appropriated for bond indebtedness	xxx	
Free and unappropriated	xxx	xxx
		xxx

Less: Treasury stock at cost	(xxx)	
Net unrealized loss on noncurrent marketable equity securities	(xxx)	
Unrealized loss from foreign currency translation	(xxx)	
Excess of minimum pension liability over unrecognized prior service cost	(xxx)	(xxx)
Total stockholders' equity		$xxx
Total liabilities and stockholders' equity		$xxx

Disclosures

(See the detailed Disclosure Checklist in the Appendix at the back of this book.)

3 Income Statement

Perspective and Issues

The income statement, also referred to as the statement of income, statement of earnings, or statement of operations, summarizes the results of an entity's economic activities for an accounting period. Since at least the early 1960s, the income statement has been widely perceived by investors, creditors, management, and other interested parties as the most important of an enterprise's basic financial statements. Investors consider the past income of a business as the most useful predictor of future earnings performance. Consequently, past income is generally considered the best indicator of future dividends and market stock price performance. Creditors look to the income statement for insight into the borrower's ability to generate the future cash flows needed to repay the obligations. Management must be concerned with the income statement by virtue of the fact that it is of concern to investors and creditors. Additionally, management uses the income statement as a gauge of its effectiveness and efficiency in combining the factors of production into the goods and/or services which it sells.

Much of current accounting theory is concerned with the measurement of income. Even with the renewed interest in the balance sheet, the income statement remains of paramount importance to the majority of financial statement users. This chapter will focus on key income measurement issues and on matters of income statement presentation and disclosure.

Sources of GAAP

ARB	_APB_	_APB Statements_	_SFAC_	_SFAS_	_TB_
43, Ch. 2	9, 11, 15, 16, 18, 20, 30	4	5, 6	4, 16, 64	85-6

Definitions of Terms

Elements of Financial Statements

Comprehensive income. The change in equity of an entity during a period from transactions and other events and circumstances from nonowner sources. It includes all changes in equity during a period, except those resulting from investments by owners and distributions to owners (SFAC 6).

Distribution to owners. Decreases in net assets of a particular enterprise resulting from transferring assets, rendering services, or incurring liabilities by the enterprise to owners.

Distributions to owners reduce the ownership interest of the receiving owners in the entity and reduce the net assets of the entity by the amount of the distribution. Such transactions are displayed in the statement of changes in equity.

Expenses. Decreases in assets or increases in liabilities during a period resulting from delivery of goods, rendering of services, or other activities constituting the enterprise's central operations (SFAC 6).

Gains. Increases in equity (net assets) from peripheral or incidental transactions of an entity and from all other transactions and other events and circumstances affecting the entity during a period except those that result from revenues or investments by owners (SFAC 6).

Investments by owners. Increases in net assets of a particular enterprise resulting from transfers to it of something valuable to obtain or increase ownership interests (or equity) in it.

Investments by owners may be in the form of assets, services, or the payment of entity liabilities. These investments are displayed in the statement of changes in equity. The purchase of an ownership interest from another owner is not a net investment because such a transfer does not increase the net assets of the entity.

Losses. Decreases in equity (net assets) from peripheral or incidental transactions of an entity from all other transactions and other events and circumstances affecting the entity during a period except those that result from expenses or distributions to owners (SFAC 6).

Revenues. Increases in assets or decreases in liabilities during a period from delivering goods, rendering services, or other activities constituting the enterprise's central operations (SFAC 6).

Other Terminology

Disposal date. The date of closing the sale if the disposal is by sale or the date that operations cease if disposal is by abandonment (APB 30).

Extraordinary item. Events and transactions that are distinguished by their unusual nature and by the infrequency of their occurrence (APB 30).

Measurement date. The date on which the management having the authority to approve the action commits itself to a formal plan to dispose of a segment of the business, whether by sale or abandonment (APB 30).

Realization. The process of converting noncash resources and rights into money or, more precisely, the sale of an asset for cash or claims to cash (SFAC 6).

Recognition. The process of formally recording or incorporating an item in the financial statements of an entity (SFAC 6).

Segment of a business. A component of an entity whose activities represent a major line of business or class of customer. A segment may be in the form of a subsidiary, a division, or a department, and in some cases, a joint venture or other non-subsidiary investee. Its assets, results of operations, and activities can be clearly distinguished, physically and operationally, and for financial reporting purposes, from the other assets, results of operations, and activities of the entity (APB 30).

Concepts, Rules, and Examples

Concepts of Income

Economists have generally adopted a wealth maintenance concept of income. Under this concept, income is the maximum amount that can be consumed during a period and still leave the enterprise with the same amount of wealth at the end of the period as existed at the beginning. Wealth is determined with reference to the current market values of the net productive assets at the beginning and end of the period. Therefore, the economists' definition of income would fully incorporate market value changes (both increases and decreases in wealth) in the determination of periodic income.

Accountants, on the other hand, have generally defined income by reference to specific events which give rise to recognizable elements of revenue and expense during a reporting period. The events that produce reportable items of revenue and expense are a subset of economic events that determine economic income. Many changes in the market values of wealth components are deliberately excluded from the measurement of accounting income, but are included in the measurement of economic income.

The discrepancy between the accounting and economic measures of income are the result of a preference on the part of accountants and financial statement users for information which is reliable. Since many fluctuations in the market values of assets are matters of conjecture, accountants have retained the historical cost model which generally precludes the recognition of market value changes until realized by a transaction. Similarly, both accountants and economists realize that the earnings process occurs throughout the various stages of production, sales, and final delivery of the product. However, the difficulty in measuring the precise rate at which this earnings process is taking place has led accountants to conclude that income should normally be recognized only when it is fully realized. Realization generally implies that the enterprise producing the item has completed all of its obligations relating to the product and that collection of the resulting receivable is assured beyond reasonable doubt. For very sound reasons, accountants have developed a reliable system of income recognition which is based on generally accepted accounting principles applied consistently from period to period. The interplay between recognition and realization generally means that values on the balance sheet are recognized only when realized through an income statement transaction.

A separate, but equally important, reason for the disparity between the accounting and economic measures of income relates to the need for periodic reporting. The economic measure of income would be relatively simple to apply on a life cycle basis. Economic income would be measured by the difference between its wealth at the termination point versus its wealth at the origination date, plus withdrawals or other distributions and minus additional investments over the course of its life. However, applying the same measurement strategy to discrete fiscal periods, as accountants do, is much more difficult. The continual earnings process, in which the earnings of a business occur throughout the various stages of production and delivery of a product, is conceptually straight-forward. Allocating those earnings to individual years, quarters, or months is substantially more difficult, requiring both estimates and judgment. Consequently, accountants have concluded that there must be unambiguous guidelines for revenue recognition. These have required recognition only at the completion of the earnings cycle.

The appropriate measurement of income is partially dependent upon the perspective of the party doing the measuring. From the perspective of the outside investors taken as a whole, income might be defined as earnings before any payments to those investors, including bondholders and preferred stockholders as well as common shareholders. On the other hand, from the perspective of the common shareholders, income might better be defined as earnings after payments to other investors, including creditors and preferred shareholders. Currently, net income is defined as earnings available for the preferred and common stockholders. However, in various statistics and special reports, a variety of these concepts is employed.

Recognition and Measurement

The definition of accounting income as a subset of economic income requires certain recognition criteria. The criteria are needed to assist accountants in determining which economic events are in the domain of items included in the measurement of income. SFAC 5 has identified four recognition criteria. They are the following:

1. **Definition**--To be recognized, the item must meet one of the definitions of an element of the financial statements. A resource must meet the definition of an asset; an obligation must meet the definition of a liability; and a change in equity must meet the definition of a revenue, expense, gain, loss, investment by owner, or distribution to owner.

2. **Measurability**--The item must have a relevant attribute that can be quantified in monetary units with sufficient reliability. Measurability must be considered in

terms of both relevance and reliability, the two primary qualitative character-istics of accounting information.

3. **Relevance**--An item is relevant if the information about it has the capacity to make a difference in investors', creditors', or other users' decisions.
4. **Reliability**--An item is reliable if the information about it is representationally faithful, verifiable, and neutral. The information must be faithful in its represen-tation, free of error, and unbiased.

In order to be given accounting recognition, an asset, liability, or change in equity would have to meet the four above-mentioned criteria.

Revenues. According to SFAC 6, para 78:

Revenues are increases in assets or decreases in liabilities during a period from delivering goods, rendering services, or other activities constituting the enterprise's central operations. Characteristics of revenues (SFAC 6, para 79) include the following:

1. *A culmination of the earnings process*
2. *Actual or expected cash inflows resulting from central operations*
3. *Inflows reported gross*

The realization concept stipulates that revenue is only recognized when the follow-ing occur:

1. The earnings process is complete or virtually complete.
2. Revenue is evidenced by the existence of an exchange transaction which has taken place.

The existence of an exchange transaction is critical to the accounting recognition of revenue. Generally, it means that a sale to an outside party has occurred, resulting in the receipt of cash or the obligation by the purchaser to make future payment for the item received.

However, an exchange transaction is viewed in a broader sense than the legal concept of a sale. Whenever an exchange of rights and privileges takes place, an ex-change transaction is deemed to have occurred. For example, interest revenue and interest expense are earned or incurred ratably over a period without a discrete trans-action taking place. Accruals are recorded periodically in order to reflect the interest realized by the passage of time. In a like manner, the percentage-of-completion method recognizes revenue based upon the measure of progress on a long-term con-struction project. The earnings process is considered to occur simultaneously with the measure of progress, e.g., the incurrence of costs.

The conditions for the timing of revenue recognition would also be varied if the production of certain commodities takes place in environments in which the ultimate realization of revenue is so assured that it can be recognized upon the completion of the production process. At the opposite extreme is the situation in which the exchange transaction has taken place, but significant uncertainty exists as to the ultimate collectibility of the amount. For example, in certain sales of real estate, where the down payment percentage is extremely small and the security for the buyer's notes is minimal, revenue is often not recognized until the time collections are actually received.

Expenses. According to SFAC 6, para 80:

> *Expenses* are decreases in assets or increases in liabilities during a period resulting from delivery of goods, rendering of services, or other activities constituting the enterprise's central operations. Characteristics of expenses (SFAC 6, para 81) include the following:
>
> 1. Sacrifices involved in carrying out the earnings process
> 2. Actual or expected cash outflows resulting from central operations
> 3. Outflows reported gross

Expenses are expired costs, or items which were assets but which are no longer assets because they have no future value. The matching principle requires that all expenses incurred in the generating of revenue should be recognized in the same accounting period as the revenues are recognized. The matching principle is broken down into three pervasive measurement principles--associating cause and effect, systematic and rational allocation, and immediate recognition.

Costs, such as materials and direct labor consumed in the manufacturing process, are relatively easy to identify with the related revenue elements. These cost elements are included in inventory and expensed as cost of sales when the product is sold and revenue from the sale is recognized. This is associating cause and effect.

Some costs are more closely associated with specific accounting periods. In the absence of a cause and effect relationship, the asset's cost should be allocated to benefiting accounting periods in a systematic and rational manner. This form of expense recognition involves assumptions about the expected length of benefit and the relationship between benefit and cost of each period. Depreciation of fixed assets, amortization of intangibles, and allocation of rent and insurance are examples of costs that would be recognized by the use of a systematic and rational method.

All other costs are normally expensed in the period in which they are incurred. This would include those costs for which no clear-cut future benefits can be identified, costs that were recorded as assets in prior periods but for which no remaining future benefits can be identified, and those other elements of administrative or general expense for which no rational allocation scheme can be devised. The general approach is first to attempt to match costs with the related revenues. Next, a method of systematic and rational allocation should be attempted. If neither of these measurement principles is beneficial, the cost should be immediately expensed.

Gains and losses. According to SFAC 6, paras 82 and 83:

*Gains (losses) are increases (decreases) in equity from peripheral trans-
actions of an entity excluding revenues (expenses) and investments by
owners (distribution to owners). Characteristics of gains and losses
(SFAC 6, paras 84-86) include the following:*

1. *Result from peripheral transactions and circumstances which
   may be beyond entity's control*
2. *May be classified according to sources or as operating and non-
   operating*

According to SFAC 5, the recognition of gains and losses should follow the principles stated below.

1. *Gains often result from transactions, and other events, that involve
   no "earnings process"; therefore, in terms of recognition, it is more
   significant that the gain be realized than earned.*
2. *Losses are recognized when it becomes evident that future economic benefits of a previously recognized asset have been reduced
   or eliminated, or that a liability has been incurred without associated
   economic benefits. The main difference between expenses and
   losses is that expenses result from ongoing major or central operations, whereas losses result from peripheral transactions that may be
   beyond the entity's control.*

Comprehensive Income. SFAC 6, para 70 summarizes the income concept by
defining comprehensive income as follows:

*Comprehensive income is the change in equity of an entity during a pe-
riod from transactions and other events and circumstances from
nonowner sources. It includes all changes in equity during a period, except those resulting from investments by owners and distributions to
owners.*

Comprehensive income arises from the following:

1. Exchange transactions between the entity and entities other than the owners
2. Production, including manufacturing, storing, transporting, lending, insurance,
   and professional services
3. Environmental activities due to the economic, legal, social, political, and physical environment (price changes and casualties)

Comprehensive income consists of two components: revenues/expenses and
gains/losses. The components are distinguished because they differ in stability, risk,
and predictability. These two components may be further divided into intermediate

measures such as gross margin, contribution margin, income from continuing operations before taxes, and income from continuing operations.

Notwithstanding the definition of comprehensive income in SFAC 6, income statements prepared in accordance with GAAP presently exclude certain changes in equity from nonowner sources. Prior period adjustments, market value changes in noncurrent portfolios of marketable equity securities, and certain currency translation gains or losses are excluded. However, these clearly represent exceptions to the general principle that all items of revenue and expense be reported in the statement of income.

Income Statement Classification and Presentation

Income statements measure economic performance for a **period of time** and, except for this variation, follow the same basic rule for headings and titles as do balance sheets. The legal name of the entity must be used to identify the financial statements and the title "Income Statement" to denote preparation in accordance with generally accepted accounting principles. If a comprehensive basis of accounting is used, such as the cash or income tax basis, the title of the statement should be modified accordingly. "Statement of Revenue and Expenses--Income Tax Basis" or "Statement of Revenue and Expense--Modified Cash Basis" are examples of such titles.

The date of an income statement must clearly identify the time period involved, such as "Year Ending March 31, 1992." This dating informs the reader of the length of the period covered by the statement and both the starting and ending dates. Dating such as "The Period Ending March 31, 1992" or "Through March 31, 1992" would be a violation of accounting principles because of the lack of precise definition in these titles. Income statements are rarely presented for periods in excess of one year but are frequently seen for shorter periods such as a month or a quarter. Entities whose operations form a natural cycle may have a reporting period end on a specific day (e.g., the last Friday of the month). These entities should head the income statement "For the 52 Weeks Ended March 28, 1992" (each week containing 7 days, beginning on a Saturday and ending on a Friday). Such entities' fiscal year only includes 364 days but is still considered an annual reporting period.

Income statements should be uniform both with respect to the appearance and the categories of income and expense accounts, from one time period through the next. Aggregation of items should not serve to conceal significant information, such as netting revenues against expenses or combining elements of interest to readers such as bad debts, depreciation, etc. The category "Other or Miscellaneous Expense" should contain, at maximum, an immaterial total amount of aggregated insignificant elements. Once this total approaches 10% of total expenses, some other aggregations with explanatory titles should be selected.

The major components and items required to be presented in the income statement are as follows:

1. Income from continuing operations

    a. Sales or revenues
    b. Cost of goods sold
    c. Operating expenses
    d. Gains and losses
    e. Other revenues and expenses
    f. Unusual or infrequent items
    g. Income tax expense related to continuing operations

2. Results from discontinued operations

    a. Income (loss) from operations of a discontinued segment (net of tax)
    b. Gain (loss) from disposal of discontinued segment (net of tax)

3. Extraordinary items (net of tax)
4. Cumulative effect of a change in accounting principles (net of tax)
5. Net income
6. Earnings per share

Income from continuing operations. This section summarizes the revenues and expenses of the company's central operations.

1. **Sales or revenues** are charges to customers for the goods and/or services provided during the period. This section should include information about discounts, allowances, and returns in order to determine net sales or net revenues.
2. **Cost of goods sold** is the cost of the inventory items sold during the period. In the case of a merchandising firm, net purchases (purchases less discounts, returns, and allowances plus freight-in) are added to beginning inventory to get cost of goods available for sale. From the cost of goods available for sale amount, the ending inventory is deducted to get cost of goods sold.

Example of Schedule of Cost of Goods Sold

ABC Merchandising Company
Schedule of Cost of Goods Sold
For the Year Ended 12/31/X4

Beginning inventory			$xxx
Add: Purchases		$xxx	
Freight-in		xxx	
Cost of purchases		xxx	
Less: Purchase discounts	$xx		
Purchase R & A	xx	(xxx)	
Net purchases			xxx
Cost of goods available for sale			xxx
Less: Ending inventory			(xxx)
Cost of goods sold			$xxx

A manufacturing company computes the cost of goods sold in a slightly different way. Cost of goods manufactured would be added to the beginning inventory to arrive at cost of goods available for sale. The ending inventory is then deducted from the cost of goods available for sale to determine the cost of goods sold. Cost of goods manufactured can be computed as follows:

Example of Schedules of Cost of Goods Manufactured and Sold

XYZ Manufacturing Company
Schedule of Cost of Goods Manufactured
For the Year Ended 12/31/X4

Direct materials inventory 1/1/X4	$xxx	
Purchases of materials (including freight-in		
and deducting purchase discounts)	xxx	
Total direct materials available	$xxx	
Direct materials inventory 12/31/X4	(xxx)	
Direct materials used		$xxx
Direct labor		xxx
Factory overhead:		
Depreciation of factory equipment	$xxx	
Utilities	xxx	
Indirect factory labor	xxx	
Indirect materials	xxx	
Other overhead items	xxx	xxx
Manufacturing cost incurred in 19X4		$xxx
Add: Work in process 1/1/X4		xxx
Less: Work in process 12/31/X4		(xxx)
Cost of goods manufactured		$xxx

XYZ Manufacturing Company
Schedule of Cost of Goods Sold
For the Year Ended 12/31/X4

Finished goods inventory 1/1/X4	$xxx
Add: Cost of goods manufactured	xxx
Cost of goods available for sale	$xxx
Less: Finished goods inventory 12/31/X4	(xxx)
Cost of goods sold	$xxx

3. **Operating expenses** are primary recurring costs associated with central operations (other than cost of goods sold) that are incurred in order to generate sales. Operating expenses are normally reported in the following two categories:

   a. Selling expenses
   b. General and administrative expenses

   Selling expenses are those expenses directly related to the company's efforts to generate sales, e.g., sales salaries, commissions, advertising, delivery expenses, depreciation of store furniture and equipment, and store supplies. General and administrative expenses are expenses related to the general administration of the company's operations, e.g., officers and office salaries, office supplies, depreciation of office furniture and fixtures, telephone, postage, accounting and legal services, and business licenses and fees.

4. **Gains and losses** stem from the peripheral transactions of the entity. These items are shown with the normal, recurring revenues and expenses. If they are material, they should be disclosed separately and shown above income (loss) from continuing operations before income taxes. Examples are writedowns of inventories and receivables, effects of a strike, and gains and losses from exchange or translation of foreign currencies.

5. **Other revenues and expenses** are revenues and expenses not related to the central operations of the company, e.g., gains and losses on the disposal of equipment, interest revenues and expenses, and dividend revenues.

6. **Unusual or infrequent** items are items which are either unusual or infrequent, but not both. They should be reported as a separate component of income from continuing operations.

7. **Income tax expense** related to continuing operations is that portion of the total income tax expense applicable to continuing operations.

Results from discontinued operations. Discontinued operations represent separately identifiable segments (components of a major class of business with separately identifiable assets, liabilities, revenues, and expenses) which are being disposed of. The discontinued operations section of an income statement consists of two components, the Income (loss) from operations and the Gain (loss) on the disposal. The first component, Income (loss) from operations, is disclosed for the current year only if the decision to discontinue operations is made after the beginning of the fiscal year for which the financial statements are being prepared. In the diagram below, the Income (loss) from operations component is determined for the time period designated by A-- the period from the beginning of the year to the date the decision is made to discontinue a segment's operations (measurement date). The second component, Gain (loss) on disposal consists of the following two elements:

1. Income (loss) from operations during the phase-out period (the period between the measurement date and disposal date), B in the diagram below
2. Gain (loss) from disposal of segment assets

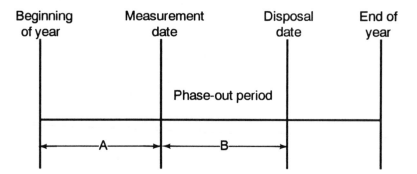

After it has been determined that certain discontinued operations constitute the disposal of a segment in accordance with APB 30, results of the discontinued segment must be segregated from normal, recurring operations. The allocation of interest to discontinued operations is permitted but not required. The maximum allocation cannot exceed the total of (a) interest on debt of the discontinued operation assumed by the buyer and (b) an allocated share of other interest not attributable to any other operations. If a loss is expected from the proposed sale or abandonment of a segment, the estimated loss should be provided for at the measurement date. If a gain is expected, it should be recognized when realized, which ordinarily is the disposal date. The results of discontinued operations should be disclosed separately as a component of income before extraordinary items and the cumulative effect of accounting changes (if applicable) as shown below.

Example of Income Statement Presentation for Discontinued Operations

Income from continuing operations before income taxes		$xxxx
Provisions for income taxes		xxx
Income from continuing operations		$xxxx
Discontinued operations (Note __):		
Income (loss) from operations of discontinued Division X (less applicable income taxes of $__)	$xxxx	
Loss on disposal of Division X, including provision of $__ for operating losses during phase-out period (less applicable income taxes of $__)	(xxxx)	xxxx
Net income		$xxxx

There are special rules for situations in which the disposal date occurs in the year after the measurement date. The problem is one of estimating the unrealized Gain (loss) on disposal for that part of the phase-out period which is in the following year and comparing it to the actual Gain (loss) on disposal that has **already been realized** at the end of the preceding year for which the financial statements are being prepared. The following two rules apply to this situation.

1. A realized Loss on disposal may be increased by an estimated loss, or it may be reduced by an estimated gain (but only to zero).
2. A realized Gain on disposal may be reduced by an estimated loss but cannot be increased due to an estimated gain.

The diagram below depicts the relationships discussed above:

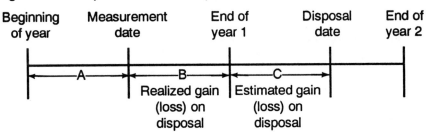

To find the year-end gain (loss), the amounts for B and C are compared and adjusted using the rules stated above.

Example of Computing the Year-End Gain (Loss) on Disposal

Assume the following:

1. Loss from operations from beginning of year to the measurement date, $699, net of taxes of $466
2. Realized loss from operations from measurement date to end of current year, $400, net of taxes of $267
3. Estimated loss from operations from year end to disposal date, $200, net of taxes of $133
   Estimated gain from disposal of assets during next year, $500, net of taxes of $333

The loss from operations of the discontinued segment represents the first component of discontinued operations and is to be shown net of tax. Items 2 and 3 above are to be reported as the second component of discontinued operations: $667 loss realized during phase-out period minus the $300 estimated **net** gain to be realized in the next period (estimated gain on disposal less the estimated loss from operations). The income statement presentation would be as follows:

Income from continuing operations before provision for income taxes	$598	
Provision for income taxes	239	
Income from continuing operations		$359
Discontinued operations:		
Loss from operations of discontinued Division Z (less applicable taxes of $466)	(699)	
Loss on disposal of Division Z including operating losses during phase-out period of $1,000 and gain on disposal of assets of $833, net of applicable taxes of $67	(100)	(799)
Net loss		$(440)

When discontinued operations are disclosed in a comparative income statement, the income statement presented for each previous year must be adjusted retroactively to enhance comparability with the current year's income statement. Accordingly, the revenues, cost of goods sold, and operating expenses (including income taxes) for the discontinued segment are removed from the revenues, cost of goods sold, and operating expenses of continuing operations. These items are netted into one figure [i.e., income (loss) from operations] which is disclosed under the discontinued operations section.

Example of Comparative Income Statement Disclosure

Assume the following:

1. The 19X4 information is from the preceding example.
2. The 19X3 information is given as shown.

	19X4	19X3
Discontinued operations:		
Loss from operations of discontinued Division Z, net of applicable taxes of $466	$699	$820
Loss on disposal of assets of discontinued Division Z, including loss during phase-out period, net of applicable taxes of $67	100	--

Example of Computing and Presenting Income from Discontinued Operations

Assume the following:

1. Income from operations is $400,000
2. The following net of tax figures are given where:

A -- is the income (loss) **from operations** of Discontinued Segment X, net of taxes, in 1992.

B_1 -- is the (loss) gain on **disposal of assets** of Discontinued Segment X, net of taxes, **excluding** operating losses or gains during the phase-out period in 1992.

B_2 -- is the **operating** (loss) gain net of taxes, during the phase-out period in 1992.

C_1 -- is the (loss) gain on **disposal of assets** of Discontinued Segment X, net of taxes, **excluding** operating losses or gains during the phase-out period in 1993.

C_2 -- is the **operating** (loss) gain during the phase-out period in 1993, net of taxes.

	Case 1	*Case 2*	*Case 3*	*Case 4*	*Case 5*	*Case 6*
A	$ 50,000	$ 50,000	$ 50,000	$(50,000)	$(50,000)	$(50,000)
B_1	100,000	100,000	(100,000)	100,000	(100,000)	(100,000)
B_2	60,000	(110,000)	(60,000)	(40,000)	110,000	90,000
C_1	(80,000)	(80,000)	80,000	80,000	60,000	(10,000)
C_2	10,000	70,000	(70,000)	(70,000)	(80,000)	80,000

The trick is to net B_1 with B_2 and C_1 with C_2 before potential netting of the B's with the C's. Then the cases simplify, as follows:

	Case 1	*Case 2*	*Case 3*	*Case 4*	*Case 5*	*Case 6*
A	$ 50,000	$ 50,000	$ 50,000	$(50,000)	$(50,000)	$(50,000)
B	160,000	(10,000)	(160,000)	60,000	10,000	(10,000)
C	(70,000)	(10,000)	10,000	10,000	(20,000)	70,000

Note that in Case 4, the $10,000 expected gain cannot be recognized since it will not be realized until 1993. The gain was recognized in Case 3 because it offset the actual loss incurred. In Case 6 when the $70,000 anticipated gain is used to offset losses, only $10,000 can be used and $60,000 is delayed until the next year.

Now income statements can be readily prepared:

	Case 1	*Case 2*	*Case 3*	*Case 4*	*Case 5*	*Case 6*
Income from contin- uing operations (net of taxes)	$400,000	$400,000	$400,000	$400,000	$400,000	$400,000
Discontinued operations (net of taxes) Income (loss) from operations of dis- continued Division X	$ 50,000	$ 50,000	$ 50,000	$ (50,000)	$ (50,000)	$ (50,000)
Gain (loss) on dis- posal of Division X, including provision for operating losses during phase-out period	90,000	(20,000)	(150,000)	60,000	(10,000)	--
Total	$140,000	$ 30,000	$(100,000)	$ 10,000	$ (60,000)	$ (50,000)
Net income (or income before extraordinary items and accounting changes) in 1992	$540,000	$430,000	$300,000	$410,000	$340,000	$350,000
Income to be reported in 1993	$ --	$ --	$ --	$ 10,000	$ --	$ 60,000

When amounts actually realized differ from estimates, differences between estimated and actual amounts shall be treated as changes in accounting estimates.
These are reported net-of-tax on the appropriate line in the "discontinued operations"
section of the income statement in the period realized. Amounts previously reported
are not revised.

In addition to the amounts that should be disclosed in the financial statements, the
notes to financial statements for the period encompassing the measurement date
should disclose the following:

1. The identity of the segment of business that has been or will be discontinued
2. The expected disposal date
3. The expected manner of disposal
4. A description of the remaining assets and liabilities of the segment at the
   balance sheet date
5. The income or loss from operations and any proceeds from disposal of the
   segment during the period from the measurement date to the balance sheet
   date

Later periods, which include the period of disposal in financial statements, should disclose items 1, 2, 3, and 4.

Extraordinary items. Both of the following criteria must be met to classify an event or transaction as an extraordinary item. APB 30, para 20 defines these criteria as follows:

Unusual nature

> *The underlying event or transaction should possess a high degree of abnormality and be of a type clearly unrelated to, or only incidentally related to, the ordinary and typical activities of the entity, taking into account the environment in which the entity operates.*

Special characteristics of the entity include the following:

1. Type and scope of operations
2. Lines of business
3. Operating policies

Infrequency of occurrence

> *The underlying event or transaction should be of a type that would not reasonably be expected to recur in the foreseeable future, taking into account the environment in which the entity operates.*

In addition, accounting pronouncements have specifically required the following items to be disclosed as extraordinary, even though they do not meet the criteria stated above:

1. Material gains and losses from the extinguishment of debt (SFAS 4, para 8). Does not apply, however, to gains and losses from extinguishments of debt made to satisfy sinking-fund requirements that an enterprise must meet within one year of the date of extinguishment (SFAS 64, para 4).
2. Profit or loss resulting from the disposal of a significant part of the assets or a separable segment of previously separate companies, provided the profit or loss is material and the disposal is within two years after a pooling of interest (APB 16, para 60).
3. Write-off of operating rights of motor carriers (SFAS 44, para 6).
4. The investor's share of an investee's extraordinary item when the investor uses the equity method of accounting for the investee (APB 18, para 19).
5. Gains of a debtor related to a troubled debt restructuring (SFAS 15, para 21).

Per FASB Technical Bulletin 85-6, neither the cost incurred by a company to defend itself from a takeover attempt nor the cost incurred as part of a "standstill" agreement meet the criteria for extraordinary classifications as discussed in para 20, SFAS 30.

Extraordinary items should be segregated from the results of ordinary operations and be shown net of taxes in a separate section of the income statement, following "discontinued operations" and preceding "cumulative effect of a change in accounting principle," if any.

Example of the Income Statement Presentation for Extraordinary Items

An extraordinary item would be presented as follows:

Income before extraordinary items	$xxx
Extraordinary items (less applicable	
income taxes of $__) (Note __)	xxx
Net income	$xxx

Accounting changes. A change in accounting principles results from adoption of a generally accepted accounting principle different from the one previously used for reporting purposes. The term **accounting principle** includes not only accounting principles and practices, but also the methods of applying them. Changes in accounting principles (or the method of applying them) must be justified by those who make the change (the firm's management), unless they are made in order to comply with a FASB position. (See Chapter 19 for a detailed discussion of accounting changes.)

Example of Disclosure for a Change in Accounting Principle

ABC Company
Income Statement
For the Year Ended December 31, 1992

	1992	1991
Income before cumulative effect of a change in accounting principle	$xxx	$xxx
Cumulative effect on prior years (to 12/31/91) of changing to (change described) (net of $__ tax)	xxx	
Net income	$xxx	$xxx
Per share amounts (simple capital structure)		
Income before cumulative effect of a change in accounting principle	$xxx	$xxx
Cumulative effect on prior years (to 12/31/91) of changing to (change described)	xxx	
Earnings per share common	$xxx	$xxx
Pro forma amounts assuming the new (change principle) is applied retroactively:		
Net income	$xxx	$xxx
Earnings per share	$xxx	$xxx

Earnings per share. Earnings per share is often used in evaluating a firm's stock price and in assessing the firm's future earnings and ability to pay dividends. Because of the importance of earnings per share, the profession has concluded that it should be disclosed on the face of the income statement.

Earnings per share is a very compact indicator of a company's performance. In order to better assess the quality of a firm's earnings, the Accounting Principles Board, through APBs 15, 20, and 30, required per share information to be disclosed for Income from continuing operations, Income before extraordinary items and cumulative effect of accounting changes, Cumulative effect of changes in accounting principles, and Net income. Per share amounts for Results from discontinued operations and extraordinary items are optional because they can be computed through simple arithmetic. A detailed discussion regarding the principles and computations involved can be found in Chapter 17.

Example of the Presentation and Computation of Earnings Per Share

Assume that 100,000 shares were outstanding throughout the year.

ABC Company
Income Statement
For the Year Ended December 31, 1992

Sales		$2,000,000
Cost of goods sold		750,000
Gross profit		$1,250,000
Selling and administrative expenses		500,000
Income from operations		$ 750,000
Other revenues and expense		
Interest income	$ 40,000	
Interest expense	(30,000)	10,000
Income before unusual or infrequent items and income taxes		$ 760,000
Unusual or infrequent items:		
Loss from permanent impairment of value of manufacturing facilities		(10,000)
Income from continuing operations before income taxes		$ 750,000
Income taxes		300,000
Income from continuing operations		$ 450,000
Discontinued operations:		
Income from operations of Division X, less applicable income taxes of $20,000	$ 30,000	
Loss on disposal of Division X, less applicable income taxes of $40,000	(60,000)	(30,000)
Income before extraordinary item and cumulative effect of accounting change		$ 420,000
Extraordinary item--loss from earthquake less applicable income taxes of $8,000		(12,000)
Cumulative effect in prior years of retroactive application of new depreciation method, less applicable income taxes of $40,000		(60,000)
Net income		$ 348,000

Per share of common stock	
Income from continuing operations	$4.50
Income before extraordinary item and cumulative effect	4.20
Cumulative effect of change in accounting principle, net of tax	(0.60)
Net income	$3.48

Format of Income Statement

There are two generally accepted formats for the presentation of income from continuing operations: the single-step and the multiple-step forms.

In the single-step form, items are classified into two groups: revenues and expenses. The operating revenues and other revenues are itemized and summed to determine total revenues. The cost of goods sold, operating expenses, and other expenses are itemized and summed to determine total expenses. The total expenses (including income taxes) are deducted from the total revenues to get net income (this title will vary depending upon the occurrence of discontinued operations, extraordinary items, or accounting changes).

Example of Single-Step Income Statement Format

ABC Company
Income Statement
For the Year Ended 12/31/X4

Revenues:		
Sales (net of discounts and returns and allowances)	$xxx	
Gain on sale of equipment	xxx	
Interest income	xxx	
Dividend income	xxx	$xxx
Expenses:		
Cost of goods sold	$xxx	
Selling expenses	xxx	
General and administrative expenses	xxx	
Interest expense	xxx	xxx
Income before unusual or infrequent items and income taxes		xxx
Unusual or infrequent items:		
Loss on sale of equipment		xxx
Income before income taxes		xxx
Income taxes		xxx
Net income		xxx
Earnings per share		$x.xx

Many accountants believe that intermediate groups and subtotals show significant relationships that assist in interpreting the income statement and advocate a multiple-step format. They believe that income statement users may be misled when operating and nonoperating activities are combined in a single-step income statement. In a multiple-step income statement, operating revenues and expenses are separated from nonoperating revenues and expenses to provide more information concerning the firm's primary activities. This format breaks the revenue and expense items into various intermediate income components so that important relationships can be shown and attention can be focused on significant subtotals. Some examples of common intermediate income components are as follows:

1. **Gross profit (margin)**--the difference between net sales and cost of goods sold.
2. **Operating income**--gross profit less operating expenses.
3. **Income from operations before income taxes**--operating income plus any other revenue items and less any other expense items.

Example of a Multiple-Step Income Statement Format

ABC Company
Income Statement
For the Year Ended 12/31/X4

Sales:			
Sales			$xxx
Less: Sales discounts		$xxx	
Sales returns and allowances		<u>xxx</u>	<u>(xxx)</u>
Net sales			$xxx
Cost of goods sold:			
Inventory, 1/1/X4		$xxx	
Purchases	$xxx		
Add transportation-in	<u>xxx</u>		
Total cost of purchases	xxx		
Less: Purchase discount	$xxx		
Purchase returns and allowances	<u>xxx</u>	<u>(xxx)</u>	
Net purchases		<u>xxx</u>	
Cost of goods available for sale		$xxx	
Less inventory, 12/31/X4		<u>(xxx)</u>	
Cost of goods sold			<u>(xxx)</u>
Gross profit			$xxx

Operating expenses:			
Selling expenses			
Sales salaries	$xxx		
Commissions	xxx		
Advertising expense	xxx		
Delivery expense	xxx		
Selling supplies expense	xxx		
Depreciation of store furniture and equipment	<u>xxx</u>	$xxx	
General and administrative expenses			
Officers' salaries	$xxx		
Office salaries	xxx		
Bad debts expense	xxx		
Office supplies expense	xxx		
Depreciation of office furniture and fixtures	xxx		
Depreciation of building	xxx		
Insurance expense	xxx		
Utilities expense	<u>xxx</u>	<u>xxx</u>	
Total operating expense			(xxx)
Operating income			$xxx
Other revenues:			
Dividend income		$xxx	
Interest income		<u>xxx</u>	xxx
Other expenses:			
Interest expense			(xxx)
Income before unusual or infrequent items and income tax			$xxx
Unusual or infrequent items:			
Write-down of inventory to market		$xxx	
Loss from permanent impairment of value of manufacturing facilities		<u>xxx</u>	(xxx)
Income from operations before income taxes			$xxx
Provision for income tax			(xxx)
Net income			<u>$xxx</u>
Earnings per share			<u>$x.xx</u>

4. **Net income**--income from operations before income tax less the income tax provision. Only the final item in the income statement can be labelled "Net Income." Titles such as "Net Income Before Extraordinary Items" are incorrect and require removal of the word "Net."

Examples of the Format for Presentation of Various Income Statement Elements

Discontinued operations and an extraordinary item

Income (loss) from continuing operations		$xxx
Discontinued operations		
Income (loss) from operations of Division Z, less applicable income taxes of $xxx	$xxx	
Income (loss) on disposal of Division Z, less applicable income taxes of $xxx	<u>xxx</u>	<u>xxx</u>
Income (loss) before extraordinary item		$xxx
Extraordinary item, less applicable income taxes of $xxx (Note __)		<u>xxx</u>
Net income		<u><u>$xxx</u></u>
Per share of common stock		
Income (loss) from continuing operations		$x.xx
Income (loss) before extraordinary item		<u>x.xx</u>
Net income		<u><u>$x.xx</u></u>

Discontinued operations and a change in accounting principle

Income (loss) from continuing operations		$xxx
Discontinued operations		
Income (loss) from operations of Division Z, less applicable income taxes of $xxx	$xxx	
Income (loss) on disposal of Division Z, less applicable income taxes of $xxx	<u>xxx</u>	<u>xxx</u>
Income (loss) before cumulative effect		$xxx
Cumulative effect on prior years (to **date of last year's income statement**) of changing to (change described), less applicable income taxes of $xxx (Note __)		<u>xxx</u>
Net income		<u><u>$xxx</u></u>
Per share of common stock		
Income (loss) from continuing operations		$x.xx
Income (loss) before cumulative effect		x.xx
Cumulative effect of change in accounting principle, net of tax		<u>x.xx</u>
Net income		<u><u>$x.xx</u></u>

Extraordinary item and a change in accounting principle

Income (loss) before extraordinary item and cumulative effect of a change in accounting principle	$xxx
Extraordinary item, less applicable income taxes of $xxx (Note __)	xxx
Cumulative effect on prior years (to **date of last year's income statement**) of changing to (change described), less applicable income taxes of $xxx (Note __)	<u>xxx</u>
Net income	<u>$xxx</u>
Per share of common stock	
Income (loss) before extraordinary item and cumulative effect of accounting change	$x.xx
Extraordinary item	x.xx*
Cumulative effect of change in accounting principle, net of tax	<u>x.xx</u>
Net income	<u>$x.xx</u>

*Not required

Statement of Income and Retained Earnings

An acceptable practice is to combine the income statement and the statement of retained earnings into a single statement called the Statement of Income and Retained Earnings. Net income is computed in the same fashion as in a multiple- or single-step income statement. The beginning balance in retained earnings is added to the net income (loss) figure. Declared dividends are deducted to obtain the retained earnings ending balance.

Example of a Comprehensive Statement of Income and Retained Earnings

Baker, Inc.
Statement of Income and Retained Earnings
For the Year Ended December 31, 19X4

Sales		$2,482
Cost of goods sold		<u>1,489</u>
Gross margin on sales		$ 993
Operating expenses		
Selling expenses	$ 220	
Administrative expenses	<u>255</u>	<u>475</u>
Income from operations		$ 518

Other revenues/gains (expenses/losses)		
Interest revenue (expense)--net	($40)	
Gain on sale of investment in ABC Company	100	
Gain on translation of foreign currencies	20	80
Income before unusual or infrequent items		$ 598
Unusual or infrequent items:		
Write-down of property and equipment	($20)	
Loss from permanent impairment of value		
of distributing facility	(50)	(70)
Income from continuing operations before		
provision for income taxes		$ 528
Provision for income taxes		211
Income from continuing operations		$ 317*
Discontinued operations:		
Loss from operations of discontinued Division Z		
(less applicable taxes of $466)	$(699)**	
Loss on disposal of Division Z including operating		
losses during phase-out period (less applicable		
taxes of $67)	(100)**	(799)
Loss before extraordinary items and cumulative		
effect of a change in accounting principle		$(482)*
Extraordinary loss from earthquake (less applicable		
income taxes of $30)		(45)**
Cumulative effect on prior years of retroactive		
application of new depreciation method (less		
applicable income taxes of $80)		(120)*
Net loss		$(647)*
Retained earnings, January 1, 19X4	$2,000	
Prior period adjustment:		
Correction of depreciation error (less		
applicable income taxes of $28)	(42)	
Adjusted retained earnings, January 1, 19X4		1,958
Total		$1,311
Deduct dividends:		
Preferred stock	$(40)	
Common stock	30	(70)
Retained earnings, December 31, 19X4		$1,241

Per share amounts (100 shares)

Income from continuing operations	$ <u>3.17</u>
Loss before extraordinary items and effect of accounting changes	<u>(4.82)</u>
Cumulative effect on prior years of retroactive application of new depreciation method	<u>(1.20)</u>
Net loss	$<u>(6.47)</u>

Note:

1. Assumes a tax rate of 40% on applicable items
2. Asterisk (*) indicates where earnings per share (EPS) amounts would be necessary. In the case of a double asterisk (**) they are optional and/or need not be shown on the face of the income statement.
3. Footnote explanation would also be required for many of the above events and transactions.

Prior Period Adjustments

SFAS 16 and APB 9 are the promulgated GAAP concerning the accounting for prior period adjustments. SFAS 16 was issued to define a prior period adjustment and clearly states that only the following shall be excluded from the determination of net income for the current period:

1. The correction of an error in the financial statements of a prior period
2. Adjustments that result from realization of income tax benefits of preacquisition operating loss carryforwards of purchased subsidiaries

APB 9 specifies the recording and presentation of a prior period adjustment. Accordingly, when prior period adjustments are recorded, the resulting effects on the net income of prior periods shall be disclosed in the year in which the adjustments are made. These effects shall be reported at both their gross amount and net of applicable income taxes. The proper presentation of these effects depends upon the nature of the statements presented. If the statements are presented for only a single period, then the beginning balance of retained earnings shall be restated to reflect the effects of the correction or change. When comparative statements are presented, corresponding adjustments should be made of the amounts of net income (and the components thereof) and retained earnings balance (as well as other affected balances) for all of the periods included in the financial statements.

An example of the accounting presentation for a prior period adjustment appears in Chapter 19, Accounting Changes and Error Correction.

Development Stage Enterprises (SFAS 7)

SFAS 7 defines a development stage enterprise as one which:

is devoting substantially all of its efforts to establishing a new business and either of the following conditions exists:

a. Planned principal operations have not commenced.
b. Planned principal operations have commenced but there has been no significant revenue.

SFAS 7 indicates that these enterprises should prepare their financial statements in accordance with the same GAAP applicable to established operating entities.

SFAS 7 indicated that specialized accounting practices are unacceptable and that development stage enterprises were to follow the same generally accepted accounting principles as those that applied to an established operating entity. SFAS 7 also provided that a development stage enterprise should disclose certain additional information which would alert readers to the fact that the company is in the development stage. Disclosure requirements include:

1. All disclosures applicable to operating entities
2. Identification of the statements as those of a development stage enterprise
3. Disclosure of the nature of development stage activities
4. A balance sheet which, in the equity section, includes the cumulative net losses since inception
5. An income statement showing current period revenue and expense as well as the cumulative amount from the inception of the entity
6. A statement of cash flows showing cash flows for the period as well as those from inception
7. A statement of stockholders' equity showing the following from the enterprise's inception:

   a. For each issuance, the date and number of equity securities issued for cash or other consideration
   b. For each issuance, the dollar amounts per share assigned to the consideration received for equity securities
   c. For each issuance involving noncash consideration, the nature of the consideration and the basis used in assigning the valuation

8. For the first period in which an enterprise is no longer a development stage enterprise, it shall be disclosed that in prior periods the entity was a development stage enterprise. If comparative statements are presented, the foregoing disclosure presentations (2-7) need not be shown.

Disclosures

(See the detailed Disclosure Checklist in the Appendix at the back of this book.)

4 Statement of Cash Flows

Perspective and Issues

The FASB has issued SFAS 95 entitled, "Statement of Cash Flows." This Statement supersedes APB 19 and establishes standards for cash flow reporting effective for years ending after July 15, 1988. The statement replaces the Statement of Changes in Financial Position (SCFP) with a Statement of Cash Flows (SCF) as a required financial statement. **The Statement of Cash Flows is similar to the SCFP prepared with cash and cash equivalents as the definition of funds and classified by operating activities, financing activities, and investing activities.**

The primary purpose of the Statement of Cash Flows is to provide information about the cash receipts and cash payments of an entity during a period. A secondary purpose is to provide information about the investing and financing activities of the entity during the period.

Specifically, the SCF should help investors and creditors assess

1. Ability to generate future positive cash flows.
2. Ability to meet obligations and pay dividends.
3. Reasons for differences between income and cash receipts and payments.
4. Both cash and non-cash aspects of entities' investing and financing transactions.

The FASB's Conceptual Framework Project, in particular SFAC 1, states that "financial reporting should provide information that is useful to present and potential investors, creditors, and other users for making rational investment and credit decisions." Since the ultimate objective of investment and credit decisions is the maximization of net cash inflows, information for assessing the amounts, timing, and uncertainty of prospective enterprise cash flows is needed. SFAC 5 gives particular attention to the statements of earnings and comprehensive income. It also addresses the question of which financial statements should be presented and the contribution of each statement to financial reporting. SFAC 5 concludes that financial statements must show cash flows during the period in order to be complete.

APB 19, Reporting Changes in Financial Position, allowed for flexibility in the form, content, and terminology used in preparing and presenting the SCFP. Although the APB concluded that the statement should encompass a broad concept of funds (all financial resources concept), the APB did not mandate a specific definition of funds to be used in arranging the changes in financial position into a meaningful format. Therefore, funds could be defined as working capital, cash, cash and short-term investments, or net monetary assets. The result of the Board's flexibility was a lack of comparability among different firms' SCFPs. Under the new SFAS, the ambiguity of the term "funds" and the resulting lack of comparability will be eliminated.

Sources of GAAP

SFAS
95

Definitions of Terms

Cash equivalents. Short-term, highly liquid investments that (a) are readily convertible to known amounts of cash and (b) are so near their maturity (original maturity of three months or less) that they present negligible risk of changes in value because of changes in interest rates. Treasury bills, commercial paper, and money market funds are all examples of cash equivalents.

Direct method. A method which derives the net cash provided by operating activities from the components of operating cash receipts and payments as opposed to adjusting net income for items not affecting funds.

Financing activities. The transactions a firm engages in to acquire and repay capital (e.g., borrowings, sale of capital stock, repayments, etc.).

Indirect (reconciliation) method. A method which derives the net cash provided by operating activities by adjusting net income for revenue and expense items not resulting from cash transactions.

Investing activities. The transactions the firm engages in which affect their investments in assets (e.g., purchase, sale).

Operating activities. The transactions not classified as financing or investing activities, generally involving producing and delivering goods or providing services.

Concepts, Rules, and Examples

Cash Basis

The Statement of Cash Flows shall include only inflows and outflows of cash and cash equivalents. Cash equivalents include any short-term highly liquid investments (see definition for criteria) used as a temporary investment of idle cash. The SCF shall exclude all transactions that do not directly affect cash receipts and payments. However, the effects of transactions not resulting in receipts or payments of cash shall be reported in a separate schedule. Under the all financial resources concept of APB 19, it was acceptable to include these items in the body of the SCFP. The reasoning for not including noncash items in the Statement of Cash Flows and placing them in a separate schedule is that it preserves the statement's primary focus on cash flows from operating, investing, and financing activities.

Classification

The Statement of Cash Flows requires classification into these three categories.

Investing activities include the acquisition and disposition of long-term productive assets or securities that are not considered cash equivalents. Investing activities also include the lending of money and collection on loans.

Financing activities include obtaining resources from and returning resources to the owners. Also included is obtaining resources from creditors and repaying the amount borrowed.

Operating activities include all transactions that are not investing and financing activities. Operating activities include delivering or producing goods for sale and providing services.

The following are examples of the Statement of Cash Flows classification.

	Operating	**Investing**	**Financing**
Cash Inflows	• Receipts from sale of goods or services	• Principal collections from loans	• Proceeds from issuing stock
	• Returns on loans (interest)	• Sale of long-term debt or equity securities	• Proceeds from issuing debt (short-term or long-term)
	• Returns on equity securities (dividends)	• Sale of plant & equipment	
Cash Outflows	• Payments for inventory	• Loans made	• Payment of dividends
	• Payments to employees	• Purchase of long-term debt or equity securities	• Repurchase of entity's stock
	• Payments of taxes	• Purchase of plant & equipment	• Repayment of debt principal
	• Payments of interest		
	• Payments to suppliers		

Example of a Classified SCF

Liquid Corporation
Statement of Cash Flows
For the Year Ended December 31, 19XX

Net cash flows from operating activities		$ xxx
Cash flows from investing activities:		
Purchase of property, plant, and equipment	$(xxx)	
Sale of equipment	xx	
Collection of notes receivable	xx	
Net cash **used** in investing activities		(xx)
Cash flows from financing activities:		
Sale of common stock	xxx	
Repayment of long-term debt	(xx)	
Reduction of notes payable	(xx)	
Net cash **provided** by financing activities		xx
Effect of exchange rate changes on cash		xx
Net increase in cash		$ xxx
Cash and cash equivalents at beginning of year		xxx
Cash and cash equivalents at end of year		$xxxx
Schedule of noncash financing and investing activities:		
Conversion of bonds into common stock		$ xxx

Operating Activities Presentation

Direct versus indirect. The operating activities section of the SCF can be presented under the direct or indirect method. However, the FASB has expressed a preference for the direct method of presenting net cash from operating activities.

The **direct method** shows the items that affected cash flow. Cash received and cash paid are presented, as opposed to converting accrual-basis income to cash flow information. Entities using the direct method are required to report the following classes of operating cash receipts and payments:

1. Cash collected from customers
2. Interest and dividends received
3. Cash paid to employees and other suppliers
4. Interest and income taxes paid
5. Other operating cash receipts and payments

The direct method allows the user to clarify the relationship between the company's net income and its cash flows. For example, payments of expenses are shown as cash disbursements and are deducted from cash receipts. In this way, the user is able to recognize the cash receipts and cash payments for the period. Formulas for conversion of various income statement amounts for the direct method presentation from the accrual basis to the cash basis are summarized below.

Accrual basis	Additions	Deductions	Cash basis
Net sales	+ Beginning A/R	- Ending A/R	= Cash received
		A/R written off	from customers
Cost of goods sold	+ Ending inventory	Depreciation	
	Beginning A/P	- and amortization[1]	= Cash paid to
		Beginning inventory	suppliers
		Ending A/P	
	Ending prepaid	Depreciation and	
	expenses	amortization	
Operating expenses	+ Beginning accrued	- Beginning prepaid	= Cash paid for
	expenses	expenses	operating
		Ending accrued	expenses
		expenses payable	

[1]Applies to a manufacturing entity only

Note that when the direct method is used, a separate schedule reconciling net income to net cash flows from operating activities must also be provided.

The **indirect method** is the most widely used presentation of cash from operating activities, primarily because it is easier to prepare. It focuses on the differences between net income and cash flows. The indirect format begins with net income, which can be obtained directly from the income statement. Revenue and expense items not affecting cash are added or deducted to arrive at net cash provided by operating activities. For example, depreciation and amortization would be added back because they reduce net income without affecting cash.

The Statement of Cash Flows prepared using the indirect method emphasizes changes in the components of most current asset and current liability accounts. Changes in inventory, accounts receivable, and other current accounts are used to determine the cash flow from operating activities. However, a short-term borrowing used to purchase equipment would not be included since it is not related to operating activities. Instead, the short-term borrowing would be classified as a financing activity. Other adjustments under the indirect method include changes in the account balances of deferred income taxes and the income (loss) from investments under the equity method.

The following diagram may facilitate understanding of the adjustments to net income necessary for converting accrual-based net income to cash-basis net income when using the **indirect method**. The diagram is simply an expanded balance sheet equation.

	Current assets*	-	Fixed assets	=	Current liabilities	+	Long-term liabilities	+	Income ____	Accrual income adjustment to convert to cash flow
1.	Increase			=					Increase	Decrease
2.	Decrease			=					Decrease	Increase
3.				=	Increase				Decrease	Increase
4.				=	Decrease				Increase	Decrease

Other than cash and cash equivalents

For example, using Row 1, a credit sale would increase accounts receivable and accrual-basis income but would not affect cash. Therefore, its effect must be removed from the accrual income in order to convert to cash income. The last column indicates that the increase in a current asset balance must be deducted from income to obtain cash flow.

Similarly, an increase in a current liability, Row 3, must be added to income to obtain cash flows (e.g., accrued wages are on the income statement as an expense, but they do not require cash; the increase in wages payable must be added back to remove this noncash flow expense from accrual-basis income).

If the **indirect method** is chosen, then the amount of interest and income tax paid shall be included in the related disclosures. Also with the indirect method, SFAS 95 permits, but does not require, separate disclosure of cash flows related to extraordinary items and discontinued operations. If an entity chooses to disclose this information, disclosure must be consistent for all periods affected.

The major drawback to the indirect method involves the user's difficulty in comprehending the information presented. This method does not show from where the cash was received or to where the cash was paid. Only adjustments to accrual basis net income are shown. In some cases the adjustments can be confusing. For instance, the sale of equipment resulting in an accrual-basis loss would require that the loss be added to net income to arrive at net cash from operating activities. (The loss was deducted in the computation of net income, but because the sale will be shown as an investing activity, the loss must be added back to net income.)

Although the **indirect method** is more commonly used in practice, the authors believe that the **direct method** is preferable. It portrays both the amounts of funds provided by and used in the firm's operations, instead of presenting net income and reconciling items. The direct method reports only the items that affect cash flow (inflows/outflows of cash) and ignores items that do not affect cash flow (depreciation, gains, etc.). Both the direct method and the indirect method are shown below.

Direct method:

Cash flows from operating activities:		
Cash received from sale of goods	$xxx	
Cash dividends received	<u>xxx</u>	
Cash provided by operating activities		$xxx
Cash paid to suppliers	(xxx)	
Cash paid for operating expenses	(xxx)	
Cash paid for taxes	<u>(xxx)</u>	
Cash disbursed for operating activities		(<u>$xxx</u>)
Net cash flows from operating activities		<u>$xxx</u>

Indirect method:

Cash flows from operating activities:	
Net income	$ xx
Add/deduct items not affecting cash	
Increase in accounts receivable	(xx)
Depreciation expense	xx
Increase in accounts payable	xx
Decrease in inventories	xx
Loss on sale of equipment	<u>xx</u>
Net cash flows from operating activities	<u>$xxx</u>

Other Requirements

Gross vs. Net Basis. The emphasis in the Statement of Cash Flows is on gross cash receipts and cash payments. For instance, reporting the net change in bonds payable would obscure the financing activities of the entity by not disclosing separately cash inflows from issuing bonds and cash outflows from retiring bonds. The Board specifies a few exceptions where netting of cash flows is allowed. Items having quick turnovers, large amounts, and short maturities may be presented as net cash flows if the cash receipts and payments pertain to 1) investments (other than cash equivalents), 2) loans receivable, and 3) debts (original maturity of three months or less).

Exchange rate effects. Foreign operations must prepare a separate statement of cash flows, and translate the statement to the reporting currency using the exchange rate in effect at the time of the cash flow (a weighted average exchange rate may be used if the result is substantially the same). This translated statement is then used in the preparation of the consolidated statement of cash flows.

Noncash exchange gains and losses recognized on the income statement should be reported as a separate item when reconciling net income and operating activities.

For a more detailed discussion about the exchange rate effects on the statement of cash flows, see Chapter 20.

Cash flow per share. This statistic shall **not** be reported in the financial statements of an enterprise.

Preparation of the Statement

Under a cash and cash equivalents basis, the changes in the cash account and any cash equivalent account is the "bottom line" figure of the SCF. Using the 19X1 and 19X2 balance sheet shown below, an increase of $22,000 can be computed. This is the difference between the totals for cash and treasury bills between 19X1 and 19X2 ($38,000 - 16,000).

When preparing the statement of cash flows using the direct method, gross cash inflows from revenues and gross cash outflows to suppliers and for expenses are presented in the operating activities section.

In preparing the reconciliation of net income to net cash flow from operating activities (indirect method), changes in all accounts other than cash and cash equivalents that are related to operations are additions to or deductions from net income to arrive at net cash provided by operating activities.

A T-account analysis may be helpful when preparing the statement of cash flows. A T-account is set up for each account, and beginning (19X1) and ending (19X2) balances are taken from the appropriate balance sheet. Additionally, a T-account for cash and cash equivalents from operating activities and a master or summary T-account of cash and cash equivalents should be used.

Example of Preparing a Statement of Cash Flows

The financial statements below will be used to prepare the SCF.

Johnson Company
Balance Sheets
December 31, 19X2 and 19X1

	19X2	*19X1*
Assets:		
Current assets		
Cash	$ 34,000	$ 10,000
Treasury Bills	4,000	6,000
Accounts receivable--net	9,000	11,000
Inventory	14,000	9,000
Prepaid expenses	10,000	13,000
Total current assets	$ 71,000	$ 49,000
Noncurrent assets		
Investment in XYZ (35%)	16,000	14,000
Patent	5,000	6,000
Property, plant, and equipment	39,000	37,000
Less accumulated depreciation	(7,000)	(3,000)
Total assets	$124,000	$103,000

Liabilities:

Current liabilities

Accounts payable	$ 5,000	$ 12,000
Notes payable--current	9,000	--
Interest payable	3,000	2,000
Dividends payable	7,000	2,000
Income taxes payable	2,000	1,000
Total current liabilities	26,000	17,000
Noncurrent liabilities		
Deferred tax liability	9,000	6,000
Bonds payable	15,000	25,000
Total liabilities	$ 50,000	$ 48,000

Stockholders' equity:

Common stock, $10 par value	$ 33,000	$ 26,000
Additional paid-in capital	11,000	3,000
Retained earnings	30,000	26,000
Total stockholders' equity	$ 74,000	$ 55,000
Total liabilities and stockholders' equity	$124,000	$103,000

Johnson Company
Statement of Earnings
For the Year Ended December 31, 19X2

Sales	$100,000
Other income	8,000
	$108,000
Cost of goods sold, excluding depreciation	60,000
Selling, general, and administrative expenses	12,000
Depreciation	8,000
Amortization of patents	1,000
Interest expense	2,000
	$ 83,000
Income before taxes	$ 25,000
Income taxes (36%)	9,000
Net income	$ 16,000

Additional information (relating to 19X2):

1. Equipment costing $6,000 with a book value of $2,000 was sold for $5,000.
2. The company received a $3,000 dividend from its investment in XYZ, accounted for under the equity method and recorded income from the investment of $5,000 which is included in other income.
3. The company issued 200 shares of common stock for $5,000.
4. The company signed a note payable for $9,000.
5. Equipment was purchased for $8,000.
6. The company converted $10,000 bonds payable into 500 shares of common stock. The book value method was used to record the transaction.
7. A dividend of $12,000 was declared.

Summary of Cash and Cash Equivalents

Inflows	Outflows	
(d) 5,000		
	8,000	(g)
(h) 5,000	7,000	(i)
(n) 9,000		
(r) 18,000		
37,000	15,000	
	22,000	Net increase in cash
37,000	37,000	

Cash and Cash Equivalents--Oper. Act.

(a) 16,000		
(b) 8,000		
(c) 1,000	3,000	(d)
(e) 3,000	5,000	(f)
(f) 3,000		
(j) 2,000		
(l) 3,000		
	5,000	(k)
(o) 1,000	7,000	(m)
(p) 1,000		
38,000	20,000	
	18,000	(r)
38,000	38,000	

Accounts Receivable

11,000		
	2,000	(j)
9,000		

Inventory

	9,000	
(k)	5,000	
	14,000	

Prepaid Expenses

13,000		
	3,000	(l)
10,000		

Investment in XYZ

	14,000	
(f)	5,000	3,000 (f)
	16,000	

Patent

6,000		
	1,000	(c)
5,000		

Prop., Plant, & Equip.

37,000		
	6,000	(d)
(g) 8,000		
39,000		

Accumulated Depr.

	3,000	
	8,000	(b)
(d) 4,000		
	7,000	

Accounts Payable

	12,000	
(m) 7,000		
	5,000	

Notes Payable

	9,000	(n)
	9,000	

Interest Payable

	2,000	
(o) 1,000	2,000	(o)
	3,000	

Dividends Payable

	2,000	
(i) 7,000	12,000	(i)
	7,000	

Income Taxes Payable

	1,000	
(p) 5,000	6,000	(p)
	2,000	

Deferred Inc. Taxes		Bonds Payable		Common Stock	
	6,000		25,000		26,000
	3,000 (e)	(h) 10,000			2,000 (h)
	9,000		15,000		5,000 (q)
					33,000

Addl. Paid-in Capital		Retained Earnings	
	3,000		26,000
	3,000 (h)		16,000 (a)
	5,000 (q)	(i) 12,000	
	11,000		30,000

Explanation of entries:

a. Cash and Cash Equivalents--Operating activities is debited for $16,000, and credited to Retained Earnings. This represents the net income figure.

b. Depreciation is not a cash flow; however, depreciation expense was deducted to arrive at net income. Therefore, Accumulated Depreciation is credited and Cash and Cash Equivalents--Operating activities is debited.

c. Amortization of patents is another expense not requiring cash; therefore, Cash and Cash Equivalents--Operating activities is debited and Patent is credited.

d. The sale of equipment (additional information, item 1) resulted in a $3,000 gain. The gain is computed by comparing the book value of $2,000 with the sales price of $5,000. Cash proceeds of $5,000 are an inflow of cash. Since the gain was included in net income, it must be deducted from net income to determine cash provided by operating activities. This is necessary to avoid counting the $3,000 gain both in cash provided by operating activities and in investing activities. The following entry would have been made on the date of sale:

Cash	5,000	
Accumulated depreciation (6,000 - 2,000)	4,000	
Property, plant, and equipment		6,000
Gain on sale of equipment (5,000 - 2,000)		3,000

Adjust the T-accounts as follows: debit Summary of Cash and Cash Equivalents for $5,000, debit Accumulated Depreciation for $4,000, credit Property, Plant, and Equipment for $6,000, and credit Cash and Cash Equivalents--Operating activities for $3,000.

e. The $3,000 increase in Deferred Income Taxes must be added to income from operations. Although the $3,000 was deducted as part of income tax expense in determining net income, it did not require an outflow of cash. Therefore, debit Cash and Cash Equivalents--Operating activities and credit Deferred Taxes.

f. Item 2 under the additional information indicates that the investment in XYZ is accounted for under the equity method. The Investment in XYZ had a net increase of
$2,000 during the year after considering the receipt of a $3,000 dividend. Dividends received (an inflow of cash) would reduce the Investment in XYZ, while the
equity in the income of XYZ would increase the investment without affecting cash.
In order for the T-account to balance, a debit of $5,000 must have been made, in-
dicating earnings of that amount. The journal entries would have been:

Cash (dividend received)	3,000	
Investment in XYZ		3,000
Investment in XYZ	5,000	
Equity in earnings of XYZ		5,000

The dividend received ($3,000) is an inflow of cash, while the equity earnings are
not. Debit Investment in XYZ for $5,000, credit Cash and Cash Equivalents--Op-
erating activities for $5,000, debit Cash and Cash Equivalents--Operating activities
for $3,000, and credit Investment in XYZ for $3,000.

g. The Property, Plant, and Equipment account increased because of the purchase of
$8,000 (additional information, item 5). The purchase of assets is an outflow of
cash. Debit Property, Plant, and Equipment for $8,000 and credit Summary of
Cash and Cash Equivalents.

h. The company sold 200 shares of common stock during the year (additional information, item 3). The entry for the sale of stock was:

Cash	5,000	
Common stock (200 shares x $10)		2,000
Additional paid-in capital		3,000

This transaction resulted in an inflow of cash. Debit Summary of Cash and Cash
Equivalents $5,000, credit Common Stock $2,000, and credit Additional Paid-in
Capital $3,000.

i. Dividends of $12,000 were declared (additional information, item 7). Only $7,000
was actually paid in cash resulting in an ending balance of $7,000 in the Dividends
Payable account. Therefore, the following entries were made during the year:

Retained Earnings	12,000	
Dividends Payable		12,000
Dividends Payable	7,000	
Cash		7,000

These transactions result in an outflow of cash. Debit Retained Earnings $12,000
and credit Dividends Payable $12,000. Additionally, debit Dividends Payable
$7,000 and credit Summary of Cash and Cash Equivalents $7,000 to indicate the
cash dividends paid during the year.

j. Accounts Receivable decreased by $2,000. This is added as an adjustment to net income in the computation of cash provided by operating activities. The decrease of $2,000 means that an additional $2,000 cash was collected on account above and beyond the sales reported in the income statement. Debit Cash and Cash Equivalents--Operating activities and credit Accounts Receivable for $2,000.

k. Inventories increased by $5,000. This is subtracted as an adjustment to net income in the computation of cash provided by operating activities. Although $5,000 additional cash was spent to increase inventories, this expenditure is not reflected in accrual-basis cost of goods sold. Debit Inventory and credit Cash and Cash Equivalents--Operating activities for $5,000.

l. Prepaid Expenses decreased by $3,000. This is added back to net income in the computation of cash provided by operating activities. The decrease means that no cash was spent when incurring the related expense. The cash was spent when the prepaid assets were purchased, not when they were expended on the income statement. Debit Cash and Cash Equivalents--Operating activities and credit Prepaid Expenses for $3,000.

m. Accounts Payable decreased by $7,000. This is subtracted as an adjustment to net income. The decrease of $7,000 means that an additional $7,000 of purchases were paid for in cash; therefore, income was not affected but cash was decreased. Debit Accounts Payable and credit Cash and Cash Equivalents--Operating activities for $7,000.

n. Notes Payable increased by $9,000 (additional information, item 4). This is an inflow of cash and would be included in the financing activities. Debit Summary of Cash and Cash Equivalents and credit Notes Payable for $9,000.

o. Interest Payable increased by $1,000, but interest expense from the income statement was $2,000. Therefore, although $2,000 was expensed, only $1,000 cash was paid ($2,000 expense - $1,000 increase in interest payable). Debit Cash and Cash Equivalents--Operating activities for $1,000, debit Interest Payable for $1,000 and credit Interest Payable for $2,000.

p. The following entry was made to record the incurrence of the tax liability:

Income tax expense	9,000	
Income taxes payable		6,000
Deferred tax liability		3,000

Therefore, $9,000 was deducted in arriving at net income. The $3,000 credit to Deferred Income Taxes was accounted for in entry (e) above. The $6,000 credit to Taxes Payable does not, however, indicate that $6,000 cash was paid for taxes. Since Taxes Payable increased $1,000, only $5,000 must have been paid and $1,000 remains unpaid. Debit Cash and Cash Equivalents--Operating activities for $1,000, debit Income Taxes Payable for $5,000, and credit Income Taxes Payable for $6,000.

q. Item 6 under the additional information indicates that $10,000 of bonds payable were converted to common stock. This is a **noncash** financing activity and should be reported in a separate schedule. The following entry was made to record the transaction:

Bonds payable	10,000	
Common stock (500 shares x $10 par)		5,000
Additional paid-in capital		5,000

Adjust the T-accounts with a debit to Bonds Payable, $10,000; a credit to Common Stock, $5,000; and a credit to Additional Paid-in Capital, $5,000.

r.   The cash and cash equivalents from operations ($18,000) is transferred to the Summary of Cash and Cash Equivalents.

Since all of the changes in the noncash accounts have been accounted for and the balance in the Summary of Cash and Cash Equivalents account of $22,000 is the amount of the year-to-year increase in cash and cash equivalents, the formal statement may now be prepared. The following classified SCF is prepared under the direct method and includes the reconciliation of net income to net cash provided by operating activities. The T-account, Cash and Cash Equivalents--Operating activities, is used in the preparation of this reconciliation. The calculations for gross receipts and gross payments needed for the direct method are shown below.

Johnson Company
Statement of Cash Flows
For the Year Ended December 31, 19X2

Cash flow from operating activities:		
Cash received from customers	$102,000*	
Dividends received	3,000	
Cash provided by operating activities		$105,000
Cash paid to suppliers	$72,000**	
Cash paid for expenses	9,000***	
Interest paid	1,000****	
Taxes paid	5,000*****	
Cash paid for operating activities		(87,000)
Net cash flow provided by operating activities		$ 18,000
Cash flows from investing activities:		
Sale of equipment	5,000	
Purchase of property, plant, and equipment	(8,000)	
Net cash used in investing activities		(3,000)
Cash flow from financing activities:		
Sale of common stock	$ 5,000	
Increase in notes payable	9,000	
Dividends paid	(7,000)	
Net cash provided by financing activities		7,000
Net increase in cash and cash equivalents		$ 22,000
Cash and cash equivalents at beginning of year		16,000
Cash and cash equivalents at end of year		$ 38,000

Calculation of Amounts for Operating Activities Section of Johnson Co.'s SCFs.

* Net sales + Beginning A/R - Ending A/R = Cash received from customers
$100,000 + $11,000 - $9,000 = $102,000

** Cost of goods sold + Beginning A/P - Ending A/P + Ending inventory - Beginning inventory = Cash paid to suppliers
$60,000 + $12,000 - $5,000 + $14,000 - $9,000 = $72,000

*** Operating expenses + Ending prepaid expenses - Beginning prepaid expenses - Depreciation expense (and other noncash operating expenses) = Cash paid for operating expenses
$12,000 + $10,000 - $13,000 = $9,000

**** Interest expense + Beginning interest payable - Ending interest payable = Interest paid
$2,000 + $2,000 - $3,000 = $1,000

***** Income taxes + Beginning income taxes payable - Ending income taxes payable + Beginning deferred income taxes - Ending deferred income taxes = Taxes paid

$9,000 + $1,000 - $2,000 + $6,000 - $9,000 = $5,000

Reconciliation of net income to net cash provided by operating activities:

Net income	$16,000
Add (deduct) items not using (providing) cash:	
Depreciation	8,000
Amortization	1,000
Gain on sale of equipment	(3,000)
Increase in deferred taxes	3,000
Equity in XYZ	(2,000)
Decrease in accounts receivable	2,000
Increase in inventory	(5,000)
Decrease in prepaid expenses	3,000
Decrease in accounts payable	(7,000)
Increase in interest payable	1,000
Increase in income taxes payable	1,000
Net cash flow provided by operating activities	$18,000

Schedule of noncash transactions

Conversion of bonds into common stock	$10,000

Disclosure of accounting policy:

For purposes of the statement of cash flows, the Company considers all highly liquid debt instruments purchased with original maturities of three months or less to be cash equivalents.

Disclosures

1. All are illustrated in the above example except the requirements that the following items shall be disclosed when only the indirect method is used for operating activities:

    a. Interest paid
    b. Income tax paid

2. Also see the detailed Disclosure Checklist in the Appendix at the back of this book.

5 Financial Instruments, Cash, Receivables, and Short-Term Investments

Perspective and Issues

SFAS 105 entitled "Disclosures of Information about Financial Instruments with Off-Balance-Sheet Risk and Financial Instruments with Concentrations of Credit Risk," is the first in a series of disclosure statements about financial instruments. The focus in the first phase of the project is on the extent, nature, and terms of financial instruments with **off-balance-sheet** credit or market risk. In addition, the statement addresses concentrations of credit risk for **all** financial instruments.

The current phase of the financial instrument project has its focus on market value disclosures. An exposure draft entitled, "Disclosures about Market Value of Financial Instruments" was issued in December, 1990. If approved, the effective date is set for December 15, 1991. Entities with total assets less than $100 million would have until December 15, 1992. Other phases of the project include (1) distinguishing between liability and equity instruments and (2) recognition and measurement issues.

Following a series of liquidity crises suffered by major corporations and banking institutions, the focus of the financial statements has returned to cash flow, liquidity, and solvency. The FASB has stated that a **primary** purpose of financial statements is to provide information useful in assessing future cash flows. SFAS 95, "Statement of Cash Flows" established standards for cash flow reporting (see Chapter 4).

One consequence of the concern with liquidity is the traditional presentation of a classified balance sheet. **Current assets** are defined as those assets which are or will become cash or will be consumed in normal business operations within a year or within one operating cycle if more than one year. **Current liabilities** are those obligations which will require the use of current assets or the incurrence of another current liability to liquidate them. Both the ratio of current assets to current liabilities (current ratio)--or, alternatively, the excess of current assets over current liabilities (working capital)--can be interpreted as a measure of an entity's liquidity. Generally, current assets are displayed in the balance sheet in the order of liquidity, beginning with cash on hand, continuing with temporary investments, receivables, inventories, and concluding with prepaid expenses.

Although a proposed interpretation that would be effective December 15, 1992 makes an exception in the case of multiple forward, swap, and similar contracts executed under master netting arrangements, offsetting of assets and liabilities is improper except where a right of setoff exists. A right of setoff is a debtor's legal right to discharge debt owed to another party by applying against the debt an amount the other party owes to the debtor. Per FASB Technical Bulletin 88-2, the conditions to be met are as follows:

1. Each of the two parties owes the other determinable amounts.
2. The reporting party has the right to setoff.
3. The reporting party intends to setoff.
4. The right of setoff is enforceable at law.

Sources of GAAP

ARB	*APB*	*SFAS*	*FASB I*	*FASB Technical Bulletins*	*EITF*
43, Ch. 3A	6, 12	6, 12, 52, 77, 80, 95, 96, 102, 105	8, 10, 11 12, 16	88-2	89-2

Definitions of Terms

Accounting loss. Accounting loss refers to the loss that may have to be recognized due to credit and market risk as a direct result of the rights and obligations of a financial instrument.

Accounts receivable. Amounts due from customers for goods or services provided to them in the normal course of the entity's business operations.

Aging the accounts. The procedure for the computation of the adjustment for anticipated uncollectible accounts receivable based upon the length of time the end-of-period outstanding accounts have been unpaid.

Assignment. The formal procedure for collateralization of borrowings through the use of accounts receivable. It normally does not involve debtor notification.

Carrying amount (value). The amount at which marketable equity securities are being carried, net of allowances. This amount is either original cost or a lower amount to which the securities were written down as a result of market declines.

Cash. Coins and currency on hand and balances in checking accounts available for immediate withdrawal.

Cash equivalents. Short-term, highly liquid investments that are readily convertible to known amounts of cash. Examples include treasury bills, commercial paper, and money market funds.

Contractual obligations. Contractual obligations encompass both those that are conditioned on the occurrence of a specified event and those that are not. All contractual obligations that are financial instruments meet the definition of a liability set forth in FASB Concepts Statement No. 6, *Elements of Financial Statements*, although some may not be recognized as liabilities in financial statements--may be "off-balance-sheet"--because they fail to meet some other criterion for recognition. For some financial instruments, the obligation is owed to or by a group of entities rather than a single group.

Contractual rights. Contractual rights encompass both those that are conditioned on the occurrence of a specified event and those that are not. All contractual rights that are financial instruments meet the definition of asset set forth in Concepts Statement 6, although some may not be recognized as assets in financial statements--may be "off-balance-sheet"--because they fail to meet some other criterion for recognition. For some financial intruments, the obligation is held by or due from a group of entities rather than a single group.

Cost (of a security). The original purchase price plus all costs incidental to the acquisition (e.g., brokerage fees and taxes) unless a new cost basis is assigned as a result of a decline in market value which is other than temporary.

Credit risk. Credit risk is the possibility that a loss may occur from the failure of another party to perform according to the terms of a contract.

Current assets. Those assets which are reasonably expected to be realized in cash or sold or consumed within a year or within the normal operating cycle of the entity.

Equity instrument. Any evidence of an ownership interest in an entity.

Factoring. The outright sale of accounts receivable to a third-party financing entity; the sale may be with or without recourse.

Financial asset. Any asset that is (a) cash, (b) a contractual right to receive cash or another financial asset from another entity, (c) a contractual right to exchange other financial instruments on potentially favorable terms with another entity, or (d) an equity instrument of another entity.

Financial instrument. A financial instrument is cash, evidence of an ownership interest in an entity, or a contract that both:

   a. Imposes on one entity a contractual obligation (1) to deliver cash or another financial instrument to a second entity or (2) to exchange financial instruments on potentially unfavorable terms with the second entity.

b. Conveys to that second entity a contractual right (1) to receive cash or another financial instrument from the first entity or (2) to exchange other financial instruments on potentially favorable terms with the first entity.

Financial instrument with off-balance-sheet risk. A financial instrument has off-balance-sheet risk of accounting loss if the risk of accounting loss to the entity may exceed the amount recognized as an asset, if any, or if the ultimate obligation may exceed the amount that is recognized as a liability in the statement of financial position.

Financial liability. Any liability that is a contractual obligation (a) to deliver cash or another financial asset to another entity or (b) to exchange financial instruments on potentially unfavorable terms with another entity.

Market risk. Market risk is the possibility that future changes in market prices may make a financial instrument less valuable or more onerous.

Marketable equity securities. Instruments representing actual ownership interest, or the rights to buy or sell such interests, and which are actively traded or listed on a national securities exchange.

Net realizable value. The amount of cash anticipated to be produced in the normal course of business from an asset, net of any direct costs of the conversion into cash.

Operating cycle. The average time intervening between the acquisition of materials or services and the final cash realization from the sale of products or services.

Percentage-of-sales method. The procedure for the computation of the adjustment for anticipated uncollectible accounts receivable based on the historical relationship between bad debts and gross credit sales.

Permanent decline. A downward movement in the value of a marketable equity security for which there are known causes. The decline indicates a remote likelihood of a price recovery.

Pledging. The process of using an asset as collateral for borrowings. It generally refers to borrowings secured by accounts receivable.

Realized gain (loss). The difference between the cost or adjusted cost of a marketable security and the net selling price realized by the seller which is to be included in the determination of net income in the period of the sale.

Recourse. The right of the transferee (factor) of accounts receivable to seek recovery for an uncollectible account from the transferor. It is often limited to specific conditions.

Risk of accounting loss. The risk of accounting loss from a financial instrument includes the (a) possibility that a loss may occur from the failure of another party to perform according to the terms of a contract (credit risk), (b) the possibility that future changes in market prices may make a financial instrument less valuable or more onerous (market risk), and (c) the risk of theft or physical loss. SFAS 105 addresses credit and market risk only.

Short-term investments. Securities or other assets acquired with excess cash, having ready marketability and intended by management to be liquidated, if necessary, within the current operating cycle.

Temporary decline. A downward fluctuation in the value of a marketable equity security that has no known causes that suggest the decline is of a permanent nature.

Unrealized gain (loss). The unrealized difference between the market value of short-term investments and their carrying value which is deemed not to be of a permanent nature.

Valuation allowance. A contra-asset account used to reduce marketable equity securities to the lower of cost or market. The offset is either a loss account (for declines in securities classified as current) or a contra-equity account (for temporary declines in noncurrent securities).

Concepts, Rules, and Examples

Financial Instruments

SFAS 105 entitled "Disclosures of Information about Financial Instruments with Off-Balance-Sheet Risk and Financial Instruments with Concentrations of Credit Risk," is the first in a series of disclosure statements about financial instruments. The focus in the first phase of the project is on the extent, nature, and terms of financial instruments with **off-balance-sheet** credit or market risk. In addition, the statement addresses concentrations of credit risk for **all** financial instruments.

The FASB believed that current disclosures in the financial statements were inadequate with regard to many newly created financial instruments and transactions. After examining accounting practices presently in effect, the Board selected the disclosures that it felt had the best balance of usefulness and cost.

SFAS 105 requires disclosure of information (1) about financial instruments with off-balance-sheet risk of accounting loss that exceeds the amount required, if any, in the statement of financial position and (2) about **all** financial instruments with concentrations of credit risk. It addresses credit and market risks only. There are specific exclusions listed in paragraphs 14 and 15 of SFAS 105.

Financial instruments include cash, ownership interest in an entity, or a contract that both:

a. Imposes a contractual obligation on one entity (1) to surrender cash or another financial instrument to a second entity or (2) to exchange financial instruments on potentially unfavorable terms with the second entity.
b. Conveys a contractual right to the second entity (1) to receive from the first entity cash or another financial instrument or (2) to exchange with the first entity other financial instruments on potentially favorable terms.

SFAS 105 limits the definition of a financial instrument. It excludes many assets because their probable future economic benefit is receipt of goods or services instead of a right to receive cash or an ownership interest in another entity. Examples of such excluded assets would be advances to suppliers and prepaid expenses. It also excludes many liabilities that contain contractual obligations because their probable economic sacrifice is delivery of goods or services instead of an obligation to deliver cash or an ownership interest in another entity. Examples of such excluded liabilities include advances from suppliers, deferred revenues, and most warranty obligations. The definition also excludes contracts that either require or **permit** settlement by the delivery of commodities.

A contractual obligation whose economic benefit or sacrifice is receipt or delivery of a financial instrument other than cash is, however, considered a financial instrument. For example, a note that is payable in U.S. Treasury bonds gives an issuer the contractual obligation to deliver and gives a holder the contractual right to receive bonds, not cash. But because the bonds represent obligations of the U.S. Treasury to pay cash they are considered financial instruments. Therefore, the note is also a financial instrument to both the holder of the note and the issuer of the note.

Another type of financial instrument is one that gives an entity the contractual right or obligation to exchange other financial instruments on potentially favorable or unfavorable terms. An example of this type of financial instrument would be a call option to purchase a U.S. Treasury note for $100,000 in 6 months. The option holder has a contractual right to exchange the financial instrument on potentially favorable terms. Six months later, if the market value of the note exceeds $100,000 the holder will exercise the option because the terms are favorable. The writer of the call option has contractual obligation to exchange financial instruments on potentially unfavorable terms if the holder exercises the option. The writer is normally compensated for this obligation. A put option to sell a Treasury note has similar but opposite effects. A bank's commitment to lend $100,000 to a customer at a fixed rate of 10% any time during the next 6 months at the customer's option is also a financial instrument.

An interest rate swap can be explained as a series of forward contracts to exchange, for example, fixed cash payments for variable cash receipts. The cash receipts would be computed by multiplying a floating-rate market index by a notional amount. An interest rate swap is both a contractual right and a contractual obligation to both parties.

Excluded from financial instrument classification are options and contracts that contain the right or obligation to exchange a financial instrument for a physical asset. For example, two entities enter a sale-purchase contract in which the purchaser agrees to take delivery of wheat or gold 6 months later and pay the seller $100,000 at the time of delivery. The contract is not considered a financial instrument because it requires the delivery of wheat or gold which are not considered financial instruments.

Also excluded from financial instrument classification are contingent items that may ultimately require the payment of cash but do not as yet arise from contracts. An example of such an item would be a contingent liability for tort judgments payable. However, when such an obligation becomes enforceable and is reduced to fixed payment schedules, it would then be considered a financial instrument.

SFAS 105 requires all entities to disclose in the body of the financial statements or in footnotes to the financial statements information about the financial instruments with **off-balance-sheet risk.** Disclosure must include the following information:

1. The face, contract, or notional principal amount
2. The nature and terms of the instruments including a discussion of (1) the credit and market risks, (2) the cash requirements, and (3) the related accounting policies (pursuant to APB 22).

A financial instrument has off-balance-sheet risk of accounting loss if the risk of accounting loss to the entity may exceed the amount recognized as an asset, if any, or if the ultimate obligation may exceed the amount that is recognized as a liability in the statement of financial position. The risk of accounting loss includes the possibility that the loss may occur from a credit risk or from a market risk. Appendix B of SFAS 105 gives numerous examples of financial instruments that both have and do not have off-balance-sheet risk of accounting loss.

For financial instruments with off-balance-sheet credit risk, an entity must disclose in the body of the statement or in notes to the statement the following information by class of financial instrument:

1. The amount of **accounting** loss the entity would incur if any party to the financial instrument failed completely to perform according to the terms of the contract and if any collateral proved worthless.
2. The entity's policy for requiring collateral on financial instruments subject to credit risks, information about access to that collateral and the nature and brief description of collateral supporting financial instruments.

Example

The Corporation might disclose the following:

Note 1: Summary of Accounting Policies
[The accounting policies note to the financial statements might include the following.]

Interest Rate Swap Agreements
The differential to be paid or received is accrued as interest rates change and is recognized over the life of the agreements.

Foreign Exchange Contracts
The Corporation enters into foreign exchange contracts as a hedge against foreign accounts payable. Market value gains and losses are recognized, and the resulting credit or debit offsets foreign exchange gains or loses on those payables.

Note X: Financial Instruments with Off-Balance Sheet Risk

In the normal course of business, the Corporation enters into or is a party to various financial instruments and contractual obligations that, under certain conditions, could give rise to or involve elements of market or credit risk in excess of that shown in the Statement of Financial Condition. These financial instruments and contractual obligations include interest rate swaps, forward foreign exchange contracts, financial guarantees, and commitments to extend credit. The corporation monitors and limits its exposure to market risk through management policies designed to identify and reduce excess risk. The Corporation limits its credit risk through monitoring of client credit exposure, reviews, and conservative estimates of allowances for bad debt and through the prudent use of collateral for large amounts of credit. The Corporation monitors collateral values on a daily basis and requires additional collateral when deemed necessary.

Interest Rate Swaps and Forward Exchange Contracts. The Corporation enters into a variety of interest rate swaps and forward foreign exchange contracts. The primary use of these financial instruments is to reduce interest rate fluctuations and to stabilize costs or to hedge foreign currency liabilities or assets. Interest rate swap transactions involve the exchange of floating rate and fixed rate interest payment of obligations without the exchange of underlying notional amounts. The company is exposed to credit risk in the unlikely event of nonper-formance by the counterparty. The differential to be received or paid is accrued as interest rates change and is recognized over the life of the agreement. Forward foreign exchange contracts represent commitments to exchange currencies at a specified future date. Gains (losses) on these contracts primarily serve to stabilize costs. Foreign currency exposure for the Corporation will result in the unlikely event that the other party fails to perform under the contract.

Financial Guarantees. Financial guarantees are conditional commitments to guarantee performance to third parties. These guarantees are primarily issued to guarantee borrowing arrangements. The Corporation's credit risk exposure on these guarantees is not material.

Commitment to Extend Credit. Loan commitments are agreements to extend credit under agreed-upon terms. The Corporation's commitment to extent credit assists customers to meet their liquidity needs. These commitments generally have fixed expiration or other termination clauses. The Corporation anticipates that not all of these commitments will be utilized. The amount of unused commitment does not necessarily represent future funding requirements.

The off-balance-sheet financial instruments are summarized as follows (in 000s):

Financial Instruments whose notional or contract amounts exceed the amount of credit risk:

	Contract or Notional Amount
Interest Rate Swap Agreements	$8,765.40
Forward Foreign Exchange Contracts	7,654.30

Financial Instruments whose contract amount represents credit risk:

	Contract or Notional Amount
Financial Guarantees	$6,543.20
Commitments to Extend Credit	5,432.10

SFAS 105 also would require disclosure of information about significant concentrations of credit risk for **all** financial instruments. Both individual and group concentrations of credit risk are to be disclosed. The following shall be disclosed about each significant concentration:

1. Information about the shared activity, region or economic characteristic that identifies the concentration.
2. The amount of accounting loss the entity would incur if any party to the financial instrument failed to completely perform and if any collateral proved worthless.
3. The entity's policy for requiring collateral on financial instruments subject to credit risks, information about access to the collateral and the nature and a brief description of collateral supporting financial instruments.

Example
Concentration of Credit Risk for Certain Entities. For certain corporations, industry or regional concentrations of credit risk may be disclosed adequately by a description of the business. Some examples are:

a. Credit risk for these off-balance-sheet financial instruments is concentrated in North America and in the Trucking Industry.
b. All financial instruments entered into by the Corporation relate to U.S. Government, international and domestic commercial airline customers.

Example

Significant Group Concentrations of Credit Risk. The Corporation grants credit to customers throughout the nation. As of December 31, 1991, the five states where the Corporation had the greatest amount of credit risk were as follows:

California	$8,765.40
Florida	7,654.30
Texas	6,543.20
New York	5,432.10
Washington	4,321.00

All of the above disclosures are in addition to other disclosure requirements prescribed by GAAP. SFAS 105 amends SFAS 77 disclosures.

In the year of transition, comparative information for previous fiscal years need not be included. For all subsequent fiscal years, the information required to be disclosed by SFAS 105 shall be included for each year for which a statement of financial position is presented for comparative purposes.

Status of Financial Instrument Project

The current phase of the financial instrument project has its focus on market value disclosures. An exposure draft entitled, "Disclosures about Market Value of Financial Instruments" was issued in December, 1990. This document would require entities to disclose the market value of **all** financial instruments, including liabilities. Pertinent descriptive information as to the value of the instrument is to be disclosed if it is not practical to estimate market values. The proposed statement excludes certain types of financial instruments including pensions, postretirement benefits, deferred compensation, defeased debt, insurance contracts, lease contracts and warranty obligations. Market value disclosure requirements specified by GAAP are acceptable for purposes of this proposed statement. The effective date is set for December 15, 1991. Entities with total assets less than $100 million would have until December 15, 1992.

Other phases of the projects include (1) distinguishing between liability and equity instruments and (2) recognition and measurement issues. A discussion memorandum (DM) on the liability-equity phase was issued in August, 1990. A DM on the recognition and measurement phase is expected in August, 1991. Both phases will be broken into subprojects and work on them will continue.

Cash

The promulgated GAAP for accounting for cash is ARB 43, Chapter 3. To be included as cash in the balance sheet, funds must be represented by actual coins and currency on hand or demand deposits available without restriction. It must be management's intention that the cash be available for current purposes. Cash in a demand deposit account which is being held for the retirement of long-term debts not maturing currently should be excluded from current assets and shown as a noncurrent investment. SFAS 6 identifies the intent of management as a key criterion in the classification of cash.

With the increased popularity of such instruments as NOW accounts and money market funds, it has become more common to see the caption "Cash and Cash Equivalents" in the balance sheet. This term includes other forms of near-cash as well as demand deposits and liquid, short-term securities. Cash equivalents must be available upon demand in order to justify inclusion.

Compensating balances. Pursuant to borrowing arrangements with lenders, an entity will often be required to maintain a minimum amount of cash on deposit (compensating balance). The purpose of this balance is to increase the yield on the loan to the lender. Since most organizations must maintain a certain working balance in their cash accounts simply to handle routine transactions and to cushion against unforeseen variations in the demand for cash, borrowers will often not find compensating balance arrangements objectionable. Nevertheless, the compensating balance is not available for unrestricted use and penalties will result if it is used. The portion of an entity's cash account which is a compensating balance must be segregated and shown as a noncurrent asset if the related borrowings are noncurrent liabilities. If the borrowings are current liabilities, it is acceptable to show the compensating balance as a **separately captioned** current asset.

Cash in savings accounts subject to a statutory notification requirement and cash in certificates of deposit maturing during the current operating cycle or within one year may be included as current assets but should be separately captioned in the balance sheet to avoid the misleading implication that these funds are available immediately upon demand. Typically, such items will be included in the **short-term investments** caption, but these could be labeled as time deposits or restricted cash deposits.

Petty cash and other imprest cash accounts are usually presented in financial statements with other cash accounts.

Receivables

Accounts receivable, open accounts, or trade accounts, are agreements by regular customers to pay for services received or merchandise obtained. Other categories of receivables include notes receivable, trade acceptances, third party instruments, and amounts due from officers, stockholders, employees, or affiliated companies. Notes receivable are formalized obligations evidenced by written promissory notes. The latter categories of receivables generally arise from cash advances but could develop from sales of merchandise or the provision of services. The basic nature of amounts due from trade customers is often different from that of balances receivable from related parties, such as employees or stockholders. Thus, generally accepted accounting principles require that these different classes of receivables be separately identified either on the face of the balance sheet or in the notes thereto.

Receivables should be presented at net realizable (i.e., realistically anticipated collectible) amounts. If the gross amount of receivables includes unearned interest or finance charges, these should be deducted in arriving at the net amount to be presented in the balance sheet (APB 6).

Deductions should be taken for amounts estimated to be uncollectible and also for the estimated returns, allowances, and other discounts to be taken by customers prior to or at the time of payment. In practice, the deductions that would be made for estimated returns, allowances, and trade discounts are usually deemed to be immaterial and such adjustments are rarely made. However, if it is known that sales are often recorded for merchandise which is shipped "on approval" and available data suggests that a **sizable** proportion of such sales are returned by the customers, then these estimated future returns must be accrued. Similarly, material amounts of anticipated discounts and allowances should be recorded in the period of sale.

The foregoing comments apply where revenues are recorded at the gross amount of the sale and subsequent sales discounts are recorded as debits (contra-revenues). An alternative manner of recording revenue, which does away with any need to estimate future discounts, is to record the initial sale at the net amount--that is, at the amount that will be remitted if the customers take advantage of the available discount terms. If the customers pay the gross amount later (they fail to take the discounts that were available to them), then this additional revenue is recorded as income when it is remitted. Notwithstanding its conceptual superiority, however, the net method of recording sales is rarely encountered in practice.

Bad Debts Expense

While the accrual of anticipated sales returns, allowances, and discounts are usually not required because of materiality, the recording of anticipated uncollectible amounts is almost always necessary. The direct write-off method, in which a receivable is charged off only when it is clear that it cannot be collected, is unsatisfactory since it results in a significant mismatching of revenues and expenses. Proper matching can only be achieved if bad debts expense is recorded in the same fiscal period as the revenues to which they are related. Since this expense is not known with certainty, an estimate must be made.

There are two popular estimation techniques. The **percentage-of-sales** method is principally oriented towards achieving the best possible matching of revenues and expenses. **Aging the accounts** is more oriented toward the presentation of the correct net realizable value of the trade receivables in the balance sheet than with the matching of revenues and expenses. Both methods are acceptable and widely employed.

Percentage of sales. Historical data are analyzed to ascertain the relationship between credit sales and bad debts. The derived percentage is then applied to the current period's sales revenues in order to arrive at the appropriate debit to bad debts expense for the year. The offsetting credit is made to an account called Allowance for Uncollectible Accounts. When specific customer accounts are subsequently deemed to be uncollectible, they are written off against this allowance.

Example of Percentage-of-Sales Method

Total **credit** sales for year:	$7,500,000
Bad debt ratio from prior years or other data source:	1.75% of sales
Computed year-end adjustment for bad debts expense:	$131,250 ($7,500,000 x .0175)

The entry required is:

Bad debts expense	131,250	
Allowance for uncollectibles		131,250

Aging the accounts. An analysis is prepared of the customer receivables at the balance sheet date. These accounts are categorized by the number of days or months they have remained outstanding. Then, based on the entity's past experience or on other available statistics, historical bad debts percentages are applied to each of these aggregate amounts, with larger percentages being applicable to the older accounts. The end result of this process is a computed total dollar amount which is the proper balance in the allowance for uncollectibles at the balance sheet date. As a result of the difference between the previous years' adjustments to the allowance for uncollectibles and the actual write-offs made to the account, there will usually be a balance in this account. Thus, the adjustment needed will be an amount other than that computed by the aging.

Example of the Aging Method

	Age of accounts			
	Under 30 days	30-90 days	Over 90 days	Total
Gross receivables	$1,100,000	$425,000	$360,000	
Bad debt ratios	0.5%	2.5%	15%	
Provision required	$5,500	$10,625	$54,000	$70,125

The credit balance required in the allowance account is $70,125. Assuming that a **debit** balance of $58,250 already exists in the allowance account (from charge-offs during the year), the necessary entry is:

Bad debts expense	128,375	
Allowance for uncollectibles		128,375

Both of the estimation techniques should produce approximately the same result. This will especially be true over the course of a number of years. Nonetheless, it must be recognized that these adjustments are based upon estimates and will never be totally accurate. When facts subsequently become available to indicate that the amount provided as an allowance for uncollectible accounts was incorrect, an adjustment classified as a change in estimate is made. Per APB 20, adjustments of this nature are never considered errors subject to subsequent correction or restatement. Only if an actual clerical or mechanical error occurred in the recording of allowance for uncollectibles would correction by means of a prior period adjustment be warranted.

Pledging, Assigning, and Factoring Receivables

An organization can alter the timing of cash flows resulting from sales to its customers by using its accounts receivable as collateral for borrowings or by selling the receivables outright. A wide variety of arrangements can be structured by the borrower and lender, but the most common are pledging, assignment, and factoring.

Pledging of Receivables. Pledging is an agreement whereby accounts receivable are used as collateral for loans. Generally, the lender has limited rights to inspect the borrower's records to achieve assurance that the receivables do exist. The customers whose accounts have been pledged are not aware of this event, and their payments are still remitted to the original obligee. The pledged accounts merely serve as security to the lender, giving comfort that sufficient assets exist which will generate cash flows adequate in amount and timing to repay the debt. However, the debt is paid by the borrower whether or not the pledged receivables are collected and whether or not the pattern of such collections matches the payments due on the debt.

The only accounting issue relating to pledging is that of adequate disclosure. The accounts receivable, which remain assets of the borrowing entity, continue to be shown as current assets in its financial statements but must be identified as having been pledged. This identification can be accomplished either parenthetically or by footnote disclosures. Similarly, the related debt should be identified as having been secured by the receivables.

Example of Proper Disclosure for Pledged Receivables

Current assets:
Accounts receivable, net of allowance for doubtful
  accounts of $600,000 ($3,500,000 of which has been
  pledged as collateral for bank loans)   8,450,000

Current liabilities:
Bank loans payable (secured by pledged accounts
  receivable)   2,700,000

A more common practice is to include the disclosure in the notes to the financial statements.

Assignment of Receivables. The assignment of accounts receivable is a more formalized transfer of the asset to the lending institution. In general, the lender will make an investigation of the specific receivables that are being proposed for assignment and will approve those which are deemed to be worthy as collateral. Customers are not usually aware that their accounts have been assigned and they continue to forward their payments to the original obligee. In some cases, the assignment agreement requires that collection proceeds be immediately delivered to the lender. The borrower is, however, the primary obligor and is required to make timely payment on the debt whether or not the receivables are collected as anticipated. The borrowing is with recourse, and the general credit of the borrower is pledged to the payment of the debt.

Since the lender knows that not all the receivables will be collected on a timely basis by the borrower, only a fraction of the face value of the receivables will be advanced as a loan to the borrower. Typically, this amount ranges from 70 to 90%, depending upon the credit history and collection experience of the borrower.

Assigned accounts receivable remain the assets of the borrower and continue to be presented in its financial statements, with appropriate disclosure of the assignment similar to that illustrated for pledging. Prepaid finance charges would be debited to a prepaid expense account and amortized to expense over the period to which the charges apply.

Factoring of Receivables. This third category of financing involving accounts receivable is the most significant in terms of accounting implications. Factoring traditionally has involved the outright sale of receivables to a financing institution known as a factor. These arrangements typically involved (1) notification to the customer to forward future payments to the factor and (2) the transfer of receivables without recourse. The factor assumes the risk of an inability to collect. Thus, once a factoring arrangement was completed, the entity had no further involvement with the accounts, except for a return of merchandise.

The classical variety of factoring provides two financial services to the business: first, it permits the entity to obtain cash earlier and, second, the risk of bad debts is transferred to the factor. The factor is compensated for each of the services. Interest is charged based on the anticipated length of time between the date the factoring is consummated and the expected collection date of the receivables sold, and a fee is charged based upon the factor's anticipated bad debt losses.

Some companies continue to factor receivables as a means of transferring the risk of bad debts, but leave the cash on deposit with the factor until the weighted-average due date of the receivables, thereby avoiding interest charges. This arrangement is still referred to as factoring, since the customer receivables have been sold. However, the borrowing entity does not receive cash but instead has created a new receivable, usually captioned "Due From Factor." This receivable, in contrast to the original customer receivables, is essentially riskless and will be presented in the balance sheet without a deduction for estimated uncollectibles.

Another variation is known as factoring with recourse. Some entities had such a poor history of uncollectible accounts that factors were only willing to purchase their accounts if a substantial fee were collected to compensate for the risk. When the company believed that the receivables were of a better quality than the factor did, a way to avoid excessive factoring fees was to sell these receivables with recourse. This variation of factoring was really an assignment of receivables with notification to the customers.

Factoring does transfer title. Where there is a no recourse provision, the removal of these receivables from the borrower's balance sheet is clearly warranted.

Merchandise returns will normally be the responsibility of the original vendor, who must then make the appropriate settlement with the factor. To protect against the possibility of merchandise returns which diminish the total of receivables to be collected, very often a factoring arrangement will **not** advance the full amount of the factored receivables (less any interest and factoring fee deductions). Rather, the factor will retain a certain fraction of the total proceeds relating to the portion of sales which are anticipated to be returned by customers. This sum is known as the factor's holdback. When merchandise is returned to the borrower, an entry is made offsetting the receivable from the factor. At the end of the return privilege period, any remaining holdback which has not been offset in this manner will become due and payable to the borrower.

Examples of Journal Entries to be Made by the Borrower in a Factoring Situation

1. Thirsty Corp. on July 1, 1991, enters into an agreement with Rich Company to sell a group of its receivables without recourse. A total face value of $200,000 accounts receivable (against which a 5% allowance had been recorded) are involved. The factor will charge 20% interest computed on the (weighted) average time to maturity of the receivables of 36 days plus a 3% fee. A 5% holdback will also be retained.
2. Thirsty's customers return for credit $4,800 of merchandise.
3. The customer return privilege period expires and the remaining holdback is paid to the transferor.

The entries required are as follows:

1.	Cash	180,055	
	Allowance for bad debts (200,000 x .05)	10,000	
	Interest expense (or prepaid) (200,000 x .20 x 36/365)	3,945	
	Factoring fee (200,000 x .03)	6,000	
	Factor's holdback receivable (200,000 x .05)	10,000	
	Bad debts expense		10,000
	Accounts receivable		200,000

(Alternatively, consistent with SFAS 77, the interest and factor's fee can be combined into a $9,945 charge to loss on sale of receivables)

2.	Sales returns and allowances	4,800	
	Factor's holdback receivable		4,800
3.	Cash	5,200	
	Factor's holdback receivable		5,200

Transfers of Receivables with Recourse

When receivables are transferred with recourse, the arrangement is a compromise between true factoring and an assignment of receivables. Past accounting practice has varied considerably because of the hybrid nature of these transactions. This varied treatment has been restricted by SFAS 77 which requires the transfer of receivables to be recognized as a sale (transfer of title) if certain specific conditions exist. These conditions are closely related to the factor's ability to put the receivables back to the borrower. If these specific conditions are met, the transferor-borrower must give immediate recognition to gains or losses arising from the transactions. If they are not met, the amount of the proceeds received as a result of the transfer is to be recorded as a liability.

Conditions. SFAS 77 applies only to the transfer of receivables which meet the conditions listed below, and not to any other borrowing situations involving receivables, such as assignments. Such agreements shall be treated as a sale, with immediate recognition of any related gains or losses, only if **all** of the following conditions are met:

1. The transferor surrenders control of the future economic benefits.
2. The transferor's obligation under the recourse provisions can be reasonably estimated.
3. The transferee cannot require the transferor to repurchase the receivables, except pursuant to the recourse provisions.

For purposes of determining whether or not control has been surrendered, SFAS 77 states that the transferor must **not** have the option to reacquire the receivables. The transferor's obligation (which must be estimated) is the expected payments under the recourse provision. Finally, the transfer is not to be recognized as a sale if the transferee has the unilateral ability to put the receivables back to the transferor.

The EITF has reached a consensus (EITF 89-2) that sale accounting would be appropriate when there is a put by the purchaser or a call by the seller to be exercised at a specified future date when outstanding balances are expected to be minor (undefined) based on the **contractual payment schedule** of the underlying receivables. Sale accounting is **not** appropriate under the above circumstances when the expected minor balances are based on the seller's estimate of prepayments and when these balances are **not** minor based on the contractual payment terms.

Gain or Loss. In computing the gain or loss to be recognized at the date of the transfer of the receivables, the borrower (transferor) must take into account the anticipated chargebacks from the transferee for bad debts to be incurred. This requires an estimate by the transferor, based on past experience. Adjustments should also be made at the time of sale for the estimated effects of any prepayments by customers (where the receivables are interest-bearing or where cash discounts are available), and for the effects of any defects in the eligibility of the transferred receivables.

If, subsequent to the sale of the receivables, the actual experience relative to the recourse terms differs from the provision made at the time of the sale, a change in an accounting estimate results and it is reflected as an additional gain or loss in the subsequent period. These changes are not corrections of errors or retroactive adjustments.

Example of Accounting for the Transfer of Receivables with Recourse

1. Thirsty Corp., on July 1, 1991, enters into an agreement with Rich Company to sell a group of receivables with a face value of $200,000 on which a 5% allowance had been recorded. Rich Company (the factor) will charge 20% interest computed on the weighted-average time to maturity of the receivables of 36 days and a 3% fee. A 5% holdback will also be retained.
2. Generally, 40% of Thirsty's customers take advantage of a 2% cash discount.
3. The factor accepts the receivables subject to recourse for nonpayment.

This situation qualifies as a sale because the Thirsty Corp. has surrendered control of the receivables, Thirsty's future obligation is reasonably estimable, and Rich Co. does not have a unilateral ability to require Thirsty to repurchase the receivables.

The entry required to record the sale is as follows:

Cash	180,055	
Loss on sale of receivables	11,545	
Allowance for bad debts	10,000	
Due to factor (200,000 x .40 x .02)		1,600
Accounts receivable		200,000

Due to factor is the sum of the anticipated amounts the factor will charge back for cash discounts ($1,600) and bad debts ($10,000) less the factor's holdback ($10,000). The accounts receivables and the allowance for bad debts (a contra-asset) are removed from the transferor's books as these have been sold. Previously accrued bad debts expense is **not** reversed, however, as the transferor still expects to incur this through the recourse provision of the factoring agreement. (Alternatively, the bad debts expense could have been reversed and the charge to loss on sale increased by $10,000.) The loss on sale of receivables is the sum of the interest charged by the factor ($3,945), the factor's fee ($6,000), and the expected chargeback for cash discounts to be taken ($1,600).

If the foregoing facts apply but the transfer does **not** qualify as a sale under the provisions of SFAS 77 because the transferee has the right to return the receivables under a wide range of circumstances, apart from default conditions, the borrower's entry will be as follows:

Cash	180,055	
Interest expense (or prepaid)	3,945	
Factoring fee	6,000	
Factor borrowing payable		190,000

The accounts receivable remain on the borrower's books. Both the accounts receivable and the factor borrowings payable should be cross-referenced in the balance sheet.

Short-Term Investments

Short-term (or temporary) investments, apart from the certificates of deposit or other restricted cash accounts discussed earlier, usually consist of marketable debt and equity securities. To be properly classified as a current asset the investment must be marketable, so that it can be liquidated readily, and management's intention must be that the investment will be liquidated within one year or the current operating cycle. Accordingly, investments that are held for purposes of control of another entity or pursuant to an ongoing business relationship--for example, stock held in a supplier-- would be excluded from current assets and would instead be listed as **other assets** or **long-term investments** (see Chapter 9).

Marketable equity securities. GAAP governing the accounting for marketable equity securities is SFAS 12. Marketable equity securities include not only stock, but also the rights to purchase stock, such as warrants or call options, and the right to sell stock, such as put options. SFAS 12 does not apply to securities accounted for by the equity method. These securities are accounted for in accordance with APB 18 and are discussed in Chapter 9.

If a classified balance sheet is to be presented, the equity securities owned by an entity shall be grouped into current and noncurrent portfolios. The determination of current or noncurrent status is to be made on the basis of whether or not the securities are considered working capital available for current operations (ARB 43, Chapter 3A). If a classified balance sheet is not presented, the marketable equity securities are to be considered noncurrent in applying the provisions of SFAS 12.

Carrying Amount. The carrying amount of a marketable equity securities portfolio is to be the lower of its aggregate cost or market value as of the balance sheet date. The lower of cost or market determination is to be made separately for both the current and noncurrent portfolio.

If the aggregate market value of the portfolio is less than its aggregate cost, the difference shall be accounted for in a valuation allowance account. This account is a contra-asset account which serves to reduce the carrying amount of the securities shown on the balance sheet to their net realizable value. The change in the valuation account, applicable to the **current** portfolio, is to be included in the determination of net income for the period. If these securities are invested to temporarily use idle cash, and if these securities are considered working capital, then management's stewardship function should be measured and evaluated by reflecting its performance on the income statement. The change in the valuation account relative to the **noncurrent** portfolio is to be included in the equity section of the balance sheet and shown separately. The unrealized loss is shown as a contra-equity account since the securities are held for the long-run and are not for sale. The income statement should not reflect changes in value since they are not relevant for performance measurement purposes in this case.

Because the allowance account exists as a result of aggregate cost exceeding aggregate market value, the effect on net income must be either a loss, or a recovery of a loss. At no time can the securities be valued above their original aggregate cost. According to SFAS 12, para 29(c), the Board does not regard the reversal of a write-down as an unrealized gain. Rather, the reversal represents a change in estimate of an unrealized loss. Thus, the income statement presentation should be stated as the recovery of an unrealized loss.

Unrealized Gain or Loss. The term unrealized gain is used by the FASB to identify a situation where the market value of the securities exceeds their cost. While this amount would not be included in the determination of net income, disclosure is required. SFAS 12 requires disclosure of the gross unrealized gains and losses in the notes to the financial statements. Note that the gross determination differs from the net determination. It is the **net** unrealized loss that would be included in current net income.

Example of Accounting for Marketable Securities

1. The year 1 current marketable equity securities portfolio is as follows:

Security	Cost	Market	Difference (cost-market)
ABC	$1,000	$ 900	$100
MNO	1,500	1,700	(200)
STU	2,000	1,400	600
XYZ	2,500	2,600	(100)
Aggregate amounts	$7,000	$6,600	$400

A $400 adjustment is required in order to recognize the decline in the aggregate market value. The entry required is:

Unrealized loss on current marketable securities	400	
Valuation allowance--current marketable securities		400

The unrealized loss would appear on the income statement as part of other expenses and losses. The balance sheet disclosure would appear as follows:

Marketable securities at cost	$7,000
Less valuation allowance to reduce marketable securities to market	(400)
Marketable securities at lower of cost or market	$6,600

In the second year the current marketable securities portfolio appeared as follows:

Year 2:

Security	Cost	Market	Difference (cost-market)
ABC	$1,000	$1,000	$ --
MNO	1,500	1,500	--
STU	2,000	1,800	200
XYZ	2,500	2,600	(100)
Aggregate amounts	$7,000	$6,900	$100

Note two important things. First, aggregate market is still less than aggregate cost, so a valuation allowance is still required. Second, while a valuation allowance of $100 is required, the present balance is $400 carried over from last year. Thus, a recovery of an **unrealized** loss of $300 is recognized in order to show the securities at a net realizable value of $6,900. The entry and associated balance sheet presentation would be:

Valuation allowance--current marketable securities	300	
Recovery of unrealized loss on marketable securities		300

The recovery of the unrealized loss would appear on the income statement as a part of other revenues and gains. The balance sheet presentation would be:

Marketable securities at cost	$7,000
Less valuation allowance to reduce marketable securities to market	(100)
Marketable securities at lower of cost or market	$6,900

If the year 2 market value had been $7,300, the journal entry amount above would have been for $400, not $300. The $400 adjustment would have reduced the valuation allowance account to zero and the securities would have been shown on the balance sheet at cost of $7,000, which is lower than the market of $7,300.

Realized Gain or Loss. Realized gains or losses result from the sale of marketable equity securities and are included in the computation of the current period net income. A realized gain or loss has no direct effect upon the computation of the valuation allowance. An indirect effect occurs because the sold security is not included in the portfolio totals at the balance sheet date when the balance in the valuation account is determined.

Example of Accounting for a Realized Gain

1. The same information as given in the above example for year 1.
2. Security XYZ was sold during year 2 for $2,700.

The entry required to record the sale is:

Cash	2,700	
Realized gain on sale of		
marketable securities		200
Marketable securities--current		2,500

The valuation allowance for year 2 would then be computed as follows:

Year 2:

Security	Cost	Market	Difference (cost-market)
ABC	$1,000	$1,000	$ --
MNO	1,500	1,500	--
STU	2,000	1,800	200
Aggregate amounts	$4,500	$4,300	$200

The entry required to adjust the allowance account to $200 (from $400) is:

Valuation allowance--current		
marketable securities	200	
Recovery of unrealized loss		200

The amounts of gross unrealized gains and losses required to be disclosed would be calculated by finding them in the last row (difference) of the cost versus market comparisons and aggregating them as to gains and losses.

If a transfer occurs between the current and noncurrent portfolios, the security shall be transferred at the lower of cost or market. If the market value of the transferred security is less than its original cost, the market value shall become its new cost basis and the difference shall be accounted for as a realized loss and included in the determination of net income in the period of transfer.

Deferred tax effects. See the discussion in Chapter 9, p. 254

Options

Call and put options have become extremely popular trading vehicles on several major exchanges. They can be effectively used as valuable hedging instruments or as highly leveraged speculative ventures. One call contract gives the **buyer** the right to **buy** 100 shares of the underlying security at a specific exercise price, regardless of the market price. The **seller** of the call, on the other hand, must **sell** the security to the buyer at that exercise price, regardless of the market price. For example, assume a Disney July 35 call has a quoted market price of $6 (per share or $600 per contract). These facts indicate that a buyer that pays six hundred dollars to a seller for a call has the right to purchase 100 shares of Disney at any time until July (typically the end of trading on the third Friday of the month quoted) for $35 per share. The buyer can exercise this right at any time until it expires. The seller of the call must stand ready to deliver 100 shares to the buyer for $35 per share until expiration. Typically, the buyer expects the market price to rise and the seller expects the market price to stay the same or to fall.

A put is the opposite of a call. A put gives the **buyer** the right to **sell** the underlying security at the exercise price regardless of the market price. It gives the **seller** the obligation to **buy** at the exercise price. Typically, the buyer expects the market price to fall and the seller expects the market price to stay the same or to rise. Strips, straps, straddles, and spreads are combinations and/or variations of the basic call and the basic put.

Example

Seller D owns 100 shares of Disney at a cost of $35 per share and sells 1 Disney July 35 call to Buyer E at $6. The following positions result if the market price:

	Position	
	Seller (D)	*Buyer (E)*
1. Stays at 35 and there is no exercise:	+$600 premium	-$600 premium

D receives the $600 premium and E pays for the right to call the stock. If the market price doesn't move, the option expires and both parties remain as they started out.

2. Rises to 55 and there is an exercise and immediate sale:	+$600 (0 + 600)	+$1,400 (2,000 - 600)

If the price rises to $55 per share and the security is called, D sells the security to E at $35 ($0 profit on the shares) and is effectively $600 (the amount of the premium) better off. E, however, buys the security at $35 per share and immediately sells it for $55 per share. E gains $2,000 from the security sale less the $600 premium and is $1,400 better off.

3. Falls to 15 and there is no exercise:	-$1,400 (- 2,000 + 600)	- $600 (0 - 600)

If the market price falls to $15 per share, D incurs an effective $2,000 decrease in value of the shares held, less the $600 premium received. E does not exercise the option and loses the premium paid.

The accounting problems revolve around whether cost or market or some combination should be used in accounting for the option itself and/or the associated underlying security. For instance, assume M buys 100 shares of XYZ at $15 per share and the security price immediately moves to $25 per share. At this point, M **buys** a November 25 put contract at 1 ($100 per contract). M has effectively hedged and guaranteed a minimum profit of $900 [(100 shares x $10) - ($1 x 100 shares)] regardless of market price movement since XYZ can be **sold** for $25 per share until the third Friday in November. If the price continues upward, the put will expire unexercised and M will continue to benefit point for point. If the price stays the same, M locks in a profit of $900. If the price falls, M has locked in a profit of $900. The question is whether these facts can be accounted for by the cost principle for option and security, by the market principle for option and security, or by some combination.

At the present time, SFAS 12 is the only definitive guidance. The AICPA has approved Issues Paper 86-2, "Accounting for Options" but because of inconsistencies with hedge accounting as specified in SFAS 52 and SFAS 80, there is considerable doubt as to whether the FASB will adopt the recommendations of the issues paper. In the meantime, the options are usually carried at the lower of cost or market. If hedge accounting is used, SFAS 80 probably provides the best guidance.

Marketable debt securities. The cost of debt securities includes brokerage fees and taxes, but accrued interest (on debt securities) at the date of purchase must be segregated as a separate asset. The selling price is considered net of brokerage fees, etc.

SFAS 12 does not apply to debt securities. ARB 43 prescribes **cost** as the carrying value for debt securities unless two conditions have occurred. The two conditions which necessitate a write-down to a value below original cost are:

1. The decline in the value of debt securities is substantial.
2. The decline in market value is not due to a temporary condition.

If both of these conditions are satisfied, then the carrying value of the securities is written down to market, and this market value becomes the new cost. The write-down is considered permanent and any recoveries are ignored.

Amortization of any premium or discount on short-term debt securities is generally ignored. The premium, or discount, on long-term debt securities is amortized. The accounting for long-term debt securities is discussed in Chapter 12.

Prepaid Expenses

Prepaid expenses are identified as a current asset by ARB 43, Chapter 3A. They are considered current not because of their anticipated conversion to cash during the current operating cycle, but rather because if they were not prepaid they would require the use of current assets during the operating cycle. The account is to be amortized to expense on a ratable basis over the life of the asset.

Disclosures

1. Financial Instruments
    a. For financial instruments with **off-balance-sheet** risk:
        1. The face, contract, or notional principal amount
        2. The nature and terms of the instruments including a discussion of
            (a) the credit and market risks,
            (b) the case requirements, and
            (c) the related accounting policies (pursuant to APB 22)
    b. For financial instruments with **off-balance-sheet** credit risk, an entity must disclose in the body of the statement or in notes to the statements the following information by class of financial instrument:
        1. The amount of **accounting** loss the entity would incur if any party to the financial instrument failed completely to perform according to the terms of the contract and if any collateral proved worthless
        2. The entity's policy for requiring collateral on financial instruments subject to credit risks, information about access to that collateral and the nature and brief description of collateral supporting financial instruments
    c. Disclosure of information is required about significant concentrations of credit risk for **all** financial instruments. Both individual and group concentrations of credit risk are to be disclosed. The following shall be disclosed about each significant concentration:
        1. Information about the shared activity, region or economic characteristic that identifies the concentration
        2. The amount of **accounting** loss the entity would incur if any party to the financial instrument failed to completely perform and if any collateral proved worthless
        3. The entity's policy for requiring collateral on financial instruments subject to credit risks, information about access to the collateral and the nature and a brief description of collateral supporting financial instruments

    All of the above disclosures are in addition to other disclosure requirements prescribed by GAAP. SFAS 105 amends SFAS 77 disclosures. In the year of transition, comparative information for previous fiscal years need not be included. For all subsequent fiscal years, the information required to be disclosed by SFAS 105 shall be included for each year for which a statement of financial position is presented for comparative purposes.

2. Cash
    a. The amount of cash restricted shall be segregated and classified according to the nature of the restriction
    b. Compensating balances shall be disclosed as to their nature and amount
    c. Overdrafts shall be presented as current liabilities

3. Receivables
    a. Receivables involving officers, employees, and other related parties shall be separated as to the amount and nature of the transactions
    b. The amount of unearned finance charges and interest shall be deducted from the face amount of the receivables
    c. The amount and nature of pledged or assigned receivables and receivables sold with recourse shall be made known
    d. The amount of the valuation allowance including the current period provision shall be made known
    e. Credit balances should be reclassified as current liabilities
4. Marketable equity securities
    a. The aggregate cost and market value shall be segregated as to current and noncurrent. Carrying value should also be identified.
    b. The gross unrealized gain or loss shall be separately disclosed for both the current and noncurrent portfolios
    c. The net realized gain or loss on marketable equity securities included in the determination of net income, and the method upon which the cost basis was determined shall be identified
    d. The change in the valuation allowance accounts included as part of equity and that included in the determination of net income shall be made known

6 Inventory

Perspective and Issues

The accounting for inventories is a major consideration for many entities because of its significance on both the income statement (cost of goods sold) and the balance sheet. Inventories are defined in ARB 43, Ch. 4 as:

> ...those items of tangible personal property which are held for sale in the ordinary course of business, are in the process of production for such sale, or are to be currently consumed in the production of goods or services to be available for sale.

The complexity of accounting for inventories arises from several factors:

1. The high volume of activity (or turnover) in the account
2. The various cost flow alternatives
3. The classification of inventories

There are two types of entities for which we must consider the accounting for inventories. The merchandising entity (generally a retailer or wholesaler) has a single inventory account which is usually titled merchandise inventory. These are the goods on hand which are purchased for resale. The other type of entity is the manufacturer. The manufacturer generally has three types of inventory: (1) raw materials, (2) work in process, and (3) finished goods. Raw materials inventory represents the goods purchased which will act as inputs in the production process leading to the finished product. Work in process (WIP) consists of the goods entered into production, but not yet completed. Finished goods inventory is the completed product which is on hand awaiting sale.

In the case of either type of entity we are concerned with satisfying the same basic questions:

1. At what point in time should the items be included in inventory (ownership)?
2. What costs incurred should be included in the valuation of inventories?
3. What cost flow assumption should be used?
4. At what value should inventories be reported (LCM)?

The promulgated GAAP which addresses these questions is ARB 43, Chapter 4. ARB 43, Chapter 4 discusses the definition, valuation, and classification of inventory. APB 28 addresses the measurement and classification of inventories during interim periods. Finally, SFAS 48 and SFAS 49 both deal with inventory-related topics; SFAS 48 concerns revenue recognition when the buyer has the right to return the product, and SFAS 49 addresses product financing arrangements.

Sources of GAAP

ARB	*APB*	*SFAS*	*EITF*
43, Chap. 4	28, 29	48, 49	86-46

Definitions of Terms

Absorption (full costing). Inclusion of all manufacturing costs (fixed and variable) in the cost of finished goods inventory, in accordance with GAAP.

Base stock. Based on the theory that a minimal level of inventory is a permanent investment, this amount is carried on the books at its historical cost.

Ceiling. In lower of cost or market computations, market is limited to net realizable value. Market (replacement cost) cannot be higher than the ceiling (net realizable value). Net realizable value is selling price less selling costs and costs to complete.

Consignments. A marketing method in which the consignor ships goods to the consignee, who acts as an agent for the consignor in selling the goods. The inventory remains the property of the consignor until sold by the consignee.

Direct (variable) costing. Inclusion of only variable manufacturing costs in the cost of ending finished goods inventory. This method is not acceptable for financial reporting purposes.

Dollar-value LIFO. A variation of conventional LIFO in which layers of inventory are priced in dollars adjusted by price indexes, instead of layers of inventory priced at unit prices.

Double-extension. A method used to compute the conversion price index. The index indicates the relationship between the base-year and current prices in terms of a percentage.

Finished goods. The completed, but unsold, products produced by a manufacturing firm.

First-in, first-out (FIFO). A cost flow assumption; the first goods purchased or produced are assumed to be the first goods sold.

Floor. In lower of cost or market computations, market is limited to net realizable value less a normal profit, called the floor. Market (replacement cost) cannot be below the floor.

Goods in transit. Goods being shipped from seller to buyer at year end.

Gross profit method. A method used to estimate the amount of ending inventory based on the cost of goods available for sale, sales, and the gross profit percentage.

Inventory. Those items of tangible property which are held for sale in the normal course of business, are in the process of being produced for such purpose, or are to be used in the production of such items.

Inventory layer. Under the LIFO method, an increase in inventory quantity during a period.

Last-in, first-out (LIFO). A cost flow assumption; the last goods purchased are assumed to be the first goods sold.

LIFO conformity rule. An IRS requirement that if the LIFO method is used for tax purposes, it must also be used for financial reporting purposes.

LIFO liquidation. Liquidation of the LIFO base or old inventory layers when inventory quantities decrease. This can distort income since old costs are matched against current revenues.

LIFO retail. An inventory costing method which combines the LIFO cost flow assumption and the retail inventory method.

Link-chain. Method of applying dollar-value LIFO by developing a single cumulative index. This method may be used instead of double-extension only when there are substantial changes in product lines over the years.

Lower of cost or market. Inventories must be valued at lower of cost or market (replacement cost). Market cannot exceed the ceiling (net realizable value) or be less than the floor (net realizable value less a normal markup).

Markdown. A decrease below original retail price. A markdown cancelation is an increase (not above original retail price) in retail price after a markdown.

Markup. An increase above original retail price. A markup cancelation is a decrease (not below original retail price) in retail price after a markup.

Moving average. An inventory costing method used in conjunction with a perpetual inventory system. A weighted-average cost per unit is recomputed after every purchase. Goods sold are costed at the most recent moving average cost.

Parking transaction. An arrangement which attempts to remove inventory and a current liability from the balance sheet. See "product financing arrangement."

Periodic. An inventory system where quantities are determined only periodically by physical count.

Perpetual. An inventory system where up-to-date records of inventory quantities are kept.

Product financing arrangements. An arrangement whereby a firm buys inventory for another firm which agrees to purchase the inventory over a certain period at specified prices which include handling and financing costs.

Purchase commitments. A noncancelable commitment to purchase goods. Losses on such commitments are recognized in the accounts.

Raw materials. For a manufacturing firm, materials on hand awaiting entry into the production process.

Replacement cost. The cost to reproduce an inventory item by purchase or manufacture. In lower of cost or market computations, the term market means replacement cost, subject to the ceiling and floor limitations.

Retail method. An inventory costing method which uses a cost ratio to reduce ending inventory (valued at retail) to cost.

Specific identification. An inventory system where the seller identifies which specific items are sold and which remain in ending inventory.

Standard costs. Predetermined unit costs, which are acceptable for financial reporting purposes if adjusted periodically to reflect current conditions.

Weighted-average. A periodic inventory costing method where ending inventory and cost of goods sold are priced at the weighted-average cost of all items available for sale.

Work in process. For a manufacturing firm, the inventory of partially completed products.

Concepts, Rules, and Examples

Ownership of Goods

The purpose of examining and determining the proper ownership of inventories is to assist in the determination of the actual physical quantity of inventory on hand. In general, a firm should record purchases and sales of inventory when legal title passes. While strict adherence to this rule is not as important in daily transactions, a proper inventory cutoff at the end of an accounting period is crucial. Thus, for accounting purposes it is necessary to determine when title has passed in order to obtain an accurate measurement of inventory quantity. The most common error made in this area is to assume that the entity has title only to the goods on hand. This may be incorrect in two ways: (1) the goods on hand may not be owned, and (2) goods that are not on hand may be owned. There are four areas which create a question as to proper ownership: (1) goods in transit, (2) consignment sales, (3) product financing arrangements, and (4) sales made with the buyer holding the right of return.

At year end, any **goods in transit** from seller to buyer must be included in one of those parties' inventories based on the conditions of the sale. Such goods are included in the inventory of the firm financially responsible for transportation costs. If goods are shipped FOB destination, transportation costs are paid by the seller, and title does not pass until the carrier delivers the goods to the buyer; thus, these goods are part of the seller's inventory while in transit. If goods are shipped FOB shipping point, transportation costs are paid by the buyer, and title passes when the carrier takes possession; thus, these goods are part of the buyer's inventory while in transit.

In **consignments,** the consignor (seller) ships goods to the consignee (buyer) who acts as the agent of the consignor in trying to sell the goods. In some consignments, the consignee receives a commission; in other arrangements, the consignee "purchases" the goods simultaneously with the sale of the goods to the customer. Goods out on consignment are included in the inventory of the consignor and excluded from the inventory of the consignee.

SFAS 49 addresses the problems involved with **product financing arrange-ments.** A product financing arrangement is a transaction in which an entity sells and agrees to repurchase inventory with the repurchase price equal to the original sales price plus the carrying and financing costs. The purpose of this transaction is to allow the seller (sponsor) to arrange financing of his/her original purchase of the inventory. The substance of the transaction is illustrated by the diagram below.

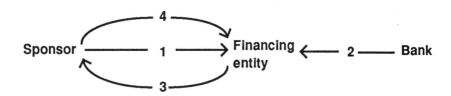

1. In the initial transaction the sponsor "sells" inventoriable items to the financing entity in return for the remittance of the sales price and at the same time agrees to repurchase the inventory at a specified price (usually the sales price plus carrying and financing costs) over a specified period of time.
2. The financing entity procures the funds remitted to the sponsor by borrowing from a bank (or other financial institution) using the newly purchased inventory as collateral.
3. The financing entity actually remits the funds to the sponsor and the sponsor presumably uses these funds to pay off the debt incurred as a result of the original purchase of the inventoriable debt.
4. The sponsor then repurchases the inventory for the specified price plus costs from the financing entity at a later time when the funds are available.

The purpose of this transaction was to enable the sponsor to acquire inventory and record sales without incurring additional reportable debt. The FASB ruled that the substance of this transaction is that of a borrowing transaction. That is, the transaction is in substance no different from the sponsor obtaining third-party financing to purchase his/her inventory. As a result, the FASB, in SFAS 49, ruled that the proper accounting is to record a liability when the funds are received for the initial transfer of the inventory in the amount of the selling price. The sponsor is then to accrue carrying and financing costs in accordance with his/her normal accounting policies. These accruals are eliminated and the liability satisfied when the sponsor repurchases the inventory. The inventory is **not** to be taken off the balance sheet of the sponsor and a sale is not to be recorded. Thus, although legal title has passed to the financing entity, for purposes of measuring and valuing inventory, the inventory is considered to be owned by the sponsor.

Another area which requires special consideration is the situation which exists when the buyer holds the **right of return**. SFAS 48 addresses the propriety of recognizing revenue at the point of sale under such a situation (this topic is discussed in detail in Chapter 7). Generally speaking, the sale is to be recorded if the future amount of the returns can be reasonably estimated. If the ability to make a reasonable estimate is precluded, then the sale is not to be recorded until the returns are unlikely. Thus, this too results in a situation where, although legal title has passed to the buyer, the seller must continue to include the goods in its measurement and valuation of inventory.

Accounting for Inventories

According to ARB 43, Chapter 4 a major objective of accounting for inventories is the matching of appropriate costs against revenues in order to arrive at the proper determination of periodic income. The accounting for inventories is done under either a periodic or perpetual system.

In a **periodic** inventory system, the inventory quantity is determined periodically by a physical count. The quantity so determined is then priced in accordance with the cost method used. Cost of goods sold is computed by adding beginning inventory and net purchases (or cost of goods manufactured) and subtracting ending inventory.

Alternatively, a **perpetual** inventory system keeps a running total of the quantity (and possibly the cost) of inventory on hand by recording all sales and purchases as they occur. When inventory is purchased, the inventory account (rather than purchases) is debited. When inventory is sold, the cost of goods sold and reduction of inventory are recorded. Periodic physical counts are necessary only to verify the perpetual records and to satisfy the tax regulations (tax regulations require that a physical inventory be taken, at least annually).

Valuation of Inventories

According to ARB 43, Chapter 4 the primary basis of accounting for inventories is cost. Cost is defined as the sum of the applicable expenditures and charges directly or indirectly incurred in bringing an article to its existing condition and location.

This definition allows for a wide interpretation of the costs to be included in inventory. For raw materials and merchandise inventory which are purchased outright, the identification of cost is relatively straightforward. The cost of these purchased inventories will include all expenditures incurred in bringing the goods to the point of sale and putting them in a salable condition. These costs include the purchase price, transportation costs, insurance, and handling costs.

It is important to note that purchases can be recorded at their gross amount or net of any allowable discount. If recorded at gross, the discounts taken represent a reduction in the purchase cost for purposes of determining cost of goods sold. On the other hand, if they are recorded at net, any lost discounts are treated as a financial expense, **not** part of cost of goods sold. The net method is considered to be theoretically preferable, but the gross method is simpler and, thus, more commonly used. Either method is acceptable under GAAP, provided that it is consistently applied.

The impact of interest costs as they relate to the valuation of inventoriable items (SFAS 34) is discussed in Chapter 8, Long-Lived Assets.

Full Absorption Costing--GAAP. As we mentioned above, the basis for valuing any inventory is cost; the basis for establishing cost in a manufacturing firm is to include both acquisition and production costs. This concept is commonly referred to as absorption or full costing. As a result, the WIP and finished goods inventory accounts are to include an appropriate portion of direct materials, direct labor, and indirect production costs (both fixed and variable). The difficulty in determining the cost for these manufacturing inventory accounts is in the allocation of indirect costs. Prior to the Tax Reform Act of 1986, production costing for GAAP and for income tax purposes was very similar. However, the Act has changed inventory costing for tax purposes by requiring certain additional indirect costs which are listed below to be capitalized rather than expensed.

ARB 43, Chapter 4 indicates that under some circumstances expenses related to an idle facility, excessive spoilage, double freight, and rehandling costs may be abnormal and, therefore, require treatment as period costs. On the other hand, there may be instances in which certain general and administrative expenses are directly related to the production process and, therefore, should be allocated to the WIP and finished goods inventory. ARB 43 also points out the fact that selling costs do not constitute inventory costs. The chart below shows items which would ordinarily be included in inventory to the extent such costs are incident to and necessary for production.

Indirect Production Costs Typically Included in Inventory Under Full Absorption

- Repairs
- Maintenance
- Utilities
- Rent
- Indirect labor
- Production supervisory wages
- Indirect materials and supplies
- Quality control and inspection
- Small tools not capitalized

Full Absorption Costing--Income Taxes. TRA 1986 requires that manufacturing firms capitalize rather than expense these additional items:

- Depreciation and amortization in excess of that reported in financial statements.

- Percentage depletion in excess of cost.
- Rework labor, scrap, and spoilage costs.
- Allocable general and administrative costs related to the production function.

For tax purposes, these costs, as well as the indirect production costs listed above for inventory costing under GAAP, will be allocated to the WIP and finished goods inventory. Examples of general and administrative costs that must be allocated include payroll department costs, wages of security guards, and the president's salary. These new capitalization rules apply to taxable years beginning after December 31, 1986. However, beginning inventories for the first year of the change must be restated as if the change had been in effect. Both the restatement of beginning inventory for tax purposes and temporary differences originating in subsequent periods will require interperiod income tax allocation.

Uniform Capitalization Rules--Tax vs. Financial. The Tax Reform Act of 1986, which established new uniform capitalization rules for inventory costs for tax purposes, has raised new accounting issues. These issues were considered by the Emerging Issues Task Force (Issue no. 86-46) and involve whether the costs capitalized for tax purposes should also be capitalized under generally accepted accounting principles and if so, whether the new costing method would be preferable for purposes of justifying a change in accounting principle.

The Task Force reached a consensus that capitalizing a cost for tax purposes does not indicate that it is preferable or appropriate to capitalize the cost for financial reporting purposes. Although the cost may be capitalized for financial purposes, an enterprise must analyze its individual facts and circumstances and determine whether to capitalize based on the nature of its operations and industry practice.

Direct costing. The alternative to absorption costing is direct costing. Direct costing is also referred to as variable costing and requires classifying only direct materials, direct labor, and variable overhead related to production as inventory costs. All fixed costs are accounted for as period costs. ARB 43, Chapter 4 indicates that the exclusion of all overhead from inventory costs does not constitute an accepted accounting procedure. This has typically been interpreted to mean that direct costing is not allowable for GAAP. Treasury regulations require the inclusion of overhead for tax purposes.

Inventory Capitalization for Retailers/Wholesalers--GAAP and Income Taxes. Retailers/wholesalers have previously recorded their inventory as the invoice price plus the cost of freight-in under both GAAP and tax law. However, the Tax Reform Act of 1986 now requires that additional costs be capitalized. These new uniform capitalization rules apply to all inventories except for the inventories of retailers/wholesalers whose average annual gross receipts do not exceed $10 million for the three preceding years. The costs which must be capitalized have been divided into two categories. The first category is direct costs and includes the inventory invoice price plus transportation. Also included in direct costs is the cost of labor for purchasing, storing, and handling inventory items. The second category is indirect costs and consists of any costs that directly benefit or are incurred because of the performance of a resale activity. The following types of indirect costs must be capitalized:

- Off-site storage or warehousing
- Purchasing
- Handling, processing, assembly, and repackaging
- Allocable general and administrative costs related
  to the above three functions

The indirect costs are allocated between inventory and cost of goods sold by using traditional methods (specific identification, standard costing methods, etc.) or one of three simplified methods. These new rules are effective for taxable years beginning after December 31, 1986, and require that the beginning inventory for the first year of application be restated to comply with the new capitalization rules. Both the restatement of beginning inventory for tax purposes and temporary differences originating in subsequent periods will require interperiod income tax allocation.

Specific Identification. The theoretical basis for valuing inventories and cost of goods sold requires assigning the production and/or acquisition costs to the specific goods to which they relate. This method of inventory valuation is usually referred to as specific identification. Specific identification is generally not practical as the product will generally lose its separate identity as it passes through the production and sales process. Exceptions to this would arise in situations involving small inventory quantities with high unit value and low turnover rate. Because of the limited applicability of specific identification, it is necessary to make certain assumptions regarding the cost flows associated with inventory. These cost flows may or may not reflect the physical flow of inventory in the organization.

Cost Flow Assumptions

According to ARB 43, Chapter 4:

> ...cost for inventory purposes shall be determined under any one of several assumptions as to the flow of cost factors; the major objective in selecting a method should be to choose the one which, under the circumstances, most clearly reflects periodic income.

The most common cost flow assumptions used are: (1) first-in, first-out (FIFO), (2) last-in, first-out (LIFO), and (3) weighted-average. Additionally, there are variations to each of these assumptions which are commonly used in practice.

In selecting the cost flow assumption to be used the entity should give thought to a variety of considerations. First of all, the industry norm should be examined as this will facilitate interfirm comparison. Recall that ARB 43 specified the major objective of such a selection "should be to choose the one which most clearly reflects periodic income." This will vary depending on the nature of the industry and the expected economic climate. The method which should be selected in a period of rising prices differs from that which is most applicable for declining prices. Each of the foregoing assumptions and their relative advantages or disadvantages are discussed below. Examples are provided to enhance the understanding of the application.

First-in, First-out (FIFO)

The FIFO method of inventory valuation assumes that the first goods purchased are the first goods used or sold, regardless of the actual physical flow. This method is thought to most closely parallel the physical flow of the units in most industries. The strength of this cost flow assumption lies in the inventory amount reported on the balance sheet. Because the earliest goods purchased are the first ones removed from the inventory account, the remaining balance is composed of items at the latest cost. This yields results similar to those obtained under current cost accounting on the balance sheet. However, the FIFO method does not necessarily reflect the most accurate income figure as historical costs are being matched against current revenues.

The following example illustrates the basic principles involved in the application of FIFO:

	Units available	Units sold	Actual unit cost	Actual total cost
Beginning inventory	100	--	$2.10	$210
Sale	--	75	--	--
Purchase	150	--	2.80	420
Sale	--	100	--	--
Purchase	50	--	3.00	150
Total	300	175		$780

Given these data, the cost of goods sold and ending inventory balance are determined as follows:

	Units	Unit cost	Total cost
Cost of goods sold	100	$2.10	$210
	75	2.80	210
	175		$420
Ending inventory	50	3.00	$150
	75	2.80	210
	125		$360

Notice that the total of the units in cost of goods sold and ending inventory, as well as the sum of their total costs, is equal to the goods available for sale and their respective total costs.

The unique characteristic of the FIFO method is that it provides the same results under either the periodic or perpetual system.

Last-in, First-out (LIFO)

The LIFO method of inventory valuation assumes that the last goods purchased are the first goods used or sold. This allows the matching of current costs with current revenue and, as proponents of the method argue, provides the best measure of periodic income which is the major objective stated in ARB 43. However, unless costs remain relatively unchanged, the LIFO method will usually misstate the ending inventory balance for balance sheet purposes because inventory usually consists of costs from earlier periods. Critics of the method also point out that LIFO does not usually follow the physical flow of merchandise or materials. However, this last argument should not affect the selection of a cost flow assumption, because the matching of physical flow is not considered to be an objective of accounting for inventories.

The LIFO method is not a promulgated accounting principle. Rather, the basis for LIFO is found in the Internal Revenue Code (the Code) §472 and, as such, is a tax concept. The treasury regulations indicate that any taxpayer who takes inventories may select LIFO application to any or all of his/her inventoriable items. This election is made with the taxpayer's tax return on Form 970 after the close of any taxable year.

Once elected, the LIFO method must continue to be used in future periods. In order to revert to another method, the taxpayer must apply for a change in accounting method on Form 3115 within the first 180 days of the taxable year during which the change is desired. A change to or from the LIFO method is an accounting change per APB 20 (see Chapter 19).

LIFO restrictions. In addition, a taxpayer must adhere to the following two significant restrictions for the portions of its inventory valued under LIFO:

1. The inventory is to be valued at cost regardless of market value (i.e., application of the lower of cost or market rule is not allowed).
2. The taxpayer may not use a different inventory method in ascertaining profit or loss of the entity for external financial reports (i.e., if LIFO is elected for tax purposes, it must also be used for accounting purposes). This is known as the LIFO conformity rule. (See the appendix to this chapter for exceptions to this rule.)

The actual implementation of LIFO requires the valuation of the quantity of ending inventory at earlier prices. The quantity of ending inventory on hand in the year of election is termed the "base layer." This inventory is valued at actual (full absorption) cost, and unit cost is determined by dividing total cost by the quantity on hand. In subsequent periods, increases in the quantity of inventory on hand are referred to as increments, or LIFO layers. These increments are valued individually by applying one of the following costs to the quantity of inventory representing a layer:

1. The actual cost of the goods most recently purchased or produced.
2. The actual cost of the goods purchased or produced in order of acquisition.
3. An average unit cost of all goods purchased or produced.
4. A hybrid method which will more clearly reflect income (this latter method must meet with the approval of the IRS Commissioner).

Thus, after using the LIFO method for five years, it is possible that an enterprise could have ending inventory consisting of the base layer and five additional layers (or increments) provided that the quantity of ending inventory increased every year.

The single goods (unit) LIFO approach is illustrated in the following example:

XYZ Co. is in its first year of operation and elects to use the periodic LIFO method of inventory valuation. The company sells only one product. XYZ will apply the LIFO method using the order of current year acquisition cost. The following data are given for years 1 through 3:

	Units	Unit cost	Total cost
Year 1			
Purchase	200	$2.00	$400
Sale	100	--	--
Purchase	200	3.00	600
Sale	150	--	--
Year 2			
Purchase	300	$3.20	$960
Sale	200	--	--
Purchase	100	3.30	330
Year 3			
Purchase	100	$3.50	$350
Sale	200	--	--
Sale	100	--	--

In year 1 the following occurred:

1. The total goods available for sale were 400 units.
2. The total sales were 250 units.
3. Therefore, the ending inventory was 150 units.

The ending inventory is valued at the earliest current year acquisition cost of $2.00 per unit. Thus, ending inventory is valued at $300 (150 x $2.00).

Another way to look at this is to analyze both cost of goods sold and ending inventory.

	Units	Unit cost	Total cost
Cost of goods sold	200	$3.00	$600
	50	2.00	100
	250		$700
Ending inventory	150	2.00	$300

Note that the base-year cost is $2.00 and that the base-year level is 150 units. Therefore, if ending inventory in the subsequent period exceeds 150 units, a new layer will be created.

Year 2	Units	Unit cost	Total cost
Cost of goods sold	100	$3.30	$330
	100	3.20	320
	200		$650
Ending inventory	150	2.00	$300
	200	3.20	640
	350		$940

Now, if ending inventory exceeds 350 units in the next period, a new layer will be created.

Year 3	Units	Unit cost	Total cost
Cost of goods sold	100	$3.50	$350
	200	3.20	640
	300		$990
Ending inventory base year	150	2.00	$300

Notice how the decrement of 200 units in year 3 eliminated the entire year 2 increment. Thus, any year 4 increase in the quantity of inventory would result in a **new** increment which would be valued at year 4 prices.

In situations where the ending inventory decreases from the level established at the close of the preceding year, the enterprise experiences a decrement or LIFO liquidation. Decrements will reduce or eliminate previously established LIFO layers. Once any part of a layer has been eliminated, it **cannot** be reinstated. For example, if in its first year after the election of LIFO an enterprise establishes a layer (increment) of 10 units, then in the next year inventory decreases by four units leaving the first layer at six units, the enterprise cannot reestablish the first layer (back up to ten units) in the year that inventory next increases. Rather, it will be forced to create a new layer for the increase. The effect of LIFO liquidations in periods of rising prices is to release costs, which are significantly below the current cost being paid, into cost of goods sold from ending inventory. Thus, the resultant effect of a LIFO liquidation is to increase income for **both** accounting and tax purposes. Because of this, LIFO is most commonly used by industries in which inventories are maintained or increased.

LIFO liquidations can take two forms, voluntary or involuntary. A voluntary liquidation exists when an enterprise decides, for one reason or another, to let inventory levels drop. Such a liquidation occurs because current prices may be too high, less inventory is needed for efficient production, or maybe because of a transition in the product lines. Involuntary LIFO liquidations stem from reasons beyond the control of the enterprise, such as a strike, shortages, shipping delay, etc. Regardless of the reason, all liquidations result in a corresponding increase in income (assuming rising prices).

To compute the effect of the liquidation, the company must compute the difference between actual cost of sales and what cost of sales would have been had the inventory been reinstated. The Internal Revenue Service has ruled that this hypothetical reinstatement must be computed under the company's normal pricing procedures for valuing its LIFO increments. In the above example the effect of the year 3 LIFO liquidation would be computed as follows:

> Inventory reinstatement:
> 200 units @ $3.50 - $3.20 = $60

Because the 200 units liquidated would have been stated at the year 3 price of $3.50 if there had been an increment, the difference between $3.50 and the actual amount charged to cost of sales for these units ($3.20) measures the effect of the liquidation.

The IRS has indicated the following to be acceptable disclosure for the LIFO liquidation:

> During 19___, inventory quantities were reduced. This reduction resulted in a liquidation of LIFO inventory quantities carried at lower costs prevailing in prior years as compared with the cost of 19___ purchases, the effect of which decreased cost of goods sold by approximately $xxx and increased net income by approximately $xx or $x per share.

An inordinate amount of record keeping is required in applying the unit LIFO method. Remember that the illustration above involved only one product. The record keeping is much greater as the number of products increases. For this reason a "pooling" approach is generally applied to LIFO inventories.

Pooling is the process of grouping items which are naturally related and then treating this group as a single unit in determining the LIFO cost. Because the quantity of ending inventory includes many more items, decreases in one item can be made up for by increases in others, whereas under the single goods unit approach a decrease in any one item results in a liquidation of LIFO layers.

The problem in applying the pooling method emanates from the tax regulations, not the practical side of application. In applying LIFO, the tax regulations state that each type of good in the opening inventory must be compared with a similar type in the closing inventory. These items must be similar as to character, quality, and price. This qualification has generally been interpreted to mean identical. The effect of this statement is to require a separate pool for each item under the unit LIFO method. The need for a simpler, more practical approach to using the LIFO concept and allowing for a greater use of the pooling concept was met by dollar-value LIFO.

Dollar-value LIFO

Use of dollar-value LIFO may be elected by any taxpayer. The dollar-value LIFO method of inventory valuation determines the cost of inventories by expressing base-year costs in terms of total dollars rather than specific prices of specific units. As discussed later, the dollar-value method also gives rise to an expanded interpretation of the use of pools. Increments and liquidations are treated the same, but are reflected only in terms of a **net** liquidation or increment for the entire pool.

Creating pools. Essentially three alternatives exist for determining pools under dollar-value LIFO: (1) the natural business unit, (2) multiple pools, and (3) pools for wholesalers, retailers, jobbers, etc.

The natural business unit is defined by the existence of separate and distinct processing facilities and operations and the maintenance of separate income (loss) records. The concept of the natural business unit is generally dependent upon the type of product, not the various stages of production for that project. Thus, the pool can (and will) contain raw materials, WIP, and finished goods. The three examples below, taken from the treasury regulations, illustrate the application of the natural business unit concept.

Example 1

A corporation manufactures, in one division, automatic clothes washers and dryers of both commercial and domestic grade as well as electric ranges, mangles, and dishwashers. The corporation manufactures, in another division, radios and television sets. The manufacturing facilities and processes used in manufacturing the radios and television sets are distinct from those used in manufacturing the automatic clothes washers, etc. Under these circumstances, the enterprise would consist of two business units and two pools would be appropriate: one consisting of all of the LIFO inventories involved with the manufacture of clothes washers and dryers, electric ranges, mangles, and dishwashers and the other consisting of all of the LIFO inventories involved with the production of radios and television sets.

Example 2

A taxpayer produces plastics in one of its plants. Substantial amounts of the production are sold as plastics. The remainder of the production is shipped to a second plant of the taxpayer for the production of plastic toys which are sold to customers. The taxpayer operates its plastics plant and toy plant as separate divisions. Because of the different product lines and the separate divisions, the taxpayer has two natural business units.

Example 3

A taxpayer is engaged in the manufacture of paper. At one stage of processing, uncoated paper is produced. Substantial amounts of uncoated paper are sold at this stage of processing. The remainder of the uncoated paper is transferred to the taxpayer's finishing mill where coated paper is produced and sold. This taxpayer has only one natural business unit since coated and uncoated paper are within the same product line.

The treasury regulations require that a pool shall consist of all items entering into the entire inventory investment of a natural business unit, unless the taxpayer elects to use the multiple pooling method.

The multiple pooling method is the grouping of substantially similar items. In determining substantially similar items, consideration should be given to the processing applied, the interchangeability, the similarity of use, and the customary practice of the industry. While the election of multiple pools will necessitate additional record keeping, it may result in a better estimation of periodic income.

According to Reg. §1.472-8(c), inventory items of wholesalers, retailers, jobbers, and distributors are to be placed into pools by major lines, types, or classes of goods. The natural business unit method may be used with permission of the commissioner.

All three methods of pooling allow for a change in the components of inventory. New items which properly fall within the pool may be added, and old items may disappear from the pool, but neither will necessarily effect a change in the total dollar value of the pool.

Computing dollar-value LIFO. The purpose of the dollar-value LIFO method of valuing inventory is to convert inventory which is priced at end-of-year prices to that same inventory priced at base-year (or applicable LIFO layer) prices. The dollar-value method achieves this result through the use of a conversion price index. The inventory at current year cost is divided by the appropriate index to arrive at the base-year cost. Thus, the main focus is on the determination of the conversion price index. There are three basic methods that can be used in the computation of the LIFO value of a dollar-value pool: (1) double extension, (2) link chain, and (3) the index method. Each of these is discussed below with examples provided where appropriate.

Double-extension method. This was the method originally developed to compute the conversion price index. It involves extending the entire quantity of ending inventory for the current year at both base-year prices and end-of-year prices to arrive at a total dollar value for each, hence the title of double extension. The end-of-year dollar total is then divided by the base-year dollar total to arrive at the index, usually referred to as the conversion price index. This index indicates the relationship between the base-year and current prices in terms of a percentage. Each layer (or increment) is valued at its own percentage. Although a representative sample is allowed (meaning that not all of the items need be double extended--this is discussed in more detail under indexing), the record keeping under this method is very burdensome. The base-year price must be kept for each inventory item. Depending upon the number of different items included in the inventory of the company, the necessary records may be too detailed to keep past the first year.

The following example illustrates the double-extension method of computing the LIFO value of inventory. The example presented is relatively simple and does not attempt to incorporate all of the complexities of inventory accounting.

Example

ABC, Inc. uses the dollar-value method of LIFO inventory valuation and computes its price index using the double-extension method. ABC has a single pool which contains two inventory items, A and B. Year 1 is the company's initial year of operations. The following information is given for years 1 through 4:

Year	Ending inventory current prices	Ending quantity (units) and current price A		B	
1	$100,000	5,000	$6.00	7,000	$10.00
2	120,300	6,000	6.30	7,500	11.00
3	122,220	5,800	6.40	7,400	11.50
4	133,900	6,200	6.50	7,800	12.00

In year 1 there is no computation of an index; the index is 100%. The LIFO cost is the same as the actual current year cost. This is our base year.

In year 2 the first step is to double extend the quantity of ending inventory at base-year and current year costs. This is illustrated below:

Item	Quantity	Base-year cost/unit	Extended	Current year cost/unit	Extended
A	6,000	$ 6.00	$ 36,000	$ 6.30	$ 37,800
B	7,500	10.00	75,000	11.00	82,500
			$111,000		$120,300*

* When using the double-extension method and extending **all** of the inventory items to arrive at the index, this number must equal the ending inventory at current prices. If a sampling method is used (as discussed under indexing) this number **divided by** your ending inventory at current prices will give you the percentage sampled.

Now we can compute the conversion price index which is:

$$\frac{\text{Ending inventory at current year prices}}{\text{Ending inventory at base-year prices}}$$

In this case: $\dfrac{120,300}{111,000} = 108.4\%$ (rounded)

Next, compute the year 2 layer at the base-year cost by taking the current year ending inventory at base-year prices (if you only extend a sample of the inventory, this number is arrived at by dividing the ending inventory at current year prices by the conversion price index) of $111,000 and subtracting the base-year cost of $100,000. In year 2 we have an increment (layer) of $11,000 at base-year costs.

The year 2 layer of $11,000 at base-year cost must be converted so that the layer is valued at the prices in effect when it came into existence (i.e., at year 2 prices). This is done by multiplying the increment at base-year cost ($11,000) by the conversion price index (1.08). The result is the year 2 layer at LIFO prices.

Base-year cost	$100,000
Year 2 layer ($11,000 x 1.084)	11,924
	$111,924

In year 3 the same basic procedure is followed.

Item	Quantity	Base-year cost/unit	Extended	Current year cost/unit	Extended
A	5,800	$ 6.00	$ 34,800	$ 6.40	$ 37,120
B	7,400	10.00	74,000	11.50	85,100
			$108,800		$122,220

There has been a decrease in the base-year cost of the ending inventory which is referred to as a decrement. A decrement results in the decrease (or elimination) of previously provided layers. In this situation, the computation of the index is not necessary as there is no LIFO layer that requires a valuation. If a sampling approach has been used, the index is needed to arrive at the ending inventory at base-year cost and thus determine if there has been an increment or decrement.

Now the ending inventory at base-year cost is $108,800. The base-year cost is still $100,000, so the total increment is $8,800. Since this is less than the $11,000 increment of year 2, no additional increment is established in year 3. The LIFO cost of the inventory is as shown below:

Base-year cost	$100,000
Year 2 layer ($8,800 x 1.084)	9,539
	$109,539

The fourth year then follows the same steps.

Items	Quantity	Base-year cost/unit	Extended	Current year cost/unit	Extended
A	6,200	$ 6.00	$ 37,200	$ 6.50	$ 40,300
B	7,800	10.00	78,000	12.00	93,600
			$115,200		$133,900

The conversion price index is 116.2% (133,900/115,200).

A current year increment exists because the ending inventory at base-year prices in year 4 of $115,200 exceeds the year 3 number of $108,800. The current year increment of $6,400 must be valued at year 4 prices. Thus, the LIFO cost of the year 4 inventory is

Base-year layer	$100,000
Year 2 layer ($8,800 x 1.084)	9,539
Year 4 layer ($6,400 x 1.162)	7,437
	$116,976

It is important to point out that once a layer is reduced or eliminated it is never replaced (as with the year 2 increment).

Link-chain method. As seen in this example, the computations for application become arduous even if only a few items exist in the inventory. Also, consider the problems that arise when there is a constant change in the inventory mix or in situations in which the breadth of the inventory is large. The link-chain method of applying dollar-value LIFO was developed to combat these problems.

Another purpose served by the link-chain method is to eliminate the problem created by a significant turnover in the components of inventory. Under the double-extension or indexing method, the regulations require that any new products added to the inventory be costed at base-year prices. If these are not available, then the earliest cost available after the base year is used. If the item was not in existence in the base year, the taxpayer may reconstruct the base cost, using a reasonable method to determine what the cost would have been if the item had been in existence in the base year. Finally, as a last resort, the purchase price can be used. While this does not appear to be a problem on the surface, imagine a base period which is 25 to 50 years in the past. The difficulty involved with finding the base-year cost may require using a more current cost, thus eliminating some of the LIFO benefit. Also imagine a situation faced by a "hi-tech" industry where inventory is continually being replaced by newer, more advanced products. The effect of this rapid change under the double-extension method (because the new products didn't exist in the base period) is to use current prices as base-year costs. Thus, when inventory has such a rapid turnover, the LIFO advantage is nonexistent as current and base-year costs are sometimes synonymous. This is the major reason for the development of the link-chain method.

This method was scheduled to be prohibited for tax purposes by the 1984 Tax Act; however, this provision was dropped in the last revision. The IRS requires that the same method of LIFO be used for both financial and tax purposes; therefore, if the method is dropped as an allowable one for tax purposes, it will no longer be used for financial purposes.

The link-chain method was originally developed for (and limited to) those companies that wanted to use LIFO but, because of a substantial change in product lines over time, were unable to recreate or keep the historical records necessary to make accurate use of the double-extension method. It is important to note that the double-extension and link-chain methods are not selective alternatives for the same situation. The link-chain election **requires** that substantial change in product line be evident over the years, and it is not electable because of its ease of application. The double-extension method must be demonstrated as impractical in order to elect the link-chain method.

The link-chain method is the process of developing a single cumulative index which is applied to the ending inventory amount priced at the beginning of the year costs. A separate cumulative index is used for each pool regardless of the variations in the components of these pools over the years. Technological change is allowed for by the method used to calculate each current year index. The index is derived by double extending a representative sample (generally thought to be between 50% and 75% of the dollar value of the pool) at both beginning-of-year prices and end-of-year prices. This annual index is then applied (multiplied) to the previous period's cumulative index to arrive at the new current year cumulative index.

An example of the link-chain method is shown below. Notice that the end-of-year costs and inventory quantity used are the same as those used in the double-extension example.

Assume the following inventory data for years 1-4. Year 1 is assumed to be the initial year of operation for the company. The LIFO method is elected on the first tax return. Assume that A and B constitute a single pool.

Product	Ending inventory quantity	Cost per unit Beg. of yr.	Cost per unit End of yr.	Extension Beginning	Extension End
Year 1:					
A	5,000	N/A	$ 6.00	N/A	30,000
B	7,000	N/A	10.00	N/A	70,000
Year 2:					
A	6,000	$ 6.00	6.30	36,000	37,800
B	7,500	10.00	11.00	75,000	82,500
Year 3:					
A	5,800	6.30	6.40	36,540	37,120
B	7,400	11.00	11.50	81,400	85,100
Year 4:					
A	6,200	6.40	6.50	39,680	40,300
B	7,800	11.50	12.00	89,700	93,600

The initial year (base year) does not require the computation of an index under any LIFO method. The base-year index will always be 1.00.

Thus, the base-year inventory layer is $100,000 (the end-of-year inventory restated at base-year cost).

The second year requires the first index computation. Notice that in year 2 our extended totals are:

	Beginning-of-year prices	End-of-year prices
A	$ 36,000	$ 37,800
B	75,000	82,500
	$111,000	$120,300

The year 2 index is 1.084 (120,300/111,000). This is the same as computed under the double-extension method because the beginning-of-the-year prices reflect the base-year price. This will not always be the case, as sometimes new items may be added to the pool, causing a change in the index.

Thus, the cumulative index is the 1.084 current year index multiplied by the preceding year index of 1.00 to arrive at a link-chain index of 1.084.

This index is then used to restate the inventory to base-year cost by dividing the inventory at end-of-year dollars by the cumulative index: $120,300/1.084 = $111,000. The determination of the LIFO increment or decrement is then basically the same as the double-extension method. In year 2 the increment (layer) at base-year cost is $11,000 ($111,000 - 100,000). This layer must be valued at the prices effective when the layer was created, or extended at the cumulative index for that year. This results in an ending inventory at LIFO cost of:

	Base-year cost	Index	LIFO cost
Base year	$100,000	1.00	$100,000
Year 2 layer	11,000	1.084	11,924
	$111,000		$111,924

The index for year 3 is computed as follows:

	Beginning-of-year prices	End-of-year prices
A	$ 36,540	$ 37,120
B	81,400	85,100
	$117,940	$122,220
	122,220/117,940 = 1.036	

The next step is to determine the cumulative index which is the product of the preceding year's cumulative index and the current year index, or 1.123 (1.084 x 1.036). The new cumulative index is used to restate the inventory at end-of-year dollars to base-year cost. This is accomplished by dividing the end-of-year inventory by the new cumulative index. Thus, current inventory at base-year cost is $108,833. In this instance we have experienced a decrement (a decrease from the prior year's $111,000). The determination of ending inventory is:

	Base-year cost	Index	LIFO cost
Base year	$100,000	1.00	$100,000
Year 2 layer	8,833	1.084	9,575
Year 3 layer	--	1.123	--
	$108,833		$109,575

Finally, perform the same steps for the year 4 computation. The current year index is 1.035 (133,900/129,380). The new cumulative index is 1.162 (1.035 x 1.123). The base-year cost of the current inventory is $115,232 (133,900/1.162). Thus, LIFO inventory at the end of year 4 is:

	Base-year cost	Index	LIFO cost
Base year	$100,000	1.00	$100,000
Year 2 layer	8,833	1.084	9,575
Year 3	--	1.123	--
Year 4 layer	6,399	1.162	7,435
	$115,232		$117,010

Notice how even though the numbers used were the same as those used in the double-extension example, the results were different (year 4 inventory under double extension was $116,976)--however, not by a significant amount. It is much easier to keep track of beginning-of-the-year prices than it is to keep base-year prices, but perhaps more importantly, it is easier to establish beginning-of-the-year prices for **new items** than to establish their base-year price. This latter reason is why the link-chain method is so much more desirable than the double-extension. However, before electing or applying this method, a company must be able to establish a sufficient need as defined in the treasury regulations.

Indexing. The last alternative available for computing the dollar-value LIFO inventory is indexing. These indexing methods can basically be broken down into two types: (1) an internal index and (2) an external index.

The internal index is merely a variation of the double-extension method. The regulations allow for a representative sample (or some other statistical method) of the inventory to be double extended. The representative index computed from the sample is then used to restate the inventory to base-year cost and to value the new layer.

The external index method involves using an index published by the Bureau of Labor Statistics (BLS) and applying this index to the inventory figures. This method was primarily limited to retailers intially; however, new regulations issued in 1981 permit these various indices to be used by small businesses (defined as three-year average sales of less than $2 million) to 100% of the change and any other businesses to 80% of the change. We do not propose to discuss this application in detail because of its complexity and limited application. The reader is referred to Reg. §1.472-8(e)(3). It should also be noted that application of the 80% method has not yet been addressed by the FASB, but the Accounting Standards Executive Committee (AcSEC) did not support its use for financial reporting purposes. Thus, larger businesses must still use one of the other alternatives in computing the dollar-value index.

The GAAP herein described for the application of LIFO has been based upon tax rules rather than on financial accounting pronouncements. ARB 43, Chapter 4 cites LIFO as an acceptable inventory method but does not provide any specific rules regarding its implementation. The tax regulations, on the other hand, do provide specific rules for the implementation of LIFO and require financial statement conformity. For this reason, tax rules have essentially defined the financial accounting treatment of LIFO inventories. In recognition of the lack of authoritative accounting guidelines in the implementation of LIFO, the AICPA's Accounting Standards Division has prepared an Issues Paper on this topic. "Identification and Discussion of Certain Financial Accounting and Reporting Issues Concerning LIFO Inventories," prepared by the Task Force on LIFO Inventory Problems, is to identify financial accounting issues resulting from the use of LIFO. This paper describes numerous accounting problems in the use of LIFO and includes advisory conclusions for these problems. Issues Papers, however, do not establish standards of financial accounting. This Issues Paper is detailed in an appendix to this chapter.

Interim Treatment of LIFO

Interim reporting problems associated with LIFO are discussed on page 587.

Weighted-average

Another method of inventory valuation involves averaging and is commonly referred to as the weighted-average method. The cost of goods available for sale (beginning inventory and net purchases) is divided by the units available for sale to obtain a weighted-average unit cost. Ending inventory and cost of goods sold are then priced at this average cost. For example, assume the following data:

	Units available	Units sold	Actual unit cost	Actual total cost
Beginning inventory	100	--	$2.10	$210
Sale	--	75	--	--
Purchase	150	--	2.80	420
Sale	--	100	--	--
Purchase	50	--	3.00	150
Total	300	175		$780

The weighted-average cost is $780/300, or $2.60. Ending inventory is 125 units at $2.60, or $325; cost of goods sold is 175 units at $2.60, or $455.

When the weighted-average assumption is applied to a perpetual inventory system, the average cost is recomputed after each purchase. This process is referred to as a moving average. Sales are costed at the most recent average. This combination is called the moving average method and is applied below to the same data used in the weighted-average example above:

	Units on hand	Purchases in dollars	Sales in dollars	Total cost	Inventory unit cost
Beginning inventory	100	$ --	$ --	$210.00	$2.10
Sale (75 units @ $2.10)	25	--	157.50	52.50	2.10
Purchase (150 units, $420)	175	420.00	--	472.50	2.70
Sale (100 units @ $2.70)	75	--	270.00	202.50	2.70
Purchase (50 units, $150)	125	150.00	--	352.50	2.82

Cost of goods sold is 75 units at $2.10 and 100 units at $2.70, or $427.50.

Comparison of Cost Assumptions

Of the three basic cost flow assumptions, LIFO and FIFO produce the most extreme results, while results from using the weighted-average method generally fall somewhere in between. The selection of one of these methods involves a detailed analysis including a determination of the organization's objectives and the current and future economic state.

As mentioned above, in periods of rising prices the LIFO method is generally thought to best fulfill the objective set forth in ARB 43, Chapter 4 of providing the clearest measure of periodic income. It does not provide an accurate estimate of the inventory value in an inflationary environment; however, this can usually be overcome by the issuance of supplementary data. In periods of rising prices a prudent business should use the LIFO method because it will result in a decrease in the current tax liability when compared to other alternatives. Yet, in a deflationary period, the opposite is true.

FIFO is a balance sheet oriented costing method as it gives the most accurate estimate of the current value of the inventory account during periods of changing prices. In periods of rising prices, the FIFO method will result in higher taxes than the other alternatives, while in a deflationary period FIFO provides for a lesser tax burden. However, a major advantage of the FIFO method is that it is not subject to all of the regulations and requirements of the tax code as is LIFO.

The average methods do not provide an estimate of current cost information on either the balance sheet or income statement. The average method will not serve to minimize the tax burden, nor will it result in the highest burden among the various alternatives.

Although price trends and underlying objectives are important in the selection of a cost flow assumption, other considerations such as the risk of LIFO liquidations, cash flow, capital maintenance, etc. are also important but were not mentioned above.

Lower of Cost or Market (LCM)

As stated in ARB 43, Chapter 4

> *...a departure from the cost basis of pricing the inventory is required when the utility of the goods is no longer as great as its cost... Where there is evidence that the utility of goods ... will be less than cost ... the difference should be recognized as a loss of the current period.*

The utility of the goods in question is generally considered to be their market value, thus the term lower of cost or market. For purposes of this calculation the term market is taken to mean the current replacement cost not to exceed a **ceiling** of the net realizable value (selling price less reasonably estimable costs of completion and disposal) nor fall below a **floor** of net realizable value adjusted for a normal profit margin.

LCM is applied regardless of the method used to determine cost with one exception: LCM is not applied in conjunction with the LIFO method of inventory valuation. This is stated in the treasury regulations as a requirement upon the adoption of the LIFO method.

LCM may be applied to either the entire inventory as a whole or to each individual inventory item. The primary objective for selecting between the alternative methods of applying the LCM rule is to select the one which most clearly reflects periodic income. Generally speaking, the rule is most commonly applied to the inventory on an item-by-item basis. The reason for this application is twofold:

1. It is required by tax purposes unless it involves practical difficulties, and
2. It provides the most conservative valuation of inventories, because decreases in the value of one item are not offset by increases in the value of another.

The application of these principles is illustrated in the example below. Assume the following information for products A, B, C, D, and E:

Item	Cost	Replacement cost	Est. selling price	Cost to complete	Normal profit percentage
A	$2.00	$1.80	$ 2.50	$0.50	24%
B	4.00	1.60	4.00	0.80	24%
C	6.00	6.60	10.00	1.00	18%
D	5.00	4.75	6.00	2.00	20%
E	1.00	1.05	1.20	0.25	12.5%

In applying the foregoing principles, you must first determine the market value and then compare this to historical cost. Market value is equal to the replacement cost, but cannot exceed the net realizable value (NRV) nor be below net realizable value less the normal profit percentage.

Market Determination

Item	Cost	Replacement cost	NRV (ceiling)	NRV less profit (floor)	Market	LCM
A	$2.00	$1.80	$2.00	$1.40	$1.80	$1.80
B	4.00	1.60	3.20	2.24	2.24	2.24
C	6.00	6.60	9.00	7.20	7.20	6.00
D	5.00	4.75	4.00	2.80	4.00	4.00
E	1.00	1.05	0.95	0.80	0.95	0.95

In the second table, NRV (ceiling) equals selling price less costs of completion (e.g., item A: $2.50 - .50 = $2.00). NRV less profit (floor) is self-descriptive [e.g., $2.50 - .50 - (24% x $2.50) = $1.40]. Market is replacement cost unless lower than the floor or higher than the ceiling. Finally, LCM is the lower of cost or market value selected in the above algorithm. Note that market must be designated before LCM is determined.

Although the rules for determining the designated market value may seem needlessly complex, there is logic behind those rules. Replacement cost is a valid measure of the future utility of the inventory item since increases or decreases in the purchase price generally foreshadow related increases or decreases in the selling price.

The ceiling and the floor provide safeguards against the recognition of either excessive profits or excessive losses in future periods in those instances where the selling price and replacement cost do not move in the same direction in a proportional manner. The ceiling avoids the recognition of additional losses in the future when the selling price is falling faster than replacement cost. Without the ceiling constraint, inventories would be carried at an amount in excess of their net realizable value. The floor avoids the recognition of abnormal profits in the future when replacement cost is falling faster than the selling price. Without the floor, inventories would be carried at a value less than their net realizable value minus a normal profit.

The loss from writing inventories down to LCM is generally reflected on the income statement in cost of goods sold. If material, the loss should be separately disclosed in the income statement. The writedown is recorded with a debit to a loss account and a credit either to an inventory or an allowance account.

Special Valuation Methods

There are instances in which an accountant must estimate the value of inventories. Whether the reason be for interim financial statements or as a check against perpetual records, the need for an inventory valuation without an actual physical count is required. Some of the methods used, which are discussed below, are the retail method, the LIFO retail method, and the gross profit method.

Retail Method. The conventional retail method is used by retailers as a method to estimate the cost of their ending inventory. The retailer can either take a physical inventory at retail prices or estimate ending retail inventory and then use the cost-to-retail ratio derived under this method to convert the ending inventory at retail to its estimated cost. This eliminates the process of going back to original invoices or other documents in order to determine the origial cost for each inventoriable item. The retail method can be used under any of the three cost flow assumptions discussed earlier: FIFO, LIFO, or average cost. As with ordinary FIFO or average cost, the LCM rule can also be applied to the retail method when either one of these two cost assumptions are used.

The key to applying the retail method is determining the cost-to-retail ratio. The calculation of this number varies depending upon the cost flow assumption selected. Essentially, the cost-to-retail ratio provides a relationship between the **cost** of goods available for sale and the **retail** price of these same goods. This ratio is used to convert the ending retail inventory back to cost. The computation of the cost-to-retail ratio for each of the available methods is described below. The use of the LIFO cost flow assumption with this method is discussed in the next section and, therefore, is not addressed in this listing.

1. FIFO cost--the concept of FIFO indicates that the ending inventory is made up of the latest purchases; therefore, beginning inventory is excluded from the computation of the cost-to-retail ratio, and the computation becomes net purchases divided by their retail value adjusted for both net markups and net markdowns.
2. FIFO (LCM)--the computation is basically the same as FIFO cost except that markdowns are excluded from the computation of the cost-to-retail ratio.
3. Average cost--average cost assumes that ending inventory consists of all goods available for sale. Therefore, the cost-to-retail ratio is computed by dividing the cost of goods available for sale (beginning inventory + net purchases) by the retail value of these goods adjusted for both net markups and net markdowns.
4. Average cost (LCM)--is computed in the same manner as average cost except that markdowns are excluded for the calculation of the cost-to-retail ratio.

A simple example illustrates the computation of the cost-to-retail ratio under both the FIFO cost and average cost methods in a situation where no markups or mark-downs exist.

	FIFO cost		Average cost	
	Cost	*Retail*	*Cost*	*Retail*
Beginning inventory	$100,000	$ 200,000	$100,000	$ 200,000
Net purchases	500,000 (a)	800,000 (b)	500,000	800,000
Total goods available				
for sale	$600,000	1,000,000	$600,000 (c)	1,000,000 (d)
Sales at retail		(800,000)		(800,000)
Ending inventory--retail		$ 200,000		$ 200,000

Cost-to-retail ratio $\quad \dfrac{(a)500,000}{(b)800,000} = 62.5\% \qquad \dfrac{(c)\ 600,000}{(d)\ 1,000,000} = 60\%$

Ending inventory--cost

200,000 x 62.5%	$ 125,000	
200,000 x 60%		$ 120,000

Note that the only difference in the two examples is the numbers used to calculate the cost-to-retail ratio.

As shown above, the lower of cost or market aspect of the retail method is a result of the treatment of net markups and net markdowns. Net markups (markups less markup cancellations) are net increases above the original retail price, which are generally caused by changes in supply and demand. Net markdowns (markdowns less markdown cancellations) are net decreases below the original retail price. An approximation of lower of cost or market is achieved by including net markups but excluding net markdowns from the cost-to-retail ratio.

To understand this approximation, assume a toy is purchased for $6, and the retail price is set at $10. It is later marked down to $8. A cost-to-retail ratio including markdowns would be $6 divided by $8 or 75%, and ending inventory would be valued at $8 times 75%, or $6 (original cost). A cost-to-retail ratio excluding markdowns would be $6 divided by $10 or 60%, and ending inventory would be valued at $8 times 60%, or $4.80 (LCM). The writedown to $4.80 reflects the loss in utility which is evidenced by the reduced retail price.

The application of the lower of cost or market rule is illustrated for both the FIFO and average cost methods in the example below. Remember, if the markups and markdowns below had been included in the previous example **both** would have been included in the cost-to-retail ratio.

	FIFO cost (LCM)		Average cost (LCM)	
	Cost	*Retail*	*Cost*	*Retail*
Beginning inventory	$100,000	$ 200,000	$100,000	$ 200,000
Net purchases	500,000 (a)	800,000 (b)	500,000	800,000
Net markups	--	250,000 (b)	--	250,000

Total goods available for sale	$600,000	1,250,000	$600,000(c)	1,250,000(d)
Net markdowns		(50,000)		(50,000)
Sales at retail		(800,000)		(800,000)
Ending inventory--retail		$ 400,000		$ 400,000

Cost-to-retail ratio   (a) $\frac{500,000}{(b)\ 1,050,000}$ = 47.6%   (c) $\frac{600,000}{(d)\ 1,250,000}$ = 48%

Ending inventory--cost

400,000 x 47.6% $ 190,400

400,000 x 48% $ 192,000

Notice that under the FIFO (LCM) method all of the markups are considered attributable to the current period purchases. While this is not necessarily accurate, it provides the most conservative estimate of the ending inventory.

There are a number of additional inventory topics and issues which affect the computation of the cost-to-retail ratio and, therefore, deserve some discussion. Purchase discounts and freight affect only the cost column in this computation. The sales figure which is subtracted from the adjusted cost of goods available for sale in the retail column must be gross sales after adjustment for sales returns. If sales are recorded at gross, then deduct the gross sales figure. If sales are recorded at net, then both the recorded sales and sales discount must be deducted to give the same effect as deducting gross sales (i.e., sales discounts are not included in the computation). Normal spoilage is generally allowed for in the firm's pricing policies, and for this reason it is deducted from the retail column **after** the calculation of the cost-to-retail ratio. Abnormal spoilage, on the other hand, should be deducted from **both** the cost and retail columns **before** the cost-to-retail calculation as it could distort the ratio. It is then generally reported as a loss separate from the cost of goods sold section. Abnormal spoilage is generally considered to arise from a major theft or casualty, while normal spoilage is usually due to shrinkage or breakage. These determinations and their treatments will vary depending upon the firm's policies.

When applying the retail method, separate computations should be made for any departments which experience significantly higher or lower profit margins. Distortions arise in the retail method when a department sells goods with varying margins in a proportion different from that purchased, in which case the cost-to-retail percentage would not be representative of the mix of goods in ending inventory. Also, manipulations of income are possible by planning the timing of markups and markdowns.

The retail method is an acceptable method of valuing inventories for tax purposes. The regulations require valuation at lower of cost or market (except for LIFO) and an annual physical inventory.

LIFO Retail Method. As with other LIFO concepts, the treasury regulations are the governing force behind the LIFO retail method. The regulations differentiate between a "variety" store which is required to use an internally computed index and a "department" store which can use a price index published by the Bureau of Labor Statistics. The computation of an internal index was previously discussed in the dollar-value LIFO section. It involves applying the double-extension method to a representative sample of the ending inventory. Selection of a published index is to be in accordance with the regulations set forth by the treasury.

The steps used in computing the value of ending inventory under the LIFO retail method are listed below and then applied to an example for illustrative purposes.

1. Calculate (or select) the current year conversion price index. Recall that in the base year this index will be 1.00.
2. Calculate the value of the ending inventory at both cost and retail. Remember, as with other LIFO methods, tax regulations **do not** permit the use of LCM, so both markups and markdowns are included in the computation of the cost-to-retail ratio. However, the beginning inventory is excluded from goods available for sale at cost and at retail.
3. Restate the ending inventory at retail to base-year retail. This is accomplished by dividing the current ending inventory at retail by the current year index determined in step 1.
4. Layers are then treated in the same fashion as they were for the dollar-value LIFO example presented earlier. If the ending inventory restated to base-year retail exceeds the previous year's amount at base-year retail, a new layer is established.
5. The computation of LIFO cost is the last step and requires multiplying each layer at base-year retail by the appropriate price index and multiplying this product by the cost-to-retail ratio in order to arrive at the LIFO cost for each layer.

The following example illustrates a two-year period to which the LIFO retail method is applied. The first period represents the first year of operations for the organization and, thus, is its base year.

Year 1

Step 1 -- Because this is the base year, there is no need to compute an index, as it will always be 1.00.

Step 2 --

	Cost	Retail
Beginning inventory	$ --	$ --
Purchases	582,400	988,600
Markups	--	164,400
Markdowns	--	(113,000)
Subtotal	$582,400	$1,040,000
Total goods available for sale	$582,400	$1,040,000
Sales--at retail		840,000

Ending year 1 inventory--
at retail $ 200,000

Cost-to-retail ratio $\frac{582,400}{1,040,000}$ = 56%

Ending inventory at cost
$200,000 x 56% $112,000

Step 3 -- Because this is the base year, the restatement to base-year cost is
not necessary; however, the computation would be $200,000/1.00
= $200,000.

Steps 4
and 5 -- The determination of layers is again unnecessary in the base year;
however, the computation would take the following format.

	Ending inventory *at base-year retail*	*Conversion* *price index*	*Cost-to-* *retail ratio*	*LIFO* *cost*
Base year ($200,000/1.00)	$200,000	1.00	0.56	$112,000

Year 2

Step 1 -- We make the assumption that the computation of an internal index
yields a result of 1.12 (obtained by double extending a representative sample).

Step 2 --

	Cost	*Retail*
Beginning inventory	$112,000	$ 200,000
Purchases	716,300	1,168,500
Markups	--	87,500
Markdowns	--	(21,000)
Subtotal	$716,300	$1,235,000
Total goods available for sale		$1,435,000
Sales--at retail		1,171,800
Ending year 2 inventory-- at retail		$ 263,200

Cost-to-retail ratio $\frac{716,300}{1,235,000}$ = 58%

Step 3 -- The restatement of ending inventory at current year retail to base-
year retail is done using the index computed in step 1. In this case
it is $263,200/1.12 = $235,000.

Steps 4
and 5 -- We know that there is a LIFO layer in year 2 because the $235,000
inventory at base-year retail exceeds the year 1 amount of
$200,000.

The computation of the LIFO cost for each layer is shown below.

	Ending inventory at base-year retail	Conversion price index	Cost-to-retail ratio	LIFO cost
Base year				
($200,000/1.00)	$200,000	1.00	0.56	$112,000
Year 2 layer	35,000	1.12	0.58	22,736
	$235,000			
Ending year 2 inventory at LIFO cost				$134,736

The treatment of subsequent increments and decrements is the same for this method as it is for the regular dollar-value method.

Gross profit method. The gross profit method is used to estimate ending inventory when a physical count is not possible or feasible. It can also be used to evaluate the reasonableness of a given inventory amount. The cost of goods available for sale is compared with the estimated cost of goods sold. For example, assume the following data:

Beginning inventory	$125,000
Net purchases	450,000
Sales	600,000
Estimated gross profit	32%

Ending inventory is estimated as follows:

Beginning inventory	$125,000
Net purchases	450,000
Cost of goods available for sale	575,000
Cost of goods sold	
[$600,000 - (32% x $600,000)]	
or (68% x $600,000)	408,000
Estimated ending inventory	$167,000

The gross profit method is used for interim reporting estimates, analyses by auditors, and estimates of inventory lost in fires or other catastrophes. The method is not acceptable for either tax or annual financial reporting purposes. Thus, its major purposes are for internal and interim reporting.

Other Cost Topics

Base stock. The base stock method assumes that a certain level of inventory investment is necessary for normal business activities and is, therefore, permanent. The base stock inventory is carried at historical cost. Decreases in the base stock are considered temporary and are charged to cost of goods sold at replacement cost. Increases are carried at current year costs. The base stock approach is seldom used in practice since it is not allowed for tax purposes, and the LIFO method gives similar results.

Standard costs. Standard costs are predetermined unit costs used by manufacturing firms for planning and control purposes. Standard costs are often incorporated into the accounts, and materials, work-in-process, and finished goods inventories are all carried at standard costs. The use of standard costs in financial reporting is acceptable if adjustments are made periodically to reflect current conditions and if its use approximates one of the recognized cost flow assumptions.

Relative sales value. Relative sales (or net realizable) values are used to assign costs to inventory items purchased or manufactured in groups. This method is applicable to joint products, subdivided assets such as real estate lots, and basket purchases.

A frequently used example is the costing of a joint product. For example, products A and B have the same processes performed on them up to the split-off point. The total cost incurred to this point is $80,000. This cost can be assigned to products A and B using their relative sales value at the split-off point. If A could be sold for $60,000 and B for $40,000, the total sales value is $100,000. The cost would be assigned on the basis of each product's relative sales value. Thus, A would be assigned a cost of $48,000 (60,000/100,000 x 80,000) and B a cost of $32,000 (400,000/100,000 x 80,000).

Other Inventory Topics

Purchase commitments. Purchase commitments generally are not recorded in the accounts because they are executory in nature. However, footnote disclosure is required for firm purchase commitments which are material in amount (ARB 43, Chapter 4).

If at year end the contract price on these commitments exceeds the market value, the estimated loss should be recognized in the accounts and reported in the income statement. Note that this results in recognition of loss before the asset is recognized on the books.

Inventories valued at selling price. In exceptional cases, inventories may be reported at sales price less disposal costs. Such treatment is justified when cost is difficult to determine, quoted market prices are available, marketability is assured, and units are interchangeable. Precious metals, certain agricultural products, and meat are examples of inventories valued in this manner (ARB 43). When inventory is valued above cost, revenue is recognized before the point of sale. Full disclosure in the financial statements is required.

Interim reporting. The principles used to determine ending inventory and cost of goods sold in annual reports are also used in interim reports, although four exceptions are allowed (APB 28). These are:

1. The gross profit method may be used to estimate cost of goods sold and ending inventory.

2. When LIFO layers are liquidated during the interim period but are expected to be replaced by year end, cost of goods sold should reflect current costs rather than old LIFO costs.
3. Temporary market decline need not be recognized if substantial evidence exists that market prices will recover. If LCM losses recorded in one interim period are recovered by year end, the recovery is recognized as a gain.
4. Planned standard cost variances expected to be offset by year end can be deferred.

Disclosures

The required disclosures for inventory include the following:

1. The dollar amount assigned to inventory
2. The cost flow assumption
3. The basis of valuation
4. Classification (materials, work in process, etc.)
5. Principles peculiar to a particular industry
6. Pledging of inventories in borrowing agreements
7. Product financing arrangements
8. Firm purchase commitments
9. Liquidation of LIFO inventories
10. Changing price information for certain corporations

APPENDIX A

LIFO Conformity Rule

As stated earlier in this chapter, Treasury Regulations require that in order to take advantage of LIFO for tax purposes, a company must also use LIFO for determining income, profit, or loss for financial statement purposes. The regulations also cite certain exceptions to this general rule. Among the exceptions allowable under the regulations are the following:

1. The use of an inventory method other than LIFO in presenting information reported as a supplement to or explanation of the taxpayer's primary presentation of income in financial reports to outside parties. [Reg. §1.472-2(e)(1)(i)]
2. The use of an inventory method other than LIFO to determine the value of the taxpayer's inventory for purposes of reporting the value of such inventory as an asset on the balance sheet. [Reg. §1.472-2(e)(1)(ii)]
3. The use of an inventory method other than LIFO for purposes of determining information reported in internal management reports. [Reg. §1.472-2(e)(1)(iii)]
4. The use of an inventory method other than LIFO for financial reports covering a period of less than one year. [Reg. §1.472- 2(e)(1)(iv)]
5. The use of lower of LIFO cost or market to value inventories for financial statements while using LIFO cost for tax purposes. [Reg. §1.472-2(e)(1)(v)]
6. For inventories acquired in a section 351 transaction, the use of the transferor's acquisition dates and costs for book purposes while using redetermined LIFO layers for tax purposes. [Reg. §1.472-2(e)(1)(vii)]
7. The inclusion of certain costs (under full absorption) in inventory for tax purposes, as required by regulations, while not including those same costs in inventory under GAAP, (full absorption) for book purposes. [Reg. §1.472-2(e)(8)(i)]
8. The use of different methods of establishing pools for book purposes and tax purposes. [Reg. §1.472-2(e)(8)(ii)]
9. The use of different determinations of the time sales or purchases are accrued for book purposes and tax purposes. [Reg. §1.472-2(e)(8)(xii)]
10. In the case of a business combination, the use of different methods to allocate basis for book purposes and tax purposes. [Reg. §1.472-2(e)(8)(xiii)]

Another important consideration in applying the LIFO conformity rule is the new law concerning related corporations. The Tax Reform Act of 1984 added a rule which states that all members of the same group of financially related corporations shall be treated as a single taxpayer when applying the conformity rule. Previously, taxpayers were able to circumvent the conformity rule by having a subsidiary on LIFO, while the non-LIFO parent presented combined non-LIFO financial statements. This practice will now be considered a violation of the conformity requirement [Sec. 472(g)], effective for years beginning after July 18, 1984.

APPENDIX B

Task Force on LIFO Inventory Problems

Most of the prescribed rules concerning the implementation of LIFO have their origins in the Internal Revenue Code and Treasury Regulations. Because authoritative financial accounting pronouncements on implementing LIFO are virtually nonexistent, GAAP has followed tax. The AICPA Task Force on LIFO Inventory problems has developed an Issues Paper to discuss certain financial accounting issues related to LIFO. Issues Papers constitute generally accepted accounting principles but are not mandatory. The key conclusions from this Issues Paper (entitled "Identification and Discussion of Certain Financial Accounting and Reporting Issues Concerning LIFO Inventories") are described below.

1. **Specific goods versus dollar value**. The Task Force believes that either the specific goods approach or dollar value approach to LIFO is acceptable for financial reporting. They also believe that it is not necessary to disclose whether the specific goods or dollar value approach is used. TRA 1986 provides an election for qualifying small businesses to account for their inventories using a simplified dollar-value LIFO method.
2. **Pricing current year purchases**. Three approaches to pricing LIFO inventory increments are available under tax regulations--earliest acquisition price, latest acquisition price, and average acquisition price. The Task Force believes that the earliest acquisition price approach is the most compatible with financial reporting objectives, but finds all three to be acceptable for financial reporting.
3. **Quantity to use to determine price**. The Task Force believes that the price used to determine the inventory increment should be based on the cost of the quantity or dollars of the increment rather than on the cost of the quantity or dollars equal to the ending inventory. They also believe that it is not necessary to disclose which approach is used.
4. **Disclosure of LIFO reserve or replacement cost**. The Task Force believes that either the LIFO reserve or replacement cost and its basis for determination should be disclosed for financial reporting.
5. **Partial adoption of LIFO**. The Task Force believes that if a company changes to LIFO, it should do so for all of its inventories. Partial adoption should only be allowed if there exists a valid business reason for not fully adopting LIFO. A planned gradual adoption of LIFO over several time periods is considered acceptable if valid business reasons exist (lessening the income statement effect of adoption in any one year is not a valid business reason). The Task Force also believes that where partial adoption of LIFO has been justified, the extent to which LIFO has been adopted should be disclosed. This can be disclosed by indicating either the portion of the ending inventory priced on LIFO or the portion of cost of sales resulting from LIFO inventories.
6. **Methods of pooling**. The Task Force addressed several issues related to

establishing pools. They believe that an entity should have valid business reasons for establishing its LIFO pools. Additionally, it is believed that the existence of a separate legal entity that has no economic substance is not reason enough to justify separate pools. It is also believed that an entity's pooling arrangements need not be disclosed.

7. **New items entering a pool**. The Task Force believes that new items should be added to the pool based on what the items would have cost had they been acquired in the base period (reconstructed cost) rather than based on their current cost. The reconstructed cost should be determined based on the most objective sources available including published vendor price lists, vendor quotes, and general industry indexes. The Task Force believes it is not necessary to disclose the way that new items are priced.

   It is also believed that, where necessary, the use of a substitute base year in making the LIFO computation is acceptable.

8. **Dollar value index**. The required index can be developed using two possible approaches, the unit cost method or the cost component method. The unit cost method measures changes in the index based on the weighted average increase or decrease to the unit costs of raw materials, work in process, and finished goods inventory. The cost component method, on the other hand, measures changes in the index by the weighted average increase or decrease in the component costs of material, labor, and overhead that make up ending inventory. The Task Force believes that either of these methods are acceptable.

9. **LIFO liquidations**. The Task Force believes that the effects on income of LIFO inventory liquidations should be disclosed in the notes to the financial statements. A replacement reserve for the liquidation should not be provided. When an involuntary LIFO liquidation occurs, the Task Force does not believe that the income effect of the liquidation should be deferred.

   When a LIFO liquidation occurs there are three possible ways to measure its effect on income:

   a. The difference between actual cost of sales and what cost of sales would have been had the inventory been reinstated under the entity's normal pricing procedure
   b. The difference between actual cost of sales and what cost of sales would have been had the inventory been reinstated at year-end replacement cost
   c. The amount of the LIFO reserve at the beginning of the year which was credited to income (excluding the increase in the reserve due to current year price changes)

   The Task Force supports the first method. It is also believed disclosure of the effect of the liquidation should give effect only to pools with decrements (i.e., there should be no netting against increments in other pools).

10. **Lower of cost or market**. The Task Force believes that the most reasonable

approach to applying the lower of cost or market rules to LIFO inventory is to base the determination on groups of inventory rather than on an item by item approach. They believe that a pool constitutes a reasonable grouping for this purpose. They also believe, however, that an item by item approach is permitted by authoritative accounting literature, particularly for obsolete or discontinued items.

For companies with more than one LIFO pool, it would be permissible to aggregate the pools in applying the lower of cost or market test if the pools are similar. It is believed that where the pools are significantly dissimilar, aggregating the pools is not appropriate.

The Task Force also believes that previous writedowns to market value of the cost of LIFO inventories should be reversed after a company disposes of the physical units of the inventory for which reserves were provided. The reserves at the end of the year should be based on a new computation of cost or market.

11. **LIFO conformity and supplemental disclosures.** The Task Force believes that a company may present supplemental non-LIFO disclosures within the historical cost framework. If nondiscretionary variable expenses (i.e., profit sharing based on earnings) would have been different based on the supplemental information, then the company should give effect to such changes. Additionally, the supplemental disclosure should reflect the same type of tax effects as required by generally accepted accounting principles in the primary financial statements.

The Task Force also believes a company may use different LIFO applications for financial reporting than it uses for income tax purposes. Any such differences should be accounted for as temporary differences with the exception of differences in the allocation of cost to inventory in a business combination. They further believe that any differences between LIFO applications used for financial reporting and those used for income tax purposes need not be disclosed beyond the requirements of APB 11.

12. **Interim reporting and LIFO.** The Task Force's conclusions on interim reporting of LIFO inventory is discussed on page 587.

13. **Different financial and income tax years**. The Task Force believes that a company which has a year end for financial reporting different from that for income tax reporting should make a separate LIFO calculation for financial purposes using its financial reporting year as a discrete period for that calculation.

14. **Business combinations accounted for by the purchase method.** Inventory acquired in a business combination accounted for by the purchase method will be recorded at fair market value at the date of the combination. The acquired company may be able to carryover its prior basis for that inventory for tax purposes, causing a difference between book and tax basis. The Task Force believes that an adjustment should be made to the fair value of the inventory only if it is reasonably estimated to be liquidated in the future. The

adjustment would be for the income tax effect of the difference between tax and book basis.

The Task Force further believes that inventory acquired in such a combination should be considered the LIFO base inventory if the inventory is treated by the company as a separate business unit or a separate LIFO pool. If instead the acquired inventory is combined into an existing pool, then the acquired inventory should be considered as part of the current year's purchases.

15. **Changes in LIFO applications**. The Task Force believes that a change in a LIFO application is a change in accounting principle under APB 20. LIFO applications refer to the approach (i.e., dollar value or specific goods), computational technique, or the numbers or contents of the pools.

The AICPA Task Force did not include intercompany transfers in the 1984 Issues Paper; however, the AICPA issued Practice Bulletin 2 in 1987 to provide guidance for this complex area.

The focus of this bulletin is the LIFO liquidation effect caused by transferring inventories which in turn create intercompany profits. This liquidation can occur when 1) two components of the same taxable entity transfer inventory, for example, when a LIFO method component transfers inventory to a non-LIFO component, or 2) when two separate taxable entities that consolidate transfer inventory--even though both use the LIFO method.

According to Practice Bulletin 2, this LIFO liquidation creates profit which must be eliminated along with the other intercompany profits eliminated in accordance with ARB 51.

7 Special Revenue Recognition Areas

Revenue should be recognized when (1) it is realized or realizable and (2) it has been earned. This is the conceptual guideline given by SFAC 5 for the recognition of revenue (see the discussion in Chapter 3). For some transactions (such as retail grocery sales) the realization principle is very easily applied. However, in some industries, accountants have a very difficult time applying these criteria. As a result, several of the professional pronouncements have concentrated on revenue recognition for certain specific areas, e.g., SFAS 48, *Revenue Recognition When Right of Return Exists*; SFAS 66, *Accounting for Real Estate Sales*; and SOP 81-1, *Accounting for Performance of Construction-Type and Certain Production-Type Contracts* (made mandatory GAAP by SFAS 56).

This chapter addresses six areas for which the circumstances of the transaction do not allow for the clear application of the revenue realization principle. These are as follows:

1. Long-term construction contracts
2. Service sales transactions
3. Sales when collection is uncertain
4. Revenue recognition when right of return exists
5. Profit recognition on nonretail sales of real estate
6. Accounting for nonrefundable fees and costs associated with originating or acquiring loans

Each of these six sections may be read as individual units.

LONG-TERM CONSTRUCTION CONTRACTS

Perspective and Issues

The basic issue in the accounting for long-term construction contracts is the determination of the point or points at which revenues should be recognized as earned and costs should be recognized as expenses. Several different accounting methods have developed because of the inherent problem of measuring the results of long-term events and allocating those results to relatively short-term accounting periods. The accounting for long-term construction contracts is complicated by the need to rely on estimates of revenues, costs, and the extent of progress toward completion.

Sources of GAAP

ARB	*Other*
45	SOP 81-1

Definitions of Terms

Back charges. Billings for work performed or costs incurred by one party that, in accordance with the agreement, should have been performed or incurred by the party billed.

Billings on long-term contracts. Accumulated billings sent to the purchaser at intervals as various points in the project are reached.

Change orders. Modifications of an original contract that effectively change the provisions of the contract without adding new provisions. (SOP 81-1, para 61)

Claims. Amounts in excess of the agreed contract price that a contractor seeks to collect from customers for customer-caused delays, errors in specifications and designs, unapproved change orders, or other causes of unanticipated costs. (SOP 81-1, para 61)

Combining contracts. Grouping two or more contracts into a single profit center for accounting purposes.

Completed-contract method. A method of accounting that recognizes income only after the contract is complete.

Construction-in-progress (CIP). An inventory account used to accumulate the construction costs of the contract project. For the percentage-of-completion method, the CIP account also includes the gross profit earned to date.

Cost-to-cost method. A percentage-of-completion method used to determine the extent of progress toward completion on a contract. The ratio of cost incurred to end of current year over total estimated costs of the project is used to recognize income.

Estimated cost to complete. The anticipated additional cost of materials, labor, subcontracting costs, and indirect costs (overhead) required to complete a project at a scheduled time.

Percentage-of-completion method. A method of accounting that recognizes income on a contract as work progresses.

Pre-contract costs. Costs incurred before a contract has been accepted (e.g., architectural designs, purchase of special equipment, engineering fees, and start-up costs).

Profit center. A unit for the accumulation of revenues and cost for the measurement of income.

Segmenting contracts. Dividing a single contract or group of contracts into two or more profit centers for accounting purposes.

Subcontractor. A second-level contractor who enters into a contract with a prime contractor to perform a specific part or phase of a construction project.

Substantial completion. The point at which the major work on a contract is completed and only insignificant costs and potential risks remain.

Concepts, Rules, and Examples

Long-term construction contract revenue may be recognized during construction rather than at the completion of the contract. This "as earned" approach to revenue recognition is justified because under most long-term construction contracts both the buyer and the seller (contractor) obtain enforceable rights. The buyer has the legal right to require specific performance from the contractor and, in effect, has ownership claim to the contractor's work in progress. The contractor, under most long-term contracts, has the right to require the buyer to make progress payments during the construction period. The substance of this business activity is that a continuous sale occurs as the work progresses (SOP 81-1).

ARB 45 describes the two generally accepted methods of accounting for long-term construction contracts.

> *The percentage-of-completion method recognizes income as work on a contract (or group of closely related contracts) progresses. The recognition of revenues and profits is generally related to costs incurred in providing the services required under the contract (para 4).*

Under this method, the construction-in-progress (CIP) account is used to accumulate costs and recognized income. When the CIP exceeds billings, the difference is reported as a current asset. If billings exceed CIP, the difference is reported as a current liability (para 5). Where more than one contract exists, the excess cost or liability should be determined on a project-by-project basis, with the accumulated costs and liabilities being separately stated on the balance sheet. Assets and liabilities should not be offset unless a right of offset exists. Thus, the net debit balances for certain contracts should not ordinarily be offset against net credit balances for other contracts. An exception may exist if the balances relate to contracts that meet the criteria for combining described in SOP 81-1.

Under the percentage-of-completion method, income should not be based on cash collections or interim billings. Cash collections and interim billings are based upon contract terms which do not necessarily measure contract performance. Costs and estimated earnings in excess of billings should be classified as a current asset. If billings exceed costs and estimated earnings, the difference should be classified as a current liability.

> The completed-contract method recognizes income only when the contract is complete, or substantially complete (para 9).

Under this method, the CIP account accumulates only the costs of contracts in process. The costs and related billings are reported as deferred items on the balance sheet until the project is complete or substantially complete. A contract can be regarded as substantially complete if remaining costs of completion are immaterial. When the accumulated costs (CIP) exceed the related billings, the excess should be shown as a current asset (inventory account). If billings exceed related costs, the difference should be shown as a current liability (para 12). This determination should also be made on a project-by-project basis with the accumulated costs and liabilities being separately stated on the balance sheet. An excess of accumulated costs over related billings should be shown as a current asset, and an excess of accumulated billings over related costs should be shown among the liabilities, in most cases as a current liability.

SOP 81-1 recommends the percentage-of-completion method as preferable when estimates are reasonably dependable and the following conditions exist:

1. Contracts executed by the parties normally include provisions that clearly specify the enforceable rights regarding goods or services to be provided and received by the parties, the consideration to be exchanged, and the manner and terms of settlement.
2. The buyer can be expected to satisfy his obligations under the contract.
3. The contractor can be expected to perform his contractual obligations.

SOP 81-1 presumes that contractors generally have the ability to produce estimates that are sufficiently dependable to justify the use of the percentage-of-completion method of accounting. Persuasive evidence to the contrary is necessary to overcome this presumption.

The principal advantage of the completed-contract method is that it is based on final results, whereas the percentage-of-completion method is dependent upon estimates for unperformed work. The principal disadvantage of the completed-contract method is that when the period of a contract extends into more than one period, there will be an irregular recognition of income (paras 13 and 14).

The Accounting Standards Division of the AICPA believes that these two methods should not be used as acceptable alternatives for the same set of circumstances. ARB 45, para 15 states that in general, when estimates of costs to complete and extent of progress toward completion of long-term contracts are reasonably dependable, the percentage-of-completion method is preferable. When lack of dependable estimates or inherent hazards cause forecasts to be doubtful, the completed-contract method is preferable.

The completed-contract method may also be acceptable when a contractor has numerous relatively short-term contracts and when the financial statement presentation does not vary materially from the presentation under the percentage-of-completion method.

Contract Costs

Contract costs are costs identifiable with or allocable to specific contracts. Generally, contract costs would include all direct costs such as direct materials, direct labor, and any indirect costs (overhead) allocable to the contracts. Contract costs can be broken down into two categories: costs incurred to date and estimated costs to complete.

The costs incurred to date would include pre-contract costs and costs incurred after contract acceptance. Pre-contract costs are costs incurred **before** a contract has been entered into, with the expectation of the contract being accepted and thereby recoverable through billings. Pre-contract costs would include architectural designs, costs of learning a new process, and any other costs which are expected to be recovered if the contract is accepted. Contract costs incurred after the acceptance of the contract are costs incurred towards the completion of the project and are also capitalized in the construction-in-progress (CIP) account.

The contract does not have to be identified before the capitalization decision is made; only the expectation of the recovery of the costs is necessary. Once the contract has been accepted, the pre-contract costs become contract costs incurred to date.

Certain costs (purchase of materials, equipment, supplies, etc.) may be deferred in anticipation of a specific contract, or for a number of identified related contracts. Pre-contract costs associated with a specific contract should **not** be included in contract costs or inventory unless the contract is accepted. These costs can be deferred; however, they are to be capitalized by the use of another account, such as Deferred Costs-Contract bid #97. Costs incurred on identified related contracts should be treated similarly to costs for a specific contract--capitalized outside of contract costs or inventory accounts.

The company may choose to defer costs related to producing excess goods in anticipation of future orders of the same item. Cost associated with excess production can be treated as inventory if the costs are considered recoverable.

A company may choose to defer the pre-contract costs for the learning, start-up, and mobilization (exclusive of R&D expenses) of an unidentified contract. These costs are treated differently than the previously mentioned pre-contract situations. If these costs are incurred with existing contracts and in anticipation of future contracts, these costs should be charged to existing contracts.

The existing contracts should absorb some portion of these pre-contract costs. Since the number of future contracts to benefit from the expenditures is unknown, the convention of conservatism prevails and the existing contracts will absorb all of the pre-contract costs incurred. If the costs were incurred for future contracts only, the costs should be accounted for as pre-contract costs for a number of contracts.

Once the outcome of the contract bid is known (acceptance or rejection), the pre-contract costs associated with it must be examined. If the contract was accepted, previously deferred pre-contract costs should be included in contract costs. If, however, pre-contract costs were charged to expense because recoverability was not probable, these costs can **not** be reinstated by crediting income. Pre-contract costs associated with rejected contracts should be expensed in the current period, unless recoverability is probable under other pending contracts.

Estimated costs to complete. These are the **anticipated costs** required to complete a project at a scheduled time. They would be comprised of the same elements as the original total estimated contract costs and would be based on prices expected to be in effect when the costs are incurred.

The latest estimates should be used to determine the progress towards completion. SOP 81-1 provides the practices to be followed when determining estimated costs to complete.

First of all, systematic and consistent procedures should be used. These procedures should be correlated with the cost accounting system and should be able to provide a comparison between actual and estimated costs. Additionally, the determination of estimated total contract costs should identify the significant cost elements.

Another procedure requires that the estimation of the costs to complete should include the same elements of costs included in accumulated costs. Additionally, the estimated costs should reflect any expected price increases. These expected price increases should not be "blanket provisions" for all contract costs, but rather specific provisions for each type of cost. Expected increases in each of the cost elements such as wages, materials, and overhead items should be taken into consideration separately.

Finally, estimates of costs to complete should be reviewed periodically to reflect new information. Estimates of costs should be examined for price fluctuations and also should be reviewed for possible future problems, such as labor strikes or direct material delays.

Accounting for contract costs is similar to accounting for inventory. Costs necessary to ready the asset for sale would be recorded in the construction-in-progress account, as incurred. CIP would include both direct and indirect costs but would usually not include general and administrative expenses or selling expenses since they are not normally identifiable with a particular contract and should therefore be expensed. However, general and administrative expenses **may** be included in contract costs under the completed contract method since a preferable allocation of revenues and costs might take place, especially in years when no contracts were completed (ARB 45, para 10).

Subcontractor costs. Since a contractor may not be able to do all facets of a construction project, a subcontractor may be engaged. The amount billed to the contractor for work done by the subcontractor should be included in contract costs. The amount billed is directly traceable to the project and would be included in the CIP account, similar to direct materials and direct labor.

Back charges. Contract costs may have to be adjusted for back charges. Back charges are billings for costs incurred, which the contract stipulated should have been performed by another party. These charges are often disputed by the parties involved.

Example of a Back Charge Situation

The contract states the subcontractor was to raze the building and have the land ready for construction; however, the contractor/seller had to clear away debris in order to begin construction. The contractor wants to be reimbursed for the work; therefore, the contractor back charges the subcontractor for the cost of the debris removal.

The contractor should treat the back charge as a receivable from the subcontractor and should reduce contract costs by the amount recoverable. If the subcontractor disputes the back charge, the cost becomes a claim. Claims are an amount in excess of the agreed contract price or amounts not included in the original contract price that the contractor seeks to collect. Claims should only be recorded as additional contract revenue if the requirements set forth in SOP 81-1, para 65 are met.

The subcontractor should record the back charge as a payable and as additional contract costs if it is probable the amount will be paid. If the amount or validity of the liability is disputed, the subcontractor would have to consider the probable outcome in order to determine the proper accounting treatment.

Types of Contracts

Four types of contracts are distinguished based on their pricing arrangements: (1) fixed-price or lump-sum contracts, (2) time-and-materials contracts, (3) cost-type contracts, and (4) unit-price contracts.

Fixed-price contracts are contracts for which the price is not usually subject to adjustment because of costs incurred by the contractor.

Time-and-materials contracts are contracts that provide for payments to the contractor based on direct labor hours at fixed rates and cost of materials.

There are two cost-type contracts: **cost-without-fee contract**--contractor is reimbursed for costs with no provision for a fee, and **cost-plus-fixed-fee contract**--contractor is reimbursed for costs plus a provision for a fee. The contract price on a cost-type contract is determined by the sum of the reimbursable expenditures and a fee. The fee is the profit margin (revenue less direct expenses) to be earned on the contract. All reimbursable expenditures should be included in the accumulated contract costs account. If a contract cost was omitted from this account, a higher fee would result. The higher fee is a result of the contract price being fixed and the accumulated contract costs being understated. The reverse is also true. If unallocable costs (i.e., general and administrative expenses) are included in accumulated contract costs, the fee or profit margin declines.

Contract costs (incurred and estimated to complete) should be used to compute the gross profit or loss recognized. Under the percentage-of-completion method, gross profit or loss would be recognized each period. The revenue recognized would be matched against the contract costs incurred (similar to cost of goods sold) to determine gross profit/loss. Under the completed contract method, the gross profit/loss is determined at the **completion** of the contract, and no revenue or contract costs are recognized until this point.

Additionally, inventoriable costs (accumulated in the CIP account) should never exceed the net realizable value of the contract. When contract costs exceed their NRV, they must be written down, requiring a contract loss to be recognized in the current period (this will be discussed in greater detail later). This is similar to accounting for inventory.

Cost-type contracts provide for reimbursement of allowable or otherwise defined costs incurred plus a fee representing profits. Some variations of cost-plus contracts are (a) cost-without-fee: no provision for a fee, (b) cost-plus-fixed-fee: contractor reimbursed for costs plus provision for a fixed fee, and (c) cost-plus-award-fee: same as (b) plus provision for award based on performance.

Unit-price contracts are contracts under which the contractor is paid a specified amount for every unit of work performed.

Revenue Measurement

In practice, various methods are used to measure the extent of progress toward completion. The most common methods are the cost-to-cost method, efforts-expended method, units-of-delivery method, and units-of-work-performed method. All of these methods of measuring progress on a contract can be identified as either an input or output measure. The input measures attempt to identify progress in a contract in terms of the efforts devoted to it. The cost-to-cost and efforts-expended methods are examples of input measures. Under the cost-to-cost method, the percentage of completion would be estimated by comparing total costs incurred to date to total costs expected for the entire job. Output measures are made in terms of results by attempting to identify progress toward completion by physical measures. The units-of-delivery and units-of-work-performed methods are examples of output measures. Under both of these methods, an estimate of completion is made in terms of achievements to date. Output measures are usually not considered as reliable as input measures.

Both input and output measures have drawbacks in certain circumstances. A significant problem of input measures is that the relationship between input and productivity is only indirect; inefficiencies and other factors can cause this relationship to change. A particular drawback of the cost-to-cost method is that start-up costs, costs of uninstalled materials, and other up-front costs may produce higher estimates of completion because of their early incurrence. These costs may be excluded or allocated over the contract life when it appears that a better measure of periodic income will be obtained. A significant problem of output measures is that the cost, time, and effort associated with one unit of output may not be comparable to that of another. For example, because of the cost of the foundation, the costs to complete the first story of a 20-story office building can be expected to be greater than the costs of the remaining 19 floors.

Because ARB 45, para 4 recommends that "recognized income (should) be that percentage of estimated total income ...that incurred costs to date bear to estimated total costs," the **cost-to-cost** method has become one of the most popular measures used to determine the extent of progress toward completion.

Under the cost-to-cost method, the percentage of **revenue** to recognize can be determined by the following formula:

$$\frac{\text{Cost to date}}{\substack{\text{Cumulative costs incurred} \\ \text{+ Estimated costs} \\ \text{to complete}}} \quad \text{x} \quad \substack{\text{Contract} \\ \text{price}} \quad - \quad \substack{\text{Revenue} \\ \text{previously} \\ \text{recognized}} \quad = \quad \substack{\text{Current} \\ \text{revenue} \\ \text{recognized}}$$

By slightly modifying this formula, current **gross profit** can also be determined.

$$\frac{\text{Cost to date}}{\substack{\text{Cumulative costs incurred} \\ \text{+ Estimated costs} \\ \text{to complete}}} \quad \text{x} \quad \substack{\text{Expected} \\ \text{total gross} \\ \text{profit}} \quad - \quad \substack{\text{Gross profit} \\ \text{previously} \\ \text{recognized}} \quad = \quad \substack{\text{Current} \\ \text{gross} \\ \text{profit}}$$

Example of Percentage-of-Completion (Cost-to-Cost) and Completed-Contract Methods With Profitable Contract

Assume a $500,000 contract that requires three years to complete and incurs a total cost of $405,000. The following data pertain to the construction period:

	Year 1	Year 2	Year 3
Cumulative costs incurred to date	$150,000	$360,000	$405,000
Estimated costs yet to be incurred at year end	300,000	40,000	--
Progress billings made during year	100,000	370,000	30,000
Collections of billings	75,000	300,000	125,000

Completed-Contracts & Percentage-of-Completion Methods

	Year 1		Year 2		Year 3	
Construction in Progress	150,000		210,000		45,000	
Cash, Payables, etc.		150,000		210,000		45,000
Contract Receivables	100,000		370,000		30,000	
Billings on Contracts		100,000		370,000		30,000
Cash	75,000		300,000		125,000	
Contract Receivables		75,000		300,000		125,000

Completed-Contract Method Only

Billings on Contracts		500,000	
Cost of Revenues Earned		405,000	
Contracts Revenues Earned			500,000
Construction in Progress			405,000

Percentage-of-Completion Method Only

	Year 1		Year 2		Year 3	
Construction in Progress	16,667		73,333		5,000	
Cost of Revenues Earned	150,000		210,000		45,000	
Contract Revenues Earned		166,667		283,333		50,000
Billings on Contracts					500,000	
Construction in Progress						500,000

Income Statement Presentation

	Year 1	Year 2	Year 3	Total
Percentage-of-completion:				
Contract revenues earned	$166,667*	$283,333**	$ 50,000***	$ 500,000
Cost of revenues earned	(150,000)	(210,000)	(45,000)	(405,000)
Gross profit	$ 16,667	$ 73,333	$ 5,000	$ 95,000
Completed-contract:				
Contract revenues earned	--	--	$ 500,000	$ 500,000
Cost of contracts completed	--	--	(405,000)	(405,000)
Gross profit	--	--	$ 95,000	$ 95,000

$$* \quad \frac{\$150,000}{450,000} \quad X \quad 500,000 = \$166,667$$

$$** \quad \frac{\$360,000}{400,000} \quad X \quad 500,000 - \quad 166,667 \quad = \$283,333$$

$$*** \quad \frac{\$405,000}{405,000} \quad X \quad 500,000 - \quad 166,667 \quad - \quad 283,333 \quad = \$50,000$$

Balance Sheet Presentation

	Year 1	Year 2	Year 3
Percentage-of-completion:			
Current assets:			
Contract receivables		$ 25,000	$ 95,000	*
Costs and estimated earnings in excess of billings on uncompleted contracts			
Construction in progress	166,667**		
Less billings on long-term contracts	(100,000)	$ 66,667	
Current liabilities:			
Billings in excess of costs and estimated earnings on uncompleted contracts, year 2 ($470,000*** - 450,000****)			$ 20,000
Completed-contract:			
Current assets:			
Contract receivables		$ 25,000	$ 95,000	*
Costs in excess of billings on uncompleted contracts			
Construction in progress	150,000		
Less billings on long-term contracts	(100,000)	$ 50,000	
Current liabilities:			
Billings in excess of costs on uncompleted contracts, year 2 ($470,000 - 360,000)			$110,000

* Since the contract was completed and title was transferred in year 3, there are no balance sheet amounts. However, if the project is complete but transfer of title has not taken place, then there would be a balance sheet presentation at the end of the third year because the entry closing out the Construction in progress account and the Billings account would not have been made yet.

** $150,000 (Costs) + 16,667 (Gross profit)

*** $100,000 (Year 1 Billings) + 370,000 (Year 2 Billings)

**** $360,000 (Costs) + 16,667 (Gross profit) + 73,333 (Gross profit)

Contract Losses

When the current estimate of total contract cost exceeds the current estimate of total contract revenue, a provision for the entire loss on the entire contract should be made. Provisions for losses should be made in the period in which they become evident under either the percentage-of-completion method or the completed-contract method (SOP 81-1, para 85). The loss provision should be computed on the basis of the **total** estimated costs to complete the contract, which would include the contract costs incurred to date plus estimated costs (use same elements as contract costs incurred) to complete. The provision should be shown separately as a current liability on the balance sheet.

In any year when a **percentage-of-completion** contract has an expected loss, the amount of the loss reported in that year can be computed as follows:

Reported loss = Total expected loss + All profit previously recognized

Example of Percentage-of-Completion and Completed-Contract Methods With Loss Contract

Using the previous information, if the costs yet to be incurred at the end of year 2 were $148,000, the total expected loss is $8,000 [$500,000 - (360,000 + 148,000)], and the total loss reported in year 2 would be $24,667 ($8,000 + 16,667). Under the completed-contract method, the loss recognized is simply the total expected loss, $8,000.

Journal entry at end of year 2	Percentage-of-completion	Completed-contract
Loss on uncompleted long-term contract	24,667	8,000
Construction in progress (or estimated loss on uncompleted contract)	24,667	8,000

Profit or Loss Recognized on Contract
(Percentage-of-Completion Method)

	Year 1	Year 2	Year 3
Contract price	$500,000	$500,000	$500,000
Estimated total costs:			
Costs incurred to date	$150,000	$360,000	$506,000*
Estimated cost yet to be incurred	300,000	148,000	--
Estimated total costs for the three-year period, actual for year 3	$450,000	$508,000	$506,000
Estimated income (loss), actual for year 3	$ 16,667	$ (8,000)	$ (6,000)
Less income (loss) previously recognized	--	16,667	(8,000)
Amount of estimated income (loss) recognized in the current period, actual for year 3	$ 16,667	$ (24,667)	$ 2,000

*Assumed

Profit or Loss Recognized on Contract
(Completed-Contract Method)

	Year 1	Year 2	Year 3
Contract price	$500,000	$500,000	$500,000
Estimated total costs:			
Costs incurred to date	$150,000	$360,000	$506,000*
Estimated costs yet to be incurred	300,000	148,000	--
Estimated total costs for the three-year period, actual for year 3	$ 50,000	$ (8,000)	$ (6,000)
Loss previously recognized	--	--	(8,000)
Amount of estimated income (loss) recognized in the current period, actual for year 3	$ --	$ (8,000)	$ 2,000

Assumed

Upon completion of the project during year 3, it can be seen that the actual loss was only $6,000 ($500,000 - 506,000); therefore, the estimated loss provision was overstated by $2,000. However, since this is a change of an estimate, the $2,000 difference must be handled prospectively; consequently, $2,000 of income should be recognized in year 3 ($8,000 previously recognized - $6,000 actual loss).

Combining and Segmenting Contracts

The profit center for accounting purposes is usually a single contract, but under some circumstances the profit center may be a combination of two or more contracts, a segment of a contract or of a group of combined contracts (SOP 81-1, para 17). The contracts must meet requirements in SOP 81-1 in order to combine, or segment; otherwise, each individual contract is presumed to be the profit center.

For accounting purposes, a group of contracts may be combined if they are so closely related that they are, in substance, parts of a single project with an overall profit margin. Per SOP 81-1, para 37, a group of contracts may be combined if the contracts

a. Are negotiated as a package in the same economic environment with an overall profit margin objective.
b. Constitute an agreement to do a single project.
c. Require closely interrelated construction activities.
d. Are performed concurrently or in a continuous sequence under the same project management.
e. Constitute, in substance, an agreement with a single customer.

Segmenting a contract is a process of breaking up a larger unit into smaller units for accounting purposes. If the project is segmented, revenues can be assigned to the different elements or phases to achieve different rates of profitability based on the relative value of each element or phase to the estimated total contract revenue. According to SOP 81-1, para 40, a project may be segmented if all of the following steps were taken and are documented and verifiable:

    a.   *The contractor submitted bona fide proposals on the separate components of the project and on the entire project.*

    b.   *The customer had the right to accept the proposals on either basis.*

    c.   *The aggregate amount of the proposals on the separate components approximated the amount of the proposal on the entire project.*

A project that does not meet the above criteria may still be segmented if all of the following (SOP 81-1, para 41) are applicable:

    a.   *The terms and scope of the contract or project clearly call for the separable phases or elements.*

    b.   *The separable phases or elements of the project are often bid or negotiated separately.*

    c.   *The market assigns different gross profit rates to the segments because of factors such as different levels of risk or differences in the relationship of the supply and demand for the services provided in different segments.*

    d.   *The contractor has a significant history of providing similar services to other customers under separate contracts for each significant segment to which a profit margin higher than the overall profit margin on the project is ascribed.*

    e.   *The significant history with customers who have contracted for services separately is one that is relatively stable in terms of pricing policy rather than one unduly weighted by erratic pricing decisions (responding, for example, to extraordinary economic circumstances or to unique customer-contractor relationships).*

    f.   *The excess of the sum of the prices of the separate elements over the price of the total project is clearly attributable to cost savings incident to combined performance of the contract obligations (for example, cost savings in supervision, overhead, or equipment mobilization). Unless this condition is met, segmenting a contract with a price substantially less than the sum of the prices of the separate phases or elements would be inappropriate even if the other conditions are met. Acceptable price variations should be allocated to the separate phases or elements in proportion to the prices ascribed to each. In all other situations a substantial difference in price (whether more or less) between the separate elements and the price of the total project is evidence that the contractor has accepted different profit margins. Accordingly, segmenting is not appropriate, and the contracts should be the profit centers.*

    g.   *The similarity of services and prices in the contract segments and services and the prices of such services to other customers contracted separately should be documented and verifiable.*

Note that the criteria for combining and segmenting should be applied consistently to contracts with similar characteristics and in similar circumstances.

Joint Ventures and Shared Contracts

Under many contracts that are obtained by long-term construction companies are those that are shared by more than one contractor. When the owner of the contract puts it up for bids, many contractors will form syndicates or joint ventures in order to bid on and successfully obtain a contract that each contractor individually could not perform under.

When this transpires, a separate set of books is maintained for the joint venture. If the percentages of interest for each of the ventures are identical in more than one contract, the joint venture might keep its records almost like another construction company. Usually, the joint venture is for a single contract and ends upon completion of that contract.

A joint venture is a form of a partnership, although a partnership for a limited purpose. An agreement of the parties and the terms of the contract successfully bid upon will determine the nature of the accounting records. Income statements are usually cumulative statements showing all totals from date of contract determination until reporting date. Each venturer records its share of the amount from the venture's income statement less its previously recorded portion of the venture's income as a single line item similar to the equity method for investments. Similarly, balance sheets of the venture give rise to a single line asset balance of investment and advances in joint ventures. In most cases, footnote disclosure is also similar to the equity method in displaying condensed financial statements of material joint ventures.

Accounting for Change Orders

Change orders are modifications of specifications or provisions of an original contract. Contract revenue and costs should be adjusted to reflect change orders that are approved by the contractor and customer. According to SOP 81-1, the accounting for the change order depends upon the scope and price of the change.

If the scope and price have both been agreed upon by the customer and contractor, contract revenue and cost should be adjusted to reflect the change order.

According to SOP 81-1, para 62, accounting for unpriced change orders depends on their characteristics and the circumstances in which they occur. Under the completed-contract method, costs attributable to unpriced change orders should be deferred as contract costs if it is probable that total contract costs, including costs attributable to the change orders, will be recovered from contract revenues. Recovery should be deemed probable if the future event or events are likely to occur.

Per SOP 81-1, para 62, the following guidelines should be followed when accounting for unpriced change orders under the percentage-of-completion method:

a. *Costs attributable to unpriced change orders should be treated as costs of contract performance in the period in which the costs are incurred if it is <u>not</u> probable that the costs will be recovered through a change in the contract price.*

b. *If it is probable that the costs will be recovered through a change in the contract price, the costs should be deferred (excluded from the cost of contract performance) until the parties have agreed on the change in contract price, or, alternatively, they should be treated as costs of contract performance in the period in which they are incurred, and contract revenue should be recognized to the extent of the costs incurred.*

c. *If it is probable that the contract price will be adjusted by an amount that exceeds the costs attributable to the change order and the amount of the excess can be reliably estimated, the original contract price should also be adjusted for that amount when the costs are recognized as costs of contract performance if its realization is probable. However, since the substantiation of the amount of future revenue is difficult, revenue in excess of the costs attributable to unpriced change orders should only be recorded in circumstances in which realization is assured beyond a reasonable doubt, such as circumstances in which an entity's historical experience provides such assurance or in which an entity has received a bona fide pricing offer from a customer and records only the amount of the offer as revenue.*

Accounting for Contract Options

Per SOP 81-1, para 64, an addition or option to an existing contract should be treated as a separate contract if any of the following circumstances exist:

a. *The product or service to be provided differs significantly from the product or service provided under the original contract.*

b. *The price of the new product or service is negotiated without regard to the original contract and involves different economic judgments.*

c. *The products or services to be provided under the exercised option or amendment are similar to those under the original contract, but the contract price and anticipated contract cost relationship are significantly different.*

If the addition or option does not meet the above circumstances, the contracts should be combined. However, if the addition or option does not meet the criteria for combining, they should be treated as change orders.

Accounting for Claims

These represent amounts in excess of the agreed contract price that a contractor seeks to collect from customers for unanticipated additional costs. The recognition of additional contract revenue relating to claims is appropriate if it is probable that the claim will result in additional revenue and if the amount can be reliably estimated. SOP 81-1, para 65 specifies that all of the following conditions must exist in order for the probable and estimable requirements to be satisfied:

a. The contract or other evidence provides a legal basis for the claim; or a legal opinion has been obtained, stating that under the circumstances there is a reasonable basis to support the claim.

b. Additional costs are caused by circumstances that were unforeseen at the contract date and are not the result of deficiencies in the contractor's performance.

c. Costs associated with the claim are identifiable or otherwise determinable and are reasonable in view of the work performed.

d. The evidence supporting the claim is objective and verifiable, not based on management's "feel" for the situation or on unsupported representations.

When the above requirements are met, revenue from a claim should be recorded only to the extent that contract costs relating to the claim have been incurred.

When the above requirements are not met, para 67 of SOP 81-1 states that a contingent asset should be disclosed in accordance with SFAS 5, para 17.

Accounting Changes

According to APB 20, a change in method of accounting for long-term construction contracts is a special change in principle requiring retroactive treatment and restatement of previous financial statements. (See Chapter 19 for further discussion.)

Revisions in revenue, cost, and profit estimates or in measurements of the extent of progress toward completion are changes in accounting estimates. Such changes should be accounted for prospectively in order for the financial statements to fully reflect the effects of the latest available estimates.

Deferred Income Taxes

Deferred taxes resulting from temporary differences should be classified in accordance with SFAS 96, *Accounting for Income Taxes.* Contract-related deferred taxes result from the use of a method of income recognition for tax purposes different from the method used for financial reporting purposes. (Refer to Chapter 14 on accounting for income taxes for further discussion of deferred taxes.)

Disclosures

In addition to the normal disclosures required in an entity's statements, the following items should be disclosed in the notes to the financial statements or in the body of the financial statements:

1. The method of recognizing income (percentage-of-completion or completed-contract)
2. If the percentage-of-completion method is used, the method of computing percentage of completion (e.g., cost-to-cost, efforts-expended)

3. If the completed-contract method is used, the justification for its use should be indicated
4. Length of the operating cycle; if greater than one year, the range of contract durations should be disclosed
5. The basis of recording inventory
6. The effect of changes in estimates
7. The accounting for deferred costs
8. The accounting for general and administrative expenses
9. Criteria for determining substantial completion (e.g., compliance with specifications, acceptance by customer)
10. Information on revenues and costs arising from claims
11. Effects of accounting changes to conform to SOP 81-1 (retroactive restatements of prior periods' financial statements)

SERVICE SALES TRANSACTIONS

Perspective and Issues

Service sales transactions represent over half of the U.S. economy's transactions; however, there are no official pronouncements that provide specific accounting standards for them. Accounting for service sales transactions has evolved primarily through industry practice. As a result, different accounting methods have developed to apply the fundamental principles of revenue and cost recognition. In fact, different accounting methods are used by similar entities for practically identical transactions. Because of these wide variations, the FASB and the AICPA combined efforts in an attempt to establish accounting standards for service transactions through their issuance of *Accounting for Certain Service Transactions*, FASB Invitation to Comment (the Invitation). The Invitation contained an AICPA draft Statement of Position that set forth conclusions on the following:

1. The guidelines to apply to transactions in which both services and products are provided
2. The appropriate manner of revenue recognition
3. The classification of costs as initial direct costs, direct costs, and indirect costs and the accounting for each
4. The accounting for initiation and installation fees

This section reflects the conclusions in the AICPA draft Statement of Position.

Sources of GAAP

Other
*

*FASB Invitation to Comment, <u>Accounting for Certain Service Transactions</u>.

Definitions of Terms

Collection method. Revenue recognized upon the collection of cash.

Completed performance method. A method that recognizes revenue after the last significant act has been completed.

Direct costs. Costs that are directly related to the performance of services.

Indirect costs. Costs that are not directly related to the negotiation or consummation of service agreements and are not directly related to the performance of services.

Initial direct costs. Costs that are directly associated with the negotiation and consummation of service agreements.

Initiation fee. A one-time, up-front charge that gives the purchaser the privilege of using the service or the use of facilities.

Installation fee. A one-time, up-front charge for the installation of equipment essential to the provision of the service.

Product transaction. A transaction between a seller and a purchaser in which the seller supplies a product to the purchaser.

Proportional performance method. A method that recognizes revenue on the basis of the number of acts performed in relation to the total number of acts to be performed.

Service transaction. A transaction between a seller and a purchaser in which the seller provides a service, or agrees to maintain a readiness to perform a service, to the purchaser.

Specific performance method. A method that recognizes revenue after one specific act has been performed.

Concepts, Rules, and Examples

The AICPA has defined service transactions as follows:

> ...transactions between a seller and a purchaser in which, for a mutually agreed price, the seller performs, agrees to perform, agrees to perform at a later date, or agrees to maintain readiness to perform an act or acts, including permitting others to use enterprise resources that do not alone produce a tangible commodity or product as the principal intended result (the Invitation, para 7).

Generally accepted accounting principles require that revenue should generally be recognized when: (1) it is **realized or realizable** and (2) it has been **earned** (SFAC 5, para 83). With respect to service transactions, the AICPA concluded:

> ...revenue from service transactions should be based on performance, because performance determines the extent to which the earnings process is complete or virtually complete (the Invitation, para 10).

In practice, performance may involve the execution of a defined act, a set of similar or identical acts, or a set of related but not similar or identical acts. Performance may also occur with the passage of time. Accordingly, one of the following four methods should serve as a guideline for the recognition of revenue from service transactions:

1. The specific performance method
2. The proportional performance method
3. The completed performance method
4. The collection method

Service vs. Product Transactions

Many transactions involve the sale of a tangible product and a service; therefore, for proper accounting treatment, it must be determined whether the transaction is primarily a service transaction accompanied by an incidental product, primarily a product transaction accompanied by an incidental service, or a sale in which both a service transaction and a product transaction occur. The following criteria are applicable:

1. If the seller offers both a service and a product in a single transaction and if the sale of the service is worded in such a manner that the inclusion or exclusion of the product would not change the total transaction price, the product is incidental to the rendering of the service; the transaction is a service transaction that should be accounted for in accordance with one of the four methods presented. For example, fixed price equipment maintenance contracts that include parts are service transactions.

2. If the seller offers both a service and a product in a single transaction and if the sale of the product is worded in such a manner that the inclusion or exclusion of the service would not change the total transaction price, the rendering of the service is incidental to the sale of the product; the transaction is a product transaction that should be accounted for as such. For example, the sale of a product accompanied by a guarantee or warranty for repair is considered a product transaction.

3. If the seller offers both a product and a service and the agreement states the product and service are separate elements such that the inclusion or exclusion of the service would vary the total transaction price, the transaction consists of two components: a product transaction that should be accounted for separately as such, and a service transaction that should be accounted for in accordance with one of the four accepted methods.

Revenue Recognition Methods

Once the sale has been identified as a service transaction, one of the following four methods should be used to recognize revenue. The method chosen should reflect the nature and extent of the service(s) to be performed.

1. **Specific performance method.** The specific performance method should be used when performance consists of the execution of a single act. Revenue is recognized at the time the act takes place. For example, a stockbroker should record sales commissions as revenue upon the sale of a client's investment.

2. **Proportional performance method.** The proportional performance method should be used when performance consists of a number of identical or similar acts.

   a. If the service transaction involves a **specified number** of **identical** or **similar** acts, an equal amount of revenue should be recorded for each act performed. For example, a refuse disposal company would recognize an equal amount of revenue for each weekly removal of a customer's garbage.

b. If the service transaction involves a specified number of defined but **not** identical or similar acts, the revenue recognized for each act should be based on the following formula:

$$\frac{\text{Direct cost of individual act}}{\text{Total estimated direct costs}} \quad \times \quad \frac{\text{Total revenues from}}{\text{complete transaction}}$$
$$\text{of the transaction}$$

For example, a correspondence school that provides lessons, examinations, and grading should use this method. If the measurements suggested in the preceding equation are impractical or not objectively determinable, revenue should be recognized on a systematic and rational basis that reasonably relates revenue recognition to service performance.

c. If the service transaction involves an **unspecified** number of acts over a fixed time period for performance, revenue should be recognized over the period during which the acts will be performed by using the straight-line method unless a better method of relating revenue and performance is appropriate. For example, a health club might recognize revenue on a straight-line basis over the life of a member's membership.

3. **Completed performance method.** The completed performance method should be used when more than one act must be done and when the final act is so significant to the entire transaction taken as a whole that performance can't be considered to have taken place until the performance of that final act occurs. For example, a moving company packs, loads, and transports merchandise; however, the final act of delivering the merchandise is so significant that revenue should not be recognized until the goods reach their intended destination. If the services are to be performed in an **indeterminable** number of acts over an **indeterminable** period of time and if an objective measure for estimating the degree to which performance has taken place can't be found, the revenue should be recognized under the completed performance method.

4. **Collection method.** The collection method should be used in circumstances when there is a significant degree of uncertainty surrounding the collection of service revenue. Under this method, revenue should not be recorded until the cash is collected. For example, personal services may be provided to a customer whose ability to pay is uncertain.

Expense Recognition

GAAP, in general, requires that costs should be charged to expense in the period that the revenue with which they are associated is recognized. Costs should be deferred only when they are expected to be recoverable from future revenues. When applying these principles to service transactions, special consideration must be given to the different types of costs that may arise. The three major classifications of costs arising from service transactions are as follows:

1. Initial direct costs
2. Direct costs
3. Indirect costs

The three types of cost classifications arising from service transactions are defined as follows (the Invitation, para 15):

1. **Initial direct costs.** Costs that are directly associated with the negotiation and consummation of service agreements. They include, but are not limited to, legal fees, commissions, costs of credit investigations, installment paper processing fees, and the portion of salespersons' and other employees' compensation, other than commissions, that is applicable to the time spent on consummated agreements. They do not include costs allocable to time spent on service transactions that are not consummated or portions of supervisory, administrative, or other indirect costs, such as rent.
2. **Direct costs.** Costs that have a clear, beneficial, or causal relationship to the services or level of services performed. For example, servicemen's labor and repair parts on a fixed price maintenance contract.
3. **Indirect costs.** All costs that cannot be classified as either an initial direct cost or a direct cost. They include provisions for uncollectible accounts, general and administrative expenses, advertising expenses, general selling expenses, the portion of salespersons' and other employees' compensation allocable to the time spent in negotiating service transactions that are not consummated, and all allocations of facility costs (depreciation, rent, maintenance, etc.).

Accounting treatment. The accounting treatment for indirect costs, initial direct costs and direct costs, and service transaction losses are discussed below.

1. **Indirect costs.** Regardless of the service revenue recognition method selected, indirect costs should always be charged to expense as incurred.
2. **Initial direct costs and direct costs.**

    a. Specific performance and completed performance methods. When service revenue is recognized under the **specific performance** or **completed performance** methods, all **initial direct costs** and **direct costs** should be recognized as expense at the time the related service revenue is recognized. Thus, any initial direct costs and direct costs incurred prior to the performance of the service should be deferred as prepayments and expensed at the time of service performance (i.e., at the point revenue is recognized).

    b. Proportional performance method. When service revenue is recognized under the **proportional performance method, initial direct costs** should be charged to expense at the time revenues are recognized. Thus, any initial direct costs incurred prior to performance should be deferred as prepayments and allocated to expense over the length of service performance in proportion to the recognition of service revenue. **Direct costs**, on the other hand, should be charged to expense as incurred because, normally, there is a close correlation between the amount of direct costs incurred and the extent of performance achieved.

    c. <u>Collection method</u>. When service revenue is recognized under the collection method (high uncertainty surrounding the realization of revenue), both **initial direct costs** and **direct costs** should be charged to expense as incurred.

   3. **Service transaction losses.** A loss on a service transaction should be recognized when initial direct costs plus estimated total direct costs of performance exceed the current estimated realizable revenue. The loss (initial direct costs + estimated total direct costs - estimated realizable revenue) should be first used to reduce any deferred costs. If an estimated loss remains, it should be credited to an estimated liability account.

Initiation and Installation Fees

Many service transactions also involve the charge of a nonrefundable initiation fee with subsequent periodic payments for future services and/or a nonrefundable fee for installation of equipment essential to the provision of future services with subsequent periodic payments for the services. These nonrefundable fees may, in substance, be partly or wholly advance charges for future services.

Initiation fees. If there is an objectively determinable value for the right or privilege granted by the initiation fee, that value should be recognized as revenue on the initiation date. Any related direct costs should be charged as expense on the initiation date. If the value of the right or privilege cannot be objectively determined, the fee should be recorded as a liability for future services and recognized as revenue in accordance with one of the recognition methods.

Installation fees. (1) If the equipment and its installation costs are essential for the service to be provided and if customers cannot normally purchase the equipment in separate transactions, the installation fee should be considered an advance charge for future services. This fee should be recognized as revenue over the estimated service period. The costs of installation and installed equipment should be amortized over the period the installation is expected to provide revenue. (2) If customers can normally purchase the equipment in a separate transaction, the installation fee is then a product transaction that should be accounted for separately as such.

Disclosures

1. The revenue recognition method used and its justification
2. Information concerning unearned revenues
3. Information concerning deferred costs
4. Periods over which services are to be performed

SALES WHEN COLLECTION IS UNCERTAIN

Perspective and Issues

Under GAAP, revenue recognition does not depend upon the collection of cash. Accrual accounting techniques normally record revenue at the point of a credit sale by establishing a receivable. When uncertainty arises surrounding the collectibility of this amount, the receivable is appropriately adjusted by establishing a contra account. In some cases, however, the collection of the sales price may be so uncertain that an objective measure of ultimate collectibility cannot be established. When such circumstances exist, APB 10 permits the seller to use either the installment method or the cost recovery method to account for installment transactions. Both of these methods allow for a deferral of gross profit until cash has been collected.

An installment transaction occurs when a seller delivers a product or performs a service and the buyer makes periodic payments over an extended period of time. Under the installment method, income recognition is deferred until the period(s) of cash collection. The seller recognizes both revenues and cost of sales at the time of the sale; however, the related gross profit is deferred to those periods in which cash is collected. Under the cost recovery method, both revenues and cost of sales are recognized at the time of the sale, but none of the related gross profit is recognized until all cost of sales has been recovered. Once the seller has recovered all cost of sales, any additional cash receipts are included in income. APB 10 does not specify when one method is preferred over the other. However, the cost recovery method is more conservative than the installment method because gross profit is deferred until all costs have been recovered; therefore, it should be reserved for situations of extreme uncertainty.

Sources of GAAP

APB
10

Definitions of Terms

Cost recovery method. The method of accounting for an installment basis sale whereby the gross profit is deferred until all cost of sales has been recovered.

Deferred gross profit. The gross profit from an installment basis sale that is deferred to future periods.

Gross profit rate. The gross profit on the installment sale divided by the revenue from the installment sale.

Installment method. The method of accounting for an installment basis sale whereby the gross profit is recognized in the period(s) the cash from the sale is collected.

Installment sale. A sales transaction for which the sales price is collected through the payment of periodic installments over an extended period of time.

Net realizable value. The fair market value of an asset less any costs of disposal.

Realized gross profit. The gross profit recognized in the current period.

Repossessions. Merchandise sold by a seller under an installment arrangement that is repossessed after the buyer defaults on the payments.

Concepts, Rules, and Examples

The installment method was developed in response to an increasing number of sales contracts that allowed buyers to make payments over several years. As the payment period becomes longer, the risk of loss resulting from uncollectible accounts increases; consequently, circumstances surrounding a receivable may lead to considerable uncertainty as to whether payments will actually be received. Under these circumstances, the uncertainty of cash collection suggests that revenue recognition should be deferred until the actual receipt of cash.

The installment method can be used in most sales transactions for which payment is to be made through periodic installments over an extended period of time and the collectibility of the sales price cannot be reasonably estimated. This method is applicable to the sales of real estate (covered in the last section of this chapter), heavy equipment, home furnishings, and other merchandise sold on an installment basis. Installment method revenue recognition is not in accordance with accrual accounting because revenue recognition should not normally be based upon cash collection; however, its use may be justified on the grounds that accrual accounting may result in "front-end loading," i.e., all of the revenue from a transaction is recognized at the point of sale with an improper matching of related costs. For example, the application of accrual accounting to transactions that provide for installment payments over periods of 10, 20, or 30 years may underestimate losses from contract defaults and other future contract costs.

Accounting Treatment

When a seller uses the installment method, both revenue and cost of sales are recognized at the point of sale, but the related gross profit is deferred to those periods over which cash will be collected. As receivables are collected, a portion of the deferred gross profit equal to the gross profit rate times the cash collected is recognized as income. When this method is used, the seller must compute each year's gross profit rate and also must maintain installment accounts receivable and deferred revenue accounts that are identified by the year of sale. All other general and administrative expenses are normally expensed in the period incurred.

The steps to use in accounting for sales under the installment method are as follows:

1. During the current year, record sales revenue and cost of sales in the regular manner. Record installment sales transactions separately from other sales.

Set up installment accounts receivable identified by the year of sale (e.g., Installment Accounts Receivable -1992).

2. Record cash collections from installment accounts receivable. Care must be taken so that the cash receipts are properly identified as to the year in which the receivable arose.

3. At the end of the current year, close out the installment sales revenue and installment cost of sales accounts into a deferred gross profit account that properly identifies the year of sale. Compute the current year's gross profit rate on installment sales as follows:

$$\text{Gross profit rate} = 1 - \frac{\text{Cost of installment sales}}{\text{Installment sales revenue}}$$

Alternatively, the gross profit rate can be computed as follows:

$$\text{Gross profit rate} = \frac{\text{Installment sales revenue - Cost of installment sales}}{\text{Installment sales revenue}}$$

4. Apply the current year's gross profit rate to the cash collections from the current year's installment sales to compute the realized gross profit from the current year's installment sales.

$$\text{Realized gross profit} = \frac{\text{Cash collections from the current year's installment sales}}{} \times \frac{\text{Current year's gross profit rate}}{}$$

5. Apply the previous years' gross profit rates to cash collections from previous years' installment sales to compute the realized gross profit from previous years' installment sales.

$$\text{Realized gross profit} = \frac{\text{Cash collections from the previous years' installment sales}}{} \times \frac{\text{Previous years' gross profit rates}}{}$$

6. Defer the current year's unrealized gross profit to future years. The deferred gross profit to carry forward to future years can be computed in the following manner:

$$\frac{\text{Deferred gross profit}}{(198X)} = \frac{\text{Ending balance installment}}{\text{account receivable (198X)}} \times \frac{\text{Gross profit}}{\text{rate (198X)}}$$

Example of the Installment Method of Accounting

Assume the following:

	1992	*1993*	*1994*
Sales on installment	$ 400,000	$ 450,000	$ 600,000
Cost of installment sales	(280,000)	(337,500)	(400,000)
Gross profit on sales	$ 120,000	$ 112,500	$ 200,000
Cash collections:			
1992 sales	$ 150,000	$ 175,000	$ 75,000
1993 sales		$ 200,000	$ 125,000
1994 sales			$ 300,000

Journal entries would be made for steps 1, 2, and 3 above using this data; the following computations are required for steps 3-6:

Step 3--Compute the current year's gross profit rate.

	1992	*1993*	*1994*
Gross profit on sales	$120,000	$112,500	$200,000
Installment sales revenue	$400,000	$450,000	$600,000
Gross profit rate	30%	25%	33 1/3%

Step 4--Apply the current year's gross profit rate to cash collections from current year's sales.

Year	*Cash collections*		*Gross profit rate*		*Realized gross profit*
1992	$150,000	X	30%	=	$ 45,000
1993	200,000	X	25%	=	50,000
1994	300,000	X	33 1/3%	=	100,000

Step 5--Apply the previous years' gross profit rates to cash collections from previous years' installment sales.

In Year 1993

From year	*Cash collections*		*Gross profit rate*		*Realized gross profit*
1992	$175,000	X	30%	=	$52,500

In Year 1994

From year	*Cash collections*		*Gross profit rate*		*Realized gross profit*
1992	$ 75,000	X	30%	=	$22,500
1993	125,000	X	25%	=	31,250
					$53,750

Step 6--Defer the current year's unrealized gross profit to future years.

12/31/92

Deferred gross profit (1992) = ($400,000 - 150,000) x 30%	= $ 75,000

12/31/93

Deferred gross profit (1993) = ($450,000 - 200,000) x 25%	= $ 62,500
Deferred gross profit (1992) = ($400,000 - 150,000 - 175,000) x 30%	= 22,500
	$ 85,000

12/31/94

Deferred gross profit (1994) = ($600,000 - 300,000) x 33 1/3%	= $100,000
Deferred gross profit (1993) = ($450,000 - 200,000 - 125,000) x 25%	= 31,250
	$131,250

Financial Statement Presentation

If installment sales transactions represent a significant portion of the company's total sales, the following three items of gross profit should, theoretically, be reported on the company's income statement:

1. Total gross profit from current year's sales
2. Realized gross profit from current year's sales
3. Realized gross profit from prior years' sales

An income statement using the previous example would be prepared as follows (assume all sales are accounted for by the installment method):

Thorsen Equipment Company
Partial Income Statement
For the Years Ending December 31

	1992	*1993*	*1994*
Sales	$400,000	$450,000	$600,000
Cost of sales	(280,000)	(337,500)	(400,000)
Gross profit on current sales	$120,000	$112,500	$200,000
Less deferred gross profit on current sales	(75,000)	(62,500)	(100,000)
Realized gross profit on current sales	$ 45,000	$ 50,000	$100,000
Plus realized gross profit on prior sales	--	52,500	53,750
Total gross profit on sales	$ 45,000	$102,500	$153,750

However, when a company recognizes only a small portion of its sales under the installment basis, the previous method of income reporting may be confusing. Therefore, in practice, some companies simply report the realized gross profit from installment sales by displaying it as a single line item on the income statement as follows:

Wisbrock Furniture Company
Partial Income Statement
For the Year Ended December 31, 1992

Sales	$ 2,250,000
Cost of sales	(1,350,000)
Gross profit on sales	$ 900,000
Realized gross profit on installment sales	35,000
Total gross profit on sales	$ 935,000

The balance sheet presentation of the installment accounts receivable will depend upon whether the installment sales are part of normal operations. If a company sells most of its products on an installment basis, the installment accounts receivable will be classified as a current asset because the operating cycle of the business is the average period of time covered by an installment contract. If the installment sales are not part of normal operations, installment accounts receivable that are not to be collected for a year or more should not be reported as current assets. In all cases, to avoid any confusion, it is generally desirable to fully disclose the year of maturity next to each set of installment accounts receivable as illustrated by the following example:

Current assets:		
Cash		$ 56,682
Receivables:		
Trade customers	$180,035	
Less allowance for uncollectible accounts	(4,200)	
	$175,835	
Installment accounts--collectible in 1993	26,678	
Installment accounts--collectible in 1994	42,234	$244,747

The accounting for the deferred gross profit account(s) is addressed in SFAC 3 which states that the deferred gross profit account is not a liability. The reason is that the seller company is not obligated to pay cash or provide services to the customer. Rather, the account arose because of the uncertainty surrounding the collectibility of the sales price. SFAC 3 goes on to say, "deferred gross profit on installment sales is conceptually an asset valuation--that is, a reduction of an asset." However, in practice, the deferred gross profit account is generally presented as either an unearned revenue classified as a current liability or a deferred credit displayed between liabilities and equity. Following the guideline given by SFAC 3, the current asset section would be presented as follows (using information from the Thorsen Equipment example and as-suming a 12/31/94 balance sheet):

Installment accounts receivable (1993)	$125,000	
Installment accounts receivable (1994)	300,000	$ 425,000
Less: Deferred gross profit (1993)	$ 31,250	
Deferred gross profit (1994)	100,000	(131,250) $293,750

Interest on Installment Contracts

The previous examples ignored interest, a major component of most installment sales contracts. It is customary for the seller to charge interest to the buyer on the unpaid installment receivable balance. Generally, installment contracts call for equal payments, each with an amount attributable to interest on the unpaid balance and the remainder to the installment receivable balance. As the maturity date nears, a smaller amount of each installment payment is attributable to interest and a larger amount is attributable to principal. Therefore, to determine the amount of gross profit to recognize, the interest must first be deducted from the installment payment and then the difference is multiplied by the gross profit rate as follows:

Realized gross profit = (Installment payment - Interest portion) x Gross profit rate

The interest portion of the installment payment should be recorded as interest revenue at the time of the cash receipt. Appropriate adjusting entries are required to accrue interest revenue when the collection dates do not correspond with the year end.

To illustrate the accounting for installment sales contracts involving interest, assume that Babich Equipment Company sold a piece of machinery on January 1, 1992 to a customer with a dubious credit history. The equipment had a cost of $3,750 and a sales price of $5,000. Terms of the agreement required that a $1,000 down payment be made on the date of the sale and that the remaining balance ($4,000) plus 10% annual interest be paid in equal installments of $1,261.88 at the end of each of the next four years.

For each cash receipt Babich must determine the amount applicable to interest revenue and the value applicable to the installment account receivable balance because gross profit is recognized only on those amounts applicable to the installment receivable balance. It can be seen in the following schedule that gross profit is recognized on the entire down payment, whereas the annual installment payments are separated into their interest and receivable portions with gross profit only being recognized on the latter portion.

Schedule of Cash Receipts

Date	Cash (debit)	Interest revenue (credit)	Installment accounts receivable (credit)	Installment accounts receivable balance	Realized gross profit
1/1/92				$5,000.00	
1/1/92	$1,000.00	$ --	$1,000.00	4,000.00	$ 250.00a
12/31/92	1,261.88	400.00b	861.88c	3,138.12d	215.47e
12/31/93	1,261.88	313.81	948.07	2,190.05	237.02
12/31/94	1,261.88	219.01	1,042.87	1,147.18	260.72
12/31/95	1,261.88	114.70	1,147.18	-0-	286.79
			Total realized gross profit		$1,250.00

Gross profit rate = 1 - $3,750/5,000 = 25%

a $1,000 x 25% = $250

b $4,000 x 10% = $400

c $1,261.88 - 400 = $861.88

d $4,000 - 861.88 = $3,138.12

e $861.88 x 25% = $215.47

Bad Debts and Repossessions

The standard accounting treatment for uncollectible accounts is to accrue a bad debt loss in the year of sale by estimating the amount that is expected to be uncollectible. This treatment is in line with the concept of accrual. However, just as income recognition under the accrual basis is sometimes abandoned for certain installment basis sales, the accrual basis of recognizing bad debts is also often abandoned.

When the installment method is used, it is usually appropriate to recognize bad debts by the direct write-off method; i.e., bad debts are not recognized until the account has been determined to be uncollectible. This practice is acceptable because most installment contracts contain a provision that allows the seller to repossess the merchandise when the buyer defaults on the installment payments. The loss on the account may be eliminated or reduced because the seller has the option of reselling merchandise. When an installment account is written off, the following three things must be accomplished:

1. The installment account receivable and the deferred gross profit must be eliminated.
2. The repossessed merchandise must be recorded at its net realizable value. Net realizable value is the resale value less any sales or reconditioning costs. The repossessed asset is recorded at this fair value because any asset acquired should be put on the books at the best approximation of its fair value.

Repossessed merchandise is inventory in the seller's hands and, therefore, should be presented in the inventory section of the balance sheet.
3. A bad debt expense, a repossession loss, or a repossession gain should be recognized. The bad debt expense or repossession gain or loss is the difference between the unrecovered cost (Installment account receivable - Deferred gross profit) and the net realizable value of the repossessed merchandise.

To illustrate, assume that the Fahey Company determined that a $3,000 installment receivable is uncollectible. The deferred gross profit ratio on the original sale was 30%; thus, $900 deferred gross profit exists ($3,000 x 30%). If the repossessed equipment has a $1,500 net realizable value, a $600 repossession loss (or bad debt expense) would need to be recorded.

Installment account receivable	$3,000
Less deferred gross profit	(900)
Unrecovered cost	$2,100
Less net realizable value	(1,500)
Repossession loss	$ 600

Fahey Company would record this loss by making the following entry:

Deferred gross profit	900	
Repossessed merchandise	1,500	
Repossession loss	600	
Installment account receivable		3,000

Cost Recovery

The cost recovery method does not recognize any income on a sale until the cost of the item has been recovered through cash receipts. Once the seller has recovered all costs, any subsequent cash receipts are included in income. The cost recovery method is used when the uncertainty of collection of the sale price is so great that even use of the installment method cannot be justified.

Under the cost recovery method, both revenues and cost of sales are recognized at the point of sale, but the related gross profit is deferred until all costs of sales have been recovered. Each installment must also be divided between principal and interest, but unlike the installment method where a portion of the principal recovers the cost of sales and the remainder is recognized as gross profit, all of the principal is first applied to recover the cost of the asset sold. After all costs of sales have been recovered, any subsequent cash receipts are realized as gross profit. The cost recovery method can be illustrated by using the information from the Babich Company example used in the interest on installment sales contract section. If Babich used the cost recovery method, gross profit would be realized as follows:

Schedule of Cash Receipts

Date	Cash (debit)	Deferred interest revenue (credit)*	Installment accounts receivable (credit)	Installment accounts receivable balance	Unrecovered cost	Realized gross profit	Realized interest revenue
1/1/92				$5,000.00	$3,750.00		
1/1/92	$1,000.00	$ --	$1,000.00	4,000.00	2,750.00	$ --	$ --
12/31/92	1,261.88	400.00	861.88	3,138.12	1,488.12	--	--
12/31/93	1,261.88	313.81	948.07	2,190.05	226.24	--	--
12/31/94	1,261.88	(713.81)	1,042.87	1,147.18	--	102.82	932.82**
12/31/95	1,261.88	--	1,147.18	-0-	--	1,147.18	114.70
	$6,047.52		$5,000.00			$1,250.00	$1,047.52

* *Interest received in 1992 and 1993 would be credited to deferred interest revenue since the cost of the asset was not recovered until 1994.*

** *Includes deferred interest revenue received in 1992 and 1993 [$713.81 (1992 and 1993) + $219.01 (1993)]. Interest revenue can only be realized after the cost of the asset is recovered (1994, in this example).*

Disclosures

1. Method and justification of accounting for installment basis sales
2. Yearly gross profit rates
3. Contractual terms such as interest and repossession provisions
4. Average length of installment contracts

REVENUE RECOGNITION WHEN RIGHT OF RETURN EXISTS

Perspective and Issues

In some industries it is common practice for customers to be given the right to return a product to the seller for a credit or refund. However, for companies that experience a high ratio of returned merchandise to sales, the recognition of the original sale as revenue is questionable. In fact, certain industries have found it necessary to defer revenue recognition until the return privilege has substantially expired. Sometimes the return privilege expires soon after the sale, as in the newspaper and perishable food industries. In other cases, the return privilege may last over an extended period of time, as in magazine and textbook publishing and equipment manufacturing. The rate of return normally is directly related to the length of the return privilege. An accounting problem arises when the recognition of the revenue occurs in one period while substantial returns occur in later periods.

SOP 75-1 was developed to reduce the diversity in the accounting for revenue recognition when the right of return exists. Before SOP 75-1, the following three alternative practices were being used:

1. The sale was recognized only after the right of return expired.
2. The sale was recognized and an allowance for estimated returns was provided.
3. A sale was recognized, but sales returns were recognized only when the product was returned (recognition of sales and sales returns possibly occurring in different periods).

The FASB extracted the specialized accounting and reporting principles and practices from SOP 75-1 and reissued them through SFAS 48, *Revenue Recognition When Right of Return Exists*.

Sources of GAAP

SFAS
5, 48

Definitions of Terms

Deferred gross profit. The gross profit from a sale that is deferred to future periods because of the uncertainty surrounding the collection of the sales price.

Return privilege. A privilege granted to a buyer by express agreement with a seller or by practice of the industry that allows the buyer to return merchandise to the seller within a stated period of time.

Concepts, Rules, and Examples

SFAS 48 provides criteria for recognizing revenue on a sale in which a product may be returned (as a matter of contract or a matter of industry practice), either by the ultimate consumer or by a party who resells the product to others. Paragraph 6 states the following:

> *If an enterprise sells its product but gives the buyer the right to return the product, revenue from the sales transaction shall be recognized at time of sale only if all of the following conditions are met:*
>
> a. *The seller's price to the buyer is substantially fixed or determinable at the date of sale.*
> b. *The buyer has paid the seller, or the buyer is obligated to pay the seller and the obligation is not contingent on resale of the product.*
> c. *The buyer's obligation to the seller would not be changed in the event of theft or physical destruction or damage of the product.*
> d. *The buyer acquiring the product for resale has economic substance apart from that provided by the seller.*
> e. *The seller does not have significant obligations for future performance to directly bring about the resale of the product by the buyer.*
> f. *The amount of future returns can be reasonably estimated. For purposes of this statement "returns" do not include exchanges by ultimate customers of one item for another of the same kind, quality, and price.*

If all of the above conditions are met, the seller should recognize revenue from the sales transaction at the time of the sale and "any costs or losses that may be expected in connection with any returns shall be accrued in accordance with SFAS 5, *Accounting for Contingencies*" (para 7). SFAS 5 states that estimated losses from contingencies shall be accrued and charged to income when it is probable that an asset has been impaired or a liability incurred and the amount of loss can be reasonably estimated.

Example of Sale with Right of Return

Assume that Lee, Inc. began the sale of its new textbook on computer programming in 1992 with the following results: On December 1, 1992, 2,000 textbooks with a sales price of $45 each and total manufacturing costs of $30 each are delivered to school bookstores on account. The bookstores have the right to return the textbooks within four months of the delivery date. The bookstores remit cash payments when the books are sold. Payment and returns for the initial deliveries are as follows:

	Cash receipts		Returns	
	Units	*Amount*	*Units*	*Amount*
December 1992	600	$27,000	--	--
January 1993	500	22,500	40	$1,800
February 1993	400	18,000	90	4,050
March 1993	300	13,500	30	1,350
	1,800	$81,000	160	$7,200

Lee, Inc. has had similar agreements with the bookstores in the past and has experienced a 15% return rate on similar sales.

Requirements for revenue recognition met. If all six of the requirements were met, the following journal entries would be appropriate:

12/1/92	Accounts receivable	90,000	
	Sales (2,000 units x $45 per unit)		90,000
	(To record sale of 2,000 textbooks)		

12/31/92	Cash (600 units x $45 per unit)	27,000	
	Accounts receivable		27,000
	(To record cash receipts for the month)		
	Cost of sales	60,000	
	Inventory (2,000 units x $30 per unit)		60,000
	(To record cost of goods sold for the month)		
	Sales (15% x 2,000 units x $45 per unit)	13,500	
	Cost of sales (15% x 2,000 units x $30 per unit)		9,000
	Deferred gross profit on estimated returns (15% x 2,000 units x $15 per unit)		4,500
	(To record estimate of returns)		

1/1/93 to 3/31/93	Cash	54,000	
	Accounts receivable		54,000
	(To record cash receipts)		
	Inventory (160 units x $30 per unit)	4,800	
	Deferred gross profit on estimated returns	2,400	
	Accounts receivable (160 units x $45 per unit)		7,200
	(To record returns)		

3/31/93	Cost of sales (140 units x $30 per unit)	4,200	
	Deferred gross profit on estimated returns	2,100	
	Sales (140 units x $45 per unit)		6,300

The revenue and cost of goods sold recognized in 1992 are based on the number of units expected to be returned, 300 (15% x 2,000 units). The net revenue recognized is $76,500 (85% x 2,000 units x $45 per unit) and the cost of goods sold recognized is

$51,000 (85% x 2,000 units x $30 per unit). The deferred gross profit balance is carried forward until the textbooks are returned or until the privilege expires.

Requirements for revenue recognition not met. If all six conditions are not met, revenue and cost of sales from the sales transactions must be deferred until either the return privilege has substantially expired or the point when all the conditions are subsequently met, whichever comes first (para 6).

In the Lee case, if any one of the six conditions is not met, the following entries would be required. The return privilege is assumed to be lost by the store when the books are sold to final customers.

12/1/92	Accounts receivable	90,000	
	Sales		90,000
	(To record sale of 2,000 units)		
12/31/92	Cash	27,000	
	Accounts receivable		27,000
	(To record cash receipts)		
	Cost of sales	60,000	
	Inventory		60,000
	(To record cost of goods sold)		
	Sales (1,400 units x $45 per unit)	63,000	
	Cost of sales (1,400 units x $30 per unit)		42,000
	Deferred gross profit		21,000
	(To defer revenue recognition on goods for which the right of return expires on 3/31/92)		
1/1/93 to 3/31/93	Cash	54,000	
	Accounts receivable (1,200 units x $45 per unit)		54,000
	(To record cash receipts)		
	Cost of sales (1,200 units x $30 per unit)	36,000	
	Deferred gross profit	18,000	
	Sales		54,000
	(To recognize revenue and cost of goods sold on cash receipts)		
	Inventory (160 units x $30 per unit)	4,800	
	Deferred gross profit	2,400	
	Accounts receivable		7,200
	(To record sales returns)		

3/31/93	Cost of sales (40 units x $30 per unit)	1,200	
	Deferred gross profit	600	
	Sales (40 units x $45 per unit)		1,800
	(To record revenue and cost of goods sold on products for which right of return expired)		

Disclosures

1. Basis for recognizing revenue and cost of sales
2. Estimated amount of returns
3. Description of return privilege granted to customers
4. Length of time covered by the return privilege

PROFIT RECOGNITION ON NONRETAIL SALES OF REAL ESTATE

Perspective and Issues

The substance of a sale of any asset is that the transaction should transfer the risks and rewards of ownership to the buyer. However, the economic substance of many real estate sales is that the risks and rewards of ownership have not been clearly transferred. The turbulent environment in the real estate market over the last 15 years has led to the evolution of many complex methods of financing real estate transactions. For example, in some transactions the seller, rather than an independent third party, finances the buyer, while in others, the seller may be required to guarantee a minimum return to the buyer or operate the property for a specified period of time. In many of these complex transactions, the seller still has some association with the property even after the property has been sold. The question that must be answered in these transactions is: At what point does the seller become disassociated enough so that profit may be recognized on the transaction?

Accounting for sales of real estate is governed by SFAS 66. This statement adopts the specialized profit recognition principles in the AICPA Industry Accounting Guide, *Accounting for Profit Recognition on Sales of Real Estate* and AICPA Statements of Position 75-6, *Questions Concerning Profit Recognition on Sales of Real Estate*, and 78-4, *Application of the Deposit, Installment, and Cost Recovery Methods in Accounting for Sales of Real Estate*. Due to the complex nature of these real estate transactions, SFAS 66 is very detailed and complex. The purpose of this section is to present the guidelines that need to be considered when analyzing nonretail real estate transactions.

Sources of GAAP
SFAS
66

Definitions of Terms

Continuing investment. Payments that the buyer is contractually required to pay on its total debt for the purchase price of the property.

Cost recovery method. A method which defers the recognition of gross profit on a real estate sale until the seller recovers the cost of the property sold.

Deposit method. A method which records payments by the buyer as deposits rather than a sale. The seller continues to report the asset and related debt on the balance until the contract is canceled or until the sale has been achieved.

First mortgage (primary debt). The debt the seller has on the property at the time the buyer purchases the property.

Full accrual method. A method which recognizes all profit from a real estate sale at the time of sale.

Initial investment. The sales value received by the seller at the point of sale. It includes cash down payment, buyer's notes supported by an irrevocable letter of credit and payment by the buyer to third parties to reduce seller indebtedness on the property.

Installment method. A method which recognizes income on the basis of payments made by the buyer on debt given to seller and payments by the buyer to the holder of primary debt. Each payment is apportioned between profit and cost recovery.

Lien. A claim or charge a creditor has on property for payment on debt by debtor.

Minimum initial investment. The minimum amount that an initial investment must equal or exceed so that the criterion for full accrual is met.

Partial sale. A sale in which the seller retains an equity interest in the property or has an equity interest in the buyer.

Property improvements. An addition made to real estate, usually consisting of buildings but may also include any permanent structure such as streets, sidewalks, sewers, utilities, etc.

Reduced profit method. A method which recognizes profit at the point of sale but only a reduced amount. The remaining profit is deferred to future periods.

Release provision. An agreement that provides for the release of property to the buyer. This agreement releases the property to the buyer free of any previous liens.

Sales value. The sales price of the property increased or decreased for other consideration in the sales transaction that are, in substance, additional sales proceeds to the buyer.

Subordination. The process by which a person's rights are ranked below the rights of others.

Concepts, Rules, and Examples

Profit from real estate sales may be recognized in full, provided the following:

1. The profit is determinable, i.e., the collectibility of the sales price is reasonably assured or the amount that will not be collectible can be estimated.
2. The earnings process is virtually complete, i.e., the seller is not obliged to perform significant activities after the sale to earn the profit (SFAS 66, para 3).

When both of these conditions are satisfied, the method used to recognize profits on real estate sales is referred to as the full accrual method. If both of these conditions are not satisfied, recognition of all or part of the profit should be postponed.

For real estate sales, the collectibility of the sales price is reasonably assured when the buyer has demonstrated a commitment to pay. This commitment is supported by a substantial initial investment, along with continuing investments that give the buyer a sufficient stake in the property such that the risk of loss through default motivates the buyer to honor its obligations to the seller. Collectibility of the sales price should also be assessed by examining the conditions surrounding the sale (e.g., credit history of the buyer; age, condition, and location of the property; and history of cash flows generated by the property).

The full accrual method is appropriate and profit shall be recognized in full at the point of sale for real estate transactions when all of the following criteria are met:

1. A sale is consummated.
2. The buyer's initial and continuing investments are adequate to demonstrate a commitment to pay for the property.
3. The seller's receivable is not subject to future subordination.
4. The seller has transferred to the buyer the usual risks and rewards of ownership in a transaction that is, in substance, a sale and does not have a substantial continuing involvement in the property.

On sales in which an independent third party provides all of the financing for the buyer, the seller should be most concerned that criterion (1) is met. For such sales, the sale is usually consummated on the closing date. When the seller finances the buyer, the seller must analyze the economic substance of the agreement to ascertain that criteria (2), (3), and (4) are also met; i.e., whether the transaction clearly transfers the risks and rewards of ownership to the buyer.

On sales in which a buyer assumes debt on property, the FASB Emerging Issues Task Force (EITF) has reached a consensus (88-24) that if the seller is not released from its liability, the seller may use the full accrual method. Proceeds from incurrence of debts secured by the property are not to be included in computing either the buyer's initial investment or cash payments under non-full accrual methods.

Consummation of a Sale

A sale is considered consummated when the following conditions are met:

1. The parties are bound by the terms of a contract.
2. All consideration has been exchanged.
3. Any permanent financing for which the seller is responsible has been arranged.
4. All conditions precedent to closing have been performed.

When a seller is constructing office buildings, condominiums, shopping centers, or similar structures, item (4) may be applied to individual units rather than the entire project. These four conditions are usually met on or after closing, not at the point the agreement to sell is signed or at a preclosing. Closing refers to the final steps of the transaction, i.e., when consideration is paid, mortgage is secured, and the deed is delivered or placed in escrow. If the consummation criteria **have not** been satisfied, the seller should use the deposit method of accounting until the sale has been consummated.

Adequacy of the Buyer's Initial Investment

Once it has been determined that the sale has been consummated, the next step is to determine whether the buyer's initial investment adequately demonstrates a commitment to pay for the property. This determination is made by comparing the buyer's initial investment to the sales value of the property. SFAS 66 specifically details items that are includable as the initial investment and the minimum percentages that the initial investment must bear as a percentage of the sales value of the property. In order to make the determination of whether the initial investment is adequate, the sale value of the property must also be computed.

Computation of Sales Value

The sales value of property in a real estate transaction can be computed by the following formula (SFAS 66, para 7):

>   Stated sales price
> \+   Proceeds from the issuance of an **exercised** purchase option
> \+   Other payments that are, in substance, additional sales proceeds (e.g., management fees, points, or prepaid interest or fees required to be maintained in advance of the sale that will be applied against amounts due to the seller at a later point)
> −   A discount that reduces the buyer's note to its present value
> −   Net present value of services seller agrees to perform without compensation
> −   Excess of net present value of services seller performs over compensation that seller will receive
> ──────────────────────────────
> =   Sales value of the property

Composition of the Initial Investment

Sales transactions are characterized by many different types of payments and commitments made between the seller, buyer, and third parties; however, the buyer's initial investment shall only include the following:

1. Cash paid to the seller as a down payment
2. Buyer's notes given to the seller that are supported by irrevocable letters of credit from independent lending institutions
3. Payments by the buyer to third parties that reduce existing indebtedness the seller has on the property
4. Other amounts paid by the buyer that are part of the sale value
5. Other consideration received by the seller that can be converted to cash without recourse to the seller, e.g., other notes of the buyer (SFAS 66, para 9)

SFAS 66 specifically states that the following items should not be included as initial investment (para 10):

1. Payments by the buyer to third parties for improvements to the property
2. A permanent loan commitment by an independent third party to replace a loan made by the seller

3. Funds that have been or will be loaned, refunded, or directly or indirectly pro-
    vided to the buyer by the seller or loans guaranteed or collateralized by the
    seller for the buyer

Size of Initial Investment

Once the initial investment is computed, its size must be compared to the sales value of the property. To qualify as an adequate initial investment, the initial investment should be equal to at least a major part of the difference between usual loan limits established by independent lending institutions and the sales value of the property. The minimum initial investment requirements for real estate sales (other than retail land sales) vary depending upon the class of property being used. The following table from SFAS 66, Appendix A provides the limits for the various properties:

Type of property	Minimum initial investment expressed as a percentage of sales value
Land	
Held for commercial, industrial, or residential development to commence within two years after sale	20
Held for commercial, industrial, or residential development to commence after two years	25
Commercial and Industrial Property	
Office and industrial buildings, shopping centers, and so forth:	
Properties subject to lease on a long-term lease basis to parties with satisfactory credit rating; cash flow currently sufficient to service all indebtedness	10
Single-tenancy properties sold to a buyer with a satisfactory credit rating	15
All other	20
Other income-producing properties (hotels, motels, marinas, mobile home parks, and so forth):	
Cash flow currently sufficient to service all indebtedness	15
Start-up situations or current deficiencies in cash flow	25
Multifamily Residential Property	
Primary residence:	
Cash flow currently sufficient to service all indebtedness	10
Start-up situations or current deficiencies in cash flow	15
Secondary or recreational residence:	
Cash flow currently sufficient to service all indebtedness	15
Start-up situations or current deficiencies in cash flow	25
Single-Family Residential Property (including condominium or cooperative housing)	
Primary residence of the buyer	5[a]
Secondary or recreational residence	10[a]

---

[a] *If collectibility of the remaining portion of the sales price cannot be supported by reliable evidence of collection experience, the minimum initial investment shall be at least 60 percent of the difference between the sales value and the financing available from loans guaranteed by regulatory bodies such as the Federal Housing Authority (FHA) or the Veterans Administration (VA), or from independent, established lending institutions. This 60-percent test applies when independent first-mortgage financing is not utilized and the seller takes a receivable from the buyer for the difference between the sales value and the initial investment. If independent first mortgage financing is utilized, the adequacy of the initial investment on sales of single-family residential property should be determined in accordance with paragraph 53.*

However, lenders' appraisals of specific properties often differ. Therefore, if the buyer has obtained a permanent loan or firm permanent loan commitment for maximum financing of the property from an independent lending institution, the minimum initial investment should be the greater of the following (SFAS 66, Appendix A):

1. The minimum percentage of the sales value of the property specified in the above table.
2. The lesser of:
   a. The amount of the sales value of the property in excess of 115% of the amount of a newly placed permanent loan or firm loan commitment from a primary lender that is an independent established lending institution.
   b. Twenty-five percent of the sales value.

To illustrate the determination of whether an initial investment adequately demonstrates a commitment to pay for property, consider the following example:

Example Determining Adequacy of Initial Investment

Krueger, Inc. exercised a $2,000 option for the purchase of an apartment building from Gampfer, Inc. The terms of the sales contract required Krueger to pay $3,000 of delinquent property taxes, pay a $300,000 cash down payment, assume Gampfer's recently issued first mortgage of $1,200,000, and give Gampfer a second mortgage of $500,000 at a prevailing interest rate.

Step 1--Compute the sales value of the property.

Payment of back taxes to reduce Gampfer's liability to local municipality	$ 3,000
Proceeds from exercised option	2,000
Cash down payment	300,000
First mortgage assumed by Krueger	1,200,000
Second mortgage given to Gampfer	500,000
Sales value of the apartment complex	$2,005,000

Step 2--Compute the initial investment.

Cash down payment	$300,000
Payment of back taxes to reduce Gampfer's liability to local municipality	3,000
Proceeds from exercised option	2,000
	$305,000

Step 3--Compute the minimum initial investment required.
   a. The minimum percentage of the sales value of the property as specified in the table is $200,500 ($2,005,000 x 10%).
   b. 1) The amount of the sales value of the property in excess of 115% of the recently placed permanent mortgage is $625,000 (sales value of $2,005,000 - $1,380,000 [115% of $1,200,000]).
      2) Twenty-five percent of the sales value ($2,005,000) is $501,250.

The lesser of b.1) and b.2) is b.2), $501,250. The greater of (a) and (b) is (b), $501,250. Therefore, to record this transaction under the full accrual method (assuming all other criteria are met), the minimum initial investment must be equal to or greater than $501,250. Since the actual initial investment is only $305,000, all or part of the recognition of profit from the transaction must be postponed.

If the sale has been consummated but the buyer's initial investment does not adequately demonstrate a commitment to pay, the transaction should be accounted for by the **installment method** when the seller is reasonably assured of **recovering the cost** of the property if the buyer defaults. However, if the recovery of the cost of the property is not reasonably assured should the buyer default or if the cost has been recovered and the collection of additional amounts is uncertain, the cost recovery or deposit methods should be used (para 22).

Adequacy of the Buyer's Continuing Investments

The collectibility of the buyer's receivable must be reasonably assured; therefore, for full profit recognition under the full accrual method, the buyer must be contractually required to pay each year on its total debt for the purchase price of the property an amount at least equal to the level annual payment that would be needed to pay that debt (both principal and interest) over a specified period. This period is no more than 20 years for land, and no more than the customary amortization term of a first mortgage loan by an independent lender for other types of real estate (SFAS 66, para 12). For continuing investment purposes, the contractually required payments must be in a form that is acceptable for an initial investment. If the seller provides funds to the buyer, either directly or indirectly, these funds must be subtracted from the buyer's payments in determining whether the continuing investments are adequate.

The indebtedness on the property does not have to be reduced proportionately. A lump-sum (balloon) payment will not affect the amortization of the receivable as long as the level annual payments still meet the minimum annual amortization requirement. For example, a land real estate sale may require the buyer to make level annual payments at the end of the first five years and then a balloon payment at the end of the sixth year. The continuing investment criterion is met provided the level annual payment required in each of the first five years is greater than or equal to the level annual payment that would be made if the receivable were amortized over the maximum 20-year (land's specified term) period.

Continuing Investment Not Qualifying

If the sale has been consummated and the minimum initial investment criteria have been satisfied but the continuing investment by the buyer does not meet the stated criterion, the seller shall recognize profit by the **reduced profit method** at the time of sale if payments by the buyer each year will at least cover both of the following:

1. The interest and principal amortization on the maximum first mortgage loan that could be obtained on the property.
2. Interest, at an appropriate rate, on the excess of the aggregate actual debt on the property over such a maximum first mortgage loan (para 23).

If the payments by the buyer do not cover both of the above, the seller may recognize profit by either the **installment** or **cost recovery** method.

Seller's Receivable Subject to Future Subordination

The seller's receivable should not be subject to future subordination. Future subordination by a primary lender would permit the lender to obtain a lien on the property, giving the seller only a secondary residual claim. This subordination criterion does not apply if either of the following occur:

1. A receivable is subordinate to a first mortgage on the property existing at the time of sale.
2. A future loan, including an existing permanent loan commitment, is provided for by the terms of the sale and the proceeds of the loan will be applied first to the payment of the seller's receivable (para 17).

If the seller's receivable is subject to future subordination, profit shall be recognized by the **cost recovery method**. The cost recovery method is justified because the collectibility of the sales price is not reasonably assured in circumstances when the receivable may be subordinated to other creditors.

Seller's Continuing Involvement

Sometimes sellers continue to be involved with property for periods of time even though the property has been legally sold. The seller's involvement often takes the form of profit participation, management services, financing, guarantees of return, construction, etc. The seller does not have a substantial continuing involvement with property unless the risks and rewards of ownership have been clearly transferred to the buyer.

If the seller has some continuing involvement with the property and does not clearly transfer substantially all of the risks and rewards of ownership, profit shall be recognized by a method other than the full accrual method. The method chosen should be determined by the nature and extent of the seller's continuing involvement. As a general rule, profit should only be recognized at the time of sale if the amount of the seller's loss due to the continued involvement with the property is limited by the terms of the sales contract. In this event, the profit recognized at this time should be reduced by the maximum possible loss from the continued involvement.

Profit-Sharing, Financing, and Leasing Arrangements

In real estate sales, it is often the case that economic substance takes precedence over legal form. Certain transactions, though possibly called sales, are in substance profit-sharing, financing, or leasing arrangements and should be accounted for as such. These include situations in which:

1. The seller has an obligation to repurchase the property, or the terms of the transaction allow the buyer to compel the seller or give an option to the seller to repurchase the property (para 26).
2. The seller is a general partner in a limited partnership that acquires an interest in the property sold and holds a receivable from the buyer for a significant part (15% of the maximum first-lien financing) of the sales price (para 27).
3. The seller guarantees the return of the buyer's investment or a return on that investment for an **extended** period of time (para 28).
4. The seller is required to initiate or support operations, or continue to operate property at its own risk for an **extended** period of time (para 29).

Options to Purchase Real Estate Property

Often a buyer will buy an option to purchase land from a seller with the hopeful intention of obtaining a zoning change, building permit, or some other contingency specified in the option agreement. Proceeds from the issue of an option by a property owner (seller) should be accounted for by the **deposit method**. If the option is exercised, the seller should include the option proceeds in the computation of the sales value of the property. If the option is not exercised, the seller should recognize the option proceeds as income at the time the option expires.

Partial Sales of Property

Per SFAS 66, para 33, "a sale is a partial sale if the seller retains an equity interest in the property or has an equity interest in the buyer." Profit on a partial sale may be recognized on the date of sale if the following occur:

1. The buyer is independent of the seller.
2. Collection of the sales price is reasonably assured.
3. The seller will not be required to support the operations of the property on its related obligations to an extent greater than its proportionate interest (para 33).

If the buyer is not independent of the seller, the seller may not be able to recognize any profit that is measured at the date of sale.

If the seller is not reasonably assured of collecting the sales price, the **cost recovery** or **installment method** should be used to recognize profit on the partial sale.

A seller who separately sells individual units in condominium projects or time-sharing interests should recognize profit by the percentage-of-completion method on the sale of individual units or interests if all of the following criteria are met:

1. Construction is beyond a preliminary stage, i.e., engineering and design work, execution of construction contracts, site clearance and preparation, excavation, and completion of the building foundation have all been completed.
2. The buyer is unable to obtain a refund except for nondelivery of the units or interest.
3. Sufficient units have been sold to assure that the entire property will not revert to rental property.
4. Sales prices are collectible.
5. Aggregate sales proceeds and costs can be reasonably estimated.

The **deposit** method would be appropriate to account for these sales up to the point all the criteria are met.

Description of the Methods of Accounting for Nonretail Sales of Real Estate

Full accrual method. This method of accounting for nonretail sales of real estate is appropriate when all four of the recognition criteria have been satisfied. The full accrual method is simply the application of the revenue recognition principle. A real estate sale is recognized in full when the profit is determinable and the earnings process is virtually complete. The profit is determinable when the first three criteria have been met, the sale is consummated, the buyer has demonstrated a commitment to pay, and the seller's receivable is not subject to future subordination. The earnings process is virtually complete when the fourth criterion has been met, the seller has transferred the risks and rewards of ownership and does not have a substantial continuing involvement with the property. If all of the criteria have not been met, the seller should record the transaction by one of the following methods as indicated by SFAS 66:

1. Deposit
2. Cost recovery
3. Installment
4. Reduced profit
5. Percentage-of-completion (see the section on Long-Term Construction Contracts in this chapter)

Profit under the full accrual method is computed by subtracting the cost basis of the property surrendered from the sales value given by the buyer. Also, the computation of profit on the sale should include all costs incurred that are directly related to the sale, such as accounting and legal fees.

Installment method. Under the installment method, each cash receipt and principal payment by the buyer on debt assumed with recourse to the seller consists of part recovery of cost and part recovery of profit. The apportionment between cost recovery and profit is in the same ratio as total cost and total profit bear to the sales value of the property sold. Therefore, under the installment method, the seller recognizes profit on each payment that the buyer makes to the seller and on each payment the buyer makes to the holder of the primary debt. When a buyer assumes debt that is without recourse to the seller, the seller should recognize profit on each payment made to the seller and on the entire debt assumed by the buyer. The accounting treatment differs because the seller is subject to substantially different levels of risk under the alternative conditions. For debt that is without recourse, the seller recovers a portion, if not all, of the cost of the asset surrendered at the time the buyer assumes the debt.

Example of the Installment Method

Assume Benson sells to Golden a plot of undeveloped land for $2,000,000. Golden will assume, with recourse, Benson's existing first mortgage of $1,000,000 and also pay Benson a $300,000 cash down payment. Golden will pay the balance of $700,000 by giving Benson a second mortgage payable in equal installments of principal and interest over the 10-year period. The cost of the land to Benson was $1,200,000 and Golden will commence development of the land immediately.

1. Computation of sales value:

Cash down payment	$ 300,000
First mortgage	1,000,000
Second mortgage	700,000
Sales value	$2,000,000

2. Computation of the initial investment:

Cash down payment	$ 300,000

3. Computation of the minimum required initial investment:

    a. $400,000 ($2,000,000 x 20%)
    b. 1) $850,000 [$2,000,000 - (115% x 1,000,000)]
       2) $500,000 ($2,000,000 x 25%)

    The minimum initial investment is $500,000 since b.2) is less than b.1) and b.2) is greater than a.

The initial investment criterion has not been satisfied because the actual initial investment is less than the minimum initial investment. Therefore, assuming the sale has been consummated and Benson is reasonably assured of recovering the cost of the land from Golden, the installment method should be used. The gross profit to be recognized over the installment payment period by Benson would be computed as follows:

Sales value	$ 2,000,000
Cost of land	(1,200,000)
Gross profit	$ 800,000

The gross profit percentage to apply to each payment by Golden to Benson and the primary debt holder is 40% ($800,000/$2,000,000).

If Golden also pays $50,000 of principal on the first mortgage and $70,000 of principal on the second mortgage in the year of sale, Benson would recognize the following profit in the year of sale:

Profit recognized on the down payment ($300,000 x 40%)	$120,000
Profit recognized on the principal payments:	
First mortgage ($50,000 x 40%)	20,000
Second mortgage ($70,000 x 40%)	28,000
Total profit recognized in year of sale	$168,000

Note that Benson recognizes profit only on the **payment** applicable to the first mortgage. This is because Benson may be called upon to satisfy the liability on the first mortgage if Golden defaults.

If Benson's first mortgage was assumed without recourse, Benson would recognize the following profit in the year of sale:

Profit recognized on the down payment ($300,000 x 40%)	$120,000
Profit recognized on Golden's assumption of Benson's first mortgage without recourse ($1,000,000 x 40%)	400,000
Profit recognized on the principal payment of the second mortgage ($70,000 x 40%)	28,000
Total profit recognized in year of sale	$548,000

The income statement (or related footnotes) for the period of sale should include the sales value received, the gross profit recognized, the gross profit deferred, and the costs of sale. In future periods when further payments are made to the buyer, the seller should realize gross profit on these payments. This amount should be disclosed as a single line item in the revenue section of the income statement.

If, in the future, the transaction meets the requirements for the full accrual method of recognizing profit, the seller may change to that method and recognize the remaining deferred profit as income at that time.

Cost recovery method. When the cost recovery method is used (e.g., when the seller's receivable is subject to subordination or the seller is not reasonably assured of recovering the cost of the property if the buyer defaults), no profit is recognized on the sales transaction until the seller has recovered the cost of the property sold. If the buyer assumes debt that is with recourse to the seller, profit should not be recognized by the seller until the cash payments by the buyer, including both principal and interest on debt due the seller and on debt assumed by the buyer, exceed the seller's cost of the property sold. If the buyer assumes debt that is without recourse to the seller, profit may be recognized by the seller when the cash payments by the buyer, including both principal and interest on debt due the seller, exceed the difference between the seller's cost of the property and the nonrecourse debt assumed by the buyer.

For the cost recovery method, principal collections reduce the seller's related receivable, and interest collections on such receivable increase the deferred gross profit on the balance sheet (para 63).

Example of the Cost Recovery Method

Assume that on January 1, 1992, Maher, Inc. purchased undeveloped land with a sales value of $365,000 from Bernard Co. The sales value is represented by a $15,000 cash down payment, Maher assumes Bernard's $200,000 first mortgage (10%, payable in equal annual installments over the next 20 years), and Maher gives Bernard a second mortgage of $150,000 (12%, payable in equal annual installments over the next 10 years). The sale has been consummated, but the initial investment is below the minimum required amount and Bernard is not reasonably assured of recovering the cost of the property if Maher defaults. The cost of the land to Bernard was $300,000. The circumstances indicate the cost recovery method is appropriate. The transaction would be recorded by Bernard as follows:

1/1/92	Notes receivable	150,000	
	First mortgage payable	200,000	
	Cash	15,000	
	Revenue from sale of land		365,000
	Revenue from sale of land	365,000	
	Land		300,000
	Deferred gross profit		65,000

Case 1 -- The first mortgage was assumed with recourse to Bernard. Immediately after the sale, the unrecovered cost of the land would be computed as follows:

Land	$300,000
Less: Cash down payment	(15,000)
Unrecovered cost	$285,000

The note (second mortgage) would be reported as follows:

| Note receivable | $150,000 | |
| Less: Deferred gross profit | (65,000) | $ 85,000 |

At the end of the year Maher would pay $26,547.64 ($8,547.64 principal and $18,000.00 interest) on the second mortgage note and $23,491.94 ($3,491.94 principal and $20,000.00 interest) on the first mortgage. At 12/31/92 the unrecovered cost of the land would be computed as follows:

Previous unrecovered cost		$285,000.00
Less: Note receivable payment	$26,547.64	
First mortgage payment	23,491.94	(50,039.58)
Unrecovered cost		$234,960.42

The receivable would be reported on the 12/31/92 balance sheet as follows:

Note receivable ($150,000 - 8,547.64)	$141,452.36	
Less: Deferred gross profit ($65,000 + 18,000)	83,000.00	$58,452.36

Case 2 -- The first mortgage was assumed without recourse to Bernard. The reporting of the note would be the same as Case 1; however, the unrecovered cost of the property would be different. Immediately after the sale, the unrecovered cost of the property would be computed as follows:

Land	$300,000
Less: Cash down payment	(15,000)
Nonrecourse debt assumed by Maher	(200,000)
Unrecovered cost	$ 85,000

After Maher makes the payments at the end of the year, the unrecovered cost would be computed as follows:

Previous unrecovered cost	$85,000.00
Less: Notes receivable payment	26,547.64
Unrecovered cost	$58,452.36

For the cost recovery method, the income statement for the year the real estate sale occurs should include the sales value received, the cost of the property given up, and the gross profit deferred. In future periods, after the cost of the property has been recovered, the income statement should include the gross profit earned as a separate revenue item.

If, after accounting for the sale by the cost recovery method, circumstances indicate that the criteria for the full accrual method are satisfied, the seller may change to the full accrual method and recognize any remaining deferred gross profit in full.

Deposit method. When the deposit method is used (e.g., when the sale is, in substance, the sale of an option and not real estate), the seller does not recognize any profit, does not record a receivable, continues to report in its financial statements the property and the related existing debt even if the debt has been assumed by the buyer, and discloses that those items are subject to a sales contract (SFAS 66, para 65). The seller also continues to charge depreciation expense on the property for which the deposits have been received. Cash received from the buyer (initial and continuing investments) is reported as a deposit on the contract. However, some amounts of cash may be received that are not subject to refund, such as interest on the unrecorded principal. These amounts should be used to offset any carrying charges on the property (e.g., property taxes and interest charges on the existing debt). If the interest collected on the unrecorded receivable is refundable, the seller should record this interest as a deposit before the sale is consummated and then include it as a part of the initial investment once the sale is consummated. For contracts that are cancelled, the nonrefundable amounts should be recognized as income and the refundable amounts returned to the depositor at the time of cancellation.

As stated, the seller's balance sheet should continue to present the debt assumed by the buyer (this includes nonrecourse debt) among its other liabilities. However, the seller should report any principal payments on the mortgage debt assumed as additional deposits, while correspondingly reducing the carrying amount of the mortgage debt.

Reduced profit method. The reduced profit method is appropriate when the sale has been consummated and the initial investment is adequate but the continuing investment does not clearly demonstrate the willing commitment to pay the remaining balance of the receivable. For example, a buyer may purchase land under an agreement in which the seller will finance the sale over a 30-year period. SFAS 66 specifically states 20 years as the maximum amortization period for the purchase of land; therefore, the agreement fails to meet the continuing investment criteria.

Under the reduced profit method, the seller recognizes a portion of the profit at the time of sale with the remaining portion recognized in future periods. The amount of reduced profit to be recognized at the time of sale is determined by discounting the receivable from the buyer to the present value of the lowest level of annual payments required by the sales contract over the maximum period of time specified for that type of real estate property (20 years for land and the customary term of a first mortgage loan set by an independent lending institution for other types of real estate). The remaining profit is recognized in the periods that lump-sum or other payments are made.

Example of the Reduced Profit Method

Assume Zarembski, Inc. sells a parcel of land to Stees Co. Zarembski receives sales value of $2,000,000. The land cost $1,600,000. Stees gave Zarembski the following consideration:

Cash down payment	$ 500,000
First mortgage note payable to an independent lending institution (payable in equal installments of principal and 12% interest, $133,887 payable at the end of each of the next 20 years)	1,000,000
Second mortgage note payable to Zarembski (payable in equal installments of principal and 10% interest, $53,039 payable at the end of each of the next 30 years)	500,000
Total sales value	$2,000,000

The amortization term of the second mortgage (seller's receivable) exceeds the 20-year maximum permitted by the statement. It is assumed that the payments by the buyer will cover the interest and principal on the maximum first mortgage loan that could be obtained on the property and interest on the excess aggregate debt on the property over such a maximum first mortgage loan; consequently, the reduced profit method would be appropriate. It is also assumed that the market interest rate on similar agreements is 14%.

The present value of $53,039 per year for 20 years at the market rate of 14% is $351,278 ($53,039 x 6.623).

The gross profit on the sale ($400,000) is reduced by the difference between the face amount of the seller's receivable ($500,000) and the reduced amount ($351,278) or $148,722. The profit recognized at the time of sale is the sales value less the cost of the land less the difference between the face amount of the receivable and the reduced amount. Therefore, the reduced profit recognized on the date of sale is computed as follows:

Sales value	$ 2,000,000
Less: Cost of land	(1,600,000)
Excess	(148,722)
Reduced profit	$ 251,278

Under the reduced profit method, the seller amortizes its receivable at the market rate, not the rate given on the second mortgage. The receivable's carrying balance is zero after the specified term expires (in this case, 20 years). The remaining profit of $148,722 is recognized in the years after the specified term expires as the buyer makes payments on the second mortgage (years 21 through 30).

Disclosures

1. None except those required by other applicable GAAP

ACCOUNTING FOR NONREFUNDABLE FEES AND COSTS ASSOCIATED WITH ORIGINATING OR ACQUIRING LOANS

Perspective and Issues

Lenders often incur a sizable number of costs directly related to the origination or purchase of loans, and normally receive different nonrefundable fees at the inception of the loans.

In accounting practice, disparate accounting procedures emerged for the accounting for these costs and fees. The FASB responded with the issuance of SFAS 91: *Accounting for Nonrefundable Fees and Costs Associated with Originating or Acquiring Loans and Initial Direct Costs of Leases.* The standard points out various examples of these costs and fees, and the different accounting for each of them.

Sources of GAAP
SFAS
91

Definition of Terms

Commitment fees. Fees charged for entering into an agreement that obligates the enterprise to make or acquire a loan or to satisfy an obligation of the other party under a specified condition. For purposes of this Statement, the term *commitment fees* includes fees for letters of credit and obligations to purchase a loan or group of loans and pass-through certificates.

Incremental direct costs. Costs to originate a loan that (a) result directly from and are essential to the lending transaction and (b) would not have been incurred by the lender had that lending transaction not occurred.

Origination fees. Fees charged to the borrower in connection with the process of originating, refinancing, or restructuring a loan. This term includes, but is not limited to, points, management, arrangement, placement, application, underwriting, and other fees pursuant to a lending or leasing transaction and also includes syndication and participation fees to the extent they are associated with the portion of the loan retained by the lender.

Concepts, Rules, and Examples

Loan origination fees and costs

Loan origination fees should be **deferred** and recognized over the life of the loan as an adjustment of interest income. If there are any related direct loan origination costs, the origination fees and origination costs should be **netted**, and only the net amount should be deferred and amortized via the interest method. Origination costs include those **incremental** costs such as credit checks and security arrangements, among others, pertaining to a specific loan.

Example 1

Debtor Corp. wishes to take out a loan with Klein Bank for the purchase of new machinery. The fair market value of the machinery is $614,457. The loan is for 10 years, designed to give Klein an implicit return of 10% on the loan. The annual payment is calculated as follows:

$$\text{Annual payment} = \frac{\$614,457}{PV_{10},\ 10\%} = \frac{614,457}{6.14457} = \$100,000$$

Unearned interest on the loan would be $385,543 [(10 x $100,000) - $614,457].

Klein also is to receive a "nonrefundable origination fee" of $50,000. Klein incurred $20,000 of direct origination costs (for credit checks, etc.). Thus, Klein has **net** nonrefundable origination fees of $30,000. The new net investment in the loan is calculated below:

Gross investment in loan (10 x $100,000)	$1,000,000
Less: Unamortized net nonrefundable origination fees	(30,000)
	970,000
Less: Unearned interest income (from above)	385,543
Net investment in loan	$ 584,457

The new net investment in the loan can be used to find the new implicit interest rate:

$$\frac{100,000}{(1+i)^1} + \frac{100,000}{(1+i)^2} + \ldots + \frac{100,000}{(1+i)^{10}} = \$584,457$$

where i = implicit rate

Thus, the implicit interest rate is 11.002%. The amortization table for the first three years is set up as follows:

(a)	(b)	(c)	(d)	(e)	(f)
			Reduction	Reduction	
	Reduction	Interest revenue	in net	in PV of	PV of
Loan	in unearned	(PV x implicit	orig. fees	net invest	net loan
payments	interest	rate of 11.002%)	(c-b)	(a-c)	investment
					$584,457
$100,000	$61,446*	$64,302	$2,856	$35,698	548,759
100,000	57,590**	60,374	2,784	39,626	509,133
100,000	53,349***	56,015	2,666	43,985	465,148

   * ($614,457 x 10%) = $61,446
  ** [$614,457 - ($100,000 - $61,446)] x 10% = $57,590
*** [$575,900 - ($100,000 - $57,590)] x 10% = $53,349

Commitment Fees and Costs

Often fees are received in advance in exchange for a **commitment** to originate or purchase a loan. These fees should be deferred and recognized upon exercise of the commitment as an adjustment of interest income over the life of the loan, as in Example 1 for origination costs and fees. If a commitment expires unexercised, the fees should be recognized as income upon expiration.

As with loan origination fees and costs, if **both** commitment fees are received and commitment costs are incurred relating to a commitment to originate or purchase a loan, the **net** amount of fees or costs should be deferred and recognized over the life of the loan.

If there is a **remote** possibility of exercise, the commitment fees may be recognized on a straight-line basis over the commitment period as "service fee income." If there is a subsequent exercise, the unamortized fees at the date of exercise shall be recognized over the life of the loan as an adjustment of interest income, as in Example 1.

In certain cases, commitment fees are determined retroactively as a percentage of available lines of credit. If the commitment fee percentage is nominal in relation to the stated rate on the related borrowing, with the borrowing earning the market rate of interest, the fees shall be recognized in income as of the determination date.

Example 2

Glass Corp. has a $2 million, 10% line of credit outstanding with Ritter Bank. Ritter charges its annual commitment fee as 0.1% of any available balance as of the end of the prior period. Ritter will report $2,000 ($2 million x 0.1%) as service fee income in its current income statement.

Fees and Costs in Refinancings or Restructurings
(Assume not a troubled-debt restructuring)

When the terms of a refinanced/restructured loan are as favorable to the lender as the terms for loans to customers with similar risks who are not in a restructuring, the refinanced loan is treated as a **new** loan, and all prior fees of the old loan are recognized in interest income when the new loan is made.

When the above situation is not satisfied, the fees or costs from the old loan become part of the net investment in the new loan.

Example 3

Jeffrey Bank refinanced a loan receivable to $1,000,000, at 10% interest, with annual interest receipts for 10 years. Jeffrey's "normal" loan in its portfolio to debtors with similar risks is for $500,000 at 9% interest for 5 years. Jeffrey had loan origination fees from the original loan of $20,000. These fees are recognized in income **immediately** because the terms of the restructuring are as favorable to Jeffrey as a loan to another debtor with similar risks.

Example 4

Assume the same facts as in Example 3 except that the refinanced terms are $500,000 principal, 7% interest for 3 years. Since the terms of the restructuring are **not** as favorable to Jeffrey as a loan to another debtor with similar risks, the $20,000 origination fees become part of the new investment in the loan and recognized in interest income over the life of the new loan, as in Example 1.

Purchase of a Loan or Group of Loans

Any fees paid or fees received when purchasing a loan or group of loans shall be considered part of the initial investment, being recognized to income over the life of the purchased loan(s) as in Example 1.

Special Arrangements

Often lenders provide demand loans (loans with no scheduled payment terms). In this case, any net fees or costs should be recognized on a straight-line basis over a period determined by mutual agreement of the parties, usually over the estimated length of the loan.

Under a revolving line of credit, any net fees or costs are recognized in income on a straight-line basis over the period that the line of credit is active. If the line of credit is terminated due to the borrower's full payment, any unamortized net fees or costs are recognized in income.

Example 5

Green Bank received $50,000 as a nonrefundable origination fee on a $2 million demand loan. Green's loan dictates that any fees are to be amortized over a period of 10 years. Therefore, $5,000 ($50,000 x 1/10) of origination fees will be recognized as an addition to interest income each year for the next ten years.

Financial Statement Presentation

The unamortized balance of origination, commitment, and other fees/costs that are recognized as an adjustment of interest income shall be reported on the balance sheet as part of the loan balance to which they relate. Except for any special cases as noted in the above paragraphs, the amount of net fees/costs recognized each period as an adjustment will be reported in the income statement as part of interest income.

Disclosures

1. None except those required by other applicable GAAP.

8 Long-Lived Assets

Perspective and Issues

Long-lived assets are those which provide an economic benefit to the enterprise for a number of future periods. Most GAAP regarding long-lived assets involves the determination of the appropriate cost at which to record the asset and the appropriate method to be used to amortize that cost over the periods benefiting.

These assets are primarily operational assets, and they may be broken down into two basic types: tangible and intangible. Tangible assets have physical substance. They may be categorized as follows:

1. Depreciable
2. Depletable
3. Other tangible assets

Intangible assets, on the other hand, have no physical substance. Their value is found in the rights or privileges which they grant to the business enterprise.

Most of the accounting problems involve proper measurement and timing of the transactions. Long-lived assets may be acquired in a multitude of ways, and adequate consideration must be given to the substance of the transaction.

Sources of GAAP

ARB	_APB_	_SFAS_	_FASB I_	_EITF_
43, Ch. 9; 44	1, 6, 17, 29	2, 34, 42, 58, 62, 68, 96	30, 33	86-29, 84-28

Other: Accounting Research Monograph 1

Definitions of Terms

Boot. The monetary consideration given or received in an asset exchange.

Depreciation. The annual charge to income that results from a systematic and rational allocation of cost over the life of a tangible asset.

Exchange. A reciprocal transfer between an enterprise and another entity that results in the enterprise acquiring assets or services or satisfying liabilities by surrendering other assets or services or incurring other obligations.

Fixed assets. Those assets which are used in a productive capacity, have physical substance, are relatively long-lived, and provide a future benefit to the enterprise which is readily measurable.

Intangible assets. Those assets which provide future economic benefit to the enterprise but have no physical substance. Examples include goodwill, patents, copyrights, etc.

Monetary assets. Assets whose amounts are fixed in terms of units of currency. Examples are cash, accounts receivable, and notes receivable.

Nonmonetary assets. Assets other than monetary assets. Examples are inventories; investments in common stock; and property, plant, and equipment.

Nonmonetary transactions. Exchanges and nonreciprocal transfers that involve little or no monetary assets or liabilities.

Nonreciprocal transfer. A transfer of assets or services in one direction, either from an enterprise to its owner or another entity or from owners or another entity to the enterprise. An enterprise's reacquisition of its outstanding stock is a nonreciprocal transfer.

Productive assets. Assets held for or used in the production of goods or services by the enterprise. Productive assets include an investment in another entity if the investment is accounted for by the equity method but exclude an investment not accounted for by that method.

Similar productive assets. Productive assets that are of the same general type, that perform the same function, or that are employed in the same line of business.

Concepts, Rules, and Examples

Fixed Assets

Fixed assets are tangible property which is to be used in a productive capacity within the business and which will benefit the enterprise for a period of more than one year. It is necessary to allocate the cost of these assets to the future periods benefited in accordance with the matching principle.

Three of the problems presented in accounting for fixed assets are:

1. The cost at which the assets should be recorded
2. The rate at which the cost should be allocated to future periods
3. The recording of the subsequent disposal of the assets

Recorded cost. All costs required to bring the asset into operable condition are recorded as part of the cost of the asset. Examples include sales taxes, finders' fees, freight costs, installation costs, breaking-in costs, and set-up costs. Thus, any reasonable cost involved in bringing the asset to the enterprise and incurred prior to using the asset in actual production is capitalized. These costs are **not** to be expensed in the period in which they are incurred.

Costs incurred subsequent to purchase. Some costs are incurred subsequent to the purchase, delivery, and set-up of the fixed asset. These costs are classified as repairs, maintenance, or betterments and are treated in one of the following ways:

1. Expensed
2. Capitalized
3. Reduced accumulated depreciation

Ordinary maintenance and repair expenditures can be anticipated to occur on a ratable basis over the life of the asset and are charged to expense.

Extraordinary repairs or maintenance increase the value (utility) of the asset or increase the estimated useful life of the asset. Those repairs which increase the value of the asset should increase the asset account, while those repairs which extend the useful life of the asset should decrease the accumulated depreciation account.

The chart on the following page summarizes the treatment of expenditures subsequent to acquisition.

Construction of assets for self use. An entity may construct its own fixed assets. All direct costs (labor, materials, and variable overhead) should be capitalized. However, a controversy exists regarding the proper treatment of fixed overhead. Two views of how to treat fixed overhead are:

1. Charge the asset with its fair share of fixed overhead (i.e., use the same basis of allocation used for inventory, possibly direct labor hours).
2. Charge the fixed asset account with only the identifiable **incremental** amount of fixed overhead.

However, the AICPA in Accounting Research Monograph 1 has suggested that:

> "...in the absence of compelling evidence to the contrary, overhead costs considered to have 'discernible future benefits' for the purposes of determining the cost of inventory should be presumed to have 'discernible future benefits' for the purpose of determining the cost of a self-constructed depreciable asset."

While this treatment is not binding, it does provide guidance in establishing consistency.

If the total cost of the fixed asset contructed exceeds the fair market value of the asset, the asset should be written down to the fair market value. The amount of the write-down is included in the determination of net income in the period that construction is completed.

Costs Subsequent to Acquisition of Property, Plant, and Equipment

| | | Normal accounting treatment | | |
| | | Capitalize | | |
Type of expenditure / *Characteristics*	*Expense when incurred*	*Charge to asset*	*Charge to accum. deprec.*	*Other*
1. Additions				
• Extensions, enlargements, or expansions made to an existing asset		X		
2. Repairs and maintenance				
a. Ordinary				
• Recurring, relatively small expenditures				
1. Maintain normal operating condition	X			
2. Do not add materially to use value	X			
3. Do not extend useful life	X			
b. Extraordinary (major)				
• Not recurring, relatively large expenditures				
1. Primarily increase the use value		X		
2. Primarily extend the useful life			X	
3. Replacements and betterments				
• Major component of asset is removed and replaced with the same type of component with comparable performance capabilities (replacement) or a different type of component having superior performance capabilities (betterment)				
a. Book value of old component is known				• Remove old asset cost and accum. deprec. • Recognize any loss (or gain) on old asset • Charge asset for replacement component
b. Book value of old component is not known		X	X	
4. Reinstallations and rearrangements				
• Provide greater efficiency in production or reduce production costs				
1. Material costs incurred; benefits extend into future accounting periods		X		
2. No measurable future benefit	X			

Depreciation of fixed assets. The method of depreciation chosen must result in the systematic and rational allocation of the cost of the asset (less its residual value) over the asset's expected useful life. The determination of the useful life must take a number of factors into consideration. These factors include technological change, normal deterioration, and actual physical usage. The method of depreciation is based on whether the useful life is determined as a function of time (e.g., technological change or normal deterioration) or as a function of actual physical usage.

Depreciation methods based on time.

1. Straight-line--depreciation expense is incurred evenly over the life of the asset.

$$\frac{\text{Cost less salvage value}}{\text{Estimated useful life}}$$

2. Accelerated methods--depreciation expense is higher in the early years of the asset's useful life and lower in the later years.

   a. Declining balance--a multiple of the straight-line rate times the book value at beginning of the year.

   $$\text{Straight-line rate} \quad = \quad \frac{1}{\text{Estimated useful life}}$$

   Example

   Double-declining balance depreciation

   2 x Straight-line rate x Book value at beginning of year

   b. Sum-of-the-years'-digits

   Applicable fraction

   $$\frac{\text{Number of years of estimated life remaining as of the beginning of the year}}{\text{Sum-of-the-years' digits*}}$$

   Sum-of-the-years' depreciation

   (Cost less salvage value) x Applicable fraction

   *Sum-of-the-years' digits $= \dfrac{n(n+1)}{2}$, where n = estimated useful life.

3. Present value methods--depreciation expense is lower in the early years and higher in the later years. The rate of return on the investment remains constant over the life of the asset. Time value of money formulas are used.

   a. Sinking fund--uses the future value of an annuity formula.
   b. Annuity fund--uses the present value of an annuity formula.

Partial-year depreciation. When an asset is either acquired or disposed of during the year, the full-year depreciation calculation is prorated between the accounting periods involved.

Example of Partial Year Depreciation

Assume the following:

XYZ, a calendar year entity, acquired a machine on June 1, 1992 which cost $40,000 with an estimated useful life of 4 years and a $2,500 salvage value. The depreciation expense for each full year of the asset's life is calculated as:

	Straight-line	*Double-declining balance*	*Sum-of-years' digits*
Year 1	37,500* ÷ 4 = 9,375	50% x 40,000 = 20,000	4/10 x 37,500* = 15,000
Year 2	9,375	50% x 20,000 = 10,000	3/10 x 37,500 = 11,250
Year 3	9,375	50% x 10,000 = 5,000	2/10 x 37,500 = 7,500
Year 4	9,375	50% x 5,000 = 2,500	1/10 x 37,500 = 3,750

*(40,000 - 2,500)

Because the first full year of the asset's life does not coincide with the company's year, the amounts shown above must be prorated as follows:

	Straight-line	*Double-declining balance*	*Sum-of-years' digits*
1992	7/12 x 9,375 = 5,469	7/12 x 20,000 = 11,667	7/12 x 15,000 = 8,750
1993	9,375	5/12 x 20,000 = 8,333	5/12 x 15,000 = 6,250
		7/12 x 10,000 = 5,833	7/12 x 11,250 = 6,563
		14,166	12,813
1994	9,375	5/12 x 10,000 = 4,167	5/12 x 11,250 = 4,687
		7/12 x 5,000 = 2,917	7/12 x 7,500 = 4,375
		7,084	9,062
1995	9,375	5/12 x 5,000 = 2,083	5/12 x 7,500 = 3,125
		7/12 x 2,500 = 1,458	7/12 x 3,750 = 2,188
		3,541	5,313
1996	5/12 x 9,375 = 3,906	5/12 x 2,500 = 1,042	5/12 x 3,750 = 1,562

As an alternative to proration, an entity may follow any one of several simplified conventions. Some alternatives are

1) Record a full year's depreciation in the year of acquisition and none in the year of disposal.
2) Record one-half year's depreciation in the year of acquisition and one-half year's depreciation in the year of disposal.

Depreciation method based on actual physical usage--units of production. Depreciation is based upon the number of units produced by the asset in a given year.

$$\text{Depreciation rate} \ = \ \frac{\text{Cost less salvage value}}{\substack{\text{Estimated number of units to be} \\ \text{produced by the asset over} \\ \text{its estimated useful life}}}$$

$$\substack{\text{Units of} \\ \text{production} \\ \text{depreciation}} \ = \ \text{Depreciation rate} \quad \text{x} \quad \substack{\text{Number of units} \\ \text{produced during} \\ \text{the current year}}$$

Tax method--MACRS. The Tax Reform Act (TRA) of 1986 maintains the Accelerated Cost Recovery System (ACRS) structure that was established by the Economic Recovery Tax Act of 1981. This system's name was changed to Modified Accelerated Cost Recovery System (MACRS) which changed the way assets were classified and depreciated under ACRS. MACRS classifies assets based on asset depreciation range (ADR) class lives--that is, the length of time the asset is expected to be used in business. Because MACRS permits companies to depreciate assets over a considerably shorter period of time than their estimated useful lives, MACRS is not considered to be an acceptable allocation method in accordance with generally accepted accounting principles. The difference between MACRS depreciation used for tax purposes and depreciation used for financial accounting purposes is a temporary difference which must be reported on a corporation's tax return as a schedule M-1 item as well as used in the calculation of deferred taxes (see Chapter 14).

The objective of this cost recovery system is to encourage investments in productive assets by permitting faster write-off. However, the alternative depreciation system may be elected which will allow corporations to deduct depreciation using straight line or 150% DB (see tables in Rev. Proc. 87-57), when high deductions in early years are not advantageous to the company's current and future tax positions.

MACRS can easily be determined by using the applicable method, period, and convention; however, optional tables have been issued by the IRS in Rev. Proc. 87-57.

Other depreciation methods.

1. Retirement method--cost of asset is expensed in period in which it is retired.
2. Replacement method--original cost is carried in accounts and cost of replacement is expensed in the period of replacement.
3. Group (Composite) method--averages the service lives of a number of assets using a weighted-average of the units and depreciates the group or composite as if it were a single unit. A group consists of similar assets, while a composite is made up of dissimilar assets.

Depreciation rate:

$$\frac{\text{Sum of the straight-line}}{\text{Total asset cost}}$$
depreciation of individual assets

Depreciation expense:

Depreciation rate x Total group (composite) cost

Gains and losses are not recognized on the disposal of an asset but are netted into accumulated depreciation.

Depletion

Depletion is the annual charge for the use of natural resources. The depletion base includes all development costs such as exploring, drilling, excavating, and other preparatory costs. The amount of the depletion base charged to income is determined by the following formula:

$$\frac{1}{\substack{\text{Total expected} \\ \text{recoverable units}}} \quad \text{x} \quad \text{Depletion base} \quad \text{x} \quad \text{Units sold}$$

The unit depletion rate is revised frequently due to the uncertainties surrounding the recovery of natural resources. The revision is made prospectively; the remaining undepleted cost is allocated over the remaining recoverable units.

Nonmonetary Transactions

APB 29 governs the accounting for nonmonetary transactions. It identifies the following three types of nonmonetary transactions:

1. Nonreciprocal transfers with owners
2. Nonreciprocal transfers with other than owners
3. Nonmonetary exchanges

The problem addressed by the Opinion is the determination of the amount assigned to the nonmonetary asset transferred to or from the enterprise.

The general rule established by APB 29 is that the accounting for nonmonetary transactions should be based on the fair values of the assets involved. The fair value to be used is that of the asset surrendered unless the fair value of the asset received is "more clearly evident." Fair value is defined in APB 29 as:

> *"...the estimated realizable values in cash transactions of the same or similar assets, quoted market prices, independent appraisals, estimated fair values of assets or services received in exchange, and other available evidence."*

While this general rule is considered adequate for most situations, the Board noted that certain modifications should be made under two specific circumstances. If the fair value is not reasonably determinable, the recorded amount (i.e., book value) may be the only amount available to measure the transaction. According to the Opinion, the fair value is to be considered not determinable within reasonable limits if:

> "...major uncertainties exist about the realizability of the value that would be assigned to an asset received in a nonmonetary transaction accounted for at fair value."

An exception to the rule is also required in the case of an exchange which is not essentially the culmination of the earnings process. The following two types of non-monetary exchanges do not result in a culmination of the earnings process:

1. An exchange of a product or property held for sale in the ordinary course of business for a product or property to be sold in the same line of business to facilitate sales to customers other than the parties to the exchange.
2. An exchange of a productive asset not held for sale in the ordinary course of business for a similar productive asset or an equivalent interest in the same or similar productive asset in the same line of business.

The FASB Emerging Issues Task Force (EITF) has reached a consensus (86-29) that a product or property held for sale exchanged for a productive asset (even in the same line of business) should be recorded at fair value.

Nonreciprocal transfers. Examples of nonreciprocal transfers with owners would include dividends-in-kind, nonmonetary assets exchanged for common stock, split-ups, and spin-offs. An example of a nonreciprocal transaction with other than the owners is a donation of property either by or to the enterprise.

The valuation of most nonreciprocal transfers should be based upon the fair market value of the asset given (or received if the fair value of the nonmonetary asset is both objectively measurable and would be clearly recognizable). However, nonmonetary assets distributed to owners of an enterprise in a spin-off or other form of reorganization or liquidation shall be based on the recorded amount. Where there is no asset given, the valuation of the transaction should be based upon the fair value of the asset received.

Example of Accounting for a Nonreciprocal Transfer

Assume the following:

1. XYZ donated property with a book value of $10,000 to a charity during the current year.
2. The property had a fair market value of $17,000 at the date of the transfer.

According to the Opinion, the transaction is to be valued at the fair market value of the property transferred, and any gain or loss on the transaction is to be recognized. Thus, XYZ should recognize a gain of $7,000 ($17,000 - 10,000) in the determination of the current period's net income. The entry to record the transaction would be as follows:

Charitable donations	17,000	
Property		10,000
Gain on transfer of property		7,000

Nonmonetary exchanges. An exchange of nonmonetary assets can take the following two basic forms:

1. Dissimilar assets may be involved in the exchange.
2. Similar assets may be involved in the exchange.

The recognition of a gain or loss on the exchange is dependent upon whether or not the gain or loss is deemed to be realized. The criterion used to make this judgment is the culmination of the earnings process. If an exchange is considered to be the culmination of the earnings process, then the resulting gain or loss will be recognized. If the exchange is not considered to be the culmination of the earnings process, the resulting gain will not be recognized.

Dissimilar Assets

An exchange is the culmination of the earnings process when dissimilar assets are exchanged. The general rule is to value the transaction at the **fair market value** of the asset given up **(unless the fair value of the asset received is more clearly evident)** and to recognize the gain or loss.

Example of an Exchange Involving Dissimilar Assets and No Boot

Assume the following:

1. Gries, Inc. exchanges an automobile with a book value of $2,500 with Springsteen & Co. for a tooling machine with a fair market value of $3,200.
2. No boot is exchanged in the transaction.
3. The fair value of the automobile is not readily determinable.

In this case, Gries, Inc. has recognized a gain of $700 ($3,200 - 2,500) on the exchange. Because the exchange involves dissimilar assets, the earnings process has culminated and the gain should be included in the determination of net income. The entry to record the transaction would be as follows:

Machine	3,200	
Automobile		2,500
Gain on exchange of automobile		700

Similar Assets

Similar assets are those that are used for the same general purpose, are of the same general type, and are employed in the same line of business. Thus, it is not necessary to exchange identical assets. The treatment described applies to those assets which are exchanged as a result of technological advancement as well as to those which are exchanged as a result of wearing out. The general rule involving the exchange of **similar** assets involving a gain is to value the transaction at the **book value** of the asset given up. In this situation, the gain is deferred over the life of the new asset by allowing a lower amount of annual depreciation.

A single exception to the nonrecognition rule for similar assets occurs when the exchange involves both a monetary and nonmonetary asset being exchanged for a similar nonmonetary asset. In such an instance, the monetary portion of the exchange is termed "boot." The EITF has reached a consensus (86-29) that when boot is at least 25% of the fair value of the exchange, it is considered a monetary transaction and both parties should record the exchange at fair value. When boot less than 25% is received in exchange, only the boot portion of the earnings process is considered to have been culminated. The portion of the gain applicable to the boot is considered realized and should be recognized in the determination of net income for the period of the exchange.

The formula for the recognition of the gain in an exchange involving boot of less than 25% of fair value can be generalized as follows:

$$\frac{\text{Boot}}{\text{Boot} + \text{Fair value of nonmonetary asset received}} \quad \times \quad \frac{\text{Total gain}}{\text{indicated}} \quad = \quad \frac{\text{Gain}}{\text{recognized}}$$

The EITF (87-29) subsequently discussed the 86-29 Consensus in the context of APB 29 and SFAS 66 and did not arrive at a consensus concerning the application of EITF 86-29 to the exchange of real estate. Pending reconsideration of this issue, the SEC is taking a case-by-case approach to resolving the accounting for exchanges of real estate with boot.

Example of an Exchange Involving Similar Assets and Boot

Assure the following:

1. ABC exchanged a casting machine for a technologically newer model. The cost of the old machine was $75,000, and the accumulated depreciation was $5,000.
2. The fair value of the machine received was $90,000.
3. Boot was received in the amount of $10,000.

A total gain of $30,000 is created by the transaction. This amount is the difference between the fair value of the assets received and the cost of the assets surrendered ($100,000 - 70,000). The amount of the gain to be recognized can be computed as shown below:

$$\frac{\$10,000}{\$10,000 + 90,000} \quad \times \quad \$30,000 \quad = \quad \$3,000$$

The entry required to record the transaction is as follows:

Cash	10,000	
New machine	63,000*	
Accumulated depreciation	5,000	
Old machine		75,000
Gain on exchange of machine		3,000

*The book value of the new machine is the book value of the old machine less the amount of boot received, plus the gain recognized.

An exchange is the culmination of the earnings process when a loss is created as a result of the exchange of similar assets. Conservatism is the basis for this latter situation being considered the culmination of the earnings process. While the earnings process is not generally considered complete when dealing with the exchange of similar assets, to record the asset at anything greater than the fair market value would be imprudent.

Summary. In some situations, the fair value of the asset cannot be determined. If the fair value is not determinable, the book values of the assets involved are to be used as the valuation measure.

The situations involving the exchange of nonmonetary assets can be summarized in the following diagram:

ACCOUNTING FOR NONMONETARY EXCHANGES

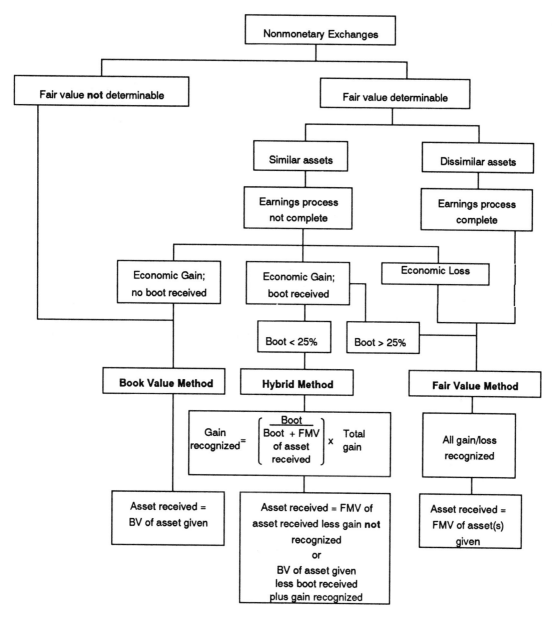

Deferred Taxes

A difference between the amount of gain or loss recognized for book purposes and that recognized for tax purposes constitutes a temporary difference. Under SFAS 96, the difference in the gain or loss will result in a difference in the basis of the asset received. Thus, the difference in the gain or loss reverses as a result of the annual charge to depreciation. The proper treatment of temporary differences is discussed in Chapter 14.

Impairment

Impairment of value occurs if the book value of fixed assets or capitalized leased assets is determined to be more than net realizable value or market value. If this happens, the carrying value may be partially reduced or totally removed. These situations result from technological obsolescence of the asset itself or the product that the asset produces (if the asset is usable only in making that product).

If the technological change results in a **partial impairment** of an asset, the asset should be written down by increasing accumulated depreciation.

> Loss due to partial impairment
> of fixed assets   xxx
>   Accumulated depreciation   xxx

If total obsolescence takes place, a **total impairment** is deemed to occur. In a total impairment the obsolete asset and related accumulated depreciation are removed from the accounts.

> Accumulated depreciation   xxx
> Loss due to permanent impair-
>   ment of fixed assets   xxx
>   Asset   xxx

The loss amount would appear on the income statement as an **unusual loss**.

The accounting problem is the lack of operational guidelines and the reliance on subjectivity to determine impairment. Proposed solutions range from requiring disclosure of fair value or realizable value of fixed assets to a lower of cost or market approach with a mandatory write down of fixed assets.

While most accountants agree in theory with the recognition of impairment and the necessity of a write down, numerous operational problems concerning timing and measurement have not been satisfactorily resolved. The AICPA has produced an Issues Paper dealing with impairment of long-lived assets, FEI has published a survey, NAA has published a research study, and the EITF has discussed impairment several times without consensus.

The only consensus that has been reached on this issue by the EITF (84-28) was that impairment of long-lived assets must be permanent in nature in order to be recognized. The FASB has now identified impairment of long-lived physical and identifiable intangible assets as an agenda project and a task force has been appointed to advise the board on this project. Issues include: (1) whether impairment should be recognized, (2) what circumstances justify recognition, (3) what measurement criteria should be used, (4) what periods should reflect recognition, (5) what groupings of assets should be considered, and (6) whether recovery of asset values should be recognized after write downs. A discussion memorandum entitled "Accounting for the Impairment of Long-Lived Assets and Identifiable Intangibles" was issued in December, 1990. An exposure draft is expected to be published in 1992.

Involuntary Conversions

Certain conditions may occur that necessitate the involuntary conversion of a non-monetary asset into a monetary asset. FASB Interpretation 30 is GAAP relative to the accounting for the involuntary conversion of a nonmonetary asset. Involuntary conversions of nonmonetary assets to monetary assets are monetary transactions, and the resulting gain or loss shall be recognized in the period of conversion. It makes no difference that the monetary assets received are immediately reinvested in nonmonetary assets. An example of such an involuntary conversion would be the condemnation of a piece of property.

This Interpretation does not apply to the involuntary conversion of LIFO inventories which are intended to be replaced but have not been replaced by the year end.

Capitalization of Interest Costs

The cost of an asset should properly include all of the costs necessary to get the asset set up and functioning properly for its intended use. As such, a question arises as to whether or not the interest incurred on debt related to the asset, during the time period in which the asset is being readied for use, should be capitalized. SFAS 34 is GAAP concerning the capitalization of interest. Other pronouncements have been issued (SFASs 42, 58, 62, and FASB Interpretation 33) which deal with the capitalization of interest in special situations.

The principal purposes to be accomplished by the capitalization of interest costs are as follows:

1. To get a more accurate original asset investment cost
2. To get a better matching of costs deferred to future periods with revenues of those future periods

In theory, all assets that require a time period to get them ready for their intended use should include a capitalized amount of interest costs. However, accomplishing this level of capitalization would usually violate a reasonable cost/benefit test because of the added accounting and administrative costs generated. In many situations, the effect of interest capitalization would be immaterial. Thus, interest costs shall only be capitalized as a part of the historical cost of the following qualifying assets when such costs are considered to be material:

1. Assets constructed for an entity's own use or for which deposit or progress payments are made.

2. Assets produced as discrete projects that are intended for lease or sale.
3. Equity method investments when the investee is using funds to acquire qualifying assets for its principal operations which have not yet begun.

Generally, inventories and land that are not undergoing preparation for intended use are not qualifying assets. When land is being developed, it is a qualifying asset. If land is developed for lots, the capitalized interest cost is added to the cost of the **land**. The interest is then matched against revenues when the lots are sold. If, however, the land is developed for a building, then the capitalized interest cost is added to the cost of the **building**. The interest is then matched against revenues as the building is depreciated.

The capitalization of interest costs does not apply to the following situations:

1. When routine inventories are produced in large quantities on a repetitive basis.
2. When effects are not material, compared to the effect of expensing interest.
3. When qualifying assets are already in use or ready for use.
4. When qualifying assets are not being used and are not awaiting activities to get them ready for use.
5. When qualifying assets are not included in a consolidated balance sheet.
6. When principal operations of an investee accounted for under the equity method have already begun.
7. When regulated investees capitalize both the cost of debt and equity capital.
8. When assets are acquired with grants and gifts restricted by the donor to the extent that funds are available from those grants and gifts.

The amount of interest capitalized. Interest cost includes the following:

1. Interest on debt having explicit interest rates
2. Interest related to capital leases
3. Interest required to be imputed on payables

The amount of interest to be capitalized is that portion which could have been avoided if the qualifying asset had not been acquired. Thus, the capitalized amount is the incremental amount of interest cost incurred by the entity to finance the acquired asset.

The most appropriate rate to use as the capitalization rate is that rate which is applicable to specific new debt that resulted from the need to finance the acquired assets. If there was no specific new debt, the capitalization rate should be a weighted-average of the rates of the other borrowings of the entity. This latter case reflects the fact that the previous debt of the entity was indirectly incurred to finance the identified qualifying asset and its interest should be part of the cost of the new asset. The selection of borrowings to be used in the calculation of the weighted-average of rates requires judgment. In resolving this problem, particularly in the case of consolidated statements, the criteria is the identification and determination of that portion of interest that could have been avoided if the qualifying assets had not been acquired.

The base (that should be used to multiply the rate by) is the average amount of accumulated net capital **expenditures** incurred for qualifying assets during the relevant time frame. Capitalized costs and expenditures are not the same terms. Theoretically, a capitalized cost financed by a trade payable for which no interest is recognized is not a capital expenditure to which the capitalization rate should be applied. Reasonable approximations of net capital expenditures are acceptable, however, and capitalized costs are generally used in place of capital expenditures unless there is a material difference.

If the average capitalized expenditures exceed the specific new borrowings for the time frame involved, then the **excess** expenditures amount should be multiplied by the weighted-average of rates and not by the rate associated with the specific debt. This requirement more accurately reflects the interest cost incurred by the entity to bring the fixed asset to a properly functioning position.

The interest being paid on the debt may be simple or compound. Simple interest is computed on the principal alone, whereas compound interest is computed on principal **and** on any interest that has not been paid. Compounding may be yearly, monthly, or daily. Most fixed assets will be acquired with debt having interest compounded.

Compound interest is found by using the compound interest tables or future amount of $1 tables. The annual interest rate is converted to the rate per period (monthly, quarterly, or daily) by dividing the annual rate by the number of compound periods. (The number of periods needs to be determined by multiplying the number of years by the total number of compound periods per year.) The interest amount is then determined by taking the table factor times the principal and subtracting the principal from this amount. Note, if interest is compounded quarterly, the interest per quarter cannot be determined from the yearly amount because the interest for the year is not evenly distributed.

The total amount of interest actually incurred by the entity during the relevant time frame is the ceiling for the amount of interest cost capitalized. Thus, the amount capitalized cannot exceed the amount actually incurred during the period involved. On a consolidated basis, the ceiling is defined as the total of the parent's interest cost plus that of the consolidated subsidiaries. If financial statements are issued separately, the interest cost capitalized should be limited to the amount that the separate entity has incurred and that amount should include interest on intercompany borrowings. The interest incurred is a gross amount and is not netted against interest earned except in cases involving tax exempt borrowings.

Example of Accounting for Capitalized Interest Costs

Assume the following:

1. On January 1, 1992, Gemini Corp. contracted with Leo Company to construct a building for $2,000,000 on land that Gemini had purchased years earlier.
2. Gemini Corp. was to make 5 payments in 1992 with the last payment scheduled for the date of completion.
3. The building was completed December 31, 1992.
4. Gemini Corp. made the following payments during 1992:

January 1, 1992	$ 200,000
March 31, 1992	400,000
June 30, 1992	610,000
September 30, 1992	440,000
December 31, 1992	350,000
	$2,000,000

5. Gemini Corp. had the following debt outstanding at December 31, 1992:

   a. A 12%, 4-year note dated 1/1/92 with interest compounded quarterly. Both principal and interest due 12/31/95 (relates specifically to building project). $850,000

   b. A 10%, 10-year note dated 12/31/88 with simple interest and interest payable annually on December 31. $600,000

   c. A 12%, 5-year note dated 12/31/90 with simple interest and interest payable annually on December 31. $700,000

The amount of interest to be capitalized during 1992 is computed as follows:

Average Accumulated Expenditures

Date	Expenditure	Capitalization period*	Average accumulated expenditures
1/1/92	$ 200,000	12/12	$200,000
3/31/92	400,000	9/12	300,000
6/30/92	610,000	6/12	305,000
9/30/92	440,000	3/12	110,000
12/31/92	350,000	0/12	--
	$2,000,000		$915,000

The number of months between the date expenditures were made and the date interest capitalization stops (December 31, 1992).

Potential Interest

Cost to be Capitalized

($850,000 x 1.12551)* - 850,000 = $106,684

 65,000 x .1108** = 7,202

$915,000 $113,886

* *The principal, $850,000, is multiplied by the factor for the future amount of $1 for 4 periods at 3% to determine the amount of principal and interest due in 1992.*

** *Weighted-average interest rate:*

	Principal	Interest
10%, 10-year note	$ 600,000	$ 60,000
12%, 5-year note	700,000	84,000
	$1,300,000	$144,000

$$\frac{\text{Total interest}}{\text{Total principal}} = \frac{\$ 144,000}{\$1,300,000} = 11.08\%$$

The actual interest is:

12%, 4-year note [($850,000 x 1.12551) - 850,000]	=	$106,684
10%, 10-year note ($600,000 x 10%)	=	60,000
12%, 5-year note ($700,000 x 12%)	=	84,000
Total interest		$250,684

The interest cost to be capitalized is the lesser of $113,886 (avoidable interest) or $250,684 (actual interest), which is $113,886. The remaining $136,798 ($250,684 - $113,886) would be expensed.

Determining the time period for interest capitalization. Three conditions must be met before the capitalization period should begin:

1. Necessary activities are in progress in order to get the asset ready to function as intended
2. Qualifying asset expenditures have been made
3. Interest costs are being incurred

As long as these conditions continue interest costs can be capitalized.

Necessary activities are interpreted in a very **broad** manner. They start with the planning process and continue until the qualifying asset is substantially complete and ready to function as intended. Brief, normal interruptions do not stop the capitalization of interest costs. However, if the entity intentionally suspends or delays the activities for some reason, interest costs shall not be capitalized from the point of suspension or delay until substantial activities in regard to the asset resume.

If the asset is completed by parts, the capitalization of interest costs stops for each part as it becomes ready to function as intended. An asset that must be entirely complete before the parts can be used as intended can continue to capitalize interest costs until the total asset becomes ready to function.

Interest costs should continue to be capitalized until the asset is ready to function as intended, even in cases where lower of cost or market rules are applicable and market is lower than cost. The required write-down should be increased accordingly.

Capitalization of interest costs incurred on tax-exempt borrowings. If qualifying assets have been financed with the proceeds from tax-exempt, **externally restricted** borrowings and if temporary investments have been purchased with those proceeds, a modification is required. The interest costs incurred from the date of borrowing must be reduced by the interest earned on the temporary investment in order to calculate the ceiling for the capitalization of interest costs. This procedure must be followed until the assets financed in this manner are ready to function as intended. When the specified assets are functioning as intended, the interest cost of the tax-exempt borrowing becomes available to be capitalized by other qualifying assets of the entity. Portions of the tax-exempt borrowings that are not restricted are eligible for capitalization in the normal manner.

Assets acquired with gifts or grants. Qualifying assets which are acquired with externally restricted gifts or grants are not subject to capitalization of interest costs. The principal reason for this treatment is the belief that there is no economic cost of financing when a gift or grant is used in the acquisition.

Summary of interest capitalization requirements. The following diagram summarizes the accounting for "interest capitalization."

SUMMARY OF ACCOUNTING FOR INTEREST CAPITALIZATION

Capitalization of Interest During
Construction

Qualifying Assets:
a. Assets constructed for use in operations
b. Assets for sale or lease which are constructed as discrete projects (ships, real estate), but not inventory

When to Capitalize Interest (All three must be met):
a. Expenditures for asset have been made
b. Activities intended to get asset ready are in progress
c. Interest cost is being incurred

Applicable Interest (Net of discounts, premiums, and issue costs):
a. Interest obligations having explicit rates
b. Imputed interest on certain payables/receivables
c. Interest related to capital leases

Amount of Interest to Capitalize:
Average accumulated expenditures

$$\begin{bmatrix} \text{Specific borrowings x} \\ \text{Applicable interest rate} \end{bmatrix} + \begin{bmatrix} \text{Other borrowings x} \\ \text{Weighted-average interest rate*} \end{bmatrix}$$

Qualifications:
a. Amount of interest to be capitalized cannot exceed total interest costs incurred during the period
b. Interest earned on temporarily invested borrowings may not be offset against interest to be capitalized

$$\text{*Weighted-average interest rate} = \frac{\text{Total interest on other borrowings}}{\text{Total principal on other borrowings}}$$

Intangible Assets

Intangible assets are noncurrent, nonphysical assets that entitle the enterprise to certain legal rights or competitive advantages. The noncurrent classification excludes such nonphysical assets as accounts receivable. Examples of intangible assets include copyrights, franchises, goodwill, leaseholds, organizational costs, patents, and trademarks. Intangibles are specifically covered by APB 17.

Intangible assets are generally acquired in one of the following ways:

1. They are purchased.
2. They are created internally.

When intangible assets are purchased, their cost should be the cash or fair market value disbursed or the present value of the liability assumed in conjunction with the exchange. This amount represents the potential earning power of the intangible asset as of the date of its acquisition.

When the intangible asset is created internally, the valuation of the asset can be very difficult because the asset may be unidentifiable. As such, the costs involved are generally expensed. Where the intangible asset is identifiable and separable from the entity, it should be valued as described in the preceding paragraph.

The intangible asset shall be amortized over the life of the asset on a straight-line basis unless some other method better matches revenues and expenses. The life to be used for the amortization period shall be the legal life if it is less than 40 years. Otherwise, it shall be determined based on numerous factors (some of which are listed below) but shall not exceed 40 years.

1. Legal, regulatory, or contractual provisions
2. Provisions for renewal or extension
3. Obsolescence, demand, competition, etc.
4. Life expectancies of employees
5. Expected actions of competitors
6. Benefits may not be reasonably projected
7. Composite of many additional factors

Research and Development Costs

Research and development (R & D) are defined in SFAS 2 as follows:

a. *Research is planned search or critical investigation aimed at the discovery of new knowledge with the hope that such knowledge will be useful in developing a new product or service or a new process or technique or in bringing about a significant improvement to an existing product or process.*

b. *Development is the translation of research findings or other knowledge into a plan or design for a new product or process or for a significant improvement to an existing product or process whether intended for sale or use.*

The following are three ways in which R & D costs are incurred by a business enterprise:

1. Through the purchase of R & D from other entities
2. Through an arrangement to develop R & D for other entities
3. Through R & D activities conducted for the benefit of the enterprise

The accounting treatment relative to R & D depends upon the nature of the cost.

SFAS 2 and SFAS 68 represent GAAP relative to research and development costs. SFAS 2 provides guidance for those R & D costs incurred in the ordinary course of operations. These costs consist of materials, equipment, facilities, personnel, and indirect costs which can be attributed to research or development activities. These costs are expensed in the period in which they are incurred unless they have alternative future uses.

Examples of R & D costs covered by SFAS 2 would include:

1. Laboratory research to discover new knowledge
2. Formulation and design of product alternatives

    a. Testing for product alternatives
    b. Modification of products or processes

3. Preproduction prototypes and models

    a. Tools, dies, etc. for new technology
    b. Pilot plants not capable of commercial production

4. Engineering activity until the product is ready for manufacture

Examples of R & D costs which are **not** covered by SFAS 2 would include:

1. Engineering during an early phase of commercial production
2. Quality control for commercial production
3. Troubleshooting during a commercial production breakdown
4. Routine, ongoing efforts to improve products
5. Adaptation of existing capacity for a specific customer or other requirements
6. Seasonal design changes to products
7. Routine design of tools, dies, etc.
8. Design, construction, startup, etc. of equipment except that used solely for R & D

Both R & D costs that are purchased from another enterprise and those that have alternative future uses are to be capitalized and amortized in accordance with APB 17. The amortization or depreciation of the asset is classified as a research and development expense. If purchased research is not determined to have future use, then its entire cost is to be expensed in the period incurred.

R & D costs incurred as a result of contractual arrangements are addressed in SFAS 68. This Statement indicates that the nature of the agreement shall dictate the accounting treatment of the costs involved. The key determinant is the transfer of the risk associated with the R & D expenditures. If the enterprise receives funds from another party to perform R & D and is obligated to repay those funds regardless of the outcome, a liability must be recorded and the R & D costs expensed as incurred. In order to conclude that a liability does not exist, the transfer of the financial risk must be substantive and genuine.

Disclosures

Fixed Assets

1. The basis of valuation
2. The method of computing depreciation
3. The amount of accumulated depreciation
4. A description of and the amount of any assets pledged as collateral

Nonmonetary Exchanges

1. The basis of accounting for the transfer of assets
2. The amount of gain or loss recognized on the transfer

Capitalization of Interest Costs

1. The total amount of interest cost incurred during the period
2. The amount which has been capitalized

Intangible Assets

1. A description of the nature of the assets
2. The amount of amortization expense for the period and the method used
3. The amortization period used
4. The amount of accumulated amortization

R & D Expenditures

1. The total research and development costs charged to expense for each period for which an income statement is presented
2. For contractual agreements:
   a. The terms of significant agreements under the R & D arrangements as of the date of each balance sheet presented
   b. The amount of compensation earned and costs incurred under contract for each period for which an income statement is presented

9 Investments

Perspective and Issues

The appropriate accounting procedures for noncurrent (long-term) investments in equity securities depend upon the investor's ownership percentage and the degree of marketability of the shares held.

For "passive" investments in marketable equity securities, generally of less than 20% of the outstanding voting common shares of the investee, SFAS 12 requires the use of the lower of cost or market method for the balance sheet presentation; any **temporary** market declines are reported as a contra-account in stockholders' equity rather than as a charge against earnings. However, **permanent** market value declines flow through earnings. (However, temporary declines in the market value of marketable equity securities held in a current [short-term] portfolio are also reflected in earnings, as described in detail in Chapter 5).

When an investor has **significant influence** over an investee--and thus is no longer a passive investor--the equity method must be used to account for the investment. Generally, significant influence is deemed to exist when the investor owns from 20 to 50% of the investee's voting shares, although APB 18 contemplates circumstances where such influence is present with under 20% ownership, or is absent with over 20% holdings. (Over 50%, of course, signals **control**, and under the provisions of SFAS 94, full consolidation of financial statements is mandatory unless one of the few exception conditions stipulated therein is met.) The equity method involves increasing the original cost of the investment by the investor's pro rata share of the investee's earnings, and decreasing it for the investor's share of the investee's losses and for dividends paid. Equity method accounting has been called "one-line consolidation," since the effect on the investor's net worth is the same as if full consolidation of the investee's financial results were accomplished. However, only a single line (or sometimes a few lines, as described later in this chapter) on the investor's statement of earnings is affected.

This chapter discusses the accounting for long-term investments in equity securities of no more than 50% of the investee's voting shares outstanding. Investments of over 50% are considered in the following chapter. The following graphic representation summarizes the levels of influence and corresponding valuation bases and balance sheet presentations prescribed by GAAP as it currently exists.

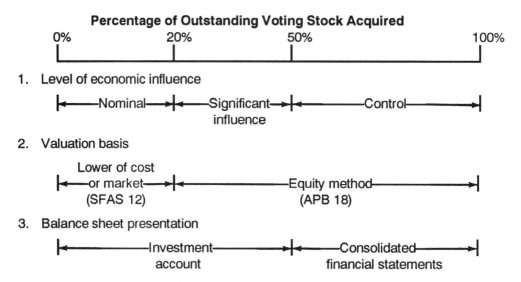

Several exceptions to these general concepts exist, as noted in the following discussion.

The FASB continues to study the various issues relating to the concept of the reporting entity, which includes consolidation policy as well as accounting for joint ventures, equity investments, and passive investments. To date, the only product of this project has been the issuance of SFAS 94 (discussed in Chapter 10). However, the Board has indicated that other major developments are forthcoming. Among other things, these may result in a definition of a reporting entity based on economic control rather than majority (voting common stock) control. The Board also intends to clarify when application of the equity method is appropriate--e.g., for certain joint ventures-- and to provide standards for disclosure of disaggregated information. The FASB has, furthermore, expressed an intention to address the foregoing issues in the context of not-for-profit entities as well. However, these matters are not being actively pursued at the present time.

Sources of GAAP

APB	*SFAS*	*FASB I*
17, 18, 24	12	4, 11, 12, 13, 35

Definitions of Terms

Corporate joint venture. A corporate business owned equally by two or more investor entities; it is typically accounted for by the equity method by the investors.

Cost method. A method of accounting for investment whereby the investor recognizes only dividends received from investee as income.

Differential. The difference between cost of common stock investment and book value of underlying net assets of the investee; it should be allocated to excess (deficiency) of fair value over (under) book value of net assets and goodwill (a negative goodwill) and amortized appropriately to earnings from investee.

Equity method. A method which includes recognition of a percentage share of income or loss, dividends, and any changes in the investment percentage in an investee by an investor. This method includes the amortization of the differential between the investment cost and book value of the investment and recognizes the effects of any intercompany transactions between the investor and investee.

Goodwill. The excess of the cost of the acquired enterprise over the sum of the amounts assigned to identifiable assets acquired less liabilities assumed.

Investee. An enterprise that issued voting stock which is held by an investor.

Investee capital transaction. The purchase or sale by the investee of its own common shares, which alters the investor's ownership interest and is accounted for by the investor as if the investee were a consolidated subsidiary.

Investor. A business enterprise that holds an investment in voting stock of another enterprise.

Significant influence. The ability of the investor to affect the financial or operating policies of the investee; it is presumed to exist when there is at least 20% voting common stock ownership by the investor.

Undistributed investee earnings. The investor's share of investee earnings in excess of dividends paid.

Concepts, Rules, and Examples

Accounting for Marketable Equity Securities

Adherence to the historical cost principle has usually meant that noncurrent assets such as long-term investments are recorded at an amount determined by an arm's-length transaction and are not adjusted for market value changes unless evidence of a **permanent** decline in value is available. However, in the past a minority of investors used either a lower of cost or market or a pure market value approach. SFAS 12 has imposed uniformity in this area and has introduced a somewhat unusual accounting approach which separates the balance sheet (valuation) issue from the income statement (realization) question.

For **noncurrent** portfolios of marketable equity securities (as defined below), SFAS 12 requires that the balance sheet account be stated at the lower of cost or market value. However, a decline from cost to market or a recovery in value to historical cost is not charged or credited to earnings when the price movement is deemed to be a temporary market fluctuation. Instead, a contra-equity account is created to accumulate the net write-down to market value.

Portfolios of **current** marketable equity securities are also accounted for by the lower of cost or market method (consistent with the net realizable value rule for all current assets), but in this case temporary market value fluctuations are reflected in earnings. Accounting for **current** investments is discussed in Chapter 5.

When an entity which presents an unclassified balance sheet has investments in marketable equity securities, these are deemed to be **noncurrent** in character for purposes of applying SFAS 12.

Declines in market value of noncurrent portfolios that are deemed to be other than temporary shall be treated as **realized** for accounting purposes by recognizing a charge against earnings. Once a portfolio is written down for such permanent impairments in value, it cannot be later written up for a recovery in market price. It should be noted that the FASB used the term **other than temporary** rather than the expression **permanent**. Thus, it would appear that there is a positive need to demonstrate that a price decline is temporary in order to justify reflecting it in stockholders' equity. In all other instances the decline would be deemed other than temporary and included in earnings.

Defining marketable equity securities. According to SFAS 12, an equity security is any instrument representing an actual ownership interest or the right to acquire or dispose of such interest (i.e., call and put options) at fixed or determinable prices. Equity securities are marketable if market prices or bid and ask quotations are regularly reported or if at least three dealers can provide such quotations. Marketability is ascertained as of the balance sheet date; however, the unavailability of a price quotation on that date does not imply nonmarketability if quotations are available for closely preceding or following days.

Temporary market price changes. In general, market price declines or recoveries of previous declines which are temporary in nature will **not** be reported in the earnings statement. Rather, these losses or gains are shown in the stockholders' equity section as a contra-equity account; i.e., the accumulated market price decline will appear as a deduction from stockholders' equity. Since an increase in market value **above** original cost cannot be recognized, the balance in this account can never be a net credit amount.

Transfers between current and noncurrent portfolios. If marketable equity securities are transferred from a current to a noncurrent portfolio, or vice versa, they are transferred at the lower of cost or market value **at the date of transfer**. If the market value is lower than cost, the decline is treated as a realized loss and charged against earnings; the market value then becomes the new cost basis for any further accounting.

The following example illustrates the accounting for a noncurrent marketable equity securities portfolio:

Example of Accounting for a Noncurrent Marketable Equity Securities Portfolio

Assume XYZ Company has the following securities in its portfolio at the end of its first year of operations:

Security	Acquisition cost	Current market	Gross unrealized gains (losses)
A preferred	$10,000	$ 9,000	$(1,000)
B common	20,000	18,000	(2,000)
C common	25,000	26,000	1,000
Aggregate amounts	$55,000	$53,000	$(2,000)

The following journal entry would be made to record the decline in aggregate market value:

Unrealized loss on decline in long-term marketable equity securities portfolio	2,000	
Allowance to reduce marketable equity securities portfolio to market		2,000

The unrealized loss of $2,000 is not charged against income; instead, it is disclosed on the balance sheet as a subtraction from total stockholders' equity. The allowance account is disclosed as a reduction from the aggregate cost of the long-term investments portfolio. In addition, the gross unrealized losses of $3,000 and the gross unrealized gain of $1,000 should be disclosed in the notes to the financial statements.

Continuing this example, assume that during XYZ's second year of operations the following events occurred:

1. It acquired D common for $35,000.
2. It sold A preferred for $12,000.
3. It received a $1,000 dividend from B common.
4. It transferred E common from its short-term marketable equity securities portfolio to its long-term portfolio when its market value was $15,000. E common was originally purchased for $18,000.

Aggregate cost and market values for XYZ's long-term marketable equity securities portfolio at the end of the second year are as follows:

Security	Acquisition cost	Current market	Gross unrealized gains (losses)
B common	$20,000	$22,000	$ 2,000
C common	25,000	21,000	(4,000)
D common	35,000	36,000	1,000
E common	15,000	12,000	(3,000)
Aggregate amounts	$95,000	$91,000	$(4,000)

Based upon the events of the second year, XYZ should make the following journal entries:

1. Investment in D common	35,000	
Cash		35,000
2. Cash	12,000	
Investment in A preferred		10,000
Gain on sale of investment		2,000
3. Cash	1,000	
Dividend revenue		1,000
4. Loss on transfer of securities between portfolios	3,000	
Investment in E common		3,000
5. Unrealized loss on decline in long-term marketable equity securities portfolio	2,000	
Allowance to reduce marketable equity securities portfolio to market		2,000

The $3,000 realized loss (entry "4") would appear in the income statement. Entry "5" is necessary to increase both the unrealized loss and allowance account by $2,000 [($4,000) amount required at end of year 2 - ($2,000) amount required at end of year 1].

Permanent decline in value. A permanent decline in the value of a noncurrent marketable equity security is deemed to be **realized**, in contrast to temporary declines which are designated as unrealized. These declines are recognized by charges against income when they occur. The amount to which the security is written down becomes the new **cost basis**, and the lower of cost or market rule is applied to this value in subsequent periods. Any increase in value above the new cost basis is ignored; a recovery of permanent decline cannot be recognized.

Example of Accounting for a Permanent Decline in Market Value

Assume the following:

5/1/92:

Q Corp. purchases 100 shares of Z Company at $38/share.

12/31/92:

The market value of Z Company is $36.

12/31/93:

Z Company declares bankruptcy in 1993, and at year end its shares are quoted over the counter at $5 each.

7/15/94:

Z Company is discharged from bankruptcy proceedings. Its shares trade at $20 each at year end.

These events would be accounted for as follows:

5/92	Investment in Z common	3,800	
	Cash		3,800
12/92	Unrealized loss on decline in long-term marketable equity securities	200	
	Allowance to reduce marketable equity securities to market		200
12/93	Loss on permanent decline in long-term marketable equity securities	3,300	
	Allowance to reduce marketable equity securities to market	200	
	Unrealized loss on decline in long-term marketable equity securities		200
	Investment in Z common		3,300
12/94	(No entry)		

Note that $5 per share is the new cost basis and that, accordingly, increases above the value cannot be recognized. Declines from that level, however, would be given appropriate recognition, either as a charge against earnings (permanent decline) or as a charge against owners' equity (temporary decline).

Changes in market value after balance sheet date. An enterprise's financial statements shall not be adjusted for realized gains or losses or for changes in market prices with respect to marketable equity securities when such gains or losses or changes occur after the date of the financial statements, but prior to their issuance. However, significant net realized and net unrealized gains and losses pertaining to marketable equity securities owned at the date of the most recent balance sheet and arising after that date, but prior to the issuance of the financial statements, shall be disclosed.

When a permanent decline is to be recognized as of the balance sheet date, information regarding the behavior of the security's price **after** the balance sheet date, while not formally recognized, can provide evidence regarding the separation of the decline into permanent and temporary portions.

Example of Permanent Versus Temporary Decline

Assume securities having a cost of $10,000 have suffered a seemingly permanent decline in value to $2,000 at year end. Subsequently (before the statements are issued) the market price of these securities recovers to $4,500. It might be determined that only a $5,500 loss should be **realized**, with the additional $2,500 decline classified as temporary and recognized by an allowance account. Of course, all the facts and circumstances must be analyzed before one could reach this conclusion in an actual situation.

Deferred tax effects. Unrealized gains or losses on marketable equity securities, whether recognized through the statement of earnings or as adjustments to the contra-equity account, are "temporary differences" as defined by SFAS 96 (see Chapter 14 for discussion). However, as a practical matter deferred taxes are rarely provided for. Since net capital losses are not deductible for tax purposes by corporations, a deferred tax benefit pertaining to an unrealized loss could generally not be justified. SFAS 96 permits recognition of deferred tax benefits only under limited circumstances. Since the projection of future capital gains to absorb the unrealized losses would not be viable (to do so would assume facts not in existence as of the balance sheet date), it follows that only if capital gains had been reported for tax purposes during the available carryback period would such recognition of the tax benefit of unrealized losses be permissible. To be consistent with the criteria set forth in SFAS 96, it would be necessary to establish that management's intent was to realize the losses for tax purposes within the remaining time available to utilize the capital loss carryback. Absent convincing support for this tax strategy, recognition of the deferred tax benefit would not be proper.

The existence of unrealized gains on other capital assets--whether or not these are given accounting recognition--can also provide the justification for the presentation of deferred tax benefits relating to losses on marketable equity securities. For example, unrealized gains on the **current** portfolio of marketable equity securities can provide the needed degree of assurance regarding realizability for recording the tax benefits of the unrealized loss on the **noncurrent** securities portfolio. Similarly, investments in nonequity securities such as bonds or in other capital assets such as stock exchange memberships can give rise to such unrealized gains. Although these unrealized gains are not given accounting recognition, they can be used to support tax-effecting the lower of cost or market adjustment to the equity securities portfolios. Finally, if other investments are accounted for by the equity method and are carried at amounts in excess of cost, this too represents an unrealized gain against which other losses may be offset. However, the maximum deferred tax benefit to be so recognized would be limited to the otherwise unrecognized deferred tax liability deriving from these unrecognized gains.

Permanent declines in noncurrent portfolios of marketable equity securities are treated for **accounting** purposes as realized. However, for **tax** purposes these losses are unrealized and thus temporary differences will arise. The recognition of the deferred tax benefit of such losses is subject to the same consideration as was noted above relative to lower of cost or market accounting for temporary declines in value. Thus, absent the extenuating circumstances described above, the tax effects of such declines are typically not provided for.

Accounting for Marketable Debt Securities

Historically, GAAP relative to marketable debt securities held as assets has not been well developed. The general practice has been to classify these investments as short-term or long-term, and to then apply a lower of cost or market valuation strategy only to the short term investment portfolio. Typically, the determination of whether investments in marketable debt securities are current or noncurrent assets is made in accordance with the stated maturity dates of the securities themselves. However, even instruments with noncurrent maturities can be classified as short term investments if management can demonstrate both the intent and the ability to dispose of them within one operating cycle.

It is likely that GAAP in this area will change in the foreseeable future. An attempt by the AICPA in 1990 to promulgate a standard pertaining to accounting for debt investments held as assets by banks became a matter of great controversy when the SEC opposed the AICPA's draft position and announced an intention to impose a market valuation requirement for banks whose financial statements are filed with the Commission. This development led to a decision by FASB to add this issue to its technical agenda as a priority item. As of mid-1991, the Board had indicated the possibility that this project may be broadened to include the accounting for other financial assets besides debt securities, and even certain liabilities, at market value. It is too early to predict how this will affect current practice, but it is probable that market value recognition will be much more widely applied than is presently the case.

Notwithstanding the foregoing, under present GAAP long-term investments in bonds should be shown on the balance sheet at cost, which includes brokerage fees, taxes, and any other acquisition costs. Unlike the case of marketable equity securities, an allowance account is **not** set up to recognize fluctuations in the market value of the investment. Rather, ARB 43 requires that debt securities are to be valued at cost unless both of the following conditions are met:

1. The decline in market value is substantial.
2. The decline in market value is not due to a temporary condition.

If both of these conditions are satisfied, then the investment shall be written down to market and the market value becomes the new cost. The write-down is included in the determination of net income for the current period. Subsequent recoveries in market value are not recognized.

Usually, a marketable debt instrument is not purchased at its face value. The resultant difference is classified as a premium (if purchased for more than the face value) or a discount (if purchased for less than the face value). The premium or discount on a marketable debt security classified as noncurrent is to be included in the determination of net income on a ratable basis over the life of the investment. The common terms used for this recognition are "amortization of the premium" and "accretion of the discount." Amortization serves to decrease net income while accretion increases net income. While accretion of the discount is includable in taxable income, amortization of the premium is not and, therefore, the premium amortization represents a temporary difference per SFAS 96. The computation of the periodic amortization or accretion shall be made using the effective interest method. The straight-line method may be used if the results produced are not materially different. Examples and discussion of this computation are presented in Chapter 12.

The Equity Method of Accounting for Investments

The equity method, sometimes referred to as "one-line consolidation," permits an entity (investor) owning a percentage of the common stock of another entity (investee) to incorporate its pro rata share of the investee's operating results into its earnings. However, rather than include its share of each component (e.g., sales, cost of sales, operating expenses, etc.) in its financial statements, the investor shall only include its share of the investee's **net** income as a separate line item in its income. However, there are exceptions to this one-line rule. The investor's share of investee extraordinary items and prior period adjustments retain their identities in the investor's income and retained earnings statements and are separately reported if material in relation to the investor's income. It should be noted that the final bottom-line impact on the investor's financial statements is **identical** whether the equity method or full consolidation is employed; only the amount of detail presented within the statements will differ.

The equity method is generally **not** a substitute for consolidation; it is employed where the investor has significant influence over the operations of the investee but lacks control. In general, significant influence is inferred when the investor owns between 20 and 50% of the investee's voting common stock. Any ownership percentage over 50% presumably gives the investor actual control, making full consolidation of financial statements necessary. The 20% threshold stipulated in APB 18 is not absolute; circumstances may suggest that significant influence exists even though the investor's level of ownership is less than 20%, or that it is absent despite a level of ownership above 20%. In considering whether significant influence exists, FASB Interpretation 35 identifies the following factors: (1) opposition by the investee, (2) agreements under which the investor surrenders shareholder rights, (3) majority ownership by a small group of shareholders, (4) inability to obtain desired information from the investee, (5) inability to obtain representation on investee board of directors, etc.

Whether contrary evidence is sufficient to negate the presumption of significant influence is a matter of judgment requiring a careful evaluation of all pertinent facts and circumstances, in some cases over an extended period of time.

In the past, in those rare instances in which the investor owned over 50% of the investee's voting common shares but consolidated statements were deemed to be inappropriate (usually because consolidated statements would mask important differences in the financial or operating characteristics of the investor-parent and investee-subsidiary), then the investor generally used the equity method. However, SFAS 94 removes this previously popular "non-homogeneity" justification for non-consolidation. This leaves only temporary control, non-control, and foreign exchange restrictions and related reasons as justifications for not consolidating majority-owned subsidiaries. While the exposure draft of this standard would have prohibited use of the equity method in such circumstances, SFAS 94 as finally promulgated is silent on this point. Accordingly, the equity method will generally continue to be appropriate for accounting for non-consolidated majority-owned subsidiaries (see Chapter 10).

Complexities in the use of the equity method arise in two areas. First, the cost of the investment to the investor might not be precisely equal to the fair value of the investor's share of investee net assets; this is analogous to the existence of goodwill in a purchase business combination. Or it may occur that the fair value of the investor's share of the investee's net assets is not equal to the book value thereof; this situation is analogous to the purchase cost allocation problem in consolidations. Since the ultimate income statement result from the use of equity method accounting must generally be the same as full consolidation, an adjustment must be made for each of these differentials.

The other major complexity relates to interperiod income tax allocation. The equity method causes the investor to reflect current earnings based on the investee's operating results; however, for income tax purposes the investor reports only dividends received and gains or losses on disposal of the investment. Thus, temporary differences result, and SFAS 96 provides guidance as to the appropriate method of computing the deferred tax effects of these differences.

In the absence of these complicating factors, the use of the equity method by the investor is straightforward: the original cost of the investment is increased by the investor's share of the investee's earnings and is decreased by its share of investee losses and by dividends received. The basic procedure is illustrated below.

Example of a Simple Case Ignoring Deferred Taxes

Assume the following information:

On January 2, 1992, R Corporation (the investor) acquired 40% of E Company's (the investee) voting common stock on the open market for $100,000. Unless demonstrated otherwise, it is assumed that R Corporation can exercise significant influence over E Company's operating and financing policies. On January 2, E's stockholders' equity is comprised of the following accounts:

Common stock, par $1, 100,000 shares authorized,
50,000 shares issued and outstanding	$ 50,000
Additional paid-in capital	150,000
Retained earnings	50,000
Total stockholders' equity	$250,000

Note that the cost of E Company common stock was equal to 40% of the book value of E's net assets. Assume also that there is no difference between the book value and the fair value of E Company's assets and liabilities. Accordingly, the balance in the investment account in R's records represents exactly 40% of E's stockholders' equity (net assets). Assume further that E Company reported a 1992 net income of $30,000 and paid cash dividends of $10,000. Its stockholders' equity at year end would be as follows:

Common stock, par $1, 100,000 shares authorized,
50,000 shares issued and outstanding	$ 50,000
Additional paid-in capital	150,000
Retained earnings	70,000
Total stockholders' equity	$270,000

R Corporation would record its share of the increase in E Company's net assets during 1992 as follows:

Investment in E Company	12,000	
Equity in E income		12,000
($30,000 x 40%)		
Cash	4,000	
Investment in E Company		4,000
($10,000 x 40%)		

When R's balance sheet is prepared at December 31, 1992, the balance reported in the investment account would be $108,000 ($100,000 + 12,000 - 4,000). This amount represents 40% of the book value of E's net assets at the end of the year (40% x $270,000). Note also that the equity in E income is reported as one amount on R's income statement under the caption "Other income and expense."

Prior to its being superceded by SFAS 96, APB 24 established the necessity of providing for the deferred tax effects of differences between the tax and financial reporting of income from investments accounted for by the equity method. In particular, these differences do not possess the attribute of indefinite reversal (as defined originally by APB 23); accordingly, non-recognition of deferred taxes can only be justified by the criteria established by SFAS 96 (e.g., because a net deferred tax benefit could not be recognized).

In computing the deferred tax effects of income recognized by the equity method, the investor must make an assumption regarding the means by which the undistributed earnings of the investee will be realized by the investor. The earnings can be realized either through later dividend receipts or by disposition of the investment at a gain. The former assumption would result in taxes at the investor's marginal tax rate on ordinary income (net of the 80% dividends received deduction permitted by the Internal Revenue Code for intercorporate investments of less than 80%) whereas the latter option would be treated as a capital gain, which is currently taxed at the full corporate tax rate, insofar as the preferential capital gain rate was eliminated by the 1986 Tax Reform.

Example of a Simple Case Including Deferred Taxes

Assume the same information as in the example above. In addition, assume that R Corporation has a combined (federal, state, and local) marginal tax rate of 34% on ordinary income and that it anticipates realization of E Company earnings through future dividend receipts. R Corporation's entries at year end 1992 will be as follows:

1. Investment in E Company   12,000
       Equity in E income   12,000

2. Income tax expense   816
       Deferred taxes   816
   (Taxable portion of investee earnings to be received in the future as dividends times marginal tax rate: $12,000 x 20% x 34% = $816.)

3. Cash   4,000
       Investment in E Company   4,000

4. Deferred taxes   272
       Taxes payable--current   272
   [Fraction of investee earnings currently taxed ($4,000/12,000) x 816 = $272]

Under prior GAAP (APB 11), the amount of deferred taxes provided ($816 in the above example) was not to be adjusted until such time as the "timing difference" reversed. At such time, any discrepancy would be adjusted through current tax expense. However, SFAS 96 is based upon an entirely different concept (the so-called "asset and liability approach"). Accordingly, the deferred tax liability, which is originally computed with reference to the **projected** tax effect of the reversal of the "temporary difference," may be subsequently adjusted for a variety of reasons, including changed tax rates and altered management expectations (see Chapter 14 for a complete discussion).

Notwithstanding SFAS 96's requirement that deferred taxes be adjusted for changed expectations at each subsequent balance sheet date, the actual tax effect of the temporary difference reversal may still differ from the deferred tax provided. This may, of course, be due to the fact that the actual tax effect is a function of the entity's other current items of income and expense (which did not enter into the calculation of the projected tax effects of the temporary differences, per SFAS 96). It may also result from a realization of the investee's earnings in a manner other than was anticipated (assuming, in particular, that tax rates on "ordinary" income differ from those on capital gains--a distinction which is **not** made by the present tax law but which generally has been made in the past and could very well be reinstituted by future tax laws).

To illustrate this last point, assume that in 1993, before any further earnings or dividends are reported by the investee, the investor sells the entire investment for $115,000. The tax impact is:

Selling price	$115,000
Less cost	100,000
Gain	$ 15,000
Capital gain rate (marginal corporate rate)	x 34%
Tax liability	$ 5,100

The entries to record the sale, the tax thereon, and the amortization of previously provided deferred taxes on the undistributed 1992 earnings are as follows:

1. Cash	115,000	
Investment in E Company		108,000
Gain on sale of investment		7,000
2. Income tax expense	4,556	
Deferred tax liability	544	
Taxes payable--current		5,100

The income tax expense of $4,556 is the sum of two factors: (a) the capital gains rate of 34% applied to the actual **book** gain realized ($115,000 selling price less $108,000 carrying value), for a tax of $2,380, and (b) the difference between the capital gains tax rate (34%) and the effective rate on dividend income (20% x 34% = 6.8%) on the undistributed 1992 earnings of E Company previously recognized as ordinary income by R Corporation [$8,000 x (34% - 6.8%) = $2,176].

Note that if the realization through a sale of the investment had been anticipated at the time the 1992 balance sheet was being prepared, the deferred tax liability account would have been adjusted (possibly to the entire $5,100 amount of the ultimate obligation), with the offsetting entry being to 1992's ordinary tax expense. This approach, mandated by SFAS 96, is radically different than that required by APB 11. The above example explicitly assumes the sale of the investment was **not** anticipated prior to 1993.

Accounting for a differential between cost and book value. The simple examples presented thus far avoided the major complexity of equity method accounting--the allocation of the **differential** between the cost to the investor and the investor's share in the net equity (net assets at book value) of the investee. Since the net impact of equity method accounting must equal that of full consolidation accounting, this differential must be analyzed into the following components and accounted for accordingly:

1. The difference between the book and fair values of the investee's net assets at the date the investment is made.
2. The remaining difference between the fair value of the net assets and the cost of the investment, which is generally attributable to goodwill.

According to APB 18, the difference between the book and fair value of the net assets should be identified and allocated to specific asset categories. These differences are then amortized to the income from investee account as appropriate--for example, over the economic lives of fixed assets whose fair values exceeded book values. The difference between fair value and cost will be treated like goodwill and, in accordance with the provisions of APB 17, amortized over a period not to exceed 40 years.

Example of Complex Case Ignoring Deferred Taxes

Assume again that R Corporation acquired 40% of E Company's shares on January 2, 1992, but that the price paid was $140,000. E Company's assets and liabilities at that date had the following book and fair values:

	Book values	Fair values
Cash	$ 10,000	$ 10,000
Accounts receivable (net)	40,000	40,000
Inventories (FIFO cost)	80,000	90,000
Land	50,000	40,000
Plant and equipment (net of accumulated depreciation)	140,000	220,000
Total assets	$320,000	$400,000
Liabilities	$ (70,000)	$ (70,000)
Net assets (stockholders' equity)	$250,000	$330,000

The first order of business is the calculation of the differential, as follows:

R's cost for 40% of E's common	$140,000
Book value of 40% of E's net assets ($250,000 x 40%)	(100,000)
Total differential	$ 40,000

Next, the $40,000 is allocated to those individual assets and liabilities for which fair value differs from book value. In the example, the differential is allocated to inventories, land, and plant and equipment, as follows:

Item	*Book value*	*Fair value*	*Difference debit (credit)*	*40% of difference debit (credit)*
Inventories	$ 80,000	$ 90,000	$10,000	$ 4,000
Land	50,000	40,000	(10,000)	(4,000)
Plant and equipment	140,000	220,000	80,000	32,000
Differential allocated				$32,000

The difference between the allocated differential of $32,000 and the total differential of $40,000 is goodwill of $8,000. Goodwill, as shown by the following computation, represents the excess of the cost of the investment over the fair value of the net assets acquired.

R's cost for 40% of E's common	$140,000
40% of the fair value of E's net assets	
($330,000 x 40%)	(132,000)
Excess of cost over fair value (goodwill)	$ 8,000

At this point, it is important to note that the allocation of the differential is not recorded formally by either R Corporation or E Company. Furthermore, R does not remove the differential from the investment account and allocate it to the respective assets, since the use of the equity method ("one-line consolidation") does not involve the recording of individual assets and liabilities. R leaves the differential of $40,000 in the investment account, as a part of the balance of $140,000 at January 2, 1992. Accordingly, information pertaining to the allocation of the differential is maintained by the investor, but this information is outside the formal accounting system, which is comprised of journal entries and account balances.

After the differential has been allocated, the amortization pattern is developed. To develop the pattern in this example, assume that E's plant and equipment have 10 years of useful life remaining and that E depreciates its fixed assets on a straight-line basis. Furthermore, assume that R amortizes goodwill over a 20-year period. R would prepare the following amortization schedule:

Item	Differential debit (credit)	Useful life	Amortization 1992	1993	1994
Inventories (FIFO)	$ 4,000	Sold in 1992	$4,000	$ --	$ --
Land	(4,000)	Indefinite	--	--	--
Plant and equipment (net)	32,000	10 years	3,200	3,200	3,200
Goodwill	8,000	20 years	400	400	400
Totals	$40,000		$7,600	$3,600	$3,600

Note that the entire differential allocated to inventories is amortized in 1992 because the cost flow assumption used by E is FIFO. If E had been using LIFO instead of FIFO, no amortization would take place until E sold some of the inventory that existed at January 2, 1992. Since this sale could be delayed for many years under LIFO, the differential allocated to LIFO inventories would not be amortized until E sold more inventory than it manufactured/purchased. Note, also that the differential allocated to E's land is not amortized, because land is not a depreciable asset.

The **amortization** of the differential is recorded formally in the accounting system of R Corporation. Recording the amortization adjusts the equity in E's income that R recorded based upon E's income statement. E's income must be adjusted because it is based upon E's book values, not upon the cost that R incurred to acquire E. R would make the following entries in 1992, assuming that

E reported net income of $30,000 and paid cash dividends of $10,000:

1.	Investment in E Company	12,000	
	Equity in E income		12,000
	($30,000 x 40%)		
2.	Equity in E income (amortization of		
	differential)	7,600	
	Investment in E Company		7,600
3.	Cash	4,000	
	Investment in E Company		4,000
	($10,000 x 40%)		

The balance in the investment account on R's records at the end of 1992 is $140,400 [$140,000 + 12,000 - (7,600 + 4,000)], and E's stockholders' equity, as shown previously, is $270,000. The investment account balance of $140,000 is not equal to 40% of $270,000. However, this difference can easily be explained, as follows:

Balance in investment account at December 31, 1992		$140,400
40% of E's net assets at December 31, 1992		108,000
Difference at December 31, 1992		$ 32,400
Differential at January 2, 1992	$40,000	
Differential amortized during 1992	(7,600)	
Unamortized differential at December 31, 1992		$ 32,400

As the years go by, the balance in the investment account will come closer and closer to representing 40% of the book value of E's net assets. After 20 years, the remaining difference between these two amounts would be attributable solely to the original differential allocated to land (a $4,000 credit). This $4,000 difference would remain until E sold the property.

To illustrate how the sale of land would affect equity method procedures, assume that E sold the land in the year 2012 for $80,000. Since E's cost for the land was $50,000, it would report a gain of $30,000, of which $12,000 ($30,000 x 40%) would be recorded by R, ignoring income taxes, when it records its 40% share of E's reported net income. However, from R's viewpoint, the gain on sale of land should have been $40,000 ($80,000 - 40,000) because the cost of the land from R's perspective was $40,000 at January 2, 1992. Therefore, besides the $12,000 share of the gain recorded above, R should record an additional $4,000 gain [($40,000 - 30,000) x 40%] by debiting the investment account and crediting the equity in E income account. This $4,000 debit to the investment account will negate the $4,000 differential allocated to land on January 2, 1992, since the original differential was a credit (the fair market value of the land was $10,000 less than its book value).

Example of Complex Case Including Deferred Taxes

The impact of interperiod income tax allocation in the foregoing example is similar to that demonstrated earlier in the simplified example. However, a complication arises with regard to the portion of the differential allocated to goodwill, since goodwill is not amortizable for tax purposes and, therefore, is a permanent (not a temporary) difference that does not give rise to deferred taxes. The other components of the differential in this example are all temporary differences.

The entries recorded by R Corporation in 1992 would be:

1.	Investment in E Company	12,000	
	Equity in E income		12,000
2.	Income tax expense	816	
	Deferred tax liability		816
	($12,000 x 20% x 34%)		
3.	Cash	4,000	
	Investment in E Company		4,000
4.	Deferred tax liability	272	
	Taxes payable--current		272
	($4,000/12,000 x 816)		
5.	Equity in E income	7,600	
	Investment in E Company		7,600
6.	Deferred tax liability	490	
	Income tax expense		490
	($7,200 x 20% x 34%)		

Note that the tax effect of the amortization of the differential is based on $7,200, not $7,600, since the $400 goodwill amortization would not have been tax deductible.

Intercompany transactions between investor and investee. Transactions between the investor and the investee **may** require that the investor make certain adjustments when it records its share of the investee earnings. The reason is that, according to the realization concept, profits can be recognized by an entity only when realized through a sale to outside (unrelated) parties in arm's-length transactions (sales and purchases) between the investor and investee, although similar problems can arise when sales of fixed assets between the parties occur. In all cases, there is **no** need for any adjustment when the transfers are made at book value, i.e., without either party recognizing a profit or loss in its separate accounting records.

In preparing consolidated financial statements, all intercompany (parent-subsidiary) transactions are eliminated. However, when the equity method is used to account for investments, only the **profit component** of intercompany (investor-investee) transactions is so eliminated. This is because the equity method does not result in the combining of all income statement accounts (such as sales and cost of sales), and therefore will not cause the financial statements to contain redundancies. In contrast, consolidated statements would include redundancies if the gross amounts of all intercompany transactions were not eliminated.

Another distinction between the consolidation and equity method situations pertains to the percentage of intercompany profit to be eliminated. In the case of consolidated statements, the entire intercompany profit is eliminated, regardless of the percentage ownership of the subsidiary. However, according to Accounting Interpretation 1 of APB 18, only the **investor's pro rata share** of intercompany profit would be eliminated in equity accounting, whether the transaction giving rise to the profit is "downstream" (a sale to the investee) or "upstream" (a sale to the investor). An exception is made when the transaction is not "arm's-length" or if the investee company was created by or for the benefit of the investor; in these cases, 100% profit elimination, unless realized through a sale to a third party before year end, would be required.

Example of Accounting for Intercompany Transactions

Continue with the same information from the previous example and also assume that E Company sold inventory to R Corporation in 1993 for $2,000 above E's cost. Thirty percent of this inventory remains unsold by R at the end of 1993. E's net income for 1993, including the gross profit on the inventory sold to R, is $20,000; E's income tax rate is 34%. R should make the following journal entries for 1993 (ignoring deferred taxes):

1. Investment in E Company   8,000
        Equity in E income   8,000
        ($20,000 x 40%)

2. Equity in E income (amortization of
        differential)   3,600
            Investment in E Company   3,600

3. Equity in E income   158
            Investment in E Company   158
        ($2,000 x 30% x 66% x 40%)

The amount in the last entry needs further elaboration. Since 30% of the inventory remains unsold, only $600 of the intercompany profit is unrealized at year end. This profit, net of income taxes, is $396. R's share of this profit ($158) is included in the first ($8,000) entry recorded. Accordingly, the third entry is needed to adjust or correct the equity in the reported net income of the investee.

Eliminating entries for intercompany profits in fixed assets are similar to those in the foregoing examples. However, intercompany profit is realized only as the assets are depreciated by the purchasing entity. In other words, if an investor buys or sells fixed assets from or to an investee at a price above book value, the gain would only be realized piecemeal over the asset's remaining depreciable life. Accordingly, in the year of sale the pro rata share (based on the investor's percentage ownership interest in the investee, regardless of whether the sale is upstream or downstream) of the unrealized portion of the intercompany profit would have to be eliminated. In each subsequent year during the asset's life, the pro rata share of the gain realized in the period would be added to income from the investee.

Example of Eliminating Intercompany Profit on Fixed Assets

Assume that Investor Co., which owns 25% of Investee Co., sold to Investee a fixed asset, having a 5-year remaining life, at a gain of $100,000. Investor Co. is in the 34% marginal tax bracket. The sale occurred at the end of 1992; Investee Co. will use straight-line depreciation to amortize the asset over the years 1993 through 1997.

The entries related to the foregoing are:

1992:

1.	Gain on sale of fixed asset	25,000	
	Deferred gain		25,000
	(To defer the unrealized portion of the gain)		
2.	Deferred tax benefit	8,500	
	Income tax expense		8,500
	(Tax effect of gain deferral)		

Alternatively, the 1992 events could have been reported by this single entry:

Equity in investee income	16,500	
Investment in Investee Co.		16,500

1993 through 1997 (each year):

1.	Deferred gain	5,000	
	Gain on sale of fixed assets		5,000
	(To amortize deferred gain)		
2.	Income tax expense	1,700	
	Deferred tax benefit		1,700
	(Tax effect of gain realization)		

The alternative treatment would be:

Investment in Investee Co.	3,300	
Equity in investee income		3,300

In the above example, the tax currently paid by Investor Co. (34% x $25,000 taxable gain on the transaction) is recorded as a deferred tax benefit in 1992 since taxes will not be due on the book gain recognized in the years 1993 through 1997. However, per SFAS 96, unless Investor Co. could demonstrate that future taxable amounts arising from existing temporary differences exist (or, alternatively, that a NOL carryback could have been elected), this deferred tax benefit could **not** be reflected in Investor Co.'s balance sheet at year end 1992. Thus, unless other temporary differences not specified in the example also existed, which provided future taxable amounts to offset the net **deductible** effect of the deferred gain (note: the deferred tax impact of an item of income for book purposes in excess of tax is the same as a deduction for tax purposes in excess of book), the deferred tax benefit might not be recognizable for financial reporting purposes.

Investee income items separately reportable by investor. In the examples thus far, the investor has reported its share of investee income, and the adjustments to this income, as a single item described as equity in investee income. However, when the investee has extraordinary items and/or prior period adjustments that are material, the investor should report its share of these items separately on its income and retained earnings statements.

Example of Accounting for Separately Reportable Items

Assume that both an extraordinary item and a prior period adjustment reported in an investee's income and retained earnings statements are individually considered material from the investor's viewpoint.

Income Statement:

Income before extraordinary item	$ 80,000
Extraordinary loss from earthquake	
(net of taxes of $12,000)	(18,000)
Net income	$ 62,000

Retained Earnings Statement:

Retained earnings at January 1, 1992 as originally reported	$250,000
Add prior period adjustment--correction of an error made in 1991 (net of taxes of $10,000)	20,000
Retained earnings at January 1, 1992, restated	$270,000

If an investor owned 30% of the voting common stock of this investee, the investor would make the following journal entries in 1992:

1. Investment in investee company   24,000
        Equity in investee income before
            extraordinary item   24,000
      ($80,000 x 30%)

2. Equity in investee extraordinary loss   5,400
            Investment in investee company   5,400
   ($18,000 x 30%)

3. Investment in investee company   6,000
            Equity in investee prior period adjustment   6,000
   ($20,000 x 30%)

The equity in the investee's prior period adjustment should be reported on the investor's retained earnings statement, and the equity in the extraordinary loss should be reported separately in the appropriate section on the investor's income statement.

Accounting for a partial sale or additional purchase of the equity investment. This section covers the accounting issues that arise when the investor sells some or all of its equity in the investee, or acquires additional equity in the investee.

Example of Accounting for a Discontinuance of the Equity Method

Assume that an investor owns 10,000 shares (30%) of XYZ Co. common stock for which it paid $250,000 ten years ago. On July 1, 1992, the investor sells 5,000 XYZ shares for $375,000. The balance in the investment in XYZ Company account at January 1, 1992, is $600,000. Assume that all the original differential between cost and book value has been amortized. In order to calculate the gain (loss) upon this sale of 5,000 shares, it is first necessary to adjust the investment account so that it is current as of the date of sale. Assuming that the investee had net income of $100,000 for the six months ended June 30, 1992, the investor should record the following entries:

1. Investment in XYZ Company   30,000
            Equity in XYZ income   30,000
   ($100,000 x 30%)

2. Income tax expense   2,040
            Deferred tax liability   2,040
   ($30,000 x 20% x 34%)

The gain upon sale can now be computed, as follows:

Proceeds upon sale of 5,000 shares	$375,000
Book value of the 5,000 shares ($630,000 x 50%)	315,000
Gain from sale of XYZ common	$ 60,000

Two entries will be needed to reflect the sale: one to record the proceeds, the reduction in the investment account, and the gain (or loss) and the other to record the tax effects thereof. Remember that the investor must have computed the deferred tax effect of the undistributed earnings of the investee that it had recorded each year, on the basis that those earnings either would eventually be paid as dividends or would be realized as capital gains. When those dividends are ultimately received or when the investment is disposed of, the previously recorded deferred tax liability must be amortized.

To illustrate, assume that the investor in this example provided deferred taxes at an effective rate for dividends (considering the 80% exclusion) of 6.8%. The realized capital gain will be taxed at an assumed 34%. For tax purposes, this gain is computed as $375,000 - 125,000 = $250,000, giving a tax effect of $85,000. For accounting purposes, the deferred taxes already provided are 6.8% x ($315,000 - 125,000), or $12,920. Accordingly, an **additional** tax expense of $72,080 is incurred upon the sale, due to the facts that an additional gain was realized for book purposes ($375,000 - 315,000 = $60,000; tax at 34% = $20,400) **and** that the tax previously provided for at dividend income rates was lower than the real capital gains rate [$190,000 x (34% - 6.8%) = $51,680 extra tax due]. The entries are as follows:

1.	Cash	375,000	
	Investment in XYZ Company		315,000
	Gain on sale of XYZ Company stock		60,000
2.	Deferred tax liability	12,920	
	Income tax expense	72,080	
	Taxes payable--current		85,000

The gains (losses) from sales of investee stock are reported on the investor's income statement in the "Other income and expense" section, assuming that a multi-step income statement is presented.

In this example, the sale of investee stock reduced the percentage owned by the investor to 15%. In such a situation, the investor should discontinue use of the equity method. The balance in the investment account on the date the equity method is suspended ($315,000 in the example) remains the balance, subject to the applicable accounting rules (lower of cost or market, per SFAS 12). This accounting principle change does **not** require the computation of a cumulative effect or any retroactive disclosures in the investor's financial statements. In periods subsequent to this principles change, the investor records cash dividends received from the investment as dividend revenue and places the security in its long-term marketable equity securities portfolio where it will be subjected to the lower of aggregate cost or market calculation. Any dividends received in excess of the investor's share of post-disposal earnings of the investee should be credits to the investment account, rather than to income.

The process of discontinuing the use of the equity method and adopting the lower of cost or market approach of SFAS 12, as necessitated by a reduction in ownership below the significant influence threshold level, does not require a retroactive restatement. However, the opposite situation--having the 20% ownership level exceeded again (or for the first time)--is more complex. APB 18 stipulates that this change in accounting principle (**to** the equity method) requires that the investment account, results of operations (all periods being presented, current and prior), and retained earnings of the investor company be retroactively adjusted.

Example of Accounting for a Return to the Equity Method of Accounting

Continuing the same example, XYZ Company reported earnings for the second half of 1992 and all of 1993, respectively, of $150,000 and $350,000; XYZ paid dividends of $100,000 and $150,000 in December of those years. In January 1994, the investor purchased 10,000 XYZ shares for $700,000, increasing its ownership to 45% and thereby necessitating a return for equity method accounting, including retroactive adjustment. The relevant entries are as follows:

1.	Cash	15,000	
	Income from XYZ dividends		15,000
2.	Income tax expense	1,020	
	Taxes payable--current		1,020
	[To record dividend income and taxes thereon at current effective tax rate ($15,000 x .068) in 1992]		
3.	Cash	22,500	
	Income from XYZ dividends		22,500
4.	Income tax expense	1,530	
	Taxes payable--current		1,530
	[To record dividend income and taxes thereon ($22,500 x .068) in 1993]		
5.	Investment in XYZ Company	700,000	
	Cash		700,000
6.	Investment in XYZ Company	37,500	
	Retained earnings		34,950
	Deferred tax liability		2,550

Entry (6) is the cumulative effect adjustment for 15% of XYZ Company's **undistributed** earnings for the second half of 1991 and all of 1992. This adjustment is computed as follows:

Income earned in 1992 subject to equity method:

1992 income ($100,000 + 150,000)	$250,000
Less income earned through June 30 which is reflected in the investment account through previous use of equity method	(100,000)
1992 income subject to equity method adjustment	$150,000
Income earned in 1993 subject to equity method	350,000
Total income subject to equity method	$500,000
Less dividends declared in 1992 and 1993	(250,000)
Increase in investee equity since suspension of equity method (undistributed income)	$250,000
Investor's equity during the period July 1, 1992, through December 31, 1993 (cumulative effect) ($250,000 x 15%)	$ 37,500

Besides showing the cumulative effect as a prior period adjustment on the retained earnings statement, the investor also must retroactively adjust the 1992 and 1993 financial statements to reflect use of the equity method. This means that the dividend income of $15,000 in 1992 and $22,500 in 1993 should be eliminated so as to reflect the equity method. Accordingly, the term "dividend income" is eliminated and "equity in investee income" is substituted. Since the equity method was used for half of the year 1992 and equity in investee income was accrued through June 30, the term should already appear on 1992's income statement. However, the equity in investee income should be increased by $22,500, the investor's share of the income for the last six months of 1992 ($150,000 x 15%). The net effect on 1992's income **before taxes** is a $7,500 increase ($22,500 increase in equity in investee income less a $15,000 decrease in dividend income). For 1993, the net effect on income before taxes is $30,000. This results from adding equity in investee income of $52,500 ($350,000 x 15%) and eliminating dividend income of $22,500. In addition to the income statement, the balance sheets at December 31, 1992 and 1993, are adjusted as follows (before income tax effects):

1. Add $7,500 to the investment in investee and the retained earnings balances at December 31, 1992.
2. Add $37,500 to the investment in investee and the retained earnings balances at December 31, 1993.

Investor accounting for investee capital transactions. According to APB 18, investee transactions of a capital nature that affect the investor's share of the stockholders' equity of the investee shall be accounted for as if the investee were a consolidated subsidiary. These transactions principally include those where the investee purchases treasury stock from, or sells unissued shares or shares held in the treasury to, outside shareholders. (If the investor participates in these transactions on a pro rata basis, its percentage ownership will not change and no special accounting will be necessary.) Similar results will be obtained when holders of outstanding options or convertible securities acquire investee common shares.

When the investee engages in one of the above capital transactions, the investor's ownership percentage is changed. This gives rise to a gain or loss, depending on whether the price paid (for treasury shares acquired) or received (for shares issued) is greater or less than the per share carrying value of the investor's interest in the investee. However, since no gain or loss can be recognized on capital transactions, these purchases or sales will affect paid-in capital and/or retained earnings directly, without being reflected in the investor's income statement. This is consistent with the treatment that would be accorded to a consolidated subsidiary's capital transaction. An exception is that, under certain circumstances, the SEC will permit income recognition based on the concept that the investor is essentially selling part of its investment.

Example of Accounting for an Investee Capital Transaction

Assume R Corp. purchases, on 1/2/92, 25% (2,000 shares) of E Corp.'s outstanding shares for $80,000. The cost is equal to both the book and fair values of R's interest in E's underlying net assets (i.e., there is no differential to be accounted for). One week later, E Corp. buys 1,000 shares of its stock from other shareholders for $50,000. Since the price paid ($50/share) exceeded R Corp.'s per share carrying value of its interest, $40, R Corp. has in fact suffered an economic loss by the transaction. Also, its percentage ownership of E Corp. has increased as the number of shares held by third parties has been reduced.

R Corp.'s new interest in E's net assets is:

$$\frac{2{,}000 \text{ shares held by R}}{7{,}000 \text{ shares outstanding}} \quad \text{x} \quad \text{E Corp. net assets}$$

.2857 x ($320,000 - 50,000) = $77,143

The interest held by R Corp. has thus been diminished by $80,000 - 77,143 = $2,857.

Therefore, R Corp. should make the following entry:

Paid-in capital (or retained earnings)	2,857	
Investment in E Corp.		2,857

R Corp. should charge the loss against paid-in capital if paid-in capital from past transactions of a similar nature exists; otherwise the debit is to retained earnings. Had the transaction given rise to a gain it would have been credited to paid-in capital only (never to retained earnings!) following the prescription in APB 6 that transactions in one's own shares cannot produce earnings.

Note that the amount of the charge to paid-in capital (or retained earnings) in the entry above can be verified as follows: R Corp.'s share of the post-transaction net equity (2/7) times the "excess" price paid ($50 - 40 = $10) times the number of shares purchased = 2/7 x $10 x 1,000 = $2,857.

Disclosures

Disclosure Requirements for Marketable Equity Securities

1. As of the date of each balance sheet presented, aggregate cost and market value (each segregated between current and noncurrent portfolios when a classified balance sheet is presented) with identification as to which is the carrying amount.
2. As of the date of the latest balance sheet presented, the following data, segregated between current and noncurrent portfolios when a classified balance sheet is presented:

    a. Gross unrealized gains representing the excess of market value over cost for all marketable equity securities in the portfolio having such an excess
    b. Gross unrealized losses representing the excess of cost over market value for all marketable equity securities in the portfolio having such an excess

3. For each period for which an income statement is presented:

    a. Net realized gain or loss included in the determination of net income
    b. The basis on which cost was determined in computing realized gain or loss (that is, average cost or other method used)
    c. The change in the valuation allowance(s) that has been included in the equity section of the balance sheet during the period and, when a classified balance sheet is presented, the amount of such change included in the determination of net income

Disclosure Requirements for Marketable Debt Securities

1. The notes to the financial statements shall disclose the nature of the carrying amount, i.e., cost or net realizable value.
2. The amount and cause of any write-down in the cost of a noncurrent investment shall be disclosed.
3. The gross unrealized gains and losses on marketable debt securities shall be disclosed in the notes to the financial statements.

Disclosure Requirements for Investments Accounted for Under the Equity Method

1. The name of each investee and the percentage of ownership of common stock should be disclosed.

2. The accounting policies with respect to each of the investments should be disclosed. The investor must explain why the equity method is not used for investments in the 20-50% range, should this be the case, and why the equity method is used for investments less than 20%. The names of the investees should also be disclosed for these last two situations.
3. The difference between the carrying amount for each investment and its underlying equity in the investee's net assets should be disclosed. The accounting treatment of the difference between these amounts must be disclosed.
4. For those investments which have a quoted market price, the aggregate value of each investment should be disclosed.
5. If investments in investees are considered to have a material effect on the investor's financial position and operating results, the investor should disclose summarized data for the investor's assets, liabilities, and results of operations.
6. If potential conversion of convertible securities and exercise of options and warrants would have material effects on the investor's percentage of the investee, these possibilities should be disclosed.

These disclosures are in addition to reporting these investments on the balance sheet and recording the equity in the investees' incomes on the income statement.

To the extent that majority-owned subsidiaries were previously accounted for by the equity method for financial reporting purposes (i.e., not consolidated) but are now to be consolidated as a result of SFAS 94, the disclosures listed above must continue to be provided. These disclosures are **not** necessary for subsidiaries previously consolidated. However, this inconsistent treatment reflects the FASB's determination that informative disclosures not be diminished vis-à-vis prior GAAP requirements, pending completion of its "reporting entity" project.

10 Business Combinations and Consolidated Financial Statements

Perspective and Issues

Regardless of its legal form, a business combination will be accounted for as either a pooling of interests or a purchase of one business by another, depending upon the facts of the specific case. A pooling of interests presumes that the ownership interests of the combining entities continue essentially unchanged in the new combined enterprise. A series of restrictive criteria must be satisfied for a combination to be accounted for as a pooling. A purchase is applicable when one entity acquires the assets, operations, or ownership interest from another enterprise or from its former owners. The majority of combinations are accounted for as a purchase.

Purchase and pooling accounting procedures, as detailed in APB 16, are applicable to combinations of entities **not** under common control. If companies under common control are combined, the accounting is similar to a pooling of interests. Examples of companies under common control are parents and subsidiaries or brother-sister affiliates. An exception exists where a minority (outside) interest in a subsidiary is acquired, which is accounted for as a purchase. In other transfers among entities under common control, where accounting as a pooling is appropriate, any purchase cost in excess of historical cost should be charged against stockholders' equity.

When a combination is to be accounted for as a purchase, the assets acquired and liabilities assumed are recorded at their fair values. If the assets and liabilities total an amount other than the total acquisition price, the excess (or deficiency) is generally referred to as goodwill (negative goodwill), for which the accounting is set forth in APB 17. Goodwill can arise only in the context of a purchase business combination. In a pooling, the assets and liabilities of the combining entities are carried forward at pre-combination book values. This is consistent with the theory that, since a pooling does not result in the acquisition of one business entity by another, a new basis of account-ability cannot be established.

When the acquired entity is **merged** into the acquiring entity or when both entities are **consolidated** into a new (third) entity, all assets and liabilities are recorded directly on the books of the surviving organization. Depending upon whether the conditions stipulated by APB 16 are met, this transaction will be treated as either a pooling or a purchase. However, when the acquirer obtains a majority (or all) of the common stock of the acquired entity, which continues a separate legal existence, the assets and lia-bilities of the acquired company will not be recorded on the acquirer's books. In this case, GAAP normally requires that consolidated financial statements be prepared; i.e., that an **accounting consolidation** be effected, and depending upon the circum-stances, either pooling or purchase accounting may be used. In certain cases **com-bined** financial statements of entities under common control (but neither of which is owned by the other) are also prepared. This process is very similar to an accounting consolidation using pooling accounting, except that the equity accounts of the combin-ing entities are carried forward intact.

The major accounting issues in business combinations and consolidated or com-bined financial statement preparation are as follows:

1. The proper accounting basis for the assets and liabilities of the combining enti-ties
2. The decision to treat a combination as a pooling or as a purchase
3. The elimination of intercompany balances and transactions in the preparation of consolidated or combined statements

Sources of GAAP

APB	*ARB*	*SFAS*	*TB*
16, 17, 18	51	79, 94	85-5, 85-6

Definitions of Terms

Accounting consolidation. The process of combining the financial statements of a parent company and one or more legally separate and distinct subsidiaries.

Acquisition. One enterprise pays cash or issues stock or debt, for all or part of the voting stock of another enterprise. The acquired enterprise remains intact as a separate legal entity. If the parent-subsidiary relationship is accounted for as a pur-chase, it is called an acquisition. If the accounting is as a pooling, the term acquisition cannot be used and the result is called a combination of interests.

Combination. Any transaction whereby one enterprise obtains control over the assets and properties of another enterprise, regardless of the resultant form of the en-terprise emerging from the combination transaction.

Combined financial statements. Financial statements presenting the financial position and/or results of operations of legally separate entities, related by common ownership, as if they were a single entity.

Consolidated financial statements. Consolidated statements present, primarily for the benefit of the shareholders and creditors of the parent company, the results of operations and the financial position of a parent company and its subsidiaries essentially as if the group were a single enterprise with one or more branches or divisions.

Consolidation. A new enterprise is formed to acquire two or more other enterprises through an exchange of voting stock. The acquired enterprises then cease to exist as separate legal entities.

Control. Ownership by one enterprise, directly or indirectly, of more than 50% of the outstanding voting shares of another enterprise.

Entity concept. A method of preparing consolidated financial statements of a parent and majority-owned subsidiary which involves restatement of net assets of the subsidiary to fair value at the date of acquisition for **both** majority and minority interests.

Goodwill. The excess of the cost of a business acquisition accounted for by the purchase method over the fair value of the net assets thereof; it must be amortized over a useful life of up to 40 years.

Merger. One enterprise acquires all of the net assets of one or more other enterprises through an exchange of stock, payment of cash or other property, or the issue of debt instruments.

Minority interest. Any remaining outstanding voting stock of a subsidiary not purchased by the acquiring enterprise.

Negative goodwill. Referred to as the "excess of fair value over cost of purchased business acquisition." This amount represents the **net** excess of fair value of the net assets of a business acquisition accounted for as a purchase, after offsetting the maximum amount against the fair value of all noncurrent assets acquired (except marketable securities).

Parent company concept. A method of preparing consolidated financial statements of a parent and majority-owned subsidiary which involves restatement of net assets of the subsidiary to fair value at the date of acquisition for **only** the majority interest.

Pooling-of-interests method. An accounting method used for a business combination which is predicated upon a mutual exchange and continuation of ownership interests in the combining entities. It does not result in the establishing of a new basis of accountability.

Purchase method. An accounting method used for a business combination which recognizes that one combining entity was acquired by another. It establishes a new basis of accountability for the acquiree.

Purchased preacquisition earnings. An account used to report the earnings of a subsidiary attributable to percentage ownership acquired at the interim date in the current reporting period.

Subsidiary. An enterprise that is controlled, directly or indirectly, by another enterprise.

Unrealized intercompany profit. The excess of the transaction price over the carrying value of an item (usually inventory or plant assets) transferred from (or to) a parent to (or from) the subsidiary (or among subsidiaries) and not sold to an outside entity. For purposes of consolidated financial statements, recognition must be deferred until subsequent realization through a transaction with an unrelated party.

Concepts, Rules, and Examples

Pooling of Interests

Business combinations have been accounted for as poolings since at least the early 1930s, although the term was not first applied until the mid-1940s. The early examples, however, generally involved affiliated entities (such as parents and subsidiaries), where the use of this method clearly made sense. The Federal Power Commission endorsed pooling accounting in 1943, and other agencies followed suit within a few years. Initially, pooling was accepted only for those mergers where the combining entities had roughly the same economic substances (so that it was difficult to discern which party was actually the acquirer). However, as time passed, pooling was accepted for a broad range of business combinations among economic unequals.

ARB 40 (1950) permitted pooling accounting when the shareholders of the combining entities continued forward as owners of the new or surviving business, and, indeed, this remains one of the clearest tests of whether a combination should be accorded pooling treatment. ARB 40 also established comparable size and management continuity as criteria, but these terms were not quantitatively defined and a wide range of combinations continued to be accounted for as poolings of interests.

This situation continued with the subsequent issuances of ARBs 43 and 48 (1953 and 1957, respectively), which failed to produce the strict guidelines that were needed. ARB 48 permitted pooling treatment even when the size relationship among the combining entities was as great as 19:1. As a result, accounting for business combinations as poolings became extremely popular in the early and mid-1960s. The major reason for pooling accounting's desirability was that the true cost (measured by the market value of the consideration--usually the acquirer's stock or debt instruments) of the acquisition was concealed, with the lower carryforward basis of the assets acquired resulting in lower amortization expense and higher reportable earnings in future periods. Also, under pooling accounting the acquirer could incorporate the acquired entity's retained earnings (subject to some limitations) into its financial statements, thereby providing further "window dressing."

The 12 pooling of interest criteria. Abuses led to pressure to narrow the range of business combinations which could receive pooling treatment. APB 16 established 12 criteria, **all of which** must be met for pooling to be used. A failure to meet all of these 12 tests makes it mandatory to use the purchase accounting method.

The criteria fall into three broad categories:

1. Those relating to the attributes of the combining entities
2. Those relating to the means by which the combination was effected
3. Those relating to the absence of specific post-acquisition planned transactions

<u>Combining companies</u>. Independent ownerships are combined to continue previously separate operations.

1. "Each of the combining companies is autonomous and has not been a subsidiary or division of another corporation within two years before the plan of combination is initiated."

   a. Plan is initiated when announced publicly to stockholders
   b. A new company meets criterion as long as it is not a successor to a nonindependent company
   c. A previously owned company divested due to government order is exempted from this criterion

2. "Each of the combining companies is independent of the other combining companies."

   a. No more than 10% of any combining company is held by any other combining company(ies)

<u>Combining of interest</u>. The combination is effected through an exchange of stock.

3. "The combination is effected in a single transaction or is completed in accordance with a specific plan within one year after the plan is initiated."

   a. Must be completed in a year unless governmental proceeding or litigation prevents completion in one year

4. "A corporation offers and issues only common stock with rights identical to those of the majority of its outstanding voting common stock in exchange for substantially all of the voting common stock interest of another company at the date the plan of combination is consummated."

   a. Cash may be distributed for partial shares, but cash cannot be given pro rata to all stockholders. However, all holders of all outstanding shares may be offered cash, and if 10% or less accept then pooling treatment would still be allowable (if all other conditions are met). If more than 10% ask for cash but a lottery system is used to select the actual recipients of cash (no more than 10%), again pooling treatment would be permitted.
   b. 90% of the acquired entity's stock outstanding at consummation must be acquired by the issuing corporation. The following shares are ex-

cluded from the shares considered acquired at consummation:

1) Stock acquired before the plan was initiated and still owned by issuing corporation
2) Stock acquired by issuing corporation, other than by issuing its own, between initiation and consummation
3) Outstanding stock of the acquired corporation after consummation
4) Shares of the issuing company held by a combining company. These shares are converted into an equivalent number of shares of the combining company and are deducted from the shares considered acquired at consummation.

  c. When more than two companies are combined, the criteria must be met for each of them

  d. An issuing company may acquire equity securities of the combining company other than common by any means **except those** issued for the combining company's stock within the prior two years (which must be acquired with common stock)

  e. The foregoing requirement may extend to more than the actual outstanding common stock of the acquired entity. If it has outstanding stock purchase warrants, these too must (within the 90% rule) be exchanged for stock of the acquirer, since warrants are "substantially identical" to common shares. On the other hand, convertible debt may be exchanged for cash.

5. "None of the combining companies changes the equity interest of the voting common stock in contemplation of effecting the combination either within two years before the plan of combination is initiated or between the dates the combination is initiated and consummated. Changes in contemplation of effecting the combination may include distributions to stockholders and additional issues, exchanges, and retirements of securities."

  a. Normal dividend distributions (as determined by past dividends) are permitted, however

6. "Each of the combining companies reacquires shares of voting common stock only for purposes other than business combinations, and no company reacquires more than a normal number of shares between the dates the plan of combination is initiated and consummated."

  a. Normal treasury stock acquisitions (as determined by past acquisitions) are permitted

  b. Acquisition by other combining companies is the same as treasury stock acquisition

7. "The ratio of the interest of an individual common stockholder to those of other common stockholders in a combining company remains the same as a result of the exchange of stock to effect the combination."

   a. No stockholder denies or surrenders his/her potential share in the issuing corporation

8. "The voting rights to which the common stock ownership interests in the resulting combined corporation are entitled are exercisable by the stockholders. The stockholders are neither deprived of nor restricted in exercising those rights for a period."

   a. Stock cannot be put into a voting trust

9. "The combination is resolved at the date the plan is consummated and no provisions of the plan relating to the issue of securities or other consideration are pending."

   a. No contingent future issuances or other consideration is permitted (including any payable through a trustee)
   b. Later settlement of contingencies existing at the date of consummation is permitted, however

Absence of planned transactions.

10. "The combined corporation does not agree directly or indirectly to retire or reacquire all or part of the common stock issued to effect the combination."

    a. The issuer may, however, retain the right of first refusal on a subsequent resale of the shares issued to effect the business combination without jeopardizing the pooling treatment

11. "The combined corporation does not enter into other financial arrangements for the benefit of the former stockholders of a combining company, such as a guaranty of loans secured by stock issued in the combination, which in effect negates the exchange of equity securities."
12. "The combined corporation does not intend or plan to dispose of a significant part of the assets of the combining companies within two years after the combination other than disposals in the ordinary course of business of the formerly separate companies and to eliminate duplicate facilities or excess capacity."

If a business combination (regardless of legal form) meets all of these 12 criteria, it must be accounted for as a pooling; otherwise, it must be treated as a purchase. A single business combination cannot be accounted for as part pooling, part purchase.

The Emerging Issues Task Force (EITF) has reached a number of consensus positions interpreting the criteria enumerated above. In one of these, the EITF stated that **common** stock, not preferred stock, of the acquirer must be issued to effect a pooling;

where control originally resides with the acquirer's preferred shareholders, it must first arrange to exchange enough common for preferred to create a controlling class of common shareholders. On the other hand, where a controlling class of preferred shareholders exists in the acquiree company, there is no problem: the acquirer simply issues its common stock in exchange for both common and preferred shares of the entity being acquired. In all cases, the issuing (i.e., acquiring) entity must issue shares of its controlling class of common stock for at least 90% of the common stock of the other (i.e., acquired) entity. Additionally, the issuing entity must issue common and preferred stock (if any) for at least 90% of the aggregate common and preferred stock of the acquiree.

The APB's pooling criteria also established the so-called "90% test" for the minimum proportion of the acquired entity's shares being exchanged for the acquirer's common stock. The EITF has established a complex series of tests to apply to situations where several entities are acquired simultaneously, particularly where a new holding company is created into which the other entities are merged. When a new company is formed to effect the combination of two or more companies, the EITF concluded that pooling treatment is required if pooling would have been indicated had **any one** of the entities been the acquirer (the "issuing company", in the language of pooling accounting).

The EITF was inclined to encourage a case-by-case evaluation regarding the potential cash acquisition of securities other than common stock of an acquiree entity in a pooling of interests. Depending on the circumstances, these securities (warrants, options, convertible debt or convertible preferred) might be deemed to be common stock equivalents--and therefore subject to the 10% limits prescribed in APB 16 if pooling treatment is to be preserved. The SEC, on the other hand, applies a stricter criterion that treats warrants and options as common stock in all instances.

Similarly, the EITF reached a consensus to the effect that the retention of a "right of first refusal" by the issuing company with regard to shares it issued to effect a pooling does not violate the rule concerning an absence of planned transactions to retire shares issued. Again, the SEC disagreed with the Task Force position. Of course, an actual intention at the time of the pooling for the acquired company to tender shares it received in the pooling would clearly violate the pooling criterion.

The EITF has considered a wide range of other purchase/pooling issues but generally has not reached consensus positions on them.

Accounting for a pooling. To illustrate the essential elements of the pooling-of-interests method of accounting, consider the following balance sheets of the combining entities:

Condensed Balance Sheets as of Date of Merger

	Company A	Company B	Company C
Assets	$30,000,000	$4,500,000	$6,000,000
Liabilities	$18,000,000	$1,000,000	$1,500,000
Common stock:			
$100 par	6,000,000	--	--
$10 par	--	3,000,000	--
$1 par	--	--	1,000,000
Additional paid-in capital	2,000,000	--	500,000
Retained earnings	4,000,000	500,000	3,000,000
Liabilities and stock-holders' equity	$30,000,000	$4,500,000	$6,000,000

Company A will acquire Companies B and C, and both B and C will tender 100% of their common shares. A will give one of its shares for each 15 shares of B stock and one of its shares for each 25 shares of C stock. Thus, A will issue 20,000 shares to acquire B and 40,000 shares to acquire C.

In a pooling of interests, the historical basis of the assets and liabilities of the combining entities is continued. No new basis of accountability is established. The assets of the combined (post-acquisition) Company A will total $40,500,000; total liabilities will be $20,500,000. Total equity (net assets) will, therefore, equal $20,000,000.

While the total stockholders' equity of the post-combination entity will equal the sum of the combining entities' individual equity accounts, the allocation between paid-in capital and retained earnings can vary. Total (post-combination) retained earnings can be equal to **or less than** the sum of the constituent entities' retained earnings but cannot be more than that amount. Consider the cases of Companies B and C.

Company A issues 20,000 shares of its stock, or an aggregate par value of $2,000,000, to substitute for Company B's $3,000,000 aggregate paid-in capital in effecting the merger with Company B. Therefore, the combined (post-acquisition) balance sheet will include $2,000,000 of par value capital stock, **plus** $1,000,000 of additional paid-in capital. Even though only $2,000,000 of stock was issued to replace Company B's $3,000,000 of aggregate par, there **can be no increase in retained earnings and no decrease in contributed capital** as a consequence of the pooling.

The Company C merger presents the opposite situation: An aggregate of $4,000,000 of Company A stock is to be issued to supersede $1,000,000 of aggregate par and $500,000 of additional paid-in capital. To accomplish this, $2,500,000 of Company C retained earnings is "capitalized," leaving only $500,000 of Company C retained earnings to be carried **as retained earnings** into the post-acquisition balance sheet. In reality, such a situation would not exist. If the pooling of interests took place simultaneously, APB 16 requires only that the combined contributed capital of all entities not be reduced. Therefore, the issuance of 60,000 shares would create an entry on A's books as follows:

Net assets	8,000,000	
Additional paid-in capital	1,500,000	
Common stock		6,000,000
Retained earnings		3,500,000

Note that the additional paid-in capital on the books of Company A is reduced by an amount sufficient to make the total increase in contributed capital of A $4,500,000 which equals the total contributed capital of both B ($3,000,000) and C ($1,500,000). In this way, all of the retained earnings of B and C are transferred to A. This accounting would hold even if A, B, and C simultaneously transferred their net assets to a new entity, D (a consolidation). The opening entry on the books of D would look the same as the consolidated balance sheet of A after the merger as presented below.

The balance sheet of Company A after the mergers are completed is as follows:

Assets	$40,500,000
Liabilities	$20,500,000
Common stock, $100 par	12,000,000
Additional paid-in capital	500,000
Retained earnings	7,500,000
Liabilities and stockholders' equity	$40,500,000

The historical basis of assets and liabilities is normally continued, but this rule has an exception: where different accounting principles were employed by the combining entities, these principles should be conformed, where possible, by retroactive adjustment. Prior period financial statements, when reissued on a pooled basis, should be restated for these changes.

If any combining entity has a deficit in its retained earnings, that deficit is continued in the combined entity (and may even be increased as a consequence of the par value changeover, as illustrated above for a nondeficit situation). It cannot be reduced or eliminated as a consequence of the combination.

Any expenses relating to a business combination accounted for as a pooling of interests (e.g., stock registration costs, finders' fees, and costs of preparing stockholders' prospectuses) must be charged against income in the period in which the combination is effected. No new assets can arise from a pooling.

Example of Pooling

To review the applicability of the pooling criteria set forth earlier and the accounting for poolings of interests, a comprehensive example will be developed here and continued in the subsequent discussion of purchase accounting.

Acquisitive Corporation (whose balance sheet is presented as Exhibit I) is about to acquire four other entities: Beta (Exhibit II), Gamma (Exhibit III), Delta (Exhibit IV), and Epsilon (Exhibit V).

1. The acquisitions will take place as follows:

a. Beta is acquired by exchanging one Acquisitive common share for each 15 of Beta common shares

b. Gamma is acquired by exchanging one Acquisitive common share for each 75 of Gamma common shares

c. Delta is acquired by paying $4,250,000 in 90-day demand notes to retire the $4.5 million bank loan, and by exchanging one Acquisitive share for each 20 of Delta common shares [except as noted in (8) below]

d. Epsilon is acquired by exchanging a new issue of $100 par, 7% preferred stock subject to a mandatory retirement plan (ending in 1994), plus common shares, for all Epsilon common stock. Shareholders of Epsilon will receive one share of Acquisitive preferred and one share of Acquisitive common for each 15 Epsilon common shares.

2. The appraised value of each acquired firm is given as follows (amounts in thousands):

	Assets acquired	Liabilities assumed	Net asset value
Beta Corporation	$78,500	$ 2,500	$76,000
Gamma Company, Inc.	42,500	6,500	36,000
Delta Corporation	37,000	2,500	34,500
Epsilon, Inc.	42,000	19,500	22,500

In each case, current assets are appraised to be worth book values as per the acquired firms' balance sheets.

3. Epsilon originally issued 8% debentures on 1/1/88 at par value. Acquisitive purchased $5.0 million (face value) of these debentures on 1/1/91 at the market price of $97.60. The discount has been regularly amortized to earnings.

4. Investments by Beta and Gamma in the common shares of Acquisitive Corporation were recorded at cost.

5. Each of the five corporations in question has been in business for at least five years, and none has ever been a subsidiary of each other or any other company.

6. The acquisition agreement with Gamma provides that, if earnings of the acquired subsidiary exceed certain amounts in each or any of the following five years, additional shares of Acquisitive will be distributed to former Gamma shareholders. Specifically, for each 50% earnings advance over 1992 levels ($2,800,000 net), an additional 10% of shares are to be issued.

7. The agreement with Epsilon provides that the purchase price of $20,000,000 is protected against market declines for two years subsequent to the merger; i.e., if the value of securities distributed to Epsilon shareholders is below $20 million as of 12/31/94, additional Acquisitive Corporation common shares will be issued at that time, in an amount sufficient to

bring the total value to the stipulated sum.

8. Holders of 5,000 shares of Delta stock angrily dissented to the merger plan, and Acquisitive agreed to pay them $25 for each share tendered instead of issuing common stock.

9. Common stock of the various firms traded on stock exchanges or were quoted in the over-the-counter market in 1992 at these prices:

	High		Low		Average		Ending	
Acquisitive Corporation	$512		$388		$495		$492	
Beta Corporation	51	7/8	28	1/2	35	1/4	35	3/4
Gamma Company, Inc.	8	3/4	7	1/2	8		8	1/8
Delta Corporation	28	1/2	14	3/8	20	1/8	20	1/2
Epsilon, Inc.	20	1/8	10	1/4	12	1/2	11	1/2

Exhibit I
Acquisitive Corporation
Condensed Balance Sheet
December 31, 1992

Sundry current assets		$ 75,000,000
Plant and equipment, net	$80,000,000	
Investment in Epsilon 8% debentures	4,900,000	84,900,000
Total assets		$159,900,000
Sundry liabilities		$ 87,000,000
Common stock, $100 par	$22,500,000	
Additional paid-in capital	12,200,000	
Retained earnings	38,200,000	72,900,000
Total liabilities and stockholders' equity		$159,900,000

Exhibit II
Beta Corporation
Condensed Balance Sheet
December 31, 1992

Sundry current assets		$ 3,900,000
Plant and equipment, net	$38,500,000	
Investment in Acquisitive common stock		
(11,250 shares)	9,800,000	48,300,000
Total assets		$52,200,000
Sundry liabilities		$ 2,500,000
Common stock, $10 par	$20,000,000	
Paid-in surplus	14,700,000	
Retained earnings	15,000,000	49,700,000
Total liabilities and stockholders' equity		$52,200,000

Exhibit III
Gamma Company, Inc.
Condensed Balance Sheet
December 31, 1992

Sundry current assets		$ 4,000,000
Plant and equipment, net	$17,400,000	
Investment in Acquisitive common stock		
(4,500 shares)	3,100,000	20,500,000
Total assets		$24,500,000
Sundry liabilities		$ 6,500,000
Common stock (no par), 3 million shares		
outstanding	$14,500,000	
Retained earnings	3,500,000	18,000,000
Total liabilities and stockholders' equity		$24,500,000

Exhibit IV
Delta Corporation
Condensed Balance Sheet
December 31, 1992

Sundry current assets		$ 4,000,000
Plant and equipment, net		24,000,000
Total assets		$28,000,000
Sundry liabilities		$ 2,500,000
Bank term loan due 1995 (6%)		4,500,000
Common stock, $1 par	$ 1,000,000	
Premium on common stock	3,500,000	
Retained earnings	16,500,000	21,000,000
Total liabilities and stockholders' equity		$28,000,000

Exhibit V
Epsilon, Inc.
Condensed Balance Sheet
December 31, 1992

Sundry current assets		$12,500,000
Plant and equipment, net		$22,000,000
Total assets		$34,500,000
Sundry liabilities		$ 7,000,000
8% debentures due 1/1/2003		12,500,000
Common stock, $10 par	$ 5,000,000	
Paid-in capital	6,200,000	
Retained earnings	3,800,000	15,000,000
Total liabilities and stockholders' equity		$34,500,000

All balance sheets are before recording mergers.

The first task is to determine which of the four mergers qualify for pooling treatment. The first company to be acquired, Beta Corporation, is to be obtained in exchange for **only** the issuing corporation's shares (which suggests a pooling); but prior to the merger Beta does own some of Acquisitive Corporation's shares, seemingly in violation of the second of APB 16's criteria. According to that requirement, each entity must be independent of the other.

However, an exception is provided for intercorporate investments of less than 10% of the total of outstanding voting shares. Therefore, the 5% of Acquisitive's shares held by Beta will not preclude the use of pooling accounting. Although in some instances an investment of **nominally** less than 10% will become an impediment (see discussion of the Gamma case, below), the situation with Beta poses no problem. Since all other pooling criteria are also satisfied, the Acquisitive-Beta merger must be handled as a pooling.

The Gamma Company, Inc. case is more complex. At first the 2% of Acquisitive shares owned by Gamma would appear, as in the Beta case, to be no problem since the 10% rule under the second pooling criterion is not violated. However, this requirement interacts with the fourth APB 16 pooling criterion (the rule that at least 90% of an acquired entity's common stock outstanding at the consummation date must be exchanged for the issuing corporation's shares, excluding shares that were acquired before the combination plan was initiated and are still owned by the acquired entity) in the following way: Using the exchange ratio, the issuing company's shares held by the acquired entity are converted into the equivalent number of acquired entity shares; these cannot exceed 10% of the total shares of the acquired entity being exchanged.

In the present instance, Gamma holds 4,500 Acquisitive shares, which at the stated exchange ratio of 1:75, are equivalent to 337,500 Gamma shares, or 11.25% of Gamma's outstanding shares. In other words, a significant part of Gamma is being obtained by Acquisitive using Gamma's own asset (its investment in the acquirer company), rather than by issuing new shares. This violates the "all at one time for the issuer's stock" requirement embodied in the fourth criterion and precludes the application of pooling accounting.

(Incidentally, the same test applied to the Beta merger has this result: 11,250 shares x 1:15 exchange ratio = 168,750 equivalent Beta shares, which is only 8.44% of Beta's outstanding stock.)

The Gamma merger would also fail to qualify for pooling treatment because the agreement provides for contingent consideration based on future earnings (violating criterion 9). Of course, as soon as any one of the 12 tests is failed, none of the others need to be applied.

The Delta Corporation merger involves both cash and stock, raising a possible red flag since poolings are, generally, purely stock swaps among the parties to the combination. However, the "only-stock" rule relates only to that which is issued by the acquirer for the acquired entity's **voting** stock; cash or other means of payment may be given in exchange for other securities (nonvoting equity or debt) of the acquired entity. Care must be exercised in dealing with this exception, since a transaction prohibited by the 12 pooling criteria cannot be finessed by making it a transaction with two steps. For example, if more than 10% of the acquired company's shares are retired in exchange for debt within two years before the merger, this debt cannot then be paid off in cash by the acquirer as part of the merger arrangement. Instead, the issuing company's common stock would have to be given to these creditors/ex-stockholders.

In the Delta case, cash is used to retire the bank loan, which was not incurred in connection with a repurchase of Delta common shares. Therefore, this is not a violation of any of the pooling criteria.

The cash exchanged for the 1/2 % common stockholding of dissenting owners of Delta also poses no problem, since substantially all of Delta's common shares (i.e., at least 90%) are obtained in exchange for Acquisitive's common stock. Accordingly, the Delta merger qualifies for pooling treatment.

Finally, consider the Epsilon, Inc. merger. Common shares of Epsilon are being obtained in exchange for a package of preferred and common Acquisitive shares, and additional common shares may be issued in the future if the market value of the shares originally given falls below a specified threshold. Also, the acquirer owns a large block of the acquired entity's debentures prior to the initiation of the merger.

The debenture ownership is not a problem since it is not an intercorporate investment in the sense of a voting interest in the future merger partner. Pooling treatment is precluded by two other factors, though.

The issuance of preferred stock that is nonvoting violates the fourth criterion, which demands that only voting common stock be used as payment for substantially all the common shares of the acquired entity. Also, the contingent future share issuance, violating the ninth criterion, would be enough to obviate the pooling method. Thus, the Epsilon merger must be accounted for as a purchase.

The necessary entries to record the Beta and Delta mergers as poolings on Acquisitive's books are as follows:

1.	Sundry current assets	3,900,000	
	Plant and equipment (net)	38,500,000	
	Treasury stock	9,800,000	
	Sundry liabilities		2,500,000
	Common stock, $100 par		13,333,300
	Additional paid-in capital		21,366,700
	Retained earnings		15,000,000
	(To record Beta acquisition by pooling)		

2.	Paid-in capital	475,000	
	Sundry current assets	4,000,000	
	Plant and equipment (net)	24,000,000	
	Sundry current assets (cash)		125,000
	Sundry liabilities		2,500,000
	Demand note payable		4,250,000
	Gain on retirement of debt		250,000
	Common stock, $100 par		4,975,000
	Retained earnings		16,375,000
	(To record Delta acquisition by pooling)		

If, instead of a merger, the combination (acquisition) form is utilized, whereby Acquisitive shares are exchanged directly for Beta and Delta shares held by the respective stockholders of those companies, Beta and Delta will continue their separate existence (albeit as wholly-owned subsidiaries of Acquisitive Corporation). The entries to record the transactions assuming a pooling are as follows:

1.	Investment in Beta common	49,700,000	
	Common stock, $100 par		13,333,300
	Additional paid-in capital		21,366,700
	Retained earnings		15,000,000
	(To record acquisition of Beta shares)		

2.	Investment in Delta common	21,000,000	
	Due from Delta	4,500,000	
	Paid-in capital	475,000	
	Notes payable		4,250,000
	Cash		125,000
	Gain on retirement of debt		250,000
	Common stock, $100 par		4,975,000
	Retained earnings		16,375,000

(To record acquisition of Delta stock, payment of bank loan, and retirement of minority shares for cash)

The purchase accounting entries will be presented in the following section, after the basic elements of this method of accounting for business combinations are discussed. Disclosure requirements for both purchases and poolings are set forth later in this chapter.

Purchase Accounting

Any business combination, of whatever legal form, involving unrelated entities (not previously under common control), that fails any of the aforementioned 12 pooling criteria **must** be treated as a purchase. Realistically, most such transactions are in fact "purchases" as that term is commonly understood (i.e., one entity has bought another, and the buyer is the surviving entity). Purchase accounting is an application of the cost principle, whereby assets obtained are accounted for at the price that was paid. A purchase transaction gives rise to a **new basis of accountability** for the purchased assets (and liabilities).

The major accounting issue relates to the allocation of the purchase cost to the various assets and liabilities acquired. Where the legal form of combination is a merger or a consolidation, the acquirer records all the assets and liabilities purchased at their **fair market values** (**not** the book values of the acquired entity). If the actual cost exceeds the fair value of the identifiable net assets acquired, this excess is recorded as an intangible asset (goodwill). A deficiency of cost under fair value is first used to reduce the fair values of all noncurrent nonmonetary assets acquired, with any balance remaining recorded as a deferred credit (erroneously called negative goodwill). Both goodwill and the deferred credit (negative goodwill) must be amortized, generally by the straight-line method, to earnings over not more than 40 years, according to APB 17.

If the acquisition form of combination is used, the acquired entity maintains a separate legal and accounting existence and all assets and liabilities remain at their premerger book values. However, when an **accounting consolidation** is performed (i.e., when consolidated financial statements are prepared), exactly the same results are obtained as those outlined above (i.e., assets and liabilities are adjusted to fair values, and goodwill is recorded). When less than 100% of the stock of the acquired entity is owned by the acquirer, a complication arises in the preparation of consolidated statements, and a minority interest (discussed below) must be computed.

The other major distinguishing characteristic of the purchase accounting method is that none of the equity accounts of the acquired entity (including its retained earnings) will appear on the acquirer's books or on consolidated financial statements. In other words, ownership interests of the acquired entity's shareholders are **not** continued after the merger, consolidation, or combination (acquisition) takes place.

Determining fair market values. The purchase method requires a determination of the fair market value for each of the acquired company's identifiable tangible and intangible assets and for each of its liabilities at the date of combination. The determination of these fair market values is crucial for proper application of the purchase method. The list below indicates specifically how this is done for various assets and liabilities:

1. **Marketable securities**--net realizable values
2. **Receivables**--present values of amounts to be received determined by using current interest rates, less allowances for uncollectible accounts
3. **Inventories**

   a. Finished goods and merchandise inventories--estimated selling prices less the sum of the costs of disposal and a normal profit
   b. Work-in-process inventories--estimated selling prices less the sum of the costs of completion, costs of disposal and a normal profit
   c. Raw material inventories--current replacement cost

4. **Plant and equipment**

   a. If expected to be used in operations--current replacement costs for similar capacity unless the expected future use of the assets indicates a lower value to the acquirer
   b. If expected to be sold--current net realizable value

5. **Identifiable intangible assets and other assets** (such as land, natural resources, and nonmarketable securities)--appraised value
6. **Liabilities** (such as notes and accounts payable, long-term debt, pensions, warranties, claims payable)--present value of amounts to be paid determined at appropriate current interest rates

Since aggregate purchase cost is allocated to the identifiable assets (and liabilities) according to their respective fair values to the acquirer, assets having no value are assigned no cost. For example, facilities of the acquired entity which duplicate those of the acquirer and which are to be disposed of should be assigned a cost equal to estimated net salvage value, or zero if no salvage is anticipated, or, in rare instances, a **negative** cost equal to the estimated costs of disposal. The EITF has approved the allocation of "holding costs" to assets to be disposed of, when debt from the business acquisition is to be paid down from the proceeds of such asset sales. In effect, this means that the value assigned to such to-be-sold assets is the present value of the estimated selling price; interest incurred on debt used to finance these assets is then charged to the asset instead of to interest expense until the disposition actually occurs. On the other hand, if facilities of the acquired entity duplicate and are superior to facilities of the purchaser, with the intention that the latter will be disposed of, fair value must be allocated to the former. Eventual disposition of the redundant facilities of the **acquirer** may later result in a recognized gain or loss. This would fall into the general category of indirect costs of acquisition--which are not capitalizable or allocable to assets acquired in the purchase business combination.

Accounting for the tax implications of purchase business combinations has changed substantially with the issuance of SFAS 96. Under prior GAAP, any existing deferred tax benefits or liabilities of the acquired entity--or any deferred tax effects created by the purchase transaction itself (e.g., due to different tax and book bases of the acquired assets or liabilities)--were not recognized **as such** in the post-acquisition consolidated balance sheet of the acquirer. Instead, these tax effects were deemed to be components of the valuation process whereby the total purchase cost was allocated to acquired indentifiable assets and liabilities and, when necessary, to goodwill or negative goodwill. Accordingly, purchased assets and liabilities were recorded on a net-of-tax basis under APB 16.

SFAS 96 has completely revised the approach under which values are assigned to purchased assets and liabilities. The net-of-tax method is prohibited; instead, values are assigned "gross", and tax effects, if any, are recorded in deferred tax accounts. Since, under the SFAS 96 "asset and liability" approach to deferred tax accounting (detailed in Chapter 14), deferred tax liabilities (and, in limited circumstances, assets) are evaluated and adjusted at the date of each balance sheet, any deferred taxes of an acquired entity, or any deferred taxes generated by the acquisition transaction itself, are now given formal recognition in recording the purchase business combination. In fact, if an acquired entity has unrecorded deferred tax benefits which can be used to offset the acquirer's deferred tax liabilities, these benefits can be recognized (to the extent allowable under SFAS 96) in the post-acquisition balance sheet. Similarly, unrecognized NOL carryforward benefits of the acquired entity may become recognizable if offsetting against the acquirer's deferred tax obligations is possible. The key issue in each of these situations is whether, employing SFAS 96's scheduling procedure, the various underlying temporary differences will reverse in such a pattern as to permit utilization of the tax benefits of one entity as offsets to the tax liabilities of the other entity.

Under prior GAAP, subsequent realization of unrecognized NOL benefits of an acquired entity necessitated reallocation of the purchase cost and possibly restatement of amortization and depreciation (and therefore net income) since the date of the purchase business combination. Under SFAS 96, only goodwill and other noncurrent intangible assets are adjusted (and then only **prospectively**, so prior earnings are never restated!) for such NOL benefits subsequently realized; benefits exceeding recorded goodwill and other tangibles are credited to income tax expense (not extraordinary income!) in the period realized for tax purposes. (See p. 317 of this chapter and Chapter 14 for details.)

Since goodwill or negative goodwill are "permanent differences" not amortizable for tax purposes, there are no deferred tax effects to be reflected for these items.

Accounting for the tax effects of purchase business combinations under the FASB's proposed replacement for SFAS 96 is addressed in Appendix D to Chapter 14.

Direct costs of the acquisition (e.g., finders' fees) are part of the cost to be allocated to tangible and intangible assets, including goodwill. However, stock registration and related expenses are offset against the proceeds (credits) of the stock issuance. Indirect costs are simply expensed in the period when the combination is effected.

In some instances, certain costs can be handled in alternative manners, influencing their treatment as either direct or indirect costs of a business acquisition. For example, if a prospective acquiree company has employee stock options outstanding, and it pays the employees to settle the options prior to the acquisition, then (per APB 25, as later interpreted by the EITF) compensation expense must be recognized. On the other hand, if the employees exercise their options and then have their shares purchased by the acquirer (or exchanged for stock in the acquirer), there is no compensation expense but instead an additional cost of the purchase.

In certain instances, allocation of purchase cost will be unclear. For example, if an acquired entity has a post-retirement benefits program, under current GAAP no liability will have been accrued by that entity although a real economic obligation exists. It is likely, however, that this obligation will have been considered in arriving at the price paid for the purchase acquisition. Therefore, the fair value of the obligation should be recorded. The EITF has failed to reach a consensus on this issue. Thus, in practice, a liability may or may not be reflected. Although this specific area of ambiguity may be eliminated when the FASB's proposed standard on post-retirement benefits other than pensions is promulgated, there will continue to be areas where the allocation of purchase costs are subject to varying interpretations.

Costs related to a takeover defense by a prospective acquiree company are not capitalized, but rather are expenses of the period incurred. However, the EITF has suggested that if the costs are related to a so-called "going private" transaction, these expenses may be classified as an extraordinary item in the statement of income.

In some takeover defense strategies, a target company will repurchase some of its own shares, generally at a price higher than that being offered by the prospective acquirer. Although generally the cost of repurchased stock is simply charged to the treasury stock account, there is the recognition that excessive repurchase costs are not always related to the "fair value" of the stock, per se. When the price paid explicitly contains consideration for the seller's agreeing to not purchase any further shares (a so-called "standstill agreement"), this excess cost must be expensed (per Technical Bulletin 85-6), with only the fair market value of the shares themselves being charged to the treasury stock account. The EITF did not reach a consensus about the treatment of excessive costs of treasury shares absent explicit payment for other services. However, the SEC favors expensing any excess costs. As a general rule, judgment should be applied in evaluating each circumstance.

Example of Accounting for a Purchase

Continuing the Acquisitive Corporation example begun in the pooling-of-interests discussion (pages 278-282), the journal entries to record the purchase of the Gamma Company, Inc. and Epsilon, Inc. shares will be presented. Tax effects are ignored in these examples.

Using the fair market value information given earlier and assuming that a legal merger (or consolidation) form is used, Acquisitive makes these entries:

1. Sundry current assets   4,000,000
   Plant and equipment   19,080,000
   Treasury stock   3,100,000
      Sundry liabilities   6,500,000
      Common stock, $100 par   4,000,000
      Additional paid-in capital   15,680,000
   (To record purchase of net assets of Gamma)

2. Sundry current assets   12,500,000
   Plant and equipment   27,000,000
      Sundry liabilities   7,000,000
      8% debentures   12,500,000
      Preferred stock, $100 par   3,333,300
      Premium on preferred   266,864
      Common stock, $100 par   3,333,300
      Additional paid-in capital   13,066,536
   (To record purchase of net assets of Epsilon)

The value of the Gamma purchase was determined by reference to the latest market value of the Acquisitive shares given ($492 per share). Notice that although the price paid was slightly greater than net **book** value ($19.68 million vs. $18 million), it was considerably less than estimated fair value ($36 million net). In other words, there was an excess of fair value over cost which, in accordance with the procedures specified by APB 16, was allocated against plant and equipment (the only noncurrent asset). Had this deficiency been large enough to reduce plant and equipment to zero, any remaining amount would have been recorded as a deferred credit (excess of fair value of net assets acquired over cost) and systematically amortized, like goodwill, over not more than 40 years (APB 17).

The total value of the Epsilon purchase was given as $20 million, and deducting the known market value of Acquisitive common shares from this revealed the apparent value assigned to the new Acquisitive preferred stock. The total price exceeded the net book value of Epsilon's identifiable assets but was lower than the fair value thereof, so again there is an excess of fair value over cost, and the noncurrent assets are recorded at less than their fair values.

If the acquisition form is used instead, the entries by the parent company would be as follows:

1. Investment in Gamma common   19,680,000
      Common stock, $100 par   4,000,000
      Additional paid-in capital   15,680,000

2. Investment in Epsilon common	20,000,000	
Preferred stock, $100 par		3,333,300
Premium on preferred		266,864
Common stock, $100 par		3,333,300
Additional paid-in capital		13,066,536

Example of Consolidation Workpaper (Date of Acquisition, 100% Ownership)

The worksheet for the preparation of a consolidated balance sheet for Acquisitive Corp. and its four wholly-owned subsidiaries at the date of the acquisitions is shown below. Remember that it is presumed that Acquisitive (the parent) acquired the common stock of each subsidiary; had it acquired the net assets directly (through a legal merger or a consolidation), this **accounting consolidation** would not be necessary.

Except for Epsilon, the entries are straightforward and need no further explanation, as they are necessary to eliminate the investment accounts of the parent and the equity accounts of the subsidiaries. Note that there are upward adjustments to the plant and equipment relative to the **purchases** of Gamma and Epsilon. The **poolings** of Beta and Delta result in their book values being carried forward.

Acquisitive Corporation and Subsidiaries
Workpapers for Consolidated Balance Sheet
As of December 31, 1992

	Acquisitive Corp.	Beta Corp.	Gamma Co., Inc.	Delta Corp.	Epsilon, Inc.	Elimination entries	Consolidated balance sheet
Current assets	$ 70,625,000	$ 3,900,000	$ 4,000,000	$ 4,000,000	$12,500,000	$ --	$ 95,025,000
Plant and equipment	80,000,000	38,500,000	17,400,000	24,000,000	22,000,000	1,680,000 c	188,580,000
						5,000,000 f	
Investments:							
Epsilon 8% debentures	4,900,000					(4,900,000)g	
Acquisitive stock		9,800,000	3,100,000			(9,800,000)b	
						(3,100,000)d	
Beta Corp.	49,700,000					(49,700,000)a	
Gamma Co., Inc.	19,680,000					(19,680,000)c	
Delta Corp.	25,500,000					(25,500,000)e	
Epsilon, Inc.	20,000,000					(20,000,000)f	
	$270,405,000	$52,200,000	$24,500,000	$28,000,000	$34,500,000		$283,605,000
Current liabilities	$ 87,000,000	$ 2,500,000	$ 6,500,000	$ 7,000,000	$ 7,000,000	$ (4,500,000)e	$105,500,000
8% debentures					12,500,000	(5,000,000)g	7,500,000
Preferred stock, $100 par	3,333,300						3,333,300
Premium on pfd. stock	266,864						266,864
Common stock							
$100 par	48,141,600						48,141,600
$10 par		20,000,000				(20,000,000)a	
No par			14,500,000			(14,500,000)c	
$1 par				1,000,000		(1,000,000)e	
$10 par					5,000,000	(5,000,000)f	
Additional paid-in capital, etc.	61,838,236	14,700,000		3,500,000	6,200,000	(14,700,000)a	61,838,236
						(3,500,000)e	
						(6,200,000)f	
Retained earnings	69,825,000	15,000,000	3,500,000	16,500,000	3,800,000	(15,000,000)a	
						(3,500,000)c	
						(16,500,000)e	69,925,000
						(3,800,000)f	
						100,000 g	
	$270,405,000	$52,200,000	$24,500,000	$28,000,000	$34,500,000		
Treasury stock (at cost)						(9,800,000)b	(12,900,000)
						(3,100,000)d	
							$283,605,000

The elimination of the investment in Epsilon debentures needs explanation. The parent paid $4,880,000 for debentures having a $5 million par on January 1, 1991. The discount has been properly amortized in 1991 and 1992, so that the carrying value at the date of acquisition of Epsilon is $4,900,000. Therefore, on a **consolidated** basis, debt of $5 million has been extinguished at a cost of $4.9 million, for a gain on retirement of $100,000. Per APB 26, this gain will appear on the consolidated statement of income and will be classified as extraordinary (SFAS 4) if material. Since the workpapers shown are only for the preparation of a consolidated balance sheet, the gain has been credited to retained earnings. This gain could also be recorded on the books of the parent, Acquisitive Corp., which would make their retained earnings equal to consolidated retained earnings.

Minority Interests in Purchase and Pooling Combinations

When a company acquires some, but not all, of the voting stock of another entity, the shares held by third parties represent a **minority interest** in the acquired company. This occurs when the acquisition form is employed. A legal merger or consolidation would give the acquirer a 100% interest in whatever assets it obtained from the selling entity. According to GAAP, if a parent company owns more than half of another entity, the two should be consolidated for financial statement purposes (unless to do so would mislead the statement users because control is temporary or the businesses are heterogeneous, etc.), and the minority interest in the assets and earnings of the consolidated entity must be accounted for.

When consolidated statements are prepared, the full amount of assets and liabilities (in the balance sheet) and income and expenses (in the income statement) of the subsidiary are generally presented. Accordingly, a contra must be shown for the portion of these items that does not belong to the parent company. In the balance sheet this contra is normally a credit item shown between total liabilities and stockholders' equity, representing the minority interest in consolidated net assets equal to the minority's percentage ownership in the net assets of the subsidiary entity. Although less likely, a debit balance in minority interest could result when the subsidiary has a deficit in its stockholders' equity **and** when there is reason to believe that the minority owners will make additional capital contributions to erase that deficit. This situation sometimes occurs where the entities are closely held and the minority owners are related parties having other business relationships with the parent company and/or its stockholders. In other circumstances, a debit in minority interest would be charged against parent company retained earnings under the concept that the loss will be borne by that company.

In the income statement, the minority interest in the income (or loss) of a consolidated subsidiary is shown as a deduction from (or addition to) the consolidated net income account. As above, if the minority interest in the net assets of the subsidiary has already been reduced to zero, and if a net debit minority interest will **not** be recorded (the usual case), then the minority's interest in any further losses should **not** be recorded. (However, this must be explained in the footnotes.) Furthermore, if past minority losses have not been recorded, the minority's interest in current profits will not be recognized until the aggregate of such profits equals the aggregate unrecognized losses. This closely parallels the rule for equity method accounting recognition of profits and losses.

Example of Consolidation Process Involving a Minority Interest

Assume the following:

Alto Company and Bass Company
Balance Sheets at 1/1/92
(Immediately before combination)

	Alto Company	Bass Company
Assets:		
Cash	$ 30,900	$ 37,400
Accounts receivable (net)	34,200	9,100
Inventories	22,900	16,100
Equipment	200,000	50,000
Less accumulated depreciation	(21,000)	(10,000)
Patents	--	10,000
Total assets	$267,000	$112,600
Liabilities and stockholders' equity:		
Accounts payable	$ 4,000	$ 6,600
Bonds payable, 10%	100,000	--
Common stock, $10 par	100,000	50,000
Additional paid-in capital	15,000	15,000
Retained earnings	48,000	41,000
Total liabilities and stockholders' equity	$267,000	$112,600

Note that the book value of the net assets of Bass Company may be computed by one of the following two methods:

1. Subtract the book value of the liability from the book values of the assets:
   $112,600 - 6,600 = $106,000
2. Add the book values of the components of Bass Company stockholders' equity:

   $50,000 + 15,000 + 41,000 = $106,000

At the date of combination, the fair values of all the assets and liabilities were determined by appraisal, as follows:

Bass Company Item	Book value (BV)	Fair market value (FMV)	Difference between BV and FMV
Cash	$ 37,400	$ 37,400	$ --
Accounts receivable (net)	9,100	9,100	--
Inventories	16,100	17,100	1,000
Equipment (net)	40,000	48,000	8,000
Patents	10,000	13,000	3,000
Accounts payable	(6,600)	(6,600)	--
Totals	$106,000	$118,000	$12,000

When a minority interest exists, as in this example, whether the consolidated balance sheet reflects the **full** excess of fair market values over book values of the subsidiary's net assets, or only the parent company's percentage share thereof, depends upon the concept employed. Under the **parent company** concept, only the parent's share of the revaluation is recognized, and minority interest is reported based on the book value of the subsidiary. If the **entity concept** is used, however, the full revaluation from book to fair value is recognized in the consolidated balance sheet, and the minority interest is based on the fair value of the subsidiary's net assets. Both techniques are acceptable.

Assume the following:

1. On January 1, 1992, Alto Company acquires a 90% interest in Bass Company in exchange for 5,400 shares of $10 par stock having a total market value of $120,600.
2. The purchase method of accounting is used for the combination.
3. Any goodwill resulting from the combination will be amortized over a period of 10 years.

The workpaper for a consolidated balance sheet at the date of acquisition is presented below. The first two columns are the trial balances from the books of Alto Company and Bass Company immediately following the acquisition.

**Alto Company and Bass Company Consolidated Working Papers
For Date of Combination--1/1/92**

Purchase accounting
90% interest

	Alto Company	Bass Company	Adjustments and eliminations Debit	Credit	Minority interest	Consolidated balances
Balance sheet, 1/1/92						
Cash	$ 30,900	$ 37,400				$ 68,300
Accounts receivable	34,200	9,100				43,300
Inventories	22,900	16,100	$ 900b			39,900
Equipment	200,000	50,000	9,000b			259,000
Accumulated depreciation	(21,000)	(10,000)		$ 1,800b		(32,800)
Investment in stock of						
Bass Company	120,600			120,600a		
Difference between cost						
and book value			25,200a	25,200b		
Excess of cost over fair						
value (goodwill)			14,400b			14,400
Patents		10,000	2,700b			12,700
Total assets	$387,600	$112,600				$404,800
Accounts payable	$ 4,000	$ 6,600				$ 10,600
Bonds payable	100,000					100,000
Capital stock	154,000	50,000	45,000a		$ 5,000	154,000
Additional paid-in capital	81,600	15,000	13,500a		1,500	81,600
Retained earnings	48,000	41,000	36,900a		4,100	48,000
Minority interest					$10,600	10,600 MI
Total liabilities and						
equity	$387,600	$112,600	$147,600	$147,600		$404,800

1. Investment on Alto Company's books

    The entry to record the 90% purchase-acquisition on Alto Company's books was:

    Investment in stock of Bass Company 120,600
       Capital stock   54,000
       Additional paid-in capital   66,600
    (To record the issuance of 5,400 shares of $10 par stock to acquire a 90% interest in Bass Company)

    Although common stock is used for the consideration in our example, Alto Company could have used debentures, cash, or any other form of consideration acceptable to Bass Company's stockholders to make the **purchase** combination.

2. Difference between investment cost and book value

     The difference between the investment cost and the parent company's equity in the net assets of the subsidiary is computed as follows:

Investment cost		$120,600
Less book value % at date of combination		
Bass Company's		
Capital stock	$ 50,000	
Additional paid-in capital	15,000	
Retained earnings	41,000	
Total	$106,000	
Parent's share of ownership	x 90%	
Parent's share of book value		95,400
Excess of cost over book value		$ 25,200

This difference is due to several undervalued assets and to unrecorded goodwill. The allocation procedure is similar to that for a 100% purchase; however, in this case, the parent company obtained a 90% interest and, thus, will recognize 90% of the difference between the fair market values and book values of the subsidiary's assets, not 100%. The allocation is presented as follows:

Allocation of the Differential

Item	*Book value (BV)*	*Fair market value (FMV)*	*Difference between BV and FMV*	*Owner-ship per-centage*	*Percentage share of difference between BV and FMV*
Cash	$ 37,400	$ 37,400	$ --		
Accounts receivable (net)	9,100	9,100	--		
Inventories	16,100	17,100	1,000	90%	$ 900
Equipment	50,000	60,000	10,000	90%	9,000
Accumulated depreciation	(10,000)	(12,000)	(2,000)	90%	(1,800)
Patents	10,000	13,000	3,000	90%	2,700
Accounts payable	(6,600)	(6,600)	--		
Total	$106,000	$118,000	$12,000		

Amount of difference between cost and book value share allocated to revaluation of net assets	$10,800
Total differential	25,200
Remainder allocated to goodwill	$14,400

The equipment has a book value of $40,000 ($50,000 less 20% depreciation of $10,000). An appraisal concluded that the equipment's replacement cost was $60,000 less 20% accumulated depreciation of $12,000 resulting in a net fair value of $48,000.

3. Elimination entries on workpaper

The basic reciprocal accounts are the investment in subsidiary account on the parent's books and the subsidiary's stockholder equity accounts. Only the parent's share of the subsidiary's accounts may be eliminated as reciprocal accounts. The remaining 10% portion is allocated to the minority interest. The entries below include documentation showing the company source for the information. The workpaper entry to eliminate the basic reciprocal accounts is as follows:

Capital stock--Bass Co.	45,000	
Additional paid-in capital--Bass Co.	13,500	
Retained earnings--Bass Co.	36,900*	
Differential	25,200	
Investment in stock of Bass Co.--Alto Co.		120,600
*($41,000 x 90% = 36,900)		

Note that only 90% of Bass Company's stockholders' equity accounts are eliminated. Also, an account called differential is debited in the workpaper entry. The differential account is a temporary account to record the difference between the cost of the investment in Bass Company from the parent's books and the book value of the parent's interest (90% in our case) from the subsidiary's books.

The next step is to allocate the differential to the specific accounts by making the following workpaper entry:

Inventory	900	
Equipment	9,000	
Patents	2,700	
Goodwill	14,400	
Accumulated depreciation		1,800
Differential		25,200

This entry reflects the allocations prepared in step 2 on the previous page and recognizes the parent's share of the asset revaluations.

The minority interest column is the 10% interest of Bass Company's net assets owned by outside, third parties. Minority interest must be disclosed because 100% of the book values of Bass Company are included in the consolidated statements, although Alto Company controls only 90% of the net assets. An alternative method to prove minority interest is to multiply the net assets of the subsidiary by the minority interest share, as follows:

Stockholders' equity of Bass Company	x	Minority interest %	=	Minority interest
$106,000	x	10%	=	$10,600

The $10,600 would be reported on the credit side of the consolidated balance sheet between liabilities and stockholders' equity.

The **parent company concept** was used above to prepare the consolidated balance sheet. If the **entity concept** had been employed, minority interest would have been as follows:

Total fair market
value of net assets   x Minority percentage = Minority interest
of Bass Company

$118,000   x   10%   = $11,800

The example does not include any other intercompany accounts as of the date of combination. If any existed, they would be eliminated to fairly present the consolidated entity. Several examples of other reciprocal accounts will be shown later for the preparation of consolidated financial statements subsequent to the date of acquisition.

If the previous example were accounted for on a push-down basis, Bass would record the following entry on its books:

Inventories	1,000	
Equipment	10,000	
Patents	3,000	
Accumulated depreciation		2,000
Paid-in capital		12,000

As a result, Alto would have an investment of $120,600 in a company whose net equity was $118,000. Then 90% x $118,000 or $106,200 contrasted with the cost of $120,600 would mean the only number unaccounted for by Alto would be goodwill of $14,400. The elimination entry on the worksheet would change only with respect to the paid-in capital of Bass as follows:

Capital stock	45,000	
Paid-in capital	24,300	
Retained earnings	36,900	
Goodwill	14,400	
Investment		120,600

This would leave $5,000 of capital stock, $2,700 of paid-in capital, and $4,100 of retained earnings as minority interest or the same $11,800 as under the entity concept.

Example of Consolidation for Pooling Involving Minority Interest

The foregoing entries are based on the combination being accounted for as a purchase. The same example will now be used to demonstrate the pooling-of-interests method applied to a minority interest situation. Assume the following:

1. On January 1, 1992, Alto Company acquired a 90% interest in Bass Company in exchange for 5,400 shares of $10 par value stock of Alto Company.
2. All criteria for a pooling have been met, and the combination is treated as a pooling of interests.

The workpaper for a consolidated balance sheet at the date of combination is presented below. Note that the first two columns are trial balances of Alto Company and Bass Company immediately after the combination was recorded by Alto Company.

1. Investment entry recorded on Alto Company's books
    The following entry was made by Alto Company to record its 90% acquisition-pooling of Bass Company:

Investment in stock of Bass Co.	95,400	
Capital stock, $10 par		54,000
Additional paid-in capital		4,500
Retained earnings		36,900

Alto Company and Bass Company Consolidated Working Papers
For Date of Combination--1/1/92

Pooling accounting
90% interest

	Alto Company	Bass Company	Adjustments and eliminations Debit	Credit	Minority interest	Consolidated balances
Balance sheet, 1/1/92						
Cash	$ 30,900	$ 37,400				$ 68,300
Accounts receivable	34,200	9,100				43,300
Inventories	22,900	16,100				39,000
Equipment	200,000	50,000				250,000
Accumulated depreciation	(21,000)	(10,000)				(31,000)
Investment in stock of						
Bass Company	95,400			$95,400a		
Patents	___	10,000				10,000
Total assets	$362,400	$112,600				$379,600
Accounts payable	$4,000	$6,600				$ 10,600
Bonds payable	100,000					100,000
Capital stock	154,000	50,000	$45,000a		$ 5,000	154,000
Additional paid-in capital	19,500	15,000	13,500a		1,500	19,500
Retained earnings	84,900	41,000	36,900a		4,100	84,900
Minority interest	___	___	___	___	$10,600	10,600 MI
Total liabilities and						
equity	$362,400	$112,600	$95,400	$95,400		$379,600

The investment entry reflects the capital mix for a pooling of less than a 100% investment. The following schedule shows the mix for our 90% combination accomplished by the issuance of 5,400 shares of Alto Company's $10 par stock:

	Bass Company	Alto Company's percentage share	Alto's share of Bass's equity
Capital stock	$ 50,000	90%	$45,000
Additional paid-in capital	15,000	90%	13,500
Retained earnings	41,000	90%	36,900
	$106,000		$95,400

The $54,000 (5,400 shares x $10 par) in new capital issued by Alto Company represents $45,000 from Bass Company's capital stock and $9,000 of the $13,500 Bass Company's additional paid-in capital. Note that the remaining $4,500 of capital and $36,900 of Bass Company's retained earnings are carried over to Alto Company's books in the combination date entry. The $10,600 of Bass's capital that is not carried over to Alto will eventually be shown as minority interest on the consolidated balance sheet.

2. Elimination entry on workpaper

   Pooling accounting uses book values as a basis of valuation; therefore, no differential will ever occur in a pooling. The reciprocal accounts in a pooling consolidated balance sheet are in the investment in stock of Bass Company account from the parent's books and the stockholders' equity accounts from the subsidiary's books. Again, note that only 90% of the equity of Bass Company is being eliminated; the 10% remainder will be recognized as minority interest. The workpaper elimination entry is:

Capital stock--Bass Co.	45,000	
Additional paid-in capital--Bass Co.	13,500	
Retained earnings--Bass Co.	36,900*	
Investment in stock of		
Bass Co.--Alto Co.		95,400
*($41,000 x 90% = $36,900)		

Consolidated Statements (Purchase and Pooling) in Subsequent Periods

The same concepts employed to prepare a consolidated balance sheet at the date of acquisition are applicable to later consolidated statements. Where a minority interest exists, income in subsequent periods must be allocated to it. The exact nature of the worksheet entries depends on whether the parent is maintaining the investment in subsidiary account on the cost, partial equity, or full equity basis (all of which are acceptable since the consolidated financial statements will be identical under any alternative). In practice, the cost and partial equity methods are most likely to be encountered. The partial equity method is used when separate, parent-only statements are expected to be prepared in addition to consolidated statements (which commonly is the case). Using the partial equity method, the parent records its share of the subsidiary's income or loss but does not amortize the differential between cost and book value against equity in the subsidiary's earnings.

In addition to the elimination entries for the parent investment account and subsidiary equity accounts, other eliminations will be needed when there are intercompany balances or transactions resulting from parent-subsidiary loans (advances), sales of inventory items (whether or not these occurred at a profit to the seller), sales of fixed assets at other than net book value, and bond transactions or transactions in stock other than voting common shares. The selected items in the following example will demonstrate the accounting issues applicable to all such intercompany items and the proper handling of these items in the consolidated workpapers.

Example of a Consolidation in Subsequent Periods

The basic facts of the Alto Company-Bass Company case have already been presented; additional information is as follows:

1. Alto Company uses the partial equity method to record changes in the value of the investment account.
2. During 1992, Alto Company sold merchandise to Bass Company that originally cost Alto Company $15,000, and the sale was made for $20,000. On December 31, 1992, Bass Company's inventory included merchandise purchased from Alto Company at a cost to Bass Company of $12,000.
3. Also during 1992, Alto Company acquired $18,000 of merchandise from Bass Company. Bass Company uses a normal markup of 25% above its cost. Alto Company's ending inventory includes $10,000 of the merchandise acquired from Bass Company.
4. Bass Company reduced its intercompany account payable to Alto Company to a balance of $4,000 as of December 31, 1992, by making a payment of $1,000 on December 30. This $1,000 payment was still in transit on December 31, 1992.
5. On January 2, 1992, Bass Company acquired equipment from Alto Company for $7,000. The equipment was originally purchased by Alto Company for $5,000 and had a book value of $4,000 at the date of sale to Bass Company. The equipment had an estimated remaining life of 4 years as of January 2, 1992.
6. On December 31, 1992, Bass Company purchased for $44,000, 50% of the outstanding bonds issued by Alto Company. The bonds mature on December 31, 1997, and were originally issued at par. The bonds pay interest annually on December 31 of each year, and the interest was paid to the prior investor immediately before Bass Company's purchase of the bonds.

The worksheet for the preparation of consolidated financial statements as of December 31, 1992, is presented below, on the assumption that purchase accounting is used for the business combination.

The investment account balance at the statement date should be reconciled to ensure the parent company made the proper entries under the method of accounting used to account for the investment. Since the partial equity method is used by Alto, the amortizations of the excess of cost over book value will be recognized only on the worksheets.

An analysis of the investment account at December 31, 1992 is as follows:

Investment in Stock of Bass Company

Original cost	120,600		
			% of Bass Co.'s dividends declared ($4,000 x 90%)
% of Bass Co.'s income ($9,400 x 90%)	8,460	3,600	
Balance, 12/31/92	125,460		

Any errors will require correcting entries before the consolidation process is continued. Correcting entries will be posted to the books of the appropriate company; eliminating entries are **not** posted to either company's books.

The difference between the investment cost and the book value of the net assets acquired was determined and allocated in the preparation of the date of combination consolidated statements presented earlier. The same computations are used in preparing financial statements for as long as the investment is owned.

The following adjusting and eliminating entries will be required to prepare consolidated financials as of December 31, 1992. Note that a consolidated income statement is required and, therefore, the nominal accounts are still open. The number or letter in parentheses to the left of the entry corresponds to the key used on the worksheet.

Step 1 --   Complete the transaction for any intercompany items in transit at the end of the year.

(1)	Cash	1,000	
	Accounts receivable		1,000

This **adjusting** entry will now properly present the financial positions of both companies, and the consolidation process may be continued.

Step 2 -- Prepare the eliminating entries.

(a) Sales   38,000
      Cost of goods sold   38,000

Total intercompany sales of $38,000 include $20,000 in a downstream transaction from Alto Company to Bass Company and $18,000 in an upstream transaction from Bass Company to Alto Company.

(b) Cost of goods sold   5,000
      Inventory   5,000

The ending inventories are overstated because of the unrealized profit from the intercompany sales. The debit to cost of goods sold is required because a decrease in ending inventory will increase cost of goods sold to be deducted on the income statement. Supporting computations for the entry are as follows:

	In ending inventory of	
	Alto Company	*Bass Company*
Intercompany sales not resold, at selling price	$10,000	$12,000
Cost basis of remaining intercompany merchandise		
From Bass to Alto (÷ 125%)	(8,000)	
From Alto to Bass (÷ 133 1/3%)		(9,000)
Unrealized profit	$ 2,000	$ 3,000

When preparing consolidated workpapers for 1993 (the next fiscal period), an additional eliminating entry will be required if the goods in 1992's ending inventory are sold to outsiders during 1993. The additional entry will recognize the profit for 1993 that was eliminated as unrealized in 1992. This entry is necessary since the entry at the end of 1992 was made only on the worksheet. The 1993 entry will be as follows:

Retained earnings--Bass Co.,
   1/1/93   2,000
Retained earnings--Alto Co.,
   1/1/93   3,000
      Cost of goods sold, 1993   5,000

(c) Accounts payable   4,000
      Accounts receivable   4,000

This eliminates the remaining intercompany receivable/payable owed by Bass Company to Alto Company. This eliminating entry is necessary to avoid overstating the consolidated entity's balance sheet. The receivable/payable is not extinguished, and Bass Company must still transfer $4,000 to Alto Company in the future.

(d)	Gain on sale of equipment	3,000	
	Equipment		2,000
	Accumulated depreciation		250
	Depreciation expense		750

This entry eliminates the gain on the intercompany sale of the equipment, eliminates the overstatement of equipment, and removes the excess depreciation taken on the gain. Supporting computations for the entry are as follows:

	Cost	At date of intercompany sale accum. depr.	1992 depr. ex.	End-of-period accum. depr.
Original basis (to seller, Alto Co.)	$5,000	($1,000)	$ 1,000	($2,000)
New basis (to buyer, Bass Co.)	7,000	--	1,750	(1,750)
Difference	($2,000)		($ 750)	$ 250

If the intercompany sale had not occurred, Alto Company would have depreciated the remaining book value of $4,000 over the estimated remaining life of 4 years. However, since Bass Company's acquisition price ($7,000) was more than Alto Company's basis in the asset ($4,000), the depreciation recorded on the books of Bass Company will include part of the intercompany unrealized profit. The equipment must be reflected on the consolidated statements at the original cost to the consolidated entity. Therefore, the write-up of $2,000 in the equipment, the excess depreciation of $750, and the gain of $3,000 must be eliminated, and the ending balance of accumulated depreciation must be shown at what it would have been if the intercompany equipment transaction had not occurred. In future periods, a retained earnings account will be used instead of the gain account; however, the other concepts will be extended to include the additional periods.

(e) Bonds payable   50,000
    Investment in bonds
      of Alto Company   44,000
    Gain on extinguishment
      of debt   6,000

This entry eliminates the book value of Alto Company's debt against the bond investment account of Bass Company. To the consolidated entity, this transaction must be shown as a retirement of debt even though Alto Company has the outstanding intercompany debt to Bass Company. SFAS 4 specifies gains or losses on debt extinguishment, if material, should be shown as an extraordinary item. In future periods, Bass Company will amortize the discount, thereby bringing the investment account up to par value. A retained earnings account will be used in the eliminating entry instead of the gain account.

(f) Equity in subsidiary's
    income--Alto Co.   8,460
      Dividends declared--Bass Co.   3,600
      Investment in stock of Alto Co.   4,860

This elimination entry adjusts the investment account back to its balance at the beginning of the period and also eliminates the subsidiary income account.

(g) Capital stock--Bass Co.   45,000
    Additional paid-in capital--
      Bass Co.   13,500
    Retained earnings--Bass Co.   36,900
    Differential   25,200
      Investment in stock of
      Bass Company--Alto Co.   120,600

This entry eliminates 90% of Bass Company's stockholders' equity at the beginning of the year, 1/1/92. Note that the changes **during** the year were eliminated in entry (f) above. The differential account reflects the excess of investment cost greater than the book value of the assets acquired.

(h)   Inventory   900
      Equipment   9,000
      Patents   2,700
      Goodwill   14,400
        Accumulated depr.   1,800
        Differential   25,200

This entry allocates the differential (excess of investment cost over the book values of the assets acquired). Note that this entry is the same as the allocation entry made to prepare consolidated financial statements for January 1, 1992, the date of acquisition.

(i)   Cost of goods sold   900
      Depreciation expense   1,800
      Other operating expenses--
        patent amortization   270
      Other operating expenses--
        goodwill amortization   1,440
          Inventory   900
          Accumulated depr.   1,800
          Patents   270
          Goodwill   1,440

The elimination entry amortizes the revaluations to fair market value made in entry (h). The inventory has been sold and, therefore, becomes part of cost of goods sold. The remaining revaluations will be amortized as follows:

	Revaluation	Amortization period	Annual amortization
Equipment (net)	$7,200	4 years	$1,800
Patents	2,700	10 years	270
Goodwill	14,400	10 years	1,440

The amortizations will continue to be made on future worksheets. For example, at the end of the next year (1993), the amortization entry (i) would be as follows:

Differential	4,410	
Depreciation expense	1,800	
Other operating expenses--		
patent amortization	270	
Other operating expenses--		
goodwill amortization	1,440	
Inventory		900
Accumulated depr.		3,600
Patents		540
Goodwill		2,880

The initial debit of $4,410 to differential is an aggregation of the prior period's charges to income statement accounts ($900 + 1,800 + 270 + 1,440). During subsequent years, some accountants prefer reducing the allocated amounts in entry (h) for prior period's charges. In this case, the amortization entry in future periods would reflect just that period's amortizations.

All the foregoing entries were based on the assumption that the acquisition was accounted for as a purchase. Had the pooling-of-interests method been used, however, book value rather than fair value would have been the basis for recording the accounting consolidation entries. Thus, entry (g) above would be different while entries (h) and (i) would **not** be made for a pooling. All other eliminating entries would be the same. The basic elimination entry (g) for a pooling, using the equity method of accounting for the investment, would be as follows:

Capital stock--Bass Co.	45,000	
Additional paid-in capital--Bass Co.	13,500	
Retained earnings--Bass Co.	36,900	
Investment in stock of Bass Co.		95,400

In adjusting for the minority interest in the consolidated entity's equity and earnings, the following guidelines should be observed:

1. Only the parent's share of the subsidiary's shareholders' equity is eliminated in the basic eliminating entry. The minority interest's share is presented separately.
2. The entire amount of intercompany reciprocal items is eliminated. For example, all receivables/payables and sales/cost of sales with a 90% subsidiary are eliminated.
3. For intercompany transactions in inventory and fixed assets, the possible effect on minority interest depends on whether the original transaction affected the subsidiary's income statement. Minority interest is adjusted only if the subsidiary is the selling entity. In this case, the minority interest is adjusted for its percentage ownership of the common

stock of the subsidiary. The minority interest is **not** adjusted for unrealized profits on downstream sales. The effects of downstream transactions are confined solely to the parent's (i.e., controlling) ownership interests.

The minority interest's share of the subsidiary's income is shown as a deduction on the consolidated income statement since 100% of the sub's revenues and expenses are combined, although the parent company owns less than a 100% interest. For our example, the minority interest deduction on the income statement is computed as follows:

Bass Company's reported income	$9,400
Less unrealized profit on an upstream	
inventory sale	(2,000)
Bass Company's income for consolidated	
financial purposes	$7,400
Minority interest share	x 10%
Minority interest on income statement	$ 740

The minority interest's share of the net assets of Bass Company is shown on the consolidated balance sheet between liabilities and controlling interest's equity. The computation for the minority interest shown in the balance sheet for our example is as follows:

Bass Company's capital stock, 12/31/92	$50,000	
Minority interest share	x 10%	$ 5,000
Bass Company's additional paid-in		
capital, 12/31/92	$15,000	
Minority interest share	x 10%	1,500
Bass Company's retained earnings, 1/1/92	$41,000	
Minority interest share	x 10%	4,100
Bass Company's 1992 income for		
consolidated purposes	$ 7,400	
Minority interest share	x 10%	740
Bass Company's dividends during 1992	$ 4,000	
Minority interest share	x 10%	(400)
Total minority interest, 12/31/92		$10,940

**Alto Company and Bass Company Consolidated Working Papers
Year Ended December 31, 1992**

Purchase Accounting
90% Owned Subsidiary
Subsequent Year, Partial Equity Method

	Alto Company	Bass Company	Adjustments and eliminations Debit	Adjustments and eliminations Credit	Minority interest	Consolidated balances
Income statements for year ended 12/31/92						
Sales	$750,000	$420,000	$38,000[a]			$1,132,000
Cost of sales	581,000	266,000	5,000[b] 900[i]	$38,000[a]		814,900
Gross margin	169,000	154,000				317,100
Depreciation and interest expense	28,400	16,200	1,800[i]	750[d]		45,650
Other operating expenses	117,000	128,400	1,710[i]			247,110
Net income from operations	23,600	9,400				24,340
Gain on sale of equipment	3,000		3,000[d]			
Gain on bonds				6,000[e]		6,000
Equity in subsidiary's income	8,460		8,460[f]			
Minority income ($7,400 x .10)					$ 740	(740)
Net income	$ 35,060	$ 9,400	$58,870	$44,750	$ 740	$ 29,600

	Alto Company	Bass Company	Adjustments and eliminations Debit	Credit	Minority interest	Consolidated balances
Statement of retained earnings for year ended 12/31/92						
1/1/92 retained earnings						
Alto Company	$ 48,000					$ 48,000
Bass Company		$ 41,000	$ 36,900g		$ 4,100	
Add net income (from above)	35,060	9,400	58,870	$ 44,750	740	29,600
Total	83,060	50,400			4,840	77,600
Deduct dividends	15,000	4,000		3,600f	400	15,000
Balance, 12/31/92	$ 68,060	$ 46,400	$ 95,770	$ 48,350	$ 4,440	$ 62,600
Balance sheet, 12/31/92						
Cash	$ 45,300	$ 6,400	$ 1,000[1]			$ 52,700
Accounts receivable (net)	43,700	12,100		$ 1,000[1] 4,000c		50,800
Inventories	38,300	20,750	900h	5,000b 900i		54,050
Equipment	195,000	57,000	9,000h	2,000d		259,000
Accumulated depreciation	(35,200)	(18,900)		250d 1,800h 1,800i		(57,950)
Investment in stock of Bass Company	125,460			4,860f 120,600g		
Differential			25,200g	25,200h		
Goodwill			14,400h	1,440i		12,960
Investment in bonds of Alto Company		44,000		44,000e		
Patents		9,000	2,700h	270i		11,430
	$412,560	$130,350				$382,990
Accounts payable	$ 8,900	$ 18,950	4,000c			$ 23,850
Bonds payable	100,000		50,000e			50,000
Capital stock	154,000	50,000	45,000g		$ 5,000	154,000
Additional paid-in capital	81,600	15,000	13,500g		1,500	81,600
Retained earnings (from above)	68,060	46,400	95,770	48,350	4,440	62,600
Minority interest					$10,940	10,940
	$412,560	$130,350	$261,470	$261,470		$382,990

The remainder of the consolidation process consists of the following work-sheet techniques:

1. Take all income items across horizontally and foot the adjustments, minority interest, and consolidated columns down to the net income line.

2. Take the amounts on the net income line (on income statement) in the adjustments, minority interest, and consolidated balances columns **down to** retained earnings items across the consolidated balances

column. Foot and crossfoot the retained earnings statement.

3. Take the amounts of ending retained earnings in each of the four columns down to the ending retained earnings line in the balance sheet. Foot the minority interest column and place its total in the consolidated balances column. Take all the balance sheet items across to consolidated balances column.

Other Accounting Problems in Business Combinations

Contingent consideration. If the terms of the acquisition include contingent consideration, the combination must be treated as a purchase. Pooling accounting cannot be used. The accounting for the subsequent payment of the added consideration depends upon whether the contingency was related to the earnings of the acquired entity or to the market value of the original consideration package given by the acquirer.

In the former instance (exemplified by the purchase of Gamma Corp. in the example presented earlier), a later payment of added cash, stock, or any other valuable consideration will necessitate a revaluation of the purchase price. This revaluation could alter the amounts allocable to noncurrent assets (where cost in the original purchase transaction was less than fair value acquired and the difference was offset against those assets), or could result in an increased amount of goodwill being recognized. The effects of a revaluation are handled prospectively--i.e., the additional amortization of goodwill and/or fixed assets is allocated to the remaining economic lives of those items, without adjustment of any post-acquisition periods' results already reported.

In the latter case (exemplified by the Epsilon Co. merger in the earlier illustration), the event triggering the issuance of additional shares is a decline in market value of the original purchase package. The total value of the purchase ($20,000,000 in the Epsilon case) would **not** be changed and, thus, no alteration of allocated amounts would be needed. However, the issuance of extra shares of common stock will require that the allocation between the common stock and the additional paid-in capital accounts would have to be adjusted. Had part of the original price been bonds or other debt, the reallocation could have affected the premium or discount on the debt, which would have an impact on future earnings as these accounts are subsequently amortized.

Net operating loss carryforward of acquired entity. An entity acquired in a purchase business combination may have a tax loss carryforward which is available for use by the acquiring entity. The accounting treatment differs between present GAAP (SFAS 96) and prior GAAP (APB 11 and 16). Prior GAAP and present GAAP **both** generally prohibit reflecting NOL benefit carryforwards in the balance sheet; the exceptions under prior rules were more liberal, however, because tax benefits of NOLs could be recognized if realization was assessed beyond a reasonable doubt. Currently, a **net** NOL benefit cannot be presented as an asset, although to the extent that temporary differences giving rise to tax liabilities exist, the NOL benefits can be offset--thus the benefits might be recognized, albeit indirectly. (The FASB's currently outstanding proposal to supersede SFAS 96 would reverse this position, and would **require** recognition of deferred tax assets arising from net operating loss carryforwards, although a valuation allowance would be provided if it was deemed "more likely than not" that the benefit would not be realized.)

The major change in GAAP relates to how the subsequent realization for tax purposes of a NOL benefit of an acquired entity will be reflected in the combined entity's financial statements. Previously, a reallocation of the purchase cost was necessitated by NOL realization: in effect, the otherwise unrecognized asset "NOL benefits" became recognized, with a corresponding decrease in the cost allocation to other tangible and intangible identifiable assets and goodwill. The precise procedure was to reduce goodwill first; after goodwill was reduced to zero, any further reductions were applied pro rata against other non-current assets. Since NOL benefits could have been realized piecemeal over several years, a number of restatements could have been required. For each restatement, earnings of all prior post-acquisition periods would have to be restated as well, as a consequence of the retrospective adjustment of goodwill amortization and/or fixed asset depreciation. However, apart from this aspect, the NOL realization had no income statement effect.

SFAS 96 limits the reallocation of purchase cost to goodwill and (if goodwill is entirely eliminated) other intangible assets (e.g., patents, customer lists, trademarks). Most significantly, prior periods' earnings are never restated; the effects on amortization are handled on a prospective basis only. If the NOL benefits realized are of such a magnitude to reduce the recorded amounts of goodwill and all other intangible assets to zero, any excess is credited to tax expense (**not** to extraordinary income) in the period realized. (Under the Board's proposed standard on accounting for income taxes, a subsequent realization of tax benefits not recognized previously would first reduce goodwill, if any, related to the acquisition, then reduce any other noncurrent **intangible** assets related to the acquisition, and finally reduce current period income tax expense.)

If a combining entity in a business combination accounted for as a pooling of interests later realizes a NOL benefit not previously recognized in the financial statements, the accounting is the same as that prescribed by SFAS 96 for other NOL realizations. Current tax expense is credited for the amount of NOL benefit realized; in contrast to prior GAAP, presentation as an extraordinary income item is no longer required or permitted.

Changes in majority interest. The parent's ownership interest can change as a result of purchases or sales of the subsidiary's common shares by the parent, or as a consequence of capital transactions of the subsidiary. The latter circumstance is generally handled precisely as was demonstrated in the equity method discussion in the previous chapter (see pages 256-257). Briefly, if the parent's relative book value interest in the subsidiary is changed, this is treated like gains or losses incurred in an entity's own treasury stock transactions. Gains are credited to paid-in capital; losses are charged to any previously created paid-in capital or to retained earnings. However, the SEC requires that when a subsidiary sells shares to outside interests at a price greater than the parent's carrying amount, the parent company should recognize a gain on the transaction.

When the parent's share of ownership increases through a purchase of additional stock, simply debit investment and credit cash for the cost. A problem occurs with consolidated income statements when the change in ownership takes place in mid-period. Consolidated statements should be prepared based on the ending ownership level.

Example of a Consolidation With a Change in the Majority Interest

Assume that Alto Company increased its ownership of Bass Company from 90% to 95% on October 1, 1992. The investment was acquired at book value of $5,452.50 and is determined as follows:

Retained earnings at 10/1/92		$50,000
Additional paid-in capital, 10/1/92		15,000
Retained earnings at 10/1/92		
Balance, 1/1/92	$41,000	
Net income for 9 months		
($9,400 x .75)	7,050*	
Preacquisition dividends	(4,000)	44,050
		$ 109,050
		x 5%
Book value acquired		$5,452.50

Assumes income was earned evenly over the year.

The consolidated net income should reflect a net of:

$$90\% \times \$9,400 \times 12/12 = \$8,460.00$$
$$\underline{\;5\%\;} \times \$9,400 \times \;\;3/12 = \underline{\$\;\;117.50}$$
$$95\% \qquad\qquad\qquad\qquad\qquad \$8,577.50$$

The interim stock purchase will result in a new account being shown on the consolidated income statement. The account is **Purchased preacquisition earnings**, which represents the percentage of the subsidiary's earnings earned, in this case, on the 5% stock interest from January 1, 1992 to October 1, 1992. The basic eliminating entries would be based on the 95% ownership as follows:

Equity in subsidiary's income--Alto Co.	8,577.50	
Dividends declared--Bass Co.		3,600.00
Investment in stock of Bass Co.		4,977.50
Capital stock--Bass Co.	47,500.00	
Additional paid-in capital--Bass Co.	14,250.00	
Retained earnings--Bass Co.	38,750.00**	
Purchased preacquisition earnings	352.50***	
Differential	25,200.00	
Investment in stock of Bass Co.--		
Alto Co.		126,052.50

* ** 95% x $41,000 beginning 1992 balance $38,950*
* Less preacquisition dividend of 5% x $4,000   (200)*
* Retained earnings available, as adjusted $38,750*
* *** 5% x $9,400 x 9/12 = $352.50*

Purchased preacquisition earnings is shown as a deduction, along with minority interest, to arrive at consolidated net income. Purchased preacquisition earnings are used only with interim acquisition under the purchase accounting method; all poolings are assumed to take place at the beginning of the period regardless of when, during the period, the acquisition was actually made.

Requirement that all majority-owned subsidiaries be consolidated. GAAP has long held that when one entity is owned outright or controlled by another entity (the "parent company"), the most meaningful representation of the economic substance of the parent company will be through consolidated financial statements. This presumption dates from ARB 51, which did not, however, absolutely require that consolidated financial reporting be employed. Over the years since the issuance of ARB 51, a number of popular exceptions to the general rule have arisen, which eventually resulted in a substantial diversity of reporting practices. This lack of comparability led the FASB to reconsider the value of consolidated financial reporting; the issuance of SFAS 94 was the first (and thus far, only) result of the Board's announced three-phase project on the reporting entity, consolidated financial statements, and the equity method.

Varied reasons were given previously for excluding some or all subsidiaries from the parent company's financial statements. Lack of absolute control over the affairs of the subsidiary--whether because of legal restrictions or due to the relationship with minority owners--was often cited as a valid justification for not consolidating the subsidiary entity in the parent's financial statements. In other situations, control was present but expected to be only temporary; to prepare consolidated statements in one reporting period would likely cause comparability problems in later, post-divestment periods.

More controversial than the foregoing reasons were the situations where so-called "off-balance sheet financing" was accomplished through the use of majority or wholly owned leasing, factoring, or other financing subsidiaries which were then excluded from the parent's financial statements. The actual justification given was that consolidation of such "non-homogeneous" operations would distort the parent's key financial and operating statistics, such as the working capital ratio and gross profit margin. This was cited particularly as the rationale for excluding highly leveraged financing subsidiaries.

The flaw in the above-noted argument is that the use of consolidated financial statements as the primary reporting vehicle never precluded the presentation of supplementary financial information--including separate subsidiary financial statements or **consolidating** financial statements--if deemed necessary to convey the true essence of a company's operations. Also, since comparability of financial data across entities has always been an important underlying postulate of accounting theory, the lack of a standardized approach by diversified entities was a major hindrance to financial analysis.

SFAS 94 significantly narrows--but does not totally eliminate--the ability of entities to exclude majority owned subsidiaries from parent company financial statements. Most importantly, the "non-homogeneity" argument cannot be employed any longer to exclude leasing, real estate, financing, insurance, or other subsidiary operations. Henceforth, unless one of the exceptions stated below applies, these operations must be included in consolidated financial statements.

The "consolidate everything" rule of SFAS 94 offers only the following exceptions:

- Control over the subsidiary is expected to be temporary in nature; or
- Control does not reside with the majority owner.

Absence of control is likely to occur only when a domestic subsidiary is in bankruptcy proceedings or when a foreign subsidiary operates in an environment of extreme exchange controls or restrictions on repatriation of earnings.

Separate financial statements of entities which are majority owned by other companies are still permitted. In fact, minority shareholders and other interested parties (creditors, vendors, or customers, as well as regulatory authorities) would receive little useful information from the parent company's consolidated financial statements in most instances. However, if the reporting subsidiary itself had one or more majority owned subsidiaries of its own, these would be consolidated in the financial statements of the first-tier subsidiary.

SFAS 94 does establish one somewhat unusual requirement. If subsidiaries were previously **not** consolidated, but rather were accounted for by the equity method, then the disclosure requirements stipulated by APB 18 are continued in effect **for those subsidiaries** even when subsequently fully consolidated. Thus, summary balance sheet and income statement information must be provided notwithstanding the consolidation of these entities into the parent's balance sheet and income statement. In an extreme case, extensive detail could be provided on relatively insignificant (and therefore formerly unconsolidated) subsidiaries, while more significant subsidiaries, always consolidated in prior financial statements, will not necessarily have similar disclosures.

The Board's reason for adopting the aforementioned rule was essentially to avoid "information loss" while it continues to deliberate on the general need for disaggregated financial information in consolidated financial statements. This project might ultimately mandate any of the following: full **consolidating** financial statements, APB 18-like summarized data for all subsidiaries, grouped disclosures on a line-of-business basis similar to that stipulated in SFAS 14 (no longer required for nonpublic entities, however), or some other mode of disclosure--or none at all. Until then, extended disclosures will only be necessary for previously unconsolidated entities, although similar disclosures can obviously be made on a voluntary basis for other subsidiaries as well.

Majority owned subsidiaries **not** consolidated (because one of the two available exception conditions applies) will generally be accounted for by the equity method. The Board's exposure draft preceding SFAS 94 would have proscribed the use of the equity method--i.e., would have required that the cost method of accounting for those investments be used. However, this was dropped from the final standard, leaving it dependent upon the specific circumstances to determine whether the equity method would be appropriate.

Combined Financial Statements

When a group of entities is under a common ownership, control, or management, it is often useful to present combined (or combining--showing the separate as well as the combined entities) financial statements. This is a situation where the economic substance of the nominally independent entities' operations may be more important to statement users than is the legal form of those enterprises. Combined statements may also be used to show the financial position, or operating results, of a group of companies which are each subsidiaries of a common parent, when consolidated statements are not being presented.

According to ARB 51, the process of preparing combined statements is virtually the same as consolidations employing the pooling-of-interests method. The major exception to this is that the equity section of the combined balance sheet will incorporate the paid-in capital accounts of each of the combining entities. However, only a single combined retained earnings account need be presented.

Example of a Combined Financial Statement

Adams Corporation and Benbow Company, Inc.
Combined Balance Sheet
December 31, 1992

Stockholders' equity
   Capital stock:
      Preferred, $100 par, authorized 90,000 shares,
        issued 5,000 shares $ 500,000
      Common, $50 par, authorized 100,000 shares,
        issued 60,000 shares   3,000,000
      Common, $10 par, authorized 250,000 shares,
        issued 100,000 shares   1,000,000
   Additional paid-in capital   650,000
   Retained earnings   3,825,000
                                         $8,975,000

Spin-Offs

Occasionally an entity disposes of a wholly or partially owned subsidiary or of an investee by transferring it unilaterally to the entity's shareholders. The proper accounting for such a transaction--generally known as a spin-off--depends upon the percentage of the company that is owned.

If the ownership percentage is relatively minor, say 25%, for example, the transfer to stockholders would be viewed as a "dividend in kind" and would be accounted for at the fair value of the property (i.e., shares in the investee) transferred.

However, when the entity whose shares are distributed is majority or wholly owned, the effect is not merely to transfer a passive investment, but actually to remove the operations from the former parent and to vest these with the parent's shareholders. This transaction is a true spin-off transaction and not merely a property dividend. APB 29 requires that spin-offs and other similar nonreciprocal transfers to owners be accounted for at the recorded book values of the assets and liabilities transferred.

If the operations (or subsidiary) being spun-off are distributed during a fiscal period, it may be necessary to estimate the results of operations for the elapsed period prior to spin-off in order to ascertain the net book value as of the date of the transfer. Stated another way, the operating results of the subsidiary to be disposed of should be included in the reported results of the parent through the actual date of the spin-off.

In most instances, the subsidiary being spun-off will have a positive net book value. This net worth represents the cost of the nonreciprocal transfer to the owners-- and, like a dividend, will be reflected as a charge against the parent's retained earnings at the date of spin-off. In other situations, the operations (or subsidiary) will have a net deficit (negative net book value). Since it is unacceptable to recognize a credit to the parent's retained earnings for other than a culmination of an earnings process, the spin-off should be recorded as a credit to the parent's paid-in capital. In effect, the stockholders (the recipients of the spun-off subsidiary) have made a capital contribution to the parent company by accepting the operations having a negative book value. As with other capital transactions, this would **not** be presented in the income statement, but only in the statement of changes in stockholders' equity (and in the statement of cash flows).

Push-Down Accounting

An unresolved issue in accounting for an entity which has had a substantial change in the ownership of its outstanding voting shares has been named "push-down" accounting. Push-down accounting reflects the revaluation of the assets and/or liabilities of the acquired company--**on its books**--based on the price paid for some or all of its shares by the acquirer. Push-down accounting has no impact on the presentation of consolidated financial statements or on the separate financial statements of the parent (investor) company. These financial statements are based on the price paid for the acquisition and not on the acquired entity's book value. However, the use of this accounting technique represents a departure in the way separate financial statements of the acquired entity are presented.

Advocates of push-down accounting point out that in a purchase business combination a new basis of accounting is established. They believe the new basis should be pushed down to the acquired entity and used to prepare its own separate financial statements, where these are presented.

While the push-down treatment has been used by a number of entities whose shares have been purchased by others, the entire area of push-down accounting remains controversial and without clear authoritative guidance. Although push-down makes some sense in the case where a major block of the investee's shares is acquired in a single free-market transaction, a series of step transactions would necessitate continually adjusting the investee's carrying values for assets and liabilities. Furthermore, it might not always be the case that the price paid for a fractional share of ownership of an investee could be meaningfully extrapolated to a value for the investee company as a whole.

Despite an AICPA recommendation on push-down accounting several years ago, the FASB has yet to issue a pronouncement on this topic. However, the SEC has in certain instances permitted or required push-down treatment, and the FASB's Emerging Issues Task Force has considered a number of push-down accounting issues.

Specifically, the SEC has held that where ownership of 100% of the entity has changed hands, the new cost basis to the acquirer should be reflected in the financial statements of the acquired entity. The SEC has yet to apply this standard to situations where less than a 100% change in ownership has occurred. A consensus on this issue within the profession has not been reached. However, a good case can be made that a **substantial** change in ownership provides the objective data needed to support a revaluation in the financial statements of the acquired entity. At the present time there is no requirement under GAAP to effect push-down accounting, absent SEC compliance, but push-down could be employed, if desired, where at least a controlling interest changed ownership.

Non-Sub Subsidiaries

An issue that has recently caused concern to accountants and the Securities and Exchange Commission is the sudden popularity of what have been called "non-sub subsidiaries." This situation arises when an entity plays a major role in the creation and financing of what is often a start-up or experimental operation, but does not take an equity position at the outset. For example, the parent might finance the entity by means of convertible debt or debt with warrants for the later purchase of common shares. The original equity partner in such arrangements most often will be the creative or managerial talent, which generally exchanges its talents for a stock interest. If the operation prospers, the parent will exercise its rights to a majority voting stock position; if it fails, the parent presumably avoids reflecting the losses in its statements.

While this strategy may seem to avoid the requirements of equity accounting or consolidation, the economic substance clearly suggests that the operating results of the subsidiary should be reflected in the financial statements of the real parent, even absent stock ownership. Until formal requirements are established in this area, an approach akin to the preparation of combined statements would seem to be reasonable.

Disclosures

Purchase Business Combination

A purchase business combination is deemed to occur on the date that assets (or the acquired company's stock, if an acquisition-form combination) are received and securities are issued, or cash (other assets) is paid by the acquirer. The precise determination of this date is important since the purchaser will record the acquired company's earnings from the date of acquisition, while earnings prior to that date will be excluded. This requirement is in contrast to a pooling of interest as discussed in the next section.

The following should be disclosed in the financial statements of the acquirer in the year of the purchase:

1. Name and description of acquired company
2. Acquisition was a purchase
3. Period that acquired results of operations are consolidated
4. Cost of acquired and shares issued
5. Plan of amortization and goodwill
6. Contingent payments

Furthermore, for public companies only (SFAS 79), the notes should include the pro forma results of operations of the current and **immediate prior** period as if the combination had taken place at the start of the prior period. Disclosures should include revenue, income before extraordinary items, net income, and earnings per share.

Nonpublic companies may also disclose these pro forma items, if so desired.

Pooling of Interests

Unlike a purchase, a pooling is reflected retroactively in all financial statements--i.e., it is deemed to have occurred at the date of the earliest financial information being presented. The first combined income statement should be reported as if the pooling had taken place at the beginning of the period, i.e., restate pooling to beginning of period to report a year of combined operations. The effect of intercompany transactions on current assets and liabilities, revenues, and cost of sales during the interim period prior to the combination should be eliminated; per share effects of nonrecurring transactions on long-term assets and liabilities should be disclosed (they need not be eliminated).

The balance sheet and other statements restated at the beginning of the period should be disclosed as being the retroactively combined individual company statements.

Revenue, extraordinary items, and net income of each of the combining companies for the interim period prior to the pooling should be disclosed in the notes to the financial statements.

A pooling should be reported when consummated. Statements of combining companies should be issued as the pooling is being initiated with disclosure of the pooling. An issuing corporation should record stock paid for in cash at cost, and stock acquired by issuing stock at the proportionate share of the net book value of the acquired company.

Until the pooling method is known to be appropriate, the investment and income account should reflect proportionate income of the acquired company. After pooling is consummated, statements on a pooling basis should be retroactively restated.

The notes of a combined company in the period of pooling should disclose the following:

1. Name and description of pooling companies
2. Pooling accounting was used
3. Description and number of shares issued
4. Details of operations of separate companies for period prior to pooling included in first year's operation
5. Accounting adjustments to achieve uniform accounting methods
6. Explanation of change in retained earnings caused by change in fiscal year
7. Reconciliation of individual company operating results to combined results

11 Current Liabilities and Contingencies

Perspective and Issues

The division of assets and liabilities into current and non-current allows working capital (current assets minus current liabilities) to be calculated. Working capital, which is the relatively liquid portion of total enterprise capital, can be used to determine the ability of an enterprise to repay obligations. Working capital assumes a going-concern concept. If the enterprise is to be liquidated in the near future, classification of assets and liabilities is inappropriate.

ARB 43, Chapter 3 defines current liabilities as those enterprise obligations whose liquidation is reasonably expected to require the use of existing resources properly classifiable as current assets or the creation of other current liabilities. This definition excludes from the current liability classification any currently maturing obligations which will be satisfied by using long-term assets and currently maturing obligations expected to be refinanced.

Offsetting of assets and liabilities is improper except where a right of setoff exists. A right of setoff is a debtor's legal right to discharge debt owed to another party by applying against the debt an amount the other party owes to the debtor. Per FASB Technical Bulletin 88-2 the conditions to be met are as follows:

1. Each of the two parties owes the other determinable amounts.
2. The reporting party has the right to setoff.
3. The reporting party intends to setoff.
4. The right of setoff is enforceable at law.

SFAS 5 and the issues related to the recognition of liabilities resulting from loss contingencies are also discussed in this chapter.

Sources of GAAP

ARB	*APB*	*SFAS*	*FASB I*	*FASB TB*	*EITF*
43, Ch. 3	6, 21	5, 6, 11, 29, 38, 43, 78	8, 14, 34	79-3, 88-2	86-5, 86-15

Definitions of Terms

Accumulated benefits. Employee benefits which can be carried over into the next year but which expire upon termination of employment.

Contingency. An existing condition, situation, or set of circumstances involving uncertainty as to possible gain or loss that will ultimately be resolved when one or more future events occur or fail to occur.

Current liabilities. Enterprise obligations whose liquidation is reasonably expected to require the use of existing resources properly classified as current assets or the creation of other current liabilities. Obligations that are due on demand or will be due on demand within one year or the operating cycle, if longer, are current liabilities. Long-term obligations callable because of the debtor's violation of a provision of the debt agreement are current liabilities unless specific SFAS 78 conditions are met.

FICA. Social security taxes levied upon both employees and employers.

FUTA. Social security tax levied upon employers to finance the administration of federal unemployment benefit programs.

Indirect guarantee of indebtedness of others. A guarantee under an agreement that obligates one enterprise to transfer funds to a second enterprise upon the occurrence of specified events under conditions whereby (1) the funds are legally available to the creditors of the second enterprise, and (2) those creditors may enforce the second enterprise's claims against the first enterprise.

Operating cycle. The average length of time necessary for an enterprise to convert inventory to receivables to cash.

Concepts, Rules, and Examples

ARB 43, Chapter 3 contains several examples of current liabilities. It also contains broad general descriptions of the types of items to be shown as current liabilities. These obligations can be divided into those where:

(1) both the amount and the payee are known;
(2) the payee is known but the amount may have to be estimated;
(3) the payee is unknown and the amount may have to be estimated; and
(4) the liability has been incurred due to a loss contingency.

Amount and Payee Known

Accounts payable arise primarily from the acquisition of materials and supplies to be used in the production of goods or in conjunction with the providing of services. APB 21, para 3a states that payables that arise from transactions with suppliers in the normal course of business which are due in customary trade terms not to exceed one year may be stated at their face amount rather than at the present value of the required future cash flows.

Notes payable are more formalized obligations which may arise from the acquisition of materials and supplies used in operations or from the use of short-term credit to purchase capital assets (APB 21, para 3a also applies to notes payable).

Dividends payable become a liability of the enterprise as soon as the board of directors declares a cash dividend. Since declared dividends are usually paid within a short period of time after the declaration date, they are classified as a current liability.

Unearned revenues or advances result from customer prepayments of either performance of services or delivery of the product. They may be required by the selling enterprise as a condition of the sale or may be made by the buyer as a means of guaranteeing that the seller will perform the desired service or deliver the product. Unearned revenues and advances should be classified as current liabilities at the balance sheet date if the services are to be performed or the products are to be delivered within one year or the operating cycle, whichever is longer.

Returnable deposits may be received to cover possible future damage to property. Many utility companies require security deposits. A deposit may be required for the use of a reusable container. Refundable deposits are classified as current liabilities if the firm expects to refund them during the current operating cycle or within one year, whichever is longer.

Accrued liabilities have their origin in the end of period adjustment process required by accrual accounting. Commonly accrued liabilities include wages and salaries payable, interest payable, rent payable, and taxes payable.

Agency liabilities result from the legal obligation of the enterprise to act as the collection agent for employee or customer taxes owed to various federal, state, or local government units. Examples of agency liabilities include sales taxes, income taxes withheld from employee paychecks, and employee FICA contributions. In addition to agency liabilities, an employer may have a current obligation for the FUTA (unemployment) tax. Payroll taxes are not legal liabilities until the associated payroll is actually paid.

Current maturing portion of long-term debt is shown as a current liability if the obligation is to be liquidated by using assets classified as current. However, if the currently maturing debt is to be liquidated by using other than current assets, i.e., by using a sinking fund which is properly classified as an investment, then these obligations should be classified as long-term liabilities.

Obligations that, by their terms, are due on demand (EITF 86-5) or will be due on demand within one year (or operating cycle, if longer) from the balance sheet date, even if liquidation is not expected to occur within that period, are classified as current liabilities. SFAS 78 also requires that long-term obligations which contain call provisions are to be classified as current liabilities, if as of the balance sheet date one of the following occurs:

1. The debtor is in violation of the agreement and this violation makes the obligation callable.
2. The debtor is in violation of the agreement and such violation, unless cured within the grace period specified in the agreement, makes the obligation callable.

Note, however, that if circumstances arise which effectively negate the creditor's right to call the obligation, then the obligation may be classified as long-term. Examples are:

1. If the creditor has waived the right to call the obligation caused by the debtor's violation or if the creditor has subsequently lost the right to demand repayment for more than one year (or operating cycle, if longer) from the balance sheet date.
2. For obligations containing a grace period for remedying the violation, and it is probable that the violation will be cured within the grace period. In these situations, the circumstances must be disclosed.

Short-term obligations expected to be refinanced may be classified as noncurrent liabilities if certain conditions are met. If an enterprise intends to refinance the currently maturing portion of long-term debt or intends to refinance callable obligations by replacing them with either new long-term debt or with equity securities, SFAS 6 must be followed. SFAS 6 states that an enterprise may reclassify currently maturing debt (other than obligations arising from transactions in the normal course of business that are due in customary terms) as long-term provided that the enterprise intends to refinance the obligation on a long-term basis **and** its intent is supported by **either** of the following:

1. Post-balance-sheet-date issuance of a long-term obligation or equity securities. After the date of the enterprise's balance sheet but before that balance sheet is issued, long-term obligations or equity securities have been issued for the purpose of refinancing the short-term obligations on a long-term basis.
2. Financing agreement. Before the balance sheet is issued, the enterprise has entered into a financing agreement that clearly permits the enterprise to refinance the short-term obligation on a long-term basis on terms that are readily determinable.

If reclassification of the maturing debt is based upon the existence of a refinancing agreement, then SFAS 6 requires the following:

1. The agreement will not expire within one year or operating cycle of the balance sheet date and is noncancelable.
2. The replacement debt will not be callable except for violation of a provision of the agreement with which compliance is objectively determinable or measurable.
3. The enterprise is not in violation of the terms of the agreement.
4. The lender or investor is financially capable of honoring the agreement.

Under the provisions of SFAS 6, the amount of currently maturing debt to be reclassified cannot exceed the amount raised by the actual refinancing nor can it exceed the amount specified in the refinancing agreement. If the amount specified in the refinancing agreement can fluctuate, then the maximum amount of debt that can be reclassified is equal to a reasonable estimate of the minimum amount expected to be available on any date from the maturing date of the maturing obligation to the end of the fiscal year. If no estimate can be made of the minimum amount available under the financing agreement, then none of the maturing debt can be reclassified as long-term. FASB Interpretation 8 states that if an enterprise uses current assets after the balance sheet date to liquidate a current obligation, and replaces those current assets by issuing either equity securities or long-term debt before the issuance of the balance sheet, the current obligation must still be classified as a current liability.

Increasing Rate Notes

Notes that mature in three months but can be continually extended for up to five years are known as "increasing rate notes." EITF Consensus 86-15 states that the outstanding term of the debt should be estimated after considering plans, ability, and intent to service the debt. Based upon this term, the borrower's periodic interest rate should be determined by the use of the interest method.

Debt interest costs should be amortized over the estimated outstanding term of the debt. Any excess accrued interest resulting from paying the debt before the estimated maturity date is an adjustment of interest expense. It is not an extraordinary item under SFAS 4.

The classification of the debt as to current or noncurrent should be based on the source of repayment. Thus, this classification need not be consistent with the period used to determine the periodic interest cost. For example, the time frame used for the estimated outstanding term of the debt could be a year or less but because of a planned long-term refinancing agreement, the noncurrent classification could be used.

Payee Known But Amount May Have to Be Estimated

Taxes payable include federal, state, and local income taxes. Due to frequent changes in the tax laws, the amount of income taxes payable may have to be estimated. That portion deemed currently payable must be classified as a current liability. The remaining amount is classified as a long-term liability.

Property taxes payable represent the unpaid portion of an entity's obligation to a state or other taxing authority which arises from ownership of real property. ARB 43,

Chapter 10 indicates that the most acceptable method of accounting for property taxes is a monthly accrual of property tax expense during the fiscal period of the taxing authority for which the taxes are levied. The fiscal period of the taxing authority referred to is the fiscal period which includes the assessment or lien date.

A liability for property taxes payable arises when the fiscal year of the taxing authority and the fiscal year of the entity do not coincide or when the assessment or lien date and the actual payment date do not fall within the same fiscal year. For example, XYZ Corporation is a calendar-year corporation which owns real estate in a state that operates on a June 30 fiscal year. In this state, property taxes are assessed and become a lien against property on July 1, although they are not payable until April 1 and August 1 of the next calendar year. XYZ Corporation would accrue an expense and a liability on a monthly basis beginning on July 1. At year end (December 31), the firm would have an expense for six months' property tax on their income statement and a current liability for the same amount.

Bonus payments may require estimation since the amount of the bonus payment may be affected by the amount of income taxes currently payable.

Compensated absences refer to paid vacation, paid holidays, and paid sick leave. SFAS 43 states that an employer shall accrue a liability for employee's compensation of future absences if all of the following conditions are met:

1. The employee's right to receive compensation for future absences is attributable to employee services already rendered.
2. The right vests or accumulates.
3. Payment of the compensation is probable.
4. The amount of the payment can be reasonably estimated.

If an employer is required to compensate an employee for unused vacation, holidays, or sick days even if employment is terminated, then the employee's right to this compensation is said to vest. Accrual of a liability for nonvesting rights depends on whether the unused rights expire at the end of the year in which earned or accumulate and are carried forward to succeeding years. If the rights expire, a liability for future absences should not be accrued at year end because the benefits to be paid in subsequent years would not be attributable to employee services rendered in prior years. If unused rights accumulate and increase the benefits otherwise available in subsequent years, a liability should be accrued at year end to the extent that it is probable that employees will be paid in subsequent years for the increased benefits attributable to the accumulated rights and the amount can be reasonably estimated.

SFAS 43 allows an exception to the application of this statement to employee paid sick days which accumulate but do not vest. No accrued liability is required for sick days which only accumulate. However, an accrual may be made. The Board stated that these amounts are rarely material and the low reliability of estimates of future illness coupled with the high cost of developing these estimates indicates that accrual is not necessary. The required accounting should be determined by the employer's actual administration of sick pay benefits. If the employer routinely lets employees take time off and allows that time to be charged as sick pay, then an accrual should be made.

Likewise, pay for employee leaves of absence that represent time off for past services should be considered compensation subject to accrual. Pay for employee leaves of absence that will provide future benefits and that are not attributable to past services rendered would not be subject to accrual. SFAS 43 does not provide guidance as to whether accruals should be based on current pay rates or expected future rates of pay and does not provide guidance regarding discounting of the accrual amounts.

Payee Unknown and the Amount May Have to Be Estimated

Premiums are usually offered by an enterprise to increase product sales. They may require the purchaser to return a specified number of box tops, wrappers, or other proofs of purchase. They may or may not require the payment of a cash amount. If the premium offer extends into the next accounting period, a current liability for the estimated number of redemptions expected in the future period will have to be recorded. If the premium offer extends for more than one accounting period, the estimated liability must be divided into a current portion and a long-term portion.

Product warranties providing for repair or replacement of defective products may be sold separately or may be included in the sale price of the product. If the warranty extends into the next accounting period, a current liability for the estimated amount of warranty expense expected in the next period must be recorded. If the warranty spans more than the next period, the estimated liability must be partitioned into a current and long-term portion.

Contingencies

SFAS 5 defines a contingency as an existing condition, situation, or set of circumstances involving uncertainty as to possible gain or loss. It will ultimately be resolved when one or more future events occur or fail to occur. SFAS 5 defines the different levels of probability as to whether or not future events will confirm the existence of a loss as follows:

1. **Probable**--the future event or events are likely to occur.
2. **Reasonably possible**--the chance of the future event or events occurring is more than remote but less than likely.
3. **Remote**--the chance of the future event or events occurring is slight.

Professional judgment is required to classify the likelihood of the future events occurring. All relevant information that can be acquired concerning the uncertain set of circumstances needs to be obtained and used to determine the classification.

SFAS 5 states that a loss must be accrued if **both** of the following conditions are met:

1. It is **probable** that an asset has been impaired or a liability has been incurred at the date of the financial statements.
2. The amount of loss can be reasonably estimated.

It is not necessary that a single amount be identified. A range of amounts is sufficient to indicate that some amount of loss has been incurred and should be accrued. The amount accrued is the amount within the range that appears to be the best estimate. If there is no best estimate, the minimum amount in the range should be accrued since it is probable that the loss will be at least this amount (FASB Interpretation 14, para 3). The maximum amount of loss should be disclosed. If future events indicate that the minimum loss originally accrued is inadequate, an additional loss should be accrued in the period when this fact becomes known. This accrual is a change in estimate, not a prior period adjustment.

When a loss is probable and no estimate is possible, these facts should be disclosed in the current period. The accrual of the loss should be made in the period in which the amount of the loss can be estimated. This accrual of a loss in future periods is a change in estimate. It is not a prior period adjustment.

If the occurrence of the loss is reasonably possible, the facts and circumstances of the possible loss and an estimate of the amount, if determinable, should be disclosed.

Guarantees. If the occurrence of the loss is remote, no accrual or disclosure is usually required. However, guarantees of indebtedness (direct or indirect), obligations under standby letters of credit, guarantees to repurchase, and guarantees with similar circumstances should be disclosed even if the possibility of loss is remote.

Unasserted Claims or Assessments. It is not necessary to disclose loss contingencies for an unasserted claim or assessment where there has been no manifestation of an awareness of possible claim or assessment by a potential claimant unless it is deemed probable that a claim will be asserted and a reasonable possibility of an unfavorable outcome exists. Under the provisions of SFAS 5, general or unspecified business risks are not loss contingencies and, therefore, no accrual is necessary. In addition, no disclosure is required. Appropriations of retained earnings may be used for these risks as long as no charge to income is made to establish the appropriation.

Loss Contingency. Loss contingencies are recognized only if there is an impairment of an asset or the incurrence of a liability as of the balance sheet date. Events which give rise to loss contingencies that occur after the balance sheet date (i.e., bankruptcy or expropriation) but before issuance of the financial statements may require disclosure so that statement users are not misled. Footnote disclosures or pro forma financial statements may be prepared as supplemental information to show the effect of the loss.

Gain Contingency. SFAS 5 leaves unchanged the provisions of ARB 50 which state that gain contingencies should not be recorded before they have been realized but that adequate disclosure of the gain contingency should be made. Such disclosure should not contain misleading implications as to the likelihood of realization.

Estimate vs. Contingency. Distinguishing between an estimate and a contingency can be difficult because both involve an uncertainty that will be resolved by future events. However, an estimate exists because of uncertainty about the amount of an event requiring an acknowledged accounting recognition. The event is known and the effect is known, but the amount itself is uncertain. For example, depreciation is an estimate, but not a contingency because the actual fact of physical depreciation is acknowledged, although the amount is obtained by an assumed accounting method.

In a contingency, whether there will be an impairment of an asset or the occurrence of a liability is the uncertainty that will be resolved in the future. The amount is also usually uncertain, although that is not an essential characteristic. Collectibility of receivables is a contingency because both the amount of loss and identification of which customer will not pay in the future is unknown. Similar logic would hold for obligations related to product warranties. Both the amount and the customer are currently unknown.

Other contingencies are rarely recognized until specific events confirming their existence occur. Every business risks loss by fire, explosion, government expropriation or guarantees made in the ordinary course of business. These are all contingencies because of the uncertainty surrounding whether the future event confirming the loss will or will not take place. The risk of asset expropriation exists, but is more likely in an unfriendly foreign country than in the United States.

Finally, the most difficult area of contingencies to account for arises from litigation. Accountants must rely on attorneys' assessments concerning the likelihood of such events. Unless the attorney indicates that the risk of loss is remote or slight, or that the loss if it occurs would be immaterial to the company, the accountant will add an explanatory paragraph regarding the contingency following the opinion paragraph of the audit report. In cases where judgments have been entered against the entity, or where the attorney gives a range of expected losses or other amounts, certain accruals of loss contingencies for at least the minimum point of the range must be made. In most cases, however, an estimate of the contingency is unknown and the contingency is reflected only in footnotes and, if material, in a modified auditor's report.

Disclosures

Accounts Payable

1. Classified according to type:

   a. Trade.
   b. Nontrade.
   c. Related parties (affiliates; investees for which the equity method is used; employee trusts; principal owners; management, immediate families of owners and management; or any party capable of significantly influencing a transaction).

Callable Obligations

1. Long-term callable obligations containing a violation of debt agreement.

   a. Description of covenants violated.
   b. In unclassified balance sheet, include surrounding circumstances with disclosure of long-term debt maturities.

Contingencies

1. Accruals **not** made because probable loss could not be estimated.
2. Upper limit of range of estimates for cases in which lower limit is accrued because **no** best estimate exists.
3. Nature of reasonably possible losses and one of the following:

   a. Estimated amount of loss.
   b. Statement that **no** estimate is possible.

4. Unasserted claims for which it is:

   a. Probable that a claim will be asserted, and
   b. Reasonably possible that an unfavorable outcome will result.

5. Events occurring after balance sheet date that may give rise to a loss contingency may be disclosed in either a footnote or pro forma presentation.
6. Gain contingencies described such that the likelihood of realization is not overstated.
7. Guarantees of affiliates' obligations.
8. Indirect guarantees of others' indebtedness.
9. Material commitments.
10. Renegotiation of government contracts.
11. Pending litigation.
12. Tax disputes.
13. Unused letters of credit.

Income Taxes Payable

1. Classified as to:

   a. Current.
   b. Deferred.

Notes Payable

1. Description of note.
2. Classified by type:

   a. Trade.
   b. Bank.
   c. Assets used as security.
   d. Related parties (see Accounts Payable, 1.c.).

Other Current Liabilities

1. Accruals.
2. Advances or deposits.
3. Current portions of long-term liabilities.

4. Compensated absences.
5. Liabilities not recorded because amounts could **not** be estimated.

Short-Term Debt Expected to Be Refinanced That Is Reclassified As Long-Term

1. General description of financing agreement.

    a. Terms of new obligation incurred or expected to be incurred.
    b. Terms of equity securities issued or expected to be issued.

12 Long-Term Debt

Perspective and Issues

Long-term debt represents future sacrifices of economic benefits to be repaid over a period of more than one year or, if longer, the operating cycle. Long-term debt includes bonds payable, notes payable, lease obligations, pension and deferred compensation plan obligations, deferred income taxes, and unearned revenue. The accounting for bonds and long-term notes is covered in this chapter. The other areas are treated in subsequent chapters.

The proper valuation of long-term debt is the present value of the future payments using the market rate of interest, either stated or implied in the transaction, at the date the debt was incurred. An exception to the use of present value (discounting) is the requirement in APB 10 that deferred income tax debits and credits should not be discounted. An exception to the use of the market rate of interest stated or implied in the transaction in valuing long-term notes occurs when it is necessary to use an imputed interest rate (APB 21).

An issue of continuing importance concerning long-term debt is that of "off-balance-sheet financing." This practice arises when funds borrowed to finance operations or capital projects do not appear on the firm's balance sheet. "Off-balance-sheet financing" is becoming even more significant now that the emphasis in accounting is shifting back to the balance sheet. By minimizing the amount of debt disclosed, a firm appears more secure than it really is because the debt/equity ratio becomes understated. Additionally, since inflation understates assets, firms look for ways to understate their liabilities. This understatement allows firms to obtain additional debt.

Debt may be kept off the balance sheet in a variety of ways. Separate trusts created to borrow funds are one possibility. Another is to sell receivables. The selling firm receives immediate funds and pays the buyer/lender the proceeds from the receivables as they are collected. If the receivables are sold with recourse and certain criteria are met, the transfer qualifies as a sale with the recourse provisions accounted for in accordance with SFAS 5. If the criteria are not met, the proceeds from the transfer are reported as a liability (SFAS 77). However, if the sale is without recourse, no liability need be disclosed. For a more complete discussion, see Chapter 5.

Through-put and take-or-pay contracts are ways in which natural resource firms disguise debt. In these situations, capital projects (e.g., factories, plants, pipelines, etc.) are built through joint ventures with other firms. The joint venture incurs the debt while the firm(s) purchase the goods or services provided by the project. The payment for the goods and services must be made whether delivery is taken or not and is at some fixed or minimum amount which covers the interest. SFAS 47 sets forth the disclosure requirements for these contracts. However, new variations of contracts are continually being created to avoid these requirements. This Statement deferred the measurement and recognition problems until a future date.

Sources of GAAP

APB	*SFAS*	*FASB I*	*FASB TB*	*EITF*
4, 14, 21, 26	4, 6, 15, 47, 64, 76, 84	8, 34	79-3, 79-6, 79-7, 80-1, 80-2, 81-6, 84-4	88-23, 89-9, 89-15

Definitions of Terms

Amortization. The process of allocating an amount to expense over the periods benefited.

Bond. A written agreement whereby a borrower agrees to pay a sum of money at a designated future date plus periodic interest payments at a specified rate on the face value to a lender.

Bond issue costs. Costs related to issuing a bond, i.e., legal, accounting, underwriting fees, and printing and registration costs.

Bonds outstanding method. The method of accounting for serial bonds which assumes the discount or premium applicable to each bond of the issue is the same dollar amount per bond per year.

Book value approach. The method of recording the stock issued from a bond conversion at the carrying value of the bonds converted.

Callable bond. A bond in which the issuer reserves the right to call and retire the bond prior to its maturity.

Carrying value. The face amount of a debt issue increased or decreased by the applicable unamortized premium or discount and issue costs.

Collateral. Asset(s) pledged to settle the obligation to repay a loan, if not repaid.

Convertible debt. Debt which may be converted into common stock at the holder's option after specific criteria are met.

Covenant. A clause in a debt contract written for the protection of the lender which outlines the rights and actions of the parties involved when certain conditions occur; e.g., when the debtor's current ratio declines beyond a specified level.

Debenture. Long-term debt not secured by collateral.

Defeasance. Extinguishment of debt by creating a trust to service it.

Discount. Created when a debt instrument sells for less than face value and occurs when the stated rate on the instrument is less than the market rate at the time of issue.

Effective interest method. The method of amortizing the discount or premium to interest expense so as to result in a constant rate of interest when applied to the amount of debt outstanding at the beginning of any given period.

Effective rate. See market rate.

Face value. The stated amount due on the maturity date.

Imputation. The process of interest rate approximation which is accomplished by examining the circumstances under which the note was issued.

Long-term debt. Probable future sacrifices of economic benefits arising from present obligations that are not currently payable within one year or the operating cycle of the business, whichever is longer.

Market rate. The current rate of interest available for obligations issued under the same terms and conditions.

Market value approach. The method of recording the stock issued from a bond conversion at the current market price of the bonds converted or the stock issued.

Maturity date. The date on which the face value (principal) of the bond or note becomes due.

Maturity value. See face value.

Premium. Created when a debt instrument sells for more than its face value and occurs when the stated rate on the instrument is greater than the market rate at the time of issue.

Principal. See face value.

Restrictive covenant. A provision in a debt contract which must be met by the borrower to avoid penalty. It is added for the protection of the lender.

Secured debt. Debt which has collateral to satisfy the obligation (i.e., a mortgage on specific property), if not repaid.

Serial bond. Debt whose face value matures in installments.

Stated rate. The interest rate written on the face of the debt instrument.

Straight-line method. The method of amortizing the premium or discount to interest expense such that there is an even allocation of interest expense over the life of the debt.

Take-or-pay contract. A contract in which a purchaser of goods agrees to pay specified fixed or minimum amounts periodically in return for products, even if delivery is not taken. It results from a project financing arrangement where the project produces the products.

Through-put agreement. An agreement similar to a take-or-pay contract except a service is provided by the project under the financing arrangement.

Troubled debt restructure. Occurs when the creditor, for economic or legal reasons related to the debtor's financial difficulties, grants a concession to the debtor (deferment or reduction of interest or principal) that it would not otherwise consider.

Unconditional purchase obligation. An obligation to transfer a fixed or minimum amount of funds in the future or to transfer goods or services at fixed or minimum prices.

Yield rate. See market rate.

Concepts, Rules, and Examples

Notes and Bonds

Long-term debt generally takes one of two forms: notes or bonds. Notes represent debt issued to a single investor without intending for the debt to be broken up among many investors. Their maturity, usually lasting one to seven years, tends to be shorter than that of a bond. Bonds also result from a single agreement. However, a bond is intended to be broken up into various sub-units, typically $1,000 each which can be issued to a variety of investors.

Notes and bonds share common characteristics. These include a written agreement stating the amount of the principal to be paid, the interest rate, when the interest and principal are to be paid, and the restrictive covenants, if any, which must be met.

The interest rate is affected by many factors, including the cost of money, the business risk factors, and the inflationary expectations associated with the business.

The stated rate on a note or bond often differs from the market rate at the time of issuance. When this occurs, the present value of the interest and principal payments will differ from the maturity, or face value. If the market rate exceeds the stated rate, the cash proceeds will be less than the face value of the debt because the present value of the total interest and principal payments discounted back to the present yields an amount which is less than the face value. Because an investor is rarely willing to pay more than the present value, the bonds must be issued at a discount. The discount is the difference between the issuance price (present value) and the face, or stated value of the bonds. This discount is then amortized over the life of the bonds to increase the recognized interest expense so that the total amount of the expense represents the actual bond yield.

Conversely, when the stated rate exceeds the market rate, the bond will sell for more than its face value (at a premium) to bring the effective rate to the market rate and will decrease the total interest expense. When the market and stated rates are equivalent at the time of issuance, no discount or premium exists and the instrument will sell at its face value. Changes in the market rate subsequent to issuance are irrelevant in determining the discount or premium or their amortization.

Notes are a common form of exchange in business transactions for cash, property, goods, and services. Most notes carry a stated rate of interest, but it is not uncommon for noninterest notes or notes bearing an unrealistic rate of interest to be exchanged. Notes such as these which are long-term in nature do not reflect the economic substance of the transaction, since the face value of the note does not represent the present value of the consideration involved. Not recording the note at its present value will misstate the cost of the asset or services to the buyer as well as the selling price and profit to the seller. In subsequent periods, both the interest expense and revenue will be misstated.

To remedy the situation APB 21 was released. **All** commitments to pay (and receive) money at a determinable future date are subject to present value techniques and, if necessary, interest imputation with the exception of the following:

1. Normal accounts payable due within one year.
2. Amounts to be applied to purchase price of goods or services or that provide security to an agreement (e.g., advances, progress payments, security deposits, and retainages).
3. Transactions between parent and subsidiary.
4. Convertible debt securities.
5. Obligations payable at some indeterminable future date (warranties).
6. Lending and depositor savings activities of financial institutions whose primary business is lending money.
7. Transactions where interest rates are affected by prescriptions of a governmental agency (e.g., revenue bonds, tax exempt obligations, etc.).

Three categories of commitments subject to APB 21 are important.

Notes issued solely for cash. When a note is issued solely for cash, its present value is assumed to be equal to the cash proceeds. The interest rate is that rate which equates the cash proceeds to the amounts to be paid in the future; i.e., **no** interest rate is to be imputed. For example, a $1,000 note due in three years which sells for $889 has an implicit rate of 4% ($1,000 x .889, where .889 is the present value factor of a lump sum at 4% for three years). This is the rate to be used when amortizing the discount.

Notes issued for cash and a right or privilege. Often when a note bearing an unrealistic rate of interest is issued in exchange for cash, an additional right or privilege is granted, such as the issuer agreeing to sell merchandise to the purchaser at a reduced rate. The difference between the present value of the receivable and the cash loaned is regarded as an addition to the cost of the products purchased for the purchaser/lender and as unearned revenue to the issuer. This treatment stems from the APB's attempt to match revenue and expense in the proper periods and to differentiate between those factors that affect income from operations and income or expense from nonoperating sources. In the situation above, the discount (difference between the cash loaned and the present value of the note) will be amortized to interest revenue or expense, while the unearned revenue or contractual right is amortized to sales and inventory, respectively. The discount affects income from nonoperational sources, while the unearned revenue or contractual right affects the gross profit computation. This differentiation is necessary because the amortization rates used differ for the two amounts.

Example of Accounting for a Note Issued for Both Cash and a Contractual Right

1. Miller borrows $10,000 via a noninterest bearing 3-year note from Krueger.

2. Miller agrees to sell $50,000 of merchandise to Krueger at less than the ordinary retail price for the duration of the note.
3. The fair rate of interest on a note such as this is 10%.

According to APB 21, para 7, the difference between the present value of the note and the face value of the loan is to be regarded as part of the cost of the products purchased under the agreement. The present value factor for an amount due in 3 years at 10% is .75132. Therefore, the present value of the note is $7,513 ($10,000 x .75132). The $2,487 ($10,000 - 7,513) difference between the face value and the present value is to be recorded as a discount on the note payable and as unearned revenue on the future purchases. The following entries would be made to record the transaction:

	Miller			*Krueger*	
Cash	10,000		Note receivable	10,000	
Discount on note payable	2,487		Contract right with supplier	2,487	
Note payable		10,000	Cash		10,000
Unearned revenue		2,487	Discount on note receivable		2,487

The discount on note payable (and note receivable) is to be amortized using the effective interest method, while the unearned revenue account and contract right with supplier account are amortized on a pro rata basis as the right to purchase merchandise is used up. Thus, if Krueger purchased $20,000 of merchandise from Miller in the first year, the following entries would be necessary:

	Miller			*Krueger*	
Unearned revenue	995		Inventory (or cost of sales)	995	
[$2,487 x (20,000/50,000)]			Contract right with supplier		995
Sales		995			
Interest expense	751		Discount on note receivable	751	
Discount on note payable		751	Interest revenue		751
($7,513 x 10%)					

The amortization of unearned revenue and contract right with supplier accounts will fluctuate with the amount of purchases made. If there is a balance remaining in the account at the end of the loan term, it is amortized to the appropriate account in that final year.

Noncash transactions. When a note is issued for consideration such as property, goods, or services, and the transaction is entered into at arm's length, the stated interest rate is presumed to be fair unless: (a) no interest rate is stated; (b) the stated rate is unreasonable; or (c) the face value of the debt is materially different from the consideration involved or the current market value of the note at the date of the transaction. According to APB 21, when the situation arises where the rate on the note is **not** considered fair, the note is to be recorded at the "fair market value of the property, goods, or services received or at an amount that reasonably approximates the market value of the note, whichever is the more clearly determinable." When this amount differs from the face value of the note, the difference is to be recorded as a discount or premium and amortized to interest expense.

Example of Accounting for a Note Exchanged for Property

1. A sells B a machine which has a fair market value of $7,510.
2. A receives a three-year noninterest-bearing note having a face value of $10,000.

In this situation, the fair market value of the consideration is readily determinable and, thus, represents the amount at which the note is to be recorded. The following entry is necessary:

Machine	7,510	
Discount on notes payable	2,490	
Notes payable		10,000

The discount will be amortized to interest expense over the three-year period using the interest rate **implied** in the transaction.

If the fair market value of the consideration or note is not determinable, then the present value of the note must be determined using an **imputed** interest rate. This rate will then be used to establish the present value of the note by discounting all future payments on the note at this rate. General guidelines for imputing the interest rate, which are provided by APB 21, paras 13 and 14, include the prevailing rates of similar instruments from creditors with similar credit ratings and the rate the debtor could obtain for similar financing from other sources. Other determining factors include any collateral or restrictive covenants involved, the current and expected prime rate, and other terms pertaining to the instrument. The objective is to approximate the rate of interest which would have resulted if an independent borrower and lender had negotiated a similar transaction under comparable terms and conditions. This determination is as of the issuance date, and any subsequent changes in interest rates would be irrelevant.

Bonds represent a promise to pay a sum of money at a designated maturity date plus periodic interest payments at a specified rate on the face value. Bonds are primarily used to borrow funds from the general public or institutional investors when a contract for a single amount (a note) is too large for any one lender to supply. Dividing up the amount needed into $1,000 or $10,000 units makes it easier to sell the bonds.

In most situations, a bond is issued at a price other than its face value. The amount of the cash exchanged is equal to the total of the present value of the interest and principal payments. The difference between the cash proceeds and the face value is recorded as a premium if the cash proceeds are greater or a discount if they are less than the face value. The journal entry to record a bond issued at a premium follows:

Cash	(proceeds)	
Premium on bonds payable		(difference)
Bonds payable		(face value)

The premium will be recognized over the life of the bond issue. If issued at a discount, "Discount on bonds payable" would be debited for the difference. As the premium is amortized, it will reduce interest expense on the books of the issuer (a discount will increase interest expense). The premium (discount) would be added to (deducted from) the related liability when a balance sheet is prepared.

The **effective interest method** is the preferred method of accounting for a discount or premium arising from a note or bond, although some other method may be used (e.g., straight-line) if the results are not materially different. While APB 21 only mandated that the effective interest method be used on notes covered by that Opinion, the profession, through the evolution of practice, has made the use of the effective interest method the only acceptable one. Under the effective interest method, the discount or premium is to be amortized over the life of the debt in such a way as to result in a constant rate of interest when applied to the amount outstanding at the beginning of any given period. Therefore, interest expense is equal to the market rate of interest at the time of issuance multiplied by this beginning figure. The difference between the interest expense and the cash paid represents the amortization of the discount or premium.

Interest expense under the **straight-line method** is equal to the cash interest paid plus the amortized portion of the discount or minus the amortized portion of the premium. The amortized portion is equal to the total amount of the discount or premium divided by the life of the debt from issuance in months multiplied by the number of months the debt has been outstanding that year.

Amortization tables are often created at the time of the bond's issuance to provide figures when recording the necessary entries relating to the debt issue. They also provide a check of accuracy since the final values in the unamortized discount or premium and carrying value columns should be equal to zero and the bond's face value, respectively.

Example of Applying the Effective Interest Method

1. A three-year, 12%, $10,000 bond is issued at 1/1/X1, with interest payments semiannually.
2. The market rate is 10%.

The amortization table would appear as follows:

Date	Credit cash	Debit int. exp.	Debit prem.	Unam. prem. bal.	Carrying value
1/1/X1				$507.61	$10,507.61[a]
7/1/X1	$ 600.00[b]	$ 525.38[c]	$ 74.62[d]	432.99[e]	10,432.99[f]
1/1/X2	600.00	521.65	78.35	354.64	10,354.64
7/1/X2	600.00	517.73	82.27	272.37	10,272.37
1/1/X3	600.00	513.62	86.38	185.99	10,185.99
7/1/X3	600.00	509.30	90.70	95.29	10,095.29
1/1/X4	600.00	504.71[g]	95.29	--	10,000.00
	$3,600.00	$3,092.39	$507.61		

[a]PV of principal and interest payments
$10,000(.74622) = $ 7,462.20
$ 600(5.07569) = 3,045.41
$10,507.61

[b]$10,000.00 x .06

[c]$10,507.61 x .05
[d]$600.00 - 525.38
[e]$507.61 - 74.62
[f]$10,507.61 - 74.62 (or $10,000 + 432.99)
[g]Rounding error = $.05

When the interest date does not coincide with the year end, an adjusting entry must be made. The proportional share of interest payable should be recognized along with the amortization of the discount or premium. **Within** the amortization period, the discount or premium should be amortized using the straight-line method.

If the bonds are issued between interest dates, discount or premium amortization must be computed for the period between the sale date and the next interest date. This is accomplished by "straight-lining" the period's amount calculated using the usual method of amortization. In addition, the purchaser prepays the seller the amount of interest that has accrued since the last interest date. This interest is recorded as a payable by the seller. At the next interest date, the buyer then receives the full amount of interest regardless of how long the bond has been held. This procedure results in interest being paid equivalent to the time the bond has been outstanding.

Costs may be incurred in connection with issuing bonds. Examples include legal, accounting, and underwriting fees; commissions; and engraving, printing, and registration costs. Although these costs should be classified as a deferred charge and amortized using the effective interest method, generally the amount involved is such that use of the simpler straight-line method would not result in a material difference. However, the FASB's position as stated in SFAC 6, para 237 is that the costs should be treated as either an expense in the period incurred or a reduction in the related amount of debt, in much the same manner as a discount. These costs do not provide any future economic benefit and, therefore, should not be considered an asset. Since these costs reduce the amount of cash proceeds, they in effect increase the effective interest rate and probably should be accounted for the same as an unamortized discount. However, because the SFACs do not constitute GAAP, bond issue costs are to be treated as deferred charges.

Short-term obligations which are expected to be refinanced and therefore classified as long-term debt per SFAS 6 are discussed in Chapter 11.

The diagram on the following page illustrates the accounting treatments for monetary assets (and liabilities) as prescribed by APB 21.

Lump-sum Payments in Union Contracts

EITF 88-23 relates solely to union contracts and not to individual employment contracts. In negotiating union contracts, lump-sum cash payments made to employees in lieu of all or a portion of a base-wage rate increase may be deferred and amortized. The Task Force's consensus requires that: (1) there is no evidence that the payment is related to past services, (2) the payment will benefit a future period in the form of a lower base-wage rate, and (3) the amortization period not extend beyond the contract period. Facts surrounding the contract and negotiations must be reviewed to determine how to account for the payment.

Extinguishment of Debt

Management may reacquire or retire outstanding debt before its scheduled maturity. This decision is usually caused by changes in present or expected interest rates or in cash flows. APB 26 was issued to provide guidance in accounting for the **early** extinguishment of debt. Subsequently, SFAS 76 has amended APB 26 to make it applicable to **all** debt extinguishments other than those currently exempted, such as debt conversions and troubled debt restructurings. According to SFAS 76, para 3, debt is now considered extinguished in the following circumstances:

1. The debtor has paid the creditor and is relieved of all obligations, regardless of whether the securities are canceled or held as so-called treasury bonds.
2. The debtor is legally released from being the primary obligor, either judicially or by the creditor, and it is probable (likely) no further payments will be required.
3. The debtor places cash or other essentially risk-free monetary assets (government or government guaranteed securities) in a trust used **solely** for satisfying both the scheduled interest payments and principal of a specific obligation that was incurred in a past time period, with the possibility of the debtor making future payments being remote (per FASB TB 84-4, the debtor is only allowed to assess the remoteness of cash flows and related risks for areas not specifically covered in SFAS 76). Note that in this situation (known as defeasance) the debt is considered extinguished even though the debtor is not legally released from being the primary obligor of the debt.

ACCOUNTING FOR MONETARY ASSETS AND LIABILITIES

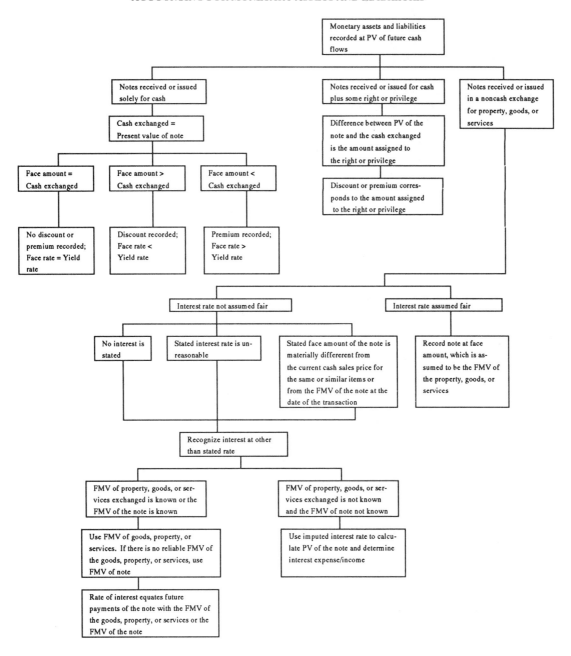

Gain or Loss. According to APB 26, para 20, the difference between the net carrying value and the acquisition price is to be recorded as a gain or loss. If the acquisition price is greater than the carrying value a loss exists. A gain is generated if the acquisition price is less than the carrying value. These gains or losses are to be recognized in the period in which the retirement took place.

The unamortized premium or discount and issue costs should be amortized to the acquisition date and recorded **prior** to the determination of the gain or loss. If the extinguishment of debt does not occur on the interest date, the interest payable accruing between the last interest date and the acquisition date must also be recorded.

Except for any gains and losses resulting from satisfying sinking fund requirements within one year of the date of the extinguishment (SFAS 64), all gains and losses from extinguishment, if material in amount, receive extraordinary item treatment (SFAS 4, para 8). (See Disclosures.)

Example of Accounting for the Extinguishment of Debt

1. A 10%, 10-year, $200,000 bond is dated and issued on 1/1/X1 at 98, with the interest payable semiannually.
2. Associated bond issue costs of $14,000 are incurred.
3. Four years later, on 1/1/X5, the entire bond issue is repurchased at $102 per $100 face value and is retired.
4. The straight-line method of amortization is used since the result is not materially different from that when the effective interest method is used.

The gain or loss on the repurchase is computed as follows:

Reacquisition price [(102/100) x $200,000]		$204,000
Net carrying amount:		
Face value	$200,000	
Unamortized discount [2% x 200,000 x (6/10)]	(2,400)	
Unamortized issue costs [14,000 x (6/10)]	(8,400)	189,200
Loss on bond repurchase		$ 14,800

The loss on bond repurchase (debt extinguishment) is treated as an extraordinary item.

Defeasance. No controversy exists in practice regarding the extinguishment of debt through actual retirement. However, debt extinguishment discussed in SFAS 76, para 3c has caused some controversy. Defeasance is the retirement of debt in substance, but not in form. The principles of defeasance are:

1. Government securities are purchased which have an interest rate, face value, and maturity date that are nearly identical to the debt being retired.
2. Both the newly purchased government securities and the old bond issue being retired are placed in an irrevocable trust. The sole purpose of the trust is to satisfy the obligations (principal and interest) of the bond issue. Note that if the debt was incurred and the assets were acquired in relatively close proximity, FASB TB 84-4 requires the transaction to be accounted for as a borrow-and-in-

vest activity and extinguishment of debt through in-substance defeasance is **not** considered to have taken place.

Once the securities are placed in the trust, the debt is considered to be extinguished. Since no financial risk is associated with the government securities, the ability of the trust assets to meet the obligations of the trust (the bond issue) is not in doubt and there is no claim on the remaining corporate assets. One exception is the fees associated with the operations of the trust. Unless specifically stated and provided for in the creation of the trust, these fees must be paid by the entity and accrued for on a regular basis.

The controversy arises because of the potential for income manipulation due to any gain that may be recognized on the extinguishment. The argument against defeasance is that it is improper to currently recognize a gain (loss) on retirement when the gain should be realized over the remaining life of the bond issue. This controversy is illustrated below:

Example Comparing the Defeasance and Retirement of a Bond Issue

1. On 1/1/X1 a 9%, 20-year, $1,000 bond was issued at par.
2. On 1/1/X5 the bond is trading at $800 due to an increase in interest rates and a deteriorating financial position.
3. On 1/1/X5 a treasury bond with the same terms as the entity's bond can be purchased for $850. The greater price is due to the decreased risk associated with U.S. Government instruments.

The following entries are required:

Defeasance		*Retirement (repurchase)*	
To purchase the bonds:			
U.S. treasury bond	850	Bonds payable	1,000
Cash	850	Cash	800
		Extraordinary gain	
		on extinguishment	200

To set up irrevocable trust:

Bonds payable	1,000	
U.S. treasury bond		850
Extrarodinary gain on		
extinguishment		150

Notice the difference in the amount of the gain under each alternative. Actual retirement provides a $200 gain, while defeasance results in a $150 gain. Two other differences also exist, however: (1) the gain on extinguishment from the retirement of the bonds is currently taxable, whereas the gain on the extinguishment arising from defeasance is not currently taxable but represents a temporary difference, and (2) it is highly unlikely that all bond holders would be willing to voluntarily submit their bonds for repurchase at such a loss. Thus, the gain obtained through retirement may not be realistic. The gain recorded through defeasance is assured.

The Board's justification for defeasance is based on the definition of liabilities found in SFAC 6, para 35: "probable future sacrifices of economic benefits arising from present obligations of a particular entity to transfer assets or provide services to other entities in the future as a result of past transactions or events." Because a debtor places essentially risk-free assets into an irrevocable trust used solely to repay the debt and because the possibility for future payments on the debt to be extinguished is remote, a transaction has been entered into which effectively satisfies the debtor's obligation. Such an arrangement ensures no "probable future sacrifices" and the liability should be removed from the debtor's balance sheet. The debt has been provided for by the trust and, in substance, the debt can be considered retired since the required payments are covered.

Offsetting the trust asset with the debt is not applicable in this situation. Offsetting is a matter of display--a presentation of existing assets and liabilities. Since the debt is considered extinguished and ceases to exist per SFAS 76, presentation is not an issue.

Critics of defeasance feel that this treatment is unsound. Gain or loss recognition should not be applicable to situations where the debtor is not legally released from being the primary obligor under the debt obligation (SFAS 76, para 3c). Recognizing these gains is merely window-dressing.

The critics point out that a liability remains until it is satisfied by a future transaction or event. The creation of a trust, even for the sole purpose of repaying the debt, does not constitute the disposition of the trust assets or the satisfaction of the liability. It simply ensures the debt will be repaid by matching up the cash flows. The assets continue to be probable future economic benefits of the debtor until the debt is actually paid. They have not yet been used to eliminate, extinguish, or satisfy the obligation. Concurrently, the liability will continue to exist until satisfied by payment or by agreement with the creditor.

However, GAAP currently allows in-substance defeasance as provided by SFAS 76. The requirements state that both the debt issue and similar risk-free instruments which will have the same cash flow as the debt issue be placed in an irrevocable trust. As a result of this action, the debt is considered extinguished and both the assets and debt are removed from the financial statements.

Debt callable by the debtor can be extinguished by in substance defeasance. FASB TB 84-4 specifies that the intent of the debtor must be known and the assets in trust must be structured to meet the cash flow requirements. If debt securities previously recognized as extinguished are acquired, the transaction is considered an investment in the future cash flows to be distributed by the trust as originally scheduled and should be reported as an asset.

Troubled Debt Restructurings

Troubled debt restructurings are defined by SFAS 15, para 2 as situations where the creditor, for economic or legal reasons related to the debtor's financial difficulties, grants the debtor a concession that would not otherwise be granted. However, in any of the following four situations, a concession granted by the creditor does not automatically qualify as a restructuring:

1. The fair value of the assets or equity interest accepted by a creditor from a debtor in full satisfaction of its receivable is at least equal to the creditor's recorded investment in the receivable.
2. The fair value of the assets or equity interest transferred by a debtor to a creditor in full settlement of its payable is at least equal to the carrying value of the payable.
3. The creditor reduces the effective interest rate to reflect a decrease in current interest rates or a decrease in the risk, in order to maintain the relationship.
4. The debtor, in exchange for old debt, issues new debt with an interest rate that reflects current market rates.

A troubled debt restructuring can occur one of two ways. The first is a settlement of the debt at less than the carrying amount. The second is a continuation of the debt with a modification of terms (i.e., a reduction in the interest rate, face amount, accrued interest owed, or an extension of the payment date for interest or face amount). Accounting for such restructurings is prescribed for both debtors and creditors. FASB TB 80-2 points out that the debtor and creditor must individually apply SFAS 15 to the specific situation since the tests are not necessarily symmetrical and it is possible for one or the other, but not both, to have a troubled debt restructuring.

Debtors. If the debt is settled by the exchange of assets, an extraordinary gain is recognized in the period of transfer for the difference between the carrying amount of the debt (defined as the face amount of the debt increased or decreased by applicable accrued interest and applicable unamortized premium, discount, or issue costs) and the consideration given to extinguish the debt. A two-step process is used: (1) a revaluation of the noncash asset to FMV with an associated recognition of an ordinary gain or loss and (2) a determination of the extraordinary restructuring gain. EITF consensus 89-15, however, concluded that an exchange of existing debt for new debt with the same creditor and with a higher interest rate (but with the new rate less than the market rate for a company with a similar credit rating) does not result in a recognized gain or loss. In this circumstance, the terms of the exchange are not representative of and are less favorable to the creditor than prevailing terms for new borrowings by companies with similar credit ratings. The result is a concession by the creditor and should be accounted for by both parties as a modification of existing obligation under SFAS 15. If stock is issued to settle the liability, the stock is recorded at its FMV (SFAS 15, paras 13 through 21).

If the debt is continued with a modification of terms, it is necessary to compare the total future cash flows of the restructured debt (both principal and stated interest) with the pre-restructured carrying value. If the total amount of future cash flows is greater than the carrying value, no adjustment is made to the carrying value of the debt. However, a new, lower effective interest rate must be computed. This rate makes the present value of the total future cash flows equal to the present carrying value of debt and is used to determine interest expense in future periods. The Statement specifies that the effective interest method must be used to compute the expense. If the total future cash flows of the restructured debt are less than the present carrying value, the current debt should be reduced to the amount of the future cash flows and an extraordinary gain should be recognized. No interest expense would be recognized in subsequent periods, since only the principal is being repaid (paras 16-18 and 21).

If the restructuring consists of part settlement and part modification of payments, the part settlement is accounted for first and then the modification of payments (para 19).

FASB TB 81-6 notes that SFAS 15 generally does not apply to debtors in bankruptcy. There is an exception in the case of a restructuring that doesn't result in a general restatement of the debtor's liabilities in bankruptcy proceedings.

Creditors. Accounting by creditors is similar to that by debtors. However, the loss to the creditor is ordinary, whereas the gain to the debtor is extraordinary.

1. Assets received in full settlement are recorded at FMV.

    a. Excess of receivable over asset FMV is an ordinary loss.
    b. Account for the assets as if purchased for cash.

    EITF consensus 89-9 concluded that collateral received in an in-substance foreclosure should be recorded at fair value, which establishes a new basis, similar to the accounting for a legal foreclosure. The collateral should not be accounted for as a valuation allowance and unrealized increases in the fair value subsequent to the in-substance foreclosure should not be recognized.

2. Modification of payments results in either a reduction of future interest revenue or recognition of a loss and no future interest revenue. The effective interest method **must** be used in determining any interest revenue.

    a. If total future interest and principal payments are greater than book value of the receivable, determine the new effective interest rate.
    b. If total future interest and principal receipts are less than book value of the receivable, then write receivable down to total cash to be received and recognize no interest revenue in the future. Note that this procedure is in contrast to the general doctrine of recognizing losses when they are evident. The prescribed procedure defers the loss (by not recognizing interest revenue in the future). FASB TB 79-7 requires that if future cash receipts exceed the recorded receivable, the excess is recognized as interest income over the remaining term of the loan. The amount of the previous direct write-down should **not** be reversed.
    c. FASB TB 79-6 requires an assessment of the collectibility of a receivable with modified terms in order to determine the need for subsequent valuation allowances. SFAS 5 applies.

3. Part settlement and part modification of payments restructurings are accounted for as follows:

a. First, as to the settlement portion.
b. Second, as to the modification of terms.

The following examples illustrate the accounting for troubled debt restructurings.

Example of Settlement of Debt

Assume the debtor company transfers land having a book value of $70,000 and a FMV of $80,000 in full settlement of its note payable. The note has a remaining life of five years, a principal balance of $90,000, and related accrued interest of $10,000. The following entries are required to record the settlement:

Debtor			*Creditor*		
Land	10,000		Land	80,000	
Gain on transfer			Loss on settlement	20,000	
of assets		10,000	Note receivable		90,000
			Interest receivable		10,000
Note payable	90,000				
Interest payable	10,000				
Land		80,000			
Extraordinary gain on					
settlement of debt		20,000			

Example of Restructuring With Gain/Loss Recognized

Assume the interest rate on the above note is 5%. The interest rate is reduced to 4%, the principal is reduced to $72,500, and the accrued interest at date of restructure is forgiven.

Future cash flows (after restructuring):	
Principal	$ 72,500
Interest (5 years x $72,500 x 4%)	14,500
Total cash to be received	$ 87,000
Amount prior to restructure	
($90,000 principal + $10,000 accrued interest)	(100,000)
Gain/loss to be recognized	
Debtor gain (extraordinary)	
Creditor loss (ordinary)	$ 13,000

The following entries need to be recorded to reflect the terms of the agreement:

Debtor			*Creditor*		

Beginning of Year 1:

Interest payable	10,000		Loss on restructure		
Note payable	3,000		of debt	13,000	
Extraordinary gain on			Loan receivable		3,000
restructure of debt		13,000	Interest receivable		10,000

End of Years 1-5:

Note payable	2,900		Cash	2,900	
Cash		2,900	Note receivable		2,900

(Note: $14,500 ÷ 5 yrs. = $2,900; No interest expense or revenue is recorded in this case)

End of Year 5:

Note payable	72,500		Cash	72,500	
Cash		72,500	Note receivable		72,500

Example of Restructuring With No Gain/Loss Recognized

Assume the $100,000 owed is reduced to a principal balance of $95,000. The interest rate of 5% is reduced to 4%.

Future cash flows (after restructuring):	
Principal	$ 95,000
Interest (5 years x $95,000 x 4%)	19,000
Total cash to be received	$ 114,000

Amount prior to restructure	
($90,000 principal + $10,000 accrued interest)	(100,000)
Interest expense/revenue over 5 years	$ 14,000

In this example, a new effective interest rate must be computed such that the present value of the future payments equals $100,000. A trial and error approach is used to calculate the effective interest rate that discounts the $95,000 principal and the $3,800 annual interest payments to $100,000, the amount owed prior to restructuring.

Trial and Error Calculation:

	(n = 5, i = 2.5%)	(n = 5, i = 3%)
PV of ordinary annuity	4.64583	4.57971
PV of 1	.88385	.86261

2.5%: (.88385 x $95,000) + (4.64583 x $3,800) = $101,620
3%: (.86261 x $95,000) + (4.57971 x $3,800) = $ 99,351

Interpolation:

$$\left[\frac{101,620 \ - \ 100,000}{101,620 \ - \ 99,351}\right] \ \times \ (3\% - 2.5\%) = \ .357$$

New effective rate = 2.5% + .357% = <u>2.857%</u>

Interest Amortization Schedule:

Year	Cash	Interest at Effective Rate	Reduction in Carrying Value	Carrying Amount
				$100,000
1	$ 3,800(a)	$2,857(b)	$ 943(c)	99,057
2	3,800	2,830	970	98,087
3	3,800	2,802	998	97,089
4	3,800	2,774	1,026	96,063
5	<u>3,800</u>	2,745	1,055	95,000*
	$19,000			

*Rounded
(a) $3,800 = $95,000 x .04
(b) $2,857 = $100,000 x 2.857%
(c) $943 = $3,800 - $2,857

The following entries are made to recognize the cash payments in the subsequent periods:

Debtor			Creditor		
End of Year 1:			**End of Year 1:**		
Note payable					
($3,800 - 2,857)	943		Cash	3,800	
Interest expense					
($100,000 x .02857)	2,857		Note receivable		943
Cash		3,800	Interest revenue		2,857
End of Year 5:			**End of Year 5:**		
Note payable	95,000		Cash	95,000	
Cash		95,000	Note receivable		95,000

According to SFAS 15, a troubled debt restructuring which involves only a modification of terms is to be accounted for prospectively. The result of this treatment is to effect no change in the carrying value of the liability **unless** the carrying amount exceeds the total future cash payments specified by the new agreement.

When the total future cash payments **may** exceed the carrying amount of the liability, no gain or loss is recognized on the books of the debtor. Rather, a new effective interest rate shall be determined which is to be the rate that equates the present value of the future cash payments with the carrying amount of the liability. Interest expense and principal reduction are then recognized as the future cash payments are made.

If the total cash payments are less than the carrying amount of the liability, the carrying amount of the liability shall be written down to the total future cash payments and the amount of the write-down is to be recognized by the debtor as a gain. This gain is to be aggregated with other gains from restructuring, and the entire amount, if material, should be reported as an extraordinary item in accordance with SFAS 4. The liability shall be reduced as the payments are made and **no** interest expense shall be recognized on the liability for any period between the restructuring and the maturity of the liability (SFAS 15, para 17). An exception exists for contingent liabilities. They generally are not included in the carrying value of the original debt. Thus, for each period that a contingent liability is both probable and reasonably estimable, interest expense shall be recognized. However, to the extent that the contingent payments were included in the total future cash payments, the payment or accrual of these contingencies should be deducted from the restructured liability.

Convertible Debt

Bonds are frequently issued with the right to convert them into common stock of the company at the holder's option when certain terms and conditions are met (i.e., a target market price is reached). Convertible debt is used for two reasons. First, when a specific amount of funds is needed, convertible debt often allows a lesser number of shares to be issued (assuming conversion) than if the funds were raised by directly issuing the shares. Thus, less dilution occurs. Second, the conversion feature allows debt to be issued at a lower interest rate and with fewer restrictive covenants than if the debt were issued without it.

This dual nature of debt and equity, however, creates a question as to whether the equity element should receive separate recognition. Support for separate treatment is based on the assumption that this equity element has economic value. Since the convertible feature tends to lower the rate of interest, a portion of the proceeds should be allocated to this equity feature. However, APB 14, para 7 argues that the debt and equity elements are inseparable. The instrument is either all debt or all equity.

Features of convertible debt typically include: (1) a conversion price 15-20% greater than the market value of the stock when the debt is issued; (2) conversion features (price and number of shares) which protect against dilution from stock dividends, splits, etc.; and (3) a callable feature at the issuer's option that is usually exercised once the conversion price is reached (thus forcing conversion or redemption).

Convertible debt also has its disadvantages. If the stock price increases significantly after the debt is issued, the issuer would have been better off by simply issuing the stock. Additionally, if the price of the stock does not reach the conversion price, the debt will never be converted (a condition known as overhanging debt).

When convertible debt is issued, no value is apportioned to the conversion feature when recording the issue (APB 14, para 12). The debt is treated as nonconvertible debt. Upon conversion, the stock may be valued at either the market value or book value of the bonds.

The **market value approach** assumes the new stock issued is valued at its cost; i.e., the market price of the stock issued or the market price of the bonds converted, whichever is more easily determinable. A gain (loss) occurs when the market value of the stocks or bonds is less (greater) than the carrying value of the bond.

Example of the Market Value Method

Assume that a $1,000 bond with an unamortized discount of $50 and a market value of $970 is converted into ten shares of $10 par common stock whose market value is $97 per share. The entry to record the conversion is:

Bonds payable	1,000	
Loss on redemption (ordinary)	20	
Discount on bonds payable		50
Common stock		100
Additional paid-in capital		870

Since conversion is initiated by the bondholder and not the firm, the loss does not qualify as an extinguishment and is therefore considered ordinary.

The fact that a gain or loss may be incurred as a result of an equity transaction is the weakness of this method. Only the existing shareholders are affected, as their equity will increase or decrease, but the firm as a whole is unaffected. For this reason, the market value approach is not widely used.

If the **book value approach** is used, the new stock is valued at the carrying value of the converted bonds. This method is widely used since no gain or loss is recognized upon conversion, and the conversion represents the transformation of contingent shareholders into shareholders. It does not represent the culmination of an earnings cycle. The primary weakness of this method is that the total value attributed to the equity security by the investors is not given accounting recognition.

Example of Book Value Method

Assume the same data as the example above. Conversion using the book value method is recorded as follows:

Bonds payable	1,000	
Discount on bonds payable		50
Common stock		100
Additional paid-in capital		850

When convertible debt is retired, the transaction is handled in the same manner as nonconvertible debt: the difference between the acquisition price and the carrying value of the bond is reported currently as a gain or loss. If material, the gain or loss is considered extraordinary.

Induced Conversion of Debt

A special situation exists in which the conversion privileges of convertible debt are modified **after** issuance. These modifications may take the form of reduced conversion prices or additional consideration paid to the convertible debt holder. The debtor offers these modifications or "sweeteners" to induce prompt conversion of the outstanding debt.

SFAS 84 specifies the accounting method used in these situations. The statement only applies when the convertible debt is converted to equity securities. Upon conversion, the debtor must recognize an expense for the **excess** of the fair value of all the securities and other consideration given over the fair value of the securities specified in the original conversion terms. The reported expense shall not be classified as an extraordinary item.

The example below illustrates the calculation and recording of the debt conversion expense.

Example of Debt Conversion Expense

1. January 1, 19X5, XYZ Company issued ten 8% convertible bonds at $1,000 par value without a discount or premium maturing December 31, 20X5.
2. The bonds are initially convertible into common stock of XYZ at a conversion price of $25.
3. On July 1, 19X9, the convertible bonds have a market value of $600 each.
4. To induce the convertible bondholders to quickly convert their bonds, XYZ reduces the conversion price to $20 for bondholders who convert before July 21, 19X9 (within 20 days).
5. The market price of XYZ Company's common stock on the date of conversion is $15 per share.

The fair value of the incremental consideration paid by XYZ upon conversion is calculated as follows for each bond converted before July 21, 19X9:

* Value of securities issued to debt holders:

Face amount	$1,000	per bond
÷ New conversion price	÷ $20	per share
Number of common shares issued upon conversion	50	shares
x Price per common share	x $15	per share
Value of securities issued	$ 750	

**Value of securities issuable pursuant to the original conversion privileges:

Face amount	$1,000	per bond
÷ Original conversion price	÷ $25	per share
Number of common shares issuable pursuant to original conversion privilege	40	shares
x Price per share	x $15	per share
Value of securities issuable pursuant to original conversion privileges	$ 600	
Value of securities issued*	$ 750	
Value of securities issuable pursuant to the original conversion privileges**	600	
Fair value of incremental consideration	$ 150	

The entry to record the debt conversion for each bond is as follows:

Convertible debt	1,000	
Debt conversion expense	150	
Common stock		1,150

Debt Issued with Stock Warrants

Warrants are certificates enabling the holder to purchase a stated number of shares of stock at a certain price within a certain time period. They are often issued with bonds to enhance the marketability of the bonds and to lower the bond's interest rate.

When bonds with **detachable** warrants are issued, the purchase price must be allocated between the debt and the stock warrants based on relative market values (APB 14, para 16). Since two separate instruments are involved, a market value can usually be determined for each. However, if one value cannot be determined, the market value of the other should be deducted from the total value to determine the unknown value.

Example of Accounting for a Bond with a Detachable Warrant

1. A $1,000 bond with a detachable warrant to buy ten shares of $10 par common stock at $50 per share is issued for $1,025.
2. Immediately after the issuance the bonds trade at $980 and the warrants at $60.
3. The market value of the stock is $54.

The relative market value of the bonds is 94% (980/1,040) and the warrant is 6% (60/1,040). Thus, $62 (6% x $1,025) of the issuance price is assigned to the warrants. The journal entry to record the issuance is:

Cash	1,025	
Discount on bonds payable	37	
Bonds payable		1,000
Paid-in capital--warrants		
(or "Stock options outstanding")		62

The discount is the difference between the purchase price assigned to the bond, $963 (94% x $1,025), and its face value, $1,000. The debt itself is accounted for in the normal fashion.

The entry to record the subsequent future exercise of the warrant would be:

Cash	500	
Paid-in capital--warrants	62	
Common stock		100
Paid-in capital		462 (difference)

Assuming the warrants are not exercised, the journal entry is:

Paid-in capital--warrants	62	
Paid-in capital--expired warrants		62

Disclosures

Notes and Bonds

1. The aggregate amount of debt shown as a long-term liability on the face of the financial statements net of the current portion due within one year and any discount or premium.
2. The detail relating to each debt issue in the notes to the financial statements, including:

    a. Nature of the liabilities.
    b. Maturity dates.
    c. Interest rates (effective and stated).
    d. Call provisions.
    e. Conversion privileges.
    f. Restrictive covenants (i.e., sinking fund requirements, restrictions on retained earnings, etc.).
    g. Assets pledged as collateral. These assets are shown in the asset section of the balance sheet.
    h. Amounts due to related parties including officers, directors, and employees, and terms of settlement (SFAS 57, para 2).
    i. Disclosure of notes or bonds issued subsequent to the balance sheet date.
    j. Amounts of unused letters of credit.

3. The current portion of the long-term debt is shown as a current liability unless other than current assets will be used to satisfy the obligation.
4. Long-term debt is classified as current if the debtor is in violation of a debt covenant at the balance sheet date which:

    a. Makes the obligation callable within one year, or
    b. Will make the obligation callable within one year if the violation is not cured within a specified grace period.

5. The debt referred to in 4 above need not be reclassified if either of the following conditions are met:

    a. The creditor has waived or has subsequently lost the right to demand repayment for one year (or, if longer, the operating cycle) from the balance sheet date.
    b. It is probable (likely) that the violation will be cured by the debtor within the grace period stated in the terms of the debt agreement, thus preventing the obligation from being called.

Induced Conversions of Convertible Debt

1. Nature of any restatement and its effect on income before extraordinary items, net income, and related per share amounts in year SFAS 84 first applied.

Extinguishment of Debt

1. Gains or losses resulting from the extinguishment of debt are to be aggregated and unconditionally classified as extraordinary items and the following information provided either on the face of the financial statements or in the notes:

    a. A description of the extinguishment transaction, including the sources of the funds used, if practicable.
    b. The income tax effect of the transaction.
    c. The per share amount of the aggregate gain or loss, net of tax (unlike other extraordinary items whose per share effect is optional per APB 15, this disclosure is mandatory).

2. Defeasance of debt requires footnote disclosure as long as that debt remains outstanding. Disclose the nature of the transaction and the amount of debt held in trust and treated as extinguished.

Troubled Debt Restructurings

1. Debtor

    a. A description of the changes in terms and/or major features of settlement.
    b. The aggregate gain on restructuring and the related tax effect.
    c. The aggregate net gain or loss on the transfer of assets recognized during the period.
    d. The per share amount of the aggregate gain on restructuring, net of tax.
    e. Information on any contingent payments.

2. Creditor

    a. For the outstanding restructured receivables:

        1) The aggregate recorded investment.
        2) The gross interest revenue that would have been recorded had there been no restructurings.
        3) The amount of interest income that was recorded on those receivables during the period.

    b. The amount of commitments to lend additional funds to debtors owing receivables whose terms have been modified by restructurings.

Unconditional Purchase Obligations (Discussed in Chapter 6)

In order to qualify as such an obligation and to be subject to disclosure, the contract must meet the following criteria:

1. It is noncancelable, or cancelable only:
    a. Upon the occurrence of some remote contingency.
    b. With the permission of the other party.
    c. If a replacement agreement is signed between the same parties.
    d. Upon payment of a penalty in an amount such that continuation of the agreement appears reasonably assured.

2. It is negotiated as part of a supplier's product financing arrangement for the facilities that will provide the contracted goods or services or for costs related to those goods or services (for example, carrying costs for contracted goods).
3. It has a remaining term in excess of one year.

If the obligation fulfills the foregoing criteria and is recorded on the balance sheet, the following disclosures are required:

1. Aggregate amount of payments to be made.
2. Aggregate amount of maturities and sinking fund requirements for all long-term borrowings.

If the obligation is **not** recorded on the balance sheet, then the following footnote disclosures are required:

1. The nature and term of the obligation(s).
2. The total amount of the fixed or determinable portion of the obligation(s) at the balance sheet date in the aggregate and for each of the next five years, if determinable.
3. The nature of any variable components of the obligation(s).
4. The amounts purchased under the obligation(s) (as in take-or-pay or through-put contracts) for each period for which an income statement is presented.

13 Accounting for Leases

Perspective and Issues

Lease transactions have grown in popularity over the years as businesses look for new ways to finance their fixed asset additions. A lease agreement involves at least two parties, a lessor and a lessee, and an asset which is to be leased. The lessor, who owns the asset, agrees to allow the lessee to use it for a specified period of time in return for periodic rent payments.

There are many economic reasons why the lease transaction is considered. They are as follows:

1. The lessee (borrower) is able to obtain 100% financing
2. Flexibility of use for the tax benefits
3. The lessor receives the equivalent of interest as well as an asset with some remaining value at the end of the lease term

The lease transaction derives its accounting complexity from the number of alternatives available to the parties involved. Leases can be structured to allow manipulation of the tax benefits associated with the leased asset. They can be used to transfer ownership of the leased asset, and they can be used to transfer the risk of ownership. In any event, the substance of the transaction dictates the accounting treatment. The lease transaction is probably the best example of the accounting profession's substance over form argument. If the transaction effectively transfers ownership to the lessee, then the substance of the transaction is that of a sale and should be recognized as such even though the transaction takes the form of a lease.

SFAS 13 is the promulgated GAAP for lease accounting. Numerous pronouncements have followed which expand upon the base set by SFAS 13. As a result of the extensive additions to the principles related to lease accounting, the FASB issued a codified restatement of SFAS 13 in May 1980. This document reflected all pronouncements issued through that date. We have used the codified restatement as the basis for our discussion. Therefore, we generally do not cite the actual pronouncements. Rather, our citations refer to the codified restatement. The reason for our using the codified restatement is that the FASB is currently rewriting this restatement to both update it and put it in a more understandable form. Thus, the codified restatement of SFAS 13 will eventually be the only source of GAAP.

Sources of GAAP

SFAS	*FASB I*	*FASB TB*
13, 22, 23, 27,	19, 21, 23,	79-10, 79-12, 79-13,
28, 29, 91, 98	24, 26, 27	79-14, 79-15, 79-16,
		79-17, 79-18, 85-3,
		86-2, 88-1

Definitions of Terms

Bargain purchase option. A provision allowing the lessee the option of purchasing the leased property for an amount which is sufficiently lower than the expected fair value of the property at the date the option becomes exercisable. Exercise of the option must appear reasonably assured at the inception of the lease.

Bargain renewal option. A provision allowing the lessee the option to renew the lease agreement for a rental payment sufficiently lower than the expected fair rental of the property at the date the option becomes exercisable. Exercise of the option must appear reasonably assured at the inception of the lease.

Contingent rentals. Rentals that represent the increases or decreases in lease payments which result from changes in the factors on which the lease payments are based occurring subsequent to the inception of the lease. However, changes due to the passthrough of increases in the construction or acquisition cost of the leased property or for increases in some measure of cost during the construction or preconstruction period should be excluded from contingent rentals. Also, provisions that are dependent only upon the passage of time should be excluded from contingent rentals. A lease payment that is based upon an existing index or rate, such as the consumer price index or the prime rate, is a contingent payment, and the computation of the minimum lease payments should be based upon the index or rate applicable at the inception of the lease.

Estimated economic life of leased property. The estimated remaining time which the property is expected to be economically usable by one or more users, with normal maintenance and repairs, for its intended purpose at the inception of the lease. This estimated time period should not be limited by the lease term.

Estimated residual value of leased property. The estimated fair value of the leased property at the end of the lease term.

Executory costs. Those costs such as insurance, maintenance, and taxes incurred for leased property, whether paid by the lessor or lessee. Amounts paid by a lessee in consideration for a guarantee from an unrelated third party of the residual value are also executory costs. If executory costs are paid by the lessor, any lessor's profit on those costs is considered the same as executory costs.

Fair value of leased property. The property's selling price in an arm's-length transaction between unrelated parties.

When the lessor is a **manufacturer or dealer**, the fair value of the property at the inception of the lease will ordinarily be its normal selling price net of volume or trade discounts. In some cases, due to market conditions, fair value may be less than the normal selling price or even the cost of the property.

When the lessor is **not a manufacturer or dealer**, the fair value of the property at the inception of the lease will ordinarily be its costs net of volume or trade discounts. However, if a significant amount of time has lapsed between the acquisition of the property by the lessor and the inception of the lease, fair value should be determined in light of market conditions prevailing at the inception of the lease. Thus, fair value may be greater or less than the cost or carrying amount of the property.

Implicit interest rate. The discount rate that, when applied to the minimum lease payments, excluding that portion of the payments representing executory costs to be paid by the lessor, together with any profit thereon, and the unguaranteed residual value accruing to the benefit of the lessor, causes the aggregate present value at the beginning of the lease term to be equal to the fair value of the leased property to the lessor at the inception of the lease, minus any investment tax credit retained and expected to be realized by the lessor (and plus initial direct costs in the case of direct financing leases).

Inception of the lease. The date of the written lease agreement or commitment (if earlier) wherein all principal provisions are fixed and no principal provisions remain to be negotiated.

Incremental borrowing rate. The rate that, at the inception of the lease, the lessee would have incurred to borrow over a similar term (i.e., a loan term equal to the lease term) the funds necessary to purchase the leased asset.

Initial direct costs.* Only those costs incurred by the lessor that are (a) costs to originate a lease incurred in transactions with independent third parties that (i) result directly from and are essential to acquire that lease and (ii) would not have been

---

* *Initial direct cost shall be offset by nonrefundable fees that are yield adjustments as prescribed in SFAS 91, Accounting for Nonrefundable Fees and Costs Associated with Originating or Acquiring Loans and Initial Direct Costs of Leases.*

incurred had that leasing transaction not occurred and (b) certain costs directly related to specified activities performed by the lessor for that lease. Those activities are: evaluating the prospective lessee's financial condition; evaluating and recording guarantees, collateral, and other security arrangements; negotiating lease terms; preparing and processing lease documents; and closing the transaction. The costs directly related to those activities shall include only that portion of the employees' total compensation and payroll-related fringe benefits directly related to time spent performing those activities for that lease and other costs related to those activities that would not have been incurred but for that lease. Initial direct costs shall not include costs related to activities performed by the lessor for advertising, soliciting potential lessees, servicing existing leases, and other ancillary activities related to establishing and monitoring credit policies, supervision, and administration. Initial direct costs shall not include administrative costs, rent, depreciation, any other occupancy and equipment costs and employees' compensation and fringe benefits related to activities described in the previous sentence, unsuccessful origination efforts, and idle time.

Lease. An agreement conveying the right to use property, plant, or equipment (land or depreciable assets or both) usually for a stated period of time.

Lease term. The fixed noncancelable term of the lease plus the following:

1. Periods covered by bargain renewal options
2. Periods for which failure to renew the lease imposes a penalty on the lessee in an amount such that renewal appears, at the inception of the lease, to be reasonably assured
3. Periods covered by ordinary renewal options during which a guarantee by the lessee of the lessor's debt directly or indirectly related to the leased property is expected to be in effect or a loan from the lessee to the lessor directly or indirectly related to the leased property is expected to be outstanding
4. Periods covered by ordinary renewal options preceding the date that a bargain purchase option is exercisable
5. Periods representing renewals or extensions of the lease at the lessor's option

However, the lease term shall not extend beyond the date a bargain purchase option becomes exercisable.

Minimum lease payments

For the **lessee**: The payments that the lessee is or can be required to make in connection with the leased property. Contingent rental guarantees by the lessee of the lessor's debt, and the lessee's obligation to pay executory costs are excluded from minimum lease payments. If the lease contains a bargain purchase option, only the minimum rental payments over the lease term and the payment called for in the bargain purchase option are included in minimum lease payments. Otherwise, minimum lease payments include the following:

1. The **minimum rental payments** called for by the lease over the lease term

2. Any **guarantee of residual value** at the expiration of the lease term made by the lessee (or any party related to the lessee), whether or not the guarantee payment constitutes a purchase of the leased property. When the lessor has the right to require the lessee to purchase the property at termination of the lease for a certain or determinable amount, that amount shall be considered a lessee guarantee. When the lessee agrees to make up any deficiency below a stated amount in the lessor's realization of the residual value, the guarantee to be included in the MLP is the stated amount rather than an estimate of the deficiency to be made up.

3. Any payment that the lessee must or can be required to make upon **failure to renew or extend** the lease at the expiration of the lease term, whether or not the payment would constitute a purchase of the leased property.

For the **lessor**: The payments described above plus any guarantee of the residual value or of the rental payments beyond the lease term by a third party unrelated to either the lessee or lessor (provided the third party is financially capable of discharging the guaranteed obligation).

Noncancelable in this context is a lease which is cancelable only upon one of the following conditions:

1. The occurrence of some remote contingency
2. The permission of the lessor
3. The lessee enters into a new lease with the same lessor
4. Payment by the lessee of a penalty in an amount such that continuation of the lease appears, at inception, reasonably assured

Nonrecourse financing. Lending or borrowing activities in which the creditor does not have general recourse to the debtor but rather has recourse only to the property used for collateral in the transaction or other specific property.

Penalty. Any requirement that is imposed or can be imposed on the lessee by the lease agreement or by factors outside the lease agreement to pay cash, incur or assume a liability, perform services, surrender or transfer an asset or rights to an asset or otherwise forego an economic benefit, or suffer an economic detriment.

Related and unrelated parties in leasing transactions.

Related parties. Entities that are in a relationship where one party has the ability to exercise significant influence over the operating and financial policies of the related party. Examples include the following:

1. A parent company and its subsidiaries
2. An owner company and its joint ventures and partnerships
3. An investor and its investees

The ability to exercise significant influence must be present before the parties can be considered related. Significant influence may also be exercised through guarantees of indebtedness, extensions of credit, or through ownership of debt obligations, warrants, or other securities. If two or more entities are subject to the significant influence of a parent, owner, investor, or common officers or directors, then those entities are considered related to each other.

Renewal or extension of a lease. The continuation of a lease agreement beyond the original lease term, including a new lease where the lessee continues to use the same property.

Sale-leaseback accounting. A method of accounting for a sale-leaseback transaction in which the seller-lessee records the sale, removes all property and related liabilities from its balance sheet, recognizes gain or loss from the sale, and classifies the leaseback in accordance with this section.

Sales recognition. Any method that is described in Section R10 in the current text of the accounting standard as a method to record a transaction involving real estate, other than the deposit method, or the methods to record transactions accounted for as financing, leasing, or profit-sharing arrangements. Profit recognition methods described in Section R10 commonly used to record transactions involving real estate include, but are not limited to, the full accrual method, the installment method, the cost recovery method, and the reduced profit method.

Unrelated parties. All parties that are not related parties as defined above.

Unguaranteed residual value. The estimated residual value of the leased property exclusive of any portion guaranteed by the lessee, by any party related to the lessee, or any party unrelated to the lessee. If the guarantor is related to the lessor, the residual value shall be considered as unguaranteed.

Concepts, Rules, and Examples

Classification of Leases--Lessee

For accounting and reporting purposes the lessee has two alternatives in classifying a lease:

1. Operating
2. Capital

The proper classification of a lease is determined by the circumstances surrounding the transaction. According to SFAS 13, if substantially all of the benefits and risks of ownership have been transferred to the lessee, the lease should be recorded as a capital lease. Substantially all of the risks or benefits of ownership are deemed to have been transferred if **any one** of the following criteria has been met:

1. The lease transfers ownership to the lessee by the end of the lease term
2. The lease contains a bargain purchase option
3. The lease term is equal to 75% or more of the estimated economic life of the leased property, and the beginning of the lease term does not fall within the last 25% of the total economic life of the leased property
4. The present value (PV) of the minimum lease payments at the beginning of the

lease term is 90% or more of the fair market value to the lessor less any investment credit retained by the lessor. This requirement cannot be used if the lease's inception is in the last 25% of the useful economic life of the leased asset. The interest rate, used to compute the PV, should be the incremental borrowing rate of the lessee unless the implicit rate is available and lower.

If a lease agreement meets none of the four criteria set forth above, it is to be classified as an operating lease on the books of a lessee.

Classification of Leases--Lessor

The four alternatives a lessor has in classifying a lease are as follows:

1. Operating
2. Sales-type
3. Direct financing
4. Leveraged

The conditions surrounding the origination of the lease determine its classification on the books of the lessor. If the lease meets **any one** of the four criteria specified below and **both** of the qualifications set forth below, the lease is classified as either a sales-type lease, direct financing lease, or leveraged lease depending upon the conditions present at the inception of the lease.

Criteria:

The same four criteria used above to differentiate a capital lease and an operating lease on the books of the lessee. However, it should be noted that per SFAS 98, para 22c, a lease involving real estate must transfer title (i.e., criteria 1 above) by the end of the lease term for the lessor to classify the lease as a sales-type lease of real estate.

Qualifications:

1. Collectibility of the minimum lease payments is reasonably predictable
2. No important uncertainties surround the amount of unreimbursable costs yet to be incurred by the lessor under the lease

If a lease transaction does not meet the criteria for classification as a sales-type lease, a direct financing lease, or a leveraged lease as specified above, it is to be classified on the books of the lessor as an operating lease. This classification process must take place prior to considering the proper accounting treatment.

Distinction Between Sales-Type, Direct Financing, and Leveraged Leases

A lease is classified as a sales-type lease when the criteria set forth above have been met and the lease transaction is structured in such a way that the lessor (generally a manufacturer or dealer) recognizes a profit or loss on the transaction in addition to interest revenue. In order for this to occur, the fair value of the property must be different from the cost (carrying value). The essential substance of this transaction is that of a sale, and thus its name. Common examples of sales-type leases: (1) when an automobile dealership opts to lease a car to its customers in lieu of making an actual sale, and (2) the re-lease of equipment coming off of an expiring lease.

A direct financing lease differs from a sales-type lease in that the lessor does not realize a profit or loss on the transaction other than interest revenue. In a direct financing lease, the fair value of the property at the inception of the lease is equal to the cost (carrying value). This type of lease transaction most often involves entities engaged in financing operations. The lessor (a bank, or other financial institution) purchases the asset and then leases the asset to the lessee. This transaction merely replaces the conventional lending transaction where the borrower uses the borrowed funds to purchase the asset. There are many economic reasons why the lease transaction is considered. They are as follows:

1. The lessee (borrower) is able to obtain 100% financing
2. Flexibility of use for the tax benefits
3. The lessor receives the equivalent of interest as well as an asset with some remaining value at the end of the lease term

In summary it may help to visualize the following chart when considering the classification of a lease:

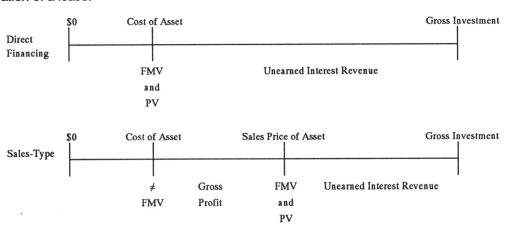

One form of a direct financing lease is a leveraged lease. This type is mentioned separately both here and in the following section on how to account for leases because it is to receive a different accounting treatment by a lessor. A leveraged lease meets all the definitional criteria of a direct financing lease, but differs because it involves at least three parties: a lessee, a long-term creditor, and a lessor (commonly referred to as the equity participant). Other characteristics of a leveraged lease are as follows:

1. The financing provided by the long-term creditor must be without recourse as to the general credit of the lessor, although the creditor may hold recourse with respect to the leased property. The amount of the financing must provide the lessor with substantial "leverage" in the transaction.
2. The lessor's net investment declines during the early years and rises during the later years of the lease term before its elimination (SFAS 13, para 42).

Accounting for Leases--Lessee

As discussed in the preceding section, there are two classifications that apply to a lease transaction on the books of the lessee. They are as follows:

1. Operating
2. Capital

Operating Leases

The accounting treatment accorded an operating lease is relatively simple; the rental payment shall be charged to expense as the payments are made or become payable. This assumes that the lease payments are being made on a straight-line basis (i.e., an equal payment per period over the lease term). If the lease agreement calls for either an alternative payment schedule or a scheduled rent increase over the lease term, the lease expense should still be recognized on a straight-line basis unless another systematic and rational basis is a better representation of the actual physical usage of the leased property. In such an instance it will be necessary to create either a prepaid asset or a liability depending upon the structure of the payment schedule. Additionally, if the lease agreement provides for a scheduled increase(s) in contemplation of the lessee's increased physical use of the leased property, the total amount of rental payments, including the scheduled increase(s) shall be charged to expense over the lease term on a straight-line basis (TB 85-3). However, if the scheduled increase(s) is due to additional leased property, recognition should be proportional to the leased property with the increased rents recognized over the years that the lessee has control over the use of the additional leased property (TB 88-1).

Notice that in the case of an operating lease there is no balance sheet recognition of the leased asset because the substance of the lease is merely that of a rental. There is no reason to expect that the lessee will derive any future economic benefit from the leased asset beyond the lease term.

Capital Leases

Recall that the classification of a lease must be determined prior to the consideration of the accounting treatment. Therefore, it is necessary to first examine the lease transaction against the four criteria (transfer of title, bargain purchase option, 75% of useful life, or 90% of net FMV). Assuming that the lease agreement satisfies one of these, it must be accounted for as a capital lease.

According to SFAS 13, para 10, the lessee shall record a capital lease as an asset and an obligation (liability) at an amount equal to the present value of the minimum lease payments at the beginning of the lease term. The asset should be recorded at the lower of the present value of the minimum lease payments or the fair market value of the asset. When the fair value of the leased asset is less than the present value of the minimum lease payments, the interest rate used to amortize the lease obligation will differ from the interest rate used in the 90% test as determined by the lessor. The interest rate used in the amortization will be the same as that used in the 90% test when the fair market value is greater than or equal to the present value of the minimum lease payments. For purposes of this computation, the minimum lease payments are considered to be the payments that the lessee is obligated to make or can be required to make excluding executory costs such as insurance, maintenance, and taxes. The minimum lease payments generally include the minimum rental payments, any guarantee of the residual value made by the lessee, and the penalty for failure to renew the lease, if applicable. If the lease includes a bargain purchase option (BPO), the amount required to be paid under the BPO is also included in the minimum lease payments. The present value shall be computed using the incremental borrowing rate of the lessee **unless** it is practicable for the lessee to determine the implicit rate computed by the lessor, **and** the implicit rate is less than the incremental borrowing rate. The lease term used in this present value computation is the fixed, noncancelable term of the lease plus the following:

1. All periods covered by bargain renewal options
2. All periods for which failure to renew imposes a penalty on the lessee
3. All periods covered by ordinary renewal options during which the lessee guarantees the lessor's debt on the leased property
4. All periods covered by ordinary renewals or extension up to the date a BPO is exercisable
5. All periods representing renewals or extensions of the lease at the lessor's option

Remember, if the amount computed as the present value of the minimum lease payments exceeds the fair value of the leased property at the inception of the lease, the amount recorded should be that of the fair value.

The amortization of the leased asset will depend upon how the lease qualified as a capital lease. If the lease transaction met the criteria as either transferring ownership, or containing a bargain purchase option, then the asset arising from the transaction is to be amortized over the estimated useful life of the leased property. If the transaction qualifies as a capital lease because it met either the 75% of useful life or 90% of FMV criteria, the asset must be amortized over the lease term. The conceptual rationale for this differentiated treatment arises because of the substance of the transaction. Under the first two criteria, the asset actually becomes the property of the lessee at the end of the lease term (or upon exercise of the BPO). In the latter situations, the title to the property remains with the lessor.

The leased asset is to be amortized (depreciated) over the lease term if title does not transfer to the lessee, while the asset is depreciated in a manner consistent with the lessee's normal depreciation policy if the title is to eventually transfer to the lessee. This latter situation can be interpreted to mean that the asset is depreciated over the useful economic life of the leased asset. The treatment and method used to amortize (depreciate) the leased asset is very similar to that used for any other asset. The amortization entry requires a debit to the lease expense and a credit to an accumulated amortization account. The leased asset shall not be amortized below the estimated residual value.

In some instances when the property is to revert back to the lessor, there may be a guaranteed residual value. This is an amount which the lessee guarantees to the lessor. If the FMV of the asset at the end of the lease term is greater than or equal to the guaranteed residual amount, the lessee incurs no additional obligation. On the other hand, if the FMV of the leased asset is less than the guaranteed residual value, then the lessee must make up the difference, usually with a cash payment. The guaranteed residual value is often used as a tool to reduce the periodic payments by substituting the lump-sum amount at the end of the term which results from the guarantee. In any event the amortization must still take place based on the **estimated** residual value. This results in a rational and systematic allocation of the expense through the periods and avoids a large loss (or expense) in the last period as a result of the guarantee.

The annual (periodic) rent payments made during the lease term are to be allocated between a reduction in the obligation and interest expense in a manner such that the interest expense represents a constant periodic rate of interest on the remaining balance of the lease obligation. This is commonly referred to as the effective interest method and was described in APB 21.

The following examples illustrate the treatment described in the foregoing paragraphs:

Example of Accounting for a Capital Lease--Asset Returned to Lessor

Assume the following:

1. The lease is initiated on 1/1/X1 for equipment with an expected useful life of three years. The equipment reverts back to the lessor upon expiration of the lease agreement.
2. The FMV of the equipment is $135,000.
3. Three payments are due to the lessor in the amount of $50,000 per year beginning 12/31/X1. An additional sum of $1,000 is to be paid annually by the lessee for insurance.
4. Lessee **guarantees** a $10,000 residual value on 12/31/X3 to the lessor.
5. Irrespective of the $10,000 residual value guarantee, the leased asset is expected to have only a $1,000 salvage value on 12/31/X3.

6. The lessee's incremental borrowing rate is 10%. (Lessor's implicit rate is unknown.)
7. The present value of the lease obligation is as follows:

PV of guaranteed residual value = $10,000 x .7513* = $ 7,513
PV of annual payments   = $50,000 x 2.4869** = 124,345
                                                            $131,858

    The first step in dealing with any lease transaction is to classify the lease. In this case, the lease term is for three years which is equal to 100% of the expected useful life of the asset. Notice that the 90% test is also fulfilled as the PV of the minimum lease payments ($131,858) is greater than 90% of the FMV ($121,500). Thus, the lease is accounted for as a capital lease.

    In number 7 (above) the present value of the lease obligation is computed. Note that the executory costs (insurance) are not included in the minimum lease payments and that the incremental borrowing rate of the lessee was used to determine the present value. This rate was used because the implicit rate was not determinable. (Note: In order to have used the implicit rate it would have to have been less than the incremental borrowing rate.) The entry necessary to record the lease on 1/1/X1 is:

Leased equipment   131,858
    Lease obligation   131,858

Note that the lease is recorded at the present value of the minimum lease payments which, in this case, is less than the FMV. If the present value of the minimum lease payments had exceeded the FMV, the lease would be recorded at FMV.

    The next step is to determine the proper allocation between interest and a reduction in the lease obligation for each lease payment. This is done using the effective interest method as illustrated below:

Year	Cash payment	Interest expense	Reduction in lease obligation	Balance of lease obligation
Inception of lease				$131,858
1	$50,000	$13,186	$36,814	95,044
2	50,000	9,504	40,496	54,548
3	50,000	5,452	44,548	10,000

The interest is calculated at 10% (the incremental borrowing rate) of the balance of the lease obligation for each period, and the remainder of the $50,000 payment is allocated to a reduction in the lease obligation. The lessee is also required to pay $1,000 for insurance on an annual basis. The entries necessary to record all payments relative to the lease for each of the three years are shown below:

---

*The present value of an amount of $1 due in three periods at 10% is .7513.
**The present value of an ordinary annuity of $1 for three periods at 10% is 2.4869.

	12/31/X1	12/31/X2	12/31/X3
Insurance expense	1,000	1,000	1,000
Interest expense	13,186	9,504	5,452
Lease obligation	36,814	40,496	44,548
Cash	51,000	51,000	51,000

The lease equipment recorded as an asset must also be amortized (depreciated). The balance of this account is $131,858; however, as with any other asset it cannot be depreciated below the estimated residual value of $1,000 (note that it is depreciated down to the actual estimated residual value, **not** the guaranteed residual value). In this case, the straight-line depreciation method is applied over a period of 3 years. This 3-year period represents the lease term, **not** the life of the asset, because the asset reverts back to the lessor at the end of the lease term. Therefore, the following entry will be made at the end of each year:

Depreciation expense	43,619	
Accumulated depreciation		43,619 [($131,858 - 1,000) ÷ 3]

Finally, on 12/31/X3 we must recognize the fact that ownership of the property has reverted back to the owner (lessor). The lessee made a guarantee that the residual value would be $10,000 on 12/31/X3; as a result, the lessee must make up the difference between the guaranteed residual value and the actual residual value with a cash payment to the lessor. The following entry illustrates the removal of the leased asset and obligation from the books of the lessee:

Lease obligation	10,000	
Accumulated depreciation	130,858	
Cash		9,000
Leased equipment		131,858

The foregoing example illustrated a situation where the asset was to be returned to the lessor. Another situation exists (under BPO or transfer of title) where the asset is expected to remain with the lessee. Remember that leased assets are amortized over their useful life when title transfers or a bargain purchase option exists. At the end of the lease, the balance of the lease obligation should equal the guaranteed residual value, the bargain purchase option price, or a termination penalty.

Example of Accounting for a Capital Lease--Asset Ownership Transferred to Lessee

Assume the following:

1. A three-year lease is initiated on 1/1/X1 for equipment with an expected useful life of five years.

2. Three annual lease payments of $50,000 are required beginning on 1/1/X1 (note that the payment at the beginning of the year changes the PV computation).
3. The lessee can exercise a bargain purchase option on 12/31/X3 for $10,000. The expected residual value at 12/31/X5 is $1,000.
4. The lessee's incremental borrowing rate is 10% (lessor's implicit rate is unknown).
5. The fair market value of the property leased is $140,000.

Once again, the classification of the lease must take place prior to the accounting for it. This lease is classified as a capital lease because it contains a BPO. In this case, the 90% test is also fulfilled.

The PV of the lease obligation is computed as follows:

$$
\begin{array}{llll}
\text{PV of bargain purchase option} & = \$10,000 \times & .7513* & = \$\ \ 7,513 \\
\text{PV of annual payments} & = \$50,000 \times & 2.7355** & = \underline{136,755} \\
& & & \underline{\underline{\$144,288}}
\end{array}
$$

Notice that the present value of the lease obligation is greater than the FMV of the asset. Because of this, the lease obligation must be recorded at the FMV of the asset leased.

1/1/X1 Leased equipment	140,000	
Obligation under capital lease		140,000

According to SFAS 13, the allocation between interest and principal is to be such that interest recognized reflects the use of a constant periodic rate of interest applied to the remaining balance of the obligation. If the FMV of the leased asset is greater than or equal to the PV of the lease obligation, the interest rate used would be the same as that used to compute the PV (i.e., the incremental borrowing rate or the implicit rate). In cases such as this when the PV exceeds the FMV of the leased asset, a new rate must be computed through a series of trial and error calculations. In this situation the interest rate used was 13.265%. The amortization of the lease takes place as follows:

Date	Cash payment	Interest expense	Reduction in lease obligation	Balance of lease obligation
Inception of lease				$140,000
1/1/X1	$50,000	$ --	$50,000	90,000
1/1/X2	50,000	11,939	38,061	51,939
1/1/X3	50,000	6,890	43,110	8,829
12/31/X3	10,000	1,171	8,829	--

---

*.7513 is the PV of an amount due in 3 periods at 10%.
2.7355 is the PV of an **annuity due for 3 periods at 10%.

The following entries are required in years X1 through X3 to recognize the payment and amortization.

		X1		X2		X3	
1/1	Obligation under capital lease	50,000		38,061		43,110	
	Accrued interest payable			11,939		6,890	
	Cash		50,000		50,000		50,000
12/31	Interest expense	11,939		6,890		1,171	
	Accrued interest payable		11,939		6,890		
	Obligation under capital lease						1,171
12/31	Depreciation expense	27,800		27,800		27,800	
	Accumulated depreciation		27,800		27,800		27,800
	($139,000 ÷ 5 years)						
12/31	Obligation under capital lease					10,000	
	Cash						10,000

Accounting for Leases--Lessor

As illustrated above, there are four classifications of leases with which a lessor must be concerned. They are as follows:

1. Operating
2. Sales-type
3. Direct financing
4. Leveraged

Operating Lease

As in the case of the lessee, the operating lease requires a less complex accounting treatment. The payments received by the lessor are to be recorded as rent revenues in the period in which the payment is received or becomes receivable. As with the lessee, if either the rentals vary from a straight-line basis or the lease agreement contains a scheduled rent increase over the lease term, the revenue is to be recorded on a straight-line basis unless an alternative basis of systematic and rational allocation is more representative of the time pattern of physical usage of the leased property. Additionally, if the lease agreement provides for a scheduled increase(s) in contemplation of the lessee's increased physical use of the leased property, the total amount of rental payments including the scheduled increase(s) shall be allocated to revenue over the lease term on a straight-line basis (TB 85-3). However, if the scheduled increase(s) is due to additional leased property, recognition should be proportional to the leased property with the increased rents recognized over the years that the lessee has control over the use of the additional leased property (TB 88-1).

The lessor shall show the leased property on the balance sheet under the caption

"Investment in leased property." This account should be shown with or near the fixed assets of the lessor, and depreciated in the same manner as the rest of the lessor's fixed assets.

Any initial direct leasing costs are to be amortized over the lease term as the revenue is recognized (i.e., on a straight-line basis unless another method is more representative). However, these costs may be charged to expense as they are incurred if the effect is not materially different from what would have occurred if the above method had not been used.

Any incentives made by the lessor to the lessee are to be treated as reductions of rent and recognized on a straight-line basis over the term of the lease (TB 88-1).

If, at the inception of the lease, the fair value of the property in an operating lease involving real estate that would have been classified as a sales-type lease except that it did not transfer title is less than its carrying amount, then the lessor must recognize a loss equal to that difference at the inception of the lease (SFAS 98, para 22j).

Sales-Type Lease

In the accounting for a sales-type lease, it is necessary for the lessor to determine the following amounts:

1. Gross investment
2. Fair value of the leased asset
3. Cost

From these amounts, the remainder of the computations necessary to record and account for the lease transaction can be made. The first objective is to determine the numbers necessary to complete the following entry:

Lease receivable	xx	
Cost of goods sold	xx	
Sales		xx
Inventory		xx
Unearned interest		xx

The gross investment (lease receivable) of the lessor is equal to the sum of the minimum lease payments (excluding executory costs) plus the **un**guaranteed residual value. The difference between the gross investment and the present value of the two components of gross investment (minimum lease payments and unguaranteed residual value) is recorded as the unearned interest revenue. The present value is to be computed using the lease term and implicit interest rate (both of which were discussed earlier). The resulting unearned interest revenue is to be amortized into income using the effective interest method. This will result in a constant periodic rate of return on the net investment (the net investment is the gross investment less the unearned income).

Recall from our earlier discussion that the fair market value (FMV) of the leased property is, by definition, equal to the normal selling price of the asset adjusted by any residual amount retained (this amount retained can be exemplified by an unguaranteed residual value, investment credit, etc.). According to SFAS 13, the adjusted selling price to be used for a sales-type lease is equal to the present value of the minimum lease payments. Thus, we can say that the normal selling price less the residual amount retained is equal to the PV of the minimum lease payments.

The cost of goods sold to be charged against income in the period of the sale is computed as the historic cost or carrying value of the asset (most likely inventory) plus any initial direct costs, less the present value of the unguaranteed residual value. The difference between the adjusted selling price and the amount computed as the cost of goods sold is the gross profit recognized by the lessor on the inception of the lease (sale). Thus, a sales-type lease generates two types of revenue for the lessor:

1. The gross profit on the sale
2. The interest earned on the lease receivable

It should be noted that if the sales-type lease involves real estate, the lessor must account for the transaction under the provisions of SFAS 66 in the same manner as a seller of the same property (SFAS 98, para 22g).

The application of these points is illustrated in the example below.

Example of Accounting for a Sales-Type Lease

XYZ Inc. is a manufacturer of specialized equipment. Many of its customers do not have the necessary funds or financing available for outright purchase. Because of this, XYZ offers a leasing alternative. The data relative to a typical lease are as follows:

1. The noncancelable fixed portion of the lease term is 5 years. The lessor has the option to renew the lease for an additional 3 years at the same rental. The estimated useful life of the asset is 10 years.
2. The lessor is to receive equal annual payments over the term of the lease. The leased property reverts back to the lessor upon termination of the lease.
3. The lease is initiated on 1/1/X1. Payments are due on 12/31 for the duration of the lease term.
4. The cost of the equipment to XYZ Inc. is $100,000. The lessor incurs cost associated with the inception of the lease in the amount of $2,500.
5. The selling price of the equipment for an outright purchase is $150,000.
6. The equipment is expected to have a residual value of $15,000 at the end of 5 years and $10,000 at the end of 8 years.
7. The lessor desires a return of 12% (the implicit rate).

The first step is to calculate the annual payment due to the lessor. Recall that present value (PV) of the minimum lease payments is equal to the selling price adjusted for the present value of the residual amount. The present value is to be computed using the implicit interest rate and the lease term. In this case, the implicit rate is given as 12% and the lease term is 8 years (the fixed noncancelable portion plus the renewal period). Thus, the structure of the computation would be as follows:

Normal selling price - PV of residual value = PV of minimum lease payment

Or, in this case,

$150,000 - (.40388* x $10,000) =   4.96764** x Minimum lease payment

$$\frac{\$145,961.20}{4.96764} = \text{Minimum lease payment}$$

$ 29,382.40   =   Minimum lease payment

Prior to examining the accounting implications of a lease, we must first determine the lease classification. Assume that there are no uncertainties regarding the lessor's costs, and the collectibility of the lease payments is reasonably assured. In this example, the lease term is 8 years (discussed above) while the estimated useful life of the asset is 10 years; thus, this lease qualifies as something other than an operating lease. [Note that it also meets the 90% of FMV criterion because the PV of the minimum lease payments of $145,961.20 is greater than 90% of the FMV which is $135,000, .90($150,000)]. Now it must be determined if this is a sales-type, direct financing, or leveraged lease. To do this, examine the FMV or selling price of the asset and compare it to the cost. Because the two are not equal, we can determine this to be a sales-type lease.

Next, obtain the figures necessary to record the entry on the books of the lessor. The gross investment is the total minimum lease payments plus the unguaranteed residual value or:

($29,382.40 x 8) + $10,000 = $245,059.20

The cost of goods sold is the historical cost of the inventory ($100,000) plus any initial direct costs ($2,500) less the PV of the unguaranteed residual value ($10,000 x .40388). Thus, the cost of goods sold amount is $98,461.20 ($100,000 + 2,500 - 4,038.80). Note that the initial direct costs will require a credit entry to some account, usually accounts payable or cash. The inventory account is credited for the carrying value of the asset, in this case $100,000.

---

*.40388 is the present value of an amount of $1 due in 8 periods at a 12% interest rate.
**4.96764 is the present value of an annuity of $1 for 8 periods at a 12% interest rate.

The adjusted selling price is equal to the PV of the minimum payments, or $145,961.20. Finally, the unearned interest revenue is equal to the gross investment (i.e., lease receivable) less the present value of the components making up the gross investment (the minimum lease payment of $29,382.40 and the unguaranteed residual of $10,000). The present value of these items is $150,000 [($29,382.40 x 4.96764) + ($10,000 x .40388)]. Therefore, the entry necessary to record the lease is:

Lease receivable	245,059.20	
Cost of goods sold	98,461.20	
Inventory		100,000.00
Sales		145,961.20
Unearned interest		95,059.20
Accounts payable (initial direct costs)		2,500.00

The next step in accounting for a sales-type lease is to determine the proper handling of the payment. Both principal and interest are included in each payment. According to SFAS 13, interest is recognized on a basis such that an equal rate is earned over the term of the lease. This will require setting up an amortization schedule as illustrated below:

Year	Cash payment	Interest	Reduction in principal	Balance of net investment
Inception of lease				$150,000.00
1	$ 29,382.40	$18,000.00	$ 11,382.40	138,617.00
2	29,382.40	16,634.11	12,748.29	125,869.31
3	29,382.40	15,104.32	14,278.08	111,591.23
4	29,382.40	13,390.95	15,991.45	95,599.78
5	29,382.40	11,471.97	17,910.43	77,689.35
6	29,382.40	9,322.72	20,059.68	57,629.67
7	29,382.40	6,915.56	22,466.84	35,162.83
8	29,382.40	4,219.57	25,162.83	10,000.00
	$235,059.20	$95,059.20	$140,000.00	

A few of the columns need to be elaborated upon. First, the net investment is the gross investment (lease receivable) less the unearned interest. Notice that at the end of the lease term, the net investment is equal to the estimated residual value. Also note that the total interest earned over the lease term is equal to the unearned interest at the beginning of the lease term.

The entries below illustrate the proper treatment to record the receipt of the lease payment and the amortization of the unearned interest in the first year:

Cash	29,382.40	
Lease receivable		29,382.40
Unearned interest	18,000.00	
Interest revenue		18,000.00

Notice that there is no entry to recognize the principal reduction. This is done automatically when the net investment is reduced by decreasing the lease receivable (gross investment) by $29,382.40 and the unearned interest account by only $18,000. The $18,000 is 12% (implicit rate) of the net investment. These entries are to be made over the life of the lease.

At the end of the lease term the asset is returned to the lessor and the following entry is required:

Asset	10,000	
Leased receivable		10,000

If the estimated residual value has changed during the lease term, then the accounting computations would have changed also to reflect this.

Direct Financing Lease

The accounting for a direct financing lease holds many similarities to that for a sales-type lease. Of particular importance is that the terminology used is much the same; however, the treatment accorded these items varies greatly. Again, it is best to preface our discussion by determining our objectives in the accounting for a direct financing lease. Once the lease has been classified, it must be recorded. In order to do this, the following numbers must be obtained:

1. Gross investment
2. Cost
3. Residual value

As mentioned earlier, a direct financing lease generally involves a leasing company or other financial institution and results in only interest revenue being earned by the lessor. This is because the FMV (selling price) and the cost are equal and, therefore, no profit is recognized on the actual lease transaction. Note how this is different from a sales-type lease which involves both a profit on the transaction and interest revenue over the lease term. The reason for this difference is derived from the conceptual nature underlying the purpose of the lease transaction. In a sales-type lease, **the manufacturer** (distributor, dealer) is seeking an alternative means to finance the sale of his product, whereas a direct financing lease is a result of the consumer's need to finance an equipment purchase. Because the consumer is unable to obtain conventional financing, he turns to a leasing company which will purchase the desired asset and then lease it to the consumer. Here the profit on the transaction remains with the manufacturer while the interest revenue is earned by the leasing company.

Like a sales-type lease, the first objective is to determine the amounts necessary to complete the following entry:

Lease receivable		xxx	
Asset			xxx
Unearned interest			xx

The gross investment is still defined as the minimum amount of lease payments exclusive of any executory costs plus the unguaranteed residual value. The difference between the gross investment as determined above and the cost (carrying value) of the asset is to be recorded as the unearned interest revenue because there is no manufacturer's/dealer's profit earned on the transaction. The following entry would be made to record initial direct costs:

Initial direct costs		xx	
Cash			xx

Net investment in the lease is defined as the gross investment less the unearned income plus the unamortized initial direct costs related to the lease. Initial direct costs are defined in the same way that they were for purposes of the sales-type lease; however, the accounting treatment is different. For a direct financing lease, the unearned lease (interest) income and the initial direct costs are to be amortized to income over the lease term so that a constant periodic rate is earned on the net investment. Thus, the effect of the initial direct costs is to reduce the implicit interest rate, or yield, to the lessor over the life of the lease.

An example follows which illustrates the preceding principles.

Example of Accounting for a Direct Financing Lease

XYZ needs new equipment to expand its manufacturing operation; however, it does not have sufficient capital to purchase the asset at this time. Because of this, XYZ has employed ABC Leasing to purchase the asset. In turn, XYZ will lease the asset from ABC. The following information applies to the terms of the lease:

Lease Information

1. A three-year lease is initiated on 1/1/X1 for equipment costing $131,858 with an expected useful life of five years. FMV at 1/1/X1 of equipment is $131,858.
2. Three annual payments are due to the lessor beginning 12/31/X1. The property reverts back to the lessor upon termination of the lease.
3. The unguaranteed residual value at the end of year 3 is estimated to be $10,000.
4. The annual payments are calculated to give the lessor a 10% return (implicit rate).
5. The lease payments and unguaranteed residual value have a PV equal to $131,858 (FMV of asset) at the stipulated discount rate.
6. The annual payment to the lessor is computed as follows:

PV of residual value   = $10,000 x .7513* = $7,513
PV of lease payments = Selling price - PV of residual value
                  = $131,858 - 7,513 = $124,345

$$\text{Annual payment} = \frac{\$124,345}{PV_{3},\ 10\%} = \frac{\$124,345}{2.4869} = \$50,000$$

*.7513 is the PV of an amount due in 3 periods at 10%.

7. Initial direct costs of $7,500 are incurred by ABC in the lease transaction.

As with any lease transaction, the first step must be to appropriately classify the lease. In this case, the PV of the lease payments ($124,345) exceeds 90% of the FMV (90% x $131,858). Assume that the lease payments are reasonably assured and that there are no uncertainties surrounding the costs yet to be incurred by the lessor.

Next, determine the unearned interest and the net investment in lease.

Gross investment in lease	
[(3 x $50,000) + $10,000]	$160,000
Cost of leased property	131,858
Unearned Interest	$ 28,142

The unamortized initial direct costs are to be added to the gross investment in the lease and the unearned interest income is to be deducted to arrive at the net investment in the lease. The net investment in the lease for this example is determined as follows:

Gross investment in lease	$160,000
Add:	
Unamortized initial direct costs	7,500
	$167,500
Less:	
Unearned interest income	28,142
Net investment in lease	$139,358

The net investment in the lease (gross investment - unearned revenue) has been increased by the amount of initial direct costs. Therefore, **the implicit rate is no longer 10%.** We must recompute the implicit rate. The implicit rate is really the result of an internal rate of return calculation. We know that the lease payments are to be $50,000 per annum and that a residual value of $10,000 is available at the end of the lease term. In return for these payments (inflows) we are giving up equipment (outflow) and incurring initial direct costs (outflows) with a net investment of $139,358 ($131,858 + $7,500). The only way to obtain the new implicit rate is through a trial and error calculation as set up below:

$$\frac{50{,}000}{(1 + i)^1} + \frac{50{,}000}{(1 + i)^2} + \frac{50{,}000}{(1 + i)^3} + \frac{10{,}000}{(1 + i)^3} = \$139{,}358$$

Where: i = implicit rate of interest

In this case, the implicit rate is equal to 7.008%.

Thus, the amortization table would be set up as follows:

(a)	(b)	(c)	(d)	(e)	(f)
		PV x	Reduction	Reduction	PVI Net
	Reduction	Implicit	in Initial	in PVI	Invest.
Lease	in Unearned	Rate	Direct Costs	Net Invest.	in Lease
Payments	Interest	(7.008%)	(b-c)	(a-b+d)	$(f)_{(n+1)} = (f)_n - (e)$
0					$139,358
1	$ 50,000	$13,186 (1)	$ 9,766	$3,420	$ 40,234	99,124
2	50,000	9,504 (2)	6,947	2,557	43,053	56,071
3	50,000	5,455 (3)	3,929	1,526	46,071	10,000
	$150,000	$28,145*	$20,642	$7,503*	$129,358	

*Rounded

(b.1) $131,858 x 10% = $13,186
(b.2) [$131,858 - ($50,000 - 13,186)] x 10% = $9,504
(b.3) [$ 95,044 - ($50,000 - 9,504)] x 10% = $5,455

Here the interest is computed as 7.008% of the net investment. Note again that the net investment at the end of the lease term is equal to the estimated residual value.

The entry made to initially record the lease is as follows:

Lease receivable** [($50,000 x 3) + 10,000]	160,000	
Asset acquired for leasing		131,858
Unearned lease revenue		28,142

When the payment (or obligation to pay) of the initial direct costs occurs, the following entry must be made:

Initial direct costs	7,500	
Cash		7,500

Using the schedule above, the following entries would be made during each of the indicated years:

	Year 1		Year 2		Year 3	
Cash	50,000		50,000		50,000	
Lease receivable**		50,000		50,000		50,000
Unearned lease revenue	13,186		9,504		5,455	
Initial direct costs		3,420		2,557		1,526
Interest revenue		9,766		6,947		3,929

Finally, when the asset is returned to the lessor at the end of the lease term, it must be recorded on the books. The necessary entry is as follows:

Used asset	10,000	
Lease receivable**		10,000

**Also the "gross investment in lease."*

Leveraged Leases

Leveraged leases are discussed in detail in Appendix A of this chapter because of the complexity involved in the accounting treatment.

Special Situations

Change in residual value. For any of the foregoing types of leases, the lessor is to review the estimated residual value on at least an annual basis. If there is a decline in the estimated residual value, the lessor must make a determination as to whether this decline is temporary or permanent. If temporary, no adjustment is required; however, if the decline is other than temporary, then the estimated residual value must be revised in line with the changed estimate. The loss that arises in the net investment is to be recognized in the period of decline. Under no circumstance is the estimated residual value to be adjusted to reflect an increase in the estimate.

Change in the provisions of a lease. In the case of either a sales-type or direct financing lease where there is a change in the provisions of a lease, the lease shall be accounted for as discussed below (by the lessor).

We are basically concerned with changes in the provisions that affect the amount of the remaining minimum lease payments. When a change such as this occurs, one of the following three things can happen:

1. The change does not give rise to a new agreement. A new agreement is defined as a change which, if in effect at the inception of the lease, would have resulted in a different classification.
2. The change does give rise to a new agreement which would be classified as a direct financing lease
3. The change gives rise to a new agreement classified as an operating lease

If either (1) or (2) occurs, the balance of the minimum lease payments receivable and the estimated residual value (if affected) shall be adjusted to reflect the effect of the change. The net adjustment is to be charged (or credited) to the unearned income account, and the accounting for the lease adjusted to reflect the change.

If the new agreement is an operating lease, then the remaining net investment (lease receivable less unearned income) is to be removed from the books and the leased asset shall be recorded at the lower of its cost, present fair value, or carrying value. The net adjustment resulting from these entries shall be charged (or credited) to the income of the period. Thereafter, the new lease shall be accounted for as any other operating lease.

Termination of a lease. The lessor shall remove the remaining net investment from his/her books and record the leased equipment as an asset at the lower of its original cost, present fair value, or current carrying value. The net adjustment shall be reflected in the income of the current period.

The lessee is also affected by the terminated agreement because s/he has been relieved of the obligation. If the lease is a capital lease, then the lessee should remove both the obligation and the asset from his/her accounts and charge any adjustment to the current period income. If accounted for as an operating lease, there is no accounting adjustment required.

Renewal or extension of an existing lease. The renewal or extension of an existing lease agreement affects the accounting of both the lessee and the lessor. SFAS 13 specifies two basic situations in this regard: (1) the renewal occurs and makes a residual guarantee or penalty provision inoperative, or (2) the renewal agreement does not do the foregoing and the renewal is to be treated as a new agreement. The accounting treatment prescribed under the latter situation for a leasee by SFAS 13 is as follows:

1. If the renewal or extension is classified as a capital lease, then the (present) current balances of the asset and related obligation should be adjusted by an amount equal to the difference between the present value of the future minimum lease payments under the revised agreement and the (present) current balance of the obligation. The present value of the minimum lease payments under the revised agreement should be computed using the interest rate that was in effect at the inception of the original lease.

2. If the renewal or extension is classified as an operating lease, then the current balances in the asset and liability accounts shall be removed from the books and a gain (loss) recognized for the difference. The new lease agreement resulting from a renewal or extension shall be accounted for in the same manner as other operating leases.

Under the same circumstances, SFAS 13 prescribes the following treatment to be followed by the lessor:

1. If the renewal or extension is classified as a direct financing lease, then the existing balances of the lease receivable and the estimated residual value accounts should be adjusted for the changes resulting from the revised agreement. (Note: Remember that an upward adjustment to the estimated residual value is not allowed.) The net adjustment should be charged or credited to an unearned income account.

2. If the renewal or extension is classified as an operating lease, then the remaining net investment under the existing sales-type lease or direct financing lease shall be removed from the books and the leased asset shall be recorded as an asset at the lower of its original cost, present fair value, or current carrying

amount. The difference between the net investment and the amount recorded for the leased asset shall be charged to income of the period. The renewal or extension should then be accounted for as any other operating lease.

3. If the renewal or extension is classified as a sales-type lease **and** it occurs at or near the end of the existing lease term, then the renewal or extension should be accounted for as a sales-type lease. (Note: A renewal or extension that occurs in the last few months of an existing lease is considered to have occurred at or near the end of the existing lease term.)

If the renewal or extension causes the guarantee or penalty provision to be inoperative, the **lessee** shall adjust the current balance of the leased asset and the lease obligation **to** the present value of the future minimum lease payments (according to SFAS 13 "by an amount equal to the difference between the PV of future minimum lease payments under the revised agreement and the present balance of the obligation"). The PV of the future minimum lease payments shall be computed using the implicit rate used in the original lease agreement.

Given the same circumstances, the **lessor** shall adjust the existing balance of the lease receivable and estimated residual value accounts to reflect the changes of the revised agreement (remember, no upward adjustments to the residual value). The net adjustment shall be charged (or credited) to unearned income.

Leases between related parties. Leases between related parties shall be classified and accounted for as though the parties are unrelated, except in cases where it is certain that the terms and conditions of the agreement have been influenced significantly by the fact that the lessor and lessee are related. When this is the case, the classification and/or accounting shall be modified to reflect the true economic substance of the transaction rather than the legal form.

If a subsidiary's principal business activity is leasing property to its parent or other affiliated companies, consolidated financial statements shall be presented.

SFAS 57 requires that the nature and extent of leasing activities between related parties be disclosed.

Accounting for leases in a business combination. A business combination, in and of itself, has no effect upon the classification of a lease. However, if, in connection with a business combination, the lease agreement is modified to change the original classification of the lease, it should be considered a new agreement and reclassified according to the revised provisions.

In most cases, a business combination that is accounted for by the pooling-of-interest method or by the purchase method will not affect the previous classification of a lease unless the provisions have been modified as indicated in the preceding paragraph.

The acquiring company shall apply the following procedures to account for a leveraged lease in a business combination accounted for by the purchase method:

1. The classification of leveraged lease should be kept.
2. The net investment in the leveraged lease should be given a fair market value

(present value, net of tax) based upon the remaining future cash flows. Also, the estimated tax effects of the cash flows should be given recognition.

3. The net investment shall then be broken down into three components: net rentals receivable, estimated residual value, and unearned income.
4. Thereafter, the leveraged lease should be accounted for as described above in the section on leveraged leases.

In a business combination where a lease is acquired that does not conform to SFAS 13 (pre-1979), the acquiring company should account for the lease by retroactively applying SFAS 13 at the date of combination.

Accounting for changes in lease agreements resulting from refunding of tax-exempt debt. If, during the lease term, a change in the lease results from a refunding by the lessor of tax-exempt debt (including an advance refunding) and (1) the lessee receives the economic advantages of the refunding and (2) the revised agreement can be classified as a capital lease by the lessee and a direct financing lease by the lessor, the change should be accounted for as follows:

1. If the change is accounted for as an extinguishment of debt:

   a. Lessee accounting. The lessee should adjust the lease obligation to the present value of the future minimum lease payments under the revised agreement. The present value of the minimum lease payments should be computed by using the interest rate applicable to the revised agreement. Any gain or loss should be recognized currently as a gain or loss on the extinguishment of debt in accordance with the provisions of SFAS 4.

   b. Lessor accounting. The lessor should adjust the balance of the lease receivable and the estimated residual value, if affected, for the difference in present values between the old and revised agreements. Any resulting gain or loss should be recognized currently.

2. If the change is not accounted for as an extinguishment of debt:

   a. Lessee accounting. The lessee should accrue any costs in connection with the debt refunding that is obligated to be refunded to the lessor. These costs should be amortized by the interest method over the period from the date of refunding to the call date of the debt to be refunded.

   b. Lessor accounting. The lessor should recognize any reimbursements to be received from the lessee, for costs paid in relation to the debt refunding, as revenue. This revenue should be recognized in a systematic manner over the period from the date of refunding to the call date of the debt to be refunded.

Sale or assignment to third parties; nonrecourse financing. The sale or assignment of a lease or of property subject to a lease that was originally accounted for as a sales-type lease or a direct financing lease will not affect the original accounting treatment of the lease. Any profit or loss on the sale or assignment should be recognized at the time of transaction except under the following two circumstances:

1. When the sale or assignment is between related parties. Apply provisions presented above under "related parties."
2. When the sale or assignment is with recourse, the profit or loss shall be deferred and recognized over the term of the lease in a rational and systematic manner (such as in proportion to the minimum lease payments).

The sale of property subject to an operating lease shall not be treated as a sale if the seller (or any related party to the seller) retains "substantial risks of ownership" in the leased property. A seller may retain "substantial risks of ownership" by various arrangements. For example, if the lessee defaults upon the lease agreement or if the lease terminates, the seller may arrange to do one of the following:

1. Acquire the property or the lease
2. Substitute an existing lease
3. Secure a replacement lessee or a buyer for the property under a remarketing agreement

A seller will **not** retain substantial risks of ownership by arrangements where one of the following occurs:

1. A remarketing agreement includes a reasonable fee to be paid to the seller
2. The seller is not required to give priority to the releasing or disposition of the property owned by the third party over similar property owned by the seller

When the sale of property subject to an operating lease is not accounted for as a sale because the substantial risk factor is present, it should be accounted for as a borrowing. The proceeds from the sale should be recorded as an obligation on the seller's books. Rental payments made by the lessee under the operating lease should be recorded as revenue by the seller even if the payments are paid to the third-party purchaser. The seller shall account for each rental payment by allocating a portion to interest expense (to be imputed in accordance with the provisions of APB 21), and the remainder will reduce the existing obligation. Other normal accounting procedures for operating leases should be applied except that the depreciation term for the leased asset is limited to the amortization period of the obligation.

The sale or assignment of lease payments under an operating lease by the lessor should be accounted for as a borrowing as described above.

Nonrecourse financing is a common occurrence in the leasing industry, whereby the stream of lease payments on a lease is discounted on a nonrecourse basis at a financial institution with the lease payments collateralizing the debt. The proceeds are then used to finance future leasing transactions. Even though the discounting is on a nonrecourse basis, TB 86-2 prohibits the offsetting of the debt against the related lease receivable unless a legal right of offset exists or the lease qualified as a leveraged lease at its inception. The SEC in a recent Staff Accounting Bulletin has also affirmed this position.

Money-Over-Money Lease Transactions. In cases where a lessor obtains nonrecourse financing in excess of the leased asset's cost, FASB TB 88-1 states that the borrowing and leasing are separate transactions and should not be offset against each other unless a right of offset exists. Only dealer profit in sales type leases may be recognized at the beginning of the lease term.

Acquisition of Interest in Residual Value (TB 86-2). Recently, there has been an increase in the acquisition of interests in residual values of leased assets by companies whose primary business is other than leasing or financing. This generally occurs through the outright purchase of the right to own the leased asset or the right to receive the proceeds from the sale of a leased asset at the end of its lease term.

In instances such as these, the rights should be recorded by the purchaser at the fair value of the assets surrendered. Recognition of increases in the value of the interest in the residual (i.e., residual value accretion) to the end of the lease term are prohibited. However, a non-temporary writedown of the residual value interest should be recognized as a loss. This guidance also applies to lessors who sell the related minimum lease payments but retain the interest in the residual value. Guaranteed residual values also have no effect on this guidance.

Leases involving government units. Leases that involve government units (i.e., airport facilities, bus terminal space, etc.) usually contain special provisions which prevent the agreements from being classified as anything but operating leases. These special provisions include the governmental body's authority to abandon a facility at any time during lease term, thus making its economic life indeterminable. These leases also do not contain a BPO or transfer ownership. The fair market value is generally indeterminable because neither the leased property nor similar property is available for sale.

However, leases involving government units are subject to the same classification criteria as nongovernment units, except when the following six criteria are met (Note: If all six conditions are met, the agreement shall be classified as an operating lease by both lessee and lessor):

1. A government unit or authority owns the leased property
2. The leased property is part of a larger facility operated by or on behalf of the lessor
3. The leased property is a permanent structure or part of a permanent structure that normally cannot be moved to another location
4. The lessor, or a higher governmental authority, has the right to terminate the lease at any time under the lease agreement or existing statutes or regulations
5. The lease neither transfers ownership nor allows the lessee to purchase or acquire the leased property
6. The leased property or similar property in the same area cannot be purchased or leased from anyone else

Accounting for a sublease. A sublease is used to describe the situation where the original lessee re-leases the leased property to a third party (the sublessee), and the original lessee acts as a sublessor. Normally, the nature of a sublease agreement does not affect the original lease agreement, and the original lessee/sublessor retains primary liability.

The original lease remains in effect, and the original lessor continues to account for the lease as before. The original lessee/sublessor shall account for the lease as follows:

1. If the original lease agreement transfers ownership or contains a BPO and if the new lease meets any one of the four specified criteria (i.e., transfers ownership, BPO, 75% test, or 90% test) and both the collectibility and uncertainties criteria, then the sublessor shall classify the new lease as a sales-type or direct financing lease; otherwise as an operating lease. In either situation, the original lessee/sublessor should continue accounting for the original lease obligation as before.

2. If the original lease agreement does not transfer ownership or contain a BPO, but it still qualified as a capital lease, then the original lessee/sublessor should (with one exception) apply the usual criteria set by SFAS 13 in classifying the new agreement as a capital or operating lease. If the new lease qualifies for capital treatment, the original lessee/sublessor should account for it as a direct financing lease, with the unamortized balance of the asset under the original lease being treated as the cost of the leased property. The one exception arises when the circumstances surrounding the sublease suggest that the sublease agreement was an important part of a predetermined plan in which the original lessee played only an intermediate role between the original lessor and the sublessee. In this situation, the sublease shall be classified by the 75% and 90% criteria as well as collectibility and uncertainties criteria. In applying the 90% criterion, the fair value for the leased property will be the fair value to the original lessor at the inception of the original lease. Under all circumstances, the original lessee should continue accounting for the original lease obligation as before. If the new lease agreement (sublease) does not meet the capitalization requirements imposed for subleases, then the new lease should be accounted for as an operating lease.

3. If the original lease is an operating lease, the original lessee/sublessor should account for the new lease as an operating lease and account for the original operating lease as before.

Sale-Leaseback Transactions

Sale-leaseback describes a transaction where the owner of property (seller-lessee) sells the property, and then immediately leases all or part of it back from the new owner (buyer-lessor). These transactions may occur when the seller-lessee is experiencing cash flow or financing problems or because the tax advantages are beneficial. The important consideration in this type of transaction is the recognition of two separate and distinct economic transactions. However, it is important to note that there is not a physical transfer of property. First, there is a sale of property, and second, there is a lease agreement for the same property in which the original seller is the lessee and the original buyer is the lessor. This is illustrated below:

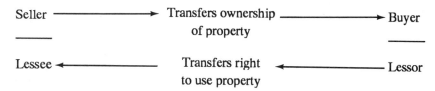

If an entity owns property and is also a lessee in it (e.g., entity invests in a partnership that owns this property), and sells the property while remaining a lessee, the transaction should be accounted for as a sale-leaseback, if the existing lease terms are modified. [FASB Emerging Issues Task Force (EITF) Consensus 88-21.]

A sales-leaseback transaction is usually structured such that the sales price of the asset is greater than or equal to the current market value. The result of this higher sales price is a higher periodic rental payment over the lease term. The transaction is attractive usually because of the tax benefits associated with it. The seller-lessee benefits from the higher price because of the increased gain on the sale of the property and the deductibility of the lease payments which are usually larger than the depreciation that was previously being taken. The buyer-lessor benefits from both the higher rental payments and the larger depreciable basis.

The accounting treatment from the seller-lessee's point of view will depend upon the degree of rights to use retained by the seller-lessee. The degree of rights to use retained may be categorized as follows:

1. Substantially all
2. Minor
3. More than minor but less than substantially all

The guideline for the determination of substantially all is based upon the classification criteria presented for the lease transaction. For example, a test based upon the 90% recovery criterion seems appropriate. That is, if the present value of fair rental payments is equal to 90% or more of the fair value of the sold asset, the seller-lessee is presumed to have retained **substantially all** of the rights to use the sold property. The test for retaining **minor** rights would be to substitute 10% or less for 90% or more in the preceding sentence.

If substantially all the rights to use the property are retained by the seller-lessee, and the agreement meets at least one of the criteria for capital lease treatment, the seller-lessee should account for the leaseback as a capital lease and any profit on the sale should be deferred and either amortized over the life of the property or treated as a reduction of depreciation expense. If the leaseback is classified as an operating lease, it should be accounted for as one, and any profit or loss on the sale should be deferred and amortized over the lease term. Any loss on the sale would also be deferred unless the loss were perceived to be a real economic loss, in which case the loss would be immediately recognized and not deferred.

If only a **minor portion** of the rights to use are retained by the seller-lessee, the sale and the leaseback should be accounted for separately. However, if the rental payments appear unreasonable based upon the existing market conditions at the inception of the lease, the profit or loss should be adjusted so the rentals are at a reasonable amount. The amount created by the adjustment should be deferred and amortized over the life of the property if a capital lease is involved or over the lease term if an operating lease is involved.

If the seller-lessee retains **more than a minor portion but less than substantially all** the rights to use the property, any excess profit on the sale should be recognized on the date of the sale. For purposes of this paragraph, excess profit is derived as follows:

1. If the leaseback is classified as an operating lease, the excess profit is the profit which exceeds the present value of the minimum lease payments over the lease term. The seller-lessee should use its incremental borrowing rate to compute the present value of the minimum lease payments. If the implicit rate of interest in the lease is known and lower, it should be used to compute the present value of the minimum lease payments.
2. If the leaseback is classified as a capital lease, the excess profit is the amount greater than the recorded amount of the leased asset.

When the fair value of the property at the time of the leaseback is less than its undepreciated cost, the seller-lessee should immediately recognize a loss for the difference. The diagram on the following page summarizes the accounting for sale-leaseback transactions.

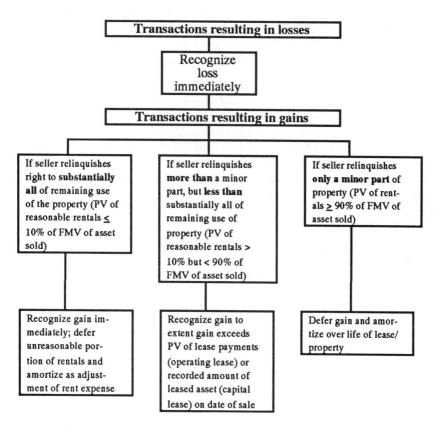

In the above circumstances, when the leased asset is land only, any amortization should be on a straight-line basis over the lease term, regardless of whether the lease is classified as a capital or operating lease.

Executory costs are not to be included in the calculation of profit to be deferred in a sale-leaseback transaction. [FASB Emerging Issues Task Force (EITF) Consensus 89-16.]

The buyer-lessor should account for the transaction as a purchase and a direct financing lease if the agreement meets the criteria of **either** a direct financing lease **or** a sales-type lease. Otherwise, the agreement should be accounted for as a purchase and an operating lease.

Sale-leaseback involving real estate. Three requirements are necessary for a sale-leaseback involving real estate (including real estate with equipment) to qualify for sale-leaseback accounting treatment. Those sale-leaseback transactions not meeting the three requirements should be accounted for as a deposit (see Chapter 7) or as a financing. The three requirements (SFAS 98, para 7) are:

1. The lease must be a normal leaseback

2. Payment terms and provisions must adequately demonstrate the buyer-lessor's initial and continuing investment in the property
3. Payment terms and provisions must transfer all the risks and rewards of ownership as demonstrated by a lack of continuing involvement by the seller-lessee

A normal leaseback involves active use of the leased property in the seller-lessee's trade or business during the lease term.

The buyer-lessor's initial investment is adequate if it demonstrates the buyer-lessor's commitment to pay for the property and indicates a reasonable likelihood that the seller-lessee will collect any receivable related to the leased property. The buyer-lessor's continuing investment is adequate if the buyer is contractually obligated to pay an annual amount at least equal to the level of annual payment needed to pay that debt and interest over no more than (a) 20 years for land, and (b) the customary term of a first year mortgage for other real estate.

Any continuing involvement by the seller-lessee other than normal leaseback disqualifies the lease from sale-leaseback accounting treatment (SFAS 98, para 10). Some examples of continuing involvement other than normal leaseback include:

1. The seller-lessee has an obligation or option (excluding the right of first refusal) to repurchase the property
2. The seller-lessee (or party related to the seller-lessee) guarantees the buyer-lessor's investment or debt related to that investment or a return on that investment
3. The seller-lessee is required to reimburse the buyer-lessor for a decline in the fair value of the property below estimated residual value at the end of the lease term based on other than excess wear and tear
4. The seller-lessee remains liable for an existing debt related to the property
5. The seller-lessee's rental payments are contingent on some predetermined level of future operations of the buyer-lessor
6. The seller-lessee provides collateral on behalf of the buyer-lessor other than the property directly involved in the sale-leaseback
7. The seller-lessee provides nonrecourse financing to the buyer-lessor for any portion of the sales proceeds or provides recourse financing in which the only recourse is the leased asset
8. The seller-lessee enters into a sale-leaseback involving property improvements or integral equipment without leasing the underlying land to the buyer-lessor
9. The buyer-lessor is obligated to share any portion of the appreciation of the property with the seller-lessee
10. Any other provision or circumstance that allows the seller-lessee to participate in any future profits of the buyer-lessor or the appreciation of the leased property

Example of Accounting for a Sale-Leaseback Transaction

To illustrate the accounting treatment is a sale-leaseback transaction, suppose that Lessee Corporation sells equipment that has a book value of $80,000 and a fair value of $100,000 to Lessor Corporation, and then immediately leases it back under the following conditions:

1. The sale date is January 1, 1992, and the equipment has a fair value of $100,000 on that date and an estimated useful life of 15 years.
2. The lease term is 15 years, noncancelable, and requires equal rental payments of $13,109 at the beginning of each year.
3. Lessee Corp. has the option to annually renew the lease at the same rental payments upon expiration of the original lease.
4. Lessee Corp. has the obligation to pay all executory costs.
5. The annual rental payments provide the lessor with a 12% return on investment.
6. The incremental borrowing rate of Lessee Corp. is 12%.
7. Lessee Corp. depreciates similar equipment on a straight-line basis.

Lessee Corp. should classify the agreement as a capital lease since the lease term exceeds 75% of the estimated economic life of the equipment, and because the present value of the lease payments is greater than 90% of the fair value of the equipment. Assuming that collectibility of the lease payments is reasonably predictable and that no important uncertainties exist concerning the amount of unreimbursable costs yet to be incurred by the lessor, Lessor Corp. should classify the transaction as a direct financing lease because the present value of the minimum lease payments is equal to the fair market value of $100,000 ($13,109 x 7.62817).

Lessee Corp. and Lessor Corp. would normally make the following journal entries during the first year:

Upon Sale of Equipment on January 1, 1992

Lessee Corp.			Lessor Corp.		
Cash	100,000		Equipment	100,000	
Equipment*		80,000	Cash		100,000
Unearned profit on					
sale-leaseback		20,000			
Leased equipment	100,000		Lease receivable		
Lease obligations		100,000	($13,109 x 15		
			= $196,635)	196,635	
			Equipment		100,000
			Unearned interest		96,635

*Assumes new equipment

To Record First Payment on January 1, 1992

Lessee Corp.			Lessor Corp.		
Lease obligations	13,109		Cash	13,109	
Cash		13,109	Lease receivable		13,109

To Record Incurrence and Payment of Executory Costs

Lessee Corp.		*Lessor Corp.*
		(No entry)
Insurance, taxes, etc. xxx		
Cash (accounts		
payable)	xxx	

To Record Depreciation Expense on the Equipment, December 31, 1992

Lessee Corp.		*Lessor Corp.*
		(No entry)
Depreciation expense 6,667		
Accum. depr. --		
capital leases		
($100,000 ÷ 15)	6,667	

To Amortize Profit on Sale-Leaseback by Lessee Corp., December 31, 1992

Lessee Corp.		*Lessor Corp.*
		(No entry)
Unearned profit on		
sale-leaseback	1,333	
Depr. expense		
($20,000 ÷ 15)	1,333	

To Record Interest for 1992, December 31, 1992

Lessee Corp.		*Lessor Corp.*	
Interest expense 10,427		Unearned interest	
		income 10,427	
Accrued interest		Interest income	10,427
payable	10,427		

Partial Lease Amortization Schedule

Date	*Cash payment*	*Interest expense*	*Reduction of obligation*	*Lease obligation*
Inception of lease				$100,000
1/1/92	$13,109	$ --	$13,109	86,891
1/1/93	13,109	10,427	2,682	84,209

Leases Involving Real Estate

Leases involving real estate can be divided into the following four categories:

1. Leases involving land only
2. Leases involving land and building(s)
3. Leases involving real estate and equipment
4. Leases involving only part of a building

Leases involving land only

<u>Lessee accounting.</u> If the lease agreement transfers ownership or contains a bargain purchase option, the lessee should account for the lease as a capital lease, and record an asset and related liability in an amount equal to the present value of the minimum lease payments. If the lease agreement does not transfer ownership or contain a bargain purchase option, the lessee should account for the lease as an operating lease.

Lessor accounting. If the lease gives rise to dealer's profit (or loss) and transfers ownership (i.e., title), SFAS 98 requires that the lease shall be classified as a sales-type lease and accounted for under the provisions of SFAS 66 in the same manner as a seller of the same property. If the lease transfers ownership, both the collectibility and no material uncertainties criteria are met, but does not give rise to dealer's profit (or loss), the lease should be accounted for as a direct financing or leveraged lease as appropriate. If the lease contains a bargain purchase option and both the collectibility and no material uncertainties criteria are met, the lease should be accounted for as a direct financing, leveraged, or operating lease as appropriate. If the lease does not meet the collectibility and/or no material uncertainties criteria, the lease should be accounted for as an operating lease.

Leases involving land and building.

Lessee accounting. If the agreement transfers title or contains a bargain purchase option, the lessee should account for the agreement by separating the land and building components and capitalize each separately. The land and building elements should be allocated on the basis of their relative fair market values measured at the inception of the lease. The land and building components are separately accounted for because the lessee is expected to own the real estate by the end of the lease term. The building should be depreciated over its estimated useful life without regard to the lease term.

When the lease agreement neither transfers title nor contains a bargain purchase option, the fair value of the land must be determined in relation to the fair value of the aggregate properties included in the lease agreement. If the fair value of the land is less than 25% of the fair value of the leased properties in aggregate, then the land is considered immaterial. Conversely, if the fair value of the land is 25% or greater of the fair value of the leased properties in aggregate, then the land is considered material.

When the land component of the lease agreement is considered immaterial (FMV land < 25% total FMV), the lease should be accounted for as a single lease unit. The lessee should capitalize the lease if one of the following occurs:

1. The term of the lease is 75% or more of the economic useful life of the real estate
2. The present value of the minimum lease payments equals 90% or more of the fair market value of the leased real estate less any lessor investment tax credit

If neither of the above two criteria is met, the lessee should account for the lease agreement as a single operating lease.

When the land component of the lease agreement is considered material (FMV land ≥ 25% total FMV), the land and building components should be separated. By applying the lessee's incremental borrowing rate to the fair market value of the land, the annual minimum lease payment attributed to land is computed. The remaining payments are attributed to the building. The division of minimum lease payments between land and building is essential for both the lessee and lessor. The lease involving the land should **always** be accounted for as an operating lease. The lease involving the building(s) must meet either the 75% or 90% test to be treated as a capital lease. If neither of the two criteria is met, the building(s) will also be accounted for as an operating lease.

Lessor accounting. The lessor's accounting depends on whether the lease transfers ownership, contains a bargain purchase option, or does neither of the two.

If the lease transfers ownership and gives rise to dealer's profit (or loss), SFAS 98, para 1 requires that the lessor shall classify the lease as a sales-types lease and account for the lease as a single unit under the provisions of FASB 66 in the same manner as a seller of the same property. If the lease transfers ownership, meets both the collectibility and no important uncertainties criteria, but does not give rise to dealer's profit (or loss), the lease should be accounted for as a direct financing or leveraged lease as appropriate.

If the lease contains a bargain purchase option and gives rise to dealer's profit (or loss), the lease should be classified as an operating lease. If the lease contains a bargain purchase option, meets both the collectibility and no material uncertainties criteria, but does not give rise to dealer's profit (or loss), the lease should be accounted for as a direct financing lease or a leveraged lease as appropriate.

If the lease agreement neither transfers ownership nor contains a bargain purchase option, the lessor should follow the same rules as the lessee in accounting for real estate leases involving land and building(s).

However, the collectibility and the no material uncertainties criteria must be met before the lessor can account for the agreement as a direct financing lease, and in no such case may the lease be classified as a sales-type lease (i.e., ownership must be transferred).

The treatment of a lease involving both land and building can be illustrated in the following examples.

Example of Accounting for Land and Building Lease Containing Transfer of Title

Assume the following:

1. The lessee enters into a 10-year noncancelable lease for a parcel of land and a building for use in its operations. The building has an estimated useful life of 12 years.
2. The FMV of the land is $75,000, while the FMV of the building is $310,000.
3. A payment of $50,000 is due to the lessor at the beginning of each of the 10 years of the lease.
4. The lessee's incremental borrowing rate is 10%. (Lessor's implicit rate is unknown.)
5. Ownership will transfer to the lessee at the end of the lease.

The present value of the minimum lease payments is $337,951 ($50,000 x 6.75902*). The portion of the present value of the minimum lease payments which should be capitalized for each of the two components of the lease is computed as follows:

FMV of land	$ 75,000
FMV of building	310,000
Total FMV of leased property	$385,000

Portion of PV allocated to land $337,951 x $\dfrac{75,000}{385,000}$ = $ 65,835

Portion of PV allocated to building $337,951 x $\dfrac{310,000}{385,000}$ =   272,116

Total PV to be capitalized $337,951

The entry made to initially record the lease is as follows:

Leased land	65,835	
Leased building	272,116	
Lease obligation		337,951

6.75902 is the PV of an annuity due for 10 periods at 10%.

Subsequently, the obligation will be decreased in accordance with the effective interest method. The leased building will be amortized over its expected useful life.

Example of Accounting for Land and Building Lease Without Transfer of Title or Bargain Purchase Option

Assume the same facts as the previous example except that title does not transfer at the end of the lease.

The lease is still a capital lease because the lease term is more than 75% of the useful life. Since the FMV of the land is less than 25% of the leased properties in aggregate, $\left(\dfrac{75,000}{385,000} = 19\%\right)$, the land component is considered immaterial and the lease will be accounted for as a single lease. The entry to record the lease is as follows:

Leased property	337,951	
Lease obligation		337,951

Assume the same facts as the previous example except that the FMV of the land is $110,000 and the FMV of the building is $275,000. Once again title does not transfer.

Because the FMV of the land exceeds 25% of the leased properties in aggregate $\left(\frac{110,000}{385,000} = 28\%\right)$, the land component is considered material and the lease would be separated into two components. The annual minimum lease payment attributed to the land is computed as follows:

FMV of land $\frac{\$110,000}{6.75902^*}$ = $16,275
PV factor

The remaining portion of the annual payment is attributed to the building.

Annual payment	$50,000
Less amount attributed to land	(16,275)
Annual payment attributed to building	$33,725

The present value of the minimum annual lease payments attributed to the building is then computed as follows:

Minimum annual lease payment attributed to building	$ 33,725
PV factor	x 6.75902*
PV of minimum annual lease payments attributed to building	$227,948

The entry to record the capital portion of the lease is as follows:

Leased building	227,948	
Lease obligation		227,948

There would be no computation of the present value of the minimum annual lease payment attributed to the land since the land component of the lease will be treated as an operating lease. For this reason, each year $16,275 of the $50,000 lease payment will be recorded as land rental expense. The remainder of the annual payment ($33,725) will be applied against the lease obligation using the effective interest method.

   *6.75902 is the PV of an annuity due for 10 periods at 10%.

Leases involving real estate and equipment. When real estate leases also involve equipment or machinery, the equipment component should be separated and accounted for as a separate lease agreement by both lessees and lessors. "The portion of the minimum lease payments applicable to the equipment element of the lease shall be estimated by whatever means are appropriate in the circumstances" (SFAS 13, para 27). The lessee and lessor should apply the capitalization requirements to the equipment lease independently of accounting for the real estate lease(s). The real estate leases should be handled as discussed in the preceding two sections. In a sale-leaseback transaction involving real estate with equipment, the equipment and land are not separated (SFAS 98, para 6).

Leases involving only part of a building. It is common to find lease agreements that involve only part of a building, as, for example, when a floor of an office building is leased, or when a store in a shopping mall is leased. A difficulty that arises in this situation is that the cost and/or fair market value of the leased portion of the whole may not be objectively determinable.

Lessee accounting. If the fair value of the leased property is objectively determinable, then the lessee should follow the rules and account for the lease as described in "Leases involving land and building." If the fair value of the leased property cannot be determined objectively, but the agreement satisfies the 75% test, the estimated economic life of the building in which the leased premises are located should be used. If this test is not met, the lessee should account for the agreement as an operating lease.

Lessor accounting. From the lessor's position, **both the cost and fair value** of the leased property must be objectively determinable before the procedures described under "Leases involving land and building" will apply. If either the cost or the fair value cannot be determined objectively, then the lessor should account for the agreement as an operating lease.

Special Situations

Wrap lease transactions. A wrap lease transaction occurs when the lessor of an asset obtains nonrecourse financing using the lease rentals and asset as collateral, sells the underlying asset and nonrecourse debt and then leases the asset back while remaining the substantive lessor under the original lease. According to FASB TB 88-1, when this occurs and the asset is real estate, SFAS 98 applies, otherwise the transaction is treated as a sales-leaseback with the lease to the end user treated as a sublease under SFAS 13.

Summary of Accounting for Selected Items (See following page)

Reporting of Current and Noncurrent Lease Receivable (Lessor) and Lease Obligations (Lessee)

The balance of lease payments receivable (lessor) and lease obligation (lessee) must be broken down between the current and noncurrent portions. First, the current portion is computed at the date of the financial statements as the present value of the next lease payment/receipt. The time period is from the date of the financial statements to the next lease payment. The noncurrent portion is computed as the difference between the current portion determined and the balance of the lease obligation at the end of the period. The conceptual justification for such treatment can be found in the fact that the total lease obligation is equal to the present value of the future minimum lease payments. Therefore, it follows that the current portion should be the present value of the next lease payment while the noncurrent portion should be the present value of all other remaining lease payments.

TREATMENT OF SELECTED ITEMS IN ACCOUNTING FOR LEASES

	Lessor		Lessee	
	Operating	Direct Financing and Sales-Type	Operating	Capital
Initial Direct Costs	Capitalize and amortize over lease term in proportion to rent revenue recognized (normally S.L. basis)	Direct financing: Record in separate account. Add to net investment in lease. Compute new effective rate that equates gross amt. of min. lease payments and unguar. residual value with net invest. Amortize so as to produce constant rate of return over lease term. Sales-type: Expense in period incurred	N/A	N/A
Investment Tax Credit Retained by Lessor	N/A	Reduces FMV of leased asset for 90% test	N/A	Reduces FMV of leased asset for 90% test
Bargain Purchase Option	N/A	Include in: Minimum lease payments 90% test	N/A	Include in: Minimum lease payments 90% test
Guaranteed Residual Value	N/A	Include in: Minimum lease payments 90% test. Sales-type: Include PV in sales revenues	N/A	Include in: Minimum lease payments 90% test
Unguaranteed Residual Value	N/A	Include In: "Gross Investment in Lease". Not included in: 90% test. Sales-type: Exclude from sales revenue. Deduct PV from cost of sales	N/A	Include in: Minimum lease payments 90% test
Contingent Rentals	Revenue in period earned	Not part of minimum lease payments; revenue in period earned	Expense in period incurred	Not part of minimum lease payments; expense in period incurred
Amortization Period	Amortize down to estimated residual value over estimated economic life of asset	N/A	N/A	[b] Amortize down to estimated residual value over lease term or estimated economic life
[a] Revenue (Expense)	Rent revenue (normally S.L. basis). Amortization (depreciation expense)	Direct financing: Interest revenue on net investment in lease (gross investment less unearned interest income). Sales-type: Dealer profit in period of sale (sales revenue less cost of leased asset). Interest revenue on net investment in lease	[c] Rent expense (normally S.L. basis)	Interest Expense and Depreciation Expense

[a] Elements of revenue (expense) listed for the above items are not repeated here (e.g., treatment of initial direct costs).

[b] If lease has automatic passage of title or bargain purchase option, use estimated economic life; otherwise, use the lease term.

[c] If payments are not on a S.L. basis, recognize rent expense on a S.L. basis unless another systematic and rational method is more representative of use benefit obtained from the property, in which case, the other method should be used.

Disclosures

1. **Lessee disclosures**

   a. For capital leases:

      1) The gross amount of assets recorded under capital leases presented by major classes according to function or nature
      2) Future minimum lease payments in the aggregate and for each of the next five fiscal years with separate deductions made for executory costs (including any profit thereon) included in the minimum lease payments, and the amount of imputed interest needed to reduce the net minimum lease payments to present value
      3) Total of minimum sublease rentals to be received in the future under non-cancelable subleases
      4) Total contingent rentals actually incurred for each period for which an income statement is presented
      5) Depreciation on capital leases should be separately disclosed

   b. For sale-leaseback transactions:

      1) In addition to requirements of SFASs 13 and 66, financials of seller-lessee shall describe terms of sale-leaseback transaction, including future commitments, obligations, provisions, or circumstances requiring or resulting in seller-lessee's involvement
      2) Where seller-lessee has accounted for transaction by deposit method or as a financing per SFAS 98, para 17:

         (a) The obligation for future minimum lease payments as of the date of the latest balance sheet presented in the aggregate and for each of the five succeeding fiscal years
         (b) The total of minimum sublease rentals, if any, to be received in the future under noncancelable subleases in the aggregate and for each of the five succeeding fiscal years

   c. For operating leases having a remaining noncancelable term in excess of one year:

      1) Future minimum lease payments in the aggregate and for each of the next five fiscal years
      2) Total of minimum rentals that will be received under noncancelable subleases

   d. For all operating leases:

      1) Present rental expense disclosing separately the amount for minimum rentals, contingent rentals, and sublease rentals

       2) Rental payments for leases with terms of a month or less that were not renewed may be excluded

   e. General description required of lessee's leasing arrangements including, but not limited to:

       1) Basis of computing contingent rental payments
       2) Existence and terms of renewal or purchase options and escalation clauses
       3) Restrictions imposed by leasing agreements such as on dividends, additional debt, and further leasing arrangements

2. Lessor disclosures

   a. For sales-type and direct financing leases:

       1) Components of the net investment in leases include the following:

          a) Future minimum lease payments to be received with separate deductions for amount representing executory costs (including any profit thereon), and the accumulated allowance for uncollectible lease payments
          b) Unguaranteed residual values accruing to benefit of lessor
          c) For direct financing leases only, initial direct costs
          d) Unearned interest revenue

       2) Future minimum lease payments to be received for each of the next five fiscal years
       3) Total contingent rentals included in income for each period for which an income statement is presented

   b. For operating leases:

       1) The cost and carrying amount (if different) of property leased or held for leasing segregated by major classes of property according to function or nature, and the total amount of accumulated depreciation
       2) Minimum rentals on noncancelable leases in the aggregate and for each of the next five fiscal years
       3) Total contingent rentals included in income for each period for which an income statement is presented

   c. A general description of the lessor's leasing arrangements

APPENDIX

Leveraged Leases

One of the more complex accounting subjects regarding leases is the accounting for a leveraged lease. Once again, as with both the sales-type and direct financing, the classification of the lease by the lessor has no impact on the accounting treatment accorded the lease by the lessee. The lessee simply treats it as any other lease and, thus, is only interested in whether the lease qualifies as an operating or capital lease. The lessor's accounting problem is substantially more complex than that of the lessee.

In order to qualify as a leveraged lease, a lease agreement must meet the following requirements, and the lessor must account for the investment tax credit (when in effect) in the manner described below (note: failure to do so will result in the lease being classified as a direct financing lease):

1. The lease must meet the definition of a direct financing lease (the 90% of FMV criterion does not apply)*
2. The lease must involve at least three parties:

   a. An owner-lessor (equity participant)
   b. A lessee
   c. A long-term creditor (debt participant)

3. The financing provided by the creditor is nonrecourse as to the general credit of the lessor and is sufficient to provide the lessor with substantial leverage
4. The lessor's net investment (defined below) decreases in the early years and increases in the later years until it is eliminated

This last characteristic poses the accounting problem.

The leveraged lease arose as a result of an effort to maximize the tax benefits associated with a lease transaction. In order to accomplish this, it was necessary to involve a third party to the lease transaction (in addition to the lessor and lessee)--a long-term creditor. The following diagram illustrates the existing relationships in a leveraged lease agreement:

The leveraged lease arrangement**

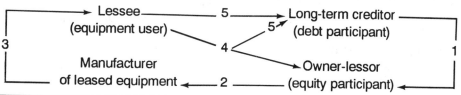

---

* A direct financing lease must have its cost or carrying value equal to the fair value of the asset at the lease's inception. So even if the amounts are not significantly different, leveraged lease accounting shall not be used (TB 88-1).

** Adapted from "A Straightforward Approach to Leveraged Leasing" by Pierce R. Smith, *The Journal of Commercial Bank Lending*, July 1973, pp. 40-47.

1. The owner-lessor secures long-term financing from the creditor, generally in excess of 50% of the purchase price. SFAS 13 indicates that the lessor must be provided with sufficient leverage in the transaction, therefore the 50%.
2. The owner then uses this financing along with his/her own funds to purchase the asset from the manufacturer
3. The manufacturer delivers the asset to the lessee
4. The lessee remits the periodic rent to the lessor
5. The debt is guaranteed by either using the equipment as collateral, the assignment of the lease payments, or both, depending on the demands established by the creditor

The FASB concluded in SFAS 13 that the entire lease agreement be accounted for as a single transaction and not a direct financing lease plus a debt transaction. The feeling was that the latter did not readily convey the net investment in the lease to the user of the financial statements. Thus, in accordance with SFAS 13, the lessor is to record the investment as a net amount. The gross investment is calculated as a combination of the following amounts:

1. The rentals receivable from the lessee, net of the principal and interest payments due to the long-term creditor
2. A receivable for the amount of the Investment Tax Credit (ITC) to be realized on the transaction*
3. The estimated residual value of the leased asset
4. The unearned and deferred income consisting of:

    a. The estimated pretax lease income (or loss), after deducting initial direct costs, remaining to be allocated to income
    b. The ITC remaining to be allocated to income over the remaining term of the lease*

The first three amounts described above are readily obtainable; however, the last amount, the unearned and deferred income, requires additional computations. In order to derive this amount, it is necessary to create a cash flow (income) analysis by year for the entire lease term. As described in (4) above, the unearned and deferred income consists of the pretax lease income (gross lease rentals - depreciation - loan interest) and the unamortized investment Tax Credit. The total of these two amounts for all of the periods in the lease term represents the unearned and deferred income at the inception of the lease.

The amount computed as the gross investment in the lease (foregoing paragraphs) less the deferred taxes relative to the difference between pretax lease income and taxable lease income is the net investment for purposes of computing the net income for

---

The investment tax credit has been repealed, effective January 1, 1986. ITC will be relevant only for property placed in service prior to this date.

the period. In order to compute the periodic net income, another schedule must be completed which uses the cash flows derived in the first schedule and allocates them between income and a reduction in the net investment.

The amount of income is first determined by applying a rate to the net investment. The rate to be used is the rate which will allocate the entire amount of cash flow (income) when applied in the years in which the net investment is positive. In other words, the rate is derived in much the same way as the implicit rate (trial and error), except that only the years in which there is a positive net investment are considered. Thus, income is recognized only in the years in which there is a positive net investment.

The income recognized is divided among the following three elements:

1. Pretax accounting income
2. Amortization of investment tax credit
3. The tax effect of the pretax accounting income

The first two shall be allocated in proportionate amounts from the unearned and deferred income included in the calculation of the net investment. In other words, the unearned and deferred income consists of pretax lease accounting income and ITC. Each of these is recognized during the period in the proportion that the current period's allocated income is to the total income (cash flow). The last item, the tax effect, is recognized in the tax expense for the year. The tax effect of any difference between pretax lease accounting income and taxable lease income is charged (or credited) to deferred taxes.

When tax rates change, all components of a leveraged lease must be recalculated from the inception of the lease using the revised after-tax cash flows arising from the revised tax rates (EITF 86-43).

If, in any case, the projected cash receipts (income) are less than the initial investment, the deficiency is to be recognized as a loss at the inception of the lease. Similarly, if at any time during the lease period the aforementioned method of recognizing income would result in a future period loss, the loss shall be recognized immediately.

This situation may arise as a result of the circumstances surrounding the lease changing. Therefore, any estimated residual value and other important assumptions must be reviewed on a periodic basis (at least annually). Any change is to be incorporated into the income computations; however, there is to be no upward revision of the estimated residual value.

The following example illustrates the application of these principles to a leveraged lease:

Example of Simplified Leveraged Lease

Assume the following:

1. A lessor acquires an asset for $100,000 with an estimated useful life of 3

years in exchange for a $25,000 down payment and a $75,000 three-year note with equal payments due on 12/31 each year. The interest rate is 18%.

2. The asset has no residual value.
3. The PV of an ordinary annuity of $1 for 3 years at 18% is 2.17427.
4. The asset is leased for three years with annual payments due to the lessor on 12/31 in the amount of $45,000.
5. The lessor uses the ACRS method of depreciation for tax purposes and elects to reduce the ITC rate to 4% as opposed to reducing the depreciable basis.
6. Assume a constant tax rate throughout the life of the lease of 40%.

Chart I analyzes the cash flows generated by the leveraged leasing activities. Chart II allocates the cash flows between the investment in leveraged leased assets and income from leveraged leasing activities. The allocation requires finding that rate of return which when applied to the investment balance at the beginning of each year that the investment amount is positive, will allocate the net cash flow fully to net income over the term of the lease. This rate can be found only by a computer program or by an iterative trial and error process. The example which follows has a positive investment value in each of the three years, and thus the allocation takes place in each time period. Leveraged leases usually have periods where the investment account turns negative and is below zero.

Allocating principal and interest on the loan payments is as follows:

$$(\$75,000 \div 2.17427 = \$34,494)$$

Year	Payment	Interest 18%	Principal	Balance
Inception of lease	$ --	$ --	$ --	$75,000
1	34,494	13,500	20,994	54,006
2	34,494	9,721	24,773	29,233
3	34,494	5,261	29,233	--

Chart I

	A	B	C	D	E	F	G	H	I
					Income				
					tax			*Cash*	
				Taxable	*payable*	*Loan*		*flow*	*Cumulative*
			Interest	*income*	*(rcvbl.)*	*principal*		*(A+G-C*	*cash*
	Rent	*Depr.*	*on loan*	*(A-B-C)*	*Dx40%*	*payments*	*ITC*	*-E-F)*	*flow*
Initial	$ --	$ --	$ --	$ --	$ --	$ --	$ --	$(25,000)	$(25,000)
Year 1	45,000	25,000	13,500	6,500	2,600	20,994	4,000	11,906	(13,094)
Year 2	45,000	38,000	9,721	(2,721)	(1,088)	24,773	--	11,594	(1,500)
Year 3	45,000	37,000	5,261	2,739	1,096	29,233	--	9,410	7,910
Total	$135,000	$100,000	$28,482	$ 6,518	$ 2,608	$75,000	$4,000	$ 7,910	

The chart below allocates the cash flows determined above between the net

investment in the lease and income. Recall that the income is then allocated between pretax accounting income and the amortization of the investment for credit.
The income tax expense for the period is a result of applying the tax rate to the
current periodic pretax accounting income.

The amount to be allocated in total in each period is the net cash flow determined in column H above. The investment at the beginning of year 1 is the initial
down payment of $25,000. This investment is then reduced on an annual basis by
the amount of the cash flow not allocated to income.

Chart II

	1	2	3	4	5	6	7
		Cash Flow Assumption				*Income Analysis*	
	Investment		*Allocated*	*Allocated*		*Income*	*Investment*
	beginning	*Cash*	*to*	*to*	*Pretax*	*tax*	*tax*
	of year	*flow*	*investment*	*income*	*income*	*expense*	*credit*
Year 1	$25,000	$11,906	$ 7,964	$3,942	$3,248	$1,300	1,994
Year 2	17,036	11,594	8,908	2,686	2,213	885	1,358
Year 3	8,128	9,410	8,128	1,282	1,057	423	648
		$32,910	$25,000	$7,910	$6,518	$2,608	$4,000

Rate of return = 15.77%

1. Column 2 is the net cash flow after the initial investment, and columns 3
   and 4 are the allocation based upon the 15.77% rate of return. The total of
   column 4 is the same as the total of column H in Chart I.
2. Column 5 allocates column D in Chart I based upon the allocations in column 4. Column 6 allocates column E in Chart I, and column 7 allocates
   column G in Chart I in the same basis.

The journal entries below illustrate the proper recording and accounting for the
leveraged lease transaction. The initial entry represents the cash down payment,
investment tax credit receivable, the unearned and deferred revenue, and the net
cash to be received over the term of the lease.

The remaining journal entries recognize the annual transactions which include
the net receipt of cash and the amortization of income.

	Year 1		Year 2		Year 3	
Rents receivable [Chart I (A-C-F)]	31,518					
Investment tax credit receivable	4,000					
Cash		25,000				
Unearned and deferred income		10,518				
[Initial investment, Chart II (5+7) totals]						
Cash	10,506		10,506		10,506	
Rent receivable		10,506		10,506		10,506
[Net for all cash transactions, Chart I (A-C-F) line by line for each year]						
Income tax receivable (cash)	4,000					
Investment tax credit receivable		4,000				
Unearned and deferred income	5,242		3,571		1,705	
Income from leveraged leases		5,242		3,571		1,705
[Amortization of unearned income, Chart II (5+7) line by line for each year]						

The following schedules illustrate the computation of deferred income tax amount. The annual amount is a result of the temporary difference created due to the difference in the timing of the recognition of income for book and tax purposes. The income for tax purposes can be found in column D in Chart I, while the income for book purposes is found in column 5 of Chart II. The actual amount of deferred tax is the difference between the tax computed with the temporary difference and the tax computed without the temporary difference. These amounts are represented by the income tax payable or receivable as shown in column E of Chart I and the income tax expense as shown in column 6 of Chart II. A check of this figure is provided by multiplying the difference between book and tax income by the annual rate.

Year 1

Income tax payable	$ 2,600	
Income tax expense	(1,300)	
Deferred income tax (Dr)		$1,300
Taxable income	$ 6,500	
Pretax accounting income	(3,248)	
Difference	$ 3,252	

$3,252 x 40% = $1,300

Year 2

Income tax receivable	$ 1,088	
Income tax expense	885	
Deferred income tax (Cr)		$1,973
Taxable loss	$ 2,721	
Pretax accounting income	2,213	
Difference	$ 4,934	

$4,934 x 40% = $1,973

Year 3

Income tax payable	$ 1,096	
Income tax expense	(423)	
Deferred income tax (Dr)		$ 673
Taxable income	$ 2,739	
Pretax accounting income	(1,057)	
Difference	$ 1,682	

$1,682 x 40% = $673

14 Accounting for Income Taxes

Perspective and Issues

The longstanding debate over accounting for income taxes remains unresolved, nine years after the topic was placed on the FASB's technical agenda and four years after the issuance of the ill-fated SFAS 96. A recently exposed standard will likely be adopted in 1992 to supersede SFAS 96. The proposed standard, while continuing most of the basic principles of SFAS 96, will nonetheless streamline the measurement of deferred income taxes and modify certain key elements of its predecessor. Because SFAS 96 is now destined to become obsolete, few additional entities will adopt it, although those that previously had done so **cannot** revert to APB 11. The new standard, if adopted as proposed, will be effective for fiscal years beginning after December 15, 1992, with earlier application available.

SFAS 96 (and its expected successor) altered the basic principles of accounting for income taxes established by APB 11. Prior GAAP was based on the **matching concept** and, accordingly, focussed primarily on the income statement effects of deferred taxes. SFAS 96 adopted the so-called asset-and-liability approach which is far more concerned with the balance sheet. This shift in emphasis was foretold when the Board adopted the Statements of Financial Accounting Concepts (SFAC), especially SFAC 6, *Elements of Financial Statements*, which necessitated a change in the measurement strategy for deferred tax assets and liabilities.

Rather than seeking to optimize the periodic measurement of revenue and expense, SFAS 96 opts for the good of ensuring that the tax effects, as measured by enacted tax laws, have been reflected for all events that have been recognized through the date of the current balance sheet. The deferred tax accounts are to be updated to incorporate those expectations that have changed since the economic events have occurred. This continual updating is only one of the major changes from APB 11.

SFAS 96 has two significant caveats: it establishes a severe limitation on the recognition of deferred tax benefits, and does not permit discounting of deferred tax assets and liabilities. The first limitation follows from the Board's conclusion that future income or expenses are not assumed and cannot be used in the calculation of the deferred tax accounts. The second limitation, prohibiting discounting, is not conceptually based but reflects the Board's desire to delay any rule-making until a comprehensive project on the use of present value measures has been completed. The proposed replacement for SFAS 96 completely removes the restriction on recognition of deferred tax assets, although under some circumstances an allowance account will need to be provided against the asset. Discounting has still not been addressed and therefore will not be permitted. Although the Board did issue a discussion memorandum on the broad issue of present value-based measures last year, resolution of that project is not anticipated to occur in the near term.

Prior to the promulgation of APB 11 in 1967, the so-called "liability method" was commonly employed. To a large extent, SFAS 96 mandates a return to the liability method from the "deferred method" used in APB 11. However, as set forth by SFAS 96, the asset and liability approach is more complex than the former liability method, and requires a more mechanistic orientation on the part of the preparer. In general, the deferred tax asset or liability cannot be computed simply by multiplying the reporting entity's aggregate "temporary differences" by its present or anticipated future marginal tax rate. Instead, a detailed scheduling by year of future reversals of all existing differences will be necessary. This is also a major departure from prior practice. This need for scheduling of temporary difference reversals was one of SFAS 96's least popular features. The proposed successor to this standard will eliminate this requirement and instead mandate that deferred tax assets and liabilities be provided at the **marginal** tax rates expected to apply to the reversals, including the future utilization of net operating loss carryforwards. This is a major change from the requirements set forth by SFAS 96.

SFAS 96 also has altered (1) the method of reporting net operating loss carryforwards that are not recognized until subsequently realized for tax purposes, (2) the balance sheet classification of deferred tax benefits and obligations, (3) the accounting for the deferred tax effects arising from purchase business combinations, and (4) the accounting for acquired net operating loss benefits. Most of these changes would be continued if the proposed successor to SFAS 96 is adopted. However, balance sheet classification of deferred tax assets and liabilities will revert to the approach employed under APB 11 and SFAS 37.

As originally promulgated, SFAS 96 was to have been effective for years beginning after December 15, 1988. However, the Board subsequently issued SFAS 100, which delayed the effective date for one year (to years beginning after December 15, 1989) while encouraging earlier adoption. SFAS 103 delayed the effective date for two additional years (to years beginning after December 15, 1991). Concurrent with its decision to expose a proposed successor to SFAS 96, the Board also proposed a further delay in the effective date of SFAS 96, to years beginning after December 15, 1992. Entities which previously did not adopt SFAS 96 will not be required to do so for the one year remaining until the new standard takes effect.

This chapter discusses accounting for income taxes under the provisions of SFAS 96, which is the preferable accounting principle under current GAAP. Appendix C discusses APB 11's provisions, while Appendix D sets forth the major provisions of the Board's proposed successor to SFAS 96.

Sources of GAAP

APB	*SFAS*	*FASB I*
2, 4, 10,	96,	18
23, 28	103	

Definitions of Terms

Deferred tax asset. The deferred tax consequences of temporary differences that will result in net tax deductions in future years.

Deferred tax liability. The deferred tax consequences of temporary differences that will result in net taxable amounts in future years.

Interperiod tax allocation. The process of apportioning income tax expense among reporting periods without regard to the timing of the actual cash payments for taxes. The objective is to reflect fully the tax consequences of all economic events reported in current or prior financial statements and, in particular, to report the expected tax effects of the reversals of temporary differences existing at the reporting date.

Intraperiod tax allocation. The process of apportioning income tax expense applicable to a given period between, income before extraordinary items, and those items required to be shown net of tax such as extraordinary items and prior period adjustments.

Operating loss carryback or carryforward. For tax purposes, an excess of tax deductions over taxable income in a given year, which may be carried back or forward to reduce taxable income in earlier or later years. For financial reporting purposes, an operating loss carryforward is the tax NOL carryforward reduced by the amount which offsets deferred tax liabilities and increased by unrecognized deferred tax benefits.

Permanent differences. Differences between pretax accounting income and taxable income as a result of the treatment accorded certain transactions by the income tax regulations which differs from the accounting treatment. Permanent differences will not reverse in subsequent periods.

Pretax accounting income. Income or loss for the accounting period as determined in accordance with GAAP without regard to the income tax expense for the period.

Tax credits. Reductions in the tax liability as a result of certain expenditures accorded special treatment under the Internal Revenue Code. Examples of such credits are: the Investment Tax Credit, investment in certain depreciable property; the Jobs Credit, payment of wages to targeted groups; the Research and Development Credit, an increase in qualifying R & D expenditures; among others.

Taxable income. The difference between the revenue and expenses as defined by the Internal Revenue Code for a taxable period without regard to the special deductions (e.g., net operating loss or contribution carrybacks and carryforwards).

Tax planning strategy. A representation by management of a planned transaction or series of transactions that would affect the particular future years in which temporary differences will result in taxable or deductible amounts.

Temporary differences. In general, differences between tax and financial reporting bases of assets and liabilities that will result in taxable or deductible amounts in future periods. Temporary differences include "timing differences" as defined by prior GAAP as well as certain other differences, such as those arising from business combinations. Some temporary differences cannot be associated with particular assets or liabilities, but nonetheless do result from events that received financial statement recognition and will have tax effects in future periods.

Concepts, Rules, and Examples

Interperiod Income Tax Allocation

Prior to the promulgation of APB 11, there was a wide-ranging debate among proponents of no allocation (reporting taxes currently payable as income tax expense), partial allocation (providing deferred taxes only for those timing differences whose net reversal could be reasonably predicted), and comprehensive allocation. APB 11 endorsed comprehensive allocation, and this position also has been adopted by the FASB in SFAS 96. (However, a major exception to comprehensive allocation, relating to unremitted earnings of subsidiaries, was created by APB 23, and was not amended by SFAS 96. Apparently, the exception will not be altered under the proposed provisions of the standard which will supersede SFAS 96.)

Comprehensive interperiod tax allocation requires the provision of income taxes for all items of income and expense reported in the statement of income, whether or not these items enter into the determination of taxes currently payable--with the exception of **permanent differences** for which deferred taxes are never provided. (An example of a permanent difference is officer's life insurance, when the cash surrender value is expected to be realized upon the death of the insured.) All **temporary differences** are subject to deferred tax accounting.

Under APB 11, the term "timing differences" referred to items of income or expense which entered into the determination of taxable income in periods different than financial reporting income. Common examples were depreciation, deferred compensation, prepaid income, bad debt reserves, and cash-versus-accrual accounting. These items are included as "temporary differences" as defined by SFAS 96. However, the newer term is more inclusive than the one it replaces. It also connotes the effects of asset basis reductions for tax credits taken, asset basis increases resulting from inflation indexing, certain intercompany transfers among entities for which consolidated financial statements but not consolidated tax returns are prepared, and certain effects of accounting for purchase business combinations.

In analyzing an item's differential tax and financial reporting treatments, it is helpful to identify the periods of **origination** and periods of **reversal**. When a presumptive temporary difference does not appear to have an expected reversal, it is possible that the difference is actually a permanent one. This approach is particularly useful when dealing with new or complex differences--as witnessed by the accounting for the basis reduction for ITC taken under the 1982 tax act (TEFRA), which many incorrectly perceived to be a permanent difference until clarification was issued by the FASB in 1983.

While the requirement for comprehensive interperiod tax allocation appears to be well understood in practice, the appropriate measurement of tax expense, including the tax effects of temporary differences, is less clear. This will be addressed in the following section.

Measurement of Expense

A number of theories have been advanced over the years regarding the computation of income tax expense when temporary differences exist. The most popular have been the **deferred method** (which was GAAP under APB 11) and the **liability method** (prohibited by APB 11, but sanctioned by SFAS 96 and its proposed successor). A third approach, the **net of tax method**, has received a good deal of academic support but was less widely employed (or understood) by practitioners. Although the deferred method was soundly based on the matching principle, it was complex to apply (as defined by the APB) and sometimes resulted in apparent distortion in the balance sheet. As attention in recent years has shifted again to the meaningful reporting of **financial position**, these issues have received renewed scrutiny. Following the promulgation of SFAC 6, it became inevitable that substantial changes in accounting for income taxes would be made. As defined in SFAC 6, the deferred charges and credits created by the proper application of APB 11 are generally **not** true assets or liabilities and do not belong on the balance sheet.

Deferred method. APB 11 required comprehensive interperiod income tax allocation. The conceptual justification supporting the deferred method of allocation appears to be found in the matching principle. Recall that the need for tax allocation is a result of differences between accounting and taxable income that will reverse. The deferred method determines the income tax expense for the period based on the accounting income while the current liability is based on taxable income. The difference between the actual current liability and the income tax expense is treated as either a deferred charge or credit which is amortized as the timing differences reverse. Timing differences that originate during the period are referred to as originating differences, while the reversal of tax effects arising from differences which originated in prior periods are referred to as reversing differences.

The tax computation which was used to determine the amount of deferred tax under APB 11 generally was referred to as the "with and without" or differential computation of income tax expense. According to APB 11, "the tax effect of a timing difference should be measured by the differential between income taxes computed with and without inclusion of the transaction creating the difference between taxable income and pretax accounting income." The purpose of the "with and without" computation was to take into account the effect of the graduated rate system. This required that the timing differences be added to (or subtracted from) taxable income and a tax on this amount was computed to determine the amount of tax had the timing difference not existed. The computation was relatively simple when there was only a single timing difference.

When many timing differences occurred in the same period, the calculation of the deferred tax adjustment became more complicated. If properly applied, APB 11 demanded that separate "with and without" computations be made for each "class" of timing difference--e.g., depreciation, prepaid income, etc. Originating and reversing differences within a given class of timing difference could be considered together if the "net change" method were used, but if the more precise "gross change" method were employed separate tax effects were to have been calculated. In practice, various shortcut methods were commonly used, often grouping **all** timing difference originations and reversals together. Frequently, the resultant deferred tax provision was different from the number prescribed by APB 11--often materially so.

In fact many accountants employed as a shortcut computation a technique that approximated the "liability method" of the pre-APB 11 era. (Of course, this clearly contradicted the requirements of APB 11.) Although SFAS 96 reestablishes the liability method as GAAP, the liability approach utilized most commonly as a shortcut under APB 11 will not be appropriate under the new standard. The specific requirements of SFAS 96 are discussed in the following pages.

Liability method--an overview. The liability method is balance sheet oriented, in direct contrast to the deferred method which is income statement oriented. The primary goal of the liability method is to present the estimated actual taxes to be payable in future periods as the income tax liability on the balance sheet. In order to accomplish this goal, it is necessary to consider the effect of certain enacted future changes in the tax rates when computing the current period's tax provision. The computation of the amount of deferred taxes is based on the rate expected to be in effect when the temporary differences reverse. The annual computation is considered a tentative estimate of the liability (or asset) which is subject to change as the statutory tax rate changes or as the taxpayer moves into other tax rate brackets.

SFAC 6 defines liabilities as "probable future sacrifices of economic benefits arising from present obligations of a particular entity to transfer assets or provide services to other entities in the future as a result of past transactions." Assets, on the other hand, are defined as "probable future economic benefits obtained or controlled by a particular entity as a result of past transactions or events." According to SFAC 6, the deferred tax credits and debits that are generated by the liability method result in liabilities or assets that meet the definitions in the SFAC. The SFAC specifically states that the deferred debits and credits generated through the use of the deferred method do not meet the definitions of assets and liabilities prescribed by the SFAC. This lack of consistency was one of the primary reasons for the FASB's reconsideration of APB 11, which culminated in the issuance of SFAS 96 in December 1987.

Application of the liability method is, in concept at least, relatively simple in comparison to the deferred method. This is a balance sheet approach. The primary concern is to state the taxes payable account as accurately as possible. This is accomplished by multiplying the aggregate unreversed temporary differences including those originating this period by the expected future rate to determine the expected future liability. This expected liability is the amount presented on the balance sheet at the end of the period. The difference between this amount and the amount on the books at the beginning of the period is the deferred tax expense for the period. (Of course, this is a gross simplification of SFAS 96's requirements, but it serves to set forth the basic notion of the liability method. The complexities of SFAS 96 are discussed beginning on page 424.)

Simplified Example of Interperiod Allocation Using the Liability Method

Gries International has no permanent differences in either years 19X3 and 19X4. The company has only two temporary differences, depreciation and prepaid rent. No consideration is given to the nature of the deferred tax account (i.e., current or long-term) as it is not considered necessary for purposes of this example. Gries has a credit balance in its deferred tax account at the beginning of 19X3 in the amount of $180,000. This balance consists of $228,000 ($475,000 depreciation temporary difference x 48% tax rate) of deferred taxable amounts and $48,000 ($100,000 prepaid rent temporary difference x 48% tax rate) of deferred deductible amounts.

For purposes of this example, it is assumed that there was a constant 48% tax rate in all of the prior periods. The pretax accounting income and the temporary differences originating and reversing in 19X3 and 19X4 are as follows:

Gries International

	19X3		19X4	
Pretax accounting income		$800,000		$1,200,000
Timing differences:				
Depreciation--originating	(180,000)		(160,000)	
reversing	60,000	(120,000)	100,000	(60,000)
Prepaid rental income--originating	75,000		80,000	
reversing	(25,000)	50,000	(40,000)	40,000
Taxable income		$730,000		$1,180,000

The tax rates for years 3 and 4 are 46% and 38%, respectively. These rates are assumed to be independent of one another and the 19X4 change in the rate was not known until it took place in 19X4.

Computation of tax provision--19X3:

Balance of deferred tax account, 1/1/X3		
Depreciation ($475,000 x 48%)		$228,000
Prepaid rental income ($100,000 x 48%)		(48,000)
		$180,000
Aggregate temporary differences, 12/31/X3		
Depreciation ($475,000 + 120,000)	$595,000	
Prepaid rental income ($100,000 + 50,000)	(150,000)	
	$445,000	
Expected future rate (19X3 rate)	x 46%	
Balance required in the deferred tax account,		
12/31/X3		204,700
Required addition to the deferred tax account		$ 24,700
Income taxes currently payable ($730,000 x 46%)		335,800
Total tax provision		$360,500

Computation of tax provision--19X4

Balance of deferred tax account, 1/1/X4		
Depreciation ($595,000 x 46%)		$273,700
Prepaid rental income ($150,000 x 46%)		(69,000)
		$204,700
Aggregate timing differences, 12/31/X4		
Depreciation ($595,000 + 60,000)	$655,000	
Prepaid rental income ($150,000 + 40,000)	(190,000)	
	$465,000	
Expected future rate (19X4 rate)	x 38%	
Balance required in the deferred tax account,		
12/31/X4		176,700
Required reduction in the deferred tax account		$(28,000)
Income taxes currently payable ($1,180,000 x 38%)		448,400
Total tax provision		$420,400

Complexities in the Liability Method--SFAS 96

Although the liability method of accounting for deferred income taxes is conceptually straightforward, under SFAS 96 the method has quite a few complexities. The Board also issued an implementation guide to answer some of the many questions which have arisen regarding certain of the complexities inherent in SFAS 96. The guidance provided therein has been incorporated in the following discussion, where appropriate. Some of this guidance will continue to be relevant under the provisions of the proposed standard which is expected to supersede SFAS 96, while other parts of it will be made obsolete when, and if, that proposal is adopted.

In the following pages, these measurement and reporting issues will be discussed in greater detail:

- Limitation on deferred tax benefit recognition
- Projection of future **originating** differences
- Need for precise schedule of future temporary differences

- Special issues re: depreciation differences
- Special issues re: lease accounting differences
- Goodwill and "negative goodwill" issues
- Treatment of other intangible assets
- Special issues re: inventory differences
- Other temporary differences resulting from "TRA '86"
- Use of tax planning strategies

A detailed, complex example of the computation of the deferred tax adjustment under SFAS 96 is presented following this discussion.

Limitation on deferred tax benefits. A key principle subscribed to by SFAS 96 is that the amount of a net deferred tax asset to be recognized is limited to the tax benefits of net deductible amounts that could be realized by means of a loss carryback to reduce taxes currently payable, or paid in prior years. The reason for this strict limitation (as contrasted to APB 11's simpler criterion that deferred tax assets be evaluated, in common with all assets, for realizability) is that no future income is assumed to be earned apart from temporary difference reversals which generate taxable amounts. Accordingly, if the scheduling exercise (described below) results in a projection of net **deductible** amounts, and the entity cannot project the opportunity to use these deductibles as either carrybacks or carryforwards, then given the requirements of U.S. tax law it must be assumed that the tax benefits of these deductible amounts will be lost. The inability to project or assume future taxable income other than that resulting from temporary differences, notwithstanding the entity's past earnings history, is a strict application of the realization concept. (However, the Board has taken an almost diametrically opposite stand on this issue in its proposal to supersede SFAS 96, which, if adopted, will permit unlimited recognition of deferred tax benefits and eliminate the need for routine scheduling of reversals of temporary differences.)

To illustrate the limitation on the recognition of deferred tax benefits under SFAS 96, consider the following simplified example:

Facts: Projected future temporary difference reversals will give rise to the following net taxable or deductible amounts:

Year	Taxable (deductible) amounts
1992	$45,000
1993	60,000
1994	50,000
1995-1996	0
1997	(60,000)

All taxable or deductible amounts will be tax effected at a 34% rate.

The taxable amounts in years 1992-94, totaling $155,000, give rise to deferred tax liabilities of $52,700 (34% of $155,000). The deductible amount projected for 1997 can only be carried back to 1994, and thus the benefit to be recognized is limited to $17,000 (34% of $50,000). The tax benefit of the remaining $10,000 deductible amount in 1996 could only be recognized if there were taxable amounts projected for years after 1996 against which the carryforward could be applied.

Although SFAS 96's limitation on net deferred tax benefits is consistent with income tax law, this became one of the new standard's most controversial features. Many reporting entities, especially banks, complained strenuously about this feature. Banks generally report net deferred tax debits because the principal temporary difference affecting them is the provision for the loan losses required under GAAP, which is non-deductible for tax purposes until actual charge-offs are made. (In its proposal to supersede SFAS 96, the Board concluded that the tax effects of Future deductible amounts are indeed recognizable assets; if adopted, this standard will require recognition of not only Future temporary difference reversals, but the benefit of net operating losses as well.)

Certain temporary difference reversals, such as depreciation, are subject to precise scheduling. Others are subject to "management intentions," and thus may be difficult to independently verify, which poses both an accounting and an auditing issue. Certain criteria for such tax planning strategies are incorporated into (or strongly implied by) SFAS 96. These are discussed later in this chapter.

The necessity for scheduling of future reversals also follows from the Board's decision that no future items of revenue and expense can be assumed--i.e., that only the reversals of past temporary differences can be anticipated. This means, from a computational standpoint, that the effects of lower bracket tax rates will impact upon the deferred tax asset or liability heavily, and in fact, all future reversals could enter deferred taxes at the lowest tax rate even though the reporting entity's taxable income is expected to be well into the top bracket every year.

Projection of future originating differences. In general, the computation of deferred tax assets or liabilities as of an entity's balance sheet date will involve the projection of reversals of temporary differences existing as of that date. This is a consequence of the essential character of most temporary differences, which are discrete originating events followed some period later by discrete reversing events. However, the so-called "asset and liability" approach endorsed by SFAS 96 does not strictly preclude the recognition of the tax effects of future **originating** temporary differences. This is because the objective of income tax accounting under this standard is the recognition of the income tax effects of all assets and liabilities presented in the balance sheet. Certain of these assets and liabilities, such as plant assets, may have predictable future temporary difference originations as well as reversals.

To schedule future temporary difference originations is **not** in any way analogous to making assumptions about future items of income or expense, which is prohibited under SFAS 96. The tax implications of future events--such as future purchases of plant, property, and equipment--are never to be projected. However, assets existing at the balance sheet date have tax attributes which must be considered in calculating the reporting entity's deferred tax position at that date. These tax attributes can include future originations as well as future reversals. As a practical matter, however, there are few assets or liabilities for which future temporary difference originations will be subject to scheduling. Plant assets and certain leases are the two categories which give rise to most projections of future temporary difference originations. These are addressed in detail below.

The need for scheduling. Under previous GAAP (APB 11, et al), deferred taxes were computed as timing differences originated by means of the calculation known as the "with and without method." These deferred tax effects were subsequently "amortized" as the timing differences actually reversed. In the interim, the deferred taxes remained on the balance sheet, immune to any revision or adjustment. Therefore, there was no need to schedule the pattern of future reversals.

The conceptual foundation for current GAAP is substantially different than prior accounting. The tax effects of assets and liabilities are very much affected by the expected timing of future reversals of existing temporary differences. This is true for several reasons: (1) expected tax rates (based on current law) may differ in the various years of future reversals; (2) since no other items of future taxable income or deductions can be assumed, the effects of graduated tax rates will vary depending upon whether scheduled reversals are spread over several years or are projected to occur simultaneously; and (3) the strict limitation on the recognition of deferred tax assets means that tax effects of future tax deductions related to existing temporary differences will achieve accounting recognition only when the pattern of their occurrence bears certain relationships to projected reversals causing taxable amounts in future years.

Accordingly, it will usually be necessary to schedule future temporary difference reversals (and certain originations also, as noted above and further explained below) on a year-by-year basis. SFAS 96 suggests that under certain circumstances scheduling can be omitted, however. This generally will be possible only when all temporary differences are susceptible (under existing tax law) to tax planning strategies: if such is the case, an "aggregate" calculation assuming the offsetting of all temporary difference reversals can be used. It should be understood that, while theoretically possible, such will rarely be justifiable. In short, scheduling will most often be a necessity of compliance with SFAS 96. The difficulty of complying with this aspect of SFAS 96 was a major reason for its being eliminated in the Board's recently exposed replacement for SFAS 96.

Depreciation. Differences in depreciation between financial reporting and tax reporting have typically been one of the major temporary differences giving rise to deferred taxes under prior GAAP. Depreciation will continue to be a factor under SFAS 96 as well. Depreciation temporary differences are easily scheduled and should include both future originations (i.e., periods when tax depreciation exceeds book depreciation) as well as reversals.

Consistent with the "asset and liability" orientation of SFAS 96, only the tax effects of assets classified as depreciable property in the balance sheet should be considered.

Accordingly, future asset acquisitions (even if supported by management intentions) are to be ignored. For this reason, construction in progress at the balance sheet date should **not** result in scheduled temporary differences, unless the construction-in-progress balance sheet account already incorporates tax-book differences. In the latter case (which is certainly a possibility, especially as a consequence of the uniform cost capitalization rules of TRA '86), the future reversals should be scheduled, but the future originations should not be, in the opinion of the EITF's implementation group.

It would seem that a similar approach should be taken in the case of plant assets which have been removed from the depreciable asset category because they have been placed on a "stand-by" status. These assets are properly reported as "other assets," not as property, plant and equipment on the balance sheet. Any temporary differences existing at the date the assets' status is redefined would reverse when the assets either are returned to service or are disposed of. Consequently, no further originations should be scheduled; the aggregate existing temporary difference, if any, should be projected to reverse in the indefinite future in the absence of convincing management intentions to the contrary.

Leases. There are at least two situations involving leases that lend themselves to detailed scheduling of future originations and reversals. The first of these is when a lease is accounted for as a capital asset for financial reporting purposes but is treated as an operating lease by the lessee for tax purposes. In such a circumstance, the lessee will report rent expense in future tax returns but will reflect depreciation and interest expense in future financial statements. Since the timing of these alternative deductions will differ, future originations and reversals can be identified with the balance sheet asset and liability (the leased asset and the related obligation). The precise tax effects will depend on several factors, including the method of (book) depreciation to be used, the depreciable life employed, and whether the value originally attributed to the leased asset was adjusted to reflect net realizable value. The depreciable life may be shorter than the lease term if useful **economic** life is deemed to be less than the non-cancelable lease term, or it may be longer than the lease term if a bargain purchase option exists and economic life is deemed to extend beyond the basic term of the lease. Again, year-by-year scheduling will generally be necessary to sort through the deferred tax implications of transactions such as these.

A second category of lease transaction potentially giving rise to deferred taxes involves operating leases which have scheduled rent increases in the primary lease term. GAAP (as set forth in Technical Bulletin 85-3) requires a "straight lining" of total rent expense recognition by the lessee and of income recognition by the lessor. For tax purposes, however, rent expense and income for the period must be recognized as stipulated in the lease agreement. Accordingly, the lessee will accumulate, in the early years, an accrued liability; the lessor will recognize a receivable for deferred rent. These liabilities and assets, respectively, have tax attributes generating deferred tax benefits and liabilities.

While it would mechanically be rather simple to schedule all future tax and book lease expenses (or income), including both future originations as well as reversals of temporary difference, this may not be appropriate. This is so because the accrued lease obligation (for the lessee) and lease receivable (for the lessor) represents only the presently existing amount which will eventually reverse; future originations do not really relate to any balance sheet account (at least for the lessee, which does not report the plant asset being leased in its balance sheet). Consequently, it would appear most consistent with SFAS 96's underlying philosophy to schedule reversals in these cases only. Of course, on a notation basis both future originations and reversals will probably be scheduled in order to ascertain precisely when the reversals phase will commence. A logical assumption (FIFO would seem most defensible) must also be made regarding the "flow" of the deferred rent obligation (i.e., do previously accumulated differences reverse before yet-unaccumulated future originations?), and once adopted this assumption should be consistently applied.

Goodwill and negative goodwill. Goodwill arises when part of the price paid in a business combination accounted for as a purchase cannot be allocated to identifiable assets; "negative goodwill" results from so-called bargain purchases. Goodwill is not deductible or amortizable for tax purposes but must be amortized (per APB 17) for financial reporting in accordance with GAAP. Since "negative goodwill" is offset against all noncurrent assets (except long-term marketable securities) for financial reporting, differences between tax and book depreciation will result.

Since goodwill (whether positive or negative) has no tax impact until the ultimate liquidation or sale of the acquired entity, SFAS 96 logically prohibits recognizing any deferred tax effects relating to goodwill. Although **ultimately** goodwill will reduce the taxable gain from the sale of the business, the going concern concept supports the Board's position that no assumption can be made that such a disposition will occur. Furthermore, absent an assumption that the sale would result in a taxable gain (which assumption cannot be made), any related deduction in the indefinite future could not generate a deferred tax benefit to be recognized currently. (The Board has continued this reasoning in its proposed standard to replace SFAS 96, with the logical but minor revision to the effect that to the extent goodwill is deductible in foreign tax jurisdictions, it is a temporary difference for which deferred taxes should be provided.)

Other nondeductible intangibles. Certain intangibles are not amortizable for tax purposes and may only be deducted upon the discontinuance of a business operation. Although this is analogous to the situation for goodwill described above, the preliminary position of the Board is different regarding the tax implications of such intangibles. The FASB staff has suggested that book and tax deductions for such intangible assets (which could include television licenses and trademarks, for example) should be fully scheduled for all future years, with the tax deduction being projected to occur in the indefinite future. Since the tax benefit of this deduction will probably not result in a recognizable deferred tax asset (unless offset by a tax liability coincidentally scheduled to occur also in the indefinite future), the net effect of this exercise will generally be to recognize only the deferred tax liability associated with the book amortization scheduled for future years.

It is not completely clear why the Board favors this approach. SFAS 96 explicitly provides that goodwill does not give rise to deferred taxes, but is silent as to other analogous intangibles. The staff of the FASB has taken that injunction to imply that the rather peculiar result described above is necessary to comply with the standard. For reporting entities having material amounts of both goodwill and other nondeductible intangibles, adequate footnote disclosure would seem to be a necessity in order to guide the user of the financial statements through this inconsistency. In the proposed standard which will, if adopted, supersede SFAS 96, the Board continues this differential treatment or goodwill and other nondeductible intangibles.

Inventories. Several categories of temporary differences arise in connection with inventories. Certain book deductions--for obsolescent or damaged goods and for excess quantities--cannot be taken for tax purposes until such time as the goods are actually disposed of, scrapped, or marketed at reduced selling prices. The scheduling of these reversals should be based on actual historical experience, such as selling obsolete goods within two years of identifying them. The resultant deferred tax benefit will be reflected as a deferred tax asset (or possibly as a reduction in the deferred tax liability) if the criteria in SFAS 96 (e.g., availability of operating loss carryback) are met.

The allocation of certain general and administrative overhead costs to inventories under the Uniform Cost Capitalization rules may also result in tax-book inventory differences. In general, where such temporary differences arise, inventories are larger for tax reporting purposes than for financial statement purposes; this will lead to projected deductible amounts in future years and a deferred tax benefit (or reduced deferred tax liability) in the reporting entity's balance sheet.

Other temporary differences resulting from TRA '86. The 1986 Tax Reform Act enacted a number of changes in accounting that require taxpayers to restate certain balance sheet accounts (such as inventories and receivables), with the adjustment being taken into taxable income over a stipulated period (generally no more than four years). Often, these mandated changes will give rise to **two** temporary differences to be scheduled over future years.

As an example, consider the new tax requirement that the specific bad debt charge-off method be used, and that the accrual of bad debt reserves (allowance for doubtful accounts) be prohibited for tax accounting purposes. If a company has previously been providing bad debt reserves for financial reporting (as required under GAAP) **and** tax, the TRA '86 change will have the following effects:

(i) Temporary differences between book provisions for doubtful accounts and tax deductions based on the specific charge-off method, must be scheduled as to the expected timing of reversals. Appropriate deferred tax benefits should be recognized subject to the usual SFAS 96 limitations. As a general observation, such charge-offs should occur within a year or two, at most, subsequent to the balance sheet date at which the reserve is provided.

(ii) The amount of the allowance account existing at the date of the change mandated by TRA '86 must be taken into taxable income over four years (generally). These are in the nature of temporary difference reversals also, and therefore logic would suggest that these should be scheduled out as well. Since these give rise to future taxable income, a deferred tax liability will typically be the consequence of this computational exercise.

Similarly, a change in inventory accounting to comply with the uniform cost capitalization (UCC) rules of TRA '86 will necessitate a restatement of beginning inventories for tax purposes, to be taken into income over four years (or fewer, depending on the specific circumstances), and will result in a deferred tax liability for financial reporting on a GAAP basis. Whether the **other** temporary difference (which is analogous to that described at (i) above) also arises depends on whether UCC is adopted for future financial reporting. If so, no future temporary differences will be anticipated, and hence there will be no tax effects to forecast. On the other hand, if UCC is not adopted or only partially adopted for financial reporting, then the reversals of amounts reflected in book inventories must be scheduled. Since tax basis inventories will exceed the corresponding book amounts, the excess will become a tax deduction when the inventory is sold and will generate future deferred tax benefits.

Although scheduling the tax effects over the four-year period would appear to be a straightforward matter, the FASB's implementation group has taken a position that further complicates this process. The FASB staff observed that TRA '86 provides that the normal four year phase-in will be accelerated in some cases if the asset giving rise to the change (e.g., inventories to which UCC is applied) is reduced in subsequent years. For example, if inventories decline by one-third, the law provides that any remaining UCC adjustment be taken into income. For this reason, given SFAS 96's insistence that no assumptions be made concerning future income, the FASB staff has stipulated that future taxable income may be assumed up to the amount that would ensue if no future inventory or receivables accumulations were made. Accordingly, the scheduling exercise should be based on (i) past experience regarding turnover as it relates to realization of assets existing at the balance sheet date, and (ii) no future asset acquisitions.

For example, assume that **most** entities will have an inventory and receivables turnover of at least one time per year. The tax effects of the reversing temporary differences should be projected to occur in the year following the balance sheet date. If the year elapses, and because declines in the asset in question do not materialize, the tax adjustment has not been fully taken into income. Then a similar scheduling assumption is again made at the next balance sheet date. The remaining adjustment (50% at the end of the second year, for example) would be projected to reverse in year three.

Other temporary differences. Logical assumptions are needed when scheduling other temporary differences. For the most part, these should be derived from the reporting entity's past experience, without assuming any future events of income or expense. For example, deferred compensation should be projected to begin reversing when the employees who will receive payments are anticipated to retire. The tax effects of discontinued operations will reverse when the anticipated disposals of assets are expected to take place. Accrued litigation losses and other contingencies should be scheduled based on prior experience--which can mean that several years will elapse before legal proceedings are to conclude. Warranty reserves should be scheduled for reversal consistent with claims experience, not extending further than the expiration of the warranty period. Long term construction-type contracts accounted for by the percentage-of-completion method for financial reporting and by the hybrid completed contract/percentage-of-completion method for tax purposes will require scheduling based on expected completion dates. Similar approaches are required for other temporary differences.

Tax strategies. Because SFAS 96 requires a year-by-year schedule of reversing and originating temporary differences, in many instances specific assumptions must be made concerning tax strategies to be employed. The most important result of making such assumptions will be to permit the offsetting of deferred tax benefits against the deferred tax liabilities.

SFAS 96 stipulates that tax planning strategies are to be used when determining the years in which temporary differences will result in taxable or deductible amounts. To qualify as a tax planning strategy, two criteria must be met: (i) it must be prudent and feasible, over which management has discretion and control; and (ii) it cannot involve significant cost to the entity, considered apart from the tax benefit to be derived. Within the bounds of these constraints, however, it is not only permissible but **required** that all available strategies be assumed for the purpose of minimizing the amount of deferred tax liabilities to be reported. There is no requirement that the entity actually carry out the strategies--they are only assumed for deferred tax computation purposes, while actual future events will determine actions to be taken by management.

In developing a tax planning strategy, management can make certain assumptions regarding the timing of future events, but it cannot assume facts not in existence at the balance sheet date. Future changes in the prices of securities or other property, for example, cannot be anticipated. The amounts entering into the deferred tax calculation are strictly limited to the differences between the tax and book bases of assets and liabilities as of the balance sheet date. Any cost of implementing the strategy must be minor and of an incidental nature; a strategy which would result in a reduction in a deferred tax liability, no matter how large, cannot be assumed if more than a trivial cost would be incurred in its implementation.

The importance of tax planning strategies to the measurement of deferred tax assets and liabilities under SFAS 96 cannot be over-emphasized. In many cases, an outside party, such as an independent accountant, will be required to evaluate the validity of the proposed tax planning strategies. To the extent that a number of different strategies with varying tax consequences are available to management, the entity may legitimately assert that a strategy having the greatest beneficial impact will be employed. The difficult aspect will be to confirm that the strategy is indeed feasible and that minimal costs would be incurred in its implementation.

The FASB staff has taken the position that management has an absolute duty to consider all available tax planning strategies in order to achieve the objective of deferred tax liability minimization. This is not optional; it is mandatory. The FASB staff has indicated its seriousness on this point by stating that as much effort be expended on this endeavor as on the measurement of any other balance sheet account. Since an entity having several classes of temporary differences might have to consider various strategies, this requirement is of no small consequence. The FASB staff has even stated that management must search for strategies that would maximize net deductible amounts in years through 1990 so as to maximize the carrybacks (for deferred tax computation purposes) to the higher-tax-rate years prior to 1988. Clearly, the search for feasible tax planning strategies is a central component of deferred tax accounting under SFAS 96.

Among the strategies management may consider are the sale and leaseback of fixed assets; the scrapping of obsolete items of inventory; the sale of loans and other investments; advance contributions to pension plans; the sale of installment receivables; an election to forego NOL carrybacks; the filing of consolidated tax returns for future periods; and the pre-funding of liabilities before payments are due.

Along with the strict limitation on net deferred tax benefits and the necessity for scheduling out all future reversals of temporary differences, the mandatory consideration of tax planning strategies was one of SFAS 96's most controversial elements. While the Board did discuss this area as part of its deliberations over problems that were identified during implementation of the new standard, it apparently has decided not to relax this requirement.

The Board's proposed replacement for SFAS 96 essentially eliminates the requirement that tax planning strategies be considered, except in the context of the valuation allowance to be established against the deferred tax asset, if any. This is discussed in greater detail in Appendix D.

Classes of Temporary Differences

APB 11 required that deferred taxes be provided for the tax effects of "timing differences." SFAS 96 expands this requirement to so-called "temporary differences." These include all the items classified as timing differences and adds several new categories. There are now nine distinct classes of temporary differences, as follows:

1. Revenues recognized for tax purposes after recognition for financial reporting--e.g., certain construction contract income; earnings from nonconsolidated affiliates and investees.
2. Revenues recognized for tax purposes before recognition for financial reporting--e.g., rent received in advance.
3. Expenses deductible for tax purposes before becoming recognized for financial reporting--e.g., accelerated depreciation under the modified ACRS system; certain pre-operating costs; certain capitalized interest costs.

4. Expenses deductible for tax purposes after recognition for financial reporting--e.g., bad debts; reserves for warranty costs; accrued contingent losses.
5. Reduction in the tax basis of assets due to ITC taken for tax purposes.
6. ITC accounted for on the deferral method for financial reporting purposes.
7. Recognition for financial reporting purposes of exchange rate fluctuation effects on assets and liabilities of foreign operations using the dollar as the functional currency.
8. Indexing of assets for tax purposes, not presently law but often discussed.
9. Business combinations accounted for as purchases, where allocations to assets and liabilities differ for tax and financial reporting purposes.

The first four classes of temporary differences are identical to common timing differences under prior GAAP. With the passing of the ITC, items 5 and 6 are less important than before. Item 9 is addressed later in this chapter. The other items are not considered here. A tenth classification was added in the Board's proposal to supersede SFAS, although it appears that the Board, at least, believes it was implicit under the requirements of SFAS 96. This relates to intercompany transfers among entities consolidated for financial reporting, but not for tax purposes.

Effect of Change in Tax Status

Prior to SFAS 96, the accounting to be accorded a change in an entity's tax status was not clearly defined under GAAP. A variety of practices had developed to account for the elimination of existing deferred tax liabilities when an S Corporation election became effective. These included (i) adjusting retained earnings in a manner similar to a correction of an error; (ii) crediting tax expense in the period of the election, on the basis that the event was essentially a change in an accounting estimate to be accounted for prospectively; and (iii) crediting paid-in capital, on the grounds that the assumption of the corporation's tax obligation by the shareholders was akin to a contribution to capital.

SFAS 96 requires that the effect of a change in an entity's tax status be reflected in current tax expense. Thus, a C Corporation electing S Corporation status will credit any balance in deferred tax liabilities to tax expense as of the date of the change in status. The Board's implementation group expressed the belief that this date is when the election has been approved by the proper authorities, or, in the case of elections that take effect automatically, the date of filing the election, even if the effective date is later. Thus, a company electing S Corporation status for years after 1991, but filing the election **before** year end 1991, would eliminate the deferred tax balance in 1991. On the other hand, a similar entity filing its change request in early 1992 could not reverse the deferred tax liability in 1991, even if knowledge of the subsequent election were obtained prior to the preparation of 1991 financial statements. In practice, however, some divergence from this view is anticipated because many will find the presentation of a deferred tax obligation on a balance sheet to be unwarranted when it is known that those liabilities will never be settled.

An entity becoming taxable must record deferred taxes based on temporary differences in existence at the date of the status change. As in the case of an election effecting a change from taxable to nontaxable status, the relevant date is when the election is approved or when filed, if approval is unnecessary. This adjustment will also flow through current tax expense. In either case, the notes to the financial statements must set forth the components of tax expense, with any portion resulting from a change in tax status (or, for that matter, a change in statutory rates) being separately captioned.

Under the tax laws, a C (taxable) Corporation electing to become an S Corporation may be determined to have a so-called "built-in gain" which will result in a tax liability, under certain circumstances, at a future date. In such cases, the S Corporation should continue to report a deferred tax liability related to the built-in gain. This follows from the definition of temporary differences under SFAS 96 as differences in the tax and financial reporting bases of assets and liabilities. All other deferred taxes should normally be eliminated when S status is elected.

Discounting

The reporting of deferred income taxes at discounted present values was not permitted under prior GAAP, and this prohibition has been continued by SFAS 96. In the past, a central argument against discounting has been that deferred tax benefits or obligations computed in accordance with the provisions of APB 11 were **not** true assets or liabilities, and thus the rationale for discounting was absent. That is, since deferred taxes were not intended to be rights to receive or liabilities to pay amounts of money at specified future dates, recognizing the time value of money would not be relevant.

Given that the failure of deferred taxes calculated by APB 11 to meet the definitions of assets and liabilities set forth in SFAC 6 was a motivating force in the Board's decision to develop SFAS 96, it would have been appropriate to require the use of discounting. However, the Board has continued the prohibition on discounting deferred tax assets or liabilities, even though the resulting undiscounted amounts do not conform to the criteria established by SFAC 6.

The decision to rule out discounting appears to have been a pragmatic one, not conceptually based. The Board has referenced APB 10's requirement that deferred taxes not be discounted, but otherwise SFAS 96 is silent on this issue. The Board published a discussion memorandum in late 1990 on the broad topic of present-value based measures in accounting. While it is not clear when, or if, new statements of financial accounting standards will result from this project, it would seem reasonable to assume that at some point the concept of discounting will be applied to deferred tax assets and liabilities. In the interim, however, discounting is **not** to be employed.

Comprehensive Example of Deferred Tax Accounting Under SFAS 96

The following example illustrates the "asset and liability approach" prescribed by SFAS 96, and in particular it focuses on the necessity for year-by-year scheduling of future book and tax revenues and expenses deriving from assets and liabilities recognized at the balance sheet date. This example will also demonstrate that a net deferred tax asset is **not** to be recognized except when it represents an amount which could be carried back against taxes paid in prior years or the current year.

Assume the following facts:

1. The FASB proposal is adopted, effective January 1992.
2. The corporate tax rate schedule, as per existing law assumed on December 31, 1992 is as follows:

Taxable Income	For 1993 through 1996	For 1997 and Subsequent Years
$ 0 - $50,000	15%	18%
$50,000 - $75,000	25%	28%
$75,000 - Up	34%	36%

NOTE: The future tax increase is hypothesized only for purposes of this example.

3. Jocelyn Corporation has temporary differences between tax and financial reporting resulting from depreciation, deferred compensation plans, and prepaid rental income. Based on transactions entered into at the balance sheet date (i.e., assuming that no new temporary differences are created by events in future years), the following taxable income or deductions are projected for future years:

    (i) For depreciation:

	Tax Deductions	Financial Reporting Expense
1993	$88,000	$56,000
1994	75,000	56,000
1995	62,000	56,000
1996	40,000	38,000
1997	28,000	38,000
1998	21,000	38,000
1999	10,000	38,000

(ii) For deferred compensation:

	Tax Deductions	Financial Reporting Expense
1993	$ --	$15,000
1994	--	15,000
1995	--	15,000
1996	14,000	10,000
1997	14,000	10,000
1998	14,000	10,000
1999	25,000	--
2000	25,000	--
2001	25,000	--

(iii) For prepaid rental income:

	Taxable Income	Financial Reporting Income
1993	$ --	$ 6,000
1994	--	1,000

4. Jocelyn Corporation had taxable income of $188,000 for the year 1990, taxable income of $90,000 in 1991, and taxable income of $122,000 in 1992, during which time the tax rate was (for this example) a flat 32%. Based on the foregoing facts, the **net** taxable or deductible amounts projected for years 1993-2001 are as follows:

	Net Taxable (Deductible) Amounts
1993	$(23,000)
1994	(5,000)
1995	9,000
1996	(6,000)
1997	6,000
1998	13,000
1999	3,000
2000	(25,000)
2001	(25,000)

The schedule below also illustrates the handling of the projected net taxable (deductible) amounts.

	1990-92	1993	1994	1995	1996	1997	1998	1999	2000	2001
Taxable income	$400,000									
Depreciation		$(32,000)	$(19,000)	$(6,000)	$(2,000)	$10,000	$17,000	$28,000		
Deferred Comp.		15,000	15,000	15,000	(4,000)	(4,000)	(4,000)	(25,000)	$(25,000)	$(25,000)
Prepaid rental income		(6,000)	(1,000)							
		$(23,000)	$ (5,000)	$ 9,000	$(6,000)	$ 6,000	$13,000	$ 3,000	$(25,000)	$(25,000)
As if carrybacks	(28,000)	23,000	5,000	(6,000)	6,000	(6,000)	(13,000)	(3,000)	22,000	
		-0-	-0-	$ 3,000	-0-	-0-	-0-	-0-	$ (3,000)	$(25,000)
	x 32%			x 15%						
	($8,960)			$ 450						
Current asset	$(7,360)									
Noncurrent asset	(1,600)	- Noncurrent liability $450 = $(1,150) Net noncurrent asset								
	$(8,960)									

These projected net taxable (deductible) amounts are handled as follows:

1993-1994

Since there was adequate taxable income during the 1990-1992 period to absorb the projected net deductible amounts in 1993 and 1994, the **tax benefits** of these deductibles can be recognized. In other words, if there are no other items of income or expense and therefore these net deductible amounts become NOLs, they could effectively be carried back to 1990 and 1991, respectively, under the existing three-year carryback rules. These are computed at the tax rates appropriate to such carrybacks, assumed to be 32% for this example.

	Net (Deductible) Amount	Recognized Tax (Benefit)
1993	$(23,000)	$(7,360)
1994	(5,000)	(1,600)

1995

A net taxable amount is projected for 1995, in the amount of $9,000. At the expected tax rate of 15% (all at lowest bracket rates, since the temporary difference does not exceed $50,000 and no other elements of income and expense can be assumed for future periods), this results in a deferred tax liability of $1,350.

1996

A net deductible of $6,000 is forecast for 1996. Since taxable income of $9,000 resulting from temporary difference reversals is forecast for 1995, the $6,000 deductible in 1996 could be carried back to 1995. At the 15% rate applied to the 1995 taxable amount, this will result in a $900 tax benefit to be associated with the 1996 deductible.

1997 - 1999

These years are projected to have net taxable amounts, with each year's amount being within the lowest tax bracket anticipated for that period. Thus,

	Net Taxable Amounts	Recognized Tax Liability
1997	$ 6,000	$ 1,080
1998	13,000	2,340
1999	3,000	540

2000

A net deductible amount of $25,000 is forecast for 2000 from temporary difference reversals. This could be carried back three years (1997-99). The net taxable amounts in those three years aggregates only $22,000, with an associated tax liability of $3,960. Accordingly, a benefit equal to this liability is associated with 2000's net deductible amount. The excess of the deductible over the available carryback amount ($25,000 - 22,000 = $3,000), is available for a carryforward, but in the present example no future taxable amounts are forecast, and therefore no tax benefit is recordable.

2001

Again a net deductible of $25,000 is forecast. However, no carryback is available and therefore no tax benefits can be recognized at December 31, 1992. Based on (benefits) liabilities for the following years:

1993	$(7,360)
1994	(1,600)
1995	1,350
1996	(900)
1997	1,080
1998	2,340
1999	540
2000	(3,960)
2001	0
	$(8,510)

The deferred portion of income tax expense would be determined by comparing the net deferred tax asset ($8,510) to be shown on the December 31, 1992 balance sheet with the beginning of year balance in the deferred tax account assumed to be $0 in this example. Total income tax expense is calculated as follows:

Total income tax expense	=	Current* portion	±	Deferred portion

*not illustrated in this example

Based on the foregoing, Jocelyn Corporation will record the following entry **for deferred taxes** in 1992:

Deferred tax asset	$ 8,510	
Tax expense		$ 8,510

The Effect of the Corporate Alternative Minimum Tax

The Corporate Alternative Minimum Tax (AMT) established by TRA '86 differs substantially from the previous add-on minimum tax, and this change dictates a new set of accounting procedures. With the provisions of SFAS 96 regarding tax planning strategies, future temporary difference reversals, and exclusion of anticipated future income, the corporate AMT has become a necessary and central part of all deferred tax calculations. This applies to corporations that never have been--and never intend to be--in a position where AMT is payable. Thus, multiple calculations of deferred taxes will be necessary for virtually all entities under SFAS 96--i.e., separate calculations for both regular tax and AMT will be required every year. Deferred taxes may be provided based on the AMT computation even though the reporting entity never becomes subject to the AMT for tax purposes.

Briefly, the corporate AMT is a separate, parallel, quasi-flat rate tax system. Entities must pay the higher of the tax computed under the regular corporate tax or the AMT. The AMT tax rate, presently 20%, is applied to a computed amount referred to as the Alternative Minimum Taxable Income, which is the corporation's regular taxable income plus and minus certain adjustments. These adjustments are principally (i) several items referred to specifically as "adjustments," which can either be additions or deductions; (ii) "preference items," which can only be additions; (iii) the "book income adjustment," which is also an addition to taxable income; (iv) the alternative minimum tax net operating loss deduction; and (v) an exemption.

"Adjustments" as defined under the AMT include the spread between accelerated depreciation under the 1986 Tax Act's modified ACRS system and that permitted for AMT purposes, certain differences between completed contract and percentage-of-completion profit recognition, installment method versus accrual recognition of earnings on certain asset sales, and a few other less commonly encountered items. "Preferences" include certain types of tax exempt interest, plus a number of other items which are normally permanent book-tax differences under the regular tax system.

The most controversial adjustment in deriving AMT taxable income is the "book income adjustment." TRA '86 decreed that (for years through 1989 only) one-half the amount by which book pre-tax income exceeds taxable income must be added back in developing AMT income. In effect, this means that one-half of what otherwise would be temporary differences is lost as a tax advantage, under certain circumstances. Whether this loss affects the entity's ultimate tax position, of course, depends on whether AMT tax exceeds regular tax, which is a function of the entire AMT computation and not merely the book income adjustment. For years after 1989 a somewhat different concept, known as "adjusted current earnings," or ACE, has been prescribed.

"Book income" for purposes of the AMT book income adjustment will usually be the pre-tax accounting income number obtained from the entity's financial statements. Where several different financial reports are prepared, the IRS has stipulated the order of priority to be applied; SEC filings and general purpose GAAP basis financial statements have the highest and next highest priorities, respectively. This requirement has encouraged some reporting entities to forego temporary differences or to switch to tax basis reporting, which of course are unintended consequences of the imposition of the AMT system. However, if GAAP-basis disclosures are included in tax-basis financial statements, these disclosures may become includable for book income adjustment purposes.

The AMT net operating loss deduction is similar to the regular NOL deduction, subject to several changes and limitations. For purposes of computing AMT taxable income, any NOL deduction included in the regular tax calculation must be replaced with the corresponding AMT NOL.

An exemption of $40,000 per year is also provided in the AMT computation. This is reduced for entities having AMT income in excess of $150,000 and is totally eliminated when AMT income reaches $310,000.

Finally, any AMT in excess of regular tax gives rise to a minimum tax credit (MTC) which can be carried forward indefinitely and used to offset future regular corporate tax in excess of AMT. This MTC is important both because it may reduce future taxes (in effect making the differential between the two parallel tax systems something akin to a timing difference) and because it will be part of the deferred tax computations. Since deferred taxes may, in a given fact situation, be computed based on the AMT even when a corporation is not really an AMT taxpayer, the MTC may also be applied in determining deferred taxes although no MTC is available to the entity for tax purposes. This result is largely due to the exclusion of all future income and expense (other than temporary differences) from the deferred tax calculation whereas actual future taxes will naturally be based on the entity's real future taxable income, not simply on the temporary differences.

An example of the AMT calculation to be made as part of the computation of deferred taxes is given below. Note that this procedure, which is required under the provisions of SFAS 96, would **not** be applicable under the proposed requirements of the standard intended to supersede SFAS 96. See Appendix D for a discussion of that proposal.

The following facts are assumed for purposes of this example:

1. The Company begins operations in 1992 and applies SFAS 96 immediately.

2. Federal income taxes are based on the following schedule for 1992 and all future years:

    Income up to $50,000   25%
    Income over $50,000   35%

    The statutory AMT rate is 20%.

3. Plant, property, and equipment costing $200,000 is acquired in 1992. Depreciation is the only temporary difference for the Company.

The Company has scheduled future depreciation to be as follows:

Year	Financial reporting	Regular tax	AMT tax	ACE tax *
1992	$ 20,000	$ 40,000	$ 30,000	$
1993	40,000	64,000	51,000	
1994	40,000	38,400	35,600	
1995	40,000	23,000	33,400	25,000
1996	40,000	23,000	33,400	25,000
1997	20,000	11,600	16,600	25,000
Totals	$200,000	$200,000	$200,000	$75,000

*   *The 1986 Tax Act stipulates that beginning in 1990 the "book income adjustment" will be replaced by the "adjusted current earnings" (ACE). The Act provides that ACE is derived by making certain adjustments to Alternative Minimum Taxable Income (AMTI). These adjustments can be either additions or subtractions; if ACE exceeds AMTI, 75% of the excess is added to AMTI before calculating tax at the AMT rate. If ACE is lower than AMTI, a negative 75% adjustment is allowed to the extent of cumulative positive adjustments of prior (post-1989) years. The ACE adjustments are principally certain otherwise nontaxable items of income (certain tax-exempt interest, for example), nondeductible expenses (e.g., penalties and fines), special rules for depreciation deductions (generally straight line, but subject to several additional computational complexities), plus a few other highly specialized items.*

4. The Company has tax exempt interest of $250,000 in 1992.

5. Book pre-tax income in 1992 is $400,000.

Based on the foregoing, the 1992 regular tax provision, before the deferred tax adjustment, is as follows:

Pre-tax accounting income	$400,000
Less:	
Tax-exempt interest	(250,000)
Excess tax depreciation	(20,000)
Regular taxable income	$130,000
Tax on $50,000 @ 25%	$ 12,500
Tax on excess @ 35%	28,000
Total regular tax	$ 40,500

The AMT provision for 1992, before any deferred tax adjustment, is computed as follows:

Regular taxable income	$130,000
AMT depreciation adjustment	10,000
Tentative AMTI	$140,000

Book income adjustment:

1/2 (Book income - TAMTI)

= 1/2 (400,000 - 140,000)	130,000
AMT Income	$270,000
Tax at 20%	$ 54,000

The actual 1992 tax liability is the higher of the regular or AMT computations; since AMT ($54,000) exceeds regular tax ($40,500), the AMT-based tax is due.

The excess ($54,000 - 40,500 = $13,500) is called the AMT credit and is available to reduce regular tax in future years, to the extent that regular tax exceeds AMT-based tax only. This **real** AMT credit may differ, however, from hypothetical AMT credits employed in the deferred tax calculation. This is discussed below.

The computation of the deferred tax adjustment at the end of 1992 necessitates the scheduling of future temporary differences (only depreciation in this example). This entails the projection of not only the regular tax effects, but the AMT tax effects as well, both on year-by-year bases. The tax effects of the scheduled temporary differences are the **higher** of the regular or AMT amounts each year.

	1992	1993	1994	1995	1996	1997
Regular tax calculation:						
Net taxable (deductible) amounts before carryback	$ 0	$(24,000)	$1,600	$17,000	$17,000	$8,400
NOL carryback*	(24,000)	24,000				
Net taxable (deductible) amounts after carryback	$(24,000)	$ 0	$1,600	$17,000	$17,000	$8,400
Regular tax (benefit)	$ (8,400)	$ 0	$ 400	$ 4,250	$ 4,250	$2,100

* *The projected excess tax depreciation in 1993 is treated as creating a NOL, which is carried back to 1992 thereby generating a tax refund based on taxes paid in 1992.*

AMT tax allocation:

Regular taxable (deductible)						
amounts before carryback	$ 0	$(24,000)	$ 1,600	$17,000	$17,000	$ 8,400
AMT depreciation adjustment	0	13,000	2,800	(10,400)	(10,400)	(5,000)
Tentative AMTI	$ 0	$(11,000)	$ 4,400	$ 6,600	$ 6,600	$ 3,400
Book income adjustment	0	5,500*	0	0	0	0
ACE adjustment**	0	0	0	6,300	6,300	(6,300)
AMTI before carryback	$ 0	$ (5,500)	$ 4,400	$12,900	$12,900	$(2,900)
NOL carryback	(5,500)	5,500	(2,900)	0	0	2,900
AMTI	$(5,500)	$ 0	$ 1,500	$12,900	$12,900	$ 0
Alternative minimum						
tax (benefit) - at 20%	$(1,100)	$ 0	$ 300	$ 2,580	$ 2,580	$ 0

* Since book income of zero is assumed for all future periods, the negative tentative AMTI in 1993 represents excess book over tax income: one-half this excess ($11,000 x .50 = $5,500) is the book income adjustment.

** Beginning in 1990, the difference between "AMT tax depreciation" and "ACE tax depreciation" is the ACE adjustment. In this example 75% of this adjustment is added (or subtracted) to tentative AMTI. Thus, in 1995 ($33,400 - $25,000) x .75 = $6,300.

Deferred tax calculation:

Regular tax	$(8,400)	$ 0	$ 400	$ 4,250	$ 4,250	$ 2,100
AMT tax	(1,100)	0	300	2,580	2,580	0
Higher of regular or AMT	$(1,100)	$ 0	$ 400	$ 4,250	$ 4,250	$ 2,100
AMT credit	0	0	(100)	(1,670)	(1,670)	(2,100)
Net deferred tax						
(benefit)	$(1,100)	$ 0	$ 300	$ 2,580	$ 2,580	$ 0

Based on the foregoing analysis, a deferred tax liability of $4,360 should be reflected in the year-end 1992 balance sheet.

Note that AMT credits are applied to years 1994-1997 in the example above. Although only $5,540 of (hypothetical) credits are absorbed, it is important to understand how much AMT credit could have been utilized for deferred tax computational purposes, at a maximum. In the present example, this maximum is given as:

Actual AMT credit created in 1992	
due to AMT tax paid	$13,500
Additional AMT credit generated by	
scheduled NOL carryback to 1992*	7,300
	$20,800

*The AMT benefit, $1,100, was lower than the regular tax benefit, $8,400, which is equivalent to a higher AMT tax.

This example, although greatly simplified versus a real life situation, is indicative of the extreme complexity to be dealt with because of the interaction between the intricate SFAS 96 requirements and the peculiarities of TRA '86.

Tax Accounting Implications of Business Combinations

SFAS 96 has mandated a series of changes, major and minor, in accounting for business combinations. Most of these changes affect business combinations accounted for as purchases, but there are required changes in accounting for combinations treated as poolings of interest as well. These will be addressed, in turn, in the following paragraphs.

Purchases. APB 11, although generally endorsing the "deferred method," required the "net-of-tax method" in allocating the tax effects of assets and liabilities acquired in a purchase business combination. Under this approach, the allocated cost assigned to identifiable assets and liabilities was an amount representing the pro rata fair values of the entire purchase (less any so-called "negative goodwill," if the transaction was a bargain purchase), net of any tax attributes deriving from differences between tax and accounting bases in those items. Thus, deferred tax benefits or liabilities were not recognized separately, but rather were only elements entering into the calculations of allocated cost.

SFAS 96 discontinues this practice and requires deferred taxes to be explicitly recognized at the time of the purchase transaction. The sole exception concerns goodwill: SFAS 96 prohibits the recognition of deferred taxes related to goodwill, even if some tax jurisdictions permit goodwill amortization for tax purposes. (Note, however, that the proposed successor to SFAS 96 will permit deferred tax accounting relating to goodwill which is deductible under other tax jurisdictions' rules.) Otherwise the usual criteria apply; accordingly, net deferred tax benefits will generally not be reported. However, if the acquired entity will file consolidated tax returns with its parent (the acquirer), and the parent has temporary differences representing future net taxable amounts, then (if the timing patterns coincide) the acquired company may be able to justify reporting net deferred tax benefits in its balance sheet.

The discontinuance of the net-of-tax method of accounting for purchase business combinations is a major change. It will improve financial reporting particularly when consolidated financial statements are presented. The past hybrid situation will no longer exist, where purchased temporary differences were accounted for differently than otherwise identical temporary differences generated by the parent or originated by the subsidiary after the acquisition date. Since the tax effect of all temporary differences will be presented explicitly (within the limitations of the computational rules of SFAS 96), the financial statements should be more comprehensible to the user.

SFAS 96 permits, but does not require, the restatement of prior years when the new standard is first adopted. If restatement is elected, then all past purchase business combinations which have taken place since the start of the earliest such period must be remeasured in accordance with the new standard. Obviously, this can be a difficult undertaking, although presumably any unamortized amounts relating to long-ago purchase combinations should be of low materiality, thus possibly mitigating the need to perform the restatement. Restatement is prohibited for purchase business combinations occurring prior to the earliest restated period presented. Thus, assets and liabilities acquired in pre-restatement business combinations are continued at net-of-tax amounts. (Here again the procedures will change if the Board's proposed replacement for SFAS 96 is ultimately adopted. See Appendix D for a discussion.)

SFAS 96 also alters the prescribed accounting for purchased net operating loss carryforwards. Under APB 11, benefits of an acquired entity's NOL carryforwards were not recognized at the date of the purchase (except for the rare instance where realization was assured beyond a reasonable doubt). When the benefits were later realized for tax purposes, that event in effect caused a re-allocation of the original purchase cost. Since typically a purchase of a company that can provide NOL carryforward benefits to the acquirer would be made at a premium over the fair value of other net assets, APB 11 required that realized NOL benefits first be used to reduce goodwill (where the excess purchase cost would have been charged). If realized tax benefits exceeded the amount of goodwill recognized on the purchase transaction, then proportional reductions of all recorded noncurrent assets were required. Further NOL benefits, exceeding even the allocated costs of all noncurrent assets, would be credited to "negative goodwill" (more properly called "excess of fair value of assets acquired over cost"). Since the goodwill and plant assets are subject to amortization and depreciation, respectively, NOL realizations in years after the purchase combination would also necessitate restatements of prior earnings. Apart from these changes, the NOL benefit realization had no impact on the income statement.

Under SFAS 96, by contrast, fixed assets are never revalued, and prior periods' earnings are never restated. Instead, unrecognized NOL benefits subsequently realized are credited to goodwill; prior periods' amortization charges are not amended, and the effect of the goodwill adjustment is handled prospectively only. Any excess NOL benefit then reduces other intangible assets (e.g., trademarks, customer lists), also on a prospective basis. If all goodwill and other intangible assets are eliminated by this process, any further NOL realization is credited to tax expense in the period the realization occurs.

The change in the treatment of purchased NOL benefits from APB 11 to SFAS 96 results in (i) more rapidly reflecting the benefits in earnings and (ii) eliminating the arduous task of restating (possibly a number of times) prior years' operating results.

Example of NOL in Purchase Method Business Combination

Chess Corporation is formed January 2, 1992 to purchase the net assets of Checkers Company. The purchase price, $85,000, is allocated to tangible assets ($95,000), liabilities ($18,000) and goodwill ($8,000). A tax loss carryforward of $35,000 is **not** recorded at the purchase date. The tax bases of the tangible assets are $12,000 lower than the allocated book value, but the tax effect of this temporary difference is ignored because if recorded the deferred tax liability would be offset by NOL benefits.

For the year ended December 31, 1992, Chess Corporation has consolidated taxable income of $24,000 and pre-tax accounting income before goodwill amortization of $29,000. Goodwill is being written off over 10 years, for an annual amortization of $800. The $5,000 excess book over tax income is due to additional temporary differences; unreversed temporary differences at December 31, 1992 are thus $12,000 + 5,000 = $17,000. Assume a tax rate of 40% for all years, and ignore AMT.

The 1992 tax provision is as follows:

Taxable income	$24,000
Tax NOL used	24,000
	- 0 -
x Tax rate	40%
Tax currently due	$ - 0 -

Remaining tax NOL is $35,000 - 24,000 = $11,000.

Book tax provision is as follows:

Pre-tax accounting income before goodwill amortization	$29,000
Taxable income before NOL	$24,000
x Tax rate	40%
Current tax expense	$ 9,600 (1)
Excess book income (represents increased temporary differences) $29,000 - 24,000	$ 5,000
x Tax rate	40%
Deferred tax expense	$ 2,000 (2)
Total (1) + (2)	$11,600

The deferred tax liability to be presented on the balance sheet is computed as follows:

Temporary differences	$17,000
Less tax NOL remaining	11,000
	$ 6,000
x Tax rate	40%
Deferred tax liability	$ 2,400

The $2,400 deferred tax liability arises from two sources: (i) the $5,000 of new temporary differences originating in 1992, and (ii) the restoration of $400 of deferred taxes previously (albeit implicitly) eliminated by NOL carryforward. Put another way, since there was only $23,000 of "book" NOL carryforward (equal to the original tax NOL of $35,000 less the temporary differences of $12,000), the excess tax NOL realized in 1992 ($24,000 - 23,000 = $1,000) is treated as restoring a portion of the deferred taxes previously offset ($1,000 x 40% = $400).

The entry to record the **consolidated** tax provision at December 31, 1992 is:

Tax expense--current	9,600	
Tax expense--deferred	2,000	
Deferred tax liability		2,400
Goodwill		7,200
NOL benefits		2,000

The "book" NOL benefits realized ($23,000 x 40% = $9,200) are credited first to goodwill ($8,000 cost less $800 amortization = $7,200 available for offset), with the excess ($9,200 - 7,200 = $2,000) being credited to NOL benefits. This reduces net tax expense in the 1992 income statement as follows:

Income before amortization		$29,000
Amortization of goodwill		800
Income before taxes		$28,200
Tax provision		
Current	$9,600	
Deferred	2,000	
NOL benefit	(2,000)	9,600
Net income		$18,600

Note the goodwill has been completely eliminated as a result of periodic amortization and the offsetting of tax benefits.

Now assume that in 1993 taxable income is $18,000 and book income is $27,500. For tax purposes, the entire remaining NOL carryforward is utilized:

Taxable income	$18,000
Tax NOL used	11,000
	7,000
x Tax rate	40%
Tax currently due	$ 2,800

For financial reporting purposes, no NOL remains to be recognized, since the full $23,000 of "book" NOL from the purchase of Checkers Company was used against 1992 income. The effect of the tax NOL realization, therefore, is entirely a restoration of deferred taxes, as follows:

Temporary differences, 12/92	$17,000
Additional temporary difference, 1993	9,500
	$26,500
x Tax rate	40%
Required deferred tax liability, 12/93	$10,600
Less existing balance	2,400
Increase in deferred tax liability	$ 8,200

The current tax expense to be recognized in the 1993 income statement is $7,200, which represents the tax currently due on **taxable** income (before NOL):

Taxable income	$18,000
x Tax rate	40%
Current tax expense	$ 7,200

Finally, the deferred tax provision results from the deferred tax effect of the incremental temporary differences arising in 1993:

Incremental temporary differences arising in 1993 ($27,500 book income - 18,000 tax income)	$ 9,500
x Tax rate	40%
	$ 3,800

The entry to record the consolidated tax provision in 1993 is therefore:

Tax expense--current	7,200	
Tax expense--deferred	3,800	
Deferred tax liability		8,200
Taxes currently payable		2,800

Poolings. The issues SFAS 96 raises in regard to combinations accounted for as poolings of interests are rather basic, in comparison to those affecting purchases. If one constituent of a pooling has an unrecognized NOL carryforward and the other has a deferred tax liability, then to the extent that the NOL can be used, under tax law, to offset the merger partner's future taxable income, it may be recognized by the combining entities. On the other hand, if only usable to offset future earnings of the entity generating the NOL, recognition is prohibited.

If one party to a pooling has adopted SFAS 96 and the other has not prior to the pooling, it may restate to conform to the procedures applied by its merger partner. Similarly, if the two entities adopted at different dates, the one adopting SFAS 96 later may restate as if it had adopted at the same date as the other entity. If one adopted the standard retroactively and the other prospectively, the latter may also adjust as if a retrospective treatment had been originally elected.

Net Operating Losses

Under present tax law, entities incurring net losses have the option of carrying the losses back to prior years--and thus gaining a refund of taxes already paid--or carrying the losses forward as offsets against future taxable income. The carryback and carryforward periods have varied as the tax laws have been revised over the years, but currently a carryback of three years and a carryforward of fifteen years are permitted. When an entity utilizes an opportunity to carry back a current period loss to obtain a refund, the tax benefit will be reported in the income statement of the loss period. Such a carryback is generally referred to as a "tax loss carryback," as distinct from a "book loss carryback," which will be considered below.

When an operating loss exceeds taxable income for the prior three years, a carry-forward benefit is available. Accounting for this tax loss carryforward has been altered by the issuance of SFAS 96. Under prior GAAP (APB 11), **in general** no financial statement recognition was given to tax loss carryforwards, on the theory that realization was not assured beyond a reasonable doubt. Instead, in the subsequent year when the loss benefit was actually realized for tax purposes (i.e., when the carryforward was used to reduce taxable income of a later year), the tax reduction was reported as an extraordinary item in the income statement.

SFAS 96 eliminates the extraordinary item treatment--which is logical, since real-ized net operating loss benefits never met the criteria for extraordinary items set forth in APB 30. Under SFAS 96, when operating loss benefits are realized in a year sub-sequent to the loss year, and the benefits were not previously recognized (see below), they simply reduce otherwise reportable tax expense. Of course, detailed disclosures on the components of tax expense, indicating the amount of NOL benefit realized cur-rently, will be presented in the notes to the financial statements.

Under APB 11, there were two circumstances under which NOL carryforwards could achieve accounting recognition in the loss period. One of these continues under present GAAP to be acceptable; the other has been eliminated. Prior GAAP permitted immediate recognition of the tax benefit of a NOL carryforward if ultimate realization was assured beyond a reasonable doubt. As a practical matter, such NOL benefits tended to be recognized when the event giving rise to the loss was of a unique, nonre-curring nature and the entity could demonstrate that existing operations would be prof-itable on an ongoing basis. For example, an uninsured loss resulting from the destruc-tion of **one** of the entity's factories by fire could have been rationalized as an unusual, infrequently occurring event which would not impair the entity's ongoing profitability from its other operations. On the other hand, a large NOL resulting from a business recession would not have supported recognition in the loss period, since business re-versals of a general nature are not unusual, extraneous events (although, arguably, with the going concern assumption and the fifteen year carryforward availability, real-ization of the loss benefit could have been anticipated with some degree of assurance).

The ability to justify the recognition of a tax loss carryforward benefit in the manner described above has been abolished by SFAS 96. Now, whatever the underlying cause of the NOL, there is no opportunity to present a net deferred tax debit (benefit) in the balance sheet, whether those debits represent the benefits of operating loss carry-forwards or the tax effects of temporary differences. The only net benefits permitted to be presented under SFAS 96 are "book loss carrybacks"--i.e., the effects of operating losses or temporary differences which could be offset against the excess of book over tax income during the statutory loss carryback period. This change has been made to eliminate the ambiguity of the previous rules, and to conform to SFAS 96's requirement that no future events be anticipated in the financial statements of a given period; recognition of unrealized tax loss carryforwards would necessarily be based on such now-prohibited assumptions.

The other exception under APB 11--which has been continued by SFAS 96--was that net operating loss carryforward benefits were recognizable by means of offsetting against existing deferred tax liabilities, within the limitation that the maximum loss benefit to be offset was the timing differences due to reverse during the statutory carry-forward period. The logic of this approach is clear: since reversals of these timing differences will, even absent no other items of future book income or expense, generate taxable income, it is valid to use this projected future income to absorb the tax NOLs. Under the provisions of SFAS 96, NOL carryforwards and deferred tax benefits have the same status: they both represent future tax deductions and can only be recorded to the extent that they would be offset or absorbed by future taxable income resulting from other temporary difference reversals.

The central role played by tax planning strategies in the basic deferred tax computations under SFAS 96 is mirrored in the NOL recognition area as well. Recall that GAAP now requires that management seek out and utilize all available tax planning strategies to minimize the deferred tax liability to be recognized in the financial statements. Similarly, SFAS 96 requires that the most beneficial strategy be chosen (hypothetically) to utilize available NOL carrybacks and carryforwards. This is particularly germane during a phase-in of new corporate tax rates, as explained in the following paragraph.

Assume that an entity has a tax loss in 1992. The law provides that this may be carried back to 1989 through 1991, when taxes were paid at (Federal) rates as high as 46%. However, in some situations management may choose to forego the carryback because the carryback would interfere with the use of foreign tax credits or for other valid reasons. In such a case, it might appear that the benefit of the loss should be projected forward to offset scheduled temporary differences generating taxable income. Given the computational requirement of SFAS 96 that only future temporary differences be scheduled, doing so may result in tax benefits of the loss being "realized" (hypothetically) at rates of only 34% or less. Notwithstanding management's intent to **really** make this election, for deferred tax computation purposes the **best** strategy (i.e., the one having the largest impact on the deferred tax liability) must be employed. This may well be to assume a carryback to prior, high effective tax rate periods.

The foregoing example illustrates once again one of the most vital features of SFAS 96: that assumptions made for tax computation purposes need not even be anticipated for actual behavior. Obviously, this will require that management spend possibly many extra hours inventing computational strategies, in addition to the time devoted to developing **real** tax strategies. This hypothetical strategy development is not limited to losses arising in the current reporting year. Any future year projected to have net tax deductibles will require that assumptions be made as to whether the resultant tax loss will be carried back or forward.

If an entity records a hypothetical NOL carryback at 46% or 40% tax rates, but actually elects to carry the loss forward, and ultimately realizes the benefit at, say, 34%, the financial statements for the two years (the loss year and the NOL realization year) will both contain what some may see as distortions. The loss of the former period will be too low (since tax benefits will be overstated due to assumed higher carryback tax rates), and the profit of the latter period will be understated (the shortfall in tax benefits previously accrued will exaggerate tax expense in the realization year). However, given SFAS 96's injunction that tax planning strategies be employed **at each reporting date** to minimize tax expense and deferred tax liabilities **at that date**, this result is to be expected, and is consistent with the underlying theory of SFAS 96.

Assume a tax rate of 40% in years 1 and 2 and 30% in years 3-5.

	Income (loss) before income taxes		Income tax expense (credit)			Cumulative net deferred tax credits
Year	Financial	Taxable	Current	Deferred	Total	
1	$30,000	$15,000	$6,000	$6,000	$12,000	$ 6,000
2	12,000	5,000	2,000	600*	2,600*	6,600*
3	40,000	18,000	5,400	6,600	12,000	13,200
4	30,000	25,000	7,500	1,500	9,000	14,700
5	(15,000)	(25,000)	(8,000)	3,000	(5,000)	17,700

Note: Deferred tax expense and cumulative net deferred tax credits in the example above were adjusted at the end of year 2 to reflect the reduction in future tax rates, which are assumed to have become law on that date. This is essentially how SFAS 96 requires periodic taxes be computed.

The refund receivable in year 5 is computed as follows:

Year	Amount carried back	Current refund (tax benefit)
2	$ 5,000	$2,000
3	18,000	5,400
4	2,000	600
		$8,000

Under SFAS 96, the deferred tax provision must be computed separately; total tax expense or benefit is then a "plugged" value derived from the sum of the current and deferred tax calculations. In the present example, in year 5 an additional $10,000 of temporary difference originates; the total **unreversed** temporary difference at the end of year 5 is $59,000. Given the future projected rate of 30%, a total of $17,700 deferred tax liability must be provided. Accordingly, an additional $3,000 deferred tax expense is accrued in year 5's income statement; the net tax benefit is thus $8,000 - 3,000 = $5,000.

The proper entry to record the year 5 carryback in situation 1 is:

Tax refund receivable	8,000	
Income tax expense--deferred	3,000	
Deferred tax liability		3,000
Income tax expense--current		8,000

Notice that it is necessary to differentiate between the current and deferred income tax expense. Presenting the book provision as a net figure (i.e., $5,000 benefit) is not sufficient. Disclosure of the current and deferred components of tax expense can be made either on the face of the income statement or in the notes thereto.

Example of Accounting for NOL Carryback-Book Loss in Excess of Tax Loss

Year	Income (loss) before income taxes		Income tax expense (credit)			Cumulative net deferred credits
	Financial	*Taxable*	*Current*	*Deferred*	*Total*	
1	$30,000	$15,000	$6,000	$6,000	$12,000	$ 6,000
2	12,000	5,000	2,000	600	2,600	6,600
3	40,000	18,000	5,400	6,600	12,000	13,200
4	30,000	25,000	7,500	1,500	9,000	14,700
5	(45,000)	(15,000)	(5,000)	(9,000)	(14,000)	5,700

In this example the same basic principles are illustrated as in the prior example, except that in this case the book loss exceeds the tax loss. The carrybacks and resultant benefits are shown below.

The refund receivable is computed as follows:

Year	*Amount carried back*	*Current refund (tax benefit)*
2	$ 5,000	$ 2,000
3	10,000	3,000
		$ 5,000

The deferred tax adjustment is computed as follows:

Aggregate unreversed temporary differences at end of year 5	$19,000
x Expected effect of reversals	30%
Deferred tax balance at year end	5,700
Balance before adjustment	14,700
Deferred tax adjustment	$ (9,000)

Total tax benefit to be reflected in year 5 is therefore the current tax benefit of $5,000 plus the reduction in the deferred tax liability of $9,000, for a total benefit of $14,000.

The required entry is:

Tax refund receivable	5,000	
Deferred tax liability	9,000	
Income tax expense--current		5,000
Income tax expense--deferred		9,000

Treatment of loss carryforward. When the book **or** the tax net operating loss exceeds the available book or tax carryback, respectively, a NOL carryforward results. Under SFAS 96, a NOL carryforward is handled exactly as would be a deferred tax benefit resulting from scheduled net deductible amounts in future years: unless these can be absorbed against net taxable amounts in future years, they cannot be reflected in the financial statements. A **net** tax benefit (apart from book or tax carrybacks) cannot be presented in the balance sheet.

To illustrate, consider the examples in the preceding section. Now, assume that the loss in year 5 exceeds the available tax carryback. Three alternative fact situations are presented, which illustrate the accounting when (i) the tax loss exceeds the book loss, but deferred tax credits are adequate to absorb the NOL; (ii) the book loss exceeds the tax loss, and again the deferred tax credits are sufficient to permit offsetting the tax loss carryforwards; and (iii) the book loss exceeds the tax loss, and deferred tax credits are insufficient to absorb the NOL carryforward.

Example of accounting for tax and book loss, with deferred tax credit available to absorb NOL:

Year	Income (loss) before income taxes		Income tax expense (credit)			Cumulative net deferred credits
	Financial	*Taxable*	*Current*	*Deferred*	*Total*	
1	$30,000	$15,000	$ 6,000	$6,000	$12,000	$ 6,000
2	12,000	5,000	2,000	600	2,600	6,600
3	40,000	18,000	5,400	6,600	12,000	13,200
4	30,000	25,000	7,500	1,500	9,000	14,700
5	(45,000)	(52,000)	(14,900)	(3,600)	(11,300)	18,300

In this example, the current tax benefit in year 5 is the amount of tax refund which will be obtained--the taxes actually paid over the prior three years. Since the loss ($52,000) exceeds taxable income for the prior three years ($48,000), a **tax** NOL carryforward exists in the amount of $4,000.

The book loss in year 5 is fully absorbed as a carryback; thus **no book** NOL carryforward exists. (The amounts and expiration dates of both tax and book basis NOL carryforwards must be disclosed in the notes to the financial statements.)

Notice that the deferred tax expense in year 5 ($3,600) is derived from an analysis of the future temporary difference reversals. Assuming a future tax rate of 30%, the $61,000 cumulative unreversed temporary difference existing at the end of year 5 will create a future tax obligation of $18,300; in conjunction with the deferred tax liability at the end of year 4 totaling $14,700, this implies a deferred tax expense in year 5 of $3,600 is needed to bring the balance in the liability account up to the necessary level.

Example of accounting for tax and book loss, with book NOL carryforward fully recognized:

In this example, the book loss exceeds not only the tax loss, but the book income for the entire statutory carryback period as well. Nonetheless, the full book NOL is recognized currently, because the entity's existing deferred tax credits are adequate to completely absorb the book NOL carryforward. (For simplicity, the schedule of future reversals is not presented, but it is assumed that all temporary differences would reverse during the statutory NOL carryforward period of 15 years.)

	Income (loss) before income taxes		Income tax expense (credit)			Cumulative net deferred
Year	Financial	Taxable	Current	Deferred	Total	credits
1	$30,000	$15,000	$ 6,000	$ 6,000	$12,000	$ 6,000
2	12,000	5,000	2,000	600	2,600	6,600
3	40,000	18,000	5,400	6,600	12,000	13,200
4	30,000	25,000	7,500	1,500	9,000	14,700
5	(90,000)	(52,000)	(14,900)	(11,400)	(26,300)	3,300

As with the previous example, the deferred tax adjustment can be directly assessed by computing the tax effects of net unreversed temporary differences at year end. At the end of year 5, the net unreversed temporary differences are $11,000; this requires a deferred tax liability of $3,300 at the anticipated rate of 30%. Given the deferred tax balance at the end of year 4, a $11,400 deferred tax benefit provision for year 5 is computed. Note that it is best not to think of the excess NOL benefit recognized as being a carryback to year 1 (which would violate the three year loss carryback rule); rather, the excess loss being recognized is the future deductible amount which will be offset against future taxable amounts in years 6, 7, etc. The fact that those future taxable amounts are, in effect, the reversals of temporary differences originating (possibly) in year 1 is irrelevant under SFAS 96.

Example of accounting for tax and book loss exceeding available deferred tax credit and NOL carryback opportunity:

Now assume the book loss in year 5 is of a magnitude to more than offset all future taxable amounts resulting from temporary differences as of the balance sheet date.

	Income (loss) before income taxes		Income tax expense (credit)			Cumulative net deferred
Year	Financial	Taxable	Current	Deferred	Total	credits
1	$ 30,000	$15,000	$ 6,000	$ 6,000	$12,000	$ 6,000
2	12,000	5,000	2,000	600	2,600	6,600
3	40,000	18,000	5,400	6,600	12,000	13,200
4	30,000	25,000	7,500	1,500	9,000	14,700
5	(125,000)	(52,000)	(14,900)	(14,700)	(29,600)	-0-

In this situation, the aggregate temporary difference at the end of year 5 (including NOLs) is a net deductible amount. However, since a benefit for future net deductible amounts cannot be recognized in the balance sheet, the excess NOL carryforward is not recorded. The **tax** NOL carryforward at the end of year 5 is $52,000 - 48,000 = $4,000. The **book** NOL carryforward is $24,000, which is equal to the book loss ($125,000) less the sum of the tax loss and the temporary differences used to absorb excess book losses ($52,000 + 49,000 = $101,000).

The foregoing discussion and examples pertain only to the provisions of SFAS 96. Accounting for the tax effects of net operating losses will change substantially if the Board adopts its proposed standard to supersede SFAS 96. See Appendix D for a discussion of the provisions of that proposed standard.

Tax Credits

Before being repealed by the 1986 tax law revisions, investment tax and other credits had been allowed under federal and some state tax laws since 1962. GAAP provided that the investment tax credit (ITC) could be recognized either when realized (i.e., when used to reduce taxes payable) or as the useful life of the asset whose acquisition generated the ITC expired. (These were known as the flow-through and deferral methods, respectively.) Until the enactment of the 1982 tax act (TEFRA), the ITC did not affect the other tax benefit of asset ownership--depreciation.

The 1982 tax revision provided that an acquirer of qualifying property could elect either reduced ITC **or** full ITC coupled with a reduction in depreciable basis in the asset. The latter course of action resulted in a timing difference when the flow-through method of recognizing ITC was employed. FASB Technical Bulletin 83-1 illustrated the appropriate accounting under these circumstances.

Under past law, ITC not utilized currently (due to a lack of taxable income) was available for carryback and carryforward, similar to an NOL. The accounting treatments generally followed those prescribed for NOLs (although ITC carryforwards subsequently realized did **not** result in extraordinary item presentation, unlike NOLs under APB 11). When ITC carryforwards were generated at a time when deferred tax liabilities existed, some or all of the ITC carryforward was recognized currently as an offset against the deferred taxes, again in a manner similar to that prescribed for NOLs by APB 11. FASB Interpretation 32 stipulated the procedures used to compute the amount of this offsetting, necessitated by the percentage limitations on utilization of ITC to reduce the tax liability.

APB 11 provided that, as with the situation where NOL carryforwards were recognized as offsets to existing deferred tax liabilities, ITC carryforwards subsequently realized for income tax purposes required a restoration of the deferred tax credits to the extent the related timing differences had not yet been reversed. Although the computational mechanics have changed with the promulgation of SFAS 96, the substance of the restoration of deferred taxes upon the realization of NOLs and ITC for tax purposes remains similar to past practice. SFAS 96 does not address ITC accounting, per se.

The 1986 tax revision rescinded the ITC retroactive to January 1, 1986. However, existing ITC carryforwards (for asset acquisitions prior to 1986) continue to be available, subject to a phased reduction, over future periods. In disclosing the amounts and expiration dates of these carryforwards, the percentage reductions mandated by the 1986 law should be stated, and, as the carryforwards remain unused in future periods, the available amounts should be reduced to reflect the phase out.

Intraperiod Tax Allocation

SFAS 96 essentially continues the procedures adopted for intraperiod tax allocation under APB 11. To the appropriate extent, tax expense or benefit must be allocated to continuing operations and also to discontinued operations, extraordinary items, cumulative effect of accounting changes, prior period adjustments and any other non-operating categories provided by present or future GAAP. An **incremental** approach is used: that is, the difference between total tax expense and tax expense on income from continuing operations is the amount to be allocated to the other income statement and/or retained earnings classifications.

A special problem arises if there are several items that are to be allocated tax effects. SFAS 96 specifies that generally these tax effects should be measured by the separate incremental effect of each such category. However, in some situations, due to certain peculiarities of the tax law, the separately determined incremental tax effects may not accumulate to the total incremental tax. In such instances, a different allocation procedure must be employed.

The statement stipulates that the incremental tax **benefits** of all loss categories (other than continuing operations) must first be determined; this is then apportioned ratably to each loss category (e.g., discontinued operations, extraordinary losses, etc.). Having done this, each gain category is allocated a ratable portion of the difference between (i) the incremental tax on all categories (gain **and** loss) other than continuing operations and (ii) the incremental benefit of all loss categories taken together.

Consider the following example.

	Amount	Tax Effect
Income from continuing operations	$ 740,000	$ 260,000
Gain on discontinuation of Widget Division	98,000	
Loss on discontinuation of Whatsis Division	(310,000)	
Extraordinary item - loss from hurricane damage	(405,000)	
Cumulative effect of change in inventory accounting method	42,000	
Net income (before tax)	$ 165,000	$ 48,000

To compute the tax effects allocable to the various non-continuing operation items, the first step is to compute the benefit of the several loss items as a group:

Income from continuing operations		$ 740,000
Loss on Whatsis Division		(310,000)
Hurricane loss		(405,000)
Total		$ 25,000
Tax thereon		$ 3,800

Thus, the tax benefit of the aggregate loss items is $260,000 - 3,800 = $256,200. This is allocated pro rata to the two loss categories in the example:

	Amount	Percent	Tax benefit
Loss on Whatsis Division	$310,000	43.36%	$ 111,088
Hurricane loss	405,000	56.64	145,112
	$715,000	100.00%	$ 256,200

The tax effect of the gain categories is next computed:

Incremental effect of **all** non-continuing operations categories:	
$260,000 - 48,000 =	$(212,000)
Less: incremental effect of loss categories (computed above)	(256,200)
Tax effect of all gain categories	$ 44,200

The total tax effect of the gain categories is then allocated to the individual gain items on a pro rata basis:

	Amount	Percent	Tax benefit
Gain on Widget Division	$ 98,000	70.00%	$30,940
Inventory accounting change	42,000	30.00	13,260
	$140,000	100.00%	$44,200

Tax Allocation for Business Investments

As noted in Chapter 9, pending forthcoming Board actions that may alter or restrict use of the equity method, there are two basic methods for accounting for investments in the common stock of other corporations: (1) the cost method and (2) the equity method. The cost method requires that the investing corporation (investor) record the investment at its purchase price, and no additional entry is made to the account over the life of the asset (this does not include any valuation contra accounts). The cost method is used in instances where the investor is not considered to have significant in-fluence over the investee. The ownership threshold generally used is 20% of owner-ship. This figure is not considered an absolute (FASB Interpretation 35), but it will be used to identify the break between application of the cost and equity methods. Under the cost method, ordinary income is recognized as dividends are declared by the in-vestee, and capital gains (losses) are recognized upon the disposal of the investment. For tax purposes, no provision is made during the holding period for the allocable undistributed earnings of the investee. There is no deferred tax computation necessary when using the cost method because there is no temporary difference.

The equity method is used whenever an investor owns more than 20% of an investee or has significant influence over its operations. The equity method calls for recording the investment at cost and then increasing this carrying amount by the allocable portion of the investee's earnings. The allocable portion of the investee's earnings is then included in pretax accounting income of the investor. Dividend payments are no longer included in pretax accounting income but are considered to be a reduction in the carrying amount of the investment. However, for tax purposes, dividends are the only revenue realized. As a result, the investor needs to recognize deferred income tax expense on the undistributed earnings of the investee that will be taxed in the future. The current promulgated GAAP in this area are APB 23 and SFAS 96, which supersede APB 24 but which continue the principles set forth therein. These are discussed below.

GAAP distinguishes between an investee and a subsidiary and prescribes different accounting treatments for each. An investee is considered to be a corporation whose stock is owned by an investor who holds more than 20% but no greater than 50% of the outstanding stock. An investee situation occurs when the investor has significant influence but not control over the corporation invested in. A subsidiary, on the other hand, exists when more than 50% of the stock of a corporation is owned by another. This results in direct control over the corporation invested in. APB 23 is the promulgated GAAP regarding the tax effects relating to the ownership of subsidiaries, and APB 24 was the promulgated GAAP on the tax effects of investments in common stock of entities other than subsidiaries and corporate joint ventures which are accounted for by the equity method until being superseded by SFAS 96.

Subsidiary undistributed earnings. According to APB 23, the inclusion of undistributed earnings of a subsidiary in the pretax accounting income of a parent company through consolidation or equity reporting (or some combination of the two) may result in a timing difference, a difference that may not reverse until indefinite future periods. It is presumed that at some point in time all of the undistributed earnings of a subsidiary will be transferred to the parent. As such, the tax effect must be recognized on the temporary difference and treated as occurring either in the form of a dividend or a capital gain. The form that the temporary difference takes (dividend or capital transaction) is dependent upon the expectation involved in the situation.

The presumption that all undistributed income will eventually be transferred to the parent can be overcome if sufficient evidence can be presented that the subsidiary will invest the undistributed earnings indefinitely or that the earnings will be distributed in a tax-free liquidation. Examples of such evidence would be the past experience of the companies involved or specific future plans of indefinite postponement. In such an instance, the Opinion requires that the following disclosures be made in the notes to the financial statements:

1. A declaration of an intention to reinvest the undistributed earnings of a sub-sidiary to support the contention that the distribution of those earnings has been indefinitely postponed or that the earnings will be distributed in the form of a tax-free liquidation.
2. The cumulative amount of undistributed earnings on which the parent company has not recognized taxes.

APB 23 provides that when a change occurs in the expectations regarding distributions of subsidiary earnings, the tax effects of the changed expectations are to be reflected in tax expense in the period the new information becomes available. In other words, the character of the change is that of an accounting estimate; it is not appropriate to treat it as either an extraordinary item or a correction of prior periods.

SFAS 96 leaves APB 23 in place, with minor amendments, as GAAP for accounting for the tax effects of investments in subsidiaries. In fact, given SFAS 96's stress on tax planning strategies, APB 23 appears to be highly appropriate as originally written. The only real change, of course, is that changes in expected future tax effects will be recognized currently (as set forth in SFAS 96), in contrast to APB 11's requirement that, once provided, deferred taxes were not subsequently revised for changes in tax rates, etc. Presumably, tax planning strategies will most often call for realization of undistributed subsidiary earnings through future dividend payments, or, if appropriate, through "indefinite reversal" to avert the need for tax accrual at all.

Investee undistributed earnings. APB 24 promulgated GAAP for situations where there is significant influence but not control. It was the difference between these two degrees of power that was the catalyst for APB 24. The fact that an investor has significant influences in the operations of an investee is not enough to determine that distribution of the investee's earnings will be postponed indefinitely. As a result, the inclusion of undistributed earnings of an investee corporation in the pretax accounting income of the parent corporation will always result in a temporary difference. Again, the facts and circumstances involved in each situation will be the final determinant as to whether the temporary difference is treated as a dividend or a capital gain.

SFAS 96 has continued the approach set forth originally in APB 24, although of course the deferred tax provision is now based on the liability approach and no longer is determined by the "with and without" calculation of APB 11.

To illustrate the application of these concepts, assume Parent Company owns 30% of the outstanding common stock of Investee Company and 70% of the outstanding common stock of Subsidiary Company. Additional data for Subsidiary and Investee Companies for the year 1992 are as follows:

	Investee Company	Subsidiary Company
Net income	$50,000	$100,000
Dividends paid	20,000	60,000

The following sections illustrate how the foregoing data are used to recognize the tax effects of the stated events.

Income Tax Effects from Investee Company

The pretax accounting income of Parent Company will include equity in investee income equal to $15,000 ($50,000 x 30%). Parent's taxable income, however, will include dividend income of $6,000 ($20,000 x 30%), and a credit of 80% of the $6,000, or $4,800, will also be allowed for the dividends received. This 80% dividends received deduction is a permanent difference between pretax accounting and taxable income and is allowed for dividends received from domestic corporations in which the ownership percentage is less than 80% but at least 20%; a lower dividend received deduction of 70% is permitted when the ownership percentage is less than 20%. A 100% credit (dividends received deduction) is allowed for dividends received from domestic corporations in which the ownership percentage is 80 to 100%. As discussed in APB 24, the originating temporary difference results from Parent's equity ($9,000) in the Investee's undistributed income of $30,000. The amount of the deferred tax credit in 1991 depends upon the expectations of Parent Company as to the manner in which the $9,000 of undistributed income will be received. If the expectation of receipt is via dividends, then the temporary difference is 20% of $9,000, or $1,800, and the deferred tax credit for this originating temporary difference in 1992 is the current tax rate times $1,800. However, if the expectation of receipt is through future sale of the investment, then the temporary difference is $9,000 and the deferred tax credit is the current capital gains rate (which in 1987 and future years is the corporation's regular marginal tax rate or alternative minimum tax rate, since the preferential capital gains rate has been ended by the 1986 tax reform) times the $9,000.

The entries below illustrate these alternatives. A tax rate of 34% is used for both ordinary income and for capital gains. Note that the amounts in the entries below relate only to Investee Company's incremental impact upon Parent Company's tax accounts.

	Expectations for Undistributed Income	
	Dividends	Capital gains
Income tax expense	1,020	3,468
Deferred tax liability	612[b]	3,060[c]
Income taxes payable	408[a]	408[a]

[a]Computation of income taxes payable:

Dividend income--30% x ($20,000)	$6,000
Less 80% dividends received deduction	(4,800)
Amount included in Parents' taxable income	$1,200
Tax liability--34% ($1,200)	$ 408

[b]Computation of deferred tax liability (dividend assumption):
Originating temporary difference:
Parent's share of undistributed income--

30% x ($30,000)	$9,000
Less 80% dividends received deduction	(7,200)
Originating temporary difference	$1,800
Deferred tax liability--34% ($1,800)	$ 612

[c]Computation of deferred tax liability (capital gain assumption):
Originating temporary difference: Parent's share

of undistributed income--30% x ($30,000)	$9,000
Deferred tax liability--34% x ($9,000)	$3,060

Although APB 24 has been superseded by SFAS 96, the accounting procedures prescribed therein are continued essentially unchanged. The one difference, of course, is that under SFAS 96 the tax effect of this (and all other) temporary difference is measured by the tax impact of the future reversal of the difference, and **not** by the "with and without" method of APB 11. The example above therefore assumes that future taxes will continue at current rates.

Income Tax Effects from Subsidiary Company

The pretax accounting income of Parent Company will also include equity in Subsidiary income of $70,000 (70% x $100,000). This $70,000 will be included in pretax consolidated income if Parent and Subsidiary issue consolidated financial statements. For tax purposes, Parent and Subsidiary cannot file a consolidated tax return because the minimum level of control, i.e., 80%, is not present. Consequently, the taxable income of Parent will include dividend income of $42,000 (70% x $60,000), and there will be an 80% dividends received deduction of $33,600. The originating temporary difference discussed in APB 23 results from Parent's equity ($28,000) in the subsidiary's undistributed earnings of $40,000. The amount of the deferred tax credit in 1992 depends upon the expectations of Parent Company as to the manner in which this $28,000 of undistributed income will be received. The same expectations can exist as previously discussed, for Parent's equity in Investee's undistributed earnings, i.e., through future dividend distributions or capital gains. In addition, however, if Parent can demonstrate that its share of Subsidiary Company's earnings will be permanently reinvested by Subsidiary, then APB 23 states that no timing difference exists and, therefore, no deferred tax credits arise. This treatment is not available for stock investments between 20 and 50%. SFAS 96 explicitly preserves the "indefinite reversal" criterion contained in APB 23. This criterion is not applicable to any other class of temporary difference.

The entries below illustrate these alternatives. A marginal tax rate of 34% is assumed. The amounts in the entries below relate only to Subsidiary Company's incremental impact upon Parent Company's tax accounts.

	Dividends	Expectations for Undistributed Income	
		Capital gains	Reinvested
Income tax expense	4,760	12,376	2,856
Deferred tax liability	1,904[b]	9,520[c]	--
Income taxes payable	2,856[a]	2,856[a]	2,856[a]

[a]Computation of income taxes payable:

Dividend income--70% x ($60,000)	$42,000
Less 80% dividends received deduction	(33,600)
Amount included in Parents' taxable income	$ 8,400
Tax liability--34% x ($8,400)	$ 2,856

[b]Computation of deferred tax liability (dividend assumption):
Originating temporary difference:

Parent's share of undistributed income-- 70% x ($40,000)	$28,000
Less 80% dividends received deduction	(22,400)
Originating temporary difference	$ 5,600
Deferred tax liability--34% x ($5,600)	$ 1,904

[c]Computation of deferred tax liability (capital gain assumption):

Originating temporary difference: Parent's share of undistributed income--70% x ($40,000)	$28,000
Deferred tax liability--34% x ($28,000)	$ 9,520

If a parent company owns 80% or more of the voting stock of a subsidiary and the parent consolidates the subsidiary for both financial and tax reports, then no temporary differences exist between pretax consolidated income and taxable income. If, in the circumstances noted above, consolidated financial statements are prepared but a consolidated tax return is not, then it should be noted that a dividends received deduction of 100% is allowed. Accordingly, the temporary difference between pretax consolidated income and taxable income is zero if the parent assumes the undistributed income will be realized in dividends.

Summary of Temporary Differences of Investees and Subsidiaries

Level of Ownership Interest

Accounting

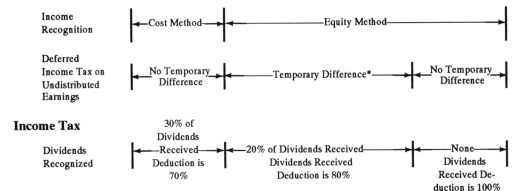

*Recognition of temporary differences

*Ownership level ≥ 20% ≤ 50%; temporary difference **must** be accounted for.*

*Ownership level > 50%; temporary difference **must** normally be accounted for, unless management intends to reinvest the subsidiary's earnings indefinitely into the future.*

Disclosures

Balance Sheet

SFAS 96 provides that the following balance sheet accounts will be presented, if appropriate:

1. Currently payable taxes
2. Currently refundable taxes
3. Net current deferred tax liability or asset
4. Net noncurrent deferred tax liability or asset

In contrast to the requirement of APB 11 (and SFAS 37), the current or noncurrent status of deferred tax assets and liabilities is determined by the traditional accounting criterion: "current" implies the obligation will be settled within one year or the current operating cycle. The previously employed approach, attempting to match the status of the deferred tax with the asset or liability giving rise to it, has been terminated.

Income Statement

The income statement disclosures under SFAS 96 are very similar to those under prior GAAP. The following components of income tax expense must be presented, typically in the notes to the financial statements:

1. Current tax expense or benefit.
2. Deferred tax expense or benefit, excluding any adjustments to the deferred accounts caused by changes in tax laws, statutory rates, or changes in the entity's tax status.
3. Investment tax credits.
4. Tax benefits of operating loss carryforwards.
5. Adjustments to the deferred tax accounts resulting from changes in tax laws, statutory rates, or the entity's tax status.

Furthermore, intraperiod tax allocation must be applied; tax must be assigned to income from continuing operations, discontinued operations, extraordinary items, cumulative effect of changes in accounting principles, and prior period adjustments, if any.

Reporting entities must provide disclosures of reconciling items between the **expected** tax (obtained by multiplying pre-tax income from continuing operations by the statutory rate) and actual tax expense. Nonpublic firms may simply disclose the nature of the reconciling items without quantifying the effect; public companies must provide a reconciling schedule with appropriate quantification of effects.

APB 11 required disclosure of **tax** NOL carryforwards plus additional information about any such carryforwards that would not impact the income statement when subsequently realized (i.e., NOL benefits already recognized as reductions to deferred tax liabilities). This requirement was often poorly complied with. SFAS 96 clarifies and strengthens this rule by mandating separate disclosure schedules for **tax** and **book** NOLs, with amounts and expiration dates for each. Other carryforwards (ITC and AMT credits, for example) are subject to similar disclosures. Also, if the entity has purchased operating loss carryforwards which will, upon realization, reduce goodwill or other assets rather than tax expense, this must be disclosed.

Finally, if an entity is using APB 23's indefinite reversal criterion to avoid accruing tax on earnings of a subsidiary, this fact and the events that would cause taxes to be accrued on previously undistributed earnings must be described in the financial statement notes. The amount of the unrecognized deferred tax liabilities must be disclosed as well.

APPENDIX A

Accounting for Income Taxes in Interim Periods

Interim Reporting

Current GAAP applicable to interim period financial reporting include APB 28 and FASB Interpretation 18. These standards have not been altered by new income tax accounting requirements of SFAS 96. Paragraph 19 of APB 28 states that:

> ...income tax provisions should be determined under the procedures set forth in APB Opinion Nos. 11, 23, and 24. At the end of each interim period the company should make its best estimate of the effective tax rate expected to be applicable for the full fiscal year. The rate so determined should be used in providing for income taxes on a current year-to-date basis. The effective rate should reflect anticipated investment tax credits, foreign tax rates, percentage depletion, capital gains rates, and other available tax planning alternatives. However, in arriving at this effective tax rate no effect should be included for the tax related to significant unusual or extraordinary items that will be separately reported or reported net of their related tax effect in reports for the interim period or fiscal year.

Below is a relatively simple example which illustrates the basic principles of the Opinion.

<u>Example of Accounting for Income Taxes in Interim Periods</u>

Hartig, Inc. estimates that pretax accounting income for the full fiscal year ending June 30, 1992 will be $400,000. The company expects amortization of goodwill for the year to be $30,000, the annual premium on an officer's life insurance policy is $12,000, and dividend income (from a less than 20% ownership interest) is expected to be $100,000. The company recognized income of $75,000 in the first quarter of the year. Tax depreciation exceeded book depreciation expense in the first quarter by $30,000. This is the company's only temporary difference.

Hartig must first calculate its estimated effective income tax rate for the year. This rate is computed using all of the tax planning alternatives available to the company (e.g., tax credits, foreign rates, capital gains rates, etc.).

Estimated pretax accounting income		$400,000
Permanent differences:		
Add: Nondeductible officer's life insurance premium	$ 12,000	
Nondeductible amortization of goodwill	30,000	42,000
		442,000
Less: Dividends received deduction ($100,000 x 70%)		(70,000)
Estimated taxable income		$372,000
Income taxes:		
Computed at rates below		$126,480
Effective tax rate ($126,480 ÷ 400,000)		31.62%

Tax rate schedule		Rate	Taxable Income	Tax
At least	Not more than			
$ --	$ 50,000	15%	$ 50,000	$ 7,500
50,000	75,000	25%	25,000	6,250
75,000	--	34%	297,000	100,980
100,000	335,000*	5%	235,000	11,750
				$126,480

* The *additional* 5% tax effectively causes entities with income over $335,000 (as in this example) to pay tax at a flat 34% rate.

The effective rate is then applied to the current quarter results as shown below.

Pretax accounting income	$75,000
Effective rate	x 31.62%
Income tax expense	$23,715
Pretax accounting income	75,000
Temporary difference	30,000
Pretax accounting income with temporary difference	45,000
Effective rate	x 31.62%
	$14,229

Therefore, the entry necessary to record the income tax expense at the end of the first quarter is as follows:

Income tax expense	23,715	
Deferred tax liability		9,486
Income taxes payable		14,229

The financial statement presentation would remain the same as has been illustrated in prior examples.

In the second quarter, Hartig, Inc. revises its estimate of income for the full fiscal year. It now anticipates only $210,000 of book income, including only $75,000 of dividend income, because of dramatic changes in the national economy. Other permanent differences are still expected to total $42,000.

Estimated pre-tax accounting income	$210,000
Add: Permanent differences	42,000
Less: Dividends received deduction	
($75,000 x 70%)	(52,500)
Estimated taxable income	$199,500
Tax thereon (see below)	61,055

Tax rate schedule			Taxable	
At least	Not more than	Rate	Income	Tax
$ --	$ 50,000	15%	$ 50,000	$ 7,500
50,000	75,000	25%	25,000	6,250
75,000	--	34%	124,500	42,330
100,000	335,000	5%	99,500	4,975
				$ 61,055

The projected effective rate is now $61,055 ÷ 210,000 = 29.07%.

Actual earnings in the second quarter were only $22,000 on a book basis; excess tax depreciation was $10,000 during the quarter.

The application of the new effective rate is shown below. Note that the results of the first quarter are **not** restated; the entire change necessary in the income tax expense year-to-date is recognized in the second quarter.

Pretax accounting income year-to-date	
($75,000 + 22,000)	$ 97,000
Effective rate	29.07%
Total tax expense year-to-date	28,198
Less first quarter provision	(23,715)
Expense provision necessary in second quarter	$ 4,483
Pretax accounting income	$ 97,000
Temporary difference ($30,000 ÷ 10,000)	40,000
Pretax accounting income year-to-date with	
temporary difference	57,000
Effective tax rate	29.07%
Total tax currently payable	16,570
Less first quarter provision	(14,229)
Current provision necessary in second quarter	$ 2,341
Total deferred ($28,198 - 16,570)	$ 11,628
Less first quarter provision	(9,486)
Deferred provision necessary in second quarter	$ 2,142

The necessary entry for the second quarter tax provision is then as follows:

Income tax expense	4,483	
Deferred tax liability		2,142
Income taxes payable		2,341

The foregoing illustrates the basic problems encountered in applying the promulgated GAAP to interim reporting. In the following paragraphs, we will provide a discussion relative to some of the items requiring a change in the approach described above.

Net Operating Losses in Interim Periods

FASB Interpretation 18 set forth the appropriate accounting when losses were incurred in interim periods or when loss carryforward benefits were realized during an interim reporting period. Given that NOL benefits realized are no longer treated as extraordinary items under SFAS 96, and given the new, more stringent limitations on the recognition of deferred tax assets, the prescriptions set forth by FASB Interpretation 18 have been revised. The changes affect (1) the calculation of the expected annual tax rate for purposes of interim period income tax provisions, and (2) the recognition of an asset for a loss carryforward.

Carryforward from prior years. Loss carryforward benefits from prior years realized in interim periods are now included in the ordinary tax provision, rather than as extraordinary gains. Interpretation 18 provided that an expected annual effective tax rate on **ordinary** income was to be calculated at each interim reporting date, and that this rate be used to provide income taxes on **ordinary** income on a cumulative basis at each interim date. The tax effects of extraordinary items, discontinued operations, and other non-operating categories were excluded from this computation; those tax effects were separately determined on a "with and without" basis as explained later in this Appendix. Since, under APB 11, NOL benefit realization was not part of operating income, it was excluded from the estimation of the annual effective tax rate.

SFAS 96 has changed this, by including the benefit of NOL carryforward realizations in operations (i.e., in the provision for income taxes relating to operating income). Accordingly, it is necessary to estimate, at each interim reporting date, the effective annual rate **including** the effect of any NOL carryforward benefits to be realized during the full fiscal year.

To illustrate, consider the following example:

The corporation has a $50,000 net operating loss carryforward; a flat 40% tax rate for current and future periods is assumed. Income for the full year (before NOL) is projected to be $80,000; in the first quarter a pre-tax loss of $10,000 will be reported.

Projected annual income	$ 80,000
NOL benefit to be realized	(50,000)
Net annual taxable income	$ 30,000
x Tax rate	40%
Projected tax liability	$ 12,000

The effective tax rate being projected for the full fiscal year is therefore:

Projected tax	$ 12,000
÷ Pre-tax book income	80,000
Effective rate	15%

Accordingly, in the income statement for the first fiscal quarter, the pre-tax operating loss of $10,000 will give rise to a tax **benefit** of $10,000 x 15% = $1,500.

If the second quarter results in a pre-tax operating income of $30,000, and the expectation for the full year remains unchanged (i.e., operating income of $80,000), the second quarter tax provision is $4,500, calculated as follows:

Cumulative pre-tax income through 2nd quarter ($30,000 - 10,000)	$20,000
x Effective rate (above)	15%
Cumulative required tax provision	$ 3,000
Less tax provision (benefit) recognized in 1st quarter	$(1,500)
Tax provision in 2nd quarter	$ 4,500

Changing the facts slightly, assume actual results through the end of the 2nd quarter are as above, but at the end the second quarter the corporation now projects full year operating income of $100,000. A new effective annual tax rate must be computed:

Projected annual income	$100,000
NOL benefit to be realized	50,000
Net annual taxable income	$ 50,000
x Tax rate	40%
Projected tax liability	$ 20,000
Projected tax	$ 20,000
÷ Pre-tax book income	100,000
Effective rate	20%

Thus, the tax provision in the 2nd quarter will be $5,500, as follows:

Cumulative pre-tax income through 2nd quarter	$20,000
x Revised effective rate	20%
Cumulative required tax provision	$ 4,000
<u>Less</u> tax provision (benefit) recognized in 1st quarter	(1,500)
Tax provision in 2nd quarter	$ 5,500

Note that the effective rate in the income statement for the second quarter is 18.33% ($5,500 ÷ 30,000).

Interpretation 18, as amended by SFAS 96, provides that the foregoing methodology be employed for normal situations where the NOL carryforward will be absorbed against operating income. If this will **not** be the case, however, and the NOL benefits will be realized as offsets against income from discontinued operations, extraordinary gains, etc., then the NOL benefits should not be included in the computation of the effective tax rate. Instead, the NOL benefits should be recognized as they are realized-- i.e., as cumulative amounts of income from discontinued operations, etc., are available to absorb the NOL. This is essentially the same procedure as Interpretation 18 had originally prescribed for NOL benefit recognition, when NOL benefits were treated as extraordinary items.

If a loss is projected for the entire year, unless there are deferred tax liabilities against which to offset a deferred tax asset resulting from the NOL carryforward, no tax benefit can be projected for the current year or any interim period thereof. This follows from the SFAS 96 prohibition against recognition of net deferred tax assets.

Estimated net loss for the year. SFAS 96 firmly establishes the principle that the tax benefit of a loss cannot be recognized until it is actually realized. As when dealing with a net operating loss at the end of a year, the tax benefit can be realized to the extent that existing deferred credits which reverse during the carryforward period can be offset.

For each of the following examples we will assume that the corporation is anticipating a loss for the fiscal year of $150,000. Deferred tax credits of $30,000 are currently recorded on the company's books; all of the credits will reverse in the 15-year carryforward period.

Example 1

Assume that the company can carry back the entire $150,000 to the preceding three years. The tax potentially refundable by the carryback **would** (remember this is only an estimate until year end) amount to $48,000 (an assumed amount). The effective rate is then 32% ($48,000/150,000).

| | Ordinary income (loss) | | Tax (benefit) expense | | |
| | | | | Less | |
Reporting period	Reporting period	Year-to date	Year-to-date	previously provided	Reporting period
1st qtr.	$ (50,000)	$ (50,000)	$(16,000)	$ --	$(16,000)
2nd qtr.	20,000	(30,000)	(9,600)	(16,000)	6,400
3rd qtr.	(70,000)	(100,000)	(32,000)	(9,600)	(22,400)
4th qtr.	(50,000)	(150,000)	(48,000)	(32,000)	(16,000)
Fiscal year	$(150,000)				$(48,000)

Note that both the income tax expense (2nd quarter) and benefit are computed using the estimated annual effective rate. This rate is applied to the year-to-date numbers just as in the previous examples, with any adjustment being made and realized in the current reporting period.

Example 2

In this case assume that the company can carry back only $50,000 of the loss and that the remainder must be carried forward. Realization of income to offset the loss is not assured beyond a reasonable doubt. The estimated carryback of $50,000 would generate a tax refund of $12,000 (again assumed). The company is assumed to be in the 40% tax bracket (a flat rate is used to simplify the example). Remember that a net operating loss carryforward existing at the same time as net deferred credits is recognized to the extent of the lesser of the tax benefit from the loss or the net deferred credits. The calculation of the estimated annual effective rate is as follows:

Expected net loss			$150,000
Tax benefit from carryback		$12,000	
Lesser of:			
Benefit of carryforward ($100,000 x 40%)	$40,000		
Net deferred credits	30,000	30,000	
Total recognized benefit			$42,000
Estimated annual effective rate ($42,000 ÷ 150,000)			28%

Reporting period	Ordinary income (loss) Reporting period	Year-to date	Tax (benefit) expense Computed	Year-to-date Limited to	Less previously provided	Reporting period
1st qtr.	$ 10,000	$ 10,000	$ 2,800	$ --	$ --	$ 2,800
2nd qtr.	(80,000)	(70,000)	(19,600)	--	2,800	(22,400)
3rd qtr.	(100,000)	(170,000)	(47,600)	(42,000)	(19,600)	(22,400)
4th qtr.	20,000	(150,000)	(42,000)	--	(42,000)	--
Fiscal year	$(150,000)					$(42,000)

As with the other examples concerning interim periods, the tax (benefit) expense is computed by multiplying the year-to-date income by the estimated annual effective rate and subtracting the provision previously provided. It makes no difference whether the current period results in net income or a loss; the same estimated rate is used. In this example, the maximum recognizable tax benefit is $42,000. If the computation described above yields as a result a tax benefit in excess of this amount, the reportable benefit must be limited to the lower figure. This is the case in the third quarter of the example. The situation arises because the year-to-date NOL exceeds our estimate of $150,000. As long as the total NOL for the year exceeds $150,000, the maximum recognizable benefit in this situation will be $42,000. The only difference which would occur as a result of changing the estimated NOL is the timing of the tax (benefit) expense recognized due to the change in the estimated rate. Thus, at the end of the year, a NOL carryforward of $25,000 exists ($100,000 less the $75,000 used when the deferred credits of $30,000 were offset), and the $30,000 of deferred credits will be reinstated in accordance with the conditions set forth in this chapter.

The foregoing examples cover most of the situations encountered in practice. The reader is referred to paras 49-55 in Appendix C of FASB Interpretation 18 for additional examples.

Operating loss occurring during an interim period. An instance may occur in which the company expects net income for the year and incurs a net loss during one of the reporting periods. In this situation, the estimated annual effective rate, which was calculated based upon the expected net income figure, is applied to the year-to-date income or loss to arrive at a total year-to-date tax provision. The amount previously provided is subtracted from the year-to-date figure to arrive at the provision for the current reporting period. If the current period operations resulted in a loss, then the tax provision for the period will reflect a tax benefit. The benefit is recognizable because realization of the loss is assumed beyond a reasonable doubt as a result of the estimation of net income for the year. This treatment has been affirmed by SFAS 96.

Tax Provision Applicable to Significant Unusual or Infrequently Occurring Items, Discontinued Operations, or Extraordinary Items Occurring in Interim Periods

Unusual, infrequent, or extraordinary items. The financial statement presentation of these items and their related tax effects are prescribed by SFAS 96. Extraordinary items and discontinued operations are to be shown net of their related tax effects. Unusual or infrequently occurring items that are part of continuing operations and will be separately disclosed in the fiscal year financial statements shall be separately disclosed as a component of pretax income, and the tax or benefit should be included in the tax provision for continuing operations.

The interim treatment accorded these items does not differ from the fiscal year-end reporting required by GAAP. However, according to APB 28, these items **are not** to be included in the computation of the estimated annual tax rate. The Opinion also requires that these items be recognized in the interim period in which they occur. Examples of the treatment promulgated by the Opinion follow later in this section.

Recognition of the tax effects of a loss due to any of the aforementioned situations is prohibited until the loss is realized or realization is assured beyond a reasonable doubt. According to FASB Interpretation 18, realization is assured beyond a reasonable doubt under any one of the following circumstances:

1. The offsetting of year-to-date ordinary income
2. The offsetting of taxable income from an unusual, infrequently occurring, or extraordinary item; from discontinued operations; or from items credited directly to stockholders' equity accounts
3. When the loss can be carried back

Although not specifically stated in either APB 28 or FASB Interpretation 18, it would appear that realization also is assured if there are existing net deferred tax credits. If a situation arises where realization is not assured beyond any reasonable doubt in the period of occurrence but becomes assured in a subsequent period in the same fiscal year, the previously unrecognized tax benefit should be reported in the same way as it would have been in the period of occurrence (FASB Interpretation 18).

The following examples illustrate the treatment required for reporting unusual, infrequently occurring, and extraordinary items. Again, these items are **not** to be used in calculating the estimated annual rate. For income statement presentation, the tax provision relating to unusual or infrequently occurring items is to be included with the tax provision for ordinary income. Extraordinary items are shown net of their applicable tax provision.

The following data apply to the next two examples:

1. The company expects fiscal year ending June 30, 1992, income to be $96,000 and net permanent differences to reduce taxable income by $25,500.
2. The company also incurred a $30,000 extraordinary loss in the second quarter of the year.

Example 1

In this case, assume that the loss can be carried back to prior periods and, therefore, the realization of any tax benefit is assured. Based on the information given earlier, the estimated annual effective tax rate can be calculated as follows:

Expected pretax accounting income	$96,000
Anticipated permanent differences	(25,500)
Expected taxable income	$70,500

Tax Calculation "Excluding" Extraordinary Item

$50,000	x	.15	=	$ 7,500
20,500	x	.25	=	5,125
$70,500				$12,625

Effective annual rate = 13.15% ($12,625 ÷ 96,000)

No adjustment in the estimated annual effective rate is required when the extraordinary, unusual, or infrequent item occurs. The tax (benefit) applicable to the item is computed using the estimated fiscal year ordinary income and an analysis of the incremental impact of the extraordinary item. The method illustrated below is applicable when the company anticipates operating income for the year. When a loss is anticipated, the company computes its estimated annual effective rate based on the amount of tax to be refunded from prior years. The tax (benefit) applicable to the extraordinary, unusual, or infrequent item is then the decrease (increase) in the refund to be received.

Computation of the tax applicable to the extraordinary, unusual, or infrequent item is as follows:

Estimated pretax accounting income	$96,000
Permanent differences	(25,500)
Extraordinary item	(30,000)
Expected taxable income	$40,500

Tax Calculation "Including" Extraordinary Item
$40,500 x .15 = $6,075

Tax "excluding" extraordinary item	$12,625
Tax "including" extraordinary item	6,075
Tax benefit applicable to extraordinary, unusual, or infrequent item	$ 6,550

| | | | Tax (benefit) applicable to | | | |
| | | | Ordinary income (loss) | | Unusual, infrequent, or extraordinary item | | |
Reporting period	Ordinary income (loss)	Unusual, infrequent, or extraordinary item	Reporting period	Year-to-date	Year-to-date	Previously provided	Reporting period
1st qtr.	$10,000	$ --	$ 1,315	$ 1,315	$ --	$ --	$ --
2nd qtr.	(20,000)	(30,000)	(2,630)	(1,315)	(6,550)	--	(6,550)
3rd qtr.	40,000	--	5,260	3,945	(6,550)	(6,550)	--
4th qtr.	66,000	--	8,680	12,625	(6,550)	(6,550)	--
Fiscal year	$96,000	$(30,000)	$12,625				$(6,550)

Example 2

Again, assume that the company estimates net income of $96,000 for the year with permanent differences of $25,500 which reduce taxable income. The extraordinary loss of $30,000 cannot be carried back and, therefore, cannot be tax effected. Because no deferred tax credits exist, the only way that the loss can be assured beyond any reasonable doubt is to the extent that current year ordinary income offsets the effect of the loss. As a result, realization of the loss is assured only as, and to the extent that, there is ordinary income for the year.

| | | | Tax (benefit) applicable to | | | |
| | | | Ordinary income (loss) | | Unusual, infrequent, or extraordinary item | | |
Reporting period	Ordinary income (loss)	Unusual, infrequent, or extraordinary item	Reporting period	Year-to-date	Year-to-date	Previously provided	Reporting period
1st qtr.	$ 5,000	$ --	$ 658	$ 658	$ --	$ --	$ --
2nd qtr.	20,000	(30,000)	2,630	3,288	(3,288)[a]	--	(3,288)
3rd qtr.	(10,000)	--	(1,315)	1,973	(1,973)[a]	(3,288)	1,315
4th qtr.	81,000	--	10,652	12,625	(6,550)[a]	(1,973)	(4,577)
Fiscal year	$96,000	$(30,000)	$12,625				$(6,550)

[a]The recognition of the tax benefit to be realized relative to the unusual, infrequent, or extraordinary item is limited to the lesser of the total tax benefit applicable to the item or the amount available to be realized. Because realization is based upon the amount of tax applicable to ordinary income during the period, the year-to-date figures for the tax benefit fluctuate as the year-to-date tax expense relative to ordinary income fluctuates. Note that at no point does the amount of the tax benefit exceed what was calculated above as being applicable to the unusual, infrequent, or extraordinary item.

Discontinued operations in interim periods. Discontinued operations, according to APB 28, are included as significant, unusual, or extraordinary items. Therefore, the computations described for unusual, infrequent, or extraordinary items will also apply to the income (loss) from the discontinued segment, including any provisions for operating gains (losses) subsequent to the measurement date.

If the decision to dispose of operations occurs in any interim period other than the first interim period, the operating income (loss) applicable to the discontinued segment has already been used in computing the estimated annual effective tax rate. Therefore, a recomputation of the **total tax** is not required. However, the total tax is to be divided into two components:

1. That tax applicable to ordinary income (loss)
2. That tax applicable to the income (loss) from the discontinued segment

This division is accomplished as follows: a revised estimated annual effective rate is calculated for the income (loss) from ordinary operations. This recomputation is then applied to the ordinary income (loss) from the preceding periods. The total tax applicable to the discontinued segment is then composed of two items:

1. The difference between the total tax originally computed and the tax recomputed on remaining ordinary income.
2. The tax computed on unusual, infrequent, or extraordinary items as described above.

Example

A corporation anticipates net income of $150,000 during the fiscal year. The net permanent differences for the year will be $10,000. The company also anticipates tax credits of $10,000 during the fiscal year. For purposes of this example, we will assume a flat statutory rate of 50%. The estimated annual effective rate is then calculated as follows:

Estimated pretax income	$150,000
Net permanent differences	(10,000)
Taxable income	140,000
Statutory rate	50%
Tax	70,000
Anticipated credits	(10,000)
Total estimated tax	$ 60,000
Estimated effective rate ($60,000 ÷ 150,000)	40%

The first two quarters of operations were as follows:

	Ordinary income (loss)		Tax provision		
Reporting period	*Reporting period*	*Year-to-date*	*Year-to-date*	*Less previously provided*	*Reporting period*
1st qtr.	$30,000	$30,000	$12,000	$ --	$12,000
2nd qtr.	25,000	55,000	22,000	12,000	10,000

In the third quarter, the company made the decision to dispose of Division X. During the third quarter, the company earned a total of $60,000. The company expects the disposal to result in a one-time charge to income of $50,000 and estimates that operating losses subsequent to the disposal will be $25,000. The company estimates revised ordinary income in the fourth quarter to be $35,000. The two components of pretax accounting income (discontinued operations and revised ordinary income) are shown below:

		Division X	
Reporting period	Revised ordinary income	Loss from operations	Provision for loss on disposal
1st qtr.	$ 40,000	$(10,000)	$ --
2nd qtr.	40,000	(15,000)	--
3rd qtr.	80,000	(20,000)	(75,000)
4th qtr.	35,000	--	--
Fiscal year	$195,000	$(45,000)	$(75,000)

The company must now recompute the estimated annual tax rate. Assume that all the permanent differences are related to the revised continuing operations. However, $3,300 of the tax credits were applicable to machinery used in Division X. Because of the discontinuance of operations, the credit on this machinery would not be allowed. Any recapture of prior period credits must be used as a reduction in the tax benefit from either operations or the loss on disposal. Assume that the company must recapture $2,000 of investment tax credit which is related to Division X.

The recomputed estimated annual rate for continuing operations is as follows:

Estimated (revised) ordinary income	$195,000
Less net permanent differences	(10,000)
	$185,000
Tax at statutory rate of 50%	$ 92,500
Less anticipated credits from continuing operations	(6,700)
Tax provision	$ 85,800
Estimated annual effective tax rate ($85,800 ÷ 195,000)	44%

The next step is to then apply the revised rate to the quarterly income from continuing operations as illustrated below:

	Ordinary income		Estimated annual effective rate	Tax provision		
Reporting period	Reporting period	Year-to-date		Year-to-date	Less previously provided	Reporting period
1st qtr.	$ 40,000	$ 40,000	44%	$17,600	$ --	$17,600
2nd qtr.	40,000	80,000	44%	35,200	17,600	17,600
3rd qtr.	80,000	160,000	44%	70,400	35,200	35,200
4th qtr.	35,000	195,000	44%	85,800	70,400	15,400
Fiscal year	$195,000					$85,800

The tax benefit applicable to the operating loss from discontinued operations and the loss from the disposal must now be calculated. The first two quarters are calculated on a differential basis as shown below:

Reporting period	Tax applicable to ordinary income		Tax (benefit) expense applicable to Division X
	Previously reported	Recomputed (above)	
1st qtr.	$12,000	$17,600	$ (5,600)
2nd qtr.	10,000	17,600	(7,600)
			$(13,200)

The only calculation remaining applies to the third quarter tax benefit pertaining to the operating loss and the loss on disposal of the discontinued segment. The calculation of this amount is made based on the revised estimate of annual ordinary income both including and excluding the effects of the Division X losses. This is shown below:

	Loss from operations of Division X	Provision for loss on disposal
Estimated annual income from continuing operations	$195,000	$195,000
Net permanent differences	(10,000)	(10,000)
Loss from Division X operations	(45,000)	--
Provision for loss on disposal of Division X	--	(75,000)
Total	$140,000	$110,000
Tax at the statutory rate of 50%	$ 70,000	$ 55,000
Anticipated credits (from continuing operations)	(6,700)	(6,700)
Recapture of previously recognized tax credits as a result of disposal	--	2,000
Taxes after effect of Division X losses	63,300	50,300
Taxes computed on estimated income before the effect of Division X losses	85,800	85,800
Tax benefit applicable to Division X	(22,500)	(35,500)
Amounts recognized in quarters one and two ($5,600 + 7,600)	(13,200)	--
Tax benefit to be recognized in the third quarter	$ (9,300)	$(35,500)

The quarterly tax provisions can be summarized as follows:

Reporting period	Pretax income (loss)			Tax (benefit) applicable to		
	Continuing operations	Operations of Division X	Provision for loss on disposal	Continuing operations	Operations of Division X	Provision for loss on disposal
1st qtr.	$ 40,000	$(10,000)	$ --	$17,600	$ (5,600)	$ --
2nd qtr.	40,000	(15,000)	--	17,600	(7,600)	--
3rd qtr.	80,000	(20,000)	(75,000)	35,200	(9,300)	(35,500)
4th qtr.	35,000	--	--	15,400	--	--
Fiscal year	$195,000	$(45,000)	$(75,000)	$85,800	$(22,500)	$(35,500)

The following income statement shows the proper financial statement presentation of these unusual and infrequent items. The notes to the statement indicate which items are to be included in the calculation of the annual estimated rate.

Income Statement
(FASB Interpretation 18, Appendix D)

*Net sales		$xxxx
*Other income		xxx
		xxxx
Costs and expenses		
* Cost of sales	$xxxx	
* Selling, general, and administrative expenses	xxx	
* Interest expense	xx	
* Other deductions	xx	
Unusual items	xxx	
Infrequently occurring items	xxx	xxxx
Income (loss) from continuing operations before income taxes and other items listed below		xxxx
+Provision for income taxes (benefit)		xxx
Income (loss) from continuing operations before items listed below		xxxx
Discontinued operations:		
Income (loss) from operations of discontinued Division X (less applicable income taxes of $xxxx)	xxxx	
Income (loss) on disposal of Division X, including provision of $xxxx for operating losses during phase-out period (less applicable taxes of $xxxx)	xxxx	xxxx
Income (loss) before extraordinary items and cumulative effect of a change in accounting principle		xxxx
Extraordinary items (less applicable income taxes of $xxxx)		xxxx
†Cumulative effect on prior years of a change in accounting principle (less applicable income taxes of $xxxx)		xxxx
Net income (loss)		$xxxx

* Components of ordinary income (loss).

+ Consists of total income taxes (benefit) applicable to ordinary income (loss), unusual items and infrequent items.

† This amount is shown net of income taxes. Although the income taxes are generally disclosed (as illustrated), this is not required.

The company had an investment credit carryforward of $5,395 at the end of 1985. This credit will expire in 1999. This credit, when recognized, will be an addition to the deferred tax credits and not a reduction in income taxes payable.

APPENDIX B

Schedule of Common Permanent and Temporary Differences

Permanent Differences

Dividends received deduction. Depending on ownership interest, a percentage of the dividends received by a corporation are nontaxable. Different rules apply to subsidiaries. See section in chapter.

Municipal interest income. 100% exclusion is permitted for investment in qualified municipal securities. Note that the capital gains applicable to these securities **are** taxable.

Officer's life insurance premiums. Premiums paid on an officer's life insurance policy on which the company is the beneficiary are not allowed as a taxable deduction, nor are any proceeds taxable.

Organization and start-up costs. Certain organization and start-up costs are not allowed amortization under the tax code. The most clearly defined are those expenditures relating to the cost of raising capital.

Goodwill. The amortization of goodwill is not allowed as a deduction for tax purposes.

Fines and penalties. Any fine or penalty arising as a result of violation of the law is not allowed as a taxable deduction.

Percentage depletion. The excess of percentage depletion over cost depletion is allowable as a deduction for tax purposes.

The portion of wages or salaries used in computing the jobs credit is not allowed as a deduction for tax purposes.

Temporary Differences

Installment sale method. Use of the installment sale method for tax purposes generally results in a timing difference because that method is not used in accordance with GAAP.

Long-term construction contracts. A temporary difference will arise if different methods (e.g., completed-contract or percentage-of-completion) are used for book and tax purposes.

Depreciation. A temporary difference will occur unless the modified ACRS method is used for financial reporting.

Estimated costs (e.g., warranty expense). Estimates or provisions of this nature are not included in the determination of taxable income until the period in which they actually occur.

Accounting for investments. Use of the equity method for financial reporting while using the cost method for tax purposes.

Prepaid income (e.g., prepaid rent). Prepaid income of this nature is includable in taxable income in the period in which it is received, while for financial purposes, it is considered a liability until the revenue is earned.

Net capital loss. The loss is recognized currently for financial reporting purposes but is carried forward to be offset against future capital gains for tax purposes.

Accrued contingent liabilities. These cannot be deducted for tax purposes until the liability becomes fixed and determinable.

Excess charitable contributions. These can be carried over to future years for tax purposes.

Mandatory change from cash to accrual. Generally one-fourth of this adjustment is recognized for tax purposes each year.

Uniform cost capitalization adjustment to beginning inventories. This also is recognized over a four year period, with exceptions, for tax purposes.

Cash basis vs. accrual basis. Use of the cash method of accounting for tax purposes and the accrual method for financial reporting is a temporary difference.

Deferred compensation. The present value of deferred compensation agreements must be accrued over the employee's remaining employment period, but cannot be deducted for tax purposes until actually paid.

APPENDIX C

Accounting for Income Taxes Under Prior GAAP (APB 11)

Promulgated in December 1987, SFAS 96, which was to be effective for fiscal years beginning after December 15, 1988, was postponed twice by SFASs 100 and 103. Statement 96 is now effective for fiscal years beginning after December 15, 1991, although entities which have already adopted the new standard are precluded from returning to the method used previously (since a change in accounting must be to a preferal accounting principle, and the existence of SFAS 96 means it, and not APB 11, is preferable as that term is defined by APB 20). Since the Board has exposed a proposed replacement for SFAS 96, it is unlikely that many entities which have not already adopted SFAS 96 will do so. Until the proposed standard is adopted, as it probably will be, those entities will continue to utilize APB 11.

This Appendix will review the principles of interperiod income tax allocation under APB 11. This standard was first promulgated in 1967 and later revised (APBs 23 and 24, SFAS 37, FASB Interpretations 18, 22, 25, 29, and 32, and FASB Technical Bulletins 83-1 and 96-1). APB 11 endorsed the so-called deferred method of interperiod tax allocation, and prohibited the liability method embraced by SFAS 96. In practice, many companies employed a short-cut approach which in effect resulted in a computation of the deferred tax liability (or asset, less commonly) in a manner akin to the prescribed liability method. The deferred tax balance was adjusted to equal the actual future tax obligation (or benefit) relating to the reversal of timing differences existing at the balance sheet date. However, the correct application of APB 11's principles will more often than not produce deferred tax balances **not** equaling such amounts. Under APB 11's "with and without" calculation, deferred taxes are to be provided based on the differential impact on taxable income of either **originating** timing differences (under the "gross change" version of the methodology prescribed in APB 11) or of the **net** timing differences (if the "net change" variation is employed). There is no attempt to revise later the amount provided, until (under the "gross change" approach) the timing difference reverses, at which point the deferred tax pertaining thereto is amortized. Thus, for example, if deferred taxes were properly provided at a 46% tax rate prior to rates being reduced to, say, 34%, deferred taxes on the unreversed timing differences would continue to be reported at the now obsolete 46% tax rate, thereby overstating the company's obligations. The opposite effect could occur during a period when tax rates were increased or the entity's earnings caused it to move into a higher tax bracket.

A detailed example of the application of APB 11 under both gross and net change approaches is given below. (Note that two variations on the gross change method are acceptable: first-in, first-out, and average tax rate.)

Example of Gross and Net Change Methods--Single Timing Difference

Assume the following:

1. The current tax rate is 34%.
2. All of the previous years' timing differences are a result of using accelerated depreciation methods for tax purposes and straight-line depreciation for book purposes.

Prior years' information:

Year	Timing difference	Tax rate	Deferred tax
1	$10,000	50%	$ 5,000
2	5,000	48%	2,400
3	6,000	48%	2,880
4	6,000	46%	2,760
	$27,000		$13,040

Average rate = 48.29% ($13,040/27,000)

Year 5

	Tax return (current)	Gross change FIFO	Gross change Average	Net change
Pretax accounting income	$200,000	$200,000	$200,000	$200,000
Timing differences:				
Current period (originating) tax depreciation in excess of book depreciation	(40,000)	--	--	--
Prior periods (reversal) book depreciation in excess of tax depreciation	20,000	--	--	--
Taxable income	180,000	200,000	200,000	200,000

Taxes:

Currently payable				
($180,000 x 34%)	61,200	61,200	61,200	61,200
Calculation of deferred:				
Net increase in timing differences [($40,000 - 20,000) x 34%]	--	--	--	6,800
Originating timing differences ($40,000 x 34%)	--	13,600	13,600	--
Reversing timing differences FIFO				
$10,000 x 50%	--	(5,000)	--	--
$ 5,000 x 48%	--	(2,400)	--	--
$ 5,000 x 48%	--	(2,400)	--	--
$20,000				
Reversing timing differences average rate ($20,000 x 48.29%)	--	--	(9,658)	--
Total taxes	$61,200	$65,000	$65,142	$68,000
Deferred tax		$ 3,800	$ 3,942	$ 6,800

The deferred tax amount is the difference between the tax computed "with" timing differences, $61,200, and tax computed "without" the timing differences.

It should be noted that this example simplifies the average rate computation. If the average rate method is to be used, a moving weighted-average rate must be computed on an annual basis for **each** group of timing differences. In the above example, only a single timing difference (depreciation) was used and all of the differences were originating. Therefore, the single weighted-average rate computed above was appropriate. However, this situation is not likely to occur. Also, once the moving average or FIFO method has been selected, it too must be used consistently. A change would result in a consistency exception in the auditor's report.

The next example illustrates the computation of income tax expense in a situation where there is more than a single timing difference using the structured tax rates in effect for years beginning on or after July 1, 1987.

Example of Gross and Net Change Methods--Multiple Timing Differences

Assume the following:

1. All prior period (originating) timing differences have entered the deferred account at a 46% marginal rate.
2. The tax rate schedule is as follows:

	Taxable income is		Tax
At least	Not more than		rate
$ --	$ 50,000		15%
50,000	75,000		25%
75,000	100,000		34%
100,000	335,000		39%*
335,000	--		34%

3. The pretax accounting income and timing differences are as given below:

H & G, Inc.

Pretax accounting income	$110,000
Timing differences:	
Tax depreciation in excess of book	
Originating	$(60,000)
Reversing	30,000
Net	(30,000)
Prepaid rental income	
Originating	15,000
Reversing	(5,000)
Net	10,000
Taxable income	$ 90,000
Taxes currently payable	$ 18,850

---

*To recapture surtax exemption.

<u>Computation of Tax Provision</u>

	Gross change	Net change
Depreciation:		
Taxable income "with" timing differences	$ 90,000	$ 90,000
Originating differences	60,000	--
Net differences	--	30,000
Taxable income "without" depreciation timing difference	$150,000	$120,000
Tax computed on "without" income[a]	41,750	30,050
Tax currently payable (from preceding page)	18,850	18,850
Deferred tax relative to depreciation differences	--	$ 11,200
Deferred tax relative to originating depreciation differences	$ 22,900	
Prepaid rental income:		
Taxable income "with" timing differences	$ 90,000	$ 90,000
Originating differences	(15,000)	--
Net differences	--	(10,000)
Taxable income "without" prepaid rental income timing difference	$ 75,000	$ 80,000
Tax computed on "without" income	13,750	15,450
Tax currently payable	18,850	18,850
Deferred tax relative to prepaid rental income	--	$ (3,400)
Deferred tax relative to originating prepaid differences	$ (5,100)	
Amortization of reversing timing differences:		
Depreciation (30,000 x .46)	$ (13,800)	--
Prepaid rental income (5,000 x .46)	2,300	--
Net reduction in deferred taxes due to amortization of timing differences	$ (11,500)	--
Tax provision:		
Addition (subtraction) to deferred balance		
Depreciation		
Originating	$ 22,900	$ --
Reversing	(13,800)	--
Net	--	11,200
Prepaid rental income		
Originating	$ (5,100)	$ --
Reversing	2,300	--
Net	--	(3,400)
Total addition to deferred tax balance	$ 6,300	$ 7,800
Taxes currently payable	18,850	18,850
Total tax provision	$ 25,150	$ 26,650

Superscripts are explained on the following page.

In the foregoing, note that the "with and without" calculations for the gross change method deal only with originating timing differences. In accordance with APB 11, originating differences enter the deferred tax account at current rates, as computed under the "with and without" method. The tax effects of reversing differences are amortized using historical rates--i.e., the deferred taxes are removed at the actual amounts that entered the deferred tax account at the time those differences originated. Although a specific identification approach would be most accurate, APB 11 permits the first-in, first-out (FIFO) and weighted average approaches as well. In the above example, since all prior periods' differences entered the accounts at 46%, the same result obtains under any of these three approaches to the calculation of the reversals.

The net change method requires that the total timing differences (originating and reversing for each group) be netted, and the tax effects of that group of timing differences be added to or removed from the deferred tax account at the current rates. The net difference for depreciation was $30,000 and for prepaid rent, $10,000.

[a]In this case, the full surtax exemption is used and the tax computation is as follows:

	Gross change	Net change
Taxable income	$150,000	$120,000
Tax rate	x 34%	x 34%
Tax at statutory rate	$ 51,000	$ 40,800
Less: Surtax exemption	(11,750)	(11,750)
Tax	$ 39,250	$ 29,050

APPENDIX D

FASB's Proposed Successor to SFAS 96

In mid-1991 the FASB exposed a draft statement intended to supersede SFAS 96. If adopted, the present plan is to have the new standard become mandatorily effective for years beginning after December 15, 1992. A companion exposure draft would delay SFAS 96's effective date, thereby effectively eliminating the need for reporting entities to adopt SFAS 96 if they have not already done so.

Basic Principle

The Board's proposal retains the basic "asset-and-liability approach" of SFAS 96, but responds to the criticisms directed at that standard by simplifying the measurement of deferred taxes substantially while lifting the prohibition against the recognition of deferred tax assets. While there are still some controversial aspects to the proposal, it is likely that financial statement preparers will be generally pleased by it and view it as being "as good as it's going to get." Consequently, it is expected that this proposal will be accepted essentially as drafted.

The proposed standard continues the principle articulated in SFAS 96 (in slightly different words), that accounting for income taxes should recognize the amount of taxes currently payable or refundable as well as the expected future tax consequences of events currently (or previously) recognized in the financial statements or tax returns. What is new, however, is the Board's interpretation of this objective and the definition (in SFAC 6) of "assets" in a manner that supports the Board's new conclusion: that future tax benefits arising in connection with net deductible amounts (i.e., temporary difference reversals) can be recognized in the financial statements. In SFAS 96, of course, the Board reached the opposite conclusion.

Deferred Tax Asset Recognition

As proposed, deferred tax assets would be recognized for all net deductible amounts expected for future years, relating to assets or liabilities reflected in the balance sheet. Deferred tax assets would also be recognized for the effects of net operating loss carryforwards.

The new standard for recognition of deferred tax assets differs from both SFAS 96 and APB 11. In terms of recognition of the tax effects of temporary differences, it is similar to the rule under APB 11, whereby deferred tax assets were recognized, subject only to the usual criterion that assets not expected to be realized (i.e., those permanently impaired) be written-off or reserved against. In contrast, SFAS 96 essentially prohibited recognition of deferred tax assets related to temporary differences. As to the tax effects of net operating losses, the proposed standard is far more liberal than APB 11, which only permitted recognition when realizability was assured beyond a reasonable doubt. SFAS 96, of course, prohibited recognition under even those limited circumstances.

The Board, in the exposure draft, addressed the asset realizability issue by requiring that a valuation allowance be provided against the deferred tax asset, to the extent that "it is more likely than not" that the benefits would not be realized. In choosing this criterion (defined as meaning a level of likelihood slightly greater than 50%) the Board deliberately rejected the SFAS 5 criteria (probable, reasonably possible, etc.) as not being applicable. SFAS 5 already dictates that losses be accrued when impairment of assets is probable and subject to reasonable estimation. The Board's proposed criterion has a much lower threshold for loss recognition (that is, the provision of a valuation allowance) than the SFAS 5 "probable" criterion would have provided. Therefore the proposed standard can be viewed as being conservative in this regard.

Tax Planning Strategies

SFAS 96 required that a broad range of tax planning strategies be considered in determining the deferred tax calculation. The need to consider these "hypothetical" actions was largely dictated by SFAS 96's prohibition against recognizing most deferred tax assets. Accordingly, it was necessary to consider how the timing of future net deductible amounts could be altered so that they could be offset or absorbed against future net taxable amounts--e.g., by using available carrybacks and carryforwards before expiration. This need is obviated by the proposal's unrestricted recognition of deferred tax assets. Consideration of tax planning strategies will only be necessary in assessing the amount, if any, of valuation allowance to be provided against the deferred tax asset. However, within this narrower scope, the proposal would still demand consideration of **all** prudent, feasible, albeit hypothetical, strategies that could be taken to prevent tax benefits from being lost. Thus, statement preparers will still be required to engage in extensive tax planning for financial statement preparation purposes, if they potentially are in a net deferred tax asset position.

Measurement of Deferred Tax Assets and Liabilities

Another major change from SFAS 96 is the proposed procedure for measurement of deferred taxes. Prior GAAP required that, for all future periods for which net taxable or net deductible amounts were projected based on temporary differences or net operating loss carryforwards, the tax effects were to be computed based on graduated tax rates, assuming **no** other items of income or expense. Thus, inevitably, at least some portion (and often most or even all) of the deferred tax liability computed in accordance with the provisions of SFAS 96 was at the lowest statutory rates. This calculation, however, could only be accomplished if year-by-year detail scheduling of reversals of temporary differences was conducted. However, elimination of such scheduling was the primary objective of replacing SFAS 96.

The Board adopted a solution requiring that all deferred taxes be provided at the **marginal** rates expected to apply to the last dollars of taxable income. While this would appear to be inconsistent with the notion that no assumptions be made about an entity's future items of income or expense, the goal of simplifying the measurement of deferred taxes was a greater concern to the Board. Expected marginal rates must be based on current enacted tax law as of the date of the financial statements, in spite of any post-balance sheet date, pre-statement issuance date changes in enacted rates applicable to future years. (Disclosure of the effect of such changes in rates would be required, if material, under existing GAAP).

Because marginal rates will be used to measure deferred tax assets and liabilities, SFAS 96's mandate that the greater of regular tax or alternative minimum tax (AMT) be reflected, on year-by-year basis, in deferred tax liability is no longer an issue. Deferred taxes, in other words, will be computed with reference only to the regular tax rates. However, a deferred tax asset will be recognized for AMT credit carryforwards existing at the balance sheet date, subject to the aforementioned criterion for provision of a valuation allowance.

APB 23 Exceptions

As discussed in the chapter, SFAS 96 continued the special provisions of APB 23, under which deferred taxes were not provided for the tax effects of undistributed earnings of subsidiaries when the "indefinite reversal" criterion was met. SFAS 96 also continued certain other highly specialized exceptions to APB 11. When SFAS 96 was promulgated, the Board stated its belief that the undistributed earnings of subsidiaries not consolidated for tax purposes were indeed temporary differences, and thus should have been subject to the provisions of SFAS 96. However, the Board bowed to popular opposition and agreed to continue the exceptions "at this time."

The present exposure draft reduces, but does not totally eliminate, these exceptions. The proposed rules would require that deferred taxes be provided on temporary differences which arose **prior** to the beginning of the fiscal year in which the new rules are applied **if** it is apparent that those differences will reverse in the "foreseeable future". Deferred taxes must be provided for most temporary differences arising **after** the new standard is first applied, except that the "indefinite reversal" criterion of APB 23 is continued only for undistributed earnings of **foreign** subsidiaries and **foreign** corporate joint ventures. The Board is taking this step in recognition of the extreme complexity of computing the hypothetical tax effects of undistributed foreign earnings. No other exceptions will be permissible.

Temporary Differences

The proposal's definition of temporary differences is essentially identical to that of SFAS 96. Accordingly the proposed definition includes "timing differences" as defined by APB 11 as well as other events creating differences in the financial reporting and tax bases of assets and liabilities. The Board has added intercompany transfers to the list of temporary differences presented in SFAS 96. Thus deferred taxes would be provided relative to gains or losses reported in separate tax returns of entities consolidated for financial reporting.

Purchase Business Combinations

The requirements established by SFAS 96 are largely continued in the Board's proposed standard. Accordingly, assets and liabilities acquired in business combinations accounted for as purchases are to be "grossed up" for the deferred tax effects of differences between book and tax bases. As with SFAS 96, however, an exception is made for goodwill, for which deferred taxes are **generally** not provided. Whereas SFAS 96 prohibited deferred tax accounting for all goodwill, the replacement standard will allow deferred taxes to the extent that it pertains to the effects of **deductible** (i.e., amortizable) goodwill, if any. This is in recognition of the fact that some foreign jurisdictions permit deductions for goodwill, although this is not true in the United States.

As was the case with SFAS 96, the Board declined to extend the exception applicable to goodwill to other classes of intangible assets which may not be amortizable for tax purposes. The logic for this position lies in goodwill's characteristic as a residual asset, unlike such other assets as customer lists which, although not amortizable, may be deductible when demonstrably worthless. This caused the Board to conclude that "grossing up" the balance sheet for goodwill and the deferred tax liability related thereto was not warranted, although doing so for other intangibles would be valid.

The current proposal differs from the requirements of SFAS 96 with regard to the restatement of prior business combinations. Both present and proposed standards require remeasurement of purchase business combinations consummated in prior years when financial statements for those prior years are to be restated. However, SFAS 96 **prohibits** remeasurement of purchase business combinations consummated prior to the earliest period restated (and therefore any remaining assets and liabilities so acquired will be presented net-of-tax, as prescribed by APB 16). The new standard will instead require that any remaining balances of assets and liabilities (except goodwill) be "grossed up" and deferred taxes recorded thereon. The Board's earlier decision arose out of a concern for comparability between enterprises, some of which would have remeasured and others which might not have done so. Now, however, the Board has concluded that the objective of representational faithfulness is more important than comparability; hence, the need to remeasure. Nonetheless, the Board recognizes that in certain instances information may be lacking or the cost to develop it may be prohibitive. In such cases, the remaining balances of all assets and liabilities obtained in a given purchase transaction must **not** be remeasured.

Financial Statement Presentation and Disclosures

The major change from SFAS 96 that would be made by the current proposal is that deferred tax assets and liabilities will be classified as current or non-current for financial reporting purposes based on the criteria established by APB 11 and SFAS 37. This change is necessitated by the elimination of the scheduling requirement of SFAS 96. Absent scheduling, it would not be simple to ascertain which deferred taxes are current, in the strict sense that realization or settlement would occur within one year from balance sheet date. Therefore, the decision was made to revert to the earlier criteria, which although less defensible, conceptually will probably not have a material effect in most instances. As under current rules, **net** current and **net** non-current deferred taxes will be presented in the balance sheet.

The proposed standard will also require supplemental disclosure of the **gross** amount of deferred tax assets and liabilities, the total valuation allowance as of the balance sheet date, and the change in the valuation allowance during the year. The types of temporary differences and carrybacks or carryforwards that give rise to significant portions of the deferred tax assets and liabilities would also be required to be disclosed. The components of income tax expense (e.g., current, deferred, etc.) will need to be disclosed, and intraperiod tax allocation would also be handled as at present. Reconciliation between statutory and effective rates would be required for public entities. Nonpublic enterprises could simply identify the nature of significant reconciling items. These requirements mirror those of SFAS 96.

SFAS 96 requires disclosure of the amounts and expiration dates of both tax and "book" operating loss carryforwards. The proposed standard would limit this to disclosure of tax NOLs, as was the case under APB 11.

Transition

If adopted, the proposal will be effective for years beginning after December 15, 1992, with earlier application permitted. Restatement of earlier periods' financial statements would be permitted as well. The effect of adoption will be a cumulative effect adjustment in the income statement of the current year (if no restatement of prior years is made) or in the earliest year being restated. Pro forma disclosure of the effects of retroactive application for prior years not being restated will **not** be required.

15 Accounting for Pensions

Perspective and Issues

In 1979, the FASB added Other Postretirement Employee Benefits (OPEB) to its employer's pension project. In 1984, it concluded that OPEB should be separated out. With the issuance of SFAS 106, the FASB has, again, joined the two projects. Although there are some major differences in terminology and measurement, the OPEB accounting basically follows the fundamental framework established for pension accounting.

SFAS 106 applies to all forms of postretirement benefits. However, in most cases, the material aspect will be the focus on postretirement health care benefits. This standard considers OPEB to be a form of deferred compensation and requires accrual accounting. The expected costs are attributed to the period that employees render services. The employer's obligation for OPEB should be fully accrued when the employee attains full eligibility for all expected benefits.

Under the SEC's Staff Accounting Bulletin (SAB) 74, employers must disclose the potential impact of the implementation of SFAS 106, if known. Reasonable estimates of impact may be required to be disclosed even before actual implementation of the standard. It is anticipated that this standard will result in significant financial statement effects for most companies.

SFAS 106 amends APB 12 and the amendment is effective for fiscal years beginning after March 15, 1991. Basically, the amendment states that the terms of the individual contract will govern the accrual of the employee's obligation for deferred compensation and the cost should be attributed over the employee service periods until full eligibility is attained. Except for the amendment, the statement is effective for fiscal years beginning after December 15, 1992. The effective date of application for small, nonpublic employers and for outside the United Stated is for fiscal years beginning after December 15, 1994.

SFAS 87 and SFAS 88 are the sources of GAAP in the pension area. Single-employer defined benefit plans are the most affected. However, multiemployer plans and defined contribution plans are also affected by some provisions.

SFAS 87 specifies the accrual basis of accounting for pension costs. This standard is considered evolutionary and transitional in nature. However, it continues three primary characteristics of APB 8:

1. Delayed recognition (changes are not recognized immediately but are subsequently recognized in a gradual and systematic way)
2. Reporting net cost (aggregates of various items are reported as one net amount)
3. Offsetting assets and liabilities (assets and liabilities are sometimes shown net)

Estimates and averages may be used as long as material differences do not result. Explicit assumptions and estimates of future events must be used for each specified variable included in pension costs.

SFAS 87 focuses directly on the terms of the plan to assist in the recognition of compensation cost over the service period of the employees. It results in earlier recognition of significant liabilities and it recognizes a minimum liability in the case of plans that are underfunded by a material amount.

The principal emphasis of SFAS 87 is the present value of the pension obligation, the fair value of plan assets, and the disclosure of the makeup of net pension costs and of the projected benefit obligation. The main accounting problems revolve around the amount to be expensed on the income statement and the amount to be accrued on the balance sheet.

SFAS 88 supersedes SFAS 74 and is closely related to SFAS 87. It establishes standards to be followed by employers of defined benefit pension plans when obligations are settled, plans are curtailed, or benefits are terminated. Some previously unrecognized amounts are required to be immediately recognized by this standard.

Sources of GAAP

APB	*SFAS*
12	35, 81, 87, 88, 106

Definitions of Terms

Accrued pension cost. Cumulative net pension cost accrued in excess of the employer's contributions.

Accumulated benefit obligation. Actuarial present value of benefits (whether vested or nonvested) attributed by the pension benefit formula to employee service rendered before a specified date and based on employee service and compensation (if applicable) prior to that date. The accumulated benefit obligation differs from the projected benefit obligation in that it includes no assumption about future compensation levels. For plans with flat-benefit or no-pay-related pension benefit formulas, the accumulated benefit obligation and the projected benefit obligation are the same.

Accumulated postretirement benefit obligation. The actuarial present value of benefits attributed to employee service rendered to a particular date. Prior to an employee's full eligibility date, the accumulated postretirement benefit obligation as of a particular date for an employee is the portion of the expected postretirement benefit obligation attributed to that employee's service rendered to that date; on and after the full eligibility date, the accumulated and expected postretirement benefit obligations for an employee are the same.

Actual return on plan assets component (of net periodic pension cost). Difference between fair value of plan assets at the end of the period and the fair value at the beginning of the period, adjusted for contributions and payments of benefits during the period.

Actuarial present value. Value, as of a specified date, of an amount or series of amounts payable or receivable thereafter, with each amount adjusted to reflect (a) the time value of money (through discounts for interest) and (b) the probability of payment (by means of decrements for events such as death, disability, withdrawal, or retirement) between the specified date and the expected date of payment.

Amortization. Usually refers to the process of reducing a recognized liability systematically by recognizing revenues or reducing a recognized asset systematically by recognizing expenses or costs. In pension accounting, amortization is also used to refer to the systematic recognition in net pension cost over several periods of previously **unrecognized** amounts, including unrecognized prior service cost and unrecognized net gain or loss.

Annuity contract. Irrevocable contract in which an insurance company* unconditionally undertakes a legal obligation to provide specified benefits to specific individuals in return for a fixed consideration or premium. It involves the transfer of significant risk from the employer to the insurance company. Participating annuity contracts provide that the purchaser (either the plan or the employer) may participate in the experience of the insurance company. The insurance company ordinarily pays dividends to the purchaser. If the substance of a participating annuity contract is such that the employer remains subject to all or most of the risks and rewards associated with the benefit obligation covered or the assets transferred to the insurance company, the purchase of the contract does not constitute a settlement.

Assumptions. Estimates of the occurrence of future events affecting pension costs, such as mortality, withdrawal, disablement and retirement, changes in compensation and national pension benefits, and discount rates to reflect the time value of money.

---

*If the insurance company is controlled by the employer or there is any reasonable doubt that the insurance company will meet its obligation under the contract, the purchase of the contract does not constitute a settlement for purposes of this statement.

Attribution. Process of assigning pension benefits or cost to periods of employee service.

Attribution period. The period of an employee's service to which the expected postretirement benefit obligation for that employee is assigned. The beginning of the attribution period is the employee's date of hire unless the plan's benefit formula grants credit only for service from a later date, in which case the beginning of the attribution period is generally the beginning of that credited service period. The end of the attribution period is the full eligibility date. Within the attribution period, an equal amount of the expected postretirement benefit obligation is attributed to each year of service unless the plan's benefit formula attributes a disproportionate share of the expected postretirement benefit obligation to employees' early years of service. In that case, benefits are attributed in accordance with the plan's benefit formula.

Career-average-pay formula (Career-average-pay plan). Benefit formula that bases benefits on the employee's compensation over the entire period of service with the employer. A career-average-pay plan is a plan with such a formula.

Contributory plan. Pension plan under which employees contribute part of the cost. In some contributory plans, employees wishing to be covered must contribute; in other contributory plans, employee contributions result in increased benefits.

Curtailment. Event that significantly reduces the expected years of future service of present employees or eliminates for a significant number of employees the accrual of defined benefits for some or all of their future services. Curtailments include (a) termination of employee's services earlier than expected, which may or may not involve closing a facility or discontinuing a segment of a business and (b) termination or suspension of a plan so that employees do not earn additional defined benefits for future services. In the latter situation, future service may be counted toward vesting of benefits accumulated based on past services.

Defined benefit pension plan. Pension plan that defines an amount of pension benefit to be provided, usually as a function of one or more factors such as age, years of service, or compensation. Any pension plan that is not a defined contribution pension plan is, for purposes of this Statement, a defined benefit pension plan.

Defined contribution pension plan. Plan that provides pension benefits in return for services rendered, provides an individual account for each participant, and specifies how contributions to the individual's account are to be determined instead of specifying the amount of benefits the individual is to receive. Under a defined contribution pension plan, the benefits a participant will receive depend solely on the amount contributed to the participant's account, the returns earned on investments of those contributions, and forfeitures of other participants' benefits that may be allocated to such participant's account.

Expected long-term rate of return on plan assets. Assumption as to the rate of return on plan assets reflecting the average rate of earnings expected on the funds invested or to be invested to provide for the benefits included in the projected benefit obligation.

Expected postretirement benefit obligation. The actuarial present value as of a particular date of the benefits expected to be paid to or for an employee, the employee's beneficiaries, and any covered dependents pursuant to the terms of the postretirement benefit plan.

Expected return on plan assets. Amount calculated as a basis for determining the extent of delayed recognition of the effects of changes in the fair value of assets. The expected return on plan assets is determined based on the expected long-term rate of return on plan assets and the market-related value of plan assets.

Explicit approach to assumptions. Approach under which each significant assumption used reflects the best estimate of the plan's future experience solely with respect to that assumption.

Fair value. Amount that a pension plan could reasonably expect to receive for an investment in a current sale between a willing buyer and a willing seller (i.e., in other than a forced or liquidation sale).

Final-pay formula (Final-pay plan). Benefit formula that bases benefits on the employee's compensation over a specified number of years near the end of the employee's service period or on the employee's highest compensation periods. For example, a plan might provide annual pension benefits equal to 1 percent of the employee's average salary for the last five years (or the highest consecutive five years) for each year of service. A final-pay plan is a plan with such a formula.

Flat-benefit formula (Flat-benefit plan). Benefit formula that bases benefits on a fixed amount per year of service, such as $20 of monthly retirement income for each year of credited service. A flat-benefit plan is a plan with such a formula.

Full eligibility (for benefits). The status of an employee having reached the employee's full eligibility date. Full eligibility for benefits is achieved by meeting specified age, service, or age and service requirements of the postretirement benefit plan. Also refer to **Full eligibility date.**

Full eligibility date. The date at which an employee has rendered all of the service necessary to have earned the right to receive all of the benefits expected to be received by that employee (including any beneficiaries and dependents expected to receive benefits). Determination of the full eligibility date is affected by plan terms that provide incremental benefits expected to be received by or on behalf of an employee for additional years of service, unless those incremental benefits are trivial. Determination of the full eligibility date is **not** affected by plan terms that define when benefit payments commence or by an employee's current dependency status.

Fund. Used as a verb, to pay over to a funding agency (as to fund future pension benefits or to fund pension cost). Used as a noun, assets accumulated in the hands of a funding agency for the purpose of meeting pension benefits when they become due.

Funding policy. Program regarding the amounts and timing of contributions by the employer(s), participants, and any other sources (for example, state subsidies or federal grants) to provide the benefits a pension plan specifies.

Gain or loss. Change in the value of either the projected benefit obligation or the plan assets resulting from experience different from that assumed or from a change in an actuarial assumption. See also **Unrecognized net gain or loss**.

Gain or loss component (of net periodic pension cost). Sum of (a) the difference between the actual return on plan assets and the expected return on plan assets and (b) the amortization of the unrecognized net gain or loss from previous periods. The gain or loss component is the net effect of delayed recognition of gains and losses (the net change in the unrecognized net gain or loss) except that it does not include changes in the projected benefit obligation occurring during the period and deferred for later recognition.

Interest cost component (of net periodic pension cost). Increase in the projected benefit obligation due to passage of time.

Market-related value of plan assets. Balance used to calculate the expected return on plan assets. Market-related value can be either fair market value or a calculated value that recognizes changes in fair value in a systematic and rational manner over not more than five years. Different ways of calculating market-related value may be used for different classes of assets, but the manner of determining market-related value shall be applied consistently from year to year for each asset class.

Measurement date. Date as of which plan assets and obligations are measured.

Mortality rate. Proportion of the number of deaths in a specified group to the number living at the beginning of the period in which the deaths occur. Actuaries use mortality tables, which show death rates for each age, in estimating the amount of pension benefits that will become payable.

Net periodic pension cost. Amount recognized in an employer's financial statements as the cost of a pension plan for a period. Components of net periodic pension cost are service cost, interest cost, actual return on plan assets, gain or loss, amortization of unrecognized prior service cost, and amortization of the unrecognized net obligation or asset existing at the date of initial application of SFAS 87. The term **net periodic pension cost** is used instead of **net pension expense** because part of the cost recognized in a period may be capitalized as part of an asset such as inventory.

Plan amendment. Change in terms of an existing plan or the initiation of a new plan. A plan amendment may increase benefits, including those attributed to years of service already rendered. See also **Retroactive benefits**.

Postretirement benefits. All forms of benefits, other than retirement income, provided by an employer to retirees. Those benefits may be defined in terms of specified benefits, such as health care, tuition assistance, or legal services, that are provided to retirees as the need for those benefits arises, such as certain health care benefits, or they may be defined in terms of monetary amounts that become payable on the occurrence of a specified event, such as life insurance benefits.

Prepaid pension cost. Cumulative employer contributions in excess of accrued net pension cost.

Prior service cost. Cost of retroactive benefits granted in a plan amendment. See also "**Unrecognized prior service cost.**"

Projected benefit obligation. Actuarial present value as of a date of all benefits attributed by the pension benefit formula to employee service rendered prior to that date. The projected benefit obligation is measured using assumptions as to future compensation levels if the pension benefit formula is based on those future compensation levels (pay-related, final-pay, final-average-pay, or career-average-pay plans).

Retroactive benefits. Benefits granted in a plan amendment (or initiation) that are attributed by the pension benefit formula to employee services rendered in periods prior to the amendment. The cost of the retroactive benefits is referred to as prior service cost.

Service. Employment taken into consideration under a pension plan. Years of employment before the inception of a plan constitute an employee's past service; years thereafter are classified in relation to the particular actuarial valuation being made or discussed. Years of employment (including past service) prior to the date of a particular valuation constitute prior service.

Service cost component (of net periodic pension cost). Actuarial present value of benefits attributed by the pension benefit formula to services rendered by employees during the period. The service cost component is a portion of the projected benefit obligation and is unaffected by the funded status of the plan.

Settlement. Transaction that (a) is an irrevocable action, (b) relieves the employer (or the plan) of primary responsibility for a pension benefit obligation, and (c) eliminates significant risks related to the obligation and the assets used to effect the settlement. Examples include making lump-sum cash payments to plan participants in exchange for their rights to receive specified pension benefits and purchasing nonparticipating annuity contracts to cover vested benefits. A transaction must meet all of the above three criteria to constitute a settlement for purposes of this statement.

Substantive plan. The terms of the postretirement benefit plan as understood by an employer that provides postretirement benefits and the employees who render services in exchange for those benefits. The substantive plan is the basis for the accounting for that exchange transaction. In some situations an employer's cost-sharing policy, as evidenced by past practice or by communication of intended changes to a plan's cost-sharing provisions, or a past practice of regular increases in certain monetary benefits may indicate that the substantive plan differs from the extant written plan.

Transition obligation. The unrecognized amount, as of the date SFAS 106 is initially applied, of (a) the accumulated postretirement benefit obligation in excess of (b) the fair value of plan assets plus any recognized accrued postretirement benefit cost or less any recognized prepaid postretirement benefit cost.

Unfunded accumulated benefit obligation. Excess of the accumulated benefit obligation over plan assets.

Unfunded accumulated postretirement benefit obligation. The accumulated postretirement benefit obligation in excess of the fair value of plan assets.

Unrecognized net gain or loss. Cumulative net gain (loss) that has not been recognized as a part of net periodic pension cost. See "**Gain or loss.**"

Unrecognized prior service cost. Portion of prior service cost that has not been recognized as a part of net periodic pension cost.

Concepts, Rules, and Examples

The principal objective of SFAS 87 is to measure the compensation cost associated with employees' benefits and to recognize that cost over the employees' service period. This Statement is concerned only with the accounting aspects of pension costs. The funding (amount paid) of the benefits is not covered and is considered to be a financial management matter.

When an entity provides benefits that can be estimated in advance to its retired employees and their beneficiaries, the arrangement is a pension plan. The typical plan is written and the amount of benefits can be determined by reference to the associated documents. The plan and its provisions can also be implied, however, from unwritten but established past practices. The accounting for most types of retirement plans is covered by SFASs 87 and 88. These plans include unfunded, insured, trust fund, defined contribution and defined benefit plans, and deferred compensation contracts, if equivalent. Independent deferred profit sharing plans and pension payments to selected employees on a case by case basis are not considered pension plans. SFAS 87 and SFAS 88 do not apply if a plan provides **only** life or health insurance benefits or both. Additionally, these statements do not **require** application to postemployment health care benefits. However, if the statements are not applied to postemployment health care benefits, related assets and obligations are excluded from consideration also.

The establishment of a pension plan represents a commitment to employees that is of a long-term nature. Although some corporations manage their own plans, this commitment usually takes the form of contributions to an independent trustee. These contributions are used by the trustee to obtain plan assets of various kinds (treasury bonds, treasury bills, certificates of deposit, annuities, marketable securities, corporate bonds, etc.). The plan assets are used to generate a return which generally is earned interest and/or appreciation in asset value. The return on the plan assets (and occasionally their liquidation) provides the trustee with cash to pay the benefits to which the employees are entitled. These benefits, in turn, are defined by the terms of the pension plan. This definition of benefits is known as the plan's benefit formula. The benefit formula incorporates many factors including employee compensation, employee service longevity, employee age, etc. and is considered to provide the best indication of pension obligations and costs. It is used as the basis for determining the pension cost recognized each fiscal year.

Net Periodic Pension Cost

It is assumed that a company will continue to provide retirement benefits well into the future. The accounting for the plan's costs should be reflected in the financial statements and these amounts should not be discretionary. All pension costs should be charged against income. No amounts should be charged directly to retained earnings.

The benefits earned and costs recognized over the employees' service period must be attributed by the pension plan's benefit formula. Net periodic pension cost consists of the sum of the following six components:

1. Service cost
2. Interest cost on projected benefit obligation
3. Actual return on plan assets
4. Gain or loss
5. Amortization of unrecognized prior service cost
6. Amortization of unrecognized net assets or net obligation existing at date of initial application of SFAS 87

Elements of pension plans that affect the determination of the above components of pension cost and amounts to be shown on the balance sheet are the accumulated benefit obligation, the projected benefit obligation, and plan assets. Both obligations are the actuarial present value of benefits attributed by the formula to service prior to a given date. The **accumulated** benefit obligation does **not** include an assumption about future compensation levels, whereas the **projected** benefit obligation does include such an assumption. Pay-related, final-pay, or career-average-pay plans are examples of plans based on future compensation levels. These plans measure benefits based on service to date but include assumptions as to compensation increases, turnover, etc. In non-pay-related or flat-benefit plans, both obligations are the same.

Example

	Start of year
Accumulated benefit obligation	$(1,500)
Progression of salary and wages	(400)
Projected benefit obligation	$(1,900)

The expected progression of salary and wages is added to the accumulated benefit obligation to arrive at the projected benefit obligation. These amounts are provided by the actuary in a pension plan report.

Plan assets include contributions and asset earnings less benefits paid. They must be segregated and effectively restricted for pension benefits.

The amount of **vested** benefit obligation must be disclosed but it does not directly figure into any of the net periodic pension cost calculations.

Service costs. This component of net periodic pension cost is the actuarial present value of benefits attributed during the current period. Under SFAS 87, the plan's benefit formula is the key to attributing benefits to employee service periods. In most cases, this attribution is straightforward.

If the benefit formula is not straightforward, the accounting for pension service costs must be based on **substantive commitment**. In some cases, this means that if an employer has committed to make future amendments to provide benefits greater than those written in the plan, that commitment shall be the basis for the accounting. The relevant facts regarding that commitment shall be disclosed.

In other cases, a disproportionate share of benefits may be attributed to later years in order to delay vesting. In this situation, instead of the benefit formula, proportions or ratios need to be used to accumulate the total projected benefit in a manner that more equitably reflects the substance of the earning of the employee benefits. If the benefit formula does not specify a relationship between services and benefits, the following applies:

a. **Includable** in vested benefits (e.g., supplemental early retirement benefit):

$$\text{Benefit accumulation} = \frac{\text{Number of completed years of service}}{\text{Number of years when benefit}}$$
$$\text{first fully vests}$$

b. **Not includable** in vested benefits (e.g., death or disability benefit):

$$\text{Benefit accumulation} = \frac{\text{Number of completed years of service}}{\text{Total projected years of service}}$$

SFAS 87 actuarial assumptions must reflect plan continuation, must be consistent as to future economic expectations, and must be the best estimate in regard to each individual assumption. It is not acceptable to determine that the aggregate assumptions are reasonable.

The discount rate used in the calculation of service costs should be the rate at which benefits could be settled. Examples include those rates in current annuity contracts, those published by Pension Benefit Guaranty Corporation (PBGC), and those that reflect returns on high quality, fixed income investments.

Future compensation will be considered in the calculation of the service cost component to the extent specified by the benefit formula. To the degree considered, future compensation would include changes due to advancement, longevity, inflation, etc. Indirect effects and automatic increases specified by the plan also need to be considered. The effect of retroactive amendments are included in the calculation when the employer has contractually agreed to them.

Example

	Start of year	Service cost
Accumulated benefit obligation	$(1,500)	$ (90)
Progression of salary and wages	(400)	(24)
Projected benefit obligation	$(1,900)	$(114) (a)*

*Component of net periodic pension cost

The current period service cost component is found in the actuarial report.

Interest cost on projected benefit obligation. This component results from multiplying the assumed settlement discount rate times the projected benefit obligation as of the start of the year. The settlement rate should be determined by an annual review and represents the time value of money. The projected benefit obligation represents the discounted present value of employee benefits earned. The result is an accumulation of interest that increases the net periodic pension cost and the projected benefit obligation.

Example

	Start of year	Service cost	Interest cost
Accumulated benefit obligation	$(1,500)	$ (90)	$(120)
Progression of salary and wages	(400)	(24)	(32)
Projected benefit obligation	$(1,900)	$(114) (a)	$(152) (b)*

*Component of net periodic pension cost

The interest cost component is calculated by multiplying the start of the year obligation balances by an assumed 8% settlement rate. This amount is found in the actuarial report.

Benefits paid to retirees are deducted from the above to arrive at the end of the year balance sheet figures for the accumulated benefit obligation and the projected benefit obligation.

Example

	Start of year	Service cost	Interest cost	Benefits paid	End of year
Accumulated benefit obligation	$(1,500)	$ (90)	$(120)	$160	$(1,550)
Progression of salary and wages	(400)	(24)	(32)	___	(456)
Projected benefit obligation	$(1,900)	$(114) (a)	$(152) (b)	$160	$(2,006)

Benefits of $160 were paid to retirees during the current year. This amount is found in the report of the pension plan trustee.

Actual return on plan assets. This component is the difference between the fair value of plan assets at the end of the period and the fair value of the plan assets at the beginning of the period adjusted for contributions and payments during the period.

Another way to express the result is that it is total (realized and unrealized) appreciation and depreciation of plan assets plus earnings from the plan assets.

Example

	Start of year	Actual return on plan assets	Funding	Benefits paid	End of year
Plan assets	$1,400	$158 (c)*	$145	$(160)	$1,543

*Component of net periodic pension cost

The actual return on plan assets of $158, cash deposited with the trustee of $145, and benefits paid ($160) are amounts found in the report of the pension plan trustee. These items increase the plan assets to $1,543 at the end of the year. The actual return on plan assets is adjusted, however, to the expected long-term rate (9% assumed) of return on plan assets ($1,400 x 9% = $126). The difference, $32, is a return on asset adjustment and is deferred as a gain (loss). The return on asset adjustment is a component of net periodic pension cost and is discussed in the following section.

Gain or loss. Gains (losses) result from (1) changes in plan assumptions, (2) changes in the amount of plan assets, and (3) changes in the amount of the projected benefit obligation. Immediate recognition of these gains (losses) is not acceptable. Also, SFAS 87 does not require that they be matched through recognition in net pension cost in the period of occurrence. Instead, unrecognized net gain (loss) is amortized if it meets certain criteria specified below.

Since actuarial cost methods are based on numerous assumptions (employee compensation, mortality, turnover, earnings of the pension plan, etc.), it is not unusual for one or more of these assumptions to be invalidated by changes over time. Adjustments will probably be necessary in order to bring prior estimates back in line with actual events. These adjustments are known as actuarial gains (losses). The accounting problem with the recognition of the actuarial adjustments is their timing. All pension costs must be charged to income. Thus, actuarial gains (losses) are not considered prior period adjustments but are considered changes in an estimate that should be recognized in current and future periods.

Plan asset gains (losses) result from both realized and unrealized amounts. They represent periodic differences between the actual return on assets and the expected return. The expected return is generated by multiplying the expected long-term rate of return and the market-related value of plan assets. This value is called market-related as opposed to fair value since it may be a calculated value. The purpose of allowing a calculated value was to enable the averaging or spreading of changes in fair value over not more than five years through a rational, systematic, and consistently applied method. Consistently applied means from year to year for each asset class (i.e., bonds, equities) since different classes of assets may have their market-related value calculated in a different manner (i.e., fair value in one case, moving average in another case). Thus, the market-related value may be fair value but it also may be other than fair value if all or a portion results from calculation.

Plan asset gains (losses) include both (1) changes in the market-related value of assets (regardless of definition) from one period to another **and** (2) any changes that aren't yet reflected in market-related value (i.e., the difference between the actual fair values of assets and the calculated market-related values). Only the former changes are recognized and amortized. The latter changes will be recognized over time through the calculated market-related values. Differences in the experienced amount of projected benefit obligation from that assumed will also result in gain (loss).

Since gains (losses) from one period may offset gains (losses) from another period, adjustments should not be recognized in a single accounting period. If they were recognized all at once, the result could be either unusually large increases or decreases (or even elimination of) net pension costs during the period. The long-term nature of pension costs must be considered, and these gains (losses) are to be accumulated as an unrecognized net gain (loss). If this unrecognized net gain (loss), however, exceeds a "corridor" of 10% of the greater of the beginning balances of the market-related value of plan assets or the projected benefit obligation, a minimum amortization is required. The **excess** over 10% should be divided by the average remaining service period of active employees and included as a component of net pension costs. Average remaining life expectancies of inactive employees may be used if that is a better measure.

Net pension costs will include only expected return on plan assets. While actual return is disclosed, any difference that results between actual and expected is deferred through the gain (loss) component of net pension cost. If actual returns are greater than expected returns, net pension costs are increased and an unrecognized gain results. If actual returns are less than expected returns, net pension costs are decreased and an unrecognized loss results. If the unrecognized net gain (loss) is large enough, it is amortized. Again, this is due to the long-term nature of pension costs. Over the long-term, the expected return should be a fairly good indicator of performance, although in any given year an unusual or infrequent result may occur.

The expected long-term rate of return used to calculate the expected return on plan assets should be the average rate of return expected to provide for pension benefits. Present rates of return and expected future reinvestment rates of return should be considered in arriving at the rate to be used.

To summarize, the net periodic pension cost includes a gain (loss) component consisting of **both** of the following:

1. As a minimum, the portion of the unrecognized net gain (loss) from previous periods that exceeds the **greater** of 10% of the beginning balances of the market-related value of plan assets **or** the projected benefit obligation, usually amortized over the average remaining service period of active employees expected to receive benefits.
2. The difference between the expected return and the actual return on plan assets.

An accelerated method of amortization of unrecognized net gain (loss) is acceptable if it is applied consistently to both gains (losses) and if the method is disclosed. In all cases, at least the minimum amount discussed above must be amortized.

Example

	Start of year	Return on asset adjustment	Amortization	End of year
Unamortized actuarial gain (loss)	$(210)	$32 (d)*	$1(d)*	$(177)

*Components of net periodic pension cost

The return on asset adjustment of $32 is the difference between the actual return of $158 and the expected return of $126 on plan assets. The actuarial loss at the start of the year ($210 assumed) is amortized if it **exceeds** a "corridor" of the larger of 10% of the projected benefit obligation ($1,900) or 10% of the fair value of plan assets ($1,400). In this example, $20 ($210 - $190) is amortized by dividing the years of average remaining service (14 years assumed), with a result rounded to $1. The straight-line method was used, and it was assumed that market-related value was fair value.

Amortization of unrecognized prior service cost. Prior service costs result from plan amendments and are accounted for as a change in estimate. These costs are measured at the amendment date by the increase in the projected benefit obligation. The service period of every active employee expected to receive benefits is to be determined, and then an equal amount of prior service cost should be assigned to each period. Consistent use of an accelerated amortization method is acceptable and must be disclosed if used.

If most of the plan's participants are inactive, remaining life expectancy should be used as a basis for amortization instead of remaining service life. If economic benefits will be realized over a shorter period than remaining service life, amortization of costs should be accelerated to recognize the costs in the periods benefited. If an amendment **reduces** the projected benefit obligation, unrecognized prior service costs should be reduced to the extent that they exist and any excess should be amortized as indicated above for benefit increases.

Example

	Start of year	Amortization	End of year
Unamortized prior service cost	$320	$(27) (e)*	$293

*Component of net periodic pension cost

Unamortized prior service cost ($320) is amortized over the years of average remaining service (12 years assumed) at the amendment date with a result rounded to $27. The straight-line method was used. These amounts are found in the actuarial report.

Amortization of unrecognized amount at date of initial SFAS 87 application. Any difference between the projected benefit obligation and the fair value of plan assets minus recognized prepaid or plus accrued pension cost at the beginning of the fiscal year of the initial SFAS 87 application is to be amortized. The amortization is to be on a straight-line basis over the average remaining active employee service period. If the average remaining service period is less than 15 years, the employer may elect to use a 15-year period. If all or almost all of a plan's participants are inactive, the employer shall use the inactive participants' average remaining expectancy period.

Example

	Start of year	Amortization	End of year
Unamortized net obligation (asset) existing at SFAS 87 application	$(30)	$3 (f)*	$(27)

Component of net periodic pension cost

The unamortized net asset ($30) existing at SFAS 87 application is amortized over the average service remaining at date of application (10 years assumed) with a result of $3. The straight-line method was used. These amounts are found in the actuarial report.

Summary of Net Periodic Pension Costs

The components that were identified in the above examples are summed to determine the one amount known as net periodic pension cost as follows:

Service cost	(a)	$114
Interest cost	(b)	152
Actual return on assets	(c)	(158)
Gain (loss)	(d)	33
Amortization of unrecognized prior service cost	(e)	27
Amortization of unrecognized net obligation (asset) existing at SFAS 87 application	(f)	(3)
Total net periodic pension cost		$165

One possible source of confusion is the return on plan assets ($158) and the loss of $33 that total $125. The actual return on plan assets reduces pension cost. This reduction, however, is adjusted by increasing pension cost by the difference between actual and expected return of $32 and the amortization of the excess actuarial loss of $1 for a total of $33. The net result is to include the **expected** return of $126 ($158 - $32) less the amortization of the excess of $1 for a total of $125 ($158 - $33).

Employer's Liabilities and Assets

Any difference between the amount funded and the amount expensed should appear on the balance sheet as a prepaid pension cost or as a liability. An additional minimum liability is also required to be recognized under SFAS 87 when plans are materially underfunded. This minimum liability results when the accumulated benefit obligation exceeds the **fair value** (not the possible calculated market-related value used for determining plan asset gains or losses) of plan assets and a liability in the amount of the difference is not already recorded as unfunded accrued pension cost. The accumulated benefit obligation is based on history of service and compensation excluding future levels and indirect effects. Fair value is determined as of the financial statement date (or not more than three months prior to that date if used consistently), and in the amount that would result from negotiations between a willing buyer and seller not in a liquidation sale. Fair value is measured in preferred order by market price, selling price of similar investments, or discounted cash flows at a rate indicative of the risk involved.

In SFAS 87, the additional minimum liability is recognized by an offset to an intangible asset up to the amount of unrecognized prior service cost. Any additional debit needed is considered a loss and is shown net of tax benefits (subject to the restrictions on recognition of deferred tax assets per SFAS 96) as a separate component reducing equity.

Several points need to be remembered in regard to the additional minimum liability. First, an asset is **not** recorded if the fair value of the plan assets exceeds the accumulated benefit obligation. Second, the calculation of the minimum liability requires consideration of any already recorded prepaid or accrued pension cost. The net liability must be at least equal to the **unfunded** accumulated benefit obligation irrespective of the starting point. A prepaid pension cost will increase the amount of the recognized additional liability. An accrued pension cost will decrease it. Third, the intangible asset is **not** amortized. Fourth, at the time of the next calculation, the amounts are either added to or reversed out with no effect on the income statement. These balance sheet entries are entirely independent of the income statement and do not affect the calculation of net pension costs. Fifth, unless a significant event occurs or measures of obligations and assets as of a more current date become available, interim financials will show the year-end additional minimum liability adjusted for subsequent contributions and accruals. In this case, previous year-end assumptions regarding net pension cost would also carryover to the interim financials.

A schedule reconciling the balance sheet amounts with the funded status of the plan is a key disclosure required by SFAS 87.

Example

	Start of year	End of year
Accumulated benefit obligation	$(1,500)	$(1,550)
Progression of salary and wages	(400)	(456)
Projected benefit obligation	(1,900)	(2,006)
Plan assets	1,400	1,543
Underfunded status	(500)	(463)
Unamortized actuarial (gain) loss	210	177
Unamortized prior service cost	320	293
Unamortized net obligation (asset) existing at SFAS 87 application	(30)	(27)
(Accrued)/prepaid pension cost	$ 0	$ (20)
Required additional liability		
Liability	(100)	0
Intangible asset	100	0

The difference between the projected benefit obligation and the plan assets indicates that the plan in this example is underfunded by **$500** at the beginning of the year. Net actuarial losses, prior service costs, and the net asset existing when SFAS 87 was first applied are the remaining reconciling items to the zero amount shown on the balance sheet. **Conceptually**, the zero balance sheet amount is a journal entry netting of the following elements that would be recognized on the employer's books if accounting under SFAS 87 mirrored the pension plan's financial statements:

Investment	1,400	
Deferred actuarial loss	210	
Deferred prior service cost	320	
Deferred asset existing at SFAS 87 application		30
Projected benefit obligation		1,900

Only the additional minimum liability in the case of seriously underfunded plans will be required on the balance sheet. This amount is the difference between the accumulated benefit obligation ($1,500) and the plan assets ($1,400) plus prepaid pension cost ($0) or minus accrued pension cost ($0). If the result exceeds the unamortized prior service cost, any excess is treated as a special equity adjustment. In the above example, the result is $100 and the journal entry follows:

Intangible asset	100	
Pension liability		100

This journal entry is entirely independent of the calculation of pension cost and has no effect on that calculation. It only affects the balance sheet and remains until adjusted at the end of the next year. At that time, it will be decreased or increased to the extent required.

Funding of $145, net periodic pension costs of $165, and benefit payments of $160 are used in order to arrive at the end of the year balance sheet amounts. An accrued pension cost of $20 ($165 - $145) is required. This difference results from funding $20 less than pension cost. **Conceptually**, this accrued amount is the netting of the following:

Investment	$1,543	
Deferred actuarial loss	177	
Deferred prior service cost	293	
Deferred assets existing at SFAS 87 application		$ 27
Projected benefit obligation		2,006
Totals	$2,013	$2,033

The excess credit is shown as an accrued pension liability of $20. Note that the additional minimum liability is no longer required since the accumulated benefit obligation ($1,550) and the plan assets ($1,543) differ by only $7 and there is already a pension liability on the balance sheet of $20. Thus, the additional minimum liability balances at the start of the year are reversed through the following journal entry:

Pension liability	100	
Intangible asset		100

This entry does not affect pension cost.

In summary, the only journal entries that are ordinarily required, if applicable, involve (1) the recording of net periodic pension cost and the associated accrued (or prepaid) pension cost, (2) the recording of the payment (funding) of the accrued (or prepaid) pension costs, and (3) the recording of any additional minimum liability and the associated intangible asset (and possible equity entry). All of the other information used to determine these amounts are provided by the actuary or worksheet entries and do not appear on the books. Thus, accounts that reflect such things as the actuarial loss and prior service costs will usually not be found in the employer's ledger.

Other Pension Considerations

If an entity has more than one plan, SFAS 87 provisions should be separately applied to each plan. Offsets or eliminations are not allowed unless there clearly is the right to use the assets in one plan to pay the benefits of another plan.

If annuity contracts and other insurance contracts that are equivalent in substance are valid and irrevocable, if they transfer significant risks to an unrelated insurance company (not a captive insurer), and if there is no reasonable doubt as to their payment, they should be excluded from plan assets and their benefits should be excluded from the accumulated benefit obligation and from the projected benefit obligation. Most other contracts are not considered annuities for SFAS 87 purposes. If a plan's benefit formula specifies coverage by **nonparticipating** annuity contracts, the service component of net pension costs is the cost of those contracts. In the case of a **participating** annuity contract, the cost of the participation right is to be recognized as an asset and measured annually at its fair value. If fair value is unestimable, it should be systematically amortized and carried at amortized cost (not to exceed net realizable value). Benefits provided by the formula beyond those provided by annuities should be accounted for in the usual SFAS 87 manner. All other insurance contracts are considered investments and are usually measured at cash surrender value, conversion value, contract value, or some equivalent.

In the typical defined contribution plan, the contribution is derived from a formula, and that amount should be the expense for that year. Benefits are generally paid from the pool of accumulated contributions. If, however, the defined contribution plan has defined benefits, the provision is calculated in the usual manner. Disclosure requirements for defined contribution plans are presented at the end of this chapter.

Participation in a multiemployer plan (two or more unrelated employers contribute) requires that the contribution for the period be recognized as net pension cost and that any contributions due and unpaid be recognized as a liability. Assets in this type of plan are usually commingled and are not segregated or restricted. A Board of Trustees usually administers these plans, and multiemployer plans are generally subject to a collective-bargaining agreement. If there is a withdrawal from this type of plan and if an arising obligation is either probable or reasonably possible, SFAS 5 applies. Disclosure requirements for multiemployer plans are presented at the end of this chapter.

Some plans are, in substance, a pooling or aggregation of single employer plans and are ordinarily without collective-bargaining agreements. Contributions are usually based on a selected benefit formula. These plans are not considered multiemployer, and the accounting is based on the respective interest in the plan.

Non-U.S. pension arrangements. The terms and conditions that define the amount of benefits and the nature of the obligation determine the substance of a non-U.S. pension arrangement. If they are, in substance, similar to pension plans, SFASs 87 and 88 apply.

Business combinations. When an entity is purchased (APB 16) that sponsors a single employer defined benefit plan, the purchaser must assign part of the purchase price to an asset if plan assets exceed the projected benefit obligation or to a liability if the projected benefit obligation exceeds plan assets. The projected benefit obligation should include the effect of any expected plan curtailment or termination. This assignment eliminates any existing unrecognized components, and any future differences between contributions and net pension cost will affect the asset or liability recognized when the purchase took place.

SFAS 88

This statement is meant to be applied within the framework of SFAS 87. It describes the accounting to be followed by obligors when all or part of defined benefit pension plans have been settled or curtailed. It also supersedes SFAS 74 and establishes employer accounting procedures in the case of benefits offered when employment is terminated. Under the provisions of SFAS 88, when one of these events occurs, some previously unrecognized amounts shall now be recognized immediately.

Settlements include both the purchase of nonparticipating annuity contracts and lump-sum cash payments. The following three criteria must all be met in order to constitute a pension obligation settlement:

1. Must be irrevocable
2. Must relieve the obligor of primary responsibility
3. Must eliminate significant risks associated with elements used to effect it

A defeasance strategy does not constitute a settlement.

Under an annuity contract settlement, an unrelated insurance company unconditionally accepts an obligation to provide the required benefits. The following criteria must be met for this type of settlement:

1. Must be irrevocable
2. Must involve transfer of material risk to the insurance company

There can be no reasonable doubt as to the ability of the insurance company to meet its contractual obligation. The substance of any **participating** annuity contract must relieve the employer of most of the risks and rewards or it does not meet the criteria.

Curtailments include early discontinuance of employee services or cessation or suspension of a plan. Additional benefits may not be earned although future service time may be counted towards vesting. Curtailments must meet the following criteria:

1. Must materially diminish present employees' future service or
2. Must stop or materially diminish the accumulation of benefits by a significant number of employees

A curtailment and a settlement can occur separately or together.

Settlements. If the entire projected benefit obligation is settled, any SFAS 87 unrecognized net gain (loss) plus any remaining unrecognized net asset existing when SFAS 87 was initially applied is immediately recognized. A pro rata portion is used in the case of partial settlement. If the obligation is settled by purchasing **participating** annuities, the cost of the right of participation is deducted from the gain (but not from the loss) before recognition.

If the total of the interest cost and service cost components of the SFAS 87 periodic pension cost is greater than or equal to the settlement costs during a given year, the recognition of the above gain (loss) is not required, but is permitted. However, a consistent policy must be followed in this regard. The settlement cost is generally the cash paid or the cost of **nonparticipating** annuities purchased or the cost of **participating** annuities reduced by the cost of the right of participation.

Curtailments. A curtailment results in the elimination of future years of service. The pro rata portion of any (1) unrecognized cost of retroactive plan amendments and (2) remaining unrecognized net obligation existing when SFAS 87 was initially applied that is associated with the eliminated years of service is immediately recognized as a loss.

If curtailment results in a decrease in the projected benefit obligation, a gain is indicated. An increase in the projected benefit obligation (excluding termination benefits) indicates a loss. This indicated gain (loss) is then netted against the loss from unrecognized prior service cost recognized in accordance with the preceding paragraph. The net result is the **curtailment gain** or **curtailment loss**. This gain (loss) is accounted for as provided in SFAS 5. A gain is recognized upon actual employee termination or plan suspension. A loss is recognized when both the curtailment is probable and the effects are reasonably estimable.

After the curtailment gain (loss) is calculated, any remaining unrecognized net asset existing when SFAS 87 was initially applied is transferred from that category and combined with the gain (loss) arising after SFAS 87 application. It is subsequently treated as a component of the new gain (loss) category.

Termination benefits. Termination benefits are accounted for in accordance with SFAS 5. Special short time period benefits require that a loss and a liability be recognized when the offer is accepted and the amount can be reasonably estimated. Contractual termination benefits require that a loss and a liability be recognized when it is probable that employees will receive the benefits and the amount can be reasonably estimated. The cost of these benefits is the cash paid and the present value of future payments. Termination benefits and curtailments can occur together.

Segment disposal. Gains (losses), as calculated above, that result because of a disposal of a business segment should be recognized according to the provisions of APB 30.

Disclosures. In the case of all (including segment disposal) gains (losses) calculated under the SFAS 88 provisions, the obligor must include in the disclosure (1) a description of the nature of the event and (2) the amount of gain (loss) recognized.

Effective date. The statement is effective in the same fiscal year that SFAS 87 is initially applied. If the obligor has previously taken part in an asset reversion transaction before SFAS 88 became effective, the gain should be recognized as the cumulative effect of a change in accounting principle when SFAS 87 is first applied. The total gain recognized is the smaller of: (1) the amount yet to be amortized or (2) unrecognized net assets existing when SFAS 87 is initially applied.

Postretirement Benefits Other Than Pensions (OPEB)

SFAS 106 rescinds FASB TB 87-1, amends APB 12, and establishes the standard for employers' accounting for other (than pension) postretirement benefits (OPEB). This standard proscribes a single method for measuring and recognizing an employer's accumulated postretirement benefit obligation (APBO). It applies to all forms of postretirement benefits, although the most material benefit is usually postretirement health care. It uses the fundamental framework established by SFAS 87 and SFAS 88. To the extent that the promised benefits are similar, the accounting provisions are similar. Only when there is a compelling reason, is the accounting different.

SFAS 106 requires accrual accounting and adopts the three primary characteristics of pension accounting:

1. Delayed recognition (changes are not recognized immediately but are subsequently recognized in a gradual and systematic way)
2. Reporting net cost (aggregates of various items are reported as one net amount)
3. Offsetting assets and liabilities (assets and liabilities are sometimes shown net)

SFAS 106 distinguishes between the **substantive** plan and **written** plan. Although generally the same, the substantive plan (the one understood as evidenced by past practice or by communication of intended changes) is the basis for the accounting if it differs from the written plan.

OPEBs are considered to be deferred compensation earned in an exchange transaction during the time periods that the employee provides services. The expected cost generally should be attributed in equal amounts (unless the plan attributes a disproportionate share of benefits to early years) over the periods from the employee's hiring date (unless credit for the service is only granted from a later date) to the date that the employee attains full eligibility for all benefits expected to be received. This accrual should be followed even if the employee provides service beyond the date of full eligibility.

The transition obligation, under SFAS 106, is the unrecognized and unfunded APBO "(accumulated postretirement benefit obligation)" for all of the participants in the plan. This obligation can either (1) be recognized immediately as the effect of an accounting change, subject to certain limitations, or (2) be recognized on a delayed basis over future service periods with disclosure of the unrecognized amount. The delayed recognition has to result in, at least, as rapid a recognition as would have been recognized on a pay-as-you-go basis.

The effective dates in SFAS 106 are for fiscal years beginning as follows:

1. After March 15, 1991 - Amendment of APB 12
2. After December 15, 1992 - SFAS 106 Employers except those in (3)
3. After December 15, 1994 - Plans outside the United States and small, nonpublic employers

Test runs by business enterprises have indicated that the collection of data required by this standard can present numerous problems. Claims cost data tends to be unavailable or incomplete.

Example

A sample illustration of the basic accounting for OPEB as established by SFAS 106 follows. Firstime Accrual Co. plans to adopt accrual accounting for OPEB as of January 1, 1992. All employees were hired at age 30 and are fully eligible for benefits at age 60. There are no plan assets. This first calculation determines the unrecognized transition obligation (UTO).

Firstime Accrual
December 31, 1991

Employee	Age	Years of Service	Total Years When Fully Eligible	Expected Retirement Age	Remaining Service to Retirement	EPBO	APBO
A	35	5	30	60	25	$ 14,000	$ 2,333
B	40	10	30	60	20	22,000	7,333
C	45	15	30	60	15	30,000	15,000
D	50	20	30	60	10	38,000	25,333
E	55	25	30	65	10	46,000	38,333
F	60	30	30	65	5	54,000	54,000
G	65	RET	--		--	46,000	46,000
H	70	RET	--		--	38,000	38,000
					85	$288,000	$226,332

Explanations

1. EPBO "(expected postretirement benefit obligation)" is usually determined by an actuary, although it can be calculated if complete data is available.
2. APBO is calculated using the EPBO. Specifically, it is EPBO x (years of service/total years when fully eligible)
3. The unrecognized transition obligation (UTO) is the APBO at 12/31/91 since there are no plan assets to be deducted. The $226,332 can be amortized over the average remaining service to retirement of 14.17 (85/6) years or an optional period of 20 years, if longer. Firstime Accrual selected the 20 year period of amortization.
4. Note that Employee F has attained full eligibility for benefits and yet plans to continue working.
5. Note that the above 1991 table is used in the calculation of the 1992 components of OPEB cost that follows.

After the establishment of UTO, the next step is to determine the benefit cost for the year ended December 31, 1992. This calculation follows the framework established by SFAS 87. The discount rate is assumed to be 10%.

Firstime Accrual
OPEB Cost
December 31, 1992

1.	Service Cost	$ 5,500
2.	Interest Cost	22,633
3.	Actual Return on Plan Assets	--
4.	Gain or Loss	--
5.	Amortization of Unrecognized Prior Service Cost	--
6.	Amortization of UTO	11,317
	Total OPEB Cost	$39,450

Explanations

1. Service cost calculation uses only employees not yet fully eligible for benefits.

Employee	12/31/91 EPBO	Total years when Fully Eligible	Service Cost
A	$14,000	30	$ 467
B	22,000	30	733
C	30,000	30	1,000
D	38,000	30	1,267
E	46,000	30	1,533
			$5,000
	Interest for 1992 ($5,000 x 10%)		500
	Total Service Cost		$5,500

2. Interest cost is the 12/31/91 APBO of $226,332 x 10% = $22,633.
3. There are no plan assets so there is no return.
4. There is no unrecognized prior service cost initially.
5. There is no gain (loss) since there are no changes yet.
6. Amortization of UTO is the 12/31/91 UTO of $226,332/20 year optional election = $11,317.

After calculation of the 1992 benefit cost, the next step is to project the EPBO and APBO for December 31, 1992. Assuming no changes, it is based on the December 31, 1991 actuarial measurement and it is calculated as shown earlier in the determination of the UTO.

Firstime Accrual
December 31, 1992

Employee	Age	Years of Service	Total Years When Fully Eligible	EPBO	APBO
A	36	6	30	$ 15,400	$ 3,080
B	41	11	30	24,200	8,873
C	46	16	30	33,000	17,600
D	51	21	30	41,800	29,260
E	56	26	30	50,600	43,853
F	61	31	--	59,400	59,400
G	66	RET	--	44,620	44,620
H	71	RET	--	36,860	36,860
				$305,880	$243,546

Changes in experience or assumptions will result in gains (losses). The gain (loss) is measured by the difference resulting in the APBO or the plan assets from that projected. However, except for the effects of a decision to temporarily deviate from the substantive plan, these gains or losses have no impact in the year of occurrence. They are deferred and amortized as in SFAS 87. Amortization of unrecognized net gain (loss) is included as a component of net postretirement cost for a year if, as of the beginning of the year, it exceeds 10% of the **greater** of the APBO or the market-related value of plan assets. The minimum amortization is the **excess** divided by the remaining average service period of active plan participants. A systematic method of amortization that amortizes a greater amount, is applied consistently to both gains and losses and is disclosed may also be used. If gains (losses) are recognized immediately, special rules of offsetting may be required.

Deferred compensation contracts. If the aggregate deferred compensation contracts with individual employees are equivalent to a pension plan, the contracts should be accounted for according to SFASs 87 and 88. All other deferred compensation contracts should be accounted for according to APB 12, para 16.

SFAS 106 amends APB 12 effective for fiscal years beginning after March 15, 1991. This amendment states that the terms of the individual contract will govern the accrual of the employee's obligation for deferred compensation and the cost should be attributed over the employee service period until full eligibility is attained.

Per APB 12, the amount to be accrued should not be less than the present value of the estimated payments to be made. This estimated amount should be accrued in a systematic and rational manner. When elements of both current and future employment are present, only the portion attributable to the current services should be accrued. All requirements of the contract, such as the continued employment for a specified period and availability for consulting services and agreements not to compete after retirement, need to be met in order for the employee to receive future payments.

One benefit which may be found in a deferred compensation contract is the period payments to employees or their beneficiaries for life, with provisions for a minimum lump-sum settlement in the event of early death of one or all of the beneficiaries. The estimated amount to be accrued should be based on the life expectancy of each individual concerned or on the estimated cost of an annuity contract, not on the minimum amount payable in the event of early death.

1974 Employee Retirement Income Security Act. Congress passed the Employee Retirement Income Security Act (ERISA) in 1974. The principal objectives of ERISA were to provide statutory law for pension plan requirements, to strengthen the financial soundness of private pension plans, to safeguard employees' pension rights, and to create the Pension Benefit Guaranty Corporation (PBGC).

Prior to ERISA, the Internal Revenue Code was the principal source of law for governing and managing pension plans. Unfortunately, the thrust of the Code was with tax considerations and the important nontax aspects of pension plans, such as vesting, funding, and employee participation were not addressed. ERISA filled the void by mandating minimum vesting, funding, employee participation, and other requirements. Virtually every private pension plan is affected by the provisions of ERISA.

The Act generally provides for full vesting of pension benefits after an employee has worked for the same employer for 15 years. Several different formulas can be used to determine when employee benefits vest. In addition, ERISA requires a minimum funding, in accordance with an acceptable actuarial method, for private pension plans. This requirement extends to the funding of past service costs over a period of 40 years or less. ERISA also established standards for employee participation and has made defined contribution plans more popular.

All of the above requirements strengthen the financial soundness of employee pension funds. To further ensure the ability of a plan to pay pension obligations and to safeguard employee rights, ERISA amended the Internal Revenue Code of 1954 to allow for the assessment of fines and the denial of tax deductions. The Act also requires that pension plans submit annual reports, provide a description of the plan, and make a full disclosure through the submission of various statements and schedules.

Prior to the enactment of ERISA, some employees lost pension benefits when plans were terminated because of bankruptcy or other reasons. In order to protect employee rights under these circumstances, ERISA created PBGC. The function of this agency is to guarantee employees, if the employer cannot pay, at least a minimum amount of benefits for their years of service. This guarantee is financed by an insurance premium charge which is levied on all employers with defined benefit plans. PBGC also has the right to administer terminated plans, to impose liens on employers' assets, and to take over employers' assets under certain specified circumstances.

For the most part, ERISA does not present any new or difficult accounting problems. It requires some additional disclosures and it has changed the tax law. Although the application of SFAS 87 is likely to produce more volatile differences than in the past between the amount shown as net periodic pension expense and the minimum or maximum (for tax purposes) amounts funded under ERISA, the Act per se has little effect on the accounting for pension plans.

Disclosures

Pensions

Defined benefit plans require the following disclosures:

1. General

   a. Description of the plan and an indication of the groups covered
   b. Statement of policy in regard to accounting and funding
   c. Types of assets held
   d. Type of benefit formula
   e. Type of any significant nonbenefit liability
   f. Acknowledgement of matters of significance that have affected the comparability of the accounting periods presented and comments as to their nature and effect. Changes in accounting methods and amendments of a plan are examples.

2. Net periodic pension cost amount, separately showing:

   a. Service cost component
   b. Interest cost component
   c. Actual return on assets
   d. Net total of other components

3. Schedule reconciling balance sheet amounts with the funded status of the plan, separately showing:

   a. Plan assets **fair value** (not the possible calculated market-related value)
   b. Projected benefit obligation, accumulated benefit obligation, and vested benefit obligation
   c. Unrecognized prior service cost amount
   d. Unrecognized net gain (loss) amount (those not yet reflected in market-related value should also be included)
   e. Unrecognized net obligation or net asset amount still remaining from that recorded at SFAS 87 date of initial application
   f. Additional minimum liability amount recorded because of underfunding
   g. Net pension asset or liability amount recognized on the balance sheet

Disclosures required above must show plans with assets in excess of the accumulated benefit obligation and those with accumulated benefit obligations in excess of plan assets separately.

4. Rates

   a. Assumed weighted-average discount rate
   b. Assumed weighted-average expected long-term rate on plan assets
   c. Assumed rate of compensation increase (if applicable) in measuring the projected benefit obligation

5. Other, if applicable

   a. Employer and related parties

      (1) Amounts and types of securities included in plan assets
      (2) Approximate amount of annual benefits covered by annuity contracts issued by the above

   b. Alternative amortization methods used
   c. Existence and nature of substantive commitments to make future plan amendments

Defined contribution plans and multiemployer plans both require the following separate disclosures:

1. Description of the plan and an indication of the groups covered
2. Acknowledgement of matters of significance that have affected the comparability of the accounting periods presented and comments as to their nature and effect
3. Amount of cost recognized during the period

Additionally, **defined contribution** plans require disclosure of the basis for determining contributions and multiemployer plans require disclosure of the type of benefits provided.

Presentation of the above data may be in the aggregation (i.e., separately by plan, in total, or in some other combination) that provides the most useful information. Unless similar economic assumptions are used, disclosure for plans inside and outside the United States should not be combined.

Settlements, Curtailments, and Termination Plans

Defined benefit plans require the following disclosures for settlements, curtailments, and termination plans:

1. Description of the nature of the event
2. The amount of gain or loss recognition

Postretirement Benefits Other than Pensions (OPEB)

1. General

   a. Description of the **substantive** plan including its nature, any modification of existing provisions, and any commitments to increase benefits.
   b. Employee groups covered
   c. Statement of policy regarding funding
   d. Types of assets held
   e. Types of benefits
   f. Types of nonbenefit liability
   g. Acknowledgement of matters of significance that have affected the comparability of the accounting periods presented and comments as to their nature and effect. Examples are the effects of divestitures or business combinations.

2. Net periodic postretirement benefit cost amount, separately showing:

   a. Service cost component
   b. Interest cost component
   c. Actual return on assets
   d. Amortization of unrecognized transition obligation (asset)
   e. Net total of other components

3. Schedule reconciling balance sheet amounts with the funded status of the plan, separately showing:

   a. Plan assets **fair value** (not the possible calculated market-related value)
   b. Accumulated postretirement benefit obligation, separately showing:

      (1) Retirees' portion
      (2) Fully eligible plan participants' portion
      (3) Other active plan participants' portion

   c. Unrecognized prior service cost amount
   d. Unrecognized net gain (loss) amount (those not yet reflected in market-related value should also be included)
   e. Unrecognized net transition obligation or net transition asset amount still remaining from that recorded at SFAS 106 date of initial application
   f. Net postretirement benefit asset or liability amount recognized on the balance sheet

4. Assumed health care trend rate(s) used to measure the expected cost of plan benefits for the following year showing:

   a. Description of direction of change in general
   b. Ultimate trend rate and when that rate is expected to be attained

5. Rates

   a. Assumed weighted-average discount rate
   b. Assumed rates of compensation increase (for pay-related plans) used to measure APBO
   c. Assumed weighted-average expected long-term rate on plan assets
   d. Assumed estimated income tax rate in rate of return on plan assets if plan income is segregated from employer's income for tax purposes

6. Based on the substantive plan and while holding all other assumptions constant, the effect of a 1% increase in health care cost trend rates for each future year on:

   a. Service and interest cost components aggregated
   b. Health care APBO

7. For plan assets, show separately:

   a. Employer and related party securities included
   b. Approximate amount of annual benefits covered by employer and related party issued insurance contracts

8. Alternative amortization methods used, if applicable
9. Settlement or curtailment gain (loss) recognized during the period with a description of the event
10. Termination benefits recognized during the period with a description of the event

16 Stockholders' Equity

Perspective and Issues

SFAC 6 defines stockholders' equity as the residual interest in the assets of an entity after deducting its liabilities. Stockholders' equity is comprised of all capital contributed to the entity plus its accumulated earnings less any distributions that have been made. Thus, there are two major categories of stockholders' equity: paid-in capital and retained earnings.

Stockholders' equity represents an **interest** in the net assets (i.e., assets less liabilities) of the entity. It is **not** a **claim** on those assets in the sense that liabilities are. Upon liquidation of the business, an obligation arises for the entity to distribute any remaining assets to the shareholders after the creditors are paid.

Earnings are not generated by transactions in an entity's own equity (e.g., by the issuance, reacquisition, or reissuance of its common or preferred shares). Depending on the laws of the jurisdiction of incorporation, distributions to shareholders may be subject to various limitations, such as to the amount of accumulated (accounting basis) earnings.

A major objective of the accounting for stockholders' equity is the adequate disclosure of the **sources** from which the capital was derived. For this reason, a number of different paid-in capital accounts may be presented in the balance sheet. The rights of each class of shareholder must also be disclosed. Where shares are reserved for future issuance, such as under the terms of stock option plans, this fact must also be made known.

Sources of GAAP

ARB	APB	FASB I	FASB TB	EITF
43, Ch. 1A, 1B,	6, 10, 12, 15,	28, 31	82-2,	88-6,
7A, 7B, 13B, 46	25, 29		85-6	88-9

Definitions of Terms

Additional paid-in capital. Amounts received at issuance in excess of the par or stated value of capital stock and amounts received from other transactions involving the entity's stock and/or stockholders. It is classified by source.

Appropriation (of retained earnings). A segregation of retained earnings for a particular purpose. The objective is to communicate the unavailability of a portion of the entity's accumulated earnings for dividend distributions.

Authorized shares. The maximum number of shares permitted to be issued by a corporation as stated in the corporate charter and by-laws.

Callable. An optional characteristic of preferred stock whereby the corporation can redeem the stock at specified future dates and at specific prices. The call price is usually at or above the original issuance price.

Compensatory stock option plans. Plans which do not meet the criteria for noncompensatory plans. Their main purpose is to provide additional compensation to officers and employees.

Constructive retirement method. Method of accounting for treasury shares which treats the shares as having been retired, thereby reverting to authorized but unissued status. The stock and additional paid-in capital accounts are relieved, with a debit to retained earnings or a credit to a paid-in capital account for the excess or deficiency of the purchase cost over or under original issuance proceeds.

Contributed capital. The amount of equity contributed by the corporation's shareholders. It consists of capital stock plus additional paid-in capital.

Convertible. An optional characteristic of preferred stock whereby the stockholders may exchange their preferred shares for common shares at a specified ratio.

Cost method. Method of accounting for treasury shares which presents aggregate cost of reacquired shares as a deduction from the total of paid-in capital and retained earnings.

Cumulative. An optional characteristic of preferred stock whereby any dividends of prior years not paid to the preferred shareholders must be paid before any dividends can be distributed to the common shareholders.

Date of declaration. The date on which the board of directors decides a dividend shall be paid. A legal liability (usually current) is created on this date in the case of cash, property, and scrip dividends.

Date of grant. The date on which the board of directors awards the stock to the employees in stock option plans.

Date of payment. The date on which the shareholders are actually paid the declared dividends.

Date of record. The date on which ownership of the shares is decided. Those owning stock on this date will be paid the previously declared dividends.

Deficit. A debit balance in the retained earnings account. Dividends may not generally be paid when this condition exists. Formally known as accumulated deficit.

Discount on capital stock. Occurs when the stock of a corporation is originally issued at a price below par value. The original purchasers become contingently liable to creditors for this difference.

Issued stock. The number of shares issued by the firm and owned by the shareholders and the corporation. It is the sum of outstanding shares plus treasury shares.

Legal capital. The aggregate par or stated value of stock. It represents the amount of owners' equity which cannot be distributed to shareholders, thus serving to protect the claims of the creditors.

Liquidating dividend. A dividend distribution which is not based on earnings. It represents a return of contributed capital and reduces the additional paid-in capital account.

Measurement date. The date on which both the number of shares under option and the option price are known. Usually this date coincides with the date of the grant.

Noncompensatory stock option plans. Plans whose primary purpose is widespread ownership of the firm among its employees and officers. They must meet four criteria (see APB 25, para 7 or the section on stock options).

No-par stock. Stock which has no par value. Sometimes a stated value is determined by the board of directors, in which case, it is accorded the same treatment as par value stock.

Outstanding stock. Stock issued by a corporation which is still in the hands of shareholders (i.e., issued shares which are not held in the treasury).

Par value method. A method of accounting for treasury shares which charges the treasury stock account for the aggregate par or stated value of the shares acquired and charges the excess of the purchase cost over the par value to paid-in capital and/or retained earnings. A deficiency of purchase cost is credited to paid-in capital.

Participating. An optional characteristic of preferred stock whereby preferred shareholders may share ratably with the common shareholders in any profit distributions in excess of a predetermined rate. Participation may be limited to a maximum rate or may be unlimited (full).

Quasi-reorganization. A procedure which reclassifies amounts from contributed capital to retained earnings to eliminate a deficit in that account. All the assets and liabilities are first revalued to their current values. It represents an alternative to a legal reorganization in bankruptcy proceedings.

Retained earnings. The undistributed earnings of a firm.

Stock options. Enables officers and employees of a corporation to purchase shares in the corporation.

Stock rights. Enables present shareholders to purchase additional shares of stock of the corporation, usually pursuant to the preemptive right granted to common shareholders by some state corporation laws.

Treasury stock. Shares of a corporation which have been repurchased by the corporation. This stock has no voting rights and receives no dividends. Some states do not recognize treasury stock. In such cases, reacquired shares are treated as having been retired.

Concepts, Rules, and Examples

Legal Capital and Capital Stock

Legal capital typically relates to that portion of the stockholders' investment in a corporation which is permanent in nature and which--theoretically, at least--represents assets which will continue to be available for the satisfaction of creditor's claims. Traditionally, legal capital was comprised of the aggregate par or stated value of common and preferred shares issued. In recent years, however, many states have eliminated the requirement that corporate shares have a designated par or stated value. Also, some states have adopted provisions of the Model Business Corporation Act which eliminated the distinction between par value and the amount contributed in excess of par.

The specific requirements regarding the preservation of legal capital are a function of the corporation laws in the state in which a particular entity is incorporated. Accordingly, any action by the corporation that could affect the amount of legal capital (e.g., the payment of dividends in excess of accumulated earnings and additional paid-in capital) must be considered in the context of the relevant laws of the state where the company is chartered.

Ownership interest in a corporation is made up of common and, optionally, preferred shares. The common shares represent the residual risk-taking ownership of the corporation after the satisfaction of all claims of creditors and senior classes of equity.

Preferred stock. Preferred shareholders are owners who have certain rights superior to those of common shareholders. These rights will pertain either to the earnings or the assets of the corporation. Preferences as to earnings exist when the preferred shareholders have a stipulated dividend rate (expressed either as a dollar amount or as a percentage) of the preferred stock's par or stated value. Preferences as to assets exist when the preferred shares have a stipulated liquidation value which indicates that, if a corporation were to wind up its affairs and liquidate, the preferred holders would be paid a specific amount before the common shareholders would have a right to participate in any of the proceeds.

In practice, preferred shares are more likely to have preferences as to earnings than as to assets. Some classes of preferred shares may have both preferential rights. Preferred shares may also have the following features: participation in earnings beyond the stipulated dividend rate; the cumulative feature affording the preferred shareholders the protection that their dividends in arrears, if any, will be fully satisfied before the common shareholders participate in any earnings distribution; and convertibility or callability by the corporation. Whatever preferences exist must be disclosed adequately in the financial statements, either on the face of the balance sheet or in the notes.

In exchange for the preferences, the preferred shareholders' rights or privileges are limited. For instance, the right to vote may be restricted to common shareholders. The most important right denied to the preferred shareholders, however, is the right to participate without limitation in the earnings of the corporation. Thus, if the corporation has exceedingly large earnings for a particular period, these earnings would tend to accrue to the benefit of the common shareholders. This is true even if the preferred stock is participating (a fairly uncommon feature) because even participating preferred stock usually has some upper limitation placed upon its degree of participation.

Occasionally, several classes of stock will be categorized as common (e.g., Class A common, Class B common, etc.). Since there can be only one class of shares that represents the true residual risk-taking investors in a corporation, it is clear that the other classes, even though described as common shareholders, must in fact have some preferential status. Typically, these preferences relate to voting rights. An example of this situation arises when a formerly closely-held corporation sells shares to the public but gives the publicly-held shares a disproportionately small capacity to exercise control over the entity. The rights and responsibilities of each class of shareholder, even if described as common, must be fully described in financial statements.

Issuance of shares. The accounting for the sale of shares by a corporation depends upon whether the stock has a par or stated value. If there is a par or stated value, the amount of the proceeds representing the aggregate par or stated value is credited to the common or preferred stock account. The aggregate par or stated value is generally defined as legal capital not subject to distribution to shareholders. Proceeds in excess of par or stated value are credited to an additional paid-in capital account. The additional paid-in capital represents the amount in excess of the legal capital which may be, under certain defined conditions, distributed to shareholders. A corporation selling stock below par value credits the capital stock account for the par value and debits an offsetting discount account for the difference between par value and the amount actually received. The discount serves to notify the actual and potential creditors of the contingent liability of those investors. As a practical matter, corporations began to avoid this problem by reducing par values to an arbitrarily low amount, eliminating the chance that shares would be sold for amounts below par. Where the Model Business Corporation Act has been adopted or where corporation laws have embraced some of the attributes of that Act, there is often no distinction made between par value and amounts in excess of par. In those jurisdictions, the entire proceeds from the sale of stock may be credited to the common stock account without distinction between the stock and the additional paid-in capital accounts. The following entries illustrate these concepts:

Facts: A corporation sells 100,000 shares of $5 par common stock for $8 per share cash.

Cash	800,000	
Common stock		500,000
Additional paid-in capital		300,000

Facts: As above, except stock has no par value.

Cash	800,000	
Common stock		800,000

Preferred stock will often be assigned a par value because in many cases the preferential dividend rate is defined as a percentage of par value (e.g., 10%, $25 par value preferred stock will have a required annual dividend of $2.50).

If the shares in a corporation are issued in exchange for services or property rather than for cash, the transaction should be reflected at the fair value of the property or services received. If this information is not readily available, then the transaction should be recorded at the fair value of the shares that were issued. Where necessary, appraisals should be obtained in order to properly reflect the transaction. As a final resort, a valuation by the board of directors of the stock issued can be utilized (APB 29, paras 18 and 25).

In certain instances, common and preferred shares may be issued to investors as a unit (e.g., a unit of one share of preferred and two shares of common can be sold as a package). Where both of the classes of stock are publicly traded, the proceeds from a unit offering should be allocated in proportion to the relative market values of the constituent securities. If only one of the securities is publicly traded, then the proceeds should be allocated to the one that is publicly traded based on its known market value, with any excess allocated to the other. Where the market value of neither security is known, resorting to appraisal information might be necessary. The imputed fair value of one class of security, particularly the preferred shares, can be based upon the stipulated dividend rate. In this case, the amount of proceeds remaining after the imputing of a value of the preferred shares would be allocated to the common stock.

The foregoing procedures would also apply if a unit offering were made up of one class of equity and a nonequity security such as convertible debentures.

Stock Subscriptions

Occasionally, particularly in the case of a newly organized corporation, a contract is entered into between the corporation and prospective investors, whereby the latter agree to purchase specified numbers of shares to be paid for over some installment period. These stock subscriptions are not the same as actual stock issuances and the accounting differs.

The amount of stock subscriptions receivable by a corporation is sometimes treated as an asset on the balance sheet and categorized as current or noncurrent in accordance with the terms of payment. However, in accordance with SEC requirements, most subscriptions receivable are shown as a reduction of stockholders' equity in the same manner as treasury stock. Since subscribed shares do not have the rights and responsibilities of actual outstanding stock, the credit is made to a stock subscribed account instead of the capital stock accounts.

If the common stock has par or stated value, the common stock subscribed account typically is credited for the aggregate par or stated value of the shares subscribed. The excess over this amount is credited to additional paid-in capital. No distinction is made between additional paid-in capital relating to shares already issued and shares subscribed for. This treatment follows from the distinction between legal capital and additional paid-in capital. Where there is no par or stated value, the entire amount of the common stock subscribed is credited to the stock subscribed account.

As the amount due from the prospective shareholders is collected, the stock subscriptions receivable account is credited and the proceeds are debited to the cash account. Actual issuance of the shares, however, must await the complete payment of the stock subscription. Accordingly, the credit to common stock subscribed is not reversed until the subscribed shares are fully paid for and the stock is issued.

The following journal entries illustrate these concepts:

(1) 10,000 shares of $50 par preferred are subscribed at a price of $65 each; a 10% down payment is received.

Cash	65,000	
Stock subscriptions receivable	585,000	
Preferred stock subscribed		500,000
Additional paid-in capital		150,000

(2) 2,000 shares of no par common shares are subscribed at a price of $85 each, with one-half received in cash.

Cash	85,000	
Stock subscriptions receivable	85,000	
Common stock subscribed		170,000

(3) All preferred subscriptions are paid, and one-half of the **remaining** common subscriptions are collected in full and subscribed shares are issued.

Cash [$585,000 + ($85,000 x .50)]	627,500	
Stock subscriptions receivable		627,500
Preferred stock subscribed	500,000	
Preferred stock		500,000
Common stock subscribed	127,500	
Common stock ($170,000 x .75)		127,500

Where the company experiences a default by the subscriber, the accounting will follow the provisions of the state in which the corporation is chartered. In some jurisdictions, the subscriber is entitled to a proportionate number of shares based upon the amount s/he has already paid on his/her subscriptions, sometimes reduced by the cost incurred by the corporation in selling the remaining defaulted shares to other stockholders. In other jurisdictions, the subscriber forfeits his/her entire investment upon default. In this case, the amount already received is credited to an additional paid-in capital account that describes its source.

Additional Paid-in Capital

Additional paid-in capital represents all capital contributed to a corporation other than that defined as legal capital (where such a distinction is made). Additional paid-in capital can arise from proceeds received from the sale of common and preferred shares in excess of their par or stated values. It can also arise from transactions relating to the following:

1. The sale of shares previously issued and subsequently reacquired by the corporation.
2. The retirement of previously outstanding shares.
3. The payment of stock dividends in a manner which justifies the dividend being recorded at the market value of the shares distributed.
4. The lapse of stock purchase warrants or the forfeiture of stock subscriptions, if these result in the retaining by the corporation of any partial proceeds received prior to forfeiture.
5. Warrants which are detachable from bonds.
6. The conversion of convertible bonds recorded at the market value of the shares issued.
7. Any other "gains" on the company's own stock, such as that which results from certain stock option plans.

Where the amounts are material, the sources of additional paid-in capital should be described in the financial statements.

Donated Capital

Donated capital should also be adequately disclosed in the financial statements. Donated capital can result from an outright gift to the corporation (e.g., if a major shareholder donates land or other assets to the company in a nonreciprocal transfer) or may result when services are provided to the corporation and the provider is compensated by a shareholder rather than by the corporation (e.g., when a shareholder pays the salary of an employee).

In these situations, historical cost is not adequate to properly reflect the substance of the transaction, since the historical cost to the corporation would be zero. Accordingly, these events should be reflected at fair market value (APB 29, para 18). If long-lived assets are donated to the corporation, they should be recorded at their fair value at the date of donation, and the amount so recorded should be depreciated over the normal useful economic life of such assets. If donations are conditional in nature, they should not be reflected formally in the accounts until the appropriate conditions have been satisfied. However, disclosure might still be required in the financial statements describing both the assets donated and the conditions required to be met.

Retained Earnings

Legal capital, additional paid-in capital, and donated capital collectively represent the contributed capital of the corporation. The other major source of capital is retained earnings, which represents the accumulated amount of earnings of the corporation from the date of inception (or from the date of reorganization) less the cumulative amount of distributions made to shareholders and other charges to retained earnings (e.g., from treasury stock transactions). The distributions to shareholders generally take the form of dividend payments but may take other forms as well, such as the reacquisition of shares for amounts in excess of the original issuance proceeds.

Retained earnings are also affected by action taken by the corporation's board of directors to appropriate a portion. This action serves to restrict dividend payments but does nothing to provide any resources for satisfaction of the contingent loss or other underlying purpose for which the appropriation has been made. Any appropriation made from retained earnings must eventually be returned to the retained earnings account. It is not permissible to charge losses against the appropriation account nor to credit any realized gain to that account. The use of appropriated retained earnings has diminished significantly over the years.

An important rule relating to retained earnings is that transactions in a corporation's own stock can result in a reduction of retained earnings (i.e., a loss on such transactions can be charged to retained earnings) but cannot result in an increase in retained earnings (any "gains" on such transactions are credited to paid-in capital, never to retained earnings). Examples of situations that may create such treatment are treasury stock transactions.

If a series of operating losses have been incurred or distributions to shareholders in excess of accumulated earnings have been made and if there is a debit balance in retained earnings, the account is generally referred to as "accumulated deficit."

Dividends

Dividends are the pro rata distribution of earnings to the owners of the corporation. The amount and the allocation between the preferred and common shareholders is a function of the stipulated preferential dividend rate, the presence or absence of (1) a participation feature, (2) a cumulative feature, and (3) arrearages on the preferred stock, and the wishes of the board of directors. Dividends--even preferred stock dividends, where a cumulative feature exists--do not accrue. Dividends only become a liability of the corporation when they are declared by the board of directors.

Traditionally, corporations were not allowed to declare dividends in excess of the amount of retained earnings. Alternatively, a corporation could pay dividends out of retained earnings **and** additional paid-in capital but could not exceed the total of these categories (i.e., they could not impair legal capital by the payment of dividends). States that have adopted the Model Business Corporation Act generally grant more latitude to the directors. Corporations can now, in certain jurisdictions, declare and pay dividends in excess of the book amount of retained earnings if the directors conclude that, after the payment of such dividends, the fair value of the corporation's net assets will still be a positive amount. Thus, directors can declare dividends out of unrealized appreciation which, in certain industries, can be a significant source of dividends beyond the realized and recognized accumulated earnings of the corporation. This action, however, represents a major departure from traditional practice and demands both careful consideration and adequate disclosure.

Three important dividend dates are:

1. The declaration date.
2. The record date.
3. The payment date.

The declaration date governs the incurrence of a legal liability by the corporation. The record date refers to that point in time when a determination is made as to which specific registered stockholders will receive dividends and in what amounts. Finally, the payment date relates to the date when the distribution of the dividend takes place. These concepts are illustrated in the following example:

On May 1, 1991, the directors of River Corp. declare a $.75 per share quarterly dividend on River Corp.'s 650,000 outstanding common shares. The dividend is payable May 25 to holders of record May 15.

May 1	Retained earnings (or Dividends)	487,500	
	Dividends payable		487,500
May 15	No entry		
May 25	Dividends payable	487,500	
	Cash		487,500

If a dividends account is used, it is closed to retained earnings at year end.

Dividends may be made in the form of cash, property, or scrip. Cash dividends are either a given dollar amount per share or a percentage of par or stated value. Property dividends consist of the distribution of any assets other than cash (e.g., inventory or equipment). Finally, scrip dividends are promissory notes due at some time in the future, sometimes bearing interest until final payment is made.

Property dividends. If property dividends are declared, the paying corporation may incur a gain or loss, if the fair value of the property is greater or less than the carrying value. Since the dividend should be reflected at the fair value of the assets distributed, the difference between fair value and book value is recorded at the time the dividend is declared and charged or credited to a loss or gain account.

Scrip dividends. If a corporation declares a dividend payable in scrip which is interest bearing, the interest is accrued over time as a periodic expense. The interest is **not** a part of the dividend itself.

Liquidating dividends. Liquidating dividends are not distributions of earnings, but rather a return of capital to the investing shareholders. A liquidating dividend is normally recorded by charging additional paid-in capital rather than retained earnings. The exact accounting for a liquidating dividend is affected by the laws where the business is incorporated, and these laws vary from state to state.

Stock dividends. Stock dividends represent neither an actual distribution of the assets of the corporation nor a promise to distribute those assets. For this reason, a stock dividend is not considered a taxable transaction.

Despite the recognition that a stock dividend is not a distribution of earnings, the accounting treatment of relatively insignificant stock dividends (defined as being less than 20% to 25% of the outstanding shares prior to declaration) is consistent with it being a real dividend. Accordingly, retained earnings are debited for the fair market value of the shares to be paid as a dividend, and the capital stock and additional paid-in capital accounts are credited for the appropriate amounts based upon the par or stated value of the shares, if any. A stock dividend declared but not yet paid is classified as such in the stockholders' equity section of the balance sheet. Since such a dividend never reduces assets, it cannot be a liability.

The selection of 20% to 25% as the threshold for recognizing a stock dividend as an earnings distribution is arbitrary, but it is based somewhat on the empirical evidence that small stock dividends tend not to result in a reduced market price per share for outstanding shares. In theory, any stock dividend should result in a reduction of the market value of outstanding shares in an inverse relationship to the size of the stock dividend. The aggregate value of the outstanding shares should not change, but the greater number of shares outstanding after the stock dividend should necessitate a lower per share price. As noted, however, the declaration of small stock dividends tends not to have this impact, and this phenomenon supports the accounting treatment.

On the other hand, when stock dividends are larger in magnitude, it is observed that per share market value declines after the declaration of the dividend. In such situations, it would not be valid to treat the stock dividend as an earnings distribution, but rather it should be accounted for as a split. The precise treatment depends upon the legal requirements of the state of incorporation and upon whether the existing par value or stated value is reduced concurrent with the stock split.

If the par value is not reduced for a large stock dividend and if state law requires that earnings be capitalized in an amount equal to the aggregate of the par value of the stock dividend declared, then the event should normally be described as a stock split effected in the form of a dividend, with a charge to retained earnings and a credit to the common stock account for the aggregate par or stated value thereof. In other cases, where the par or stated value is reduced in recognition of the split and state laws do not require treatment as a dividend, there is no formal entry to record the split but merely a notation that the number of shares outstanding has increased and the per share par or stated value has decreased accordingly.

Treasury Stock

Treasury stock consists of a corporation's own stock which has been issued, subsequently reacquired by the firm and not yet reissued or cancelled. Treasury stock does not reduce the number of shares issued but does reduce the number of shares outstanding, as well as total stockholders' equity. These shares are not eligible to receive dividends of any sort. Treasury stock is **not** an asset although, in some circumstances, it may be presented as an asset if adequately disclosed (ARB 43, Ch. 1A). Reacquired stock which is awaiting delivery to satisfy a liability created by the firm's compensation plan or reacquired stock held in a profit-sharing trust is still considered outstanding and would not be considered treasury stock. In each case, the stock would be presented as an asset with the accompanying footnote disclosure. Accounting for excesses and deficiencies on treasury stock transactions is governed by ARB 43, Ch. 1B, and APB 6, paras 12 and 13.

Three approaches exist for the treatment of treasury stock: the **cost, par value,** and **constructive retirement** methods.

Cost method. Under the cost method, the gross cost of the shares reacquired is charged to a contra-equity account (treasury stock). The equity accounts which were credited for the original share issuance (common stock, paid-in capital in excess of par, etc.) remain intact. When the treasury shares are reissued, proceeds in excess of **cost** are credited to a paid-in capital account. Any deficiency is charged to retained earnings (unless paid-in capital from previous treasury share transactions exists, in which case the loss is charged to that account, with any excess charged to retained earnings). If many treasury stock purchases are made, a cost flow assumption (e.g., FIFO or specific identification) should be adopted to compute excesses and deficiencies upon subsequent share reissuances. The advantage of the cost method is that it avoids identifying and accounting for amounts related to the original issuance of the shares and is, therefore, the simpler, more frequently used method. The cost method is most consistent with the one-transaction concept. This concept takes the view that the classification of stockholders' equity should not be affected simply because the corporation was the middle "person" in an exchange of shares from one stockholder to another. In substance, there is only a transfer of shares between two stockholders. Since the original balances in the equity accounts are left undisturbed, its use is most acceptable when the firm acquires its stock for reasons other than retirement, or when its ultimate disposition has not yet been decided.

Par value method. Under the second approach, the par value method, the treasury stock account is charged only for the aggregate par (or stated) value of the shares reacquired. Other paid-in capital accounts (excess over par value, etc.) are relieved in proportion to the amounts recognized upon the original issuance of the shares. The treasury share acquisition is treated almost as a retirement. However, the common (or preferred) stock account continues at the original amount, thereby preserving the distinction between an actual retirement and a treasury share transaction.

When the treasury shares accounted for by the par value method are subsequently resold, the excess of the sale price over par value is credited to paid-in capital. A reissuance for a price **below** par value does not create a contingent liability for the purchaser. It is only the original purchaser who risks this obligation to the entity's creditors.

Constructive retirement method. The constructive retirement method is similar to the par value method, except that the aggregate par (or stated) value of the reacquired shares is charged to the stock account rather than to the treasury stock account. This method is superior when (1) it is management's intention not to reissue the shares within a reasonable time period or (2) the state of incorporation defines reacquired shares as having been retired. In the latter case, the constructive retirement method is probably the only method of accounting for treasury shares that is **not** inconsistent with the state Business Corporation Act, although the state law does not necessarily dictate such accounting. Certain states require that treasury stock be accounted for by this method.

The two-transaction concept is most consistent with the par value and constructive retirement methods. First, the reacquisition of the firm's shares is viewed as constituting a contraction of its capital structure. Second, the reissuance of the shares is the same as issuing new shares. There is little difference between the purchase and subsequent reissuance of treasury shares and the acquisition, retirement, and issuance of new shares.

Treasury shares originally accounted for by the cost method can subsequently be restated to conform to the constructive retirement method. If shares were acquired with the intention that they would be reissued and it is later determined that such reissuance is unlikely (due, for example, to the expiration of stock options without their exercise), then it is proper to restate the transaction.

Example of Accounting for Treasury Stock

Assume the following:

1. 100 shares ($50 par value) which were originally sold for $60 per share are later reacquired for $70 each.
2. All 100 shares are subsequently resold for a total of $7,500.

To record the acquisition, the entry is:

Cost method			Par value method			Constructive retirement method		
Treasury stock	7,000		Treasury stock	5,000		Common stock	5,000	
Cash		7,000	Additional paid-in			Additional paid-in		
			capital--common			capital-common		
			stock	1,000		stock	1,000	
			Retained earnings	1,000		Retained earnings	1,000	
			Cash		7,000	Cash		7,000

To record the resale, the entry is:

Cost method			Par value method			Constructive retirement method		
Cash	7,500		Cash	7,500		Cash	7,500	
Treasury stock		7,000	Treasury stock		5,000	Common stock		5,000
Additional paid-in			Additional paid-in			Additional paid-in		
capital--treasury			capital--common			capital--common		
stock		500	stock		2,500	stock		2,500

If the shares had been resold for $6,500, the entry is:

Cost method			Par value method			Constructive retirement method		
Cash	6,500		Cash	6,500		Cash	6,500	
*Retained earnings	500		Treasury stock		5,000	Common stock		5,000
Treasury stock		7,000	Additional paid-in			Additional paid-in		
			capital--common			capital--common		
			stock		1,500	stock		1,500

"Additional paid-in capital--treasury stock" or "Additional paid-in capital--retired stock" of that issue would be debited first to the extent it exists.

Alternatively, under the par or constructive retirement methods, any portion of or the **entire** loss on the treasury stock acquisition may be debited to retained earnings without allocation to paid-in capital. Any gains would always be credited to an "Additional paid-in capital--retired stock" account.

The laws of some states govern the circumstances under which a corporation may acquire treasury stock and may prescribe the accounting for the stock. For example, a charge to retained earnings may be required in an amount equal to the treasury stock's total cost. In such cases, the accounting per the state law prevails. Also, some states (including those that have adopted the Model Business Corporation Act) define excess purchase cost of reacquired (i.e., treasury) shares as being "distributions" to shareholders which are no different in nature than dividends. In such cases, the financial statement presentation should adequately disclose the substance of these transactions (e.g., by presenting both dividends and excess reacquisition costs together in the retained earnings statement).

When a firm decides to formally retire the treasury stock, the journal entry is dependent on the method used to account for the stock. Using the original sale and reacquisition data from the illustration above, the following entry would be made:

Cost method			*Par value method*		
Common stock	5,000		Common stock	5,000	
Additional paid-in			Treasury stock		5,000
capital--common stock	1,000				
*Retained earnings	1,000				
Treasury stock		7,000			

"Additional paid-in capital--treasury stock" may be debited to the extent it exists.

If the constructive retirement method were used to record the treasury stock purchase, no additional entry would be necessary upon the formal retirement of the shares.

After the entry is made, the pro rata portion of all paid-in capital existing for that issue (i.e., capital stock and additional paid-in capital) will have been eliminated. If stock is purchased for immediate retirement (i.e., not put into the treasury) the entry to record the retirement is the same as that made under the constructive retirement method.

In the case of donated treasury stock, the intentions of management are important. If the shares are to be retired, then the capital stock account is debited for the par or stated value of the shares, "Donated capital" is credited for the fair market value, and "Additional paid-in capital--retired stock" is debited for the difference. If the intention of management is to reissue the shares, then three methods of accounting are available. The first two methods, cost and par value, are analogous to the aforementioned treasury stock methods except that "Donated capital" is credited at the time of receipt and debited at the time of reissuance. Under the cost method, the current market value of the stock is recorded (an apparent contradiction), while under the par value method, the par or stated value is used. The last method is the memo method, where only a memorandum entry indicating the number of shares received is made. No journal entry is made at the time of receipt. At the time of reissuance, the entire proceeds are credited to "Donated capital." The method actually used is generally dependent on the circumstances involving the donation and the preference of the firm.

Other Equity Accounts

There are other adjustments to balance sheet accounts which are accumulated and reflected as separate components of stockholders' equity. At present, GAAP provides for three of the situations, relating respectively, to the accumulated unrealized **loss** on noncurrent marketable equity securities (SFAS 12); to the accumulated **gain or loss** on translation of foreign currency denominated financial statements (SFAS 52); and to the net loss not recognized as pension cost (SFAS 87).

Stock Options

Stock options allow employees the right to purchase common stock at a specified price over a stipulated period of time. The accounting requirements applicable to options are set forth in ARB 43, Ch. 13B and APB 25, and may be altered by the results of the FASB's current project, "Accounting for Compensation Plans Involving Certain Rights Granted to Employees." Two types of stock option plans exist: noncompensatory and compensatory. Noncompensatory plans spread ownership of the firm among its employees and raise equity capital. Conversely, compensatory plans compensate the employees for their services.

Noncompensatory plans. These are the most common and require no difficult entries since compensation expense does not exist. Exercise is simply accounted for as a normal issuance and is recorded at the option price. Accounting for noncompensatory plans will probably be altered by the FASB's current project on compensatory stock option plans. There is tentative agreement that the APB 25 criteria should not be retained.

Compensatory plans. Compensation expense is usually measured and recorded as the dollar value difference between the option price and the market price if the option price is below the market price. There is one exception to the foregoing statement: if shares are acquired (i.e., repurchased) specifically to be used to meet the requirements of a stock option plan and are delivered to option holders shortly thereafter, compensation cost is measured with reference to the share purchase cost instead of market value at the date of measurement.

For financial reporting purposes, compensation is measured on the measurement date--the date on which **both** the number of shares the individual employee is entitled to and the option or purchase price are known. The measurement date is usually, though not always, the date of grant (APB 25, para 10b). This date of grant was chosen as the date of measurement over others such as the date of the plan's adoption or the date the options were first exercised because at this date it may be presumed that the employer had a value in mind. This date also represents the date the corporation foregoes an alternative use of the shares placed under the option agreement.

Many options are granted at a price equal to or greater than the market price when the option is granted for a fixed number of shares. Thus, there is no compensation expense and no journal entry involving compensation expense is recorded. Disclosure, however, as to the options outstanding, is required. When the employee acquires stock under these circumstances, the corporation debits cash for the option price and credits common stock for par and paid-in capital for the difference.

If the measurement date is the grant date and deferred compensation is recorded, it is amortized over the periods in which the employee provides the services for which the option contract is the reward.

Example of Accounting for Stock Options--Measurement and Grant Date the Same

Assume an option is granted to a corporate officer to purchase 100 shares of $1 par common at $52 when the market price is $58. The entry to record the granting of the option is:

Deferred compensation expense	600	
Stock options outstanding		600

Deferred compensation expense is subtracted from stock options outstanding in the paid-in capital section of owner's equity to indicate the amount of net contributed services on any date [i.e., on the grant date nothing has yet been contributed by the option holder ($600 - 600 = $0)]. As the employee provides services to earn the option, an entry is made assigning compensation expense to years 1-5 (assuming a five-year period):

Compensation expense	120	($600 ÷ 5 years)
Deferred compensation expense	120	

When the option is exercised, cash is received and the stock is issued as reflected in the following entry (assume exercise after the five-year period):

Cash	5,200	(option price)
Stock options outstanding	600	
Common stock	100	(par)
Additional paid-in capital	5,700	(excess)

If the options are forfeited as a result of the employee failing to fulfill an obligation (e.g., staying with the company), compensation expense is credited in the year of forfeiture. The amount credited reflects the total compensation expense previously charged to the income statement for the employee who forfeited the options. In the above example, assume the officer leaves the company in year 3, two years before the options can be exercised. The result is handled as a change in an accounting estimate and the following entry is made in year 3:

Stock options outstanding	600	
Deferred compensation expense	360	
Compensation expense	240	

If the measurement date follows the grant date, it is necessary to assume compensation expense based on the market values of the common stock that exist at the end of each period until the measurement date is reached. Per FASB Interpretation 28, changes in the market value of stock between the date of grant and the measurement date are adjustments to compensation expense in **the period the market value of the stock changes**. The effect of such changes is **not** spread over future periods.

Example of Accounting for Stock Options--Measurement and Grant Date Different

1. On 1/1/X0, a company grants an option to purchase 100 shares of common stock at 90% of the market price at 12/31/X2 and that the compensation period is **four years**. The total compensation amount per share is represented by the difference between the current market price and the estimated purchase price granted by the option (90% x market price) or simply 10% of the current market price.
2. Observe that at 1/1/X0, the number of shares is determinable, but the option price is unknown.
3. The market values of the common stock are as follows:

12/31/X0	$10
12/31/X1	13
12/31/X2	15

The following entries for compensation expense are recorded:

	19X0	*19X1*	*19X2*	*19X3*
Compensation expense	25	40	47.50	37.50
Stock options outstanding	25	40	47.50	37.50

19X0: ($10 x 10% x 100 shares x 1/4) = $25

19X1: ($13 x 10% x 100 shares x 2/4) - expense recognized to date = $40

19X2: ($15 x 10% x 100 shares x 3/4) - expense recognized to date = $47.50

19X3: ($15 x 10% x 100 shares x 4/4) - expense recognized to date = $37.50

The expense recorded from 19X1 and 19X2 results from a change in estimate. Note that the market value of the stock at the end of 19X0 and 19X1 is used as the estimate of the market price of the stock at 12/31/X2 and that the total amount of compensation expense previously accrued is subtracted from the latest estimate of cumulative expense.

A time line depicting the actual and estimated compensation expense would appear as follows:

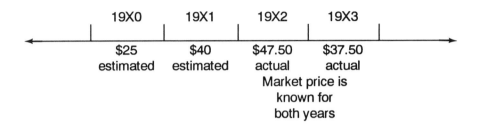

Stock Appreciation Rights

Stock appreciation rights (SARs) allow employees to receive stock or cash equal in amount to the difference between the market value and some predetermined amount per share for a certain number of shares. SARs allow employees to receive share appreciation without having to make the cash outlay that is usually required in stock option plans.

The accounting treatment for SARs is prescribed by FASB Interpretation 28. Compensation expense is recorded in each period prior to exercise based on the excess of the market value at the end of each period over the predetermined amount multiplied by the number of SARs outstanding. This excess represents the best estimate of the true compensation expense. Compensation expense is adjusted up or down as the market value of the stock changes before the measurement date (which is the exercise date). Therefore, compensation expense could be credited if the stock's market value drops from one period to the next. The total (estimated) compensation expense is allocated over the employee's period of service. Notice, however, that the allocation process for SARs is not like the deliberate allocation performed under stock option plans. Rather, it is a by-product of the volatile market price. If the market price never changes, the entire compensation expense resulting from the SARs would be recorded in the first year.

Example of Accounting for SARs

Assume the following:

1. A company grants 100 SARs, payable in cash, to an employee on 1/1/X1.
2. The predetermined amount for the SAR plan is $50 per right, and the market value of the stock is $55 on 12/31/X1, $53 on 12/31/X2, and $61 on 12/31/X3.

Compensation expense recorded in each year would be:

	Total expense		Expense previously accrued		Current expense
19X1 100($55-50) =	$ 500	-	$ 0	=	$ 500
19X2 100($53-50) =	$ 300	-	$500	=	$(200)
19X3 100($61-50) =	$1,100	-	$300	=	$ 800

The total expense recognized over the three-year period is $1,100 [100($61 - 50)]. The required journal entries would be as follows:

<table>
<tr><td colspan="3">19X1</td></tr>
<tr><td>Compensation expense</td><td>500</td><td></td></tr>
<tr><td>   Liability under SAR plan</td><td></td><td>500</td></tr>
<tr><td colspan="3">19X2</td></tr>
<tr><td>Liability under SAR plan</td><td>200</td><td></td></tr>
<tr><td>   Compensation expense</td><td></td><td>200</td></tr>
<tr><td colspan="3">19X3</td></tr>
<tr><td>Compensation expense</td><td>800</td><td></td></tr>
<tr><td>   Liability under SAR plan</td><td></td><td>800</td></tr>
</table>

If the SARs were to be redeemed in common stock, "Stock rights outstanding" (a paid-in capital account) would replace the liability account in the above entries.

The example assumes no service or vesting period, which is a period of time until the SARs become exercisable. If the above plan had a two-year service period, 50% of the total expense would be recognized at the end of the first year and 100% at the end of the second year and thereafter until exercise. The compensation would be accrued as follows:

$$19X1\ (\$\ 500\ x\ \ \ 50\%) = \$\ \ 250 - \ \ 0\ \ = \underline{\$250}$$
$$19X2\ (\$\ 300\ x\ 100\%) = \$\ \ 300 - 250 = \$\ \underline{\ 50}$$
$$19X3\ (\$1,100\ x\ 100\%) = \$1,100 - 300 = \underline{\$800}$$

Often stock option plans and SARs are combined, thus making accounting for them more complex. On the basis of the available facts each period, a determination must be made as to which one of the compensation plans has the higher likelihood of exercise. Once determined, this is the plan accounted for with the other plan being ignored. In the absence of evidence to the contrary, however, the presumption is that the SARs, not the options, will be exercised.

Example of Accounting for a Combined Stock Option and Stock Appreciation Rights

To illustrate the accounting for a combined SAR and stock option plan, consider the following facts:

1/1/X1   Plan adopted; market price is $100, option price is $95; 1,000 shares exercisable on 1/1/X5 **or** 1,000 SARs payable in cash on 1/1/X5 on increase over 1/1/X1 market value.

Market prices are as follows:

12/31/X1	$ 98
12/31/X2	110
12/31/X3	108
12/31/X4	125

Two cases are presented simultaneously, representing two alternative fact situations.

Case 1:   It is assumed that only SARs will be exercised.

Case 2:   It is assumed that 1/2 SARs, 1/2 options will be exercised.

The appropriate journal entries are as follows:

	Case 1		*Case 2*		
12/31/X1	No entry		Compensation expense	625	
			Deferred compensation	1,875	
			Stock options out-		
			standing		
			(500 shares x $5)		2,500

Compensation expense is 1/4 of projected four-year total relating to expected option exercise in Case 2.

No SAR liability is accrued since the market price is below the base price.

	Case 1			*Case 2*		
12/31/X2	Compensation expense	10,000		Compensation expense	5,625	
	Liability under SAR			Deferred compensation		625
	plan ($10 x			Liability under SAR plan		
	1,000 SARs)		10,000	($10 x 500 SARs)		5,000

Deferred compensation relating to options amortized ratably over option period ($2,500 x 1/4).

SAR liability recognized for difference between year-end market value and base price for number of expected SARs exercisable.

12/31/X3	Liability under SAR			Liability under SAR plan	1,000	
	plan	2,000		Compensation expense		375
	Compensation ex-			Deferred compensation		625
	pense		2,000			
12/31/X4	Compensation expense	17,000		Compensation expense	9,125	
	Liability under SAR			Deferred compensation		625
	plan		17,000	Liability under SAR plan		
				($12,500 - $5,000 + $1,000)		8,500

The option holders may exercise either the options or the SARs in ratios other than those presumed as the basis for the accounting. Assume that either (a) holders elect 100% SARs; (b) holders elect 50% SARs, 50% stock; or (c) they elect to exercise only the stock options. For each of the cases above, the entries under each assumed exercise ratio are as follows:

	Case 1			*Case 2*		
(a)	Liability under SAR			Liability under SAR		
(all cash)	plan	25,000		plan	12,500	
	Cash		25,000	Stock options		
				outstanding	2,500	
				Compensation expense	10,000	
				Cash		25,000

	Account	Debit	Credit	Account	Debit	Credit
(b) (1/2 cash, 1/2 stock)	Liability under SAR plan	25,000		Liability under SAR plan	12,500	
	Cash ($47,500 - $12,500)	35,000		Stock options outstanding	2,500	
	Common stock--			Cash	35,000	
	$20 par		10,000	Common Stock--$20 par		10,000
	Additional paid-in capital		50,000	Additional paid-in capital		40,000
(c) (all stock)	Liability under SAR plan	25,000		Liability under SAR plan	12,500	
	Cash	95,000		Stock option outstanding	2,500	
	Common stock--			Cash	95,000	
	$20 par		20,000	Common stock--$20 par		20,000
	Additional paid-in capital		100,000	Additional paid-in capital		90,000

Notice that the proceeds of the stock issuance vary. When stock options are exercised but SARs were accrued, the cost of the shares includes the accrued SAR liability. On the other hand, when the expectation was that options would be exercised but SARs are exercised instead, additional compensation expense will be recorded (as in Case 2a). Since this is due to a change in estimate and not an accounting error, no prior period adjustment can be recorded.

An additional complication arises when the **vesting** is not immediate, as assumed here, but is partial over the years of the option/SAR plans. In such cases, the amount of compensation expense and/or liability under the SAR plan is based on the fraction of vesting at each reporting period. This has the effect of deferring much of the cost to later periods.

Essentially the same accounting procedures are employed for interim financial reporting. If in subsequent periods the presumed ratio of SAR exercise to stock option exercise in combination (or tandem) plans changes, compensation expense accrued in connection with the anticipated SAR exercise is **not** reduced even though the expected number of SARs to be exercised is diminished. On the other hand, a reduced expectation of stock option exercise may result in a reversal of compensation expense.

The expense recorded for compensation is deductible for tax purposes. The deduction is limited to the amount the employees record as income and is allowed in the period in which it is included in their taxable income. The amount of the compensation expense deduction used in computing the firm's taxable income may be different from the amount used in determining book income. This difference can be broken down into two sources. First, the compensation expense may be deductible for tax purposes in a period other than the period in which it is recorded as an expense for book purposes. The book expense is recorded during the period the employees perform the related services. For tax purposes, the expense may be deducted at the exercise date if the stock option had no ascertainable value at the date of grant. If, on the other hand, the stock option had an ascertainable value at the date of grant then the tax compensation deduction exists at the grant date. This portion of the difference results in a temporary difference.

The other source is similar to a permanent difference and arises from the difference between the total compensation expense recorded for book purposes and the total deduction taken for tax purposes in each period. This difference results because the measured compensation for book purposes (market value minus the option price at the measurement date) is not likely to equal the allowable tax deduction (market value minus the option price at the exercise date) due to price fluctuations in the stock between the two dates. When this source of the difference exists and the allowable compensation tax deduction is greater than the related expense, the tax effect of the difference is credited to a separate paid-in capital account. The FASB Implementation Group has taken the position that it would not be feasible to estimate the deductions the company would get if all nonqualified options were exercised at the market price on the balance sheet date due to the difficulty of making assumptions concerning the intentions of the option holders. Thus, the accounting prescribed by APB 25 remains in effect. Conversely, if the deduction is lower than the expense, paid-in capital is debited to the extent it exists from previous credits (APB 25, para 17). If the paid-in capital account does not exist or is not sufficient enough to absorb these debits, it would seem most appropriate to reduce retained earnings for the amount not charged to paid-in capital. This treatment is similar to that accorded treasury stock and stock retirements in certain instances. No guidance is provided by the Opinion.

Example of Accounting for the Tax Ramifications of Stock Options

An option to purchase 10 shares at $80 per share is granted to a key employee when the market price is $100 per share. The following entry is made to record the deferred compensation:

Deferred compensation expense	200	[10 x ($100 - 80)]
Stock options outstanding	200	

Compensation is associated with employee service in years 1-4. The annual entry to recognize the expense is:

Compensation expense	50
Deferred compensation expense	50

Assume the tax rate remains constant at 40% and income before stock option compensation expense for years 1-5 is $400. The compensation expense is not deductible for tax purposes until the option is exercised. The entry to record the taxes and tax effects for years 1-4 is:

Tax expense	140
Deferred tax asset	20
Tax payable	160

Recognition of the deferred tax asset is subject to the restrictions of SFAS 96 as explained in Chapter 14. In year 5, the options are exercised at the option price of

$80 per share when the market price per share is $115. Thus, the compensation expense deductible for tax purposes in year 5 is $350 [10 shares x ($115 - 80)]. No additional compensation expense is allowed as a deduction in the determination of net income. The result is a permanent difference of $150 ($350 - 200). The current year tax expense is $160 ($400 x 40%). The current year taxes payable is $20 [($400 - 350) x 40%]. The $140 difference represents the tax effects of the $200 reversing temporary difference ($80) and the $150 permanent difference ($60). The journal entry is as follows:

Tax expense	160	
Paid-in capital		60
Deferred tax asset		80
Tax payable		20

Convertible Preferred Stock

The treatment of convertible preferred stock at its issuance is no different than that of nonconvertible preferred. When it is converted, the book value approach is used to account for the conversion. Use of the market value approach would entail a gain or loss for which there is no theoretical justification since the total amount of contributed capital does not change when the stock is converted. When the preferred stock is converted, the "Preferred stock" and related "Additional paid-in capital--preferred stock" accounts are debited for their original values when purchased, and "Common stock" and "Additional paid-in capital--common stock" (if an excess over par or stated value exists) are credited. If the book value of the preferred stock is less than the total par value of the common stock being issued, retained earnings is charged for the difference. This charge is supported by the rationale that the preferred shareholders are offered an additional return to facilitate their conversion to common stock. Many states require that this excess instead reduce additional paid-in capital from other sources.

Preferred Stock With Mandatory Redemption

A mandatory redemption clause requires the preferred stock to be redeemed (retired) at a specified date(s). This feature is in contrast to callable preferred stock, which is redeemed at the issuing corporation's option.

The mandatory redemption feature, when combined with a cumulative dividend preference, causes the preferred stock to have characteristics much like debt, especially when the stock is to be redeemed in 5-10 years. The dividend payments represent interest and redemption is the repayment of principal. However, there is one important difference. The dividend payments do not receive the same tax treatment as interest payments. They are not deductible in determining taxable income.

Despite these debt-like characteristics, this class of preferred stock currently receives no special treatment under GAAP. It is treated as any other stock upon issuance and, upon redemption, the stock is treated as an ordinary retirement.

For disclosure purposes, the stock is treated as equity and it is presented within the stockholders' equity portion of the balance sheet. Note that this presentation puts legal form over substance, which is in contrast with SFAC 2's qualitative characteristic of representational faithfulness. SFAS 47, however, does require disclosure of the amounts and timing of any redemption payments for each of the five years following the balance sheet date.

The SEC, conversely, does recognize the debt characteristics of mandatory redeemable preferred stock. According to ASR No. 268, the stock may not be presented under the heading "Stockholders' Equity." Rather, the amounts pertaining to this type of stock may be presented either as long-term debt or between long-term debt and stockholders' equity.

Note that neither GAAP nor the SEC have completely considered the full effect of this issue. A question of the proper treatment of the dividend payments exists. To be consistent with the representational faithfulness concept, the dividend payments should be charged to operations much like interest expense. Additionally, there is the conceptual question of the treatment of the redeemable stock (equity vs. liability, including current maturities).

Book Value Stock Plans

The EITF (88-6) concluded that book value stock plans of public companies should be considered performance plans and should be accounted for like SARs. The SEC staff will require the redemption amount of the book value stock to be presented outside stockholders' equity on the balance sheet (similar to redeemable preferred stock) if there are any conditions under which the company must redeem the stock with the payment of cash.

Put Warrant

A detachable put warrant can either be put back to the debt issuer for cash or can be exercised to acquire common stock. The Emerging Issues Task Force has concluded (EITF 88-9) that these instruments should be accounted for in the same manner as mandatory redeemable preferred stock. The proceeds applicable to the put warrant ordinarily are to be classified as equity and should be presented between the liability and equity sections in accordance with SEC ASR 268.

In the case of a warrant with a put price substantially higher than the value assigned to the warrant at issuance, however, the proceeds should be classified as a liability since it is likely that the warrant will be put back to the company.

The original **classification** should not be changed because of subsequent economic changes in the value of the put. The value assigned to the put warrant at issuance, however, should be adjusted to its highest redemption price, starting with the date of issuance until the earliest date of the warrants. Changes in the redemption price before the earliest put dates are changes in accounting estimates and changes after the earliest put dates should be recognized in income. If the put is classified as equity, the adjustment should be reported as a charge to retained earnings, and if the put is classified as a liability the adjustment is reported as interest expense.

Regardless of how the put is classified on the balance sheet, the primary and fully diluted EPS should be calculated on both an equity basis (warrants will be exercised) and on a debt basis (put will be exercised) and the more dilutive of the two methods should be used.

Corporate Bankruptcy and Reorganizations

The going concern assumption is one of the basic principles underlying the primary financial statements (Balance Sheet, Income Statement, and Statement of Cash Flows). However, this assumption of continued existence is threatened in corporations that are in severe financial trouble.

In bankruptcy, the accounting and financial reporting must present the information necessary for the liquidation of the business. A **Statement of Affairs** is compiled which presents the current market or liquidation values of the firm's assets. These values become the most relevant measure as the firm enters bankruptcy since the historical cost values are relevant only in cases where the going concern assumption applies. The statement also presents, in order of preference, the status of the various categories of the claims on these assets, i.e., secured, partially secured, and unsecured. The legal rights of each creditor are determined by the terms of the credit agreement each has with the company and by the National Bankruptcy Act. In addition, the anticipated costs of liquidation should be recognized.

The Statement of Affairs begins with the present book values of the company's assets. After relating the projected proceeds from the liquidation of the assets to the various equity interests, the statement concludes with the estimated dollar amount of unsecured claims that cannot be paid (the estimated deficiency). Stockholders' equity balances generally have no significance in this statement.

The existence of severe financial troubles does not mean bankruptcy proceedings should automatically be initiated. The troubles a firm is experiencing may be due to overvalued assets, which when taken to the income statement (in the form of depreciation, cost of goods sold, etc.) cause large losses and possibly an accumulated deficit in retained earnings. The deficit precludes the payment of dividends. The firm will now find it harder to raise outside funds. When the troubles are not due to net negative cash flows or operational difficulties, such as the situation described above, a **quasi-reorganization** may be more appropriate.

Quasi-reorganization. Generally, this procedure is applicable during a period of declining price levels. It is termed "quasi" since the accumulated deficit is eliminated at a lower cost and with less difficulty than a legal reorganization.

Per ARB 43, Ch. 7A, the procedures in a quasi-reorganization involve the:

1. Proper authorization from stockholders and creditors where required
2. Revaluation of assets to their current values. All losses are charged to retained earnings, thus increasing any deficit.
3. Elimination of any deficit by charging paid-in capital

    a. First, additional paid-in capital to the extent it exists

b. Second, capital stock when additional paid-in capital is insufficient. The par value of the stock is reduced, creating the extra additional paid-in capital to which the remaining deficit is charged.

No retained earnings may be created by a reorganization. Any excess created by the reduction of par value is credited to "Paid-in capital from quasi-reorganization."

ARB 46, para 2 requires that retained earnings be dated for 10 years (less than 10 years may be justified under exceptional circumstances) after a quasi-reorganization takes place. Disclosure similar to "since quasi-reorganization of June 30, 19XX" is appropriate.

Disclosures

The stockholders' equity section of the balance sheet provides information to interested parties concerning the stewardship function and the efficiency of the firm's management. In addition, it provides information concerning the historical and prospective economic interests of the groups holding a specific or general interest in the firm. The following should be disclosed:

1. The sources of capital supplied to the firm
2. The legal restrictions on the distribution of invested capital
3. The legal, contractual, managerial, and financial restrictions on the distribution of dividends to stockholders
4. The priorities of the classes of stockholders in a partial or final liquidation

Capital Stock and Additional Paid-in Capital

1. For each class of stock

    a. Par, stated, or assigned value
    b. Number of shares authorized, issued, and outstanding
    c. Number of shares held in treasury
    d. Conversion terms of preferred, if applicable, including call prices, rates, and dates. Additionally, the amount of redemption requirements for all issues of stock that are redeemable at fixed or determinable prices on fixed or determinable dates must be disclosed for each of the five years following the date of the latest balance sheet presented.
    e. Changes in the number of shares authorized, issued, and outstanding during the year and changes in the equity accounts
    f. Liquidation values, if different than par, in the aggregate for preferred
    g. For preferred, any dividend preferences, special privileges, etc.
    h. Any unusual voting rights

2. The amount of cumulative dividends in arrears, per share and in aggregate
3. Aggregate securities issuable under rights or warrants, as well as their prices, and exercise and expiration dates
4. Any discount on capital stock
5. The amount of subscribed shares not yet issued

6. Deferred compensation expense offset against the paid-in capital account, "Stock options outstanding" (see 23)
7. Stock dividends distributable in total or at par or stated value with the excess included in additional paid-in capital. Also acceptable is deferment of their recording until issuance. However, disclosure is necessary in the notes.
8. The amount of capital stock issued in business combinations (purchase or pooling) or agreements to issue additional shares at a later date
9. Transactions affecting equity subsequent to the date of the financial statements (recapitalization, sales of stock, etc.)
10. Additional paid-in capital, listed by source, along with any changes during the period
11. Any changes in the capital accounts of partners or sole proprietors

Retained Earnings

12. Appropriation and segregation of retained earnings should be disclosed in the equity section, as well as their nature, cause, and amount. Changes in these accounts should be disclosed.
13. Nature and dollar amounts of restrictions on retained earnings (treasury stock, lease covenants, etc.)
14. Date retained earnings for 10 years following quasi-reorganization
15. Increase/decrease results from combination by pooling of interests (revenues, expenses, extraordinary items, and net income)
16. Prior period adjustments, net of tax and in gross. For correction of an error, in the period discovered:

   a. Nature of the error on previous statements
   b. Effect of correction on income before extraordinary items, net income, and related per share amounts

Dividends

17. Dividends in aggregate and per share as well as the nature and extent of any restrictions on retained earnings limiting availability of dividends
18. The amount of dividends in arrears, per share and in aggregate
19. Dividends declared after balance sheet date, prior to opinion date, should be disclosed unless a long-established history of regular payment dates exists and the dividend is not abnormal in amount
20. For stock dividends and stock splits, disclosure of the amounts capitalized, per share and in total. Historical presentations of earnings per share should be restated in an equivalent number of shares so the figures are presented on a comparable basis.

Treasury Stock

21. Treasury stock, cost method: Present total cost of treasury stock as a deduction from total stockholders' equity. Disclose number of shares held in treasury.

22. Treasury stock, par value method: Present par value of treasury stock as a deduction from par value of issued shares of same class. Any related additional paid-in capital from treasury stock is netted with corresponding additional paid-in capital without separate disclosure. Disclose number of shares held in treasury.

Compensatory Stock Plans

23. The net earned compensation under a stock option plan, presented as additional paid-in capital. For example:

Stock options outstanding	xx
Less deferred compensation expense	(xx)
	xx

24. Stock purchase and stock option plans--as a minimum, the following should be disclosed:

    a. Status of the plan at balance sheet date

       1) Number of shares under option
       2) Option price
       3) Number of shares as to which options were exercisable

    b. Activity during period as to

       1) Number of shares involved in options exercised
       2) Option price of shares exercised

    c. Transactions after balance sheet date but prior to issuance of report should be disclosed in the notes.

25. Stock appreciation rights--parallels requirements for stock purchase and stock option plans

APPENDIX

Financial Statement Presentation

This appendix provides an illustration of the various financial statements which may be required to be presented and are related to the stockholders' equity section of the balance sheet.

Stockholders' Equity Section of a Balance Sheet (figures assumed)

Capital stock:

Preferred stock, $100 par, 7% cumulative, 30,000 shares authorized, issued, and outstanding		$ 3,000,000
Common stock, no par, stated value $10 per share, 500,000 shares authorized, 415,000 shares issued		4,150,000
Total capital stock		$ 7,150,000
Additional paid-in capital:		
Issued price in excess of par value--preferred	$ 150,000	
Issued price in excess of stated value--common	845,000	995,000
Total paid-in capital		$ 8,145,000
Donated capital		100,000
Retained earnings:		
Appropriated for plant expansion	$2,100,000	
Unappropriated	2,275,000	4,375,000
Total capital and retained earnings		$12,620,000
Less 10,000 common shares held in treasury, at cost		(120,000)
Total stockholders' equity		$12,500,000

Retained Earnings Statement

Statement of Retained Earnings
(figures assumed)

Balance at beginning of year, as reported	$ 3,800,000
Prior period adjustment - correction of an error in method of depreciation (less tax effect of $77,000)	115,000
Balance at beginning of year, restated	$ 3,915,000
Net income for the year	748,000
Cash dividends declared during the year	
Preferred stock	(210,000)
Common stock	(78,000)
Balance at end of year	$ 4,375,000

Statement of Changes in Stockholders' Equity (including Retained Earnings Statement) (figures assumed)

	Preferred stock		Common stock		Additional paid-in capital	Donated capital	Retained earnings	Treasury stock (common)	Total stockholders' equity
	Shares	Amount	Shares	Amount					
Balance, 12/31/X0, as reported	--	--	400,000	$4,000,000	$840,000	$100,000	$3,800,000	$(120,000)	$ 8,620,000
Correction of an error in method of depr.	--	--	--	--	--	--	115,000	--	115,000
Balance, 12/31/X0, restated	--	--	400,000	$4,000,000	$840,000	$100,000	$3,915,000	$(120,000)	$ 8,735,000
Preferred stock issued in public offering	30,000	$3,000,000	--	--	150,000	--	--	--	3,150,000
Stock options exercised	--	--	15,000	150,000	5,000	--	--	--	155,000
Net income	--	--	--	--	--	--	748,000	--	748,000
Cash dividends declared:									
Preferred, $7.00 per share	--	--	--	--	--	--	(210,000)	--	(210,000)
Common, $.20 per share	--	--	--	--	--	--	(78,000)	--	(78,000)
Balance, 12/31/X1	30,000	$3,000,000	415,000	$4,150,000	$995,000	$100,000	$4,375,000	$(120,000)	$12,500,000

17 Earnings Per Share

Perspective and Issues

Earnings per share (EPS) is an index which is widely used by both actual and prospective investors to gauge the profitability of a corporation. Its purpose is to indicate how effective an enterprise has been in using the resources provided by common shareholders. In its simplest form, EPS is net income (loss) divided by the number of shares of outstanding common stock. The EPS computation becomes difficult with existence of securities that are not common stock but have the potential of causing additional shares of common stock to be issued (e.g., convertible preferred stock or convertible debt, and options or warrants). The computation of an EPS number which ignores these potentially dilutive securities can be very misleading. In addition, a lack of standardization in the way in which these securities are included in an EPS computation makes comparisons among corporations extremely difficult.

The profession's first attempt to provide guidance in this area was Accounting Research Bulletin 49 (1958). However, this pronouncement was generally ignored, and most firms still computed EPS by dividing net income minus preferred stock dividends by a weighted-average of the number of common shares outstanding. The distortion inherent in an EPS number computed without regard for potentially dilutive securities was highlighted by the merger and acquisition activity of the 1960s. Many of these mergers, which resulted in larger earnings for the combined entity, were accomplished by the issuance of convertible securities, options, or warrants and by the retirement of the common stock of the merged company. Thus, an entity which disregarded outstanding dilutive securities when computing EPS could show an increase in EPS without a corresponding increase in profitability. The increase was due to larger combined earnings being divided by a smaller number of common shares.

APB 9 (1966) advised corporations with potentially dilutive securities (convertible preferred stock, convertible debt, or outstanding options or warrants) that if "potential dilution was material, supplementary pro forma computations of earnings per share should be furnished, showing what the earnings would be if conversions or contingent issuances took place."

APB 15 (1969) expanded and more clearly defined those securities which have the potential to dilute EPS, provided more specific guidance in computational matters, and delineated the correct reporting and display requirements. This opinion is not applicable to nonprofit corporations, government-owned corporations, registered investment companies, mutual companies without common stock or common stock equivalents, or nonpublic enterprises as defined in SFAS 21. However, if any of these entities present EPS information, it must be prepared and displayed in conformity with the requirements of APB 15.

Sources of GAAP

APB	*SFAS*	*FASB I*	*FASB TB*	*AICPA AIN*
15, 30	21, 55, 85	28, 31	79-8	15, 20

Definitions of Terms

There are a number of terms used in discussion of earnings per share which have special meanings in that context. When used, they are intended to have the meanings given in the following definitions.

Antidilution. An increase in earnings per share or reduction in net loss per share resulting from the inclusion of a potentially dilutive security in EPS calculations.

Call price. The amount at which a security may be redeemed by the issuer at the issuer's option.

Common stock. A stock which is subordinate to all other stocks of the issuer.

Common stock equivalent. A security which, because of its terms or the circumstances under which it was issued, is in substance equivalent to common stock.

Contingent issuance. A possible issuance of shares of common stock that is dependent upon the exercise of conversion rights, options or warrants, the satisfaction of certain conditions, or similar arrangements.

Conversion price. The price that determines the number of shares of common stock into which a security is convertible. For example, $100 face value of debt convertible into 5 shares of common stock would be stated to have a conversion price of $20.

Conversion rate. The ratio of (a) the number of common shares issuable upon conversion to (b) a unit of convertible security. For example, a preferred stock may be convertible at the rate of 3 shares of common stock for each share of preferred stock.

Conversion value. The current market value of the common shares obtainable upon conversion of a convertible security, after deducting any cash payment required upon conversion.

Dilution (Dilutive). A reduction in earnings per share or an increase in net loss per share resulting from the assumption that convertible securities have been converted or that options and warrants have been exercised or other shares have been issued upon the fulfillment of certain conditions.

Dual presentation. The presentation with equal prominence of two types of earnings per share amounts on the face of the income statement--one is primary earnings per share; the other is fully diluted earnings per share.

Earnings per share. The amount of earnings attributable to each share of common stock. For convenience, the term is used in APB 15 to refer to either net income (earnings) per share or net loss per share. It should be used without qualifying language only when no potentially dilutive convertible securities, options, warrants, or other agreements providing for contingent issuances of common stock are outstanding.

Effective yield. The implicit or market value rate reflected in the transaction at the date of issuance. The effective yield test modifies the cash yield test by including any original issuance premiums or discount and any call premium or discount in the computation of the yield rate. For convertible bonds, this rate is their market rate of interest at the time of issuance. For preferred stock, the effective and cash yield is the cash received by the holder of the stock as a distribution of accumulated or current earnings or as a contractual payment for return on the amount invested, without regard to the par of the stock. For example, 4% preferred stock (par $100) and a market value of $80 at issuance would have an effective and cash yield of 5% (4% of $100 is $4 ÷ 80 = 5%).

Exercise price. The amount that must be paid for a share of common stock upon exercise of a stock option or warrant.

Fully diluted earnings per share. The amount of current earnings per share reflecting the maximum dilutions that would have resulted from conversions, exercises, and other contingent issuances that individually would have decreased earnings per share and in the aggregate would have had a dilutive effect. All such issuances are assumed to have taken place at the beginning of the period (or at the time the contingency arose, if later).

If-converted method. A method of computing earnings per share data that assumes conversion of convertible securities as of the beginning of the earliest period reported (or at time of issuance, if later).

Investment value. The price at which it is estimated a convertible security would sell if it were not convertible, based upon its stipulated preferred dividend or interest rate and its other senior security characteristics.

Market parity. A market price relationship in which the market price of a convertible security and its conversion value are approximately equal.

Option. The right to purchase shares of common stock in accordance with an agreement upon payment of a specified amount, including but not limited to options granted to and stock purchase agreements entered into with employees. Options are considered "securities" in APB 15.

Primary earnings per share. The amount of earnings attributable to each share of common stock outstanding, including common stock equivalents.

Redemption price. The amount at which a security is required to be redeemed at maturity or under a sinking fund arrangement.

Security. The evidence of a debt or ownership or related right. For purposes of APB 15, it includes stock options and warrants, as well as debt and stock.

Senior security. A security having preferential rights and which is not a common stock or common stock equivalent, e.g., nonconvertible preferred stock.

Supplementary earnings per share. A computation of earnings per share, other than primary or fully diluted earnings per share, which gives effect to conversions, etc., that took place during the period or shortly thereafter as though they had occurred at the beginning of the period (or date of issuance, if later).

Time of issuance. The time of issuance generally is the date when agreement as to terms has been reached and announced, even though such agreement is subject to certain further actions, such as directors' or stockholders' approval.

Treasury stock method. A method of recognizing the use of proceeds that would be obtained upon exercise of options and warrants in computing earnings per share. It assumes that any proceeds would be used to purchase common stock at current market prices.

Two-class method. A method of computing earnings per share that treats common stock equivalents as though they were common stocks with different dividend rates from that of the common stock.

Warrant. A security giving the holder the right to purchase shares of common stock in accordance with the terms of the instrument, usually upon payment of a specified amount.

Weighted-average number of shares. The number of shares determined by relating (a) the portion of time within a reporting period that a particular number of shares of a certain security has been outstanding to (b) the total time in that period. For example, if 100 shares of a certain security were outstanding during the first quarter of a fiscal year and 300 shares were outstanding during the balance of the year, the weighted-average number of outstanding shares would be 250[(100 x 1/4) + (300 x 3/4)].

Concepts, Rules, and Examples

Simple Capital Structure

According to APB 15, simple capital structures are those that "either consist of only common stock or include no potentially dilutive securities, options, warrants, or other rights that upon conversion or exercise could in the aggregate dilute earnings per common share." Dilutive securities are essentially those that exhibit the rights of debtholders (including warrants and options) and which have the potential upon their issuance to reduce the earnings per share. APB 15 also indicates that the capital structure is still simple if these dilutive securities exist, but their exercise would result in a reduction in the EPS amount of less than 3%. If the dilutive effect of these securities is greater than 3%, the capital structure is considered to be complex.

Computational guidelines. In its simplest form the EPS calculation is net income divided by the weighted-average number of common shares outstanding. The objective of the EPS calculation is to determine the amount of earnings available to each common share which provided capital to generate the earnings. Complexities arise because net income does not necessarily represent the earnings available to the common shareholder, and a simple weighted-average of common shares outstanding does not necessarily reflect the true nature of the situation.

Numerator. The net income figure used as the numerator in any of the EPS computations must reflect any claims against it by **senior securities**. The justification for this reduction is that the claims of the senior securities must be satisfied before any income is available to the common shareholder. These securities are usually in the form of preferred stock, and the deduction from income is the amount of the dividend declared during the year on the preferred stock. If the preferred stock is cumulative, the dividend is to be deducted from income (added to the loss) whether it is declared or not. Dividends in arrears do not affect the calculation of EPS in the current period as they have been included in the prior periods. However, the amount in arrears should be disclosed, as should all of the effects of the rights given to senior securities on the EPS calculation.

Denominator. The weighted-average computation is used so that "the effect of increases or decreases in outstanding shares of EPS data is related to the portion of the period during which the consideration affected operations" (APB 15, para 27). The difficulty in computing the weighted-average exists because of the effect that various transactions have on the computation of common shares outstanding. While it is impossible to analyze all the possibilities, APB 15 provides discussion of some of the more common transactions affecting the number of common shares outstanding. The theoretical construct set forth in these relatively simple examples is to be followed in all other situations.

If a **company reacquires its stock** (treasury stock), the number of shares reacquired should be excluded from their date of acquisition. The same theory holds for the issuance of common stock during the period. The number of shares newly issued is included only in the computation for the period after their issuance date. The logic for this treatment is that the consideration for the shares was not available to generate earnings until the shares were issued. This same logic applies to the reacquired shares because the consideration relative to those shares was no longer available to generate earnings after the acquisition date.

A **stock dividend or split** does not generate additional consideration, but it does increase the number of shares outstanding. APB 15 states that the increase in shares as a result of a stock split or dividend, or decrease in shares as a result of a reverse split, should be given retroactive recognition as an appropriate equivalent charge for all periods presented. Thus, even if a stock dividend or split occurs at the end of the period, it is considered outstanding for the entire period of **each** period presented. The reasoning is that a stock dividend or split has no effect on the ownership percentage of the common stockholder. As such, to show a dilution in the EPS reported would erroneously give the impression of a decline in profitability when in fact it was merely an increase in the shares outstanding due to the stock dividend or split. APB 15 carries this one step further by requiring the retroactive adjustment of outstanding shares for stock dividends or splits occurring after the end of the period, but before the release of the report. The reason given is that the primary interest of the financial statement user is considered to be the current capitalization. If this situation occurs, disclosure of both the end-of-year outstanding shares and those used to compute EPS is required.

Complications also arise when a **business combination** occurs during the period. The treatment of the additional shares depends upon the nature of the combination. If the business combination is recorded as a pooling of interests, then the additional shares are assumed to have been issued at the beginning of the year, regardless of when the combination occurred. Conversely, if the combination is accounted for as a purchase, the shares are considered issued and outstanding as of the date of acquisition. The reason for this varied treatment lies in the income statement treatment accorded a pooling and a purchase. In a pooling, the income of the acquired company is included in the statements for the entire year, whereas in a purchase, the income is included only for the period after acquisition.

WEIGHTED-AVERAGE (W/A) COMPUTATION

Transaction	*Effect on W/A Computation*
• Common stock outstanding at the beginning of the period	• Increase number of shares outstanding by the number of shares
• Issuance of common stock during the period	• Increase number of shares outstanding by the number of shares issued times the portion of the year outstanding
• Conversion into common stock	• Increase number of shares outstanding by the number of shares converted times the portion of the year outstanding
• Company reacquires its stock	• Decrease number of shares outstanding by number of shares reacquired times portion of the year outstanding
• Stock dividend or split	• Increase number of shares outstanding by number of shares issued or increased due to the split
• Reverse split	• Decrease number of shares outstanding by decrease in shares
• Pooling of interest	• Increase number of shares outstanding by number of shares issued
• Purchase	• Increase number of shares outstanding by number of shares issued times portion of year since acquisition

---

These do not characterize all of the possible complexities arising in the EPS computation; however, most of the others occur under a complex structure. The complications arising under a complex capital structure are discussed in detail later in this chapter. The illustration below applies the foregoing concepts to a simple capital structure.

Example of EPS Computation--Simple Capital Structure

Assume the following information:

Numerator information		*Denominator information*	
a.	Income from continuing operations before extra-ordinary items $130,000	a.	Common shares outstanding 1/1/92 100,000
b.	Extraordinary loss (net of tax) 30,000	b.	Shares issued for cash 4/1 20,000
c.	Net income 100,000	c.	Shares issued in 10% stock dividend declared in July 12,000
d.	6% cumulative preferred stock, $100 par, 1,000 shrs. issued and outstanding 100,000	d.	Shares of treasury stock purchased 10/1 10,000

When calculating the amount of the numerator, the claims of senior securities (i.e., preferred stock) should be deducted to arrive at the earnings attributable to common shareholders. In this example, the preferred stock is cumulative. Thus, regardless of whether or not the board of directors declares a preferred dividend, holders of the preferred stock have a claim of $6,000 (1,000 shares x $100 x 6%) against 1992 earnings. Therefore, $6,000 must be deducted from the numerator to arrive at the net income attributable to common shareholders. Note that any cumulative preferred dividends in arrears are ignored in computing this period's EPS since they would have been incorporated into previous periods' EPS calculations. Also note that this $6,000 would have been deducted for **non**cumulative preferred only if a dividend of this amount had been declared during the period.

The EPS calculations follow:

Earnings per common share:

On income from continuing operations before extraordinary item

$$\frac{\$130,000 - 6,000}{\text{Common stock outstanding}}$$

On net income

$$\frac{\$100,000 - 6,000}{\text{Common shares outstanding}}$$

The computation of the denominator is based upon the weighted-average number of common shares outstanding. Recall that a simple weighted-average is not considered appropriate because of the various complexities. The table below illustrates one way of computing the weighted-average number of shares outstanding.

Table I

Item	Number of shares actually outstanding	Fraction of the year outstanding	Shares times fraction of the year
Number of shares as of beginning of the year 1/1/92	110,000 [100,000 + 10%(100,000)]	12/12	110,000
Shares issued 4/1/92	22,000 [20,000 + 10%(20,000)]	9/12	16,500
Treasury shares purchased 10/1/92	(10,000)	3/12	(2,500)
Weighted-average number of common shares outstanding			124,000

Recall that the stock dividend declared in July is considered to be retroactive to the beginning of the year. Thus, for the period 1/1 through 4/1, 110,000 shares are considered to be outstanding. When shares are issued, they are included in the weighted-average beginning with the date of issuance. The stock dividend applicable to these newly issued shares is also assumed to have existed for the same period. Thus, we can see that of the 12,000-share dividend, 10,000 shares relate to the beginning balance and 2,000 shares to the new issuance (10% of 100,000 and 20,000, respectively). The purchase of the treasury stock requires that these shares be excluded from the calculation for the remainder of the period after their acquisition date. The figure is subtracted from the calculation because the shares were purchased from those outstanding prior to acquisition.

To complete the example, we divided the previously derived numerator by the weighted-average number of common shares outstanding to arrive at EPS.

Earnings per common share:

On income from continuing operations before extraordinary item
$$\frac{\$130,000 - 6,000}{124,000 \text{ common shares}} = \$1.00$$

On net income
$$\frac{\$100,000 - 6,000}{124,000 \text{ common shares}} = \$.76$$

Reporting a $.24 loss per share ($30,000 ÷ 124,000) due to the extraordinary item is optional. The numbers computed above are required to be presented on the face of the income statement.

Complex Capital Structure

The computation of EPS under a complex capital structure involves all of the complexities discussed under the simple structure and many more. By definition, a complex capital structure is one that has securities which have the potential to be exercised and **reduce** EPS by more than 3% (dilutive securities). Any antidilutive securities (those that increase EPS) would not be included in this "3% test" or any other computation of EPS. The "3% test" is generally required to be performed first in order to determine the nature of the capital structure. Dilutive securities fall into two categories:

(1) those that are common stock equivalents (CSEs), and (2) those that are not CSEs. Note that a complex structure requires dual presentation of both primary EPS (PEPS) and fully diluted EPS (FDEPS). The common stock outstanding and CSEs are used to compute PEPS, while the common stock, CSEs, and all other dilutive securities are used to compute FDEPS.

Primary earnings per share (PEPS). PEPS has been identified as the earnings attributable to each share of common stock plus CSEs. The computation of PEPS requires that the following steps be performed:

1. Identify all potentially dilutive securities.
2. Determine which of the dilutive securities are CSEs.
3. Compute the effect (dilution) of the CSEs on net income and common shares outstanding.

Identification of potentially dilutive securities. The first step requires that we identify all potentially dilutive securities. As defined earlier, dilutive securities are those which have the potential of being exercised and reducing the EPS figure. Some examples of dilutive securities identified by APB 15 are convertible debt, convertible preferred stock, options, warrants, participating securities, two-class common stocks, and contingent shares.

Determination of common stock equivalents. The second step requires that we determine which dilutive securities are CSEs. According to APB 15, para 25 a CSE is "a security which is not, in form, a common stock but which usually contains provisions to enable its holder to become a common stockholder and which, because of its terms and the circumstances under which it was issued, is in substance equivalent to a common stock." In other words, a CSE gives its holder the right to acquire common shares through exercise or conversion. Another characteristic common to most CSEs is that the value of the CSE is tied to the value of the common stock.

The CSE determination requires that the security in question be a potentially dilutive security. Additionally, APB 15 mandates that the determination of whether a dilutive security is a CSE is to be made upon the issuance of the security and this status should not be changed so long as the security remains outstanding. There are two exceptions to this rule: (1) if a convertible security is issued and determined to be a CSE and a similar security exists that exhibits the same characteristics of the newly issued security but was not originally considered a CSE, the old security should be given CSE status, and (2) if a convertible security is considered issued and an approximation must be used as the market price for determining the effective yield, the result (i.e., status as a CSE or not) may be adjusted to reflect the actual market price at issuance. Sometimes referred to as a third exception is the fact that in the computation of PEPS (as well as FDEPS), only dilutive securities are to be considered. Thus, while a security will almost always maintain its CSE status, it may or may not be included in the computation of PEPS depending upon whether it is dilutive or antidilutive in the period being reported. As a result, a CSE may be included in the computation of PEPS in one period and not another.

The determination of common stock equivalent status which is to be done at the time of issuance varies depending upon the nature of the security. The date of issuance is generally considered to be the date when agreement has been reached as to the terms of the issuance although approval may still be needed. No specific guide-lines can be set for determining CSE status because of the numerous possibilities that exist. Rather, the determination should involve review of all of the characteristics of the security in question which may affect its status.

Convertible securities. A convertible security is one type of potentially dilutive security that may qualify as a CSE. The Board determined in APB 15 that the de-termination of whether or not a convertible security is a CSE should be based upon the relationship between its cash yield (based on its current market price or fair market value) and another easily identifiable, common interest rate (originally the bank prime rate). SFAS 55 specified that a convertible security is considered to be a CSE if its cash yield is less than 66-2/3% of the average Aa corporate bond yield. It was also noted that some securities are issued with scheduled dividend or interest rate changes. APB 15 states that for any security issued with such provisions scheduled in the first five years, the lowest scheduled rate is to be used for the purpose of computing the cash yield.

For all securities issued after March 31, 1985, SFAS 85 specifies that an "effective yield" test should now be used to test for common stock equivalency. The effective yield test modifies the cash yield test by including any original issuance premium or discount and any call premium or discount in the computation of the yield rate. The justification for this change was a better test for zero-coupon or deep-discount bonds. Under the cash yield test, these types of bonds were always CSEs.

The effective yield rate is the implicit or market rate reflected in the transaction at the date of issuance. The lower of the effective yield to a call date or the effective yield to maturity should be used. For securities without a stated maturity date (e.g., convert-ible preferred stock), the effective yield test is the same as the cash yield test (the ratio of the security's stated annual interest or dividend payments over the market price at issuance).

The APB developed the effective yield test for common stock equivalency in order to resolve the dual nature inherent in a convertible security. Convertibles are com-prised of two distinct elements, the right to receive interest **and** the right to potentially participate in earnings by becoming a common shareholder. Which of these elements most influenced the purchase? The Board believed that if the effective yield was less than 2/3 of the average Aa bond yield, then the security was purchased primarily for its conversion feature. Conversely, if the effective yield was greater than 2/3 of the av-erage Aa bond yield, then the security was purchased primarily for the interest ele-ment.

The conversion must be exercisable within five years of the financial statement date in order to be included in the PEPS computation. If the conversion is exercisable within five to ten years, it is included in the FDEPS computation only.

CONVERTIBLE SECURITIES AS CSE
Effective Yield < 2/3 average corporate Aa bond yield rate

<u>Effective Yield</u>

       Convertible Bond: Market rate
       Convertible Preferred Stock: Annual dividend ÷
                               Amount received at issuance

Options and warrants. Specific mention is also given to **options, warrants, and their equivalents**. Because options and warrants generally have no effective yield, their entire value is derived from the right to obtain common stock at specified prices over an extended period of time. Therefore, as concluded in APB 15, these securities shall **always** be considered CSEs. As with convertible securities, the exercise must be within five years in order to be included in PEPS. If exercisable within five to ten years, it is included in FDEPS.

Participating securities and two-class common stocks. Participating securities and two-class common stocks are to be considered CSEs if the nature of their characteristics is such that they share in the earnings of the corporation on substantially the same basis as the common stockholders. Participating dividends do not necessarily result in CSE status; therefore, all of the characteristics of the security must be examined.

Contingent issuances of common stock. Also mentioned are **contingent issuances of common stock** (e.g., stock subscriptions). If shares are to be issued in the future with no restrictions on issuance other than the passage of time, they are to be considered issued and treated as CSEs. Other issuances that are dependent upon certain conditions being met are to be evaluated in a different respect. APB 15 uses as examples the maintenance of current earnings levels and the attainment of specified earnings increases. If the contingency is to merely maintain the earnings levels currently being attained, then the shares are considered to be CSEs and outstanding for the entire period. If the requirement is to increase earnings over a period of time, the shares are not considered to be CSE because of the lack of certainty involved with the future issuance. However, these securities are still included in the computation of FDEPS, which will be discussed in a subsequent section. Previously reported EPS should not be restated to give recognition to shares issued as a result of the earnings level attainment. If the term of the contingency expires, the shares should not be considered outstanding and the prior periods' EPS should be restated to reflect the expiration. If a contingent issuance is based upon the lapsing of time **and** the market price of the stock (generally affects the number of shares issued), the number of shares treated as CSEs should be based on the market price at the end of the period being reported on. Fluctuations in the market price will cause the prior periods' EPS presented in comparative statements to be restated.

<u>Computation of PEPS</u>. The third step in the process is the actual computation of PEPS and determining how to account for CSEs. There are basically two methods

used to incorporate the effects of CSEs and EPS (excluding participating and two-class common securities):

(1) the treasury stock method and
(2) the if-converted method

The treasury stock method. The treasury stock method which is used for the exercise of most warrants or options requires that EPS be computed as if the options or warrants were exercised at the beginning of the period (or date of issuance, if later), and that the funds obtained from the exercise were used to purchase common stock at the average market price for the period. For example, if a corporation has warrants outstanding for 1,000 shares of common stock exercisable at $10 per share and the average market price of the common stock is $16 per share, the following would occur: the company would receive $10,000 (1,000 x $10) and issue 1,000 shares from the exercise of the warrants which would enable it to purchase 625 shares ($10,000 ÷ $16) in the open market. The net increase in the denominator (which effects a dilution in EPS) is 375 shares (1,000 issued less 625 repurchased). If the exercise price is greater than the average market price, the exercise should not be assumed since the result of this would be antidilutive. Additionally, the Board recommended that exercise only be assumed after the average market price had exceeded the exercise price for a minimum of three consecutive months. In this case, EPS of prior periods presented in comparative form should **not** be restated to reflect a change in market price.

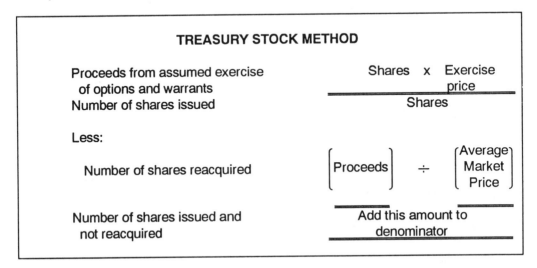

Modified treasury stock method. The modified treasury stock method is used when the exercise of all of the warrants and options potentially exercisable would result in a more than 20% increase in the number of shares outstanding at the end of the period. This is commonly referred to as the "20% test." If the 20% test is met, all of the options and warrants are assumed to be exercised and their total proceeds are to be applied in two steps:

1. The first step is to apply the funds to be received from the exercise to the

repurchase of outstanding common shares at the average market price up to the 20% limit.

2. Next, the remainder of the funds should first be applied to any short-term or long-term borrowings and any balance should be considered as being invested in U.S. government securities or commercial paper. The reduction in expense or increase in income should be recognized net of the related tax effect.

These steps should be performed and then the options and warrants in the aggregate should be judged as dilutive or antidilutive. Only if the effect is dilutive should it enter into the computation.

SYNOPSIS OF MODIFIED TREASURY STOCK METHOD

If number of shares reacquired ≥ 20% x number of shares outstanding,

Then use modified treasury stock method.
Apply proceeds in following sequences:
1. To reacquire 20% x number of shares outstanding
2. To reduce existing short-term or long-term debt
3. To purchase securities or commercial paper

MODIFIED TREASURY STOCK METHOD

Numerator

Net income recomputed to reflect retirement
of debt or income from investments
- Add interest expense less tax effects
- Add income from investments less tax
effects

- -

Denominator

Common stock outstanding + number of shares
not acquired with proceeds from options
and warrants

The if-converted method. The if-converted method is used for those securities which are currently sharing in the earnings of the company through the receipt of interest or dividends as senior securities, but which have the **potential** for sharing in the earnings as common stock. The if-converted method logically recognizes that the convertible security only can share in the earnings of the company as one or the other, not both. Thus, the dividends or interest less tax effects applicable to the convertible security as a senior security are not recognized in the net income figure used to compute EPS and the weighted-average number of shares is adjusted to reflect the conversion as of the beginning of the year (or date of issuance, if later). See the example of the if-converted method for illustration of treatment of convertible securities when they are issued during the period and, therefore, were not outstanding for the entire year.

IF-CONVERTED METHOD

Numerator

Net income recomputed to reflect conversion
- Add back interest expense less tax effects
- Convertible preferred dividends no longer subtracted
- Add back other expenses attributable to convertible issues

- -- - - - - - - - - - - - -

Denominator

Common stock outstanding if convertible securities were converted at beginning or date of issuance, if later

---

Summary. Generally speaking, the if-converted method is used for convertible securities, while the treasury stock method is used for options and warrants. There are some situations specified by APB 15 for which this does not hold true:

1. When warrants contain provisions which permit or require that debt or other securities of the issuer be tendered for all or a portion of the exercise price, the if-converted method should be used.
2. If the terms of the warrants require that the proceeds from the exercise are to be used to retire existing debt, the if-converted method should be used.
3. For convertible securities which require cash payment upon conversion, and are, therefore, considered equivalent to warrants, the treasury stock method should be used.
4. If the number of shares of common stock obtainable through the exercise of the warrants or options exceeds 20% of the outstanding common stock at the close of the period being reported on, a modified treasury stock method should be used.

Fully Diluted Earnings Per Share (FDEPS). FDEPS is a pro forma presentation which reflects the dilution of EPS that would have occurred if **all** contingent issuances of common stock that would individually reduce EPS had taken place at the beginning of the period (or the date issued, if later). The concept of the dual earnings per share presentation distinguishes between probable dilution and potential dilution. Primary earnings per share is computed including common stock equivalents because they are substantively equivalent to common stock. Since these securities are by their terms or by the market deemed to be economically common stock, the dilution in earnings per share that will transpire upon their exercise is **probable**. Therefore, primary earnings per share anticipates this dilution. Fully diluted earnings per share assumes that all issuances that have the legal right to become common stock exercise that right (unless such exercise would be antidilutive) and therefore, anticipates and measures all **potential** dilution. The dual presentation of both PEPS and FDEPS is to be prominently disclosed on the face of the financial statements. The underlying basis for the computation is that of conservatism. The FDEPS considers only those securities which are dilutive, and the inclusion of those securities is not limited to those which are CSEs. Thus, in most cases, the FDEPS is less than the PEPS. An exception occurs when no dilutive securities exist aside from the CSEs. The FDEPS can never be greater than the PEPS because of these characteristics, but it could possibly be the same if all of the dilutive securities were CSEs.

For the most part, the FDEPS is calculated in the same manner as the PEPS. However, in order to reflect maximum dilution, a change is made in the application of the treasury stock method. If the market price of the shares at the close of the period in question is higher than the average price of the shares during the period, the market price at the end of the period should be used to calculate the number of shares repurchased. By so doing, a lower number of shares will be assumed to have been repurchased, thereby increasing the number of shares assumed to be outstanding. As a result, dilution will be maximized.

Examples of EPS Computation--Complex Capital Structure

Each of the following independent examples is presented to illustrate the foregoing principles. The procedural guidelines are detailed so as to allow the reader to understand the computation without referring back to the text.

Example of the Treasury Stock Method

Assume that the net income is $50,000 and the weighted-average number of common shares outstanding has been computed as 10,000. Additional information regarding the capital structure is given as:

1. 4% nonconvertible, cumulative preferred stock, par $100, 1,000 shares issued and outstanding the entire year.
2. Options and warrants to purchase 1,000 shares of common stock at $8 per share. The average market price of common stock during the year was $10, and the closing market price was $12 per share. The options and warrants were outstanding all year.

The first step in the solution of this problem is the determination of the EPS on the weighted-average of common shares outstanding. This calculation appears as follows:

$$\frac{\text{Net income - Preferred dividends}}{\substack{\text{Weighted-average number of} \\ \text{common shares outstanding}}} = \frac{\$50,000 - 4,000}{10,000 \text{ shares}} = \$4.60$$

The reason for this calculation is to determine if the dilutive securities are significant enough to result in a complex capital structure and dual presentation. For purposes of this discussion, we will refer to the EPS on the weighted-average common shares as the "benchmark" EPS. If either PEPS or FDEPS $\leq$ $4.46 ($4.60 x 97%), the capital structure is complex and a dual presentation of EPS is required.

Recall that the calculation of PEPS includes the weighted-average number of shares of outstanding common stock and CSEs. In this example, the only potentially dilutive securities are the options, and these are always considered CSEs. Also remember that only dilutive options (market price > exercise price) are included in the computation unless the number of shares issuable under all options and warrants > 20%. The treasury stock method used to compute the number of shares to be added to the denominator is illustrated below.

Proceeds from assumed exercise of options and warrants (1,000 shares x $8)	$8,000
Number of shares issued	1,000
Number of shares reacquired ($8,000 ÷ $10)	800
Number of shares assumed issued and not reacquired	200*

*An alternative approach that can be used to calculate this number for primary EPS is demonstrated below:

$$\frac{\text{Average market price - Exercise price}}{\text{Average market price}} \times \substack{\text{Number of shares under} \\ \text{options/warrants}} = \substack{\text{Shares not} \\ \text{reacquired}}$$

$$\frac{\$10 - 8}{\$10} \times 1,000 \text{ shares} = 200 \text{ shares}$$

Primary EPS can now be calculated as follows, including the effects of applying the treasury stock method:

$$\frac{\text{Net income - Preferred dividends}}{\substack{\text{Weighted-average of common} \\ \text{shares outstanding + Number of} \\ \text{shares not reacquired with} \\ \text{proceeds from options and warrants}}} = \frac{\$50,000 - 4,000}{10,200 \text{ shares}} = \$4.51$$

Note the incremental effects of the treasury stock method when the number of shares issuable < 20% of the outstanding common; there was no effect on the numerator of the EPS calculation, while there were 200 shares added to the denominator. Note also that the options and warrants are dilutive, as EPS is reduced from $4.60 to $4.51.

The calculation of fully diluted EPS is based upon outstanding common stock, dilutive CSEs, and other dilutive securities. This example does not contain any other dilutive securities. The options and warrants are the only potentially dilutive securities in the example, and it has been shown that these securities are dilutive CSEs. However, the application of the treasury stock method differs for fully diluted EPS if the closing market price is higher than the average market price. When this occurs, use the closing market price in applying the treasury stock method in the calculation of fully diluted EPS.

The computation below illustrates this difference:

Proceeds from assumed exercise of options and warrants (1,000 shares x $8)	$8,000
Number of shares issued	1,000
Number of shares reacquired ($8,000 ÷ $12)	667
Number of shares assumed issued and not reacquired	333

Fully diluted EPS is calculated as follows:

$$\frac{\text{Net income - Preferred dividends}}{\substack{\text{Weighted-average of common,}\\ \text{shares outstanding + Number of,}\\ \text{shares not acquired with,}\\ \text{proceeds from options and warrants}}} = \frac{\$50,000 - 4,000}{10,333 \text{ shares}}$$

Since fully diluted EPS satisfies the 3% test (the "benchmark" $4.60 x 97% = $4.46), a dual presentation of EPS is required (primary EPS = $4.51 and fully diluted = $4.45). Table II summarizes the calculations made for the first example involving complex capital structures.

Table II
Computations of Primary and Fully Diluted Earnings Per Share

Items	EPS on outstanding common stock (the "benchmark" EPS) Numerator	Denominator	Primary Numerator	Denominator	Fully diluted Numerator	Denominator
Net income	$50,000		$50,000		$50,000	
Preferred dividend	(4,000)		(4,000)		(4,000)	
Common shs. outstanding		10,000 shs.		10,000 shs.		10,000 shs.
Options and warrants	___	___	___	200	___	333
Totals	$46,000 ÷	10,000 shs.	$46,000 ÷	10,200 shs.	$46,000 ÷	10,333 shs.
EPS	$4.60		$4.51		$4.45	

Example of the Modified Treasury Stock Method

Assume that the company has net income of $50,000 and that the weighted-average number of common shares outstanding was computed as 10,000. The company has an effective income tax rate of 40%. The following additional information is given regarding the capital structure:

1. 4% nonconvertible, cumulative preferred stock, par $100, 1,000 shares issued and outstanding the entire year.
2. Options and warrants to purchase 1,000 shares of common stock at $8 per share.
3. Options to purchase 2,000 shares of common stock at $13 per share.
4. All options and warrants were outstanding all year. The average market price of common stock during the year was $10 and the closing market price was $12 per share.
5. $5,000 short-term 10% note payable, outstanding the entire year.
6. $40,000 long-term 8% mortgage payable, outstanding the entire year.

Again, the first step is to compute the "benchmark" EPS. This results in a figure of $4.60 ($50,000 - 4,000/10,000). Thus, either the FDEPS or PEPS must fall below $4.46 ($4.60 x 97%) in order for this to be considered a complex capital structure. The capital structure needs to be examined for potentially dilutive securities, and then these must be reviewed for CSE status. In this case, the only potentially dilutive securities are the options and warrants, and as noted earlier, these are always considered CSEs. The 20% test is next performed to determine if the treasury stock method or the modified treasury stock method is to be used. Remember that only dilutive options (market price > exercise price) are included in the computation unless the number of shares issuable under all options and warrants > 20%. Because exercise of **all** the options and warrants would result in an additional 3,000 shares being issued and because this number is 30% ($\geq$ 20%) of the common shares outstanding at year end, the modified treasury stock method is used.

The steps in applying the modified treasury stock method require that we assume **all** of the options and warrants are exercised and that the proceeds are first applied to repurchase stock (up to 20% of the outstanding shares at year end) and next applied to debt reduction and then invested in government securities. The effect on net income of the last two applications is to be included in the numerator net of tax. The application of these principles to this example is illustrated below:

Number of shares issued	3,000
Number of shares reacquired (20% x 10,000)	(2,000)
Number of shares issued but not reacquired	1,000
Proceeds from assumed exercise of options and warrants:	
1,000 shares @ $8	$ 8,000
2,000 shares @ $13	26,000
Total assumed proceeds	$34,000

Application of proceeds:

To reacquire 2,000 shares (2,000 shares @ $10)	$20,000
To retire short-term debt	5,000
To retire a portion of long-term debt	9,000
Total application of proceeds	$34,000

Net income effects of debt retirement, net of tax:

Interest on short-term debt, assumed not paid, of $500 ($5,000 x 10%) net of tax	$300
Interest on long-term debt, assumed not paid, of $720 ($9,000 x 8%) net of tax	432
Total assumed increase in net income	$732

Primary EPS is then calculated as follows:

$$\frac{\text{Net income - Preferred dividends} + \text{Interest expense (net of tax)}}{\text{Weighted-average of common shares outstanding} + \text{Number of shares not acquired with proceeds from options and warrants}} = \frac{\$50,000 - 4,000 + 732}{10,000 + 1,000} = \$4.25$$

Notice that the PEPS of $4.25 is less than the "benchmark" EPS and, therefore, the options are dilutive. The PEPS is also less than the 3% reduction of the "benchmark" EPS and, thus, the capital structure is complex and FDEPS must be computed and presented.

Remember, the determination of whether or not the options and warrants were dilutive in this case was based upon the aggregate result. There was no way that only a part of the options and warrants would have been included in the computation. If the aggregate result had been antidilutive, the options and warrants would not have been included in the computation of the reported figure.

The application of the modified treasury stock method in the computation of EPS is basically the same except that the repurchase of the common shares is assumed to take place at the year-end price because it is greater. FDEPS is computed below:

Number of shares issued	3,000
Number of shares reacquired	(2,000)
Number of shares issued but not reacquired	1,000
Proceeds from assumed exercise of options and warrants	
1,000 shares @ $8	$ 8,000
2,000 shares @ $13	26,000
Total assumed proceeds	$34,000
Application of proceeds:	
To reacquire 2,000 shares (2,000 shares @ $12)	$24,000
To retire short-term debt	5,000
To retire a portion of long-term debt	5,000
Total application of proceeds	$34,000

Net income effects of debt retirement, net of tax:

Interest on short-term debt, assumed not paid,
of $500 net of tax $300

Interest on long-term debt, assumed not paid,
of $400 ($5,000 x 8%) net of tax   240

Total assumed increase in net income $540

Fully diluted EPS can now be calculated as follows:

$$\frac{\text{Net income - Preferred dividends + Interest expense (net of tax)}}{\text{Weighted-average of common shares outstanding + Number of shares not acquired with proceeds from options and warrants}} = \frac{\$50,000 - 4,000 + 540}{11,000} = \$4.23$$

Table III summarizes the calculations under the modified treasury stock method.

Table III
Computation of Primary and Fully Diluted Earnings Per Share

Items	EPS on outstanding common stock (the "benchmark" EPS) Numerator	Denominator	Primary Numerator	Denominator	Fully diluted Numerator	Denominator
Net income	$50,000		$50,000		$50,000	
Preferred dividend	(4,000)		(4,000)		(4,000)	
Common shs. outstanding		10,000 shs.		10,000 shs.		10,000 shs.
Options and warrants			732	1,000 shs.	540	1,000 shs.
Totals	$46,000 ÷	10,000 shs.	$46,732 ÷	11,000 shs.	$46,540 ÷	11,000 shs.
EPS	$4.60		$4.25		$4.23	

Example of the If-Converted Method

Again we will assume a net income of $50,000 and a weighted-average number of common shares outstanding of 10,000. The following information is provided regarding the capital structure:

1. 7% convertible debt, 200 bonds each convertible into 40 common shares. The bonds were outstanding the entire year. The average Aa corporate bond yield was 10% at the date the bonds were issued. The income tax rate is 40%. The bonds were issued at par ($1,000 per bond). No bonds were converted during the year.

2. 4% convertible, cumulative preferred stock, par $100, 1,000 shares issued and outstanding. Each preferred share is convertible into two common shares. The preferred which was issued at par was outstanding the entire year, and the average Aa corporate bond yield at the date the preferred was issued was 10%. No shares were converted during the year.

Once again the first step is to compute the "benchmark" EPS. As with the other examples, this figure is $4.60 and, thus, the FDEPS or PEPS must be less than $4.46 ($4.60 x 97%) in order for the capital structure to be considered complex.

The next step is the computation of primary EPS. Unlike options and warrants, convertible securities are not automatically CSEs. An effective yield test must be performed on each convertible security to determine its CSE status. If the effective yield of the convertible security (market or discount rate) at the date of issuance is < 2/3 of the average Aa corporate bond yield (SFAS 55), the convertible security is a CSE; otherwise, it is not a CSE.

In the present example, the convertible bonds are not common stock equivalents because the effective yield at date of issuance of 7% is larger than 6.7% (2/3 x 10%). On the other hand, the convertible preferred is a CSE because its effective yield of 4% is less than 6.7%. Thus, the computation of PEPS will include the convertible preferred if it is dilutive.

To determine the dilutive effect of the preferred stock, an assumption (called the if-converted method) is made that all of the preferred stock is converted at the earliest date that it could have been during the year. In this example, the date would be January 1. The effects of this assumption are twofold. One, if the preferred is converted, there will be no preferred dividends of $4,000 for the year; and, two, there will be an additional 2,000 shares of common outstanding during the year (the conversion rate is 2 for 1 on 1,000 shares of preferred). Primary EPS is computed, as follows, reflecting these two assumptions:

$$\frac{\text{Net Income}}{\substack{\text{Weighted-average of common shares} \\ \text{outstanding + Shares issued upon} \\ \text{conversion of preferred}}} = \frac{\$50,000}{12,000 \text{ shares}} = \$4.17$$

The convertible preferred is dilutive because it reduced EPS from $4.60 to $4.17. Furthermore, primary EPS is lower than $4.46 ($4.60 x 97%); thus, a dual presentation of EPS is required.

Fully diluted EPS includes dilutive CSEs and other non-CSE dilutive securities. In the example, the convertible bonds are also assumed to have been converted at the beginning of the year. Again, the effects of the assumption are twofold. One, if the bonds are converted, there will be no interest expense of $14,000 (7% x $200,000 face value); and two, there will be an additional 8,000 shares (200 bonds x 40 shares) of common stock outstanding during the year. One note of caution, however, must be mentioned; namely, the effect of not having $14,000 of interest expense will increase income, but it will also increase tax expense. Consequently, the net effect of not having interest expense of $14,000 is $8,400 ([1 - .40] x $14,000). Fully diluted EPS is computed as follows, reflecting the dilutive preferred and the effects noted above for the convertible bonds.

$$\frac{\text{Net income + Interest expense (net of tax)}}{\substack{\text{Weighted-average of common shares} \\ \text{outstanding + Shares issued upon} \\ \text{conversion of preferred and} \\ \text{conversion of bonds}}} = \frac{\$50,000 + 8,400}{20,000 \text{ shares}} = \$2.92$$

The convertible debt is also dilutive as it reduces EPS from $4.17 to $2.92. Together the convertible bonds and preferred reduced EPS from $4.60 to $2.92. Table IV summarizes the computations made for this example.

Table IV

Computations of Primary and Fully Diluted Earnings Per Share

Items	EPS on outstanding common stock (the "benchmark" EPS) Numerator	Denominator	Primary Numerator	Denominator	Fully diluted Numerator	Denominator
Net income	$50,000		$50,000		$50,000	
Preferred dividend	(4,000)					
Common shs. outstanding		10,000 shs.		10,000 shs.		10,000 shs.
Conversion of preferred				2,000		2,000
Conversion of bonds					8,400	8,000
Totals	$46,000	÷ 10,000 shs.	$50,000	÷ 12,000 shs.	$58,400	÷ 20,000 shs.
EPS	$4.60		$4.17		$2.92	

In the preceding example all of the potentially dilutive securities were outstanding the entire year and no conversions or exercises were made during the year. If a potentially dilutive security was not outstanding the entire year, then the numerator and denominator effects would have to be "time-weighted." For instance, suppose the convertible bonds in the above example were issued during the current year on July 1. If all other facts remain unchanged, fully diluted EPS would be computed as follows:

$$\frac{\text{Net income + Interest expense (net of tax)}}{\substack{\text{Weighted-average of common shares outstanding +} \\ \text{Shares issued upon conversion of preferred} \\ \text{and conversion of bonds}}} = \frac{\$50,000 + 1/2(8,400)}{\substack{10,000 + 2,000 + \\ 1/2(8,000)}} = \$3.39$$

In this case, the convertible debt is dilutive whether or not it is outstanding the entire year.

If actual conversions or exercises take place during a period, the common shares issued will be outstanding from their date of issuance and, therefore, will be included in the computation of the weighted-average number of common shares outstanding. These shares are then weighted from their respective times of issuance. Assume that all the bonds in the above example are converted on July 1 into 8,000 common shares; the following effects should be noted:

1. The weighted-average of common shares outstanding will be increased by (8,000)(.5) or 4,000. Income will increase $4,200 net of tax, because the bonds are no longer outstanding.
2. The if-converted method is applied to the period January 1 to July 1 because it was during this period that the bonds were potentially dilutive. The interest expense, net of tax, of $4,200 is added to the income, and 4,000 shares (.5 of 8,000) are added to the denominator.

3. Interestingly, the net effect of items 1 and 2 is the same for the period whether these dilutive bonds were outstanding the entire period or converted during the period.

Presentation. The reason for the differentiation between simple and complex capital structures is that APB 15 requires different financial statement presentation for each. Various pronouncements have mandated that EPS be shown on the face of the income statement for each of the following items (when applicable):

1. Income from continuing operations.
2. Income before extraordinary items and/or cumulative effect of a change in accounting principle.
3. Cumulative effect of a change in accounting principle net of tax.
4. Net income.

(Notice that while EPS is often presented for an extraordinary item, it is optional and not required.)

These requirements must be fulfilled regardless of whether the structure is simple or complex. The difference in the two structures is that a simple capital structure requires presentation of only a single EPS number for each item, while a complex structure requires the dual presentation of both primary EPS (PEPS) and fully diluted EPS (FDEPS) for each item.

Disclosures

Captions for the income statement

1. For simple capital structures--Earnings per common share
2. For complex capital structures

   a. Primary--Earnings per common and common equivalent share.
   b. Fully diluted--Earnings per share, assuming full dilution.

Additional disclosures for complex capital structure EPS

1. A schedule explaining the EPS figures should be presented disclosing common stock equivalents, underlying assumptions, and number of shares issued upon conversion, warrants, etc.
2. If potential dilution exists in any of the periods, both PEPS and FDEPS should be presented for all periods.   .

   a. Gives the reader understanding of the trend in potential dilution.
   b. If earnings of a prior period presented have been restated, the EPS data should be revised and effect of restatement in EPS should be disclosed in year of restatement.

3. Supplementary EPS figures should be presented when

   a. Conversions during or after the period would have affected PEPS. Note that PEPS should not be retroactively adjusted for conversions.

      b. Sale of common or common stock equivalents and the proceeds are used to retire debt, preferred, etc.

For both simple and complex capital structures, as the case may be, the financial statements should summarize the rights or equity issues outstanding which include

1. Dividend and liquidation preferences.
2. Participation rights.
3. Call prices and dates.
4. Conversion or exercise prices and dates.
5. Sinking fund requirements.
6. Unusual voting rights.

APPENDIX A

Comprehensive Example

The examples within the text used a simplified approach for determining whether or not options, warrants, convertible preferred stock, or convertible bonds have a dilutive effect on either primary or fully diluted EPS. This approach compared a "benchmark" EPS with an EPS number which reflected the effects of conversion or issuance of additional shares of common stock. If the EPS number computed was lower than the "benchmark" EPS, the security was considered dilutive. This approach is adequate so long as the firm has only **one** potentially dilutive security. If this is not the case and the firm has more than one potentially dilutive security, a more complex ranking procedure must be employed (interpretation of APB 15).

For example, assume the following facts concerning the capital structure of a firm:

1. Net income is $50,000.
2. Weighted-average number of common shares outstanding is 10,000 shares.
3. Tax rate is 40%.
4. Options to purchase 1,000 shares of common stock at $8 per share. The options were outstanding all year.
5. Options to purchase 2,000 shares of common stock at $13 per share. The average market price of common stock during the year was $10 and the closing market price was $12 per share.
6. 7% convertible bonds, 200 bonds each convertible into 40 common shares. The bonds were outstanding the entire year. The average Aa corporate bond yield was 10% at the date the bonds were issued. The bonds were issued at par and no bonds were converted during the year.
7. 4% convertible, **cumulative** preferred stock, par $100, 1,000 shares issued and outstanding the entire year. Each preferred share is convertible into one common share. The average Aa corporate bond yield was 10% at the date the stock was first issued. The preferred stock was issued at par and no shares were converted during the year.

Note that in the application of the procedures set forth below, reference is made to some of the tables included in the body of the chapter because the facts above represent a combination of the facts used for the examples in the chapter.

In order to determine both primary and fully diluted EPS, the following procedures must be performed:

1. Calculate an EPS number as if the capital structure were simple ("benchmark" EPS).
2. Identify which potentially dilutive securities are common stock equivalents.

Steps 3 through 5 must be performed separately for PEPS and FDEPS.

3. Calculate the per share effects of assuming issuance or conversion of each potentially dilutive security on an individual basis.
4. Rank the per share effects from smallest to largest.

5. Recalculate the simple EPS (step 1 above) adding the potentially dilutive securities one at a time in order, beginning with the one with the smallest per share effect.

6. Continue adding potentially dilutive securities until all have been added or until the addition of a security increases EPS (antidilution) from its previous level.

Applying these procedures to the facts above:

1. "Benchmark" EPS:

$$\frac{\text{Net income - Preferred dividends}}{\substack{\text{Weighted-average number of} \\ \text{common shares outstanding}}} = \frac{\$50,000 - 4,000}{10,000} = \$4.60$$

2. Identification of CSEs:

    a. Options and warrants are automatically CSEs.
    b. 7% convertible bonds are **not** CSEs; the effective yield of 7% > 6.7% (2/3 of 10% Aa bond yield).
    c. 4% convertible preferred stock **is** a CSE; the effective yield of 4% ≤ 6.7% (2/3 of 10% Aa bond yield).

Primary EPS

3. Per share effects of conversion or exercise of the CSEs:

    a. Options and warrants--the total cash which would be raised by the exercise of the options is $34,000. $20,000 is used to repurchase 2,000 shares; the remainder is used to reduce the debt. This latter use results in an increase in net income after tax of $732 (see Table III).

$$\frac{\text{Increase/decrease in net income}}{\substack{\text{Increase in weighted-average} \\ \text{number of shares}}} = \frac{\$732}{1,000} = \$.73$$

    b. 4% convertible preferred stock--the outstanding shares increase by 1,000 when all shares are converted. This results in the total dividends of $4,000 not being paid (see Table IV).

$$\frac{\text{Increase/decrease in net income}}{\substack{\text{Increase in weighted-average} \\ \text{number of shares}}} = \frac{\$4,000}{1,000} = \$4.00$$

    c. 7% convertible bonds do not affect PEPS computation as they are not CSEs.

4. Ranking of the per share effects from smallest to largest:

    a. Options and warrants $ .73
    b. 4% convertible preferred   4.00

5. Recalculate the simple EPS adding in rank order one CSE at a time:

a. Primary EPS--options and warrants added

$$\frac{\text{Net income - Preferred dividends + Interest expense (net of tax)}}{\text{Weighted-average number of common stock outstanding + Shares not acquired with proceeds of options and warrants}} = \frac{\$50,000 - 4,000 + 732}{11,000 \text{ shs.}} = \$4.25$$

b. Primary EPS--options and warrants and 4% convertible preferred added

$$\frac{\text{Net income + Interest expense (net of tax)}}{\text{Weighted-average number of common stock outstanding + Shares not acquired with proceeds of options and warrants + Shares issued on preferred stock}} = \frac{\$50,000 + 732}{12,000 \text{ shs.}} = \$4.23$$

Primary EPS = $4.23

Fully diluted EPS

3. Per share effects of conversion or issuance of CSEs and other non-CSEs but potentially dilutive securities:

a. Options and warrants (using closing market price--Table III)

$$\frac{\text{Increase/decrease in net income}}{\text{Increase in weighted-average number of common shares outstanding}} = \frac{\$540}{1,000 \text{ shs.}} = \$54$$

b. 4% convertible preferred (Table IV)

$$\frac{\text{Increase/decrease in net income}}{\text{Increase in weighted-average number of common shares outstanding}} = \frac{\$4,000}{1,000 \text{ shs.}} = \$4.00$$

c. 7% convertible bonds

$$\frac{\text{Increase/decrease in net income}}{\text{Increase in weighted-average number of common shares}} = \frac{\$8,400}{8,000 \text{ shs.}} = \$1.05$$

4. Rank the per share effects:

a. Options and warrants $ .54
b. 7% convertible bonds   1.05
c. 4% convertible preferred stock 4.00

5. Recalculate the simple EPS adding in rank order one CSE or potentially dilutive security at a time:

   a. Fully diluted EPS--options and warrants added

$$\frac{\text{Net income - Preferred dividends + Interest expense (net of tax)}}{\text{Weighted-average number of common stock outstanding + Shares not acquired with proceeds of options and warrants}} = \frac{\$50,000 - 4,000 + 540}{11,000 \text{ shs.}} = \$4.23$$

   b. Fully diluted EPS--options and warrants and 7% convertible bonds added

$$\frac{\text{Net income - Preferred dividends + Interest expense (net of tax)}}{\text{Weighted-average number of common stock outstanding + Shares of acquired with proceeds of options and warrants + Shares issued upon conversion of bonds and common stock}} = \frac{\$50,000 - 4,000 + 8,400 + 540}{19,000 \text{ shs.}} = 2.89$$

   c. Fully diluted EPS--options and warrants, 7% convertible bonds and 4% convertible preferred added

$$\frac{\text{Net income + Interest expense (net of tax)}}{\text{Weighted-average number of common stock outstanding + Shares not acquired with proceeds of options and warrants + Shares issued upon conversion of bonds and common stock}} = \frac{\$50,000 + 8,400 + 540}{20,000 \text{ shs.}} = \$2.95$$

Fully diluted EPS = $2.89

Since the addition of the 4% convertible preferred stock raises fully diluted EPS from $2.89 to $2.95, the 4% convertible preferred is antidilutive and is, therefore, excluded from the fully diluted EPS. Note that under this ranking procedure, the 4% convertible preferred is dilutive for primary EPS but is antidilutive for fully diluted EPS. Therefore, it is included in primary EPS but excluded from fully diluted EPS.

A dual presentation of primary and fully diluted EPS is required because both primary EPS of $4.23 and fully diluted EPS of $2.89 are lower than 97% of simple EPS (simple EPS of $4.60 x 97% = $4.46). The dual presentation on the face of the income statement would appear as follows:*

Net income	$50,000
Earnings per common share and common share equivalent** (Note X)	$4.23
Earnings per common share, assuming full dilution	$2.89

Note X - Earnings Per Share

Earnings per common share and common share equivalent were computed by dividing net income by the weighted-average number of common shares and common share equivalents outstanding during the year. All of the options and the 4% cumulative preferred stock are considered to be common stock equivalents. Consequently, the net income figure is adjusted to reflect the elimination of the preferred dividend; and the number of common shares issuable assuming full conversion of the preferred stock, and complete exercise of the options as of the beginning of the year, were added to the number of common shares outstanding.

Fully diluted earnings per share was computed assuming the conversion of all options and the 7% convertible bonds.

---

* Assuming there are no discontinued operations or changes in accounting principle.
** Primary earnings per share and fully diluted earnings per share may be substituted, respectively.

APPENDIX B

Contingent Issuances

If an issuance of common stock in the future is based upon some condition existing in the future, the treatment in earnings per share presentations of the potential issuance can be difficult. If the issuance in the future is probable based upon current information or economic results, then the issuance is assumed to have taken place for the purposes of computing primary earnings per share. Otherwise, such an issuance would be assumed only for fully diluted earnings per share provided that the issuance would be dilutive and assuming the future condition exists.

Example

Net income	$10,000
Common shares outstanding	1,000

1. If net income next year is $9,000, then an additional 250 shares will be issued. Since issuance appears probable, primary earnings per share would be:

$$\frac{\$10,000}{1,000 + 250} = \$8$$

2. If net income next year is $11,000, then an additional 250 shares will be issued. Since issuance is not probable, primary earnings per share would be:

$$\frac{\$10,000}{1,000} = \$10$$

Fully diluted earnings per share would be:

$$\frac{\$10,000 + 1,000}{1,000 + 250} = \frac{\$11,000}{1,250} = \$8.80$$

3. If net income next year is $15,000, then an additional 250 shares will be issued. Since adding $5,000 to the numerator of earnings per share and 250 shares to the denominator would cause earnings per share to rise, the result is antidilutive. Accordingly, the contingent issuance would not affect earnings per share presentations.

18 Interim and Segment Reporting

Perspective and Issues

Interim financial reporting is financial reporting for periods of less than a year, generally for a period of three months (quarterly reporting). The purpose of quarterly reports is to provide financial statement users with more timely information for investment and credit decisions. Additionally, quarterly reports can yield significant information concerning business points and seasonality, both of which could be "buried" in annual reports.

For over 60 years, the New York Stock Exchange has required quarterly financial reporting in its listing agreement. Since 1970, the SEC has required companies subject to its periodic reporting requirements to file quarterly financial information on a form 10-Q. Until 1973, however, there was no promulgated GAAP for publicly-held companies issuing interim reports to their stockholders. The general guidelines are now set forth in APB 28, SFAS 3, and FASB Interpretation 18. Today, interim reporting generally takes the form of quarterly earnings reports.

The basic objective of interim reporting is to provide frequent and timely assessments of enterprise performance. However, interim reporting has inherent limitations. As the reporting period is shortened, the effects of errors in estimation and allocation are magnified. The proper allocation of annual operating expenses is a major problem. Because progressive tax rates are applied to total annual income and various tax credits may arise, the determination of quarterly income tax expense is often difficult. Other annual operating expenses are often concentrated in one interim period, yet benefit the entire year's operations. Examples include advertising expenses and major repairs or maintenance of equipment. The effects of seasonal fluctuations and temporary market conditions further limit the reliability, comparability, and predictive value of interim reports. Because of this reporting environment, the issue of independent auditor association with interim financial reports is subject to continuing controversy.

Two distinct views of interim reporting have developed. Under the first view, the interim period is considered to be an **integral** part of the annual accounting period. Annual operating expenses are estimated and then allocated to the interim periods based on forecasted annual activity levels such as sales volume. The results of subsequent interim periods must be adjusted to reflect estimation errors. Under the second view, the interim period is considered to be a **discrete** accounting period. Thus, there are no estimations or allocations different from those used for annual reporting. The same expense recognition rules apply as under annual reporting, and no special interim accruals or deferrals are applied. Annual operating expenses are recognized in the interim period incurred, irrespective of the number of interim periods benefited.

Proponents of the **integral** view argue that the unique expense recognition procedures are necessary to avoid misleading fluctuations in period-to-period results. Using the **integral** view results in interim earnings which are indicative of annual earnings and, thus, useful for predictive purposes. Proponents of the **discrete** view argue that the smoothing of interim results for purposes of forecasting annual earnings has undesirable effects. For example, a turning point during the year in an earnings trend may be obscured.

In response to inconsistencies in interim reporting practices and problems in implementing interim reporting GAAP, the FASB undertook a comprehensive study of the issue. In 1978, the FASB Discussion Memorandum, *Interim Financial Accounting and Reporting*, was issued. A fundamental objective of this project was to resolve the **integral/discrete** debate. However, the FASB has made no recommendations and removed the project from its agenda.

Sources of GAAP

APB	*SFAS*	*FASB I*	*FASB TB*	*EITF*
28	3, 16, 69	18	79-9	86-13

Definitions of Terms

Discrete view. An approach to measuring interim period income by viewing each interim period separately.

Estimated annual effective tax rate. An expected annual tax rate which reflects estimates of annual earnings, tax rates, tax credits, etc.

Integral view. An approach to measuring interim period income by viewing each interim period as an integral part of the annual period: Expenses are recognized in proportion to revenues earned through the use of special accruals and deferrals.

Interim reporting. Financial reporting for a period of less than a year, generally for a period of three months.

Last-twelve-months reports. Financial reporting for the twelve-month period which ends on a given interim date.

Liquidation of LIFO inventories. The situation which occurs when quarterly sales exceed purchases and base-period costs are released into cost of goods sold.

Seasonality. The normal, expected occurrence of a major portion of revenues or costs in one or two interim periods.

Year-to-date reports. Financial reporting for the period which begins on the first day of the fiscal year and ends on a given interim date.

Concepts, Rules, and Examples

Revenues

Revenues are to be recognized as earned during an interim period using the same basis followed in annual reports. This rule applies to both product sales and service revenues. For example, product sales cut-off procedures should be applied at the end of each quarter as is done at year end, and revenue from long-term construction contracts should be recognized at interim dates using the same method used at year end.

Product Costs and Direct Costs

Product costs (and costs directly associated with service revenues) should be treated in interim reports as they are in annual reports (the discrete approach). However, APB 28 provides for four integral exceptions, described below.

1. The gross profit method may be used to estimate cost of goods sold and ending inventory for interim periods.
2. When inventory consisting of LIFO layers or a portion of the base-period is liquidated at an interim date, but is expected to be replaced by year end, cost of sales should include the expected cost of replacing the liquidated inventory.
3. An inventory market decline reasonably expected to be restored by year end (i.e., a decline deemed to be **temporary** in nature) need not be recognized in the interim period. The Emerging Issues Task Force (Issue no. 86-13) has reached a consensus that situations not requiring a writedown are generally limited to seasonal price fluctuations. If an inventory loss from a market decline that is recognized in one period is followed by a market price recovery, such reversal should be recognized as a gain. Recognition of this gain is limited to the extent of loss previously recognized, in the later interim period.
4. Firms using standard cost accounting systems ordinarily should report purchase price, wage rate, and usage or efficiency variances in the same manner as used at year end. Planned purchase price and volume variances should be deferred if expected to be absorbed by year end.

The reason for the first exception above is to eliminate the need for a physical inventory count at the interim date. The other three exceptions attempt to synchronize the quarterly statements with the annual report. For example, consider the LIFO liquidation exception. Without this exception, interim cost of goods sold could include low base-period costs, while annual cost of goods sold would include only current-year costs.

Several additional problems are encountered when using LIFO for interim reporting.

1. What is the best approach to estimating interim LIFO cost of sales?
2. As noted above, when an interim liquidation occurs that is expected to be replaced by year end, cost of sales should include the expected cost of replacement. How should this adjustment be treated on the interim balance sheet?
3. How should an interim liquidation that is **not** expected to be replaced by year end be recorded?

These problems are not addressed in APB 28. The only literature related to these problems is the AICPA Task Force Issues Paper, *Identification and Discussion of Certain Financial Accounting and Reporting Issues Concerning LIFO Inventories.*

The Issues Paper describes two acceptable approaches to measuring the interim LIFO cost of sales. The first approach makes specific quarterly computations of the LIFO effect based on year-to-date amounts. This is accomplished by reviewing quarterly price level changes and inventory levels. The second approach projects the expected **annual** LIFO effect and then allocates that projection to the quarters. The allocation can be made equally to each quarter or can be made in relation to certain operating criteria per quarter.

The Issues Paper also describes two acceptable approaches to treating the interim liquidation replacement on the balance sheet. The first approach is to record the adjustment for the pretax income effect of the replacement as a deferred credit in the current liabilities section. The second approach is to instead record the adjustment as a credit to inventory.

When an interim LIFO liquidation occurs that is not expected to be reinstated by year end, the Task Force believes that a company should recognize the effect of the liquidation in the period in which it occurs to the extent that this can reasonably be determined. They also believe, however, that a company using dollar value LIFO may allocate the expected effect of the liquidation to the quarters.

Other Costs and Expenses

Most other costs and expenses are recognized in interim periods as incurred. However, an expenditure which **clearly benefits** more than one interim period (e.g., annual repairs or property taxes) may be allocated among the periods benefited. The allocation is to be based on estimates of time expired, benefit received, or activity related to the periods. Such allocation procedures should be consistent with those used by the firm at year-end reporting dates. However, if cost or expense cannot be readily associated with other interim periods, such costs should not be arbitrarily assigned to those periods. Application of these interim reporting expense principles is illustrated in the examples below:

1. Costs expensed at year-end dates that benefit two or more interim periods

(e.g., annual major repairs) should be assigned to interim periods through use of deferrals or accruals.

2. Quantity discounts given customers based on annual sales volume should be apportioned to interim periods on the basis of sales to customers during the interim period relative to estimated annual sales.
3. Property taxes (and like costs) may be deferred or accrued at a year-end date to reflect a full year's charge to operations. Charges to interim periods should follow similar procedures.
4. Advertising costs may be deferred to subsequent interim periods within the same fiscal year if such costs clearly benefit the later interim periods. Advertising costs may be accrued and charged to interim periods preceding the time the service is received if there is an advertising program clearly implicit in the sales arrangement.

Costs and expenses subject to year-end adjustment, such as bad debts expense and discretionary bonuses, should be estimated and assigned to interim periods in a reasonable manner.

Income Taxes

At each interim date, the company should make its best estimate of the effective tax expected for the full fiscal year. This estimate should reflect expected federal and state tax rates, tax credits, and other tax planning techniques. However, changes in tax legislation are reflected only in interim periods after the effective date of the legislation.

The tax effect of losses in early quarters of the year should be recognized only when such losses can be carried back, or when the realization of the carryforward is reasonably assured. An established seasonal pattern of early-year losses offset by income later in the year constitutes reasonable assurance, in the absence of contrary evidence.

The accounting for income taxes in interim periods is treated extensively in Appendix A to Chapter 14, Accounting for Income Taxes.

Discontinued Operations and Extraordinary Items

Extraordinary items and the effects of disposal of a segment should be reported separately in the interim period in which they occur. The same treatment is given to other unusual or infrequently occurring events. No attempt should be made to allocate such items over the entire fiscal year. Materiality is determined by relating the item to the annual results of operations.

Accounting Changes

Retroactive type changes in accounting principle are handled on the same basis as in annual reports. Previously issued interim financial statements are retroactively restated.

When a cumulative effect type change occurs in the first quarter, the cumulative effect is included in the first quarter net income. However, if the cumulative effect type change occurs in later quarters, it is treated as if it occurred in the first quarter (to conform with the annual treatment). Therefore, previous quarters' financial statements are restated to reflect the change, and the cumulative effect as of the beginning of the year is included in the first quarter net income.

The treatment of accounting changes in interim reports is covered extensively in the Appendix to Chapter 19, Accounting Changes.

Earnings Per Share

The same procedures used at year end are used for earnings per share computations and disclosures in interim reports. Note that annual earnings per share generally will not equal the sum of the interim earnings per share amounts, due to such factors as stock issuances during the year and market price changes.

Contingent Items

In general, contingencies at an interim date should be accrued or disclosed in the same manner required for annual reports. The materiality of the contingency is to be evaluated in relation to the expected annual results.

Certain items which are adjustments related to prior interim periods, such as a settlement of litigation or an income tax dispute, are accorded special treatment in interim reports. If such items are material, directly related to prior interim periods of the current fiscal year, and become reasonably estimable in the current interim period, they should be reported as follows:

1. The portion directly related to the current interim period is included in that period's income.
2. Prior interim periods are restated to reflect the portions directly related to those periods.
3. The portion directly related to **prior years** is recognized in the restated first quarter income of the current year.

Seasonality

The operations of many businesses are subject to material seasonal variations. Such businesses should disclose the seasonality of their activities to avoid the possibility of misleading interim reports. APB 28 also suggests that such businesses supplement their disclosures with information for twelve-month periods ending at the interim date of the current and preceding year.

Fourth Quarter Adjustments

When the fourth quarter results are not separately reported, material year-end adjustments as well as disposals of segments, extraordinary items, and unusual or infrequently occurring items for the quarter should be disclosed in a footnote to the annual report.

Disclosures

Certain minimum disclosures are required by APB 28 when publicly-traded entities report summarized interim financial information. These required disclosures are:

1. Sales or gross revenues, provision for income taxes, extraordinary items, cumulative effect of a change in principle, and net income.
2. Primary and fully diluted earnings per share.
3. Seasonal revenues, costs, and expenses.
4. Significant changes in income tax estimates.
5. Discontinued operations and extraordinary, unusual, or infrequently occurring items.
6. Contingencies.
7. Changes in accounting principles or estimates.
8. Significant changes in financial position.

When summarized financial information is reported on a regular quarterly basis, the above disclosures should be presented for the current year and the current year-to-date (or preceding 12 months), with comparable data for the preceding year.

SEGMENT REPORTING

Perspective and Issues

Segment reporting, the disclosure of information about an enterprise's operations in different industries, its foreign operations and export sales, and its major customers, is a relatively recent development in financial reporting.

During the late 1960s, a large number of business combinations resulted in highly diversified corporations. Some of these companies voluntarily disclosed segment financial information in their annual reports, but the extent and nature of the disclosure varied widely. APB Statement No. 2, issued in 1967, recommended further voluntary disclosure. In addition, professional organizations, such as the FEI and the NAA, sponsored research studies that generally supported the desirability and feasibility of segment reporting.

Although the SEC began requiring "line-of-business" information in registrants' 10-K reports in 1970, many diversified companies still had no segment information in their annual reports issued to stockholders. By 1974, the SEC required registrants to include some of the line-of-business information in their annual reports to stockholders. Other companies began segmental disclosure to gain the approval of investors. SFAS 14, issued in December 1976, established specific guidelines for the required disclosure of segment information on financial reports issued to stockholders. SFAS 18 suspended the requirement for segment reporting in interim reports, and SFAS 21 further limited the required disclosures to the annual reports of publicly-held companies. It should be noted that previous pronouncements dealt indirectly with information on a less than total-enterprise basis. APB 18, for example, requires information on unconsolidated equity investees, and APB 30 requires information on discontinued segment operations.

The primary benefit of segment reporting is the release of "hidden data" from consolidated financial information. The different industry segments and/or geographic areas may possess different levels of profitability, risk, and growth. This important information is merged in the consolidated amounts. Assessing the amounts of future cash flows and their associated risks can be aided by segmental data. For example, knowledge of the level of enterprise operations in a growth or declining industry can help cash-flow predictions, while knowledge of the level of enterprise operations in an unstable geographic area can help assessment of risk. In general, information about the nature and relative size of an enterprise's various businesses is considered useful.

Still, several arguments, listed below, have been offered against segment reporting.

1. Comparison of segment results between companies is misleading due to the wide variety of measurement techniques in use.
2. Lack of user knowledge could render segment information meaningless or misleading.

3. Disclosure of such information to competitors, labor unions, etc. could harm the enterprise.
4. Such disclosure may discourage management from taking reasonable business risks to avoid reporting unsatisfactory segment data.
5. The investor invests in the entire company and has no right to expect segment information.
6. Accounting classification and allocation problems are inherent to segment reporting.
7. Information overload--financial reports have become too detailed and complex for the average user.
8. Information on an organizational unit (rather than industry) basis is more useful for evaluating divisional management.

Despite the disadvantages listed above, segment reporting has become more important as the number and size of conglomerates increase, as foreign operations increase, and as companies continue to diversify.

Sources of GAAP

APB	*SFAS*	*FASB TB*
18	14, 18, 21, 24, 30, 69	79-4, 79-5, 79-8

Definitions of Terms

Capital expenditures. Additions to an industry segment's property, plant, and equipment.

Common costs. Operating expenses incurred by the enterprise for the benefit of more than one industry segment.

Complete set of financial statements. A set of financial statements (including necessary footnotes) that present financial position, results of operations, and changes in financial position in conformity with generally accepted accounting principles.

Consolidated financial information. Aggregate (financial) information relating to an enterprise as a whole whether or not the enterprise has consolidated subsidiaries.

Corporate assets. Assets maintained for general corporate purposes and not used in the operations of any industry segment.

Dominant segment. An industry segment which accounts for at least 90% of an enterprise's revenue, operating profit or loss, and identifiable assets, while no other segment meets any of the 10% tests.

Export sales. Sales to customers in foreign countries by an enterprise's domestic operations.

Financial report. Includes any compilation of information that includes one or more complete sets of financial statements, such as in an annual report to stockholders or in a filing with the Securities and Exchange Commission.

Foreign operations. Operations located outside of the enterprise's home country that generate either unaffiliated or intraenterprise revenues.

General corporate expenses. Expenses incurred for the benefit of the corporation as a whole, which cannot be reasonably allocated to any segment.

Geographic areas. Individual countries or groups of countries established to appropriately reflect the nature of the enterprise's operations.

Identifiable assets. Those tangible and intangible assets used by an industry segment, including those the segment uses exclusively, and an allocated portion of assets used jointly by more than one segment.

Identifiable assets test. One of the three 10% tests; used to determine reportability of industry segments, foreign operations, and geographic areas.

Industry segment. A component of an enterprise engaged in providing a product or service or a group of related products or services primarily to unaffiliated customers for a profit.

Intersegment sales. Transfers of products or services, similar to those sold to unaffiliated customers, between industry segments or geographic areas of the enterprise.

Intrasegment sales. Transfers within an industry segment or geographic area.

Major customer. A customer responsible for at least 10% of an enterprise's revenues.

Nonpublic enterprise. An enterprise other than one (a) whose debt or equity securities trade in a public market on a foreign or domestic stock exchange or in the over-the-counter market (including securities quoted only locally or regionally) or (b) that is required to file financial statements with the Securities and Exchange Commission. An enterprise is no longer considered a nonpublic enterprise when its financial statements are issued in preparation for the sale of any class of securities in a public market. Nonpublic enterprises include certain mutual associations, cooperatives, nonbusiness organizations, and partnerships that often make their financial statements available to a broad class, such as insurance policyholders, depositors, members, contributors, or partners.

Operating profit or loss. An industry segment's revenue minus all operating expenses, including an allocated portion of common costs.

Operating profit and loss test. One of the three 10% tests; used to determine reportability of industry segments.

Profit center. Those components of an enterprise that sell primarily to outside markets and for which information about revenue and profitability is accumulated. They are the smallest units of activity for which revenue and expense information is accumulated for internal planning and control purposes.

Reportable geographic areas. Geographic areas considered to be significant to an enterprise's operations; passed one of two 10% tests.

Reportable industry segments. Industry segments considered to be significant to an enterprise's operations; passed one of three 10% tests.

Revenue. Revenue from sales to unaffiliated customers and from intersegment sales or transfers.

Revenues test. One of three 10% tests; used to determine reportability of industry segments, foreign operations, geographic areas, export sales, and major customers.

Segment reporting. Disclosure of information on an enterprise's operations in different industries, its foreign operations and export sales, and its major customers.

75% test. A test used to determine whether the reportable segments of an enterprise represent a substantial portion of the enterprise's total operations.

Transfer pricing. The pricing of products or services between industry segments or geographic areas.

Concepts, Rules, and Examples

Applicability of SFAS 14

Originally SFAS 14 applied to all reports of all enterprises. However, as amended by SFAS 18 (suspending segment reporting in interim reports) and SFAS 21 (suspending segment reporting for nonpublic enterprises), SFAS 14 now applies primarily to the annual financial reports of publicly-held companies. However, all companies must disclose economic dependency such as a major customer when such disclosure may be necessary for fair presentation and full disclosure.

SFAS 24 limits segment reporting requirements for financial statements that are presented in another enterprise's financial report. Examples of such statements are "parent company only" statements presented in addition to the consolidated statements, or the financial statements of an unconsolidated subsidiary presented in the footnotes to the parent's statements. Segment reporting is not required for parent-only statements, but is required for the statements of unconsolidated subsidiaries if that information is significant in relation to the financial statements of the primary reporting entity.

Industry Segments

In SFAS 14, an industry segment is defined as:

> *A component of an enterprise engaged in providing a product or service, or a group of related products and services, primarily to unaffiliated customers for a profit.*

This general definition leaves it up to management's judgment to determine industry segment classifications. The breakdown into segments should be designed to yield meaningful reported segment information. The FASB in SFAS 14, para 100 suggests three factors to be considered in determining industry segments:

1. *The nature of the product. Related products or services have similar purposes or end uses. Thus, they may be expected to have similar rates of profitabilty, similar degrees of risk, and similar opportunities for growth.*

2. *The nature of the production process. Sharing of common or inter-*

changeable production or sales facilities, equipment, labor force, or service group or use of the same or similar basic raw materials may suggest that products or services are related. Likewise, similar degrees of labor-intensiveness or similar degrees of capital-intensiveness may indicate a relationship among products or services.

3. *Markets and marketing methods. Similarity of geographic marketing areas, types of customers, or marketing methods may indicate a relationship among products or services.... The sensitivity of the market to price changes and to changes in general economic conditions may also indicate whether products and services are related or unrelated.*

Reportable Industry Segments

An industry segment is considered to be reportable if it is significant to the enterprise as a whole. A segment is to be regarded as significant if it satisfies **one** of the three **10% tests** described below.

Revenues test--Segment revenue (unaffiliated and intersegment) is at least 10% of the combined revenue (unaffiliated and intersegment) of all the industry segments.

Operating profit and loss test--The absolute amount of segment operating profit or loss is at least 10% of the **greater**, in absolute amount, of:

1. Combined operating **profits** of all segments reporting a profit.
2. Combined operating **losses** of all segments reporting a loss.

Identifiable assets test--Segment identifiable assets are at least 10% of combined identifiable assets of all segments. Operating profit (loss) is revenues minus operating expenses. Both revenues and operating expenses consist of unaffiliated and intersegment components. Identifiable assets are those assets used exclusively by the segment and an allocated portion of assets shared by two or more segments. Assets held for general corporate purposes are not assigned to segments.

Interperiod comparability must be considered in conjunction with the results of the 10% tests. If a segment fails to meet the tests, but has satisfied the tests in the past and is expected to in the future, it should be considered reportable in the current year for the sake of comparability. Similarly, if a segment which rarely passes the tests does so in the current year as the result of an unusual event, that segment may be excluded to preserve comparability.

After the 10% tests are completed, a 75% test must be performed. The combined **unaffiliated** revenue of all **reportable** segments must be at least 75% of the combined unaffiliated revenue of all segments. If the 75% test is not satisfied, additional segments must be designated as reportable until the test is satisfied. The purpose of this test is to ensure that reportable segments account for a substantial portion of the entity's operations.

The following example illustrates the three 10% tests and the 75% test.

Segment	Unaffiliated revenue	Intersegment revenue	Total revenue	Operating profit (loss)	Identifiable assets
A	$ 90	$ 90	$ 180	$ 20	$ 70
B	120		120	10	50
C	110	20	130	(40)	90
D	200		200	0	140
E	330	110	440	(100)	230
F	380	—	380	60	260
Total	$1,230	$220	$1,450	$ (50)	$840

Revenues Test: (10%)($1,450) = $145

   Reportable segments: A, D, E, F

Operating profit or loss test: (10%)($140) = $14

   Reportable segments: A, C, E, F

   [Note: Total operating loss ($140) is greater than total operating profit ($90)]

Identifiable assets test: (10%)($840) = $84

   Reportable segments: C, D, E, F

Reportable segments are those which pass **at least one** of the 10% tests. Segments A, C, D, E, and F are reportable in this example.

75% test: (75%)($1,230) = $922.50

Segments A, C, D, E, and F have total unaffiliated revenue of $1,110, which is greater than $922.50. The 75% test is satisfied; no additional segments need be reported.

Two other factors must be considered when identifying reportable segments. First, the number of reportable segments should not be so great as to decrease the usefulness of segment reporting. As a rule of thumb, the FASB suggests that if the number of reportable segments exceeds ten, segment information may become too detailed. In this situation, the most closely related industry segments should be combined into broader reportable segments.

Another consideration is the possible presence of a **dominant segment**. A segment is dominant when its revenue, operating profit or loss, and identifiable assets all exceed 90% of the combined totals and no other segment meets any of the 10% tests. In this case, the industry in which a dominant segment operates must be identified, but detailed segment reporting is not required.

Accounting Problems

Since segment revenue as defined by SFAS 14 includes intersegment sales, **transfer pricing** becomes an issue. Rather than establishing a basis for setting transfer prices, the FASB required companies to use the same transfer prices for segment reporting purposes as are used internally. Since most segments are organizational profit centers, internal transfer prices would generally reflect market prices.

Another problem in determining operating profit or loss is the **allocation of common costs.** Common costs are operating expenses incurred by the enterprise for the benefit of more than one industry segment. These costs must be allocated on a reasonable basis to those segments which derive the benefits. Examples of allocation bases include revenues, operating profit before common costs, or tangible assets.

Items which would have to be allocated on an arbitrary basis are **not** included in the computation of operating profit or loss. These items include:

1. Revenue earned at the corporate level.
2. General corporate expenses.
3. Interest expense (unless the segment's operations are primarily of a financial nature).
4. Income taxes.
5. Equity in income of unconsolidated investees.
6. Gains or losses on discontinued operations.
7. Extraordinary items.
8. Minority interest.
9. The cumulative effect of a change in accounting principle.

A problem can arise in distinguishing common costs from general corporate expenses. General corporate expenses are not operating expenses from the point of view of any segment; they are incurred for the benefit of the corporation as a whole and cannot be reasonably allocated to any segment.

Information About Foreign Operations, Geographic Areas, and Export Sales

An enterprise's domestic operations are those operations located in the enterprise's home country that generate either unaffiliated or intraenterprise revenues. The enterprise's foreign operations are similar operations located outside of the enterprise's home country.

The enterprise's foreign operations are considered reportable (in aggregate or possibly by geographic area) if one of two 10% tests described below is satisfied.

Revenues test. Unaffiliated revenue is at least 10% of consolidated revenue.

Identifiable assets test. Identifiable assets are at least 10% of consolidated total assets.

If the enterprise functions in two or more foreign **geographic areas**, the above tests are also applied to each area to determine if any individual areas are reportable. A geographic area is defined as an individual country or group of countries as appropriate in the enterprise's circumstances. Factors to be considered include proximity, economic affinity, similarities in business environments, and the interrelationship of the enterprise's operations in different countries.

Information to be disclosed for foreign operations in aggregate or foreign geographic areas individually includes:

1. Unaffiliated and intraenterprise revenue.
2. Operating profit or loss, or net income, or some similar measure of profitability.
3. Identifiable assets.

Each of these disclosures must also be made for domestic operations, and each must be reconciled to related amounts in the consolidated statements. The reason for the flexibility in the profitability disclosure is that a pretax measure can often be misleading due to differences in foreign tax structures.

Similar to the foreign operations disclosures are required disclosures for export sales by the enterprise's domestic operations. Export sales are defined as sales to customers in foreign countries from domestic production. If the amount of export sales to unaffiliated customers is at least 10% of consolidated revenue, that amount is to be separately reported, in aggregate and by appropriate geographic areas.

Information About Major Customers

If an enterprise earns 10% or more of its revenue on sales to a single customer, that fact and the amount of revenue from each such customer must be disclosed. Also, the industry segment making these sales must be disclosed.

A group of customers under common control, such as subsidiaries of a parent, is regarded as a single customer. Similarly the various agencies of a government are considered to be a single customer. An insuring entity (such as Blue Cross) should not be considered the customer unless that entity (rather than the patient) controls the decision as to the doctor, type of service, etc.

Restatement of Previously Reported Segment Information

Segment reporting is required on a comparative basis, and therefore the information must be restated to preserve comparability, when:

1. The enterprise's statements have been restated for a change in accounting principle or a change in entity.
2. The enterprise has changed the industry or geographic grouping of its operations.

Disclosures

Certain disclosures are required for each reportable segment and in the aggregate for the remainder of the industry segments. These disclosures can be classified as revenue information, profitability information, identifiable assets information, and other disclosures.

Revenue information. Both unaffiliated and intersegment revenues must be disclosed. These are to be reconciled to consolidated revenue.

Profitability information. Operating profit or loss must be disclosed. It shall be reconciled to pretax income from continuing operations on the consolidated income statement.

Identifiable assets information. The aggregate carrying amount of identifiable assets must be disclosed and reconciled to total consolidated assets.

Other disclosures. These disclosures include the aggregate amount of depreciation, depletion, and amortization; the amount of capital expenditures; equity in unconsolidated but vertically integrated subsidiaries and their geographic location; and the effect of a change in accounting principle on segment income.

The above segmental disclosures may be presented within the body of the financial statements (with appropriate footnote explanation), entirely in the footnotes to the financial statements, or in a separate schedule that is included as an integral part of the financial statements.

Other general disclosures include the type of products and services produced by each segment, specific accounting policies, the basis used to price intersegment transfers, the method used to allocate common costs, and the nature and amount of any unusual or infrequent items added to or deducted from segment operation profit.

19 Accounting Changes and Correction of Errors

Perspective and Issues

Financial statements are the results of choices among different accounting principles and methodology. Companies select those principles and methods that they believe depict, in their financial statements, the economic reality of their financial position, results of operations, and changes in financial position. Changes take place because of changes in the assumptions and estimates underlying the application of these principles and methods, changes in the acceptable principles by a promulgating authority, or other types of changes.

Accounting for and reporting of these changes is a problem which has faced the accounting profession for years. Much financial analysis is based on the consistency and comparability of annual financial statements. Any type of accounting change creates an inconsistency; thus, a primary focus of management in making the decision to change should be to consider its effect on financial statement comparability. APB 20 was issued so that these accounting changes could be reported and disclosed in a manner that would improve analysis and understanding of the financial statements.

In APB 20 the Board defined an accounting change as being a change in:

1. Accounting principle
2. Accounting estimate
3. Reporting entity

Even though the correction of an error in previously issued financial statements is not considered to be an accounting change, it is discussed in the Opinion and, therefore, will be covered in this chapter.

The Board concluded that in the preparation of the financial statements there is an underlying presumption that an accounting principle, once adopted, should not be changed in accounting for events and transactions of a similar type. This consistent use of accounting principles was felt to enhance the utility of the financial statements. The presumption that an entity should not change an accounting principle may be overcome only if the enterprise justifies the use of an alternative acceptable accounting principle on the basis that it is preferable.

APB 20 contained no definition of preferability or criteria by which to make assessments. Because there was no universally agreed-upon set of objectives for external financial reporting, what was preferable to one industry or company was not necessarily considered preferable to another. This led to some of the same consistency problems in reporting that existed prior to the issuance of APB 20. However, this consistency problem did not cause great concern in the accounting profession because the justification of preferability rested with the enterprise. The independent accountant was responsible only for reviewing the rationale for preferability and determining its reasonableness.

In September of 1975 the Securities and Exchange Commission (SEC) radically changed the accounting profession's view of preferability by issuing Accounting Series Release (ASR) 177. In this ASR, the SEC mandated that each change in accounting principle, for purposes of SEC filing, must be accompanied by a letter from the independent accountant "...indicating whether or not the change is to an alternative principle which in his judgment is preferable under the circumstances." The lack of a uniform set of objectives for external reporting, necessitated making individual determinations as to the preferability of accounting principles. In order to avoid this practice, accountants began using industry audit guides to assist in their decision because this was indicated as acceptable practice in APB 20. The FASB formalized this process by issuing SFAS 32 in 1979. This statement indicated that certain Statements of Position (SOP) and Industry Audit Guides were to be considered preferable accounting principles (these are listed in the appendixes of SFAS 32 and 56).

SFAS 56 amended SFAS 32 to include additional SOPs and many of the recent SFASs have been issued in order to set single, acceptable accounting policies for various industries so as to eliminate the preferability question. The promulgating bodies of the accounting profession are attempting to narrow the broad range of acceptable accounting principles, but until they are successful the accountant will be called upon to implement accounting changes made by management.

Sources of GAAP

APB	*SFAS*	*FASB I*
8, 20, 28	3, 16, 32, 56, 63, 73	1, 20

Definitions of Terms

Change in accounting estimate. A revision of an accounting measurement based on new events, additional experience, subsequent developments, better insight, and improved judgment. Such revisions are an inherent part of the accounting process.

Change in accounting principle. A switch from one generally accepted accounting principle to another generally accepted accounting principle including the methods of applying these principles. This does not include selection of an accounting principle to account for events occurring for the first time.

Change in reporting entity. A special type of change in accounting principle that results in financial statements which, in effect, are those of a different reporting entity. Financial statements are prepared for an entity that is different from the one reported on in previous financial statements.

Comparability. The quality of information that enables users to identify similarities in and differences between two sets of economic phenomena. Normally, comparability is a quantitative assessment of a common characteristic.

Consistency. Conformity from period to period with unchanging policies and procedures. Enhances the utility of financial statements to users by facilitating analysis and understanding of comparative accounting data.

Cumulative effect. The difference between the beginning retained earnings balance of the year in which the change is reported and the beginning retained earnings balance that would have been reported if the new principle had been applied retroactively for all prior periods which would have been affected.

Error. Results from mathematical mistakes, mistakes in applying accounting principles, oversight or misuse of available facts, and use of unacceptable GAAP.

Pro forma. "As if" basis. Disclosure of the required numbers computed on the assumption that certain events have transpired.

Restatement of financial reports. The recasting of a previously determined and published balance sheet or operating statement and its republication where there has been a substantial change in accounting principles or policies.

Concepts, Rules, and Examples

APB 20 describes three ways of reporting accounting changes and the type of change for which each should be used. These are:

1. Retroactively
2. Currently
3. Prospectively

Retroactive treatment requires an adjustment to all current and prior period financial statements for the effect of the accounting change. Prior period financial statements presented currently are to be restated on a basis consistent with the newly adopted principle.

Current treatment requires reporting the cumulative effect of the accounting change in the current year's income statement as a special item. Prior period financial statements are **not** restated.

Prospective treatment of accounting changes requires **no** restatement of prior financial statements and **no** computing or reporting of the accounting change's cumulative effect in the current period's income statement. Only current and/or future periods' financial report data will reflect the accounting change.

Each of the types of accounting changes and the proper treatment prescribed for them is discussed in detail in the following sections.

Change in Accounting Principle

According to APB 20 the term "accounting principle" includes the accounting principles and practices used as well as the methods of applying them. FASB Interpretation 1 sets a base for the application of this statement by ruling that a change in the components used to cost a firm's inventory is considered a change in accounting principle. The Interpretation also stated that the preferability assessment must be made from the perspective of financial reporting basis and not from the income tax perspective. The Opinion indicates that changes in accounting principles should be accounted for currently using the cumulative effect method; however, there are exceptions to this general rule in a few specific instances. One of these occurs when an authoritative body issues a new standard. The adoption of the standard will require accounting for the change as prescribed by the new pronouncement. Each new FASB has its own transition rules. However, APB 20 requires that the cumulative effect method be used for most changes in accounting principles, and no restatement is to occur in the prior period financial statements.

The cumulative effect method is to be applied as follows:

1. Previously issued financial statements are **not** to be restated.
2. The cumulative effect of changing to the new accounting principle on the amount of retained earnings at the beginning of the period in which the change occurs should be included in the net income of the period of the change.
3. The effect of adopting the new principle on income before extraordinary items and net income, including per share amounts of the period of change, should be disclosed in the notes to the statements.
4. Income before extraordinary items and net income computed on a pro forma basis (defined below) should be shown on the face of the income statements for all periods presented as if the newly adopted principle had been applied during all periods affected. The nature of and justification for the change shall be disclosed in the financial statements in which the change is made.

According to the Board's conclusions, **income for the period of the change is to be computed using the newly adopted principle** while all other periods are to be presented as they originally appeared (step 1). **Restatement will occur only in the disclosures and the pro forma calculations.**

The cumulative effect of a change in accounting principle is to appear as a single amount on the income statement between extraordinary items and net income (step 2). The amount shown should be the difference between:

1. The amount of retained earnings at the beginning of the period, and

2. The amount of retained earnings that would have been reported at that date if the new accounting principle had been applied retroactively to all prior periods affected.

The cumulative effect is generally determined by first calculating income before taxes for both the new principle and the old principle for all prior periods affected. Second, the difference between the two incomes for each prior period is determined. Third, these differences are adjusted for tax effects. Finally, the net of tax differences for each prior period are totaled. This total represents the cumulative effect adjustment at the beginning of the current period. The cumulative effect will either be an addition to or a subtraction from current income depending on how the change to the new principle affects income. Generally, only the direct effects of the change and the related income tax effect should be included in the cumulative effect calculation (i.e., if the company changes its method of computing depreciation, only the effects of the change in depreciation expense, net of tax, are considered to be direct effects). Indirect effects, such as the effect on a profit sharing contribution or bonus payments that would have occurred as a result of the change in net income, are not included in the cumulative effect computation unless these are to be recorded by the firm (i.e., the expense is actually incurred).

Step 3 requires that the effects of the change on income before extraordinary items and net income be disclosed for the year of the change. This is the difference between the old principle and the new principle on an after tax basis. The amount shall be disclosed for both the total effect and the per share amounts. In addition, the nature of and justification for the change must be disclosed, clearly indicating why the newly adopted principle is preferable.

The computation of income on a pro forma basis must be made for each period currently presented. The objective is to present income before extraordinary items and net income as if the new principle were being applied. This is achieved by adjusting each period's income before extraordinary items as previously reported (i.e., applying the old principle). The adjustment is made by adding or subtracting the difference in income net of tax for the period to income before extraordinary items as previously reported. The difference, net of tax is the change in income that occurs when the new principle is applied instead of the old principle. This results in an income before extraordinary items figure that reflects the application of the new principle. Net income is then calculated as normally done from the adjusted income before extraordinary items. The per share amounts required are based upon the pro forma income before extraordinary items and net income amounts.

The pro forma calculation required by step 4 differs from that of the cumulative effect. It is to include both the direct effects of the change and the "nondiscretionary" adjustments of items **based** on income before taxes or net income. Examples of nondiscretionary items would be profit sharing expense or certain royalties. Both of these expenses are in some way based on net income, generally as a specified percentage. The related tax effects should be recognized for **both** the direct and nondiscretionary adjustments. The pro forma calculation is to be shown on the face of the financial statements for income before extraordinary items and net income. The earnings per share amounts (both primary and fully diluted as defined in APB 15) for both should also be computed and shown. According to APB 20, if space is not available on the face of the financial statements, the pro forma information may be disclosed prominently in the notes to the financial statements.

The following example will illustrate the computations and disclosures necessary when applying the **cumulative effect** method. This particular example is adapted from the one which is included in Appendix A of APB 20.

Example of Cumulative Effect (Example from APB 20, Appendix A)

ABC Co. decides in 19X5 to adopt the straight-line method of depreciation for plant equipment. The straight-line method will be used for all new acquisitions as well as for previously acquired plant equipment for which depreciation had been provided on an accelerated method.

The following assumptions are being made:

1. The direct effect of the change is limited to the change in accumulated depreciation.
2. The tax rate is a constant 40%.
3. The executive incentive bonus is the only nondiscretionary item affected by the change. It is 10% of the pretax accounting income.
4. There are 1,000,000 shares of common stock outstanding throughout the entire period affected by the change.
5. An additional 100,000 shares would be issued if all the outstanding bonds, which are not common stock equivalents, were converted. Annual interest on this bond obligation is $25,000 (net of tax).
6. For 19X4 and 19X5 the income before extraordinary item is given as $1,100,000 and $1,200,000 respectively. There is an extraordinary item in each year amounting to $100,000 for 19X4 and ($35,000) for 19X5. The extraordinary items are included to illustrate the proper positioning of the cumulative effect adjustment on the income statement.

Year	Excess of accelerated depreciation over straight-line depreciation	Direct effects of change, net of tax	Nondiscretionary item, net of tax	Pro forma amounts
Prior to 19X1	$ 20,000	$ 12,000	$ 1,200	$ 10,800
19X1	80,000	48,000	4,800	43,200
19X2	70,000	42,000	4,200	37,800
19X3	50,000	30,000	3,000	27,000
19X4	30,000	18,000	1,800	16,200
Total at beg. of 19X5	$250,000	$150,000	$15,000	$135,000

The following narrative is provided to assist you in grasping the computational aspects of the information given above. The "excess of...depreciation" is given in this example. It is generally determined by recomputing the depreciation under the new method and obtaining the difference between the two methods. The "direct... tax" represents the effect of the actual change (i.e., depreciation) upon income before extraordinary items adjusted for the tax effects. For example, in the years prior to 19X1 the change in depreciation methods (from accelerated **to** straight-line) resulted in a $20,000 reduction in depreciation expense (or an increase in income). The net of tax number is $12,000 because the $20,000 increase in income is reduced by an $8,000 (40% x $20,000) increase in income tax expense.

The "nondiscretionary item, net of tax" represents the income statement items affected indirectly as a result of the change. In this case, we were given the fact that the executive incentive bonus equal to 10% of pretax accounting income was the only "nondiscretionary item" affected. Thus, in years prior to 19X1, when pre-tax accounting income increased by $20,000, the bonus expense would have been $2,000 higher ($20,000 x 10%). APB 20 indicates that this should also be computed net of tax, and because the expense would have increased by $2,000, the taxes would have decreased by $800 ($2,000 x 40%). The net of tax increase in expense is $1,200. The "pro forma" amounts are to include both the direct and indirect effects of the change. The computation for this example is as follows:

	Increase (decrease) in net income
Reduction in depreciation expense	$20,000
Increase in taxes (depreciation)	(8,000)
Increase in compensation expense	(2,000)
Reduction in taxes (compensation)	800
	$10,800

The pro forma amount is needed for disclosure purposes so that 19X4 income can be shown on a comparative basis with 19X5 net income (i.e., adding the 19X4 income before the change. The pro forma increase or decrease will result in an income figure which reflects the same accounting principles as the 19X5 income figure).

Below are the necessary disclosures required by APB 20 for the aforementioned situation.

On the Face of the Income Statement

	19X5	19X4
Income before extraordinary item and cumulative effect of a change in accounting principle	$1,200,000	$1,100,000
Extraordinary item (description)	(35,000)	100,000
Cumulative effect on prior years (to December 31, 19X4) of changing to a different depreciation method	150,000	--
Net income	$1,315,000	$1,200,000
Per share amounts:		
Earnings per common share--assuming no dilution:		
Income before extraordinary item and cumulative effect of a change in accounting principle	$1.20	$1.10
Extraordinary item	(0.04)	0.10
Cumulative effect on prior years (to December 31, 19X4) of changing to a different depreciation method	0.15	--
Net income	$1.31	$1.20
Earnings per common share--assuming full dilution:		
Income before extraordinary item and cumulative effect of a change in accounting principle	$1.11	$1.02
Extraordinary item	(0.03)	0.09
Cumulative effect on prior years (to December 31, 19X4) of changing to a different depreciation method	0.14	--
Net income	$1.22	$1.11
Pro forma amounts assuming the new depreciation method is applied retroactively:		
Income before extraordinary item	$1,200,000	$1,116,200
Earnings per common share--assuming no dilution	$1.20	$1.12
Earnings per common share--assuming full dilution	$1.11	$1.01
Net income	$1,165,000	$1,216,200
Earnings per common share--assuming no dilution	$1.17	$1.22
Earnings per common share--assuming full dilution	$1.08	$1.11

In the Notes to the Financial Statements
Note A--Change in Depreciation Method for Plant Equipment

During 19X5 the company decided to change its method of computing depreciation on plant equipment from sum-of-the-years' digits (SYD) to the straight-line method. The company made the change because the straight-line method better matches revenues and cost amortization and, therefore, is a preferable accounting principle. The new method has been applied retroactively to equipment acquisitions of prior years. The effect of the change in 19X5 was to increase income before extraordinary items by approximately $10,000 (or $.01 per share). The adjustment of $150,000 (net of $100,000 in taxes) included in 19X5 income is the cumulative effect of applying the new method retroactively. The pro forma amounts shown on the income statement have been adjusted for the effect of the retroactive application of the new depreciation method, the change in the provisions for incentive compensation which would have been made had the new method been used, and the related income taxes for both.

If the company elected to disclose the pro forma amounts in notes to the financial statements and not on the face of the income statement, the following disclosure would have been included as part of Note A.

The following pro forma amounts show the effect of the retroactive application of the change from the SYD to straight-line method of depreciation.

	Actual	*Pro forma*
19X5		
Income before extraordinary items	$1,200,000	$1,200,000
Primary earnings per share	$1.20	$1.20
Fully diluted earnings per share	$1.11	$1.11
Net income	$1,315,000	$1,165,000
Primary earnings per share	$1.31	$1.17
Fully diluted earnings per share	$1.22	$1.08
19X4		
Income before extraordinary items	$1,100,000	$1,116,200
Primary earnings per share	$1.10	$1.12
Fully diluted earnings per share	$1.02	$1.01
Net income	$1,200,000	$1,216,200
Primary earnings per share	$1.20	$1.22
Fully diluted earnings per share	$1.11	$1.11

Notice how in the above example the four steps provided in APB 20 are followed:

Step 1 -- No restatement takes place on the face of the income statements. The 19X4 figures provided for comparative purposes are the same as those originally reported.

Step 2 -- The cumulative effect of the change is included on the face of the income statement as a single amount. The $150,000 shown in 19X5 represents the total direct effect net of tax for all years prior to 19X5. The effect of the change in 19X5 is included in the computation of ordinary income for 19X5.

Step 3 -- The required disclosure of the 19X5 effects of the change, both in total and the per share amounts, is usually done in the notes to the financial statements. This is assumed to be $10,000 in the example above or $.01 per share.

Step 4 -- The pro forma amounts are used to make the statements from the two years comparable. 19X4 income before extraordinary items is increased by $16,200 to $1,116,200. This is the amount found in the original table across from 19X4. Notice also how the 19X5 net income figure no longer contains a cumulative effect adjustment. This is because 19X5 and 19X4 earnings, under the pro forma computations, are derived using the same accounting principles.

As was mentioned earlier, there are several cases for which the (FASB) APB has determined that a change in accounting principle should be accounted for retroactively in the financial statements. There are five instances which require retroactive treatment.

1. Change from LIFO to another inventory method (APB 20, para 27)
2. A change in the method of accounting for long-term contracts (APB 20, para 27)
3. A change to or from the full cost method of accounting for exploration costs in the extractive industries (APB 20, para 27)
4. Any change made by a company first issuing financial statements for the purpose of obtaining additional equity capital, effecting a business combination, or registering securities (APB 20, para 29)
5. Any changes mandated by authoritative pronouncements (while this case is not specified by APB 20, the promulgating bodies have in most instances thus far required that the change be made retroactively). FASB Interpretation 20 has also indicated that AICPA SOPs may mandate the treatment given the change.

The process of restating the financial statements in these situations was favored because it did not require that the cumulative effect of the change be included in net income. Rather, each of the years presented is adjusted to reflect the new accounting principle. The cumulative effect is calculated in the same manner shown earlier for accounting changes receiving nonretroactive treatment. **The cumulative effect of all periods prior to such period presented is treated as an adjustment to beginning retained earnings of the period.** The net income of each period presented is recomputed applying the new principle. Thus, the adjustment to beginning retained earnings includes all income effects prior to each period presented, and the recomputed net income includes the effect of the new principle on income for each period presented. Together these two adjustments restate the retained earnings ending balance for the period presented to the amount it would have been had the new principle always been applied. This restatement process is consistently followed for all periods presented. According to APB 20, the nature of and justification for the change must be disclosed in the year that the change is made. In addition, the effect of the change on income before extraordinary items, net income, and the related per share amounts should be disclosed for all periods presented. Again, subsequent financial statements do not need to repeat the disclosures.

The restatement need only reflect the direct effects of the change in accounting principle. The exception to this statement arises if the direct effect results in a change in a nondiscretionary item that will be recorded on the books. For example, assume that profit sharing expense is based on net income. The company changes its method of accounting for long-term construction contracts which results in an increase in income in all of the prior years. This increase in income would have changed the amount of the profit sharing expense required during the applicable years. However, the expense would only be changed for the purpose of the restatement if it is to be paid. If the profit sharing agreement does not require an adjustment to the actual contribution, the increase in expense would not be recognized on the restated financial statements.

The following illustration is an adaption of Appendix B in APB 20 and illustrates the proper restatement in a situation where the company changes its method of accounting for long-term construction contracts. As mentioned above, this is one of the five situations for which APB 20 requires retroactive treatment.

Example of Retroactive Treatment (Example from APB 20, Appendix B)

During 19X5 XYZ Company decided to adopt the percentage-of-completion method in accounting for all of its long-term construction contracts. The company had used the completed contract method in previous years and had maintained records which were adequate to retroactively apply the percentage-of-completion method.

The following assumptions are made for this example:

1. A constant tax rate of 40%.
2. There are 1,000,000 common shares outstanding in all periods affected by the change.
3. An additional 100,000 shares would be issued if all of the outstanding bonds, which are not common stock equivalents, were converted. The annual interest on this bond obligation is $15,000 (net of tax).

| | Pretax accounting income | | Difference in income | |
Year	Percentage-of-completion method	Completed contract method	Direct	Net of tax effect
Prior to 19X1	$1,800,000	$1,300,000	$500,000	$300,000
19X1	900,000	800,000	100,000	60,000
19X2	700,000	1,000,000	(300,000)	(180,000)
19X3	800,000	600,000	200,000	120,000
19X4	1,000,000	1,100,000	(100,000)	(60,000)
Total at beg. of 19X5	$5,200,000	$4,800,000	$400,000	$240,000
19X5	1,100,000	900,000	200,000	120,000
Total	$6,300,000	$5,700,000	$600,000	$360,000

Following is the proper method of disclosing this type of change as prescribed by APB 20.

On the Face of the Income Statement

	19X5	As adjusted See Note A 19X4
Income before extraordinary item	$ 660,000	$ 600,000
Extraordinary item (description)	--	(80,000)
Net income	$ 660,000	$ 520,000
Per share amounts:		
Earnings per common share--assuming no dilution:		
Income before extraordinary item	$.66	$.60
Extraordinary item	--	(.08)
Net income	$.66	$.52
Earnings per common share--assuming full dilution:		
Income before extraordinary item	$.61	$.56
Extraordinary item	--	(.07)
Net income	$.61	$.49

On the Statement of Retained Earnings

	19X5	As adjusted See Note A 19X4
Balance at beginning of year, as previously reported	$17,910,000	$17,330,000
Add adjustment for the cumulative effect on prior years of applying retroactively the new method of accounting for long-term contracts (Note A)	240,000	300,000*
Balance at beginning of year	$18,150,000	$17,630,000
Net income	660,000	520,000
Balance at end of year	$18,810,000	$18,150,000

*This is the resultant amount of the change less the tax effect through 19X3.

In the Notes to the Financial Statements

Note A--Change in Method of Accounting for Long-term Construction Contracts

In 19X5 the company changed its method of accounting for long-term construction contracts from the completed contract method to the percentage-of-completion method. The change was made because the company felt that the new method resulted in a more accurate recognition of revenue and a better matching of revenue and costs. The financial statements of prior periods have been restated to apply the new method retroactively. The company will continue to use the completed contract method for income tax purposes. The effect of the accounting change in income of 19X5 and on income previously reported for 19X4 is:

	Increase (decrease)	
	19X5	*19X4*
Effect on:		
Income before extraordinary item and net income	$120,000	$(60,000)
Earnings per common share--no dilution	.12	(.06)
Earnings per common share--full dilution	.11	(.05)

The balances of retained earnings for 19X4 and 19X5 have been adjusted for the effect (net of income taxes) of retroactively applying the new method of accounting.

Notice that the income statement does not highlight the change. This lack of disclosure has been the major argument surrounding the use of this method. While both periods reflect the increase in income resulting from the change, it is assumed that the average user of the financial statements may not refer to the notes in order to understand the change.

The only change shown "on" the financial statements is the cumulative adjustment which is part of the Statement of Retained Earnings. This amount is determined by totaling the effect of the change for all periods prior to the period presented in the financial statements. This amount is reflected as an adjustment to the beginning balance of Retained Earnings.

The notes to the financial statements must disclose the nature of and reason for the change. In addition, the effect of the change on income before extraordinary items and net income including the related per share amounts should be disclosed for all of the years presented. In this case, the change for 19X5 and 19X4 is to increase (decrease) net income by $100,000 and ($50,000), respectively.

Cumulative effect not determinable. The Board also realized that there would be certain circumstances in which the pro forma accounts or the cumulative effect amount would not be available. If the pro forma amounts cannot be determined or reasonably estimated for the individual prior periods, the cumulative effect should be shown on the income statement and the reason for not showing the pro forma amounts disclosed in the notes to the financial statements. In an instance where the cumulative effect cannot be determined disclosure will be limited to showing the effect of the change on the results of operations for the period of the change (including per share data) and to explaining the reason for omitting accounting for the cumulative effect and disclosure of pro forma results. The Board specified the change from the FIFO to LIFO method of inventory pricing as one circumstance under which it would be impossible to determine the cumulative effect.

Example of Change from FIFO to LIFO

During 1992 Ramirez, Inc. decided to change the method used for pricing its inventories from FIFO to LIFO. The inventory values are as listed below for both FIFO and LIFO cost. Sales for the year amounted to $15,000,000 and the company's total purchases were $11,000,000. Other expenses amounted to

$1,200,000 for the year. The company had 1,000,000 shares outstanding throughout the year.

Inventory values:

	FIFO	LIFO
12/31/91	2,000,000	N/A
12/31/92	4,000,000	1,800,000

The computations would be as follows:

	FIFO	LIFO
Net income:		
Sales	$15,000,000	$15,000,000
Less: Cost of goods sold	9,000,000	11,200,000
Gross margin	$ 6,000,000	$ 3,800,000
Other expenses	1,200,000	1,200,000
Net income	$ 4,800,000	$ 2,600,000

The following footnote would be an example of the required disclosure in this circumstance:

Note A--Change in Method of Accounting for Inventories

During 1992, the company changed its method of accounting for all of its inventories from first-in, first-out (FIFO) to last-in, first-out (LIFO). The change was made because management believes that the LIFO method provides a better matching of costs and revenues. In addition, the adoption of LIFO conforms the company's inventory pricing policy to the one which is predominate in the industry. The change and its effect on net earnings ($000 omitted except for per share) and earnings per share for 1992 are as follows:

	Net earnings	Earnings per share
Net earnings before the change	$4,800	$4.80
Reduction of earnings by the change	2,200	2.20
Net earnings	$2,600	$2.60

There is no cumulative effect of the change on prior years because beginning inventory on January 1, 1992 at LIFO is the same as that which was reported on a FIFO basis at December 31, 1991. As a result of this change, the current period's financial statements are not comparable with those of any prior periods.

The current cost of inventories valued at LIFO exceeds the carrying amount by $2,200,000 at December 31, 1992.

Change in amortization method. Another special case in accounting for a change in principle takes place when a company chooses to change the systematic pattern of amortizing the costs of long-lived assets to expense. When a company adopts a new method of amortization for newly acquired identifiable long-lived assets and uses that method for all new assets of the same class without changing the method used previously for existing assets of the same class, there is a change in accounting principle. Obviously, there is no adjustment required to the financial statements or any cumulative type adjustment. In these special cases, a description of the nature of the method changed and the effect on net income, income before extraordinary items, and related per share amounts should be disclosed in the period of the change. Should the new method be adopted for all assets, both old and new, then the change in accounting principle would be the usual one and would require a cumulative effect adjustment.

Change in Accounting Estimate

The preparation of financial statements requires frequent use of estimates for such items as asset service lives, salvage values, collectibility of accounts receivable, warranty costs, pension costs, etc. These future conditions and events and their effects cannot be perceived with certainty; therefore, changes in estimates will be inevitable as new information and more experience is obtained. APB 20 requires that changes in estimates be handled currently and prospectively. "The effect of the change in accounting estimate should be accounted for in (a) the period of change if the change affects that period only or (b) the period of change and future periods if the change affects both." For example, on January 1, 1992, a machine purchased for $10,000 was originally estimated to have a 10-year life. On January 1, 1997 (six years later), the asset is expected to last another 10 years. As a result, both the current period and the subsequent periods are affected by the change. The annual depreciation charge over the remaining life would be computed as follows:

$$\frac{\text{Book value of asset - Salvage value}}{\text{Remaining useful life}} = \frac{\$5,000 - 0}{10 \text{ yrs.}} = \$500/\text{yr.}$$

A permanent impairment affecting the cost recovery of an asset should not be handled as a change in accounting estimate but should be treated as a loss of the period. (See the discussion in Chapter 8.)

The Board concluded that a change in accounting estimate that is in essence effected by a change in accounting principle should be reported as a change in accounting estimate, the rationale being that the effect of the change in accounting principle is inseparable from the effect of the change in estimate. For example, a company may change from deferring and amortizing a cost to recording it as an expense when incurred because the future benefits of the cost have become doubtful. In this instance, the company is changing its accounting principle (from deferral to immediate recognition) because of its change in the estimate of the future value of a particular cost. The amount of the cumulative effect would be the same as that attributable to the current or future periods. Because the two are indistinguishable, changes of this type are to be considered changes in estimates according to APB 20. However, the change must be clearly indistinguishable to be combined. The ability to compute each element independently would preclude combining them as a single change. Also, for generally accepted auditing standards such a change is deemed a change in accounting principle for purposes of applying the consistency standard.

Change in Reporting Entity

An accounting change which results in financial statements that are, in effect, the statements of a different reporting entity should be reported by restating the financial statements of all prior periods presented in order to show financial information for the new reporting entity for all periods. The following qualify as changes in reporting entity:

1. Consolidated or combined statements in place of individual statements
2. Change in group of subsidiaries for which consolidated statements are prepared
3. Change in companies included in combined statements
4. Business combination accounted for as a pooling of interests

Correction of an Error

While good internal control and the exercise of due care will serve to minimize the number of errors made, these safeguards cannot be expected to completely eliminate errors in the financial statements. As a result, it was necessary for the accounting profession to promulgate standards that would insure uniform treatment of accounting for error corrections. APB 20 and SFAS 16 are the promulgated GAAP regarding the accounting for error corrections. APB 20 identifies examples of some errors and indicates that they are to be treated as prior period adjustments. SFAS 16 reiterates this treatment for accounting errors and provides guidance for the disclosing of prior period adjustments.

APB 20, para 13 identifies examples of errors as resulting from mathematical mistakes, mistakes in the application of accounting principles, or the oversight or misuse of facts known to the accountant at the time the financial statements were prepared. APB 20 also states that the change from an unacceptable (or incorrect) accounting principle to a correct principle **is** considered a correction of an error, not a change in accounting principle. This should not be confused with the preferability dilemma discussed earlier which involves two or more acceptable principles. While errors occur that affect both current and future periods, we are primarily concerned with the reporting of the correction of an error occurring in previously issued financial statements. Errors affecting current and future periods require correction but do not require disclosure as they are presumed to be discovered prior to the issuance of financial statements. According to APB 20, the correction of an error in the financial statements of a prior period discovered subsequent to their issuance should be reported as a prior period adjustment. The essential distinction between a change in estimate and the correction of an error depends upon the availability of information. An estimate requires correction because by its nature it is based upon incomplete information. Later data will either confirm or contradict the estimate and any contradiction will require correction. An error **misuses** existing information available at the time of the decision and is discovered at a later date. However, this discovery is not a result of additional information.

The required disclosure regarding the correction of an error is set forth by APB 20 and includes the nature of the error and the effect of its correction on income before extraordinary items, net income, and the related per share amounts in the period in which the error was discovered and corrected. This disclosure does not need to be repeated in subsequent periods.

The major criterion for determining whether or not to report the correction of the error is the materiality of the correction. According to APB 20, there are many factors to be considered in determining the materiality of the error correction. Materiality should be considered for each correction individually, as well as for all corrections in total. If the correction is determined to have a material effect on income before extraordinary items, net income, or the trend of earnings, it should be disclosed in accordance with the requirements set forth in the preceding paragraph.

Thus, the prior period adjustment should be presented in the financial statements as follows:

Retained earnings, 1/1/8X, as previously reported	xxx
Correction of error (description) in prior period(s) (net of $___ tax)	xxx
Adjusted balance of retained earnings at 1/1/8X	xxx
Net income	xxx
Retained earnings, 12/31/8X	xxx

In comparative statements, prior period adjustments should also be shown as adjustments to the beginning balances in the retained earnings statements. The amount of the adjustment on the earliest statement shall be the cumulative effect of the error on periods prior to the earliest period presented. The later retained earnings statements presented should also show a prior period adjustment for the cumulative amount as of the beginning of the period being reported on.

Example of Prior Period Adjustment

Assume that ABC Company had overstated its depreciation expense by $50,000 in 1990 and $40,000 in 1991, both due to a mathematical mistake. The errors which affected both the income statement and the tax return in 1990 and 1991 are found in 1992.

The following prior period adjustment would be required in 1992 to correct the accounts (assuming a 40% tax rate):

Accumulated depreciation	90,000	
Income taxes payable		36,000
Retained earnings		54,000

Assuming that we are presenting two-year comparative statements, the resulting effects of the prior period adjustment should be included in each statement presented. The comparative statement of retained earnings would appear as follows (all figures other than corrections are assumed):

	1992	1991
Retained earnings, 1/1 (as previously reported)	$305,000	$250,000
Adjustments (See Note 1)	54,000	30,000
Restated as of 1/1	$359,000	$280,000
Net income	90,000	104,000
	$449,000	$384,000
Dividends	45,000	25,000
Retained earnings	$404,000	$359,000

Note 1

The balance of retained earnings at the end of 1991 has been restated from amounts previously reported to reflect a retroactive credit of $54,000 ($90,000 net of $36,000 tax) for overstatement of depreciation in the previous periods. Of this amount, $24,000 ($40,000 net of $16,000 tax) is applicable to 1991 and has been reflected as an increase in income for that year, and the balance (applicable to years prior to 1991) has been credited to 1991 beginning retained earnings.

The retained earnings as previously reported in 1991 and as it would have appeared in 1992 if no adjustments were made is as follows:

	1992	1991
Retained earnings, 1/1	$305,000	$250,000
Net income	90,000	80,000
	$395,000	$330,000
Dividends	45,000	25,000
Retained earnings, 12/31	$350,000	$305,000

Disclosures

(See the Summary of Accounting for Accounting Changes and Error Correction on the following page.)

SUMMARY OF ACCOUNTING FOR ACCOUNTING CHANGES AND ERROR CORRECTION

	Footnote disclosures		Reporting on financial statements				Recording in books	
			Effect on income before X-items, NI, EPS		Statement disclosures			
	Nature of item	Justification*	Current yr. only	All periods presented	Retroactive treatment: previous financial statements restated	Cumulative effect treatment: pro formas shown for all years	Direct dr./cr. to retained earnings	Cumulative effect account
ACCOUNTING CHANGES								
In Principle								
General—change in principle or method of application from one acceptable GAAP to another. (Change from unacceptable GAAP is correction of error.)	X	X	X			X		X
Special	X	X		X	X		X	
• LIFO to another method								
• Change in method of accounting for long-term construction contracts.								
• Change to or from "full cost" method of accounting in the extractive industries.								
Special Exemptions for closely held corporation when it changes principles before its initial public offering.	X	X			X		X	
FASB Mandated Examples: equity method, R&D costs, inflation accounting.	X			X	X		X	
In Estimate** Natural occurences because judgment is used in preparation of statements. New events, more experience, and additional information affect earlier good faith estimates.				X***				
In Reporting Entity*** Includes consolidated or combined statements in place of individual statements, change in group of subsidiaries for which consolidated statements are prepared, change in companies included in combined statements, and business combination accounted for as a pooling of interests.	X	X		X	X			
ERROR CORRECTION Mathematical mistakes, mistakes in applying principles, oversight or misuse of available facts, change from unacceptable to acceptable GAAP.	X			X	X		X	

*Should clearly explain why the newly adopted accounting principle is preferable.

**Change in estimate effected by a change in principle is accounted for as a change in estimate.

***For material changes affecting more than just the current year.

APPENDIX

Accounting Changes In Interim Periods

APB 28 is concerned with interim reporting. APB 28 indicates that accounting changes are to be reported in interim periods in accordance with the provisions set forth in APB 20. The FASB then issued SFAS 3 in order to clarify the interim treatment of an accounting change and to provide examples. Of particular concern in SFAS 3 was the treatment to be accorded cumulative effect type accounting changes (including a change to LIFO for which no cumulative effect can be determined) and accounting changes made in the fourth quarter by publicly-traded companies.

The treatment of a cumulative effect change in an interim period depends upon the quarter in which the change is made. If the cumulative effect type accounting change is made in the first quarter, then the cumulative effect on the beginning balance of retained earnings should be included in the net income of the first quarter. Again, the income for the first quarter of the current period is computed using the newly adopted method, and the cumulative effect of the change shall be shown on the income statement after extraordinary items and before net income. In accordance with APB 20, the comparative periods are not to be restated.

If the cumulative effect type accounting change is made in a period other than the first quarter, then no cumulative effect of the accounting change should be included in the net income of the period. Rather, the pre-change interim periods of the year in which the change is made should be restated to reflect the newly adopted accounting principle. The cumulative effect on the beginning balance of retained earnings is then shown in the first interim period of the year in which the change is made. This includes any year-to-date or other financial statements that include the first interim period.

SFAS 3 requires that the following disclosures be made regarding a cumulative effect type accounting change in an interim period in addition to the treatment described above for the actual amount of the cumulative effect:

1. In the financial statements for the period in which the change is made, the nature and justification of the change
2. Disclosure of the effect of the change on income from continuing operations, net income, and related per share amounts for the interim period in which the change is made. If the change is made in other than the first interim period, then they shall also disclose the effect of the change on income from continuing operations, net income, and related per share amounts for each pre-change interim period, and income from continuing operations, net income, and related per share amounts for each pre-change interim period restated.
3. In the period in which the change is made, the pro forma amounts for income from continuing operations, net income, and the related per share amounts should be disclosed for:

    a. The interim period in which the change is made.

b. Any interim periods of prior years for which financial information is presented.

If no prior year fiscal information is presented, then disclosure should be made, in the period of the change, of the actual and pro forma amounts of income from continuing operations, net income, and related per share amounts for the interim period of the immediately preceding fiscal year that corresponds to the interim period in which the change is made. The pro forma amounts are to be calculated in accordance with APB 20 (discussed earlier).

4. The same disclosures described in (1) and (2) above shall be made regarding any year-to-date or last-twelve-months financial statements that include the period of the change.
5. For a post-change interim period (same fiscal year), disclosure shall be made of the effect of the change on income from continuing operations, net income, and the related per share amounts for the post-change period.

As mentioned earlier, a change to the LIFO method of pricing inventories generally results in a situation where the cumulative effect is not determinable. If such a change occurs in the first interim period, then the same disclosures described above for the cumulative effect type accounting change shall be made with the exception of the pro forma amounts. If the change is made in a period other than the first interim period, the disclosures should include those mentioned above **and** restatement of the financial information presented for pre-change interim periods of that year reflecting the adoption of the new accounting principle.

The following examples will illustrate the foregoing principles relative to a cumulative effect type accounting change made in both the first interim period and other than the first period. We will use the same facts and assumptions for both examples.

Example of Accounting Change in First Interim Period

In 19X5 ABC Company decided to adopt the straight-line method of depreciation for plant equipment. The new method was to be used for both new acquisitions and previously acquired plant equipment. In prior periods, the company had used an accelerated method of computing depreciation on plant equipment. The following assumptions are made:

1. The effects of the change are limited to the direct effect on depreciation and the indirect effect on the incentive compensation, as well as the related tax effects.
2. The incentive compensation is 10% of pretax accounting income.
3. There is a constant tax rate of 50%.
4. There were 1,000,000 shares issued and outstanding throughout the periods covered, with no potential for dilution.
5. The company presents comparative interim statements.

6. Assume that the following information is given for years 19X4 and 19X5:

Period	Net income on the basis of old accounting principle (accelerated depreciation)	Gross effect of change to straight-line depreciation	Gross effect less income taxes	Net effect after incentive compensation and related income taxes
Prior to first qtr. 19X4		$ 20,000	$ 10,000	$ 9,000
First quarter 19X4	$1,000,000	30,000	15,000	13,500
Second quarter 19X4	1,200,000	70,000	35,000	31,500
Third quarter 19X4	1,100,000	50,000	25,000	22,500
Fourth quarter 19X4	1,100,000	80,000	40,000	36,000
Total at beg. of 19X5	$4,400,000	$250,000	$125,000	$112,500
First quarter 19X5	$1,059,500*	$ 90,000	$ 45,000	$ 40,500*
Second quarter 19X5	1,255,000	100,000	50,000	45,000
Third quarter 19X5	1,150,500	110,000	55,000	49,500
Fourth quarter 19X5	1,146,000	120,000	60,000	54,000
	$4,611,000	$420,000	$210,000	$189,000

In the first example we apply the SFAS 3 criteria applicable to a change made in the first quarter. Notice that in interim reporting the same principles are followed as were set for annual financial reporting. The cumulative effect is considered to be a change in the beginning balance of Retained Earnings and, therefore, effective at the beginning of the year. To include the cumulative effect in any interim period other than the first, or year-to-date including the first, would be misleading. In this case we are dealing with the first period and the $125,000, representing the direct effects net of tax, is presented on the face of the income statement. Also, as with the annual reporting, the pro forma amounts reflecting the direct and indirect effects of the change are also presented. In this case the 19X5 number already reflects the change, and from the given information we can see that the total effect on the first quarter of 19X4 was to increase net income by $13,500.

The notes, as required, state the nature and justification of the change. Also included in the notes are the total cumulative effect, the effect on the earnings of the first quarter of the year in which the change is made (this disclosure makes allowable a comparison between statements), and the nature of the pro forma amounts. Essentially, if the change is made in the first quarter, the reporting and disclosure requirements are very similar to those in the annual financial statements.

The net income for 19X5 has been broken down into income based on the old accounting principle and the effect of the change. These numbers are unrealistic in the sense that the 19X5 income figure would be computed based on the new principle (e.g., the 1st quarter net income is $1,100,000 which is $1,059,500 + 40,500).

The following quarterly financial statements and note illustrate the foregoing principles:

	Three months ended March 31,	
	19X5	*19X4*
Income before cumulative effect of a change in accounting principle	$1,100,000	$1,000,000
Cumulative effect on prior years (to December 31, 19X4) of changing to a different depreciation method (Note A)	125,000	--
Net income	$1,225,000	$1,000,000
Amounts per common share:		
Income before cumulative effect of a change in accounting principle	$1.10	$1.00
Cumulative effect on prior years (to December 31, 19X4) of changing to a different depreciation method (Note A)	0.13	--
Net income	$1.23	$1.00
Pro forma amounts assuming the new depreciation method is applied retroactively (Note A):		
Net income	$1,100,000	$1,013,500
Net income per common share	$1.10	$1.01

Note A--Change in Depreciation Method for Plant Equipment

During the first quarter of 19X5, the company decided to change the method of computing depreciation on plant assets from the accelerated method used in previous periods to the straight-line method. The change was made to better match the amortized cost of the asset to the revenue produced by it. The retroactive application of the new method resulted in a cumulative effect of $125,000 (net of $125,000 in income taxes) which is included in the income for the first quarter of 19X5. The effect of the change on the first quarter of 19X5 was to increase income before cumulative effect of a change in accounting principle by $40,500 ($.04 per share) and net income by $165,500 ($.17 per share). The pro forma amounts reflect the effect of retroactive application on depreciation, the change in provisions for incentive compensation that would have been made in 19X4 had the new method been in effect, and the related income taxes.

Example of Accounting Change in Other Than First Interim Period

In this case, we assume that the change is made in the third quarter of the year and that the company is presenting comparative financial information for both the current quarter and year-to-date. As mentioned above, the cumulative effect is not necessarily to be presented in the period of the change because it relates to the beginning of the year. Thus, in the illustration below the three months ended September 30 do not include an amount for the cumulative effect; however, the nine-month statements do. The presentation of the three-month statements reflects the effect of the accounting change for 19X5 and does not reflect this change for 19X4. The 19X4 statement is the same as it was presented in the prior year. The pro forma amounts and the disclosure in the notes provide the information necessary to make these two interim periods comparable.

The nine-month statement for 19X5 reflects the effect of the change for the entire nine-month period. Thus, the results of the six-month period for 19X5 added to the three-month results would not equal the amounts shown in the nine-month statement. This is because the prior statement for the six-month period would not have reflected the new principle that the three-month and nine-month figures do. Again, the 19X4 numbers are presented as they were in the previous year. The remainder of the example is really no different from the disclosure required by another accounting change, with one exception. The exception is that the effect of the change on the preceding interim periods must also be disclosed. Note that the cumulative effect is included in the first period. The total of the three individual quarters will now equal the total income shown in the nine-month statement.

| | Three months ended September 30, | | Nine-months ended September 30, | |
	19X5	*19X4*	*19X5*	*19X4*
Income before cumulative effect of a change in accounting principle	$1,200,000	$1,100,000	$3,600,000	$3,300,000
Cumulative effect on prior years (to December 31, 19X4) of changing to a different depreciation method (Note A)	--	--	125,000	--
Net income	$1,200,000	$1,100,000	$3,725,000	$3,300,000
Amounts per common share:				
Income before cumulative effect of a change in accounting principle	$1.20	$1.10	$3.60	$3.30
Cumulative effect on prior years (to December 31, 19X4) of changing to a different depreciation method (Note A)	--	--	0.13	--
Net Income	$1.20	$1.10	$3.73	$3.30
Pro forma amounts assuming the new depreciation method is applied retroactively (Note A):				
Net income	$1,200,000	$1,122,500	$3,600,000	$3,367,500
Net income per common share	$1.20	$1.12	$3.60	$3.37

Note A--Change in Depreciation Method for Plant Equipment

During the third quarter of 19X5, the company decided to change the method of computing depreciation on plant assets from the accelerated method used in previous periods to the straight-line method. The change was made to better match the amortized cost of the asset to the revenue produced by it. The retroactive application of the new method resulted in a cumulative effect of $125,000 (net of $125,000 in income taxes) which is included in the income for the nine months ended September 30, 19X5. The effect of the change on the three months ended September 30, 19X5, was to increase net income by $49,500 ($.05 per share); the effect of the change on the nine months ended September 30, 19X5, was to increase income before cumulative effect of a change in accounting principle by $135,000 ($.14 per share) and net income by $260,000 ($.26 per share). The pro forma amounts reflect the effect of retroactive application on depreciation, the change in the provisions for incentive pay that would have been made in 19X4 had the new method been in effect, and the related income taxes.

The effect of the change on the first and second quarters of 19X5 is as follows:

	Three months ended	
	March 31, 19X5	*June 30, 19X5*
Net income as originally reported	$1,059,500	$1,255,000
Effect of change in depreciation method	40,500	45,000
Income before cumulative effect of a change in accounting principle	1,100,000	1,300,000
Cumulative effect on prior years (to December 31, 19X4) of changing to a different depreciation method	125,000	--
Net income as restated	$1,255,000	$1,300,000
Per share amounts:		
Net income as originally reported	$1.06	$1.26
Effect of change in depreciation method	0.04	0.04
Income before cumulative effect of a change in accounting principle	1.10	1.30
Cumulative effect on prior years (to December 31, 19X4) of changing to a different depreciation method	0.13	--
Net income as restated	$1.23	$1.30

20 Foreign Currency

Perspective and Issues

Since World War II, international activity by U.S. corporations has increased significantly. Not only are transactions consummated with independent foreign entities, but also with foreign subsidiaries of U.S. firms. In order for the users of these firms' financial statements to properly analyze the foreign involvement, the transactions entered into must be expressed in terms the users can understand, i.e., U.S. dollars. The generally accepted accounting principles governing the translation of foreign currency financial statements and foreign currency transactions into U.S. dollars are found primarily in SFAS 52, which superseded both SFAS 8 and 20. Additional guidance in this area is provided by FASB Interpretation 37. As stated in SFAS 52, these principles apply to the translation of:

1. Foreign currency transactions (e.g., exports, imports, and loans) which are denominated in other than a company's functional currency.
2. Foreign currency financial statements of branches, divisions, subsidiaries, and other investees which are incorporated in the financial statements of a U.S. company by combination, consolidation, or the equity method.

The objectives of translation are to provide:

1. Information relative to the expected economic effects of rate changes on an enterprise's cash flows and equity.
2. Information in consolidated statements relative to the financial results and relationships of each individual foreign consolidated entity as reflected by the functional currency of each reporting entity.

Sources of GAAP

SFAS	*FASB I*
52	37

Definitions of Terms

Conversion. The exchange of one currency for another.

Current exchange rate. The current exchange rate is the rate at which one unit of a currency can be exchanged for (converted into) another currency. For purposes of translation of financial statements referred to in SFAS 52, the current exchange rate is the rate as of the end of the period covered by the financial statements or as of the dates of recognition in those statements in the case of revenues, expenses, gains, and losses.

Discount or premium on a forward contract. The foreign currency amount of the contract multiplied by the difference between the contracted forward rate and the spot rate at the date of inception of the contract.

Foreign currency. A currency other than the functional currency of the entity being referred to (for example, the dollar could be a foreign currency for a foreign entity). Composites of currencies, such as the Special Drawing Rights on the International Monetary Fund (SDRs), used to set prices or denominate amounts of loans, etc., have the characteristics of foreign currency for purposes of applying SFAS 52.

Foreign currency statements. Financial statements that employ as the unit of measure a functional currency that is not the reporting currency of the enterprise.

Foreign currency transactions. Transactions whose terms are denominated in a currency other than the entity's functional currency. Foreign currency transactions arise when an enterprise (a) buys or sells on credit goods or services whose prices are denominated in foreign currency, (b) borrows or lends funds and the amounts payable or receivable are denominated in foreign currency, (c) is a party to an unperformed forward exchange contract, or (d) for other reasons, acquires or disposes of assets or incurs or settles liabilities denominated in foreign currency.

Foreign currency translation. The process of expressing in the reporting currency of the enterprise those amounts that are denominated or measured in a different currency.

Forward exchange contract. An agreement to exchange at a specified future date currencies of different countries at a specified rate (forward rate).

Functional currency. An entity's functional currency is the currency of the primary economic environment in which the entity operates; normally, that is the currency of the environment in which an entity primarily generates and expends cash.

Local currency. The currency of a particular country being referred to.

Monetary items. Cash, claims to receive a fixed amount of cash, and obligations to pay a fixed amount of cash.

Nonmonetary items. All balance sheet items other than cash, claims to cash, and cash obligations.

Remeasurement. If an entity's books and records are not kept in its functional currency, remeasurement into the functional currency is required. Monetary balances are translated by using the current exchange rate, and nonmonetary balances are translated by using historical exchange rates. If the U.S. dollar is the functional currency, remeasurement into the reporting currency (the U.S. dollar) obviates translation.

Reporting currency. The currency in which an enterprise prepares its financial statements.

Reporting enterprise. An entity or group whose financial statements are being referred to. In this Statement, those financial statements reflect (a) the financial statements of one or more foreign operations by combination, consolidation, or equity accounting; (b) foreign currency transactions; or (c) both of the foregoing.

Spot rate. The exchange rate for immediate delivery of currencies exchanged.

Transaction date. The date at which a transaction (for example, a sale or purchase of merchandise or services) is recorded in accounting records in conformity with generally accepted accounting principles. A long-term commitment may have more than one transaction date (for example, the due date of each progress payment under a construction contract is an anticipated transaction date).

Transaction gain or loss. Transaction gains or losses result from a change in exchange rates between the functional currency and the currency in which a foreign currency transaction is denominated. They represent an increase or decrease in (a) the actual functional currency cash flows realized upon settlement of foreign currency transactions and (b) the expected functional currency cash flows on unsettled foreign currency transactions.

Translation adjustments. Translation adjustments result from the process of translating financial statements from the entity's functional currency into the reporting currency.

Concepts, Rules, and Examples

Translation of Foreign Currency Financial Statements

Selection of the functional currency. Before the financial statements of a foreign branch, division, or subsidiary are translated into U.S. dollars, the management of the U.S. company must make a decision as to which currency is the functional currency of the foreign entity. Once chosen, the functional currency cannot be changed unless it is clear that economic facts and circumstances have changed. Additionally, previously issued financial statements are not restated for any changes in the functional currency. The functional currency decision is crucial because different translation methods are applied which may have a material effect on the U.S. company's financial statements.

The Financial Accounting Standards Board defines functional currency but does not list definitive criteria which, if satisfied, would result in the selection of an entity's functional currency. Rather, realizing that such criteria did not exist, the Board listed various factors which were intended to give management guidance in making the functional currency decision. These factors include:

1. Cash flows (Do the foreign entity's cash flows directly affect the parent's cash flows and are they immediately available for remittance to the parent?).
2. Sales prices (Are the foreign entity's sales prices responsive to exchange rate changes and to international competition?).
3. Sales markets (Is the foreign entity's sales market the parent's country or are sales denominated in the parent's currency?).
4. Expenses (Are the foreign entity's expenses incurred in the parent's country?).
5. Financing (Is the foreign entity's financing primarily from the parent or is it denominated in the parent's currency?).
6. Intercompany transactions (Is there a high volume of intercompany transactions between the parent and the foreign entity?).

If the answers to the questions above are predominantly yes, the functional currency is the reporting currency of the parent company, i.e., the U.S. dollar. If the answers are predominantly no, the functional currency would most likely be the local currency of the foreign entity, although it is possible for a foreign currency other than the local currency to be the functional currency.

Translation methods. In deciding upon the method used to translate assets and liabilities of a company's foreign subsidiary, the Board had four from which to choose. The primary distinction among the methods was the classification of assets and liabilities which would be translated at either the current or historical rate.

The first method is known as the **temporal method.** This method translates cash, receivables, payables, and assets and liabilities carried at present or future values at the current rate, with the remaining assets and liabilities carried at historical costs translated at the applicable historical rates. In essence, the accounting principles used to measure the assets and liabilities in the foreign statements are retained. However, the foreign exchange gains or losses which arise from this method do so because of this method and not because the economic events which affect the foreign entity's operations are reflected.

In most cases, the temporal method produces the same results as the second approach, the **monetary/nonmonetary method.** The remeasurement technique, required per SFAS 52 when the books and records are not maintained in the functional currency, is essentially the same as the monetary/nonmonetary method. This method translates nonmonetary assets and liabilities at the proper historical rates.

Under this method, it is the characteristics of assets and liabilities which are used as the basis for classification rather than the method of accounting, as under the first approach. It is by mere coincidence that assets and liabilities are measured on bases which approximately coincide with the monetary/nonmonetary classification which produces the aforementioned similar results. A problem with this method is that not all items may be classified as monetary or nonmonetary, and some arbitrary decisions must be made.

The third method is the **current/noncurrent method,** which, as implied, stresses balance sheet classification as the basis for translation. Current assets and liabilities are translated at the current rate and noncurrent assets and liabilities at the applicable historical rates. A major weakness under this approach is the treatment of inventory and long-term debt. Inventory, a current asset, would be translated at its current cost, a major departure from traditional GAAP. The translation of foreign-denominated long-term debt under this approach would be misleading to users, as it would be translated at its historical value. If the dollar weakens internationally, it will take more dollars to repay this obligation, a fact which would not be apparent from the parent's financial statements. Furthermore, some balance sheets are not classified and variations between current and noncurrent classifications of classified balance sheets may be arbitrarily based upon management's intentions.

The last approach is known as the **current rate method** and is the approach mandated by SFAS 52 when the functional currency is the foreign currency. All assets and liabilities are translated at the current rate. The basis of this method is the "net investment concept" wherein the foreign entity is viewed as a separate entity which the parent invested into, rather than it being considered as part of the parent's operations. The Board's reasoning was that users can benefit most when the information provided about the foreign entity retains the relationships and results created in the environment (economics, legal, and political) in which the entity operates.

Under this approach, the reasoning follows that foreign-denominated debt is used to purchase assets which create foreign-denominated revenues. These assets act as a hedge against the debt from changes in the exchange rate. The excess (net) assets will, however, be affected by this foreign exchange risk, and this is the effect which is recognized by the parent.

If the foreign entity's local currency is the functional currency, the Board requires the current rate method when translating the foreign entity's financial statements. If, on the other hand, the U.S. dollar is the functional currency, the Board requires the remeasurement method when translating the foreign entity's financial statements. Both of these methods will be illustrated below.

Application of the Current Rate Method

Assume that a U.S. company has a 100% owned subsidiary in Germany that commenced operations in 1991. The subsidiary's operations consist of leasing space in an office building. This building, which cost 500 deutsche marks (DM), was financed primarily by German banks. All revenues and cash expenses are received and paid in deutsche marks. The subsidiary also maintains its books and records in DM. As a result, management of the U.S. company has decided that the DM is the functional currency.

The subsidiary's balance sheet at December 31, 1991, and its combined statement of income and retained earnings for the year ended December 31, 1991, are presented below in DM.

German Company
Balance Sheet
At December 31, 1991

Assets:			*Liabilities and stockholders' equity:*		
Cash	DM	50	Accounts payable	DM	30
Note receivable		20	Unearned rent		10
Land		100	Mortgage payable		400
Building		500	Common stock		40
Accumulated depreciation		(10)	Additional paid-in capital		160
			Retained earnings		20
			Total liabilities and		
Total assets	DM	660	stockholders' equity	DM	660

German Company
Combined Statement of Income and Retained Earnings
For the Year Ended December 31, 1991

Revenues	DM	200
Operating expenses (including depreciation expense of 10)		170
Net income	DM	30
Add retained earnings, January 31, 1991		--
Deduct dividends		(10)
Retained earnings, December 31, 1991	DM	20

Various exchange rates for 1991 are as follows:

1 DM = $.40 at the beginning of 1991 (when the common stock was issued and the land and building were financed through the mortgage)
1 DM = $.43 weighted-average for 1991
1 DM = $.42 at the date the dividends were declared and the unearned rent was received
1 DM = $.45 at the end of 1991

Since the DM is the functional currency, the German Company's financial statements must be translated into U.S. dollars by the **current rate method**. This translation process is illustrated below.

German Company
Balance Sheet Translation
(DM is the functional currency)
At December 31, 1991

Assets:	DM	Exchange rate	U.S. dollars
Cash	DM 50	.45	$ 22.50
Accounts receivable	20	.45	9.00
Land	100	.45	45.00
Building (net)	490	.45	220.50
Total assets	DM 660		$297.00

Liabilities and stockholders' equity:			
Accounts payable	DM 30	.45	$ 13.50
Unearned rent	10	.45	4.50
Mortgage payable	400	.45	180.00
Common stock	40	.40	16.00
Additional paid-in capital	160	.40	64.00
Retained earnings	20	See income statement	8.70
Translation adjustments	--	--	10.30
Total liabilities and stockholders' DM equity	660		$297.00

German Company
Combined Income and Retained Earnings
Statement Translation
For the Year Ended December 31, 1991

	DM	Exchange rate	U.S. dollars
Revenues	DM 200	.43	$86.00
Expenses (including DM10 depreciation expense)	170	.43	73.10
Net income	DM 30	.43	$12.90
Add retained earnings, January 1	--	--	--
Deduct dividends	(10)	.42	(4.20)
Retained earnings, December 31	DM 20		$ 8.70

German Company
Statement of Cash Flows
For the Year Ended December 31, 1991

		Local Currency	_Exchange rate_	_Reporting Currency_
Operating activities:				
Net income	DM	30	.43	$12.90
Adjustments to reconcile net income				
to net cash provided by operating				
activities:				
Depreciation		10	.43	4.30
Increase in accounts receivable		(20)	.43	(8.60)
Increase in accounts payable		30	.43	12.90
Increase in unearned rent		10	.42	4.20
Net cash provided by				
operating activities		60		$25.70
Investing activities:				
Purchase of land		(100)	.40	$ (40.00)
Purchase of building		(500)	.40	$(200.00)
Net cash used by				
investing activities		(600)		$(240.00)
Financing activities:				
Common stock issue		200	.40	$ 80.00
Mortgage payable		400	.40	160.00
Dividends paid		(10)	.42	(4.20)
Net cash provided by financing		590		$235.80
Effect on exchange rate changes on cash		N/A		1.00
Increase in cash and equivalents	DM	50		22.50
Cash at beginning of year		-0-		-0-
Cash at end of year	DM	50	.45	$ 22.50

The following points should be noted concerning the current rate method:

a. All **assets and liabilities** are translated using the current exchange rate at the balance sheet date (1 DM = $.45). All revenues and expenses should be translated at the rates in effect when these items are recognized during the period. Due to practical considerations, however, weighted-average rates can be used to translate revenues and expenses (1 DM = $.43).

b. **Stockholders' equity** accounts are translated by using historical exchange rates. Common stock was issued at the beginning of 1991 when the exchange rate was 1 DM = $.40. The translated balance of retained earnings is the result of the weighted-average rate applied to revenues and expenses and the specific rate in effect when the dividends were declared (1 DM = $.42).

c. **Translation adjustments** result from translating all assets and liabilities at the current rate, while stockholders' equity is translated by using historical and weighted-average rates. The adjustments have no direct effect on cash flows; however, changes in exchange rate will have an indirect effect upon sale or liquidation. Prior to this time the effect is uncertain and remote. Also, the effect is due to the net investment rather than the subsidiary's operations. For these reasons, the translation adjustments balance is reported as a separate component in the stockholders' equity section of the U.S. company's consolidated balance sheet. This balance essentially equates the total debits of the subsidiary (now expressed in U.S. dollars) with the total credits (also in dollars). It also may be determined directly, as shown next, to verify the translation process.

d. The translation adjustments credit of $10.30 is calculated as follows:

Net assets at the beginning of 1991 (after common stock was issued and the land and building were acquired through mortgage financing)	200 DM (.45 - .40) =	$10.00 credit
Net income	30 DM (.45 - .43) =	.60 credit
Dividends	10 DM (.45 - .42) =	.30 debit
Translation adjustment		$10.30 credit

e. The translation adjustments balance that appears as a separate component of stockholders' equity is cumulative in nature. Consequently, the change in this balance during the year should be disclosed in the financial statements. In the illustration, this balance went from zero to $10.30 at the end of 1991. The analysis of this change was presented previously. In addition, assume the following occurred during 1992:

German Company
Balance Sheet
December 31

Assets:		1992		1991		Increase/(Decrease)
Cash	DM	100	DM	50	DM	50
Accounts receivable		-0-		20		(20)
Land		150		100		50
Building (net)		480		490		(10)
	DM	730	DM	660	DM	70

Liabilities and Stockholders' Equity:

Accounts payable	DM	50	DM	30	DM	20
Unearned rent		-0-		10		(10)
Mortgage payable		450		400		50
Common stock		40		40		-0-
Additional paid-in capital		160		160		-0-
Retained earnings		30		20		10
Total liabilities & stockholders' equity	DM	730	DM	660	DM	70

German Company
Combined Statement of Income and Retained Earnings
For the Year Ended December 31, 1992

Revenues	DM	220
Operating expenses (including depreciation exp. of DM 10)		170
Net income	DM	50
Add: Retained earnings, Jan. 1, 1992		202
Deduct dividends		(40)
Retained earnings, Dec. 31, 1992	DM	30

Exchange rates were:
   1 DM = $.45 at the beginning of 1992
   1 DM = $.48 weighted-average for 1992
   1 DM = $.50 at the end of 1992
   1 DM = $.49 when dividends were paid in 1992 and land bought by incurring mortgage

The translation process for 1992 is illustrated below.

German Company
Balance Sheet Translation
(DM is the functional currency)
At December 31, 1992

Assets:	*DM*		*Exchange rate*	*U.S. dollars*
Cash	DM	100	.50	$ 50.00
Land		150	.50	75.00
Building		480	.50	240.00
	DM	730		$365.00

Liabilities & Stockholders' Equity:

Accounts payable	DM 50	.50	$ 25.00
Mortgage payable	450	.50	225.00
Common stock	40	.40	16.00
Addl. paid-in capital	160	.40	64.00
Retained earnings	30	(see income statement)	13.10
Translation adjustments	--		21.90
Total Liabilities & Stockholders' Equity	DM 730		$365.00

German Company
Combined Income and Retained Earnings
Statement Translation
For the Year Ended December 31, 1992

	DM	Exchange rate	U.S. dollars
Revenues	DM 220	.48	$105.60
Operating expenses (including depreciation of DM 10)	170	.48	81.60
Net income	DM 50	.48	$ 24.00
Add: Retained earnings 1/1/92	20	--	8.70
Less: Dividends	(40)	.49	(19.60)
Retained earnings 12/31/92	DM DM 30		$ 13.10

German Company
Statement of Cash Flows
For the Year Ended December 31, 1992

	Local Currency	Exchange Rate	Reporting Currency
Operating activities:			
Net income	DM 50	.48	$24.00
Adjustments to reconcile net income to net cash provided by operating activities:			
Depreciation	10	.48	4.80
Decrease in accounts receivable	20	.48	9.60
Increase in accounts payable	20	.48	9.60
Decrease in unearned rent	(10)	.48	(4.80)
Net cash provided by Operating Activities	DM 90		$43.20
Investing activities:			
Purchase of land	(50)	.49	(24.50)
Net cash used by investing activities	(50)		$(24.50)

Financing activities:

Mortgage payable		50	.49	$24.50
Dividends		(40)	.49	(19.60)
Net cash provided by financing	DM	10		$ 4.90

Effect of exchange rate changes on cash		NA		3.90

Increase in cash and equivalents	DM	50		$27.50
Cash at beginning of year	DM	50		$22.50
Cash at end of year	DM	100	.50	$50.00

Using the analysis that was presented before, the translation adjustment attributable to 1991 would be computed as follows:

Net assets at January 1, 1992	220 DM(.50 - .45)= $ 11.00 credit
Net income for 1992	50 DM(.50 - .48)= 1.00 credit
Dividends for 1992	40 DM(.50 - .49)= .40 debit
Total	$11.60 credit

The balance in the translation adjustment account at the end of 1992 would be $21.90. ($10.30 from 1991 and $11.60 from 1992.)

    f.   The use of the equity method by the U.S. company in accounting for the subsidiary would result in the following journal entries based upon the information presented above:

	1991		*1992*	
Original Investment:				
Investment in German subsidiary	80*		--	
Cash		80		--

*[$.40 x common stock of 40 DM plus additional paid-in capital of 160 DM]

Earnings pickup:				
Investment in German subsidiary	12.90		24**	
Equity in subsidiary income		12.90		24

**[$.48 x net income of 50 DM]

Dividends received:				
Cash	4.20		19.60	
Investment in German subsidiary		4.20		19.60

Translation adjustments:				
Investment in German subsidiary	10.30		11.60	
Translation adjustments		10.30		11.60

Note that the stockholders' equity of the U.S. company should be the same whether or not the German subsidiary is consolidated (APB 18, para 19). Since the subsidiary does not report the translation adjustments on its financial statements, care should be exercised so that it is not forgotten in the application of the equity method.

g. If the U.S. company disposes of its investment in the German subsidiary, the translation adjustments balance becomes part of the gain or loss that results from the transaction and must be eliminated. For example, assume that on January 2, 1993, the U.S. company sells its entire investment for 300 DM. The exchange rate at this date is 1 DM = $.50. The balance in the investment account at December 31, 1992 is $135 as a result of the entries made previously.

	Investment in German subsidiary	
1/1/91	80.00	
	12.90	4.20
	10.30	
Total	103.20	4.20
1/1/92	99.00	
	24.00	
	11.60	19.6
Total	115.00	

The following entries would be made to reflect the sale of the investment:

Cash (300 DM x $.50)	150	
Investment in German subsidiary		115
Gain from sale of subsidiary		35
Translation adjustments	21.90	
Gain from sale of subsidiary		21.90

If U.S. company had sold a portion of its investment in the German subsidiary, only a pro rata portion of the translation adjustments balance would have become part of the gain or loss from the transaction (FASB Interpretation 37). To illustrate, if 80% of the German subsidiary was sold for 250 DM on January 2, 1993, the following journal entries would be made:

Cash	125	
Investment in German subsidiary (.8 x $115)		92
Gain from sale of subsidiary		33
Translation adjustments (.8 x $21.90)	17.52	
Gain from sale of subsidiary		17.52

Application of the Remeasurement Method

In the previous situation, the DM was the functional currency because the German subsidiary's cash flows were primarily in DM. Assume, however, that the financing of the land and building was in U.S. dollars instead of DM and that the mortgage payable is denominated in U.S. dollars, i.e., must be paid in U.S. dollars. Although the rents collected and the majority of the cash flows for expenses are in DM, management has decided that, due to the manner of financing, the U.S. dollar is the functional currency. The books and records, however, are maintained in DM.

The translation of the German financial statements is accomplished by use of the **remeasurement method** (also known as the monetary/nonmonetary method). This method is illustrated below using the same information that was presented before for the German subsidiary.

German Company
Balance Sheet Translation (Remeasurement Method)
(U.S. dollar is the functional currency)
At December 31, 1991

Assets:	_DM_	_Exchange rate_	_U.S. dollars_
Cash	DM 50	.45	$ 22.50
Note receivable	20	.45	9.00
Land	100	.40	40.00
Building (Net)	490	.40	196.00
Total assets	DM 660		$267.50
Liabilities and stockholders' equity:			
Accounts payable	DM 30	.45	$ 13.50
Unearned rent	10	.42	4.20
Mortgage payable	400	.45	180.00
Common stock	40	.40	16.00
Additional paid-in capital	160	.40	64.00
Retained earnings	20	See income statement	(10.20)
Total liabilities and stockholders' equity DM	660		$267.50

German Company
Combined Income and Retained Earnings Statement Translation
(Remeasurement Method)
(U.S. dollar is the functional currency)
For the Year Ended December 31, 1991

	_DM_	_Exchange rate_	_U.S. dollars_
Revenues	DM 200	.43	$86.00
Expenses (not including depreciation)	(160)	.43	(68.80)
Depreciation expense	(10)	.40	(4.00)
Translation loss	--	See analysis below	(19.20)
Net income (loss)	DM 30	--	$ (6.00)
Retained earnings, January 1	--	--	--
Dividends paid	(10)	.42	(4.20)
Retained earnings, December 31	DM 20		(10.20)

German Company
Translation (Remeasurement Method) Loss
For the Year Ended December 31, 1991

	DM Debit	DM Credit	Exchange rate	U.S. dollars Debit	U.S. dollars Credit
Cash	DM 50		.45	$22.50	
Note receivable	20		.45	9.00	
Land	100		.40	40.00	
Building (net)	490		.40	196.00	
Accounts payable		DM 30	.45		$ 13.50
Unearned rent		10	.42		4.20
Mortgage payable		400	.45		180.00
Common stock		40	.40		16.00
Additional paid-in capital		160	.40		64.00
Retained earnings	--	--	--		--
Dividends declared	10		.42	4.20	
Revenues		200	.43		86.00
Operating expenses	160		.43	68.80	
Depreciation expenses	10		.40	4.00	
Totals	DM 840	DM 840		$344.50	$363.70
Loss from remeasurement				19.20	
Totals				$363.70	$363.70

The following observations should be noted about the remeasurement method:

a. **Assets and liabilities** which have historical cost balances (nonmonetary assets and liabilities) are translated by using historical exchange rates, i.e., the rates in effect when the transactions occurred. Monetary assets and monetary liabilities, on the other hand, are translated by using the current exchange rate at the balance sheet date.

b. **Revenues and expenses** that occur frequently during a period are translated, for practical purposes, by using the weighted-average exchange rate for the period. Revenues and expenses that represent allocations of historical balances (e.g., depreciation) are translated by using historical exchange rates. Note that this is a different treatment as compared to the current rate method. Note also that in 1992, the unearned rent from 1991 of 10 DM would be translated at the rate of 1 DM = $.42. The unearned rent at the end of 1991 is not considered a monetary liability. Therefore, the $.42 historical exchange rate should be used for all applicable future years. See the appendix at the end of this chapter for a listing of accounts that are translated using historical exchange rates.

c. If the functional currency is the U.S. dollar rather than the local foreign currency, the amounts of specific line items presented in the reconciliation of net income to net cash flow from operating activities will be different for nonmonetary items (e.g., depreciation). Note, however, that the **net** cash flow from operating activities will be the same in the reporting currency regardless of the applicable functional currency.

d.   The calculation of the translation gain (loss), in a purely mechanical sense, is the amount needed to make the dollar debits equal the dollar credits in the German company's trial balance.

e.   The translation loss of $19.20 is reported on U.S. Company's consolidated income statement because the U.S. dollar is the functional currency. When the reporting currency is the functional currency, as it is in this example, it is assumed that all of the foreign entity's transactions occurred in U.S. dollars. Accordingly, translation gains and losses are taken immediately to the income statement in the year in which they occur as they can be expected to have direct cash flow effects. They are not deferred in a translation adjustments account as they were when the functional currency was the DM (current rate method).

f.   The use of the equity method of accounting for the subsidiary would result in the following entries by U.S. Company during 1991:

Original Investment:

Investment in German subsidiary	80	
Cash		80

Earnings (loss) pickup:

Equity in subsidiary loss	6	
Investment in German subsidiary		6

Dividends received:

Cash	4.20	
Investment in German subsidiary		4.20

Note that translation gains and losses are included in the subsidiary's net income (net loss) as determined in U.S. dollars before the equity pickup is made by the U.S. company.

g.   In highly inflationary economies, those in which cumulative inflation is greater than 100% over a three-year period, the functional currency is the reporting currency, i.e., the U.S. dollar (SFAS 52, para 11). The remeasurement method must be used in this situation even though the factors indicate the local currency is the functional currency. The Board made this decision in order to prevent the evaporation of the foreign entity's fixed assets, a result that would occur if the local currency was the functional currency.

Summary of Current Rate and Remeasurement Methods

1.   Before foreign currency financial statements can be translated into U.S. dollars, management of the U.S. entity must select the functional currency for the foreign entity whose financial statements will be incorporated into theirs by consol-

idation, combination, or the equity method. As the example illustrated, this decision is crucial because it may have a material effect upon the financial statements of the U.S. company.

2. If the functional currency is the local currency of the foreign entity, the current rate method is used to translate foreign currency financial statements into U.S. dollars. All assets and liabilities are translated by using the current exchange rate at the balance sheet date. This method insures that all financial relationships remain the same in both local currency and U.S. dollars. Owners' equity is translated by using historical rates, while revenues (gains) and expenses (losses) are translated at the rates in existence during the period when the transactions occurred. A weighted-average rate can be used for items occurring numerous times throughout the period. The translation adjustments (debit or credit) which result from the application of these rules are reported as a separate component in owners' equity of the U.S. company's consolidated balance sheet (or parent-only balance sheet if consolidation was not deemed appropriate).

3. If the functional currency is the reporting currency (the U.S. dollar), the foreign currency financial statements are remeasured into U.S. dollars. All foreign currency balances are restated to U.S. dollars using both historical and current exchange rates. Foreign currency balances which reflect prices from past transactions are translated by using historical rates, while foreign currency balances which reflect prices from current transactions are translated by using the current exchange rate. Translation gains/losses that result from the remeasurement process are reported on the U.S. company's consolidated income statement.

The above summary can be arranged in tabular form as shown below:

Functional currency	Functional currency determinants	Translation method	Reporting
Local currency of foreign company[a]	a. Operations not integrated with parent's operations b. Buying and selling activities primarily in local currency c. Cash flows not immediately available for remittance to parent d. Financing denominated in local currency	Current rate (all assets/liabilities translated using current exchange rate; revenues/ expenses use weighted-average rate; equity accounts use historical rates)	Translation adjustments are reported in equity section of U.S. Company's consolidated balance sheet. Analysis of changes in accumulated transaction adjustments disclosed via footnote or separate schedule
U.S. dollar	a. Operations integrated with parent's operations b. Buying and selling activities primarily in the U.S. and/or U.S. dollars c. Cash flows immediately available for remittance to parent d. Financing denominated in U.S. dollars	Remeasurement (monetary assets/ liabilities use current exchange rate; historical cost balances use historical rates; revenues/expenses use weighted-average rates and historical rates, the latter for allocations like depr. exp.).	Translation gain/loss is reported on the U.S. company's consolidated income statement.

[a]The functional currency could be a foreign currency other than the local currency. If this is the case, the foreign currency statements are first remeasured in the functional currency before the current rate method is applied.

Foreign Operations in the U.S.

With the world economy as interconnected as it is, entities in the U.S. are sometimes the subsidiaries of parent companies domiciled elsewhere in the world. The financial statements of the local company may be presented separately in the U.S. or may be combined as part of the financial statements in the foreign country.

In general, financial statements of U.S. companies are prepared in accordance with U.S. generally accepted accounting principles. However, adjustments may have to be made to these statements in order to conform them to the accounting principles where they will be combined or consolidated into local companies.

Translation of Foreign Currency Transactions

According to SFAS 52, a foreign currency transaction is a transaction " ... denominated in a currency other than the entity's functional currency." Denominated means that the amount to be received or paid is fixed in terms of the number of units of a particular foreign currency regardless of changes in the exchange rate. From the viewpoint of a U.S. company, a foreign currency transaction results when it imports or exports goods or services to a foreign entity or makes a loan involving a foreign entity and agrees to settle the transaction in currency other than the U.S. dollar (the functional currency of the U.S. company). In these situations, the U.S. company has "crossed currencies" and directly assumes the risk of fluctuating exchange rates of the foreign currency in which the transaction is denominated. This risk may lead to recognition of foreign exchange transaction gains or losses in the income statement of the U.S. company. Note that transaction gains or losses can result only when the foreign currency transactions are denominated in a foreign currency. When a U.S. Company imports or exports goods or services and the transaction is to be settled in U.S. dollars, the U.S. company will incur neither gain nor loss because it bears no risk due to exchange rate fluctuations.

The following example will illustrate the terminology and procedures applicable to the translation of foreign currency transactions. Assume that U.S. Company, an exporter, sells merchandise to a customer in Germany on December 1, 1992 for 10,000 DM. Receipt is due on January 31, 1993, and U.S. Company prepares financial statements on December 31, 1992. At the transaction date (December 1, 1992), the spot rate for immediate exchange of foreign currencies indicates that 1 DM is equivalent to $.50. To find the U.S. dollar equivalent of this transaction, the foreign currency amount, 10,000 DM, is multiplied by $.50 to get $5,000. At December 1, 1992, the foreign currency transaction should be recorded by U.S. Company in the following manner:

Accounts receivable--Germany	5,000	
Sales		5,000

The accounts receivable and sales are measured in U.S. dollars at the transaction date using the spot rate at the time of the transaction. While the accounts receivable is measured and reported in U.S. dollars, the receivable is denominated or fixed in DM. This characteristic may result in foreign exchange transaction gains or losses if the spot rate for DM changes between the transaction date and the date the transaction is settled (January 31, 1993).

If financial statements are prepared between the transaction date and the settlement date, all receivables and liabilities which are denominated in a currency other than the functional currency (the U.S. dollar) must be restated to reflect the spot rates in existence at the balance sheet date. Assume that, on December 31, 1992, the spot rate for DM is 1 DM = $.52. This means that the 10,000 DM are now worth $5,200 and that the accounts receivable denominated in DM should be increased by $200. The following journal entry would be recorded as of December 31, 1992:

Accounts receivable--Germany	200	
Foreign currency transaction gain		200

Note that the sales account, which was credited on the transaction date for $5,000, is not affected by changes in the spot rate. This treatment exemplifies the two-transaction viewpoint adopted by the FASB. In other words, making the sale is the result of an operating decision, while bearing the risk of fluctuating spot rates is the result of a financing decision. Therefore, the amount determined as sales revenue at the transaction date should not be altered because of a financing decision to wait until January 31,

1993, for payment of the account. The risk of a foreign exchange transaction loss can be avoided either by demanding immediate payment on December 1 or by entering into a forward exchange contract to hedge the exposed asset (accounts receivable). The fact that U.S. Company, in the example, did not act in either of these two ways is reflected by requiring the recognition of foreign currency transaction gains or losses in its income statement (reported as financial or nonoperating items) in the period during which the exchange rates changed. This treatment has been criticized, however, because both the unrealized gain and/or loss are recognized in the financial statements, a practice which is at variance with traditional GAAP. Furthermore, earnings will fluctuate because of changes in exchange rates and not because of changes in the economic activities of the enterprise.

On the settlement date (January 31, 1993), assume the spot rate is 1 DM = $.51. The receipt of 10,000 DM and their conversion into U.S. dollars would be journalized in the following manner:

Foreign currency	5,100	
Foreign currency transaction loss	100	
Accounts receivable--Germany		5,200
Cash	5,100	
Foreign currency		5,100

The net effect of this foreign currency transaction was to receive $5,100 from a sale which was measured originally at $5,000. This realized net foreign currency transaction gain of $100 is reported on two income statements--a $200 gain in 1992 and a $100 loss in 1993. The reporting of the gain in two income statements causes a temporary difference between pretax accounting and taxable income. This results because the transaction gain of $100 is not taxable until 1993, the year the transaction was completed or settled. Accordingly, interperiod tax allocation is required for foreign currency transaction gains or losses.

Intercompany Transactions and Elimination of Intercompany Profits

Gains or losses from intercompany transactions should be reported on the U.S. Company's consolidated income statement unless settlement of the transaction is not planned or anticipated in the foreseeable future. In this case, gains and losses arising from intercompany transactions should be reflected in the translations adjustments component of the U.S. entity's stockholders' equity. In the typical situation, i.e., gains and losses reported on the U.S. entity's income statement, note that gains and losses result whether the functional currency is the U.S. dollar or the foreign entity's local currency. When the U.S. dollar is the functional currency, foreign currency transaction gains and losses result because of one of the two situations below:

1. The intercompany foreign currency transaction is denominated in U.S. dollars. In this case, the foreign subsidiary has a payable or receivable denominated in

U.S. dollars. This may result in a foreign currency transaction gain or loss which would appear on the foreign subsidiary's income statement. This gain or loss would be translated into U.S. dollars and would appear on the U.S. entity's consolidated income statement.

2. The intercompany foreign currency transaction is denominated in the foreign subsidiary's local currency. In this situation, the U.S. entity has a payable or receivable denominated in a foreign currency. Such a situation may result in a foreign currency transaction gain or loss that should be reported on the U.S. entity's income statement.

The above two cases can be easily altered to reflect what happens when the foreign entity's local currency is the functional currency.

The elimination of intercompany profits due to sales and other transfers between related entities should be based upon exchange rates in effect when the sale or transfer occurred. Reasonable approximations and averages are allowed to be used if intercompany transactions occur frequently during the year.

Hedging

Foreign currency transaction gains or losses on assets and liabilities, which are denominated in a currency other than the functional currency, can be hedged if the U.S. Company enters into a forward exchange contract. Hedges and other futures contracts that are not entered into with respect to a foreign currency transaction are accounted for in accordance with SFAS 80, "Accounting for Futures Contracts" (See Chapter 22). In the previous example, which illustrated the accounting for foreign currency transactions, the U.S. Company could have entered into a forward exchange contract on December 1 to sell 10,000 DM for a negotiated amount to a foreign exchange broker for future delivery on January 31, 1993. This forward contract is a hedge against the exposed asset position created by having an account receivable denominated in DM.

The negotiated rate referred to above is called a futures or forward rate. In most cases, this futures rate is not identical to the spot rate at the date of the forward contract. The difference between the futures rate and the spot rate at the date of the forward contract is referred to as a discount or a premium. Any discount or premium must be amortized over the term of the forward contract, generally on a straight-line basis (SFAS 52, para 18). The amortization of discount or premium is reflected in a separate revenue or expense account, not as an addition or subtraction to the foreign currency transaction gain or loss amount. It is important to observe that under this treatment, no net foreign currency transaction gains or losses result if assets and liabilities denominated in foreign currency are completely hedged at the transaction date.

To illustrate a hedge of an exposed asset, consider the following additional information for the German transaction:

On December 1, 1992, U.S. Company entered into a forward exchange contract to sell 10,000 DM on January 31, 1993 at $.505 per DM. The spot rate on December 1 is $.50 per DM.

The journal entries which reflect the sale of goods and the forward exchange contract appear as follows:

Sale transaction entries			*Forward exchange contract entries (futures rate 1 DM = $.505)*		
12/1/92 (spot rate 1 DM = $.50)					
Accounts receivable--			Due from exchange broker	5,050	
Germany	5,000		Due to exchange broker		5,000
Sales		5,000	Premium on forward contract		50
12/31/92 (spot rate 1 DM = $.52)					
Accounts receivable--			Foreign currency transaction loss	200	
Germany	200		Due to exchange broker		200
Foreign currency transac-			Premium on forward contract	25	
tion gain		200	Financial revenue		
			($25 = $50/2 months)		25
1/31/93 (spot rate 1 DM = $.51)					
Foreign currency	5,100		Due to exchange broker	5,200	
Foreign currency transac-			Foreign currency		5,100
tion loss	100		Foreign currency transaction		
Accounts receivable--			gain		100
Germany		5,200	Cash	5,050	
			Due from exchange broker		5,050
			Premium on forward contract	25	
			Financial revenue		25

The following points should be noted from the entries above:

1. The net foreign currency transaction gain or loss is zero. The account "Due from exchange broker" is fixed in terms of U.S. dollars, and this amount is not affected by changes in spot rates between the transaction and settlement dates. The account "Due to exchange broker" is fixed or denominated in DM. The U.S. company owes the exchange broker 10,000 DM, and these must be delivered on January 31, 1993. Because this liability is denominated in DM, its amount is determined by spot rates. Since spot rates change, this liability changes in amount equal to the changes in accounts receivable because both of the amounts are based on the same spot rates. These changes are reflected as foreign currency transaction gains and losses which net out to zero.

2. The premium on forward contract is fixed in terms of U.S. dollars. This amount is amortized to a financial revenue account over the life of the forward contract on a straight-line basis.

3. The net effect of this transaction is that $5,050 was received on January 31, 1993 for a sale originally recorded at $5,000. The $50 difference was taken into income via amortization.

SFAS 52 does not require a forward exchange contract in order for a hedge to take place. For example, it is possible for a foreign currency transaction to act as an economic hedge against a parent's net investment in a foreign entity if

1. The transaction is designated as a hedge.
2. It is effective as a hedge.

To illustrate, assume that a U.S. parent has a wholly owned British subsidiary which has net assets of 2 million pounds. The U.S. parent can borrow 2 million pounds to hedge its net investment in the British subsidiary. Assume further that the British pound is the functional currency and that the 2 million pound liability is denominated in pounds. Fluctuations in the exchange rate for pounds will have no net effect on the parent company's consolidated balance sheet because increases (decreases) in the translation adjustments balance due to the translation of the net investment will be offset by decreases (increases) in this balance due to the adjustment of the liability denominated in pounds.

Disclosures

The financial statement or footnote disclosures required by SFAS 52, paras 30 to 32 consist of the following:

1. Aggregate transaction gain or loss that is included in the entity's net income.
2. Analysis of changes in accumulated translation adjustments which are reported as a separate component of the entity's owners' equity. At a minimum, the disclosures should include:

   a. The beginning and ending amounts of the translation adjustments account.
   b. The aggregate adjustment for the period resulting from translation adjustments and gains and losses from certain hedges and intercompany balances.
   c. The amount of income taxes for the period allocated to translation adjustments.
   d. The amounts transferred from the translation adjustments account and included in determining net income as a result of the (partial) sale or liquidation of the foreign operation.

3. Significant rate changes subsequent to the date of the financial statements including effects on unsettled foreign currency transactions. Rate changes subsequent to the balance sheet date are not incorporated into the financial statements for the period just ended.

APPENDIX

Accounts to be Remeasured Using Historical Exchange Rates

1. Marketable securities carried at cost

   a. Equity securities
   b. Debt securities not intended to be held until maturity

2. Inventories carried at cost
3. Prepaid expenses such as insurance, advertising, and rent
4. Property, plant, and equipment
5. Accumulated depreciation on property, plant, and equipment
6. Patents, trademarks, licenses, and formulas
7. Goodwill
8. Other intangible assets
9. Deferred charges and credits, except deferred income taxes and policy acquisition costs for life insurance companies
10. Deferred income
11. Common stock
12. Preferred stock carried at issuance price
13. Revenues and expenses related to nonmonetary items

    a. Cost of goods sold
    b. Depreciation of property, plant, and equipment
    c. Amortization of intangible items such as goodwill, patents, licenses, etc.
    d. Amortization of deferred charges or credits, except deferred income taxes and policy acquisition costs for life insurance companies

Source: SFAS 52, para 48.

21 Personal Financial Statements

Perspective and Issues

AICPA Statement of Position (SOP) 82-1, *Personal Financial Statements,* addresses the preparation and presentation of personal financial statements, or, more specifically, financial statements of individuals or groups of related individuals (i.e., family). Personal financial statements are generally prepared to organize and plan an individual's financial affairs on a more formal basis. Specific purposes deal with the obtaining of credit, income tax planning, retirement planning, gift and estate planning, or the public disclosure of financial affairs. The aforementioned purposes are such that the users of personal financial statements rely on them in determining whether to grant credit, in assessing the financial activities of individuals, in assessing the financial affairs of public officials and candidates for public office, and for similar purposes.

The 1968 AICPA Industry Audit Guide, *Audits of Personal Financial Statements,* used historical cost as the primary basis of measurement for personal financial statements. However, the guide recommended the presentation of estimated current values as additional information. The increasing use of personal financial statements created the need to reassess the conclusions found in the Industry Audit Guide due to the purposes for which personal financial statements are prepared, the users to whom they are directed, and the ways in which they are used. That reassessment resulted in SOP 82-1 which is discussed and illustrated in this chapter.

Sources of GAAP
SOP
82-1

Definitions of Terms

Estimated current value of an asset. The amount for which an item could be exchanged between a buyer and a seller, each of whom is well informed and willing, and neither of whom is compelled to buy or sell.

Estimated current amount of liabilities. Payables and other liabilities should be presented at the discounted amounts of cash to be paid. The discount rate should be the rate implicit in the transaction in which the debt was incurred. If, however, the debtor is able to discharge the debt currently at a lower amount, the debt should be presented at the lower amount.

Concepts, Rules, and Examples

Personal financial statements may be prepared for an individual, husband and wife, or family. Personal financial statements consist of

1. Statement of financial condition--presents estimated current values of assets, estimated current amounts of liabilities, estimated income taxes and net worth at a specified date
2. Statement of changes in net worth--presents main sources of increases (decreases) in net worth and is **optional**

Assets and liabilities, including changes therein, should be recognized using the accrual basis of accounting. In the Statement of Financial Condition, assets and liabilities should be listed by order of liquidity and maturity, not on a current/noncurrent basis.

In personal financial statements, **assets** should be presented at their estimated current value. This is an amount at which the item could be exchanged assuming both parties are well informed, neither party is compelled to buy or sell, and material disposal costs are deducted to arrive at current values. A specialist may have to be consulted in the determination of the current value of certain types of assets (e.g., works of art, jewelry, restricted securities, investments in closely held businesses, and real estate). **Liabilities** should be presented at the lesser of the discounted amount of cash to be paid or the current cash settlement amount. The use of recent transactions involving similar types of assets and liabilities, in similar circumstances, constitutes a satisfactory means of determining the estimated current value of an asset and the estimated current amount of a liability. If recent information cannot be obtained, other methods can be used (e.g., capitalization of past or prospective earnings, the use of liquidation values, the adjustment of historical cost based on changes in a specific price index, the use of appraisals, and the use of the discounted amounts of projected cash receipts and payments). The methods used should be followed consistently from period to period unless the facts and circumstances dictate a change to different methods. Income taxes payable should include unpaid income taxes for completed tax years and the estimated amount for the elapsed portion of the current tax year. Additionally, personal financial statements should include the estimated income tax on the difference between the current value (amount) of assets (liabilities) and their respective tax bases as if they had been realized or liquidated. The table below summarizes the methods of determining "estimated current values" for assets and "estimated current amounts" for liabilities.

Assets and liabilities	Discounted cash flow	Market price	Appraised value	Other
• Receivables	X			
• Marketable securities		X		If traded on valuation day: closing price. If not traded: valuation must fall in range (bid and asked price)
• Options--securities		X		Difference between exercise price and current value of asset; if material, discount the difference
• Options--other assets*				
• Investment in life insurance				Cash value less outstanding loans
• Investment in closely held business	X		X	Liquidation value, multiple of earnings, reproduction value, adjustment of book value or cost
• Real estate	X		X	Sales of similar property
• Intangible assets	X			Net proceeds from current sale or discounted cash flows from asset; otherwise, may use cost of asset
• Future interests (non-forfeitable rights)**	X			
• Payables and other liabilities	X			Discharge amount if lower than discounted amount
• Noncancelable commitments***	X			
• Income taxes payable				Unpaid income tax for completed tax years and estimated income tax for elapsed portion of current tax year to date of financial statements
• Estimated income tax on difference between current values of assets and current amounts of liabilities and their respective tax bases				Computed as if current value of assets and liabilities had been respectively realized or liquidated considering applicable tax laws and regulations, recapture provisions and carryovers.
• Uncertain obligations*				Not covered by SOP 82-1; follow SFAS 5

*Taken from: "Personal Financial Statements," Michael D. Kinsman and Bruce Samuelson, *Journal of Accounting*, September, 1987, pp. 138-148.

**Rights have all of the following attributes: (1) are for fixed or determinable amounts; (2) are not contingent on holder's life expectancy or occurrence of a particular event (e.g., disability/death), and (3) do not require future performance of service by holder

***Commitments have all of the following attributes: (1) are for fixed or determinable amounts; (2) are not contingent on others' life expectancies or occurrence of a particular event (e.g., disability/death); and (3) do not require future performance of service by others.

Business interests which comprise a large portion of a person's total assets should be shown separately from other investments. An investment in a separate entity which is marketable as a going concern (e.g., closely held corporation) should be presented as one amount. If the investment is a limited business activity, not conducted in a separate business entity, separate asset and liability amounts should be shown (e.g., investment in real estate and related mortgage; of course, only the person's beneficial interest in the investment is included in their personal financial statements).

The CPA must decide whether to valuate the net investment him/herself or to defer valuation to a specialist. Because of the risk of litigation and the liability coverage limitations on valuation functions many CPAs prefer using a specialist. If the CPA does the valuation s/he must ensure that s/he has attained a sufficient level of competence to perform the engagement. The possible valuation methods available are: discounted cash flow, appraised value, liquidation value, multiple of earnings, reproduction value, adjustment of book value (e.g., equity method) or cost.

Disclosures

Personal financial statements should have sufficient disclosure in order to make the statements adequately informative. Disclosures can be made in either the body of the financial statements or in the notes. The following enumeration, as found in SOP 82-1, is not intended to be all-inclusive but simply indicative of the information that ordinarily should be disclosed:

a. A clear indication of the individuals covered by the financial statements
b. That assets are presented at their estimated current values and liabilities are presented at their estimated current amounts
c. The methods used in determining estimated current values of major assets and estimated current amounts of major liabilities or major categories of assets and liabilities, since several methods are available, and changes in methods from one period to the next
d. If assets held jointly by person and by others are included in statements, nature of the joint ownership
e. If person's investment portfolio is material in relation to his or her other assets and is concentrated in one or a few companies or industries, names of the companies or industries and estimated current values of securities
f. If person has a material investment in a closely held business, at least the following:

  • Name of company and person's percentage of ownership
  • Nature of the business
  • Summarized financial information about assets, liabilities, and results of operations for most recent year based on financial statements of business, including information about the basis of presentation (for example, GAAP, income tax basis, or cash basis) and any significant loss contingencies

g. Descriptions of intangible assets and their estimated useful lives

h. Face amount of life insurance the individuals own
i. Nonforfeitable rights that do not have all attributes listed in first note to table presented earlier (e.g., pensions based on life expectancy)
j. The following tax information:

- Methods and assumptions used to compute estimated income taxes on the differences between estimated current values of assets and estimated current amounts of liabilities and their tax bases, and a statement that the provision will probably differ from amounts of income taxes that might eventually be paid because those amounts are determined by timing and method of disposal, realization, or liquidation and tax laws and regulations in effect at time of disposal, realization, or liquidation
- Unused operating loss and capital loss carryforwards
- Other unused deductions and credits, with their expiration periods, if applicable
- The differences between estimated current values of major assets and estimated current amounts of major liabilities or categories of assets and liabilities and their tax bases

k. Maturities, interest rates, collateral, and other pertinent details relating to receivables and debt
l. Noncancelable commitments that do not have all attributes listed in second note to the table presented earlier (e.g., operating leases)

An example set of personal financial statements complete with footnotes appears in the Appendix to this chapter.

APPENDIX
Hypothetical Set of Personal Financial Statements

Marcus and Kelly Imrich
Statements of Financial Condition
December 31, 19X2 and 19X1

	19X2	*19X1*
Assets		
Cash	$ 381,437	$ 207,621
Securities		
Marketable (Note 2)	128,787	260,485
Tax-Exempt Bonds (Note 3)	1,890,222	986,278
Certificate of deposit	20,000	10,000
Loans receivable (Note 4)	262,877	362,877
Partnership and venture interests (Note 5)	935,000	938,000
Real estate interests (Note 6)	890,000	2,500,000
David Corporation (Note 7)	2,750,687	2,600,277
Cash surrender value of life insurance (Note 8)	388,000	265,000
Personal residences (Note 9)	2,387,229	2,380,229
Deferred losses from partnerships	68,570	60,830
Vested interest in David Corporation		
Benefit Plan	545,960	530,960
Personal jewelry and furnishings (Note 10)	513,000	6,700
Total assets	$11,161,769	$11,109,257
Liabilities		
Mortgage Payable (Note 11)	$ 254,000	$ 267,000
Security deposits--rentals	--	5,700
Income taxes payable--current year balance	9,800	10,680
Total liabilities	263,800	283,380
Estimated income taxes on difference		
between estimated current values of assets		
and estimated current amounts of		
liabilities and their tax bases (Note 12)	555,400	731,000
Net Worth	10,342,569	10,094,877
Total liabilities and net worth	$11,161,769	$11,109,257

Marcus and Kelly Imrich
Statement of Changes in Net Worth
For the Years Ended December 31, 19X2 and 19X1

	Year ended December 31,	
	19X2	19X1
Realized increases in net worth		
Salary and bonus	$ 200,000	$ 175,000
Dividends and interest income	184,260	85,000
Distribution from limited partnerships	280,000	260,000
Gain on sales of marketable securities	58,240	142,800
	722,500	662,800
Realized decreases in net worth		
Income taxes	180,000	140,000
Interest expense	25,000	26,000
Real estate taxes	21,000	18,000
Personal expenditures	242,536	400,000
	468,536	584,000
Net realized increase in net worth	253,964	78,800
Unrealized increases in net worth		
Marketable securities (net of realized gains on securities sold)	37,460	30,270
Benefit plan--David Corporation	15,000	14,000
Personal jewelry and furnishings	20,000	18,000
	72,460	62,270
Unrealized decrease in net worth		
Estimated income taxes on the difference between the estimated current values of assets and the estimated current amounts of liabilities and their tax bases	78,732	64,118
Net unrealized decrease in net worth	(6,272)	(1,848)
Net increase in net worth	247,692	76,952
Net worth at the beginning of year	10,094,877	10,017,925
Net worth at the end of year	$10,342,569	$10,094,877

Marcus and Kelly Imrich
Notes to Financial Statements

Note 1. The accompanying financial statements include the assets and liabilities of Marcus and Kelly Imrich. Assets are stated at their estimated current values, and liabilities at their estimated current amounts.

Note 2. The estimated current values of marketable securities are either (a) their quoted closing prices or (b) for securities not traded on the financial statement date, amounts that fall within the range of quoted bid and asked prices.

Marketable securities consist of the following:

	December 31, 19X2		December 31, 19X1	
	Number of shares	*Estimated current values*	*Number of shares*	*Estimated current values*
Stocks				
Susan Schultz, Inc.			1,000	$122,000
Ripley Robotics Corp.	500	$ 51,927	1,000	120,485
L.A.W. Corporation	300	20,700	100	5,000
Jay & Kelly Corp.	300	20,700	200	5,000
J.A.Z. Corporation	200	35,460	200	8,000
		$128,787		$260,485

Note 3. The interest income from state and municipal bonds is not subject to federal income taxes but is, except in certain cases, subject to state income tax.

Note 4. The loan receivable from Carol Parker, Inc. matures January, 19X9 and bears interest at the prime rate.

Note 5. Partnership and venture interests consist of the following:

	Percent Owned	*Cost*	*Estimated Current Value 12/31/X2*	*Estimated Current Value 12/31/X1*
East Third Partnership	50.0%	$ 50,000	100,000	100,000
631 Lucinda Venture	20.0	10,000	35,000	38,000
27 Wright Partnership	22.5	10,000	40,000	50,000
Eannarino Partnership	10.0	40,000	60,000	50,000
Sweeney Venture	30.0	100,000	600,000	600,000
Kelly Parker Group	20.0	20,000	100,000	100,000
707 Lucinda Venture	50.0	(11,000)	--	--
			$935,000	$938,000

Note 6. Mr. and Mrs. Imrich own a one half interest in an apartment building in DeKalb, Illinois. The estimated fair market value was determined by Mr. and Mrs. Imrich. Their basis in the apartment building was $1,000,000 for both 19X2 and 19X1.

Note 7. Kelly Imrich owns 75% of the common stock of the David Corporation. A condensed statement of assets, liabilities and stockholders' equity (income tax basis) of David Corporation as of December 31, 19X2 and 19X1 is summarized below.

	19X2	19X1
Current assets	$2,975,000	$3,147,000
Investments	200,000	200,000
Property and equipment (net)	145,000	165,000
Loans receivable	110,000	120,000
Total assets	$3,430,000	$3,632,000
Current liabilities	$2,030,000	$2,157,000
Other liabilities	450,000	400,000
Total liabilities	2,480,000	2,557,000
Stockholder's equity--	950,000	1,075,000
Total liabilities and stockholder's equity	$3,430,000	$3,632,000

Note 8. At December 31, 19X2 and 19X1, Marcus Imrich owned a $1,000,000 whole life insurance policy.

Note 9. The estimated current values of the personal residences are their purchase prices plus their cost of improvements. Both residences were purchased in 19X0.

Note 10. The estimated current values of personal effects and jewelry are the appraised values of those assets, determined by an independent appraiser for insurance purposes.

Note 11. The mortgage (collateralized by the residence) is payable in monthly installments of $1,083 a month, including interest at 10% a year through 20X8.

Note 12. The estimated current amounts of liabilities at December 31, 19X2, and December 31, 19X1, equaled their tax bases. Estimated income taxes have been provided on the excess of the estimated current values of assets over their tax bases as if the estimated current values of the assets had been realized on the statement date, using applicable tax laws and regulations. The provision will probably differ from the amounts of income taxes that eventually might be paid because those amounts are determined by the timing and the method of disposal or realization and the tax laws and regulations in effect at the time of disposal or realization.

The estimated current values of assets exceeded their tax bases by $1,850,000 at December 31, 19X2, and by $1,770,300 at December 31, 19X1. The excess of estimated current values of major assets over their tax bases are:

	December 31,	
	19X2	19X1
Investment in David Corporation	$1,400,000	$1,350,000
Vested interest in benefit plan	350,000	300,000
Investment in marketable securities	100,000	120,300

22 Specialized Industry GAAP

The FASB undertook a project in FASB Statement No. 32 (SFAS 32) to promulgate and establish accounting principles unique to specialized industries. The purpose of this chapter is to serve as a reference source for these FASB pronouncements, for AICPA Statements of Position, Industry Audit Guides, Audit and Accounting Guides, and Issues Papers of the Accounting Standards Division.

Banking and Thrift (APB 23; SFASs 32, 72, 83, 91, 96, 104; FASB Interpretation 9; FASB Technical Bulletin 85-1)

These pronouncements adopt the Audit and Accounting Guide, *Savings and Loan Associations* (1979), the *Audits of Banks* (Audit Guide, 1983), and SOP 83-1, *Reporting by Banks of Investment Securities Gains or Losses*, as preferable accounting principles. Special accounting rules are stated that permit an accelerated method of amortization for goodwill arising from the purchase of a savings and loan association if certain conditions are met. An accelerated method may be used if goodwill represents amounts paid for items for which there is not a satisfactory basis for assigning amounts to individual factors and the benefits from these factors decline over their expected lives. The period of amortization should not be longer than the discount on long term interest bearing assets acquired and recognized as interest income. The statement also prohibits providing deferred taxes on the differences between tax and financial reporting income attributable to the bad debt reserve. In the cash flow statement, banks, savings institutions and credit unions are not required to report gross amounts of cash receipts and payments for deposits and withdrawals with other financial institutions, time deposits activities and loans made and loan payments received from customers.

Broadcasting (SFAS 63)

This statement establishes accounting and reporting standards for broadcasters. Broadcasters will account for a license agreement for program material as a purchase of rights. A licensee will report an asset and a liability, at either present value or gross amount of the liability, when the license period begins, and all of the following conditions have been met:

   a. The cost of each program is known or reasonably determinable.

   b. The program material has been accepted by the licensee in accordance with the conditions of the license agreement.

   c. The program is available for showing or broadcast.

The asset and liability should be segregated on the balance sheet. The asset is divided into current and noncurrent based upon estimated time of usage while the liability is segregated based on the payment terms. The asset should be valued at the lower of unamortized cost or net realizable value.

Also established are standards for barter transactions and network affiliation agreements.

Cable Television (SFAS 51)

This statement presents standards applicable to the construction and operation of a cable television system. The standards provide that while a cable television system is in the prematurity period (a period while the system is partially under construction and partially in service), costs incurred that relate to both current and future operations will be partially capitalized and partially expensed. The prematurity period will usually not exceed two years and will frequently be shorter. If only a portion of the cable system is in the prematurity period, that portion, if it can be clearly distinguished from the remainder of the system, should be accounted for separately. Such a portion would have geographical, mechanical, timing of operations or investment differences and have separate accounting or accountability records. Costs of the cable plant are capitalized and subscriber related costs are expensed. Programming and other systems costs should be allocated between current and future operations based upon the relationship of current subscribers to future expected subscribers at the end of the prematurity period.

Computer Software (SFASs 2 and 86)

The accounting for the costs of computer software (both developed internally and purchased) to be sold, leased, or otherwise marketed, as a separate product or as part of a product or as a process, is covered by these pronouncements. Costs incurred internally in creating a computer software product are charged to expense as incurred until completion of a detail program design or completion of a working model. Thereafter, all software production costs are capitalized and valued at the lower of unamortized cost or net realizable value. Capitalized costs are amortized based upon current and future revenue for each product with a minimal annual amortization determined by the straight line method over remaining estimated economic life.

Construction-Type Contracts (ARB 45; SFASs 32 and 56)

These pronouncements establish accounting and reporting standards for long-term contracts and evaluate the percentage-of-completion and completed-contract methods. The percentage-of-completion method is preferred if estimates of costs to complete and extent of progress toward completion of long-term contracts are reasonably dependable. If dependable estimates are lacking or other inherent hazards exist, then the completed-contract method is preferred.

Educational Organizations (SFAS 32)

The specialized accounting and reporting principles and practices contained in *Audits of Colleges and Universities* (Audit Guide, 1973) and SOP 74-8, *Financial Accounting and Reporting by Colleges and Universities*, are preferable accounting principles for purposes of justifying a change in accounting principle.

Employee Benefit Plans (SFASs 32 and 83)

The Audit Guide, *Audits of Employee Benefit Plans* (1983), contains preferable accounting principles for purposes of justifying a change in accounting principles for such plans.

Finance Companies (SFASs 32 and 91)

The specialized accounting and reporting principles and practices contained in *Audits of Finance Companies* (Audit Guide, 1973) are preferable accounting principles for purposes of justifying a change in accounting principles.

Franchising and Accounting by Franchisors (SFAS 45)

This pronouncement establishes that franchise fee revenue from franchise sales will be recognized only when all material services or conditions relating to the sale have been substantially performed by the franchisor. Also covered are standards for continuing franchising fees, continuing product sales, agency sales, franchising costs, repossessed franchises, commingled revenues, and other transactions. Continuing franchise fees are revenue as earned and receivable from the franchisee. To the extent the franchisee can purchase equipment or supplies from the franchisor at a bargain, a portion of the initial franchise fee should be deferred and accounted for as an adjustment of the selling price of such products. Direct and incremental franchise costs should be deferred until revenue is recognized but should not exceed anticipated revenue less additional related costs. Indirect costs should be expensed as incurred.

Government Contracts (ARB 43, Chapter 11; SFASs 32 and 56)

The accounting and income recognition problems concerning cost plus fixed fee and fixed price supply contracts are covered by these pronouncements. The fees under government cost plus fixed fee contracts may be recognized as income on the basis of partial performance if there is reasonable assurance of realization. Fees may also be accrued as they are billable unless this accrual is not reasonably related to the proportionate performance of total work to be performed.

Health Care Industries: Hospitals (SFASs 32 and 56)

The specialized principles contained in the Hospital Audit Guide (1972); SOP 78-1, *Accounting by Hospitals for Certain Marketable Equity Securities*; SOP 78-7, *Financial Accounting and Reporting by Hospitals Operated by a Governmental Unit*; and SOP 81-2, *Reporting Practices Concerning Hospital Related Organizations* are preferable accounting principles for purposes of justifying a change in accounting principles.

Insurance (SFASs 5, 60, 91, 96 and 97)

These pronouncements apply to insurance enterprises other than mutual life insurance companies, assessment enterprises, and fraternal benefit societies. Standards are established to classify insurance contracts as short-duration or long-duration and provide for recognition of premium revenue based on certain criteria. Claim costs, including incurred but not reported claims, are recognized when insured events occur. Acquisition costs and accounting for investments are also covered within these pronouncements.

Investment Companies (SFASs 32, 54 and 102)

The specialized accounting and reporting principles and practices contained in *Audits of Investment Companies* (Audit Guide, 1987); SOP 74-11, *Financial Accounting and Reporting by Face-Amount Certificate Companies*; SOP 77-1, *Financial Accounting and Reporting by Investment Companies*; and SOP 79-1, *Accounting for Municipal Bond Funds*, are preferable accounting principles for purposes of justifying a change in accounting principles. Highly liquid investment companies may be exempt from the requirement to provide a statement of cash flows as part of a full set of financial statements. The conditions for exemption are being subject to the Investment Company Act of 1940 or having essentially the same characteristics as those subject to the 1940 Act or being a common trust fund, variable annuity account or similar fund.

Mortgage Banking Activities (SFASs 65, 91 and FASB Technical Bulletin 87-3)

Mortgage loans and mortgage-backed securities held for sale, origination costs, premiums paid to acquire mortgage loans, loan organization fees, and other fees are accounted for in accordance with these pronouncements. This also applies to other companies, such as commercial banks, that conduct operations similar to the operations of a mortgage banking entity. However, this pronouncement does not apply to the normal lending activities of those other enterprises. Mortgage loans and mortgage backed securities held for sale are valued at the lower of cost or market. Loan origination fees and related direct loan costs for loans held for sale are capitalized as part of the related loan while those fees and costs for loans held for investment are deferred and recognized as an adjustment to the yield.

Motion Picture (SFAS 53)

This pronouncement concerns accounting and reporting standards for producers and distributors of motion picture films. Producers and distributors that license film exhibition rights will recognize revenue on the dates of exhibition. The sale of exhibition rights for television program material is recognized when the license period begins and certain other conditions have been met. Costs to produce a film are capitalized as film cost inventory and amortized using the individual film forecast computation method. Exploitation costs are also capitalized as film cost inventory if they clearly benefit future periods. Inventory is valued at lower of unamortized cost or net realizable value.

Not-for-profit Organizations (SFASs 32 and 93)

The specialized accounting and reporting principles contained in *Audits of Voluntary Health and Welfare Organizations* (Audit Guide, 1974) and SOP 78-10, *Accounting Principles and Reporting Practices for Certain Nonprofit Organizations*, are preferable accounting principles for the purpose of justifying a change in accounting principles.

Oil and Gas Producing Activities (SFASs 19, 25, 69, 95 and 96; FASB Interpretation 36)

These pronouncements describe certain accounting and reporting requirements for entities with such activities. The pronouncement requires entities to disclose the method of accounting for costs incurred. Production payments payable in cash are classified as debt and comprehensive income tax allocation is required to be followed. In addition, a preferable but not required form of the successful efforts method of accounting for oil and gas producing activities is presented.

Pension Funds (SFASs 35, 75 and 102)

These pronouncements present accounting and reporting standards for the annual financial statements of a defined benefit pension plan.

Real Estate (SFASs 32, 66, 67 and 98)

Statement 66 concerns accounting standards for profit recognition on all sales of real estate without regard to the seller's principal business. The statement also defines the difference between retail land sales and other sales of real estate and explains how differences in terms of sales and selling procedures will lead to different profit recognition methods. The provisions of SFAS 66 are covered in the last section of Chapter 7.

The specialized accounting and reporting principles and practices contained in SOP 75-2, *Accounting Practices of Real Estate Investment Trusts,* SOP 78-2, *Accounting Practices of Real Estate Investment Trusts,* and SOP 78-9, *Accounting for Investments in Real Estate Ventures*, are preferable accounting principles.

Statement 67 established standards for accounting and reporting of acquisition, development, construction, selling and rental costs associated with real estate projects.

In addition, the accounting for initial rental operations of real estate projects is discussed.

Records and Music (SFAS 50)

Accounting and reporting standards for licensors and licensees in the record and music industry are presented in this pronouncement. The statement permits recognition of the licensing fee as revenue if the licensing agreement is substantially a sale and collectibility of the fee is reasonably assured. Also discussed are accounting standards for minimum guarantees, artist compensation cost, and cost of record masters.

Regulated Operations (SFASs 71, 87, 90, 92, 96, 98, 101 and 106; FASB Technical Bulletin 87-2)

These statements contain accounting and reporting standards for most public utilities and for other enterprises with regulated operations that meet specified criteria. The type of regulation referred to in this pronouncement permits an entity to charge rates that are intended to produce revenue equal to the estimated costs of providing regulated services.

Stockbrokerage (SFASs 32 and 83)

The specialized accounting and reporting principles and practices contained in *Audits of Brokers and Dealers in Securities* (Audit Guide, 1985) are preferable accounting principles for purposes of justifying a change in accounting principles.

Title Plant (SFAS 61)

This pronouncement applies to enterprises such as title insurance companies, title abstract companies, and title agents that use a title plant in their operations. The standard provides that costs directly incurred to construct a title plant should be capitalized when the entity can use the title plant to do title searches and that such capitalized costs are not normally depreciated. The statement also requires that the costs of maintaining a title plant and doing title searches be expensed as incurred.

Preferrable Accounting Principles

There are also other Statements of Position, Industry Audit Guides, and Audit and Accounting Guides, which have been designated as preferable accounting principles pending action by the FASB to abstract from them the principles and practices that are generally accepted and issue a FASB Standard. These are as follows:

Statements of Position

SOP 74-8   Financial Accounting and Reporting by Colleges and Universities
SOP 74-11 Financial Accounting and Reporting by Face-Amount Certificate Companies
SOP 75-2   Accounting Practices of Real Estate Investment Trusts
SOP 76-3   Accounting Practices for Certain Employee Stock Ownership Plans

SOP 77-1   Financial Accounting and Reporting by Investment Companies
SOP 78-1   Accounting by Hospitals for Certain Marketable Equity Securities
SOP 78-2   Accounting Practices of Real Estate Investment Trusts
SOP 78-9   Accounting for Investments in Real Estate Ventures
SOP 78-10 Accounting Principles and Reporting Practices for Certain Nonprofit Organizations
SOP 79-1   Accounting for Municipal Bond Funds
SOP 81-1   Accounting for Performance of Construction-Type and Certain Production-Type Contracts
SOP 81-2   Reporting Practices Concerning Hospital-Related Organizations
SOP 83-1   Reporting by Banks of Investment Securities Gains or Losses

Industry Audit Guides

Audits of Banks, 1984 (SFAS 83)
Audits of Colleges and Universities, 1975 (also refer to SOP 74-8)
Audits of Finance Companies, 1988
Audits of Government Contractors, 1983
Audits of Investment Companies, 1987 (also refer to SOPs 74-11, 77-1, and 79-1)
Audits of Voluntary Health and Welfare Organizations, 1974
Audits of Hospitals, 1985 (also refer to SOPs 78-1 and 78-7)

Audit and Accounting Guides

Savings and Loan Associations, 1985
Construction Contractors, 1981 (SFAS 56)
Brokers and Dealers in Securities, 1985
Employee Benefit Plans, 1983 (SFAS 83)

The remaining pronouncements issued by either the Accounting Standards Division or the Auditing Standards Division are as follows:

March 1978- Clarification of Accounting, Auditing, and Reporting Practices Relating to Hospital Malpractice Loss Contingencies--Statement of Position of the Auditing Standards Division
SOP 85-1   Financial Reporting by Not-For-Profit Health Care Entities for Tax-Exempt Debt and Certain Funds Whose Use is Limited
SOP 85-2   Accounting for Dollar Repurchase-Dollar Reverse Repurchase Agreements by Sellers-Borrowers
SOP 85-3   Accounting by Agricultural Producers and Agricultural Cooperatives
SOP 86-1   Reporting Repurchase--Reverse Repurchase Agreements and Mortgage-Backed Certificates by Savings and Loan Associations
SOP 87-1   Accounting for Asserted and Unasserted Medical Malpractice Claims of Health Care Providers and Related Issues
SOP 87-2   Accounting for Joint Costs of Informational Materials and Activities of Not-For-Profit Organizations That Include a Fund Raising Appeal

SOP 88-1   Accounting for Developmental and Preoperating Costs, Purchases and Exchanges of Take-Off and Landing Slots, and Airframe Modifications

SOP 89-5   Financial Accounting and Reporting by Providers of Prepaid Health Care Services

SOP 90-3   Definition of the Term "Substantially the Same" for Holders of Debt Instruments, as Used in Certain Audit Guides and a Statement of Position

SOP 90-7   Financial Reporting by Entities in Reorganization under the Bankruptcy Code

SOP 90-8   Financial Accounting and Reporting by Continuing Care Retirement Communities

SOP 90-11   Disclosure of Certain Information by Financial Institutions about Debt Securities Held as Assets

Audits of Agricultural Procedures and Agricultural Cooperatives, 1987
Audits of Airlines, 1988
Audits of Casinos, 1984
Audits of Certain Nonprofit Organizations, 1988
Audits of Credit Unions, 1986
Audits of Entities with Oil and Gas Producing Activities, 1986
Audits of Fire and Casualty Insurance Companies, 1982
Audits of Stock Life Insurance Companies, 1985
Personal Financial Statements Guide, 1983

Issues Papers of the Accounting Standards Division

Issues Papers of the AICPA's Accounting Standards Division primarily identify financial accounting and reporting issues that the Division believed needed addressing by the Financial Accounting Standards Board. These pronouncements constitute generally accepted accounting principles but are not mandatory.

Title	Date Issued
Accounting for Changes in Estimates	12/15/78
Accounting for Uncertainties	12/20/78
Reporting Finance Subsidiaries in Consolidated Financial Statements	12/27/78
The Meaning of "In Substance a Repossession or Foreclosure" and Accounting for Partial Refinancings of Troubled Real Estate Loans Under FASB Statement No. 15	1/15/79
Accounting for Allowances for Losses on Certain Real Estate and Loans and Receivables Collateralized by Real Estate	6/21/79
Joint Venture Accounting	7/17/79
Accounting by Investors for Distributions Received in Excess of Their Investment in a Joint Venture (An Addendum to the July 17, 1979 Issues Paper on Joint Venture Accounting)	10/8/79
Accounting for Grants Received from Governments	10/16/79
"Push Down" Accounting	10/30/79
Accounting for Vested Pension Benefits Existing or Arising When a Plant is Closed or a Business Segment is Discontinued	2/5/80
Accounting in Consolidation for Issuances of a Subsidiary's Stock	6/3/80
Accounting for Lease Brokers	6/20/80
Accounting for an Inability to Fully Recover the Carrying Amounts of Long-Lived Assets	7/15/80
Accounting for Forward Placement and Standby Commitments and Interest Rate Future Contracts	12/16/80
Certain Issues that Affect Accounting for Minority Interest in Consolidated Financial Statements	3/17/81
Accounting for Installment Lending Activities of Financial Companies	6/25/81
Accounting for Joint Costs of Multi-Purpose Informational Materials and Activities of Nonprofit Organizations	7/16/81
Depreciation of Income Producing Real Estate	11/16/81
The Acceptability of "Simplified LIFO" for Financial Reporting Purposes	10/14/82
Accounting for Employee Capital Accumulation Plans	11/4/82

Title	Date Issued
Computation of Premium Deficiencies in Insurance Enterprises	3/26/84
Accounting for Key-Person Life Insurance	10/31/84
Identification and Discussion of Certain Financial Accounting and Reporting Issues Concerning LIFO Inventories	11/30/84
Accounting by Health Maintenance Organizations and Associated Entities	6/1/85
Accounting for Options	3/6/86
Software Revenue Recognition	4/21/87
The Use of Discounting in Financial Reporting for Monetary Items with Uncertain Terms Other Than Those Covered by Existing Literature	9/9/87

Practice Bulletins

1. Purpose and Scope of AcSEC Practice Bulletins and Procedures for their Issuance

Title	Date Issued
ACRS Lives and GAAP	11/23/81
Accounting by Colleges and Universities for Compensated Absences	9/13/82
Mortgage Banking Activities	6/27/83
Interest as a Holding Cost	10/10/83
Bank Loan Disclosures	12/26/83
Accounting and Disclosures for Reinsurance Transactions	1/23/84
Deposit Float	9/24/84
Accounting for Foreign Loan Swaps	5/27/85
ADC Arrangements	2/10/86

2. Elimination of Profits Resulting from Intercompany Transfers of LIFO Inventories
3. Prepayments into the Secondary Reserve of the FSLIC and Contingencies Related to Other Obligations of the FSLIC
4. Accounting for Foreign Debt/Equity Swaps
5. Income Recognition on Loans to Financially Troubled Countries
6. Amortization of Discounts on Certain Acquired Loans
7. Criteria for Determining Whether Collateral for a Loan has been In-Substance Foreclosed

APPENDIX

Simplified Disclosure Checklist

The simplified disclosure checklist presented below provides a quick reference to the disclosures common to the financial statements of most business enterprises. **The checklist is not intended to be a comprehensive restatement of all required disclosures.**

Disclosure Index

General

A. Basis of Reporting
B. Accounting Policies
C. Accounting Changes
D. Related Parties
E. Contingencies and Commitments
F. Nonmonetary Transactions
G. Subsequent Events

Balance Sheet

A. Cash
B. Receivables
C. Marketable Equity Securities
D. Marketable Debt Securities
E. Inventories
F. Investments--Equity Method
G. Other Investments
H. Property, Plant, and Equipment
I. Intangibles
J. Current Liabilities
K. Deferred Tax Assets and Liabilities
L. Notes Payable and Debt
M. Disclosures of Information about Financial Instruments
N. Pensions
O. Employers' Accounting for Postretirement Benefits other than Pensions
P. Leases--Lessees
Q. Leases--Lessors
R. Other Liabilities
S. Stockholders' Equity

Income Statement

   A. Income Taxes
   B. Extraordinary Items
   C. Discontinued Operations
   D. Special Reporting
   E. Foreign Currency
   F. Business Combinations and Consolidations
   G. Earnings per Share

Statement of Cash Flows

   A. Basis
   B. Format

General

A. Basis of Reporting

1. Name of entity for whom statements are being presented
2. Titles of statements should be appropriate (certain titles denote GAAP statements; other titles denote comprehensive basis of accounting)
3. Dates and periods covered should be clearly stated
4. If comparative statements are presented, repeat footnotes from prior years to extent appropriate
5. Differences between "economic" entity and entity being presented (e.g., consolidated or not? subsidiaries included and excluded, combined statements?, etc.) Disclose summarized financial information for previously unconsolidated subsidiaries

B. Accounting Policies

1. Description of business unless otherwise apparent from statements themselves
2. Description of all significant accounting policies involving inventory; marketable securities and investments; property, plant, and equipment; income taxes; revenue recognition; and cost allocation schemes

C. Accounting Changes

1. Nature and justification of change and its effects on statements
2. Change in principle: regular

   a. Cumulative effect adjustment between extraordinary items and net income on income statement
   b. Pro forma effects on net income, income before extraordinary items, and per share

    c. Effect of new principle on current and future income

3. Change in principle: retroactive

    a. Restate prior period for the following changes: from LIFO; in long-term contract accounting; to or from full cost in extractive industries; in connection with initial public offering; in accounting entity

    b. Follow transition rules in all SFASs which might vary from APB 20

4. Change in principle: no cumulative effect (such as change in depreciation method for current and future asset acquisitions):

    Statement that cumulative effect either does not exist or cannot be computed

5. Change in estimate:

    Effect on current and future income, if material

6. Correction of error--adjust retained earnings

    a. Nature of error

    b. Effect on income before extraordinary item, net income and per share amounts

D. Related Parties

1. Nature of relationship and amounts due to or from related parties with terms and matter of settlement

2. For each income statement: description and dollar amounts of transactions

3. Economic dependency and significant customers

E. Contingencies and Commitments

1. Nature and amount of accruals made

2. Nature and estimate of possible losses not accrued

3. Guarantees and commitments

4. Gain contingencies

5. Purchase obligations (SFAS 47)

F. Nonmonetary Transactions

1. Nature of transaction

2. Gain or loss and basis of accounting for assets transferred

G. Subsequent events:

    If material, adjust financial statements for conditions existing at balance sheet date and disclose for conditions subsequent

Balance Sheet

A. Cash and Cash Equivalents

1. The amount of cash restricted shall be segregated and classified according to the nature of the restriction
2. Compensating balances should be disclosed as to their nature and amount
3. Overdrafts shall be presented as a current liability

B. Receivables

1. Receivables involving officers, employees, and other related parties shall be separated as to the amount and nature of the transactions
2. The amount of unearned finance charges and interest deducted from the face amount of the receivables shall be disclosed
3. The amount and nature of pledged or assigned receivables and receivables sold with recourse shall be disclosed
4. The amount of the valuation allowance including the current period provision shall be disclosed
5. Negative balances should be reclassified as a current liability

C. Marketable Equity Securities

1. As of the date of each balance sheet presented, aggregate cost and market value (each segregated between current and noncurrent portfolios when a classified balance sheet is presented) with identification as to which is the carrying amount
2. As of the date of the latest balance sheet presented, the following data, segregated between current and noncurrent portfolios when a classified balance sheet is presented:

   a. Gross unrealized gains representing the excess of market value over cost for all marketable equity securities in the portfolio having such an excess
   b. Gross unrealized losses representing the excess of cost over market value for all marketable equity securities in the portfolio having such an excess

3. For each period for which an income statement is presented:

   a. Net realized gain or loss included in the determination of net income
   b. The basis on which cost was determined in computing realized gain or loss (that is, average cost or other method used)
   c. The change in the valuation allowance(s) that has been included in the equity section of the balance sheet during the period and, when a classified balance sheet is presented, the amount of such change included in the determination of net income

4. Income tax effects

D. Marketable Debt Securities

1. The notes to the financial statements shall disclose the nature of the carrying amount, i.e., cost or net realizable value
2. The amount and cause of any write-down in the cost of a noncurrent investment
3. The gross unrealized gains and losses on marketable debt securities

E. Inventories

1. Basis for valuation (cost, lower of cost or market, etc.)
2. Cost flow assumption (LIFO, FIFO, etc.)
3. Classes of inventory
4. Liquidation of LIFO layers
5. Inventories pledged in borrowing and product financing arrangements

F. Investments--Equity Method

1. The name of each investee and the percentage of ownership of common stock
2. The accounting policies with respect to each of the investments
3. The difference between the carrying amount for each investment and its underlying equity in the investee's net assets and the accounting treatment of the difference between these amounts
4. For those investments which have a quoted market price, the aggregate value of each investment
5. If investments in investees are considered to have a material effect on the investor's financial position and operating results, summarized data for the investor's assets, liabilities, and results of operations
6. If potential conversion of convertible securities and exercise of options and warrants would have material effects on the investor's percentage of the investee

G. Other Investments

1. For equity securities: basis of accounting, any valuation accounts in stockholders' equity and income statement effects
2. For nonequity securities: basis of accounting and income statement effects

H. Property, Plant, and Equipment

1. Basis of valuation
2. Classified by nature or function
3. Depreciation expense, accumulated depreciation, and depreciation methods by class
4. Capitalized interest cost

I. Intangibles

1. A description of the nature of the assets
2. The amount of amortization expense for the period and the method used
3. The amortization period used
4. The amount of accumulated amortization

J. Current Liabilities

1. Bank overdrafts
2. Obligations due on demand
3. Short-term obligations awaiting refinancing
4. Compensated absences
5. Special termination benefits
6. Credit balances in accounts receivable

K. Deferred Tax Assets and Liabilities

1. Assets are limited to amounts that could be realized by loss carrybacks segregated by tax jurisdiction
2. Liabilities are recognized for temporary differences that result in net taxable amounts in future years
3. Classify as current if related to asset or liability that is current or will result in net taxable or deductible amounts next year. Otherwise classify as non-current.

L. Notes Payable and Debt

1. Interest rate, maturities, covenants and other restrictions
2. Troubled debt restructurings
3. Extinguished debt

    a. By repayment
    b. By defeasance

4. Unconditional obligations: nature and maturities over next 5 years
5. Conversion features

M. Disclosure of Information about Financial Instruments

1. Extent, nature, and terms of financial instruments with off-balance-sheet risk

    a. Face or contract amount (or notional principal amount if there is no face or contract amount)
    b. Credit and market risk
    c. Cash requirements
    d. Related accounting policy pursuant to the requirements of APB 22

    e.   To be disclosed by class of financial instrument in body of FSs or in the accompanying notes

    f.   Exceptions

       (1) Insurance contracts, other than financial guarantees and investment contracts, as discussed in SFAS 60 and SFAS 97

       (2) Unconditional purchase obligations subject to SFAS 47

       (3) Employers' and plans' obligations for pension benefits, post retirement health care and life insurance benefits, and employee stock option and stock purchase plans, as reported by SFASs 35, 43, 81, and 87, as well as APBs 12 and 25

       (4) Financial instruments of a pension plan, when subject to SFAS 87

       (5) Substantively extinguished debt subject to SFAS 76

       (6) Lease contracts, as defined in SFAS 13

       (7) Payables and obligations denominated in foreign currencies and included in the statement of financial position at translated or remeasured amounts according to SFAS 52, Foreign Currency Translation, except

          (a) Obligations that have additional off-balance-sheet risk from other risks, and

          (b) Obligations under foreign currency exchange contracts

2. Disclosure of credit risk of financial instruments with off-balance-sheet credit risk

    a.   Amount of accounting loss entity would incur should any party to the financial instrument fail to perform according to terms of the contact and collateral or security, if any, is of no value

    b.   Entity's policy of requiring collateral or security, entity's access to that collateral or security, and the nature and brief description of collateral or security

    c.   To be disclosed by class of financial instrument in the body of the FSs or in the accompanying notes

    d.   Exceptions: Same as in 1.f. above

3. Disclosure of concentrations of credit risk of all financial instruments

    a.   Disclose all significant concentrations of credit risk from **all** financial instruments, whether from an individual counterparty or groups of counterparties

    b.   Group concentrations exist if a number of counterparties are engaged in similar activities and have similar economic characteristics such that they would be similarly affected by changes in conditions

    c.   Disclose for each significant concentration

        (1)   Information about the (shared) activity, region, or economic characteristics

        (2)   Same as 2.a.

        (3)   Same as 2.b.

    d. Exceptions: Same as 1.f.(1)--1.f.(5)

N. Pensions

1. Defined benefit plans require the following disclosures:

    a. General

        (1)   Description of the plan and an indication of the groups covered

        (2)   Statement of policy in regard to accounting and funding

        (3)   Types of assets held

        (4)   Type of benefit formula

        (5)   Type of any significant nonbenefit liability

        (6)   Acknowledgement of matters of significance that have affected the comparability of the accounting periods presented and comments as to their nature and effect. Changes in accounting methods and amendments of a plan are examples.

    b. Net periodic pension cost amount and separately showing:

        (1)   Service cost component

        (2)   Interest cost component

        (3)   Actual return on assets

        (4)   Net total of other components

    c. Schedule reconciling balance sheet amounts with the funded status of the plan, separately showing:

        (1)   Plan assets fair value

        (2)   Projected benefit obligation, accumulated benefit obligation, and vested benefit obligation

        (3)   Unrecognized prior service cost amount

        (4)   Unrecognized net gain (loss) amount (those not yet reflected in market-related value should also be included)

        (5)   Unrecognized net obligation or net asset amount still remaining from that recorded at SFAS 87 date of initial application

        (6)   Additional minimum liability amount recorded because of underfunding

        (7)   Net pension asset or liability amount recognized on the balance sheet

    d. Rates

        (1) Assumed weighted-average discount rate
        (2) Assumed weighted-average expected long-term rate on plan assets
        (3) Assumed rate of compensation increase (if applicable) in measuring the projected benefit obligation

    e. Other, if applicable

        (1) Employer and related parties

            (a) Amounts and types of securities included in plan assets
            (b) Approximate amount of annual benefits covered by annuity contracts issued by the above

        (2) Alternative amortization methods used
        (3) Existence and nature of substantive commitments to make future plan amendments

    f. Settlements, curtailments, and terminations

  2. Defined contribution plans require the following separate disclosures:

    a. Description of the plan and an indication of the groups covered
    b. Basis for determining contributions
    c. Acknowledgement of matters of significance that have affected the comparability of the accounting periods presented and comments as to their nature and effect
    d. Amount of cost recognized during the period
    e. For multi-employer plans: types of benefits provided

  3. Postretirement Health Care and Life Insurance Benefits (SFAS 81)

    a. A description of the benefits and of the employee groups covered
    b. A description of the accounting and funding policies
    c. The cost of the period benefits recognized. If separate postretirement benefits cannot be reasonably calculated, the total cost of these benefits, the number of active employees, and the number of retirees covered by the plan shall be disclosed.
    d. The acknowledgement of matters of significance that have affected the comparability of the accounting periods presented and comments as to their nature and effect

O. Employers' Accounting for Postretirement Benefits other than Pensions

  1. Description of plan
  2. Any modifications of cost-sharing provisions and any commitments toward benefits

3. The amount of net periodic postretirement benefit cost showing separately the service cost component, the interest cost component, the actual return on plan assets for the period, amortization of the unrecognized transition obligation or transition asset, and the net total of other components.
4. A schedule reconciling the funded status of the plan(s) with amounts reported in the employer's statement of financial position, showing separately:

   a. The fair value of plan assets
   b. The accumulated postretirement benefit obligation, identifying separately the portion attributable to retirees, other fully eligible plan participants, and other active plan participants
   c. The amount of unrecognized prior service cost
   d. The amount of unrecognized net gain or loss (including plan asset gains or losses not yet reflected in market-related value)
   e. The amount of any remaining unrecognized transition obligation or transition asset
   f. The amount of net postretirement benefit asset or liability recognized in the statement of financial position, which is the net result of combining the preceding five items

5. The assumed health care cost trend rate used to measure the expected cost of benefits covered by the plan for the next year and a general description of the direction and pattern of change in the assumed trend
6. The weighted-average of the assumed discount rate and rate of compensation increase used
7. The effect of a one-percentage-point increase in the assumed health care cost trend rates for each future year on (1) the aggregate of the service and interest cost components of net periodic postretirement health care benefit cost and (2) the accumulated postretirement benefit obligation for health care benefits
8. The amounts and types of securities of the employer and related parties included in plan assets, and the approximate amount of future annual benefits of plan participants covered by insurance contracts issued by the employer and related parties
9. The amount of gain or loss recognized during the period for a settlement or curtailment and a description of the nature of the event
10. The cost of providing special or contractual termination benefits recognized during the period and a description of the nature of the event

P. Leases--Lessees

1. Nature of leasing arrangements
2. For capital leases

    a. Gross amounts of leased assets by class of property

    b. Future minimum lease payments for each of the next 5 years and in the aggregate

    c. Contingent rentals and amounts paid for each year for which an income statement is presented

3. For operating leases

    a. Future minimum lease payments for each of the next 5 years and in the aggregate

    b. Contingent rentals and rent expense for each year

4. Subleases

Q. Leases--Lessors

1. Nature of leasing arrangements
2. For sales-type and trust financing type leases

    a. Net investment

    b. Future minimum lease payments for each of the next 5 years and in the aggregate

    c. Contingent rentals

3. For operating leases

    a. Amounts of assets leased out or held for leasing

    b. Future minimum lease payments for each of the next 5 years and in the aggregate

    c. Contingent rentals

4. Leveraged leases

R. Other Liabilities

1. Deferred compensation
2. Minimum pension obligations (SFAS 81)

S. Stockholders' Equity

Capital Stock and Additional Paid-in Capital

1. For each class of stock

    a. Par, stated, or assigned value

    b. Number of shares authorized, issued, and outstanding

    c. Number of shares held in treasury

    d. Conversion terms of preferred, if applicable, including call prices, rates, and dates. Additionally, the amount of redemption requirements for all issues of stock that are redeemable at fixed or determinable prices on fixed or determinable dates must be disclosed for each of the five years following the date of the latest balance sheet presented.

   e.   Changes in the number of shares authorized, issued, and outstanding during the year and changes in the equity accounts

   f.   Liquidation values, if different than par, in the aggregate for preferred

   g.   For preferred, any dividend preferences, special privileges, etc.

   h.   Any unusual voting rights

2.   The amount of cumulative dividends in arrears, per share, and in aggregate

3.   Aggregate securities issuable under rights of warrants, as well as their prices, and exercise and expiration dates

4.   Any discount on capital stock

5.   The amount of subscribed shares not yet issued

6.   Stock dividends payable in total or at par or stated value with the excess included in additional paid-in capital

7.   The amount of capital stock issued in business combinations (purchase or pooling) or agreements to issue additional shares at a later date

8.   Transactions affecting equity subsequent to the date of the financial statements (recapitalization, sales of stock, etc.)

9.   Additional paid-in capital, listed by source, along with any changes in it during the period

10.   Any changes in the capital accounts of partners or sole proprietors

Retained Earnings

11.   Appropriation and segregation of retained earnings should be disclosed in the equity section, as well as their nature, cause, and amount. Changes in these accounts should be disclosed.

12.   Nature and dollar amounts of restrictions on retained earnings (treasury stock, lease covenants, etc.)

13.   Date retained earnings for 10 years following quasi-reorganization

14.   Increase/decrease results from combination by pooling of interests (revenues, expenses, extraordinary items, and net income)

15.   Prior period adjustments, net of tax and in gross. For correction of an error, in the period discovered:

   a.   Nature of the error on previous statements

   b.   Effect of correction on income before extraordinary items, net income, and related per share amounts

Dividends

16.   Dividends in aggregate and per share as well as the nature and extent of any restrictions on retained earnings limiting availability of dividends

17.   The amount of dividends in arrears, per share and in aggregate

18. Dividends declared after balance sheet date, prior to opinion date, should be disclosed unless a long-established history of regular payment dates and the dividend is not abnormal in amount

19. For stock dividends and stock splits, disclosure of the amounts capitalized, per share and in total. Historical presentations of earnings per share should be restated in an equivalent number of shares so the figures would be presented on a comparable basis.

Treasury Stock

20. Treasury stock, cost method: Present total cost of treasury stock as a deduction from total stockholders' equity. Disclose number of shares held in treasury.

21. Treasury stock, par value method: Present par value of treasury stock as a deduction from par value of issued shares of same class. Any related additional paid-in capital from treasury stock is netted with corresponding additional paid-in capital without separate disclosure. Disclose number of shares held in treasury.

Compensatory Stock Plans

22. The net earned compensation under a stock option plan, presented as additional paid-in capital. For example:

Stock options outstanding	xx
Less deferred compensation expense	(xx)
	xx

23. Stock purchase and stock option plans--as a minimum, the following should be disclosed:

    a. Status of the plan at balance sheet date

       (1) Number of shares under option
       (2) Option price
       (3) Number of shares as to which options were exercisable

    b. Activity during period as to

       (1) Number of shares involved in options exercised
       (2) Option price of shares exercised

    c. Transactions after balance sheet date but prior to issuance of report should be disclosed in the notes

24. Stock appreciation rights--parallels requirements for stock purchase and stock option plans

Income Statement

A. Income Taxes

1. State if entity is not subject to income taxes because income is taxed directly to owners. State the net difference between tax and book bases of assets and liabilities.
2. State amounts allocated to:

   a. Current tax expense or benefit
   b. Deferred tax expense or benefit
   c. Investment tax credits
   d. Operating loss carryforward benefits
   e. Rate change effects
   f. Tax status change effects
   g. Government grants effects

3. Amounts allocated to:

   a. Continuing operations
   b. Discontinued operations
   c. Extraordinary items
   d. Cumulative effect of accounting changes
   e. Prior period adjustments
   f. Gains and losses included in comprehensive income but excluded from net income
   g. Capital transactions

4. Reconcile statutory tax rates to actual rates for significant items (non-public enterprises need only disclose the nature of significant reconciling items)
5. Amounts and expiration dates for operating loss and tax credit carryforward for financial reporting
6. If consolidated return filed, separately issued financial statements should state:

   a. Amount of current and deferred tax expense for each income statement
   b. Tax-related balances due to or from affiliates for each balance sheet
   c. The method of allocating consolidated amounts of current and deferred tax expense and effects of any change in that methodology

7. Effect of adopting new pronouncement for restated prior years' financial statements
8. Cumulative effect of change (similar to change in accounting principle) for earliest restated financial statements

B. Extraordinary Items

  1. Segregated and shown net of tax
  2. Adequate explanations of nature
  3. Infrequent or unusual items shown separately although not extraordinary; not shown net of tax

C. Discontinued Operations

  1. Assets and operations segregated
  2. Gain/loss from disposal
  3. Expected loss on future disposal

D. Special Reporting

  1. Interim financial information
  2. Segment data
  3. Development stage enterprises
  4. Research and development expenditures
  5. Research and development arrangements
  6. Sales where collection is uncertain
  7. Revenue recognition when right of return exists
  8. Financing arrangements--real estate and product financing
  9. Real estate sales
  10. Futures contracts

E. Foreign Currency

  1. Exchange gain or loss
  2. Change in cumulative translation adjustment amount in stockholders' equity
  3. Significant changes in foreign operations
  4. Disclose foreign customers and/or foreign operations adequately

F. Business Combinations and Consolidations

  1. Nature and policy of combination
  2. Intercompany eliminations
  3. Detailed purchase disclosures--cost of acquisition, goodwill, contingencies, income consolidated, net operating loss carryforward
  4. Detailed pooling disclosures--shares issued, changes in income and retained earnings, combined operations
  5. Remeasure purchase combinations for prior year financial statements restated for deferred income taxes payable
  6. Summarize disclosures of balance sheets and income statements previously provided for formerly unconsolidated majority-owned subsidiaries

G. Earnings Per Share

1. Captions for the income statement

   a. For simple capital structures--Earnings per common share
   b. For complex capital structures

      (1) Primary--Earnings per common and common equivalent share
      (2) Fully diluted--Earnings per share, assuming full dilution

2. Additional disclosures for complex capital structure EPS

   a. A schedule explaining the EPS figures should be presented disclosing common stock equivalents, underlying assumptions, and number of shares issued upon conversion, warrants, etc.
   b. If potential dilution exists in any of the periods, both PEPS and FDEPS should be presented for all periods

      (1) Gives the reader understanding of the trend in potential dilution
      (2) If earnings of a prior period presented have been restated, the EPS data should be revised and effect of restatement in EPS should be disclosed in year of restatement.

   c. Supplementary EPS figures should be presented when

      (1) Conversions during or after the period would have affected PEPS. Note that PEPS should not be retroactively adjusted for conversions
      (2) Sale of common or common equivalents and the proceeds are used to retire debt, preferred, etc.

Statement of Cash Flows

A. Basis

1. Definition of cash and cash equivalents adopted
2. Summarize noncash investing and financing activities

B. Format

1. Reconcile net income to net cash flow
2. If direct method used, display major categories of gross cash receipts and cash payments

   a. Cash receipts

      (1) Cash receipts from sale of goods or services
      (2) Interest and dividends received
      (3) Other operating cash receipts

    b. Cash payments

        (1) Payments to employees and other suppliers of goods or services
        (2) Income taxes paid
        (3) Interest paid
        (4) Other operating cash payments

3. If indirect method used, state both interest and income taxes paid

Feedback to Authors

We invite your suggestions, corrections, typographical errors, etc. Please send these to Patrick R. Delaney, c/o CPA Examination Review of John Wiley & Sons, Inc., P.O. Box 886, DeKalb, Illinois 60115 before June 1, 1992, for inclusion in the 1992 Edition.

1.

2.

3.

4.

5.

6.

7.

8.

9.

10.

11.

12.

13.